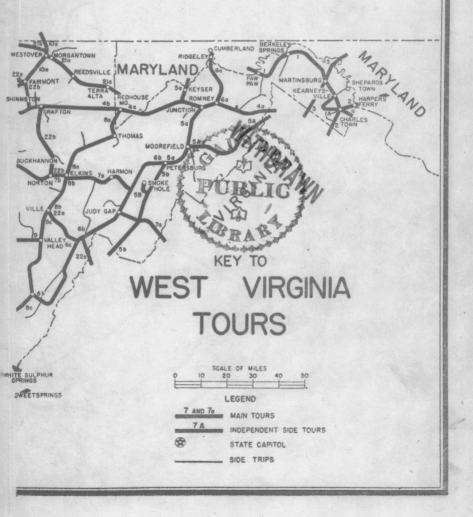

KEY TO

WEST VIRGINIA
TOURS

SCALE OF MILES

| 0 | 10 | 20 | 30 | 40 | 50 |

LEGEND

7 AND 7a — MAIN TOURS

7 A — INDEPENDENT SIDE TOURS

⊛ — STATE CAPITOL

—— — SIDE TRIPS

WEST VIRGINIA

A Guide to the Mountain State

WEST VIRGINIA

A GUIDE TO THE MOUNTAIN STATE

↑↑

*Compiled by workers of the Writers' Program
of the Work Projects Administration in the
State of West Virginia*

AMERICAN GUIDE SERIES

ILLUSTRATED

Sponsored by the Conservation Commission of West Virginia

OXFORD UNIVERSITY PRESS · NEW YORK

WEST VIRGINIA STATE BOARD OF EDUCATION
State-wide Sponsor of the
West Virginia Writers' Project

FEDERAL WORKS AGENCY
JOHN M. CARMODY, *Administrator*

WORK PROJECTS ADMINISTRATION
HOWARD O. HUNTER, *Commissioner*
FLORENCE KERR, *Assistant Commissioner*
JOSEPH N. ALDERSON, *State Administrator*

ʃʃʃ

Preface

West Virginia: A Guide to the Mountain State represents the work of many minds over a period of several years. West Virginia's activities are as diversified as its topography and borders are irregular; but finally the multitude of facts was reduced to order and the *West Virginia Guide* reached completion. The director, editors, writers, research workers, draftsmen, consultants, typists, and all others who had part in its compilation take pride in presenting the book to the public as the first comprehensive picture of the State's varied life.

The development of West Virginia from a backward frontier State to one of the most highly industrialized areas in the Nation is portrayed in text and illustrations. This development has been so extensive, diversified, and rapid that many West Virginians themselves have not been fully aware of it; to them no less than to visitors it is hoped the *Guide* will be all its name implies. In the Tours, important but little-known phases of activity and incidents of history are recorded for perhaps the first time in print. In this section and in descriptions of cities, an attempt has been made to treat each community adequately, with relation to its background.

Because of the word limit, some of the smaller cities, among them Bluefield and Beckley, are not included in the cities section, but are handled at length in the tour division and represented in the picture folios. Separate treatment is given Shepherdstown because of its historic interest.

As the 1940 population figures were not available while the *Guide* was being written, 1930 figures are used throughout the text, except in 'Population and Its Distribution.' There is, however, an alphabetical list of the final 1940 figures in the Appendices.

Grateful acknowledgment is due many individuals and organizations for assistance in the preparation of the book. In addition to aid given by the State Conservation Commission, valuable services were rendered by other State agencies, including the State Road Commission, Department of Education, Department of Agriculture, Department of Labor,

v

Department of Mines and Department of Archives and History, and by the United States Forest Service. Much assistance was received also from West Virginia University and other colleges, Kanawha County Public Library, the State Chamber of Commerce, city chambers of commerce, and many private corporations. The staff is particularly grateful to Dr. Roy Bird Cook, who was an ever-ready consultant on historical matters, and to Professor Rexford Newcomb, dean of the School of Fine and Applied Arts at the University of Illinois, who contributed the essay on architecture. For contributions and criticisms thanks are due Dr. P. D. Strausbaugh, Dr. A. B. Brooks, Dr. Frank Gilbert, Dr. Fred M. Smith, Dr. J. B. Edworthy, Right Reverend W. L. Gravatt, Dr. W. W. Trent, Stanley Dadisman, Paul Olejar, N. P. Rinehart, Dr. Paul H. Price, Professor Maurice Brooks, Professor Creel Cornwell, Professor L. W. Chappell, and to John L. Stender, former State Director of the project.

We are indebted to the West Virginia Art Project for the art work.

BRUCE CRAWFORD, *State Supervisor.*
PAUL H. BECKER, *Assistant State Supervisor.*

February 1, 1941

Contents

Part I. The General Background

Part II. Cities

Part III. Tours

X CONTENTS

Part IV. Appendices

Illustrations

List of Maps

General Information

Railroads: Baltimore & Ohio R.R., Chesapeake and Ohio Ry., Norfolk and Western Ry., New York Central System, Pennsylvania R.R., Virginian Ry., Western Maryland Ry.

Highways: 16 US highways; 2,243 miles of Federal Aid highways; 33,163 miles of State roads, including Federal Aid and local roads under State control, of which 5,011 miles are surfaced. State police patrol highways regularly; inspection of driver's license and registration. Gasoline filling stations numerous on all main highways. Federal gas tax 1¢, State gas tax 5¢ (total tax 6¢). Red Cross first-aid stations and State-maintained drinking fountains at frequent intervals.

Bus Lines: Interstate: Greyhound Lines, Blue Ridge Lines, Lincoln Trailways, Penn-Ohio Coach Lines Co., Red Star Way Lines, Tennessee Coach Co., Consolidated Bus Lines, Arcodel System. Intrastate: West Virginia Transportation Co., Reynolds Transportation Co. Many local lines serve parts of State.

Air Lines: American Airlines, Inc. (between Washington, D. C., and Cincinnati, Ohio), stops at Elkins, Charleston, and Huntington. Pennsylvania Central Airlines (between Pittsburgh, Pa., and Birmingham, Ala.), stops at Charleston.

Traffic Regulations: Certificate of registration required for each motor vehicle operated on highways, and driver's license required of all persons driving same; driver's license issued to persons over 15 years of age, after examination by the (superintendent of) department of public safety; vehicle registered or operator licensed in any other State that grants reciprocal privilege is exempted for period not to exceed three months. Maximum speed 45 m.p.h. on open country road, 25 m.p.h. on suburban streets or at any railway crossing where view is not obstructed, 20 m.p.h. in any business district, and 15 m.p.h. in school zones; speed not to be greater than reasonable and prudent, considering traffic and hazards. Make full stop before entering or crossing main routes marked by STOP signs. Right and left turns are indicated by signs at intersections. In case of accident in which anyone is injured, the nearest State police detachment should be notified. Hand signals required for turns and stops; full stop 5 feet from busses or streetcars while they are stopped for passengers to enter or alight; projections extending 5 feet or more from vehicle require red flag by day, red light by night; light required at left front end of trailers; no more than 3 persons in front seat of any motor vehicle; cut-outs and passing other vehicles on curve or on top of hill prohibited.

Road Maps: Issued bi-monthly; may be secured from State Road Commission in Charleston and from most hotels.

Information Bureaus: West Virginia Chamber of Commerce, Great Kanawha Bldg., Charleston; West Virginia State Road Commission, 1340 Wilson St., Charleston; West Virginia Dept. of Agriculture, Capitol Bldg., Charleston; State Conservation Commission, Capitol Bldg., Charleston; American Automobile Association in principal cities.

State Police Service: State police maintain detachments in cities, larger towns, and keypoints for heavy traffic. To call State police: From dial telephones, dial *O* (operator) and ask for State police; from all other telephones lift receiver and ask for State police.

Accommodations: Tourist accommodations of all types are available in most parts of the State. Inns, hotels, tourist homes, and cabins located at frequent intervals, except where otherwise noted in tours; rates 75¢ up.

Climate and Equipment: Summer travelers should expect moderately warm weather, with infrequent hot and muggy days. Winter visitors should be prepared for subfreezing to near-zero weather, occasional snowstorms and dangerous ice; driving hazardous until highways are cindered.

Poisonous Plants and Reptiles: Poison ivy, or three-leafed mercury, is common throughout State, growing on trees and stream banks and over stone walls and old buildings. Poison sumac found near Cowen in Webster County and Elkins in Randolph County. Rattlesnakes in most parts of the State but more numerous in Pocahontas and Greenbrier Counties and in vicinity of New River Gorge. Copperheads throughout the State. Boots or puttees should be worn when hiking in mountains.

Plant Regulations: Picking flowers and shrubs within 300 feet of highway is prohibited, and likewise the transportation of flowers and shrubs picked elsewhere without permission of property owner.

Fishing: Game fish are defined as trout, black bass, green bass, white bass, willow bass, white salmon, landlocked salmon, jack salmon, walleyed pike, muskellunge, pickerel, and perch. Seasons usually range from mid-April to November 30, but regulations are frequently changed, and fishermen should obtain latest fish and game bulletins on season dates, minimum length of fish, and daily catch limits from State Conservation Commission in Charleston or from county clerk where license is purchased. Fishing by means other than rod and line is prohibited, except that small seines may be used for securing bait minnows.

Hunting: Small game is defined as squirrel (gray, black, and fox), ruffed grouse, quail, rabbit, raccoon, opossum, skunk, red fox, muskrat, and waterfowl. Large game, whitetail deer, wild turkey and black bear. Seasonal regulations sometimes changed, and hunters should secure latest hunting bulletin on season dates, daily and season limit from State Conservation Commission.
Prohibited: Transporting game birds or game fish out of State (except that nonresident licensee may transport own catch or kill not to exceed limit taken in any two days); sale or purchase of squirrels, any game bird or game animal and any but a few species of fish.
Licenses: Required of all persons above 15 years of age. Fees: Resident: combined hunting and fishing license $2. Nonresident: combined hunting and fishing license $15, fishing license $5, tourist license, fishing only, 24 hours, $1. (No hunting license issued to nonresidents unless combined with fishing.)

Hiking: Most State parks and forests have well-marked trails.

Riding: Larger cities and most smaller communities have stables where saddle horses may be rented. Several hundred miles of dirt and gravel roads available, where traffic is light and where riders can explore the back country. Fine horses and riding trails are available in most State parks.

Horse Shows and Racing Meets: Horse shows held each year in Huntington, Wheeling, Lewisburg, Elkins, Charles Town, and Parkersburg and at some annual county fairs. Two race tracks: Wheeling Downs, Wheeling, and Charles Town Race Track, Charles Town, where racing meets are held each spring and fall, with betting legalized under parimutuel system.

Mountain Climbing: No guides, instructors, or special facilities for mountain climbing are available.

Bicycling: Bicycles may be rented at most State parks. Light on front and reflector on rear required at night. A few cities require license fee of 25¢ or 50¢.

Golfing: There are about 50 golf courses, one within a short distance of practically every large community.

Tennis: Ample facilities for tennis in or near most large communities; courts also in some State parks.

Swimming: In central and southern parts of State, swimming is confined to commercial pools (about 45 in State); a few public beaches on northern rivers.

State Parks: Babcock State Park, 10 m. W. of East Rainelle on State 41; Blackwater Falls State Park, 2.6 m. E. of Thomas on State 32; Cacapon State Park, 9 m. S. of Berkeley Springs on State 38; Hawks Nest State Park, 2 m. W. of Ansted (43 m. E. of Charleston) on US 60; Lost River State Park, 3 m. W. of Mathias; Pinnacle Rock State Park, 6.7 m. NW. of Bluefield on US 52; Tomlinson Run State Park, just W. of Pughtown on State 2; Watoga State Park, 8 m. E. of Huntersville on graveled road.

State Monuments and Historical Sites: Berkeley Springs; Carnifex Ferry Battlefield, 10 m. W. of Summersville on US 19, thence 6 m.

SE. from Drennen on secondary paved road; Corrick's Ford State Monument, S. of Parsons; Droop Mountain Battlefield, 26 m. N. of Lewisburg on US 219; Morgan-Morgan State Monument, Bunker Hill; Nancy Hanks State Monument, N. of Ridgeville to Antioch, then 4 m. W.; State 4-H Camp (memorial to General Jackson) NW. of Weston at Jackson's Mill; Tu-Endie-Wei State Monument, Point Pleasant.

State Forests: Cabwaylingo, 45 miles S. of Huntington on US 52 and E. of Missouri Branch; Cooper's Rock, 10 miles NE. of Morgantown on both sides of SR 73, immediately adjacent to Cheat River; Kumbrabow, 4 miles W. of Elkwater (Randolph County, US 219) on State Forest gravel road; Seneca, 10 miles NE. of Huntersville, Pocahontas County, on Brown's Creek secondary gravel road; Greenbrier, 3 miles S. of White Sulphur Springs on Hart's Run secondary gravel road; Kanawha, 3 miles W. of Hernshaw (US 119, Kanawha County) on secondary gravel road.

Recreation Areas

(For location of West Virginia recreation areas see reverse side of State map in back pocket, on which they are numbered as below.)

West Virginia's recreation system is being rapidly developed, with vacation cabins and incidental facilities being completed in many parks and forests. The vacation cabins are built of log, native stone or clapboard and are conveniently equipped for housekeeping with hot and cold water, shower, modern sanitary facilities and practical cooking ranges. The cabins range in size from normal accommodations for 2 persons to similar accommodations for 6 persons, with rates starting at $10 per week. Reservations must be made in advance through the Conservation Commission, Division of State Parks, Charleston, West Virginia. A check or money order in the amount of $5, to apply on rental charge, must accompany application. Application forms are available by writing the address above.

Cots for auxiliary sleeping accommodations are available at 35¢ per night.

The U. S. Forest Service has developed a number of recreation areas in the Monongahela National Forest, but the emphasis is on camp grounds and swimming places. No cabins are available in U. S. Forest Service areas. Camping permits may be obtained from the supervisor's office at Elkins, or, for the George Washington National Forest, from headquarters at Harrisonburg, Virginia.

1. CACAPON STATE PARK, 9 m. S. of Berkeley Springs on State 38 (*see Tour* 1). Comprises 5,400 acres of low but rugged and forested mountain area with superb view of 4 States and of a picturesque bend of the Potomac River. Fine picnic area with large parking area, 31 picnic tables, 21 outdoor fireplaces, and 1 picnic shelter; 13 cabins. Bicycling. Boating on 6-acre lake at nominal hourly charge. Fishing in lake for trout; bathing beach. Hiking and riding with 24 miles of trails; lodge for overnight accommodations and meals.

2. HAWKS NEST STATE PARK, 43 m. E. of Charleston on US 60 (*see Tour* 15). Notable view from Hawks Nest, 585 feet above New River, of picturesque gorge. Park area of 41 acres, contains museum with pioneer exhibits, parking facilities, picnic area with shelter, completely equipped picnicking units and hiking trails. Concession and sanitary toilets along main highway.

3. LOST RIVER STATE PARK, 3 m. W. of Mathias (town on State 259) (*see Tour* 5*A*). Magnificent view of mountain country from Big Ridge (elevation 3,200 feet) reached by steep park road. Seventeen mile drive to park from Moorefield affords superb views of Moorefield valley. Old Lee White Sulphur Spring restored for use. Park contains 3,760 acres. Developed area contains grills, 16 cabins, picnicking facilities, bicycling, hiking over 10 miles of trail, swimming in concrete pool. Deer and turkey abound in developed area.

4. SENECA STATE FOREST, 5 m. E. of Marlinton on State 28 thence N. on gravel road (*see Tour* 6). Wooded foothill country, 11,049 acres, along Greenbrier River, between Allegheny and Back Allegheny Mountains. Forest has many deer, and timber stand improvement projects are under way. Numerous game food and cover patches have been established. Fire tower at highest point on forest. 8 cabins; picnic facilities; boating and swimming in artificial lake; hiking over mountain trails.

5. WATOGA STATE PARK, 5 m. E. of Marlinton on State 28, thence 8 m. from Huntersville on gravel road. Ferry entrance from Seebert. Largest State park, 10,960 acres in area. Rugged foothill country along Greenbrier River with altitudes to 3,264 feet. A natural refuge territory, the park has deer, turkey, grouse, and other small game. Brooks Memorial Arboretum denotes an abundance of varied flower growth. 25 cabins; picnic site, fully equipped; restaurant concession; bicycling; horseback riding at a reasonable charge; boating and fishing (on 12-acre lake) form the recreation nucleus of the park. Swimming, beach, on Greenbrier River. Concrete pool now being constructed.

6. BABCOCK STATE PARK, 10 m. W. of Rainelle on US 60, thence 2 m. S. on State 41 (*see Tour* 15). 3,230 acres of rugged scenic mountain land and gorge territory with altitudes to 2,650 feet, affording many thrilling views. Vacation cabins, restaurant and concession, overnight accommodations, picnic area with fireplaces, tables, shelter, water, sanitary facilities. Fishing (in season) in Manns and Glade Creeks, rainbow trout, artificial lure only. Hiking and riding over 25 miles of foot and horse trail. Horses available at reasonable charge. Swimming in mountain pool; bathhouse in administration building.

7. TOMLINSON RUN STATE PARK, entrance 4 m. N. of New Cumberland on State 2 (*see Tour* 19*a*). Area of 1,224 acres now (1941) being developed. Will have play areas, picnic area, motor roads, hiking trails, swimming beach and fishing.

8. CABWAYLINGO STATE FOREST, 42 m. S. of Huntington on US 52, thence 3 m. E. on dirt road (*see Tour* 18*b*). Forested area, 6,483 acres in rugged country up to 1,250 feet elevation. Fine view of surrounding area, including Kentucky and Ohio, from Tick Ridge fire tower. 13 cabins; two picnic areas. Fishing, swimming in Twelvepole Creek. Hiking on mountain trails.

9. KANAWHA STATE FOREST, 10 m. S. of Charleston at Olcott. Wooded hill country, 6,705 acres in area. Being developed as a game

refuge and recreation area. Picnic areas. Dam being constructed will provide a beach for swimming.

10. PINNACLE ROCK STATE PARK, 6.7 m. NW. of Bluefield on US 52 (*see Tour 18a*). A towering rock promontory with an altitude of 2,764 feet, rising from a mountain ridge, this point of vantage provides a magnificent view of mountain country in West Virginia and Virginia. An area of some 30 acres, centering around the rock, is being developed as a picnicking ground.

11. CARNIFEX FERRY BATTLEFIELD, 12 m. S. of Summersville on State 41 or 25 m. NE. of Gauley Bridge on US 19 (*see Tour 10b*). An area of 218 acres on Gauley River to be developed as an historical monument with picnicking facilities.

12. BLUE BEND FOREST CAMP (U. S. Forest Service), 6 m. W. of White Sulphur Springs on US 60 (*see Tour 15a*). Recreation area, in Monongahela National Forest, built around the blue water of a swimming hole in Anthony Creek, between steep ranges of Greenbrier and Allegheny Mountains. Camp sites, picnic facilities, fireplaces, shelters. Swimming (free); lifeguard attendant.

13. DROOP MOUNTAIN BATTLEFIELD STATE PARK, 27 m. N. of Lewisburg on US 219 (*see Tour 8b*). A battlefield area of 265 acres (altitude 3,060 ft.), commanding views of rugged mountain country; lookout tower. 3 cabins, picnic area, foot paths to memorabilia of a battle in the War between the States (1863). Guide service.

14. KUMBRABOW STATE FOREST, 6 m. W. of Valley Head on State 15, thence 6 m. N. on improved road (*see Tour 9*). Area of 9,425 acres on slopes of Point Mountain, being reforested by State. Has trout nursery and is a game refuge. Recreational facilities being developed.

15. HOLLY RIVER STATE PARK, 33 m. S. of Buckhannon on State 20 (*see Tour 20b*). 6,000 acres of rugged forest country on tributaries of Holly River. Game refuge, interesting wild life. 9 cabins, picnic area, swimming in concrete pool (bathhouse adjacent), wading pool for children, hiking, tennis. Holly River was developed by the Resettlement Administration of the U. S. Department of Agriculture.

16. STUART FOREST CAMP (U. S. Forest Service), 6 m. E. of Elkins on US 33 (*see Tour 7a*). A recreational area built around a natural swimming hole, in a loop of Shavers Fork of Cheat River, with mountain ranges to east and west. Bathhouses and sand beach, swimming (free), lifeguard attendant; picnicking areas, tent and trailer sites; open meadow for sports. 3½ miles north of camp on one-way Stuart Memorial Drive is BICKLE KNOB FOREST CAMP, an improved picnic ground (spring water) and short distance from fire tower (4,008 ft.) with view of surrounding country. 3½ miles east of Bickle Knob Camp, on the same one-way forest road, is ROOSEVELT FOREST CAMP, at the junction with US 33. Picnic sites with tables, fireplaces and comfort stations are provided free. A strong flowing spring provides good water.

17. BLACKWATER FALLS STATE PARK, 3 m. E. of Thomas to

Davis on State 32, thence 1.2 m. S. on cindered road (*see Tour 8a*) 447 acres of leased land on tableland in excess of 3,000 ft. altitude. Railed walks and steps provide fine view of 63-foot Blackwater Falls. Excellent views of Blackwater Canyon from its rim. Picnicking arrangements and free guide service. Fishing (trout) in Blackwater River.

18. HORSESHOE FOREST CAMP (U. S. Forest Service), about 5 m. N. of Parsons on Horseshoe Forest Road. On Horseshoe Run, a branch of Cheat River and surrounded by forested mountains. Tent and trailer sites, picnic areas; swimming in improved natural swimming hole, bathhouse, lifeguard.

19. COOPERS ROCK STATE FOREST, 11 m. E. of Morgantown on US 119 and State 73 (*see Tour 21a*). 13,000 acres of forest land on Cheat Mountain make it the largest of the State forests, with fine view of Cheat River Gorge from Coopers Rock. Swimming and boating in 2,000-acre artificial lake on adjacent Cheat River. Picnicking, hiking; fishing for bass and pan fish in Cheat River.

20. SMOKE HOLE FOREST CAMP (U. S. Forest Service), 17 m. S. of Petersburg on US 220, thence about 5 m. NW. on improved forest road. Recreation area in Monongahela National Forest in cliff-bordered gorge of South Branch of Potomac River. Picnic facilities; tent and trailer sites; hiking, bass fishing and swimming in South Branch.

21. GRANDVIEW STATE PARK, 12 m. E. of Beckley on graded road, an area of 52 acres affording a magnificent view of the New River Gorge. To be developed with picnicking facilities.

22. GREENBRIER STATE FOREST, 3 miles S. of White Sulphur Springs on Hart's Run secondary gravel road, an area of 5,400 acres on Kate's Mountain. This State Forest affords excellent picnicking on 2 developed sites, one on Hart's Run and the other on the summit of Kate's Mountain. The forest, at present, has 4 overnight cabins available for public use and construction of others is contemplated. A 12-mile sky line loop drive from White Sulphur Springs over Kate's Mountain and down Hart's Run provides some of the finest panorama scenery in the State. The forest is administered as a State Game Refuge.

Calendar of Events

MARCH

No fixed date	at Morgantown	State High School Basketball Tournament

APRIL

Second Friday	State-wide	Arbor Day
Easter Sunday	at Wheeling	Easter Sunrise Service
No fixed date	at Wheeling	Music Festival

MAY

No fixed date	at Wheeling	Ohio Valley Arbor Day
No fixed date	at Charleston	May Music Festival
No fixed date	at Parkersburg	School Children's Field Day
No fixed date	at Parkersburg	Spring Flower Show
No fixed date	at Wheeling	Wheeling Downs Horse Racing Meet, 22 days
No fixed date	at Charles Town	Racing Meet; Charles Town Jockey Club, extending to July 4

JUNE

No fixed date	at Buckhannon	Central West Virginia Strawberry Festival, two days
No fixed date	at Huntington	Junior League Horse Show, three days
No fixed date	at Morgantown	Commencement, West Virginia University

JULY

Midmonth	at White Sulphur Springs	State Open Tennis Championship, men and women, six days
No fixed date	at Webster Springs	Rhododendron Festival, three days
No fixed date	at White Sulphur Springs	State Amateur Golf Championship, men and women, six days
No fixed date	at Arthurdale	Folk Festival

AUGUST

Last week	at Lewisburg	Horse Show
No fixed date	at Charles Town	Horse Show; Charles Town Horse Show Association
No fixed date	at White Sulphur Springs	Mason-Dixon Golf Tournament
No fixed date	at Point Pleasant	Mason County Potato Festival
No fixed date	at Flat Top Mountain, Mercer County	Lilly Family Reunion, accommodations for 70,000 persons
No fixed date	at Mouth of Seneca	Seneca-Smoke Hole Association Riding Tournament
No fixed date	at Fairmont	Dahlia Show
No fixed date	at Richwood	Spud and Splinter Homecoming and Festival, three days
No fixed date	at Bluefield	Southern Appalachian Industrial Exhibit
No fixed date	at Wheeling, Oglebay Park	Panhandle Regional 4-H Fair
No fixed date	at Marlinton	Pocahontas County Fair, six days
No fixed date	at Parsons	Tucker County Fair, four days
No fixed date	at Lewisburg	Greenbrier Valley Fair; horse show, six days

No fixed date	at Summersville	Nicholas County Fair, four days
No fixed date	at Fayetteville	Fayette County Fair, two days
No fixed date	at Jackson's Mill	State Dairy Cattle Show, three days
No fixed date	at Ripley	Jackson County Fair, five days
No fixed date	at Pennsboro	Ritchie County Fair, four days

SEPTEMBER

First week	at Weirton	Festival of Nations, two days
First Sat.	at Charleston	State 4-H Free Fair, nine days
Second week	at Charleston	Dog Show
Second week	at White Sulphur Springs	Dahlia Show
Third week	at Charleston	Dahlia Show
Midmonth	at Sutton	Braxton County Fair
Midmonth	at Petersburg	Tri-County Fair; riding tournaments, rodeo, three days
Midmonth	at Oak Hill	Fayette County Negro Fair, two days
Midmonth	at Helvetia	Helvetia Community Fair, three days
No fixed date	at Philippi	Barbour County Fair, four days
No fixed date	at Cowen	Webster County Fair, six days
No fixed date	at Glenville	Gilmer County Fair, four days
No fixed date	at Moundsville	Marshall County Fair, three days
No fixed date	at Berkeley Springs	Tomato Festival, three days
No fixed date	at Clay	Clay County Fair, four days
No fixed date	at Jackson's Mill	4-H Fair, four days

No fixed date	at Parkersburg	Dahlia Show
No fixed date	at Union	Dahlia Show
No fixed date	at Ravenswood	Ohio River Festival
No fixed date	at Wheeling	Song Festival

OCTOBER

No fixed date	at Elkins	Mountain State Forest Festival; pageant, horse show, rodeo, riding tournament, industrial exhibits, wood chopping contest, four days
No fixed date	at Huntington	Bible Pageant; parade and floats by various churches
No fixed date	at Morgantown	West Virginia Fox Hunters' Association Bench and Field Show, eight days

NOVEMBER

Midmonth	at Huntington	Tobacco Festival; exhibits and prizes for tobacco growers, six days
No fixed date	variable	Safety Day; contest among coal miners' first aid and rescue teams
No fixed date	at Martinsburg	Apple Harvest Festival

DECEMBER

| No fixed date | at Charles Town | Racing Meet of Charles Town Jockey Club |

SEASONAL EVENTS

Spring

No fixed date	at Morgantown	Spring Music Festival
No fixed date	at Charleston	Rose Show
No fixed date	at Huntington	Band Music Festival; high school bands

| No fixed date | at Bluefield | Spring Flower Show |
| No fixed date | at Wheeling | Dog Show |

Summer

| No fixed date | at Parkersburg | Horse Show |
| No fixed date | at Morgantown | Lantern Parade |

Fall

No fixed date	at Morgantown	Fall Music Festival
No fixed date	at Charles Town	Fall Flower Show
No fixed date	at Shepherdstown	Homecoming at Shepherd State Teachers College
No fixed date	at Charleston	West Virginia University *vs.* Washington & Lee football game
No fixed date	at Bluefield	Fall Flower Show

PART I
The General Background

The Way West Virginians Are

THE belief long persisted outside the State that West Virginia was a rough, untamed wilderness. The natural ruggedness of the terrain and the attendant circumstance that much of the region until recent years has been inaccessible to automobile traffic have lent credibility to this misconception. In addition, highly dramatized stories of pioneer days obscure the present.

Nicholas County once was famed for the incredible feats of its giant lumberjacks. They shaved with the bits of their axes; they felled a tree and with the trunk drove a two-foot splinter into the earth; they spat tobacco juice into a headwind in summertime 19 feet from stand. Today, Nicholas County holds an annual Spud and Splinter Festival to celebrate its two principal products—potatoes and clothespins. The bandsaws still sing their shrill tunes, but the lyrics have been expurgated by the inevitable blue pencil of civilization.

Time was, on the Tug Fork of the Big Sandy River that divides southern West Virginia and eastern Kentucky, when a boatman had only to yell Warfield! or Naugatuck!—battle cries of two small Kentucky and West Virginia towns—to be greeted by a salvo of sticks, stones, and fists. But that, again, belongs to the saga of a State that has conserved the evidences and spirit of its youth only where they will perform some useful service.

In isolated instances the traveler meets, deep in the hills, picturesque individuals with the speech and social customs of the earliest Anglo-Saxon colonists. Perhaps it is a mountain preacher quoting tirelessly, hour after hour, from the Scriptures, with only a copy of Chaucer's *Canterbury Tales* open in front of him (the book merely for show; whether he can read or not, his Scriptural quotations are culled from his capacious memory). Perhaps it is a railroading Negro, retelling stories of John Henry that the phonograph companies have not yet put on the records.

These, it is true, are rare types, the passing of which is more to be

3

regretted than hailed with provincial joy. They add their diminishing quota to the State's many contrasts, but are no longer typical of the whole. With the longer-lingering family reunion and country general store, they emphasize the distance the State has journeyed since the time when such were the rule instead of the exception. Even today, many family reunions are held annually. The widely publicized Lilly Reunion raises questioning editorial eyebrows in newspapers from Washington to Florida, when attendance figures of over 50,000 are quoted by the Associated Press. At such affairs persons of no family connection welcome each other like long lost brothers, and fraternity rises to a peak at the barbecue pit and cider jug.

West Virginia presents striking contrasts, not only among the individuals who live there and in their ways of living, but also in its industrial development and widely varying topography. Families that stem back to America's beginnings live side by side with aliens who have just taken out their first citizenship papers. Ancient water mills operate within sight of coal conveyors that are the acme of modern industrial ingenuity. The State's chief products may be arranged in such unusual groupings as coal and clothespins, pop bottles and potatoes, plate glass and chlorine, steel plates and bluing, petroleum and coin nickel, box cars and gasoline. In contrast to these utilitarian commodities, some of the finest art work in stained glass is created in West Virginia.

The scenery, too, is unusual and interesting in its diversity: high mountains are broken by broad level valleys, narrow gorges, or swiftly falling rivulets that form shining miniature falls and cascades; sloping foothills and rolling valleys are ribboned by broad rivers; bare peaks rise above forested hills and field-dotted plateaus. At the base of Ice Mountain in the Eastern Panhandle, ice formed by natural refrigeration may be found on the hottest summer day. Forests and parks with the beauty and grandeur of the wilderness are but short distances from modern cities complete with all the conveniences of the industrial age. Little Edens, where sylvan tranquillity replaces the rush of machines and where one can ride, camp, swim, hike, or just be lazy, are operated by the State government in a wide program of recreational development.

The scenic delights and recreational facilities of the Mountain State attract West Virginians themselves to a degree extraordinary in this day of long-distance driving. Aside from proximity, two explanations for this phenomenon may be suggested: urban dwellers find the interior of the State a hitherto unopened book, because many of the most interesting sections have been made accessible to automobile traffic only in recent years; and the growth of cities, removing a large part of the population from any direct contact with the natural aspects of the State, has given charm and strangeness to ordinary geographical features. The West Virginian finds it thoroughly novel as well as enjoyable to run up to Greenbrier Valley for some week-end fishing or to Lost River Park for a camping trip, instead of hieing himself away to playgrounds in other States.

This reversal of the old adage about the greener fields has inspired also the West Virginian's pride in his $72,000,000 educational plant and its 500,000 pupils. The rapid growth of educational facilities from the Ichabod Crane period of the one-room log cabin to the present fully equipped, consolidated school has been aided by the increasing tendency toward concentration in industrial centers as well as by a State program of highway construction that has made transportation of pupils an easy matter.

Cities in general have grown up wherever industry found a favorable site: Charleston because of the chemical industry; Wheeling because of steel, tobacco, and flour; Huntington as a rail center and wholesale distributing point; Fairmont, Bluefield, and Beckley because of coal and railroads and the wholesale business. This growth in city population has given West Virginia another vivid contrast: while urban centers developed, the rural counties, for the most part, retained their early customs and ways of living until community characteristics now range from rural self-containment and semi-rural lethargy to the bustling, jostling vitality of the metropolis.

Individual West Virginians vary as much as the geographical divisions and industrial occupations. From other States and from every part of the world the stream of immigration has brought its load of custom and habit into the State. Here each element has been set free to work its way into the composite life of West Virginia, to act as a leaven or to be submerged and obliterated. In many cases, the racial or national culture persists in its original form.

The earliest human stock of West Virginia, the Indian, was replaced by a pioneer breed that was chiefly Anglo-Saxon and North European. This group introduced the Negro slaves. Later, immigrants came from Middle and South Europe, from Asia, and from Africa. Economic opportunity for unskilled labor in the mines brought an influx of southern Negroes after the War between the States. At the same time, mining also attracted many of the poor whites of the South as well as Kentucky, Tennessee, and North Carolina mountaineers. More recently industrial progress in chemicals and other fields brought new immigration from western, northern, and eastern States.

West Virginia has never been of the North, the South, the East, or the West. Today the State more closely resembles Pennsylvania than Virginia; but one section, the Eastern Panhandle, cannot be differentiated from the Old Dominion. The farmer of this section shows few of the traits of the southern miner, who may be of mixed Irish, Italian, and Hungarian extraction. On the other hand, the southern mountaineer is usually of unmixed national heritage and does not intermarry with other stocks; frequently he does not know why he refuses to mix; he just feels that way. In a single community one can listen to all the dialects of America. Side by side live families and individuals whose former homes have been in Minnesota, California, Texas, Georgia, New York, Massachusetts, Maryland, Mississippi, Colorado, Nevada, Canada, Nova Scotia, Mexico, and the South and Central American nations. Economic opportunity has lured them to West Virginia, and they continue to come, bringing with them their contrasting backgrounds, personalities, and ways of living.

True, there are representative types in West Virginia: the southern miner, his face and overalls coated with coal dust, slow of speech yet cursing fluently to pad his thin conversation, tenaciously holding to the ideas of his fathers in religion, and striking boldly for what he considers justice in social, economic, and political life; the hillbilly, shunning too much modern comfort, going barefoot in summer, rejecting newfangled educational theories for his young, and convinced of man's inheritance of the image of God; the new industrial worker, living urbanely in town and commuting to work in outlying factories, slick-haired and neatly dressed, newspaper-read, opinionated; the farmer, easygoing, hard-working, taciturn, and indifferent to superficial success, trusting to Providence, the weather, and his own hard muscles.

And there are members of the professions and occupations to be found everywhere, but modified by conditions peculiar to the State: the editor of a so-called independent newspaper, parroting even in private life the ideas that the owner of the paper has decided are appropriate for public consumption; the small-town merchant, wavering between support of the union or the employer, not quite sure on which side of his bread he will find more butter. Then, of course, there is the West Virginian of substance, who is educated, successful in business or the professions, and a leader in public affairs, but who is little different from his kind elsewhere; he may be an aristocrat, with an unbroken line of successful forbears, but more likely he is a bottom rail on the top of the fence, raised to eminence by his own innate ability or by fortuitous circumstances. These, and many others, are here. But there is no single type that may be called the West Virginian.

Natural Setting

LATERALLY and vertically, the most marked physical characteristic of West Virginia is its irregularity. The word rugged ap-
plies with unusual appropriateness to both its outline and its
surface configuration.

The State's 1,170-mile boundary, which for the most part follows
the course of rivers or the line of mountain ranges, encloses a total
area of only 24,170 square miles, of which 148 are water surface.
Fortieth in size among the States of the Union, West Virginia, nevertheless, extends its panhandles over a surprisingly wide range of latitude and longitude. The easternmost tip has the same longitude as
Rochester, New York, and the most westerly as Port Huron, Michigan; the Northwest Panhandle pushes into a latitude well north of
that of Pittsburgh, Pennsylvania, while in the opposite direction the
State dips farther south than Richmond, Virginia. Because of this pecu-
liarity and the fact that the State is in the very heart of the Appalachian Plateau, West Virginia has been described as 'the most southern
of the northern, the most northern of the southern, and the most
western of the eastern, and the most eastern of the western States.'

For a distance of 277 miles the northwestern bank of the Ohio
River forms the northwestern boundary between West Virginia and
Ohio; and the Big Sandy and Tug Fork Rivers divide the State from
Kentucky and Virginia for about 114 miles on the south and west.
High water, high spirits, and southern hospitality probably placed this
line where it is today. When Kentucky was formed, the Big Sandy
River was recognized as the boundary between the State and what
is now West Virginia, but the main branch of the river had never
been properly defined until the Virginia-Kentucky boundary commis-
sion met, in 1799, where the Levisa and Tug Rivers join the Big
Sandy. It was the commission's purpose to determine the larger of
the two branches and designate it the boundary between the States.
History is vague about details, but it is recorded that Tug Fork, nor-

8

mally much the smaller of the streams, was flooded by heavy rains, which at the same time drove the commission to seek amusement indoors. With whisky and weather both working in its favor, the Tug was adjudged the principal stream and became the boundary. By this decision an area of about 1,000 square miles was lost to West Virginia.

This loss was offset in part, however, by gains on the Maryland side. By fixing the Potomac and its North Branch as the streams that separate West Virginia and Maryland for 218 miles, the United States Supreme Court saved to West Virginia the land lying between the North Branch and the South Branch of the Potomac River. Maryland had claimed the area on grounds that the South Branch—the greater of the two—was the proper boundary. A crooked line following the crests of Dividing Ridge and the Allegheny Mountains for 365 miles would roughly mark the boundary between West Virginia and Virginia on the south and east.

The remainder of the State's boundary, some 200 miles in extent, is principally man-made. The grant of Pennsylvania to William Penn in 1681 provided for a southern boundary 'extending from the Delaware River five degrees west.' In conformity with this Royal charter, the Mason-Dixon Line, completed in 1784, stopped short of the Ohio River by about 16 miles; and thus was created the Northern Panhandle of West Virginia, which reaches fingerlike 64 miles northward from the main area of the State. The Deakins line (named for its early surveyor), running northward from the source of the Potomac to the Mason-Dixon Line, forms the eastern boundary between West Virginia and Maryland. The Eastern Panhandle in the Potomac section, the easternmost part of the State, is almost entirely surrounded by Maryland and Virginia; it is joined to the rest of West Virginia by a narrow neck of land only 15 miles wide.

Topographically, West Virginia is as irregular as it is in outline. The range in elevation from 240 feet near Harpers Ferry to 4,860 feet on Spruce Knob gives it a mean altitude of 1,500 feet, the highest of any State east of the Mississippi River. The divide areas are usually sharp and the valleys narrow and V-shaped.

Most of West Virginia's larger rivers and numerous streams flow toward the Ohio, which with its important tributary systems—the Monongahela, the New, and the Kanawha—drains about 21,000 square miles of the State's territory. Drainage in the northeastern section of the State is through the Potomac River by way of the James, the North and the South Branches, and other smaller streams. The New River, with its source in the Blue Ridge Mountains of North Carolina, crosses the southern boundary line between Virginia and West Virginia and is joined by the Gauley River at Gauley Bridge to form the Great Kanawha. The New and the Great Kanawha together make up a stream that flows across the entire State. Northern Pocahontas County is a major divide area in which rise the headwaters of many large streams; here is the source of the South Branch of the Potomac, and the sources of the Gauley, Elk, Cheat, Greenbrier, and Tygarts Valley Rivers, all tributaries of the Ohio.

The State is divided into two physiographic provinces by an escarpment known as the Allegheny Front, which extends in an irregular line from Keyser, on the West Virginia-Maryland boundary, southwestward to Bluefield, on the West Virginia-Virginia Line.

East of the Front is the Appalachian Valley and Ridge Province. The drainage of this portion of West Virginia, 4,000 square miles in extent, is of the trellis pattern characteristic of such strongly folded areas. Weathering and erosion have etched into bold relief the strong and massive sandstone strata and at the same time have created valleys in the weaker limestones and shales. In this manner parallel ridges and valleys have been formed, with a general northeast-southwest trend. Some streams flow in a trough or valley for 40 or 50 miles, cross a ridge through a water gap, and then resume the original direction in a parallel valley. The rectangular pattern thus formed is known as trellis drainage. Most of the Valley and Ridge Province of West Virginia is drained by the Potomac River. A little of the western part of this area is in the Ohio River watershed, and a section of about 80 square miles in Monroe County drains into the James River.

West of the Front, covering an area of more than 20,000 square miles, is a part of the Appalachian Plateau Province known as the Allegheny Plateau. The drainage of the Allegheny Plateau is dendritic (treelike), a type of drainage occurring where rock strata are nearly horizontal and the guidance of streams is slight. The drainage waters of this part of the State eventually reach the Ohio River.

Rough and rugged, West Virginia comes honestly by its name, the Mountain State. Moses Bennett, whose home on Spruce Knob is the highest habitation in the State, is credited with the comment that 'It's right spread out, and it's mighty rough; but it's a damned good State for the shape it's in.' There is little flat land other than the narrow flood plains of the river bottoms, the broadest of which, in the Ohio Valley, is at no place more than two miles wide. The exceptions are a few limited plateaus atop the Cheat and Allegheny ranges and the rolling country of the Eastern Panhandle, where the Valley of Virginia, overspreading State lines, includes the whole of Jefferson County and the larger part of Berkeley.

CLIMATE

The climate of West Virginia is of the humid continental type, with hot summers and cool to cold winters. Because of the wide range of altitudes, rainfall and temperature vary greatly from section to section. Prevailing winds are from the southwest, and the area is affected by the constant succession of the high and low pressure areas of the prevailing westerlies. The Eastern Panhandle is influenced by proximity to the Atlantic Ocean and has the climate of the Atlantic Slope.

According to the U. S. Weather Bureau: The mean annual temperature of various stations in West Virginia ranges from 56° in the southwestern counties to 48° in the higher parts of the mountain counties. For the greater part of the State, the mean is about 52° to 53°. The coldest temperature recorded was 35° below zero at Lost Creek, Harrison County, in February, 1899. However, temperatures lower than 15° below zero or above 100° are quite unusual. In normal years, the mean January temperature is between 30° to 35°; the mean July temperature, about 75°.

As the atmosphere reaches higher elevations in moving from west to east across the State, it is cooled, and precipitation occurs. Therefore, in general, the heaviest rainfall is in regions of highest altitude. East of the high ridges and in the larger valleys of the eastern part of the State the rainfall is somewhat less than in the State as a whole. Distribution of precipitation throughout the year is quite uniform. Normally, July is the wettest month. The mean annual precipitation for West Virginia is about 45 inches. Differences in precipitation east and west of the Allegheny Front are marked. The region of Pickens, Randolph County, has an annual rainfall of approximately 60 inches, while on the eastern side of the Allegheny Front the village of Upper Tract in Pendleton County has an annual rainfall of only about 29 inches, which is less than that of Michigan and somewhat more than that of Nebraska.

Snow usually lasts only a few days in the lowlands but may persist for months in the highlands. The effect of altitude upon temperature is clearly demonstrated by a comparison of Terra Alta and Morgantown, between which the air-line distance is less than 30 miles and the difference in elevation is about 2,000 feet; the growing season of lowland Morgantown is about two weeks longer than that of upland Terra Alta, and several times every winter rain may be falling in Morgantown when snow is blocking the highways at Terra Alta.

GEOLOGIC HISTORY

More directly and more manifestly than are most States, West Virginia is the product of its geological foundation—the determining factor in the State's social development and industrial growth as well as the source of its great natural beauty. The inaccessibility of this mountainous region left it an eastern frontier long after the westward sweep of settlement; the mineral wealth in coal, oil, gas, iron, limestone, and brine ultimately led to industrial development; and the rugged surface, with its forest-clad valleys and mountains, leaves much of the State today a lovely wilderness.

With the exception of a few acres of crystalline rock in the eastern part of the State, the 30,000-foot layer of rock that covers West Virginia was deposited as sediment during the Paleozoic era. At the beginning of this era, which lasted some 340,000,000 years and ended at least 200,000,000 years ago, a long trough, or geosyncline, extended from the present Alabama northeastward to the area of New Brunswick, Canada. East of this geosyncline was a continent known to historical geologists as Old Appalachia, because of the high mounts from which eroded sediments were carried by streams to the Appalachian trough.

During most of the Paleozoic era sediments were deposited in an arm of the ocean that extended into the trough. Marine fossils in the rocks are evidence that sea water was present. The character of the sedimentary rocks shows that the area covered by the continental sea varied greatly from time to time; thus a formation that is hundreds of feet thick in one place may be very thin in another and absent entirely from a third.

It is apparent that in the early periods of the Paleozoic, the gradients of the streams flowing from the land area east of the Appalachian geosyncline were low, for the sediments were very fine. After an initial sand deposition, lime and clay were deposited during the first two periods. Thousands of feet of limestone of this age outcrop in eastern West Virginia.

At times swampy conditions prevailed in the Appalachian area and vegetation thrived. Successive layers of peat, formed by the partial decomposition of vegetable matter, buried by sediments through millions of years, changed gradually into bituminous coal, West Virginia's greatest natural resource. The Carboniferous period, during which the coal measures were laid, occurred near the close of the Paleozoic era. The sea disappeared from the Appalachian region and the era closed with conditions no longer favorable for the formation of peat.

In the beginning, when sediments from Old Appalachia and other higher lands were carried to the geosyncline, the area was depressed by the weight of the material. A shift occurred at a great depth, masses of rock were forced upward, and erosion was so increased that there was a nearly continual deposition of material in the geosyncline. The process continued with slight disturbances of the beds until in places thirty or forty thousand feet of sediments were laid down. The old rock beneath was pushed into the earth so far that the Appalachian geosynclinal area became a zone of weakness. Toward the end of the Paleozoic era, because of lateral pressure on the earth's crust, the strata were folded and forced upward, and great faults occurred on the eastern side of the geosyncline. This major disturbance, known as the Appalachian Revolution, began in the Pennsylvanian period and lasted through the Permian period, which terminated the Paleozoic era.

During the succeeding Mesozoic and Cenozoic eras the West Virginia region was alternately worn down to a plain and uplifted. Although the land must have been appreciably warped from time to time, there is no evidence that pronounced folding has taken place since the Permian period. During the early part of the Tertiary period of the Cenozoic, the period preceding the ice age, West Virginia and the surrounding area were eroded to a nearly featureless peneplain. Then the region was again uplifted with slight warping. Erosive forces etched into relief the more resistant rocks and formed valleys in the weaker strata. No doubt bold ridges and narrow plateaus capped with sandstone and conglomerate characterized the topography in eastern West Virginia at this time. The upper Carboniferous rocks, being weaker, were eroded more than the underlying rock, and the western part of the State was again reduced to a low-lying plain near sea level. Streams meandered over the land, forming wide flood plains. Near the close of the Tertiary period, the region was uplifted a second time and streams sculptured the landscape we see today. Many of the ancient meanders have been preserved, although the streams have worn channels hundreds of feet below the levels of the old flood plains.

Although the Pleistocene continental ice sheets did not touch any portion of West Virginia, they did cause a modification of drainage within the area. Frank Leverett, I. C. White, and other eminent geologists have pointed out the effect of glaciation on a majority of the streams of the Allegheny Plateau. Before the ice age, Lake Erie was not in existence. The streams of western West Virginia flowed across the present course of the Ohio River across the area of Ohio to the Erie Basin, and thence to the ancient St. Lawrence River. The ice extended over the larger part of Ohio and into Pennsylvania as far south as Beaver Falls. The Monongahela River followed essentially its present course as far as Pittsburgh. From here it flowed down the present valley of the Ohio to the mouth of what is now the Beaver River, thence to the Erie Basin. When ice blocked the flow of the Monongahela at Beaver Falls, water was impounded in the Monongahela Valley to a depth of about 1,100 feet, and the great lake thus formed overflowed to the southward. There are evidences of two overflow channels into the Little Kanawha drainage near Weston and of one channel near Salem. The fourth low divide through which the lake waters poured was between the present locations of New Martinsville, West Virginia, and Sardis, Ohio, on the Ohio River. Owing chiefly to the steeper gradient of the south-flowing stream, this overflow channel was lowered more rapidly than its three competitors and finally became the sole outlet of Lake Monongahela. Fishing Creek, with other streams, apparently had formed a valley that reached the ancient Monongahela at a point where this river turned northward to pass through the present Beaver Valley. As the waters of Lake Monongahela receded, the channel of the Ohio River was formed. South of the divide near New Martinsville the drainage followed somewhat the course of the present Ohio. With later advances of the ice, the stream bed was further modified as the Ohio became a marginal glacial stream.

As Lake Monongahela subsided it formed terraces in the various valleys. These terraces, marking successive levels of the old lake, may be observed along the Monongahela River from Clarksburg, West Virginia, to Pittsburgh, Pennsylvania.

An unusual physiographic feature in the southwestern part of the State is Teays Valley, a trough extending from Scary on the Kanawha River to Huntington on the Ohio River. The floor of the valley is only about 100 feet above the flood plain of the Kanawha. It is evident that the Teays Valley was at one time the course of the Kanawha, but the cause of the diversion of the river has not been fully explained; possibly the valley was only an emergency outlet for the Kanawha, and the river resumed its former course when some temporary barrier was removed. In recent geologic time the Kanawha drainage system has been robbed of the eastward-flowing streams of the Atlantic Slope as erosion has moved the divide westward. Owing in part to the recency of the uplift of the land and in part to the resistant Carboniferous sandstones, the New River in West Virginia has entrenched itself in a gorge far below the old peneplain level.

ANIMAL LIFE

Pronounced differences in altitude, annual rainfall, and topography have fostered an extraordinary number of floral species and have favored a great variety of fauna in the State.

No fewer than 56 species and subspecies of mammals and 268 similar groupings of birds have been identified in West Virginia; they range from the denizens of the Canadian life zone, who nest and breed in the higher elevations of the Alleghenies, to the Carolinian zone species, who congregate in the lower altitudes after migrating from the south through the valleys of the Ohio and Potomac Rivers.

The larger mammals that menaced the pioneers are extinct, except for the great black bear and the bay lynx, or wildcat, which still haunt the deep reaches of mountain timber covering the Allegheny ridges on the State's eastern boundary. The gray timber wolf, the panther, the elk, and the American bison have entirely disappeared, one of the last bison having been killed at the mouth of the Tygarts Valley River in 1825, long after the roaming herds had crossed the Ohio River for the last time in search of new pasturage.

The smaller fur-bearing mammals that provided food, clothing, and revenue for early settlers, trappers, and wilderness scouts are greatly diminished in number and variety; some, like the beaver and otter, are nearly extinct. The raccoon, mink, skunk, woodchuck, opossum, and gray and red fox are still numerous, as are smaller species, such as the squirrels, mice, moles, shrews, rabbits, and hares. Six species of bats may be found hanging in grisly clusters in mountain caves.

The steady increase of population has slowly driven the large mammals into the more inaccessible areas of the State's 9,000,000 acres of forest land, and has resulted in total destruction of depredatory species and the near extinction of game animals, except those protected by closed seasons. White-tailed deer, however, are plentiful and are hunted enthusiastically by sportsmen during the open season; deep in the heavy pine forests and in the matted underbrush of cut-over timberland, numerous black bears are taken each year.

Red foxes and raccoons are hunted regularly throughout the State, while the big gray fox is common in the southern border counties. The wildcat of the eastern and southern mountain slopes is fair prey at all times. Hares occur and cottontails are plentiful, the larger hares being found in the forests at higher elevations, the cottontails in the brush piles of farm country, especially in the Ohio Valley and on the rolling flats between ranges of hills. Squirrels inhabit hardwood forests and stands of oak timber throughout the State. These, and quail, ruffed grouse, and blue pike, bass, and trout, offer the outdoor man a variety of sport.

The avifauna of the State is thriving and varied because of the considerable food sources, the extensive timbered regions, and the numerous rivers and clear-flowing small streams. The rivers and small lakes attract brownish-grey grebes, popularly called hell-divers, great black diving loons with laughing maniacal call, ducks, and geese during migration perods. Long-winged gulls and terns and slate-colored cormorants driven inshore by sea storms rest on inland streams. The great blue heron, green heron, and American bittern come up annually from the southern swamps after nesting season. Plover, quail, woodcock, snipe, and sandpipers are found in the woodlots of agricultural sections, along the banks of streams, and in the underbrush of second-growth timberlands. Predatory birds ,such as the great horned owl and his numerous cousins, ten species of hawks, the bald eagle, and occasionally even the rare golden eagle, falcons, and ospreys take an annual toll of rodents and small game, while the turkey vulture or buzzard plans his scavenging from a vantage point high over the fields and woods.

Songsters and birds of gorgeous plumage add melody and color to the pageant of wildlife. The call of the whipporwill mingles with the staccato tattoo of any of seven brilliantly marked woodpeckers. The Baltimore oriole, bobolink, purple finch, scarlet and black tanager, indigo bunting, cardinal, and numerous vireos brighten with flecks of color the hues of woods and field. Warblers, mocking birds, bluebirds, robins, and thrushes, the last the best known of American songbirds, add their melodies to the overtones of sighing winds and the undertones of rustling branches. Comparatively silent and unnoticed but omnipresent are wrens, nuthatches, and sparrows.

West Virginia's streams tempt the angler with brook, rainbow, and Loch Leven trout, muskellunge, smallmouthed and largemouthed bass, and walleyed pike among the game fish, and with carp, rock bass, catfish, perch, sunfish, bluegills, suckers, and eels. The lean, bony gar, known for its vicious nature and long pointed head, is found in the State's larger streams.

Numerous amphibia of interest to the naturalist, including several species of frogs, toads, and salamanders, the last commonly called 'mud puppies,' are widely distributed, as are the many reptiles. Several species of turtles and a few of lizards are plentiful in streams and marshes, and two poisonous reptiles, the timber rattlesnake and the copperhead, are shunned by campers. More numerous are the nonpoisonous snakes, such as the puff adder or blowing viper, the black racer, the green snake, the common water snake, the black snake, the garter snake, and other smaller species.

PLANT LIFE

The plant life of West Virginia is abundant and highly diversified. It is abundant because more than half of the State's area is still forested, and diversified because the topography varies so much in elevation that it furnishes a natural habitat for plants from three life zones, the Canadian, Alleghenian, and Carolinian. Although the State has the highest average altitude east of the Rockies, its numerous heights and depressions and the extremes of annual rainfall in the different sections provide favorable living conditions for more than 3,400 known species, ranging from the great spruce of the higher elevations to the prickly-pear cactus and other semidesert plants found in the South Branch Valley.

The mountain peaks are capped with evergreen growths that tower in serried splendor over surrounding areas of deciduous forest; mountain glades suggestive of the great northern tundra are mottled with cranberries, chokeberries, and round-leaved sundew; while mosses, ferns, and liverworts abound in the shade of near-by rock gorges. On moist mountain slopes and in low-altitude ravines thrive the beech, hemlock, and maple, shouldering great growths of oak and hickory, the dominant forest types of the State. As one descends from the heights to the lowlands, he reaches first the old flood plains, on which sugar maples are the most prominent, then the young flood plains where the willow, sycamore, and river maple predominate.

Red cedar, yellow poplar, black walnut, hickory, beech, ash, cottonwood, hemlock, buckeye, maple, pitch pine, aspen, butternut, chinquapin, and gum trees are distributed throughout the State where climate and soil are most conducive to their growth. On Scott's Mountain a stand of 2,280 acres, consisting largely of gum, is famous for its heavy burden of mistletoe, two carloads being shipped from this section each year.

The extent and variety of flowering-plant growth have made the State a botanist's paradise. Although botanists have discovered a number of rare and peculiar species, certain plants receive much attention for their seasonal dominance, such as the rhododendron, which is the official State flower, the laurel, the blueberry, and the huckleberry, the last two being of some economic importance. Along with the everchanging panorama of wild floral beauty, more than 200 flowering trees and shrubs provide an impressive spectacle, among which the pink blossom of the wild crabapple, in contrast to the green of budding vegetation in early April, is most conspicuous, alternating with the white-blossomed hawthorn; both flourish everywhere in the State on mountain slopes and in river valleys. Spring also brings the white or creamy blossoms of the dogwood, the pinkish flowers of the redbud, and the catkins of the pussywillow. The yellow poplar and linden produce attractive blossoms with a sweet fragrance; the latter is called the 'bee tree' because of the swarms of bees that seek its nectar.

The official herald of spring, though not the first flower to bloom, is the spring beauty, a small white flower striped with lavender, which often shoots up before the last snows of March have melted, and gives a hint of the enveloping beauty to come. Following its lead, the gleaming white bloodroot, the yellow dogtooth violet, the white and pale-blue blossoms of the hepatica, and the softly colored, tiny bluets arrive to open the season. As the meadows turn green, the dark- and light-blue, yellow, and white violets mingle with the green and gold buttercups in mantling fields and hillsides.

The full flush of floral beauty is first reached in April and May. A brilliant pageant of wild flowers begins its seasonal procession, with the wakerobin, the golden ragwort, the purplish pink and white trailing arbutus, and the yellow and orange wild azalea forming the advance guard, accompanied by the white anemone, the tangy wild ginger, and the blue violet growing in azure masses in mountain dells and along stream beds. These are closely followed by tripetaled brilliantly colored trilliums, bright yellow dandelions, snowy white strawberry blossoms, purple-hued wild geraniums, and the golden cinquefoil. The cliffs begin to display a brilliant appearance as warm weather approaches and the wild columbine and azalea bloom. On the hillsides the jack-in-the-pulpit rears its white-and-purple head, and in humid woodland spots the crested iris of imperial hue and the pink ladyslipper come to life. The 36 species of orchids native to the State blossom from early spring to late fall in the more mountainous regions, where 60 species of ferns are found on windswept slopes and in cool, moist, wooded dells.

Midsummer bedecks the mountain slopes with unending acres of pink-and-white and rose-purple rhododendron. The meadows burst into living glory with the blossoming of the black-eyed Susan and the sprightly white and yellow daisies. The smaller and earlier field flowers are replaced by these and by the stately, columnar field lily and the wild rose. Blooms of the St.-John's-wort, blue lobelia, orange milkweed, white meadow rue, and virgin's-bower add variety and richness to the lush beauty of the dominant flower forms.

The waning summer brings a final burst of climbing and twining morning glories of mingling colors, blue, purple, and white asters, ironweed, joe-pye weed, and shining goldenrod, which blooms until November in some sections of the State.

As might be expected, rare forms are often found among this mass of floral growth. The box huckleberry, believed to be one of the oldest plants, if not the oldest, in existence, is found in Summers, Greenbrier, and Monroe Counties, where it was first discovered in 1892. It was for years thought to be a native of this area alone, but has since been discovered elsewhere. The dainty yellow coltsfoot, a native of the northern latitudes, is found only at Greer in Monongalia County. The thornless blackberry, a shade form of the mountain blackberry, has mystified scientists, as it produces berries on a thornless bush when growing wild but develops thorns when cultivated. The southern chain fern, a native of the Carolinas, has established itself on Droop Mountain, as has the delicate creamy-white grass-of-Parnassus, a member of the saxifrage family.

The red pine grows naturally on North Fork Mountain, the farthest south it has ever been discovered, as does the three-toothed cinquefoil, a plant at home as far north as Greenland. The extremely rare Phymosia was discovered near the Virginia-West Virginia Line in 1927; it is a native to only one other known place in the world, a small island in the Kankakee River in Illinois. In contrast, the eastern prickly pear, representative of a desert family, grows in central and northeastern counties.

Trees notable for their historic association or record-breaking size are plentiful in the State. The Mingo Oak, when it was cut down in 1938, was the largest white oak in the world, and was 576 years old. Growing near Williamson in Mingo County, the tree was 145 feet in height and 30 feet, 9 inches in circumference at the base. A cross section may be seen in the Museum in Charleston. The largest trees known in the eastern United States were the Washington Sycamores on Three Brother Island. When he visited the Ohio Valley in 1771, George Washington was amazed at their size, and estimated in his diary that one of the group was 61 feet in circumference at the base. A Tygarts Valley apple tree, the largest known of its species, produces 100 bushels of fruit each season and has a recorded total yield of 6,000 bushels. The Marlinton Corner Oak, or King George's Oak, in Pocahontas County is famed as the boundary marker used by surveyors in 1751 in locating a 100,000-acre grant in the Greenbrier River Valley, granted by King George to the Greenbrier Company.

The hillsides and ravines at varying altitudes offer many species of edible berries, all of which are picked, though few are used commercially. Blueberries are found on a 20-mile ridge in Randolph County in such great quantities that the crop is never gleaned, regardless of the number of pickers, while blackberries, raspberries, huckleberries, and cranberries flourish in other sections of the State.

An extensive assortment of unusual flora is found in the Cranberry Glades in Pocahontas County. Once a lake bed, the terrain now resembles that of a northern glacial bog, with alder thickets, sedges, mosses, and lichens covering spongy soil. Here are found red spruce, hemlock, and various hardwood species bordering large bogs in which two varieties of cranberries grow in abundance. A giant hawthorn, 40 feet in height and thought to be the largest of its species known, was observed here by a scientist in 1927. Terrestrial orchids and the sundew, one of the few carnivorous plants, are also found here. These, with the buck bean, bog rosemary, and other flowers springing from the carpet of mosses, lichens, and low shrubs, form a patchwork quilt of gray, green, rose and brown, laid within a forest of red spruce, hemlock, and northern hardwoods.

Natural Resources and Conservation

RICH mineral deposits are responsible for most of West Virginia's industrial development; tremendous water power, actual and potential, exists in the steep gradients of its many rivers; despite early waste and exploitation, millions of acres of forest land under the present conservation program again rank among the State's most valuable assets; and in cultivation of the fertile soil of the river bottoms and the limited rolling land a fifth of the gainfully employed find their livelihood.

West Virginia is the most important bituminous coal-producing State in the Union. It leads not only in annual production and in extent of reserves, but also in quality of coal produced. Investigations by the State geological survey indicate that the total coal resources, three or more feet in seam thickness and recoverable under present methods, originally amounted to about 50,000,000,000 tons. Total coal removed by the end of 1933 was approximately 2,860,000,000 tons, leaving 47,140,000,000 minable tons in the ground, or enough to last at the present rate of production for approximately 400 years. Thinner seams will provide an additional total of probably 12,000,000,000 tons, which would be profitably recoverable under improved systems of mining. Of the 24,170 square miles within the State's limits, a total of 9,500 square miles, or 38.8 per cent, is underlaid with coal. This area covers 43 of the 55 counties in whole or in part, and coal is mined in commercial quantities in 34 counties. Coal formations exist in nearly 100 separate seams, of which 60 show minable possibilities, 41 are of practical minable thickness, and 30 are being worked at the present time.

More than two-thirds of the State lies within the Appalachian bituminous area, which extends from Pennsylvania to Alabama, and the bituminous and semibituminous coals mined from its seams are well adapted for all fuel purposes and the manufacture of by-products. That this natural resource has inestimable potentialities is further evidenced by the fact that the State ranks first in the production of bituminous coal but only eighth in the value of its coal by-products.

Other outstanding mineral resources in West Virginia, listed according to their relative commercial importance in 1938, are natural gas, petroleum, natural gasoline, limestone, brine, sand and gravel, clays, and building stone.

The producing area for natural gas is, roughly, the western half of the State. This most nearly perfect fuel—so described because it can easily be transported through pipe lines and because it leaves no residue when burned—is the product of prehistoric vegetable and animal matter, buried under the earth by volcanic disturbances millions of years ago. About 1930, geologists estimated that West Virginia's supply probably would be exhausted in 30 to 40 years, but fields were discovered in 1937 and 1938. In any event, the State still has vast potential wealth in this resource, especially if the development of by-products continues. One of the newer developments is polymerization—commonly known as cracking—of one of the principal elements of the gas, butane, to produce gasoline of exceptional anti-knock efficiency; and at the present rate of production West Virginia's natural gas could be turned into 40,000,000 gallons of this gasoline annually. Almost all the State's natural gas is now consumed either as a raw fuel or natural-gas gasoline. By processing and refining, it would be possible to increase the value several times.

West Virginia's petroleum-bearing sands lie in the same general area as its natural gas fields—in 33 counties extending from the tip of the Northern Panhandle to the State's southernmost borders. Like natural gas, petroleum has by-products of great value; both may be processed to produce numerous organic chemicals, such as olefins, alcohols, ketones, esters, glycols, and glycol ethers.

One of the great and comparatively undeveloped resources in West Virginia is limestone, found in what geologists describe as almost unlimited quantities in the Eastern Panhandle and in a half dozen counties extending along the eastern edge of the State. Jefferson and Berkeley counties are large producers of metallurgical limestone and dolomites for fluxing purposes in the steel industry in the Pittsburgh area, but their utilization for the production of Portland cement, chemicals, rock-wool, agricultural lime, road-ballast and road-surfacing materials, concrete aggregates, and other commodities has been developed only slightly. In 1938 the State had only two cement plants, and only one producing mineral-wool, which is used extensively in the rapidly expanding insulating industry.

Salt production was one of the first important industries in West Virginia, especially in the Kanawha Valley; and salt brines, used in the comparatively new chemical industry, have again attained importance. The chief constituent of these brines is sodium chloride, the raw material for production of sodium carbonate, or soda ash, and of chlorine, now in demand for bleaching pulpwood in the southern paper industry. Valuable by-products include calcium and magnesium chlorides and bromine. Twenty of the 55 counties can produce salt brine of good quality, and rock salt is found in large quantities in the northwestern part of the State.

Extensive beds of building sands and gravel are found throughout West Virginia, and in some areas, principally in Morgan, Preston, Monongalia, Randolph, and Upshur Counties, are virtually unlimited sources of fine-quality glass sands, ranging from 98 to 100 per cent pure silica. Large quantities of molding sand are available along the flood plains of the Ohio and Big Sandy Rivers. While the State has vast supplies of natural nonrefractory clays and of shales that may be ground into clays suitable for such manufactures as face brick, paving brick, and tile, it possesses only a limited reserve of high-grade refractory clays; and most of the materials used in the china and clay-products industries are imported—one of the few instances in which West Virginia is a large producer of a finished product from non-native materials.

Every county in the State has at least one large horizon of sandstone that has been, or could be, quarried for building stone. The stone—red, pink, brown, or gray in color—varies from massive to flaggy in type and from coarse-grained to fine-grained in texture. There is one large deposit of marble in Pocahontas County, and some West Virginia limestone is used for building purposes.

The State's estimated reserve of 300,000,000 tons of iron ore lies for the most part in the mountainous regions, and commercial production is not regarded as likely to be profitable until the exhaustion of the more easily minable deposits around Lake Superior and near Birmingham, Alabama. Some manganese is mined in Greenbrier and Monroe Counties, and lead has been found in the Appalachian area, although not in sufficient quantities to warrant mining operations.

West Virginia's soil derives primarily from its native limestones and sandstones; and although as many as 11 types of soil are found in a single county, their principal element is either sand or lime, sometimes both. The Eastern Panhandle and the eastern part of the State in general have soils especially rich in lime content. The soils of central West Virginia, with more sandstones and shales, contain less lime, but the combination of elements provides a soil that covers most of the bluegrass area. There is still less limestone in the western counties, but in the river valleys the lack of lime as a natural fertilizer is offset by the presence of shales and alluvial deposits providing fertile soils.

Although the greater part of West Virginia's first-growth timber has been depleted, the second-growth forests and reforested areas will supply a substantial lumber industry for many years. The hardwoods, listed in order of approximate commercial importance, include white oak, yellow poplar, red oak, sugar maple, chestnut oak, black cherry, black birch, yellow birch, basswood, red maple, white ash, beech, chestnut, cucumber, black locust, hickory, gum, buckeye, ironwood, and white walnut. The conifers, usually found on the high mountain ridges and plateaus and in the deep river gorges, include red spruce, white pine, hemlock, balsam fir, and scrub pine. There are several other native varieties, although in stands too small for commercial use, and some not indigenous to the State are being introduced by Civilian Conservation Corps reforestation projects.

West Virginia has one national forest entirely within its borders—the Monongahela, embracing a purchase area of 1,700,000 acres. The George Washington lies partly in Virginia but has 94,000 acres in four West Virginia counties. There are six State forests: Cooper's Rock, 13,000 acres; Seneca, 11,049 acres; Kumbrabow, 9,422 acres; Cabwaylingo, 7,000 acres; Kanawha, 6,705 acres; and Greenbrier, 5,000 acres. In addition 5,500,000 acres of forest lands are privately owned.

With its broken topography providing numerous natural channels, with an inestimable number of deep-hidden springs, and with an annual average rainfall of more than 43 inches, West Virginia is virtually covered with a network of rivers and smaller streams. The larger waterways are a valuable part of the State's transportation system, and rapid progress is being made in harnessing them for hydroelectric power. In 1938 West Virginia had 11 hydroelectric generating plants in operation, with a total capacity of 343,800 horsepower. It is estimated that the streams of the State are capable of producing 1,250,000 horsepower, a greater potential total than that of any other State east of the Continental Divide with the exception of New York.

West Virginia has a number of mineral springs the waters of which are highly valued for medicinal uses. Only two, Berkeley and White Sulphur, are now developed as health resorts and vacation centers, but mineral waters are bottled and shipped from some of the others, including Capon Springs, which has a daily flow of 240,000 gallons of water with a lithia content. The possibilities for development and wider utilization of these springs make them a valuable natural resource.

CONSERVATION

Conservation in West Virginia comes under four general classifications: (1) forestry and reforestation, (2) fish and game protection and propagation, (3) soil erosion prevention, and (4) flood control and stream pollution elimination. All are handled under Federal and State agencies in co-operation, with semiofficial and private organizations assisting in the work in many instances.

The earliest record of any kind of conservation in the State was made in 1699, when the Virginia House of Burgesses forbade the burning of brush to drive deer into the open. In 1849 Virginia adopted a simple code of game laws—freely ignored because no means of enforcement was provided—which was adopted by West Virginia when the new State was created in 1863. The West Virginia legislature during the next 34 years adopted various laws intended to protect certain species of game, fish, and birds, but no State enforcement was provided until the office of fish and game warden was created in 1901. Forest protection was added to his duties in 1909, and in 1913 the Federal and State governments started a combined forest-fire protection program. The State established a game and fish commission in 1921; and in 1933 a law was enacted creating the present State Conservation Commission, which took over the functions of the earlier body. At the same time, the conservation, fish, game, and forestry laws were revised, chiefly to permit co-operation with the Federal Government in emergency conservation work.

The commission is charged with the conservation and development of lands, forests, and plant and animal life and the protection of natural scenic wonders. Its forestry division supervises a large force of fire wardens, observers, and rangers and operates a large forest tree nursery. The commission also supervises extensive educational work among sportsmen and in the public schools. Its revenue is derived from hunting and fishing licenses, Federal aid, State legislative appropriations, and an assessment of 1 cent per acre for fire protection from private forest land. The law stipulates that 10 per cent of all license fees must be set aside for purchase of lands for forest parks and for game and fish refuges.

In forestry the commission lays special stress on fire protection rather than on reforestation, under the theory that if present forests are protected and allowed to grow, nature will take care of reforesting. In 1938 the division had 5 district foresters, 51 observers, and 140 rangers to provide protection in 5,500,000 acres of privately owned forests and 52,000 acres of State forests. In actual fire fighting this force was augmented by the personnel of the eight CCC camps in the State. The observers and rangers operated 51 fire towers and about 1,200 miles of State-owned telephone lines.

The 20-acre State forest nursery operated at Greenbottom, near Huntington, in 1938 distributed 1,015,343 trees for reforestation. Its potential annual production is estimated at 5,000,000. The trees are sold at less than cost to farmers, coal companies, and other buyers interested in the work, and seedlings are given free to 4-H Clubs and State institutions.

Similar fire-protection and reforestation activities are carried on by the National Forest Service at Monongahela National Forest. The service established a 67-acre nursery near Parsons in Tucker County in 1928, and ten years later approximately 4,000,000 trees were being produced annually for reforestation purposes.

The national and State services co-operate in supervising protection of privately owned forests, and receive, besides aid from the CCC, assistance from such organizations as the Central West Virginia Fire Protective Association and the Southern West Virginia Fire Protective Association, whose memberships are comprised of firms and individuals interested in saving timberlands, and from volunteer fire fighters who are paid by the State for their services.

Besides reforestation, the CCC has engaged in other conservation activities in West Virginia. It has been of great service in the improvement of State parks, helping in the construction of trails, dams, and vacation cabins. Other Federal organizations, including the Work Projects Administration and the Soil Conservation Service, have figured importantly in the broadening of the State's general conservation program.

In 1939 the State had 18 State parks and forests, ranging in size from 30 acres (Pinnacle Rock) to 12,915 acres (Cooper's Rock), with a total area of 75,000 acres. (*See Recreational Areas.*) These regions of great natural beauty serve as refuges for wildlife and provide recreational facilities for tourists and vacationists.

The State Conservation Commission's principal source of revenue comes from the sale of hunting and fishing licenses (178,562 licenses brought in $256,179 in 1937–8). Its program contemplates increasing facilities for sportsmen by the maintenance of game refuges on all State-owned lands, replenishment of fish and game stock, and protection of fish and game through the establishment of closed seasons. In 1937–8 a total of 9,841 animals—deer, raccoon, and cottontail rabbits —and 7,656 bobwhite quail and wild turkeys were released. A program is followed whereby deer and beaver are live-trapped in areas that are overstocked and transplanted to areas needing restocking. The State is divided into 6 game districts, under the supervision of 56 game wardens; in 1937–8 the wardens made 1,351 arrests and obtained 1,157 convictions, with fines totaling $24,350. The National Forest Service assists in restocking activities in the Monongahela Forest, where it has 23,000 acres set aside in refuges.

Of the 11 most valuable species of fur-bearing animals in the State, only the raccoon and beaver are included in the commission's restocking program. On the other hand, the commission condones the killing of certain predatory animals, birds, fish, and reptiles; 147,509 of these were killed in vermin-control activities in 1937–8. Trappers in West Virginia reported a 1937–8 catch of 308,196 pelts, marketed for $188,653.

The commission operates three fish hatcheries and one hatchery rearing station, and in 1937–8 its workers aided by the CCC planted 3,341,334 fish, principally trout, in West Virginia streams. An additional 498,509 were planted from the Federal hatcheries at White Sulphur Springs, and Leetown.

No comprehensive attempt to solve the soil erosion problem in West Virginia had ever been made until the Federal Government began its soil-conservation program in 1933. A survey revealed that accelerated soil erosion existed on 90 per cent of the State's land surface, and that nearly 10,000,000 acres had lost between 25 and 75 per cent of their top soil, and 4,000,000 acres more than 75 per cent.

The Soil Conservation Service has developed a plan of erosion control that includes reforestation, pasture improvement, improved crop rotation, contour strip cropping, contour cultivation, and construction of permanent and temporary mechanical erosion controls. Under this plan, in which most of the labor involved in tree planting and other necessary work is performed by the CCC, the farmer agrees to follow the methods outlined for at least five years. The SCS provides from its own nurseries the trees needed in the reforestation phase of the program.

Two large projects, one near Spencer in Roane County, involving 441 farm owners and 64,401 acres of land, and one in Marshall County, with 135 owners and 12,517 acres, were inaugurated for watershed demonstration purposes. In addition, 672 agreements covering 101,947 acres had been effected by October 1, 1938, for special control work in five other counties; this work was to include all or part of the complete program as conditions warranted.

In 1938 approximately 50,000 West Virginia farmers, participating in the benefits of the U. S. Soil Conservation and Allotment Act, obtained bonuses for conserving soil and for improving crops and farm practices. Although the main purpose of this act is the regulation of farm production, soil specialists believe that its greatest value in this State may be in the resultant soil improvement and water conservation.

Except for the watershed protection gained through Federal and State reforestation, flood control in West Virginia in 1938 was largely in the projected stage. The U. S. Flood Control Act of 1936 authorized the building of five large reservoirs in the State, at an estimated cost of $43,257,320; but only one of these, the $18,600,000 Tygarts River Dam near Grafton, had been constructed, and none of the other projects had been finally approved.

With the exception of the Ohio River, West Virginia's major streams create a greater flood problem for other States than for West Virginia itself. For this reason flood control has been left to a large extent in the hands of the Federal Government, although some communities have adopted local flood-control measures. One of the most modern and costly structures built under a local program is a $6,000,000 floodwall under construction at Huntington.

Sewage disposal, wastes from industrial plants, and acid seepage from abandoned coal mines have combined to produce serious stream pollution, detrimental to public health, to fish propagation, and agriculture. Only since 1933—when funds became available under a Federal emergency works program—has there been any determined attempt to solve the problem.

Surveys in 1930 showed that sewage from a population of 600,000 was draining untreated into West Virginia streams. This condition has been appreciably improved by the work of the Public Works Administration and other relief agencies, which, between 1933 and 1938, have constructed eight new sewerage systems with disposal plants, three new disposal plants for existent systems, three complete new sewerage systems, and many hundreds of miles of additions and improvements to previously built sewerage systems.

During the same period, considerable progress was made in reducing the volume of industrial wastes. A number of the larger industries, co-operating with the State Department of Health and the State Water Commission, installed effective means of reclaiming their wastes or of removing harmful elements. By October 1, 1938, a program supervised by the U. S. Public Health Service had resulted in the sealing of 664 out of 1,755 abandoned mines, thus reducing seepage by 855,277 pounds of acid daily or 39 per cent of the previous daily acid load. The health departments of West Virginia, Ohio, Pennsylvania, Indiana, and Kentucky are co-operating under the Ohio River Interstate Stream Conservation Agreement to reduce the disposal of domestic sewage and industrial wastes in the Ohio River Basin.

History

LYING within the great valley drained by the Ohio River, West Virginia shares the rich history of that region. More interesting still, periods of national significance frequently have been pointed up by happenings in this State—the only one, as J. M. Callahan notes, 'that was formed as a result of the sectionalism which existed in every state crossed by the Appalachians.' The isolated backwoodsman in the West Virginia hills typified the westward-moving pioneer. John Brown at Harpers Ferry, self-consecrated to an act of madness or of glory, focused the thought of his time upon the problem of slavery. The turn from an agrarian to an industrial economy brought the railroads and the swift development of natural resources to West Virginia.

BEFORE THE WHITE MAN

The first known inhabitants of West Virginia were the early ancestors of the present Indians, the Mound Builders. Evidence of their occupancy has been found along the Ohio River and in the Kanawha Valley, where mounds and enclosures, containing human skeletons, weapons of flint and bone, clay pipes and pottery, shell and ivory beads, copper bracelets, and other relics, testify to their presence. The structures take three characteristic forms: the conical earthern mound, the earthern wall or enclosure, and the rock enclosure with cairns.

Most numerous are the conical mounds. Many of these have been almost or quite obliterated by the weathering of centuries, but traces of about 300 have been reported, many have been positively identified, and a few have been carefully excavated. Largest of these is the Grave Creek Mound at Moundsville (*see Tour* 22), which is 79 feet high and 900 feet in circumference at the base. When it was explored in 1838, a tunnel from the northern side to the center and a perpendicular shaft from the top disclosed, at the center of the base, a vault 8 feet wide and 12 feet long, lined with stakes driven vertically along the sides, their ends sharpened by fire. The top had been constructed of arched poles covered with rocks, most of which had fallen in. The vault contained two human skeletons. One was without ornament, but the other had suspended from its neck 650 discoidal beads and an ivory pendant, six inches long and more than an inch wide, tapering to the ends. Above this vault, about midway of the center shaft, a second vault of similar construction and in a much better state of preservation contained the skeleton of a woman. About her neck were 1,700 ivory beads and 500 shell ornaments, and on her arms five copper bracelets.

Culturally this mound has the same affiliation as the Beach Bottom Mound (*see Tour 19a*), excavated by Charles Bache and Linton Satterhwaite. The presence of copper and of Gulf Coast shell, the forms of tubes and blades, and the form of the mounds place them in one of the cultures of the upper Mississippi area. The absence of certain characteristic features, however, excludes the Hopewell and the Fort Ancient cultures and associates them rather with the Adena, 'a third prehistoric mound culture in the Ohio area still in process of definition.' The great size, careful construction, and conical symmetry of the mounds, the uncremated burials, the tubular tobacco pipes, and the round sculpture of objects found in the vaults are characteristic of these as of the mounds in the Great Kanawha Valley. Artifacts found in excavation of the 33-foot mound at South Charleston (*see Tour 15*) definitely associate the culture represented with that of the Grave Creek and Beach Bottom mounds.

Of the earthen enclosures, the Huddleson enclosure opposite Mount Carbon (*see Tour 15b*), circular in form and 1,344 feet in circumference, lies on a smooth river terrace above high water mark. On opposite sides of the earthen wall of surface soil and mussel shells are a stone cist and an ash pit. The wall, once three or four feet high, has been reduced by long cultivation to a mere trace. The irregular South Charleston enclosure (*see Tour 15c*) of 20 acres and the elaborate Long Reach enclosure (*see Tour 19b*), like many others of varying shape and size, have been almost completely obliterated.

The Long Reach formations are among the most extensive in the State. Two parallel walls of earth about 120 feet apart, originally from 6 to 10 feet high, begin near the northern end of the present town and, extending northward almost to Long Reach, curve back toward Ben's Run in a course corresponding to the contour of the nearest foothill. The outer wall is about 4½ miles and the inner, about 4 miles in length. A cross wall bisects the area enclosed by the inner wall. Two well preserved mounds occupy the upper sections thus formed, and two parallel curved walls about 300 feet apart divide the lower portion into three enclosures. Outside the enclosure is a platform about 120 feet long and 35 feet wide bordered by stones laid on edge.

Of the stonework enclosures, which are closely related to the earthen enclosures and probably owe their difference to the building materials available at different sites, the Mount Carbon ruins (*see Tour 15b*) are characteristic. The crumbling wall of loose rock, difficult of access because of heavy underbrush, circles the top of the mountain to form an enclosure about three miles in length and varying in width from a few hundred yards to more than a mile. A cross wall divides the enclosure equally.

Cairns, carefully founded on the base rock, have been found within the enclosures. Some, about 8 feet high and with a base diameter of 40 feet, have triangular vaults entirely enclosed. Skeletal remains, rude pottery, and flint weapons were found in the vaults.

For the Indians who followed their mound-building ancestors, the greater part of what is now West Virginia was only a hunting ground. On the map prepared by the Bureau of American Ethnology showing the distribution of Amerindian linguistic groups in North America, West Virginia, with the exception of the area south of the Great Kanawha River, appears as a blank, unclassified region; none of the tribes (Algonquian, Iroquoians, and Siouan) that had come into this region had ever claimed it or made it their permanent habitat.

Three great Indian trails traversed the region. The Scioto-Monongahela, which roughly followed a course from Pennsylvania through the present towns of Morgantown and Fairmont and thence westward to Parkersburg on the Ohio River; the Seneca Trail, which is closely paralleled by the present US 219 from Maryland to Virginia, with its principal fork that followed the South Branch of the Potomac from its mouth to Seneca Rocks and thence westward to the present town of Elkins; and the Kanawha or Canoy Trail, which is roughly paralleled today by the Midland Trail (US 60) between White Sulphur Springs and Huntington. The northern branch of this path followed the Great Kanawha to its mouth on the Ohio. Over these paths the surrounding tribes hunted and fought, but never came to rest.

With the arrival of white settlers on the seaboard and the westward movement of the tribes of the coastal plains, more or less permanent villages were established within the State. But even then it was a land of passage, and during the French and Indian Wars became the ground on which were fought some of the bloodiest battles, and where was waged the most constant warfare between the white man and the Indian in the struggle for possession of the Ohio country.

COLONIAL HISTORY

When Jamestown, Virginia, was settled by English colonists in 1607, it was thought that it could serve as a base for finding a short route by water to the Pacific Ocean. Excited by the will-o'-the-wisp of a route to the 'Western Ocean,' early explorers climbed through clefts in the washboard ridges of the Blue Ridge and Alleghenies, through the valley of the South Branch of the Potomac, to the New, the Greenbrier, and, later, the Monongahela Rivers—only to find that a greater river carried their waters to the south and that a seemingly endless expanse of land lay before them. In time the wish to penetrate the wilderness for the fur trade supplanted the vain hope of finding a short waterway. The first explorations resulted in the discovery of New River by Walter Chiles, Rice Hoe, Walter Austin, and Joseph Johnson in 1641.

Sir William Berkeley, governor of Virginia, sent John Lederer on three expeditions westward, on one of which, in 1669, he reached a point near Harpers Ferry. In 1671 Thomas Batts and Robert Fallam, sent out by Colonel Abraham Wood, a fur trader, explored the New River region of what is now West Virginia as far west as Kanawha Falls. Their object was partly 'for finding out the ebbing and flowing of ye South Sea,' which they believed they had discovered at the Falls of the Great Kanawha. When they gazed at the land west of the Alleghenies they did not know that they were looking at a country the Indians found too rugged to live in the year round. They and others who followed them through the gaps and into the canoe-shaped valleys were to learn this soon enough.

With the exception of a few Tuscarora, Mingo, Shawnee, and Delaware living on the fringes of the territory of what is now West Virginia, the region was uninhabited; so far as the Indians were concerned, this was just a good region for hunting, fishing, and gathering salt.

Energetic Lieutenant Governor Alexander Spotswood, western Virginia's first publicity agent, came in 1716, looked, and returned home to hand out souvenir golden horseshoes and interviews praising the fertility of the land he saw. It is thought he either saw from a distance or actually reached Pendleton County.

John Van Meter came in 1724 to barter with the Indians for furs, but his sons, whom he advised regarding the fertile lands of the South Branch of the Potomac, were not to be the first white men to establish a home in what is now West Virginia.

While there is evidence that settlers were near the site of present Shepherdstown as early as 1719, Morgan ap Morgan is credited with being the first white man to build a permanent home in this State. Having received Virginia patents to 1,000 acres of land in western Virginia, he took possession in 1726-7, building a log cabin in the vicinity of Bunker Hill, on Mill Creek, in what is now Berkeley County. However he does not seem to have taken up permanent residence there, with his family, until 1730. Morgan (born 1688), a native of Wales, came as a young man to Penn's province, settling in the Lower counties (Delaware) at Christiana as a merchant. In 1727 he was a magistrate of New Castle County, Delaware, and seven years later a 'Gentleman Justice' of Orange County, Virginia.

The stubbornness of two men in a lawsuit contributed more to the westward movement than Spotswood's advertising. Joist Hite and 15 other families cut their way through the wilderness from York, Pennsylvania, in 1732 and, crossing the Potomac two miles above Harpers Ferry, proceeded to the vicinity of Winchester. Hite became involved in a lawsuit with Lord Fairfax (1736), which rendered the validity of land titles in the lower Shenandoah Valley so doubtful that many families moved farther west into the New, Greenbrier, and Kanawha Valleys. The suit was settled after both men were dead.

Threatened with confinement to a thin strip along the Atlantic Coast, the English attempted to open the territory to the west, to halt encroachment on the land which the French claimed all the way to the Mississippi. In 1722 the Iroquois had relinquished their claims to the lands between the Alleghenies and the Blue Ridge, and settlement was thus made safer.

It is known that frugal, homeseeking Germans, driven from Pennsylvania by dissension with William Penn's heirs, followed the valleys down into the Eastern Panhandle after 1730; one of their settlements grew into a village called Mecklenburg—later Shepherdstown. In 1735 the first settlement in the South Branch Valley started in Hampshire County, and by 1748 the population of the valley totaled 200.

Pendleton County's first settlers located about a mile below the site of Brandywine in 1745. Others came in 1747, and six years later newcomers of Dutch, German, Scotch, Irish, and English descent had swelled the region's population to 200, equally divided between the

Upper Tract and the South Branch. With the growth of the latter region, it became evident that a local seat of government was needed. Hampshire County, the oldest county in West Virginia, was formed from parts of Frederick and Augusta Counties in 1753. The first presiding justice, Thomas Bryan Martin, a nephew of Lord Fairfax, began his court at Romney. In 1762 the Virginia General Assembly passed an act incorporating several towns, among them Romney and Mecklenburg, in what is now West Virginia.

Direct incentive for the venturing of settlers into the New River region was possibly the glowing accounts Christopher Gist gave of the country after he returned from his Ohio exploring trip in 1750. Those who had been fretting in the settlements of the Shenandoah crossed the mountains into the Greenbrier and New River Valleys.

Perhaps the first recorded settlement west of the Alleghenies was made by two New Englanders, Jacob Marlin and Stephen Sewell, in Pocahontas County in 1749. The two had a difference of opinion over religion and Sewell went to live in a near-by tree, although it is said they remained good friends. They were found there in 1751 by General Andrew Lewis, agent of the Greenbrier Land Company, which had obtained a grant of land to be sold for settlement.

In 1753 Andrew Culbertson settled on Crumps Bottom in what is now Summers County. Settlers continued to pour into the region. They came from the north by way of the Shenandoah and the South Branch of the Potomac, and from the coast by way of the James River.

In 1747–8 young George Washington stopped at 'ye famed Warm Springs at Bath' (Berkeley Springs). In 1756 Lord Fairfax gave to Virginia the land and springs at Bath so that 'these healing waters might be forever free to the publick, for the welfare of suffering humanity' (see Berkeley Springs).

Among the first white settlements made in the New River Valley was Draper's Meadows, founded by the Draper and Ingles families in 1748, near what is now Blacksburg, Montgomery County, Virginia.

On Sunday, July 8, 1755, this settlement was surprised by a band of marauding Shawnee from beyond the Ohio and most of the settlers were killed or captured. William Ingles was in the woods near by at the time and managed to make his escape, but his wife, Mary Ingles, was captured. She was carried away by the raiders, who moved down to Bluestone, up the Bluestone River to the head of Paint Creek, thence to Campbells Creek and across the Ohio. On this journey Mary Ingles was forced to make salt for her Indian captors, the first made by a white person in West Virginia. She escaped in the latter part of the same year and after incredible hardships found her way back and rejoined her husband. She furnished valuable information to the white settlers in frustrating other Indian raids.

The wave of settlement trickled over into the Tygarts River Valley in 1753. Robert Files and David Tygart built cabins within three miles of one another near Beverly; but, unfortunately, they had established their homes on the Seneca War Trail. The Indians killed Files and scared Tygart back into the South Branch Valley.

Three years later the Eckarlys settled on the Cheat River at Dunkard's Bottom in Preston County, and Thomas Decker and others built homes in 1758 near the mouth of Decker's Creek in Monongalia County. These settlements were broken up by the Indians and there were no permanent ones made in this region until after the French and Indian War. The territory had an estimated population of 10,000 whites and 400 Negroes, concentrated in the Eastern Panhandle.

These people became the first-line troops in the struggle for a continent waged so savagely by the French and British that its ferocity threatened to wipe out years of progress by the settlers against the wilderness and the Indians. Bloody raids by the Indians decimated the isolated settlements. Washington's unsuccessful expedition in 1754 and Braddock's defeat in 1755 heightened the confidence of the Indians and they menaced settlers along the entire frontier line. Governor Dinwiddie sent Captain Andrew Lewis against the Indians in 1756, but the severe winter weather broke up his expedition near the junction of the Tug and Levisa forks of the Big Sandy River, and the savages, further encouraged, continued their assaults until 1763.

Forts sprang up along the northern frontier to stem the Indian raids. In most cases, these were but feeble efforts. The fate of the trans-Allegheny region hung in the balance until the fall of Fort Duquesne in 1758; this defeat of the Indians' allies, the French, apparently reopened the territory for settlement. The roads through the wilderness left by the forces of Braddock and Forbes provided an important aid.

It now became a violation of the law to settle in trans-Allegheny. George III, desiring to leave the territory to the Indians, issued a proclamation forbidding the colonists to grant warrants, surveys, or patents in the territory until treaties with the Indians permitted peaceful acquirement of land. This voided all titles beyond a line established by the proclamation.

However, the Dutch and Germans could not read English, and the

Scotch-Irish ignored the proclamation. They pushed into the forbidden territory to secure squatter's rights (sometimes called tomahawk rights because their boundaries were marked on trees with axes or tomahawks), followed this up with settlement rights, and in this manner pushed the frontier to the Ohio River, while an order from England to remove all settlers west of the proclamation line went unexecuted.

A second treaty was entered into with the Iroquois at Fort Stanwix in 1768 whereby they ceded all claims to land between the Alleghenies and the Ohio River, and following this concession came the near-formation of a fourteenth colony out of what is now West Virginia. The plan had been proposed by Governor Dinwiddie as early as 1756. Definite action was taken on the proposal in 1771 when Thomas Walpole and Benjamin Franklin submitted a petition to the king asking for the new colony. The proposal met with royal approval, but the action necessary to carry it out was halted by the Revolution. For some unknown reason, the new colony, whose formation might have saved considerable trouble 80 years later, was to have been named Vandalia.

Difficulty with titles established at this time arose partly from the haphazard manner of laying claims to land. Along with this was the speculation carried on in land, whereby a settler might buy land sight-unseen from an eastern Virginia speculator and arrive on his plot only to find some other already on it with a squatter's claim. To add to the confusion, claims were filed in the names of children, hogs, cats, and dogs, as well as of the settlers themselves. This unsettled condition of land titles was responsible for the sparse settlement of some parts of the new territory.

Emigrants, desirous of owning their own home and land, scuttled in droves over the mountains after the Treaty of Fort Stanwix. By 1775 the estimated population of trans-Allegheny Virginia was 30,000 persons, grouped in a rough circle about a heavily timbered area that remained unpenetrated for two decades. The settlements followed the streams and the Indian trails. The larger the streams and the more navigable, the greater the number and the larger the size of settlements.

By 1769 settlers began to push up the Greenbrier River to form a way-station for future settlers moving to the west down the Kanawha to the Ohio, and over the divide into the Monongahela watershed. The first permanent settlement in Greenbrier County started at Frankfort in 1769; the building of the old Savannah Fort at Lewisburg took place in 1770; and within the next four years six other settlements sprang up near by. Settlements along the Great Kanawha River were made at about the same time. Levi Morris located in 1770 on the site of Montgomery. Settlements were started at the mouth of Kellys Creek by 1774, and in 1775 the site of Charleston was surveyed for Colonel Thomas Bullitt. The Kelly settlement became the jumping-off place for later settlers leaving by boat for the West, and boatyards started here built river craft for many years.

By 1772 nearly all of the land in the Tygarts Valley had been located, although few patents were obtained for it until several years later. Similarly, the rest of the Monongahela watershed received the flood of settlers from the South Branch of the Potomac and Pennsylvania River Valleys. Wheeling had its origin in 1769 when it was settled by Colonel Ebenezer Zane and two brothers, who came from the South Branch Valley. Strategically located, it offered a rallying point for standing off repeated Indian raids and a gathering point in later years for settlers going farther west when it became the western end of the National Road.

Conflicting claims of Pennsylvania and Virginia over the location of the boundary between the two was aggravated by Virginia's desire to have Pittsburgh within its borders, and for sometime there were two city governments in that town. In 1767 the surveyors of the Mason and Dixon Line proceeded west until they were stopped at Dunkard Creek by the Shawnee and Delaware, who laid claim to this territory. The boundary dispute was stopped only by the Revolution.

Western Virginia history has its focal point in Lord Dunmore's War of 1774. In it fought the men who planted American institutions beyond the Appalachian barrier and who later became the rear guard of the Revolution. Hostilities arose from widespread alarm of the Indians over the tenacious land-grabbing of the 'Long Knives' and the depletion of their favorite hunting grounds.

The overt act arousing them to warfare resulted from the brutal slaughter of the family of Logan, a friendly Mingo chief, at Yellow Creek, Hancock County, by drunken whites. Logan swore vengeance and all of the tribes joined in a campaign against the settlement. Lord Dunmore carried the fight to the Indians to divert Virginians from the trouble brewing with England.

He led an expedition down the Ohio River from Pittsburgh to meet another under General Andrew Lewis, advancing down the Greenbrier and Big Kanawha to the Ohio. While Lewis awaited him at Point Pleasant, the Indians under Cornstalk decided to attack first, on October 10, 1774, while the white forces were divided. The resulting all-day battle ended in an important victory for the frontiersmen. Sometimes called the 'first battle of the Revolution,' it was distinctly an American victory and was a deciding factor in keeping the Indians quiet for the first two years of the Revolution, and could almost be said to have won the Northwest for the Colonial side. It is not improbable that the Treaty of 1783 with England would have fixed the western boundary of the United States at the Alleghenies had not this region been held by white settlers.

Possibly preventing a general Indian war on the frontier, a peace treaty was signed with seven tribes at Pittsburgh in September 1775. It at least secured a pledge of neutrality for two years, thus permitting western Virginians to cross the mountains to aid Revolutionary forces and to consolidate firmer defenses against later attacks.

The primary causes of the Revolution were of little interest to the frontiersmen, but they were entirely sympathetic toward the colonist cause. In order to cripple frontier chances in the coming conflict with England, Lord Dunmore's last official acts were to order the evacuation of Fort Dunmore and Fort Blair. The former, at Pittsburgh, was seized by the frontiersmen, and the latter, at Point Pleasant, was later replaced by Fort Randolph.

At about the same time, the District of West Augusta was set up as a separate area, with vaguely defined boundaries roughly extending from the Alleghenies westward to the Ohio River and northward to Pittsburgh, according to conflicting reports. In 1776 this district was subdivided into three counties: two, Ohio and Monongalia, were in what is now West Virginia; Greenbrier County was established in 1778. From the location of the forts, it is evident that the greater part of the Northern Panhandle, the Valley of the West Fork, and the Greenbrier Valley, with some in-between territory, had been occupied.

British agents succeeded in stirring the Indians up again and the 'bloody year of the three 7's' was one long remembered on the frontier for the ferocity of the attacks. The war was brought on by constant friction with the Indians, an aggravated instance being the murder of Chief Cornstalk. Large-scale operations in western Virginia during the Revolution extended from September 1777 to September 1782. During this period, British-led Indian armies made three major invasions. For the first time, Indian raids were confined to the west of the Alleghenies —the frontier had moved west.

The Indians attacked Fort Henry at Wheeling and Fort Randolph at Point Pleasant in 1777. They made an extended invasion of the

Greenbrier and Kanawha Valleys in 1778, made another assault on Fort Henry in 1782, and raided as far east as Tucker County. In 1778 the Monongahela region was attacked three times, and once the next year. In 1780 the Greenbrier region was raided. However, George Rogers Clark's expedition against Fort Vincennes in 1779 cut the raids to a minimum. Their ardor dampened by this bold thrust deep into their territory, the Indians suffered also from the capture of General 'Hair Buyer' Hamilton, which removed British influence to a great extent.

Older settlements grew during the Revolution and new ones appeared. Population expanded in the Eastern Panhandle. Shepherdstown became a busy center of trade for the area. Berkeley County (now Berkeley, Jefferson, and Morgan Counties) was formed from Frederick in 1772. Bath (Berkeley Springs) was incorporated in 1776, and Martinsburg in 1778.

While Continental forces fought with the British in the East, frontier Virginians held off the Indians at the colony's back door. At the beginning of the war, there were 6 forts along the Ohio River, 4 on Cheat, 9 on the Monongahela, 2 on the Greenbrier, and 3 on the Great Kanawha. During the Revolution, 14 forts were erected on the Ohio, 14 on the Monongahela, 5 on the Cheat, 3 more on the Greenbrier, 2 others on the Great Kanawha—60 forts in all by the middle of the Revolution.

WESTERN VIRGINIA, 1778–1863

After the war, the desire for a strong central government to quell the Indians and force the opening of the Mississippi River for export of their products influenced the delegates from western Virginia to vote almost unanimously for ratification of the Constitution of the United States. With General 'Mad Anthony' Wayne's decisive victory at the battle of Fallen Timbers in 1794, the Indians were effectively quelled. The opening of the Mississippi came through the treaty with Spain in 1795, and the Louisiana Purchase of 1803 made control by the United States permanent. Until 1796, the British continued to occupy Detroit and abet the Indians in their raids.

Toward the close of the eighteenth century the sound of the settlers' axes clearing their claims first penetrated the wilderness, remote from the main stream of migration through the passes and down the rivers. Wirt County's first homeseekers arrived in 1796 and Wood County was organized in 1798.

As late as 1791, Daniel Boone, for some time a leading citizen of the Kanawha Valley, reported: 'From the pint [Point Pleasant] to Elke [Elk River], no inhabitence, from Elke to the Bote yards [Kellys Creek] 20 miles all inhabited.' The region ultimately embraced in Cabell, Putnam, and Lincoln Counties in the southwestern part of western Virginia remained unsettled until after 1796 and the counties south of the Great Kanawha were to remain sparsely settled until the coming of the railroads late in the next century.

In the older regions of the State, population increased rapidly. The first Federal census of 1790 enumerated 55,873 persons living in what is now West Virginia. The 1800 census revealed that the population had increased to 78,592. Division of the original counties followed the increases. In 1784 Harrison County was formed from the southern area of Monongalia County; Hardy from Hampshire in 1786; Randolph from Harrison in 1787; Pendleton from Augusta, Rockingham, Hardy and Bath in 1788, and Kanawha from Greenbrier and Montgomery in 1789.

Older towns established and incorporated before the close of the century were: Lewisburg in 1782; Clarksburg in 1785; Morgantown in 1785; Charles Town in 1786; Frankfort in 1787; Middletown and West Liberty in 1787.

Religion reached the scattered settlers through the efforts of such tireless and zealous men as the Reverend Francis Asbury, later a Methodist Episcopal bishop, whose circuit extended from Florida to Pennsylvania and west. He traveled through every part of settled America before 1786, organizing and building churches, and he took his sleep, his food, and his audience where he happened to find them.

Perhaps the first church established in western Virginia was Morgan's Chapel at Bunker Hill, built by Morgan ap Morgan, the first permanent settler in West Virginia, Joist Hite, Dr. John Briscoe, and other settlers in 1740. It was Episcopal. In the southern part of the State, the first church seems to have been the old Rehoboth Church (1786), near Union, Monroe County. Bishop Asbury preached here at what is believed to be the oldest church of the Methodist Episcopal denomination west of the mountains. It is still standing. The 'Old Stone Church' at Lewisburg, still in use, was built by Presbyterians in 1796.

Early settlers waged a nip-and-tuck struggle with nature for food. During the first years, they were necessarily eaters of meat, especially during late winter and early spring. 'Greenup' time would find them eagerly looking for fresh green food. One early settler wrote:

I remember how narrowly the children watched the growth of the potato tops, pumpkins and squash vines, hoping from day to day to get something to answer in place of bread. How delicious was the taste of young potatoes when we got them. What a jubilee when we were permitted to pull the young corn for roasting ears. Still more so when it acquired sufficient hardness to be made into Johnny Cakes by the aid of the tin grater. We then became healthy, vigorous and contented with our situation, poor as it was.

For some time after the first settlements in western Virginia, there was scanty law enforcement of any sort. Uncertain whether it was in Virginia or Pennsylvania, Monongalia County had little law and order of any kind. Adding to the confusion were proposals for the new colony of Vandalia, and, later, for a new State to be called Westsylvania. In addition, there was much uncertainty of land tenure, because of the claims of the Ohio and, later, the Indiana land-speculating companies.

The formation of new counties by Virginia in 1776 served only to complicate matters, and confusion continued until the establishment of a land office in 1779. Final adjustment did not come until 1784, when the location of the Mason-Dixon Line was established as part of the Pennsylvania-Virginia division line.

Meanwhile, the residents in this part of Virginia were a law unto themselves. With the Anglo-Saxon faculty for maintaining social organization even in the most primitive environment, the settlers preserved a rough civil discipline. Violators of common rights were 'hated out' of the neighborhood. Whipping was a common punishment and in many cases the injured party took the law in his own hands.

Infant industries had been started by 1797. The saw mill replaced the adze; the gristmill took the place of the mortar, the grater, and the sweep. In 1797 Elisha Brooks began manufacturing salt for commercial purposes on the Great Kanawha, thus making the settlers independent of the east for this important commodity. Powder was made in Monongalia County, and Wheeling had boatyards and rope walks. Most families became skilled in making domestic products and in many regions remained self-sufficient for about 100 years.

With the nineteenth century, a new era opened in western Virginia. A new type of settler began to take the initiative in affairs of the region; and the true pioneer, intolerant of crowding, forged ahead into the spacious west, where he could find more elbow room.

Roaming all over the State and finding himself crowded out everywhere, Adam O'Brien, a roving pioneer, gave up in disgust; with his parting comment upon the new settlers, he spoke for his brethren:

'He is a poor man and has got behind-hand and when that's the case, there is no staying in the settlements; for those varmints, the sheriffs and constables, are worse than the Indians, because you can kill Indians and you dare not kill the sheriffs.' He remarked that the settlers 'lived quite happy before the Revolution, for then there was no law, no courts and no sheriffs and they agreed pretty well, but after awhile the people began to come and made settlements and then there was need for laws; and then came the lawyers and next the preachers, and from that time they never had any peace anymore.'

O'Brien lamented that 'the lawyers persuaded them to sue when not paid, and the preachers converted one half and they began to quarrel with the other half because they would not take care of their own souls, and from that time they never had any peace for body or soul,' and that 'the sheriffs were worse than wild cats and "painters" [panthers] and would take the last coverlet from your wife's straw bed or turn you out in a storm.' He swore: 'I would rather take my chances and live among the savages than live among justices and sheriffs and lawyers who, with all their civility, have no natural feeling in them.'

The opening of the Mississippi River stimulated the commercial activity of western Virginia, since it provided an outlet for products denied by the mountain barrier to the east. Immediately after the river's opening came the first steamboat on the Ohio (1811). The *New Orleans* was built at Pittsburgh by Nicholas J. Roosevelt, Robert Fulton's agent, who hoped to establish a monopoly in transportation on inland waters.

Some doubt existed at first as to the practicability of steamboats' breasting the river's currents, but this was dispelled with the construction of the first really successful river steamboat, the *Washington*, at Wheeling (1817) by Captain Henry Shreve, long a picturesque figure in the history of inland transportation. Bucking the current, he brought the *Washington* back from New Orleans to Louisville in 25 days—and lived to see it done in 5 days.

The completion of the National, or Cumberland, Road from Cumberland to Wheeling in 1818, together with the steamboat, opened up the West and benefited western Virginia. Although traveling but a short distance through western Virginia, this road closely paralleled the northern boundary and its influence was strongly felt. It meant an early start for Wheeling in its fight with Pittsburgh for chief honors on the upper Ohio.

With the coming of river improvements, boats began to travel up the Kanawha as far as Red House shoals and later to Charleston. The cry of 'Steamboat down at the bend' abruptly shifted Morgantown's population to the river bank one rainy Sunday morning in 1826. Congregations poured from the churches, with their pastors close on their heels, and scurried to see their first steamboat. The development of steamboat and barge building boomed the lumber trade and boatyards sprang up along the Ohio, some of which are still active.

Freight and land-hungry migrants poured over the National Road from the east and traffic on the Ohio flourished. All sorts of traffic was seen on the road: lumbering 'Mountain wagons,' fast express wagons, and the traveling coaches, realistically called 'shake-guts' by the travelers, which 'tore' along at breakneck speed. In the other direction went livestock for the eastern markets.

The James River and Kanawha Turnpike filled the early transportation need of western Virginians in the south-central part of the State. Leading over the mountains and down the Great Kanawha, this crude road was kept almost impassable for other traffic by east-bound livestock herds. Supplying the herds with food provided the farmers along the road a convenient income.

The banking situation constantly irritated the residents of this rapidly filling part of Virginia. In 1812 there were only two banks in Virginia and both of these were in Richmond. Along with those of neighboring States, they had suspended specie payment and left western Virginia with almost no medium of exchange other than some rare coins that were given little circulation. As the result of agitation against this condition, two banks were established west of the mountains in 1817, one at Winchester and the other at Wheeling; these banks were allowed to establish branches in near-by towns. Demands for redistribution of representation in the General Assembly and suffrage for non-freeholders aided this action.

The impelling force behind the agitation for the banks was the growth of infant industries in western Virginia. On the Great Kanawha the salt industry began to make strong headway under David and Joseph Ruffner (1808). With deep wells and improved casing, more and better brine was secured. The discovery of coal in Kanawha County in 1817, and its use by the Ruffners as fuel to evaporate their brine into salt crystals, gave impetus to the salt industry. The Kanawha Salt Company, said to be 'the first trust in the United States,' was organized in 1817. The Kanawha salt came into general use throughout the Ohio Valley.

Primarily an agricultural State, rural West Virginia nevertheless became a region of small mills processing the wool for a growing sheep-raising industry. Merino sheep were the dominant breed in the early years. The carding and weaving mills and other small industries, located at small cross-roads communities, remained in operation until after the beginning of the twentieth century.

The development of steam navigation contributed to a new industrial order. An increased demand for raw and finished products continued to increase with the opening of the War of 1812. Cannon balls manufactured at the Tarr Iron Works in the Northern Panhandle battered British frigates at the Battle of Lake Erie. Iron manufacturers prospered during this era in Monongalia and near-by counties as well as in the Eastern Panhandle. Wheeling had an iron foundry, a woolen mill, and glass, paper, and pottery plants, while boatyards at Wheeling, Point Pleasant, Kellys Creek, and other places filled the growing need for boats.

In 1823 the Virginia assembly directed surveys to be made for a Staunton-Parkersburg road, but on account of financial difficulties and the necessity of changing the route to avoid natural barriers it was not completed until 1847. The road was macadamized, and a section that later became an important oil and gas region was opened for settlement. The Northwestern Turnpike was incorporated in 1827 and built from Winchester to Parkersburg in competition with the National Road, reaching Parkersburg in 1838 over the shortest possible route, disregarding communities off its path.

In 1827 the Baltimore & Ohio Railroad was started from Baltimore to the Ohio River. During the 26 years it took the railroad to reach Wheeling, eastern Virginia interests fought with all their power in the General Assembly to impede its progress. The attempts of these interests to frustrate more tapping of the region by the B&O were circumvented shortly afterward by a thinly disguised B&O sponsorship of the railroad from Parkersburg to Grafton. A short time after its completion in 1857, the Grafton-Parkersburg railroad became a part of the B&O.

Agriculturally and industrially, western Virginia sprang to life with the coming of the railroad. Potential natural resources were tapped for the first time. Towns doubled and trebled in population and new ones sprang into being where wilderness had been a few years before. Coal mines were opened in Hampshire, Mineral, Marion, and other counties along the road. In fact, Wheeling was leading Pittsburgh in the race for growth. River traffic on the Ohio boomed and new lines were started.

While the railroad boomed the communities in the northern section, it took trade from the Kanawha Valley region. The speedier, more economical transportation by rail diverted a considerable portion of the James River and Kanawha Turnpike traffic up the river by boat for transshipment by the railroad at Wheeling. Northwestern Virginia continued to grow in this way for 40 years, at the expense, to some extent, of the southern part of the State.

By 1830 trans-Allegheny Virginia had become comparatively prosperous, with transportation facilities increasingly bettered until thousands of persons crossed the region from east to west. Many newspapers were established. Doughty observers of the times, the newspaper editors and publishers of this early day recorded, from week to week, events that present-day historians laboriously seek to find among the yellowed pages of these old chronicles. Printed on a 9 by 15 inch page, the first newspaper published in what is now West Virginia was the *Potomak Guardian and Berkeley Advertiser,* founded by Dr. Thomas Henry at Shepherdstown in 1789.

As the country opened up, more irritation was felt with the eastern part of the State. There were three major political reasons why the people of western Virginia complained of eastern domination and the discrimination directed at their part of the State of Virginia.

In the first place, they complained of inequality in taxation. The constitution provided that taxation of all property should be uniform and according to its value, except in the case of slaves. This allowed a slave to be taxed at a lower rate than a beast of the field. As the settlers of western Virginia did most of their own work and employed few slaves, this provision worked to the advantage of the slave-owning eastern Virginians.

Secondly, representation in the legislature was apportioned on what was called a mixed basis—slave population being taken into consideration as a certain percentage in arriving at a suffrage basis. In spite of the preponderance of white population in the western part of the State in later years, there never existed an equality of representation in the General Assembly.

Finally, there was the unequal distribution of funds for public works by which the eastern part of the State was favored. Nearly all government buildings were in the east.

Disgusted with the treatment they were getting, the people of the west arranged for the calling of a constitutional convention in 1829. Acting with the residents of the Valley of Virginia, they hoped to get equal manhood suffrage in the place of freehold qualification; representation based on white population instead of on the property-owning basis; the reform of the county court system to provide an elective set of county officials; and a more responsible State executive instead of the puppet selected by the ruling clique of the General Assembly.

The convention was a farce. Elected on the old basis, the delegates showed a large majority for the east. The question of manhood suffrage was compromised, although requirements were reduced and tenants who paid taxes were allowed to vote. Proposals for free public education and popular election of sheriffs met with thumbs down.

Defeated at every turn, the delegates from the west showed their opinion of the new constitution when they voted on it. All of them voted against it except one—who was too ill to be present. The vote in the western counties was likewise heavily against it, and from this time on the talk of separation from the east gained momentum.

Continued indignation in the western counties resulted in a new constitutional convention in 1850. Sensing the determination of the western delegates to withdraw if they failed to get some concessions, eastern delegates compromised. They allowed representation in the lower house on a white population basis and arbitrarily set apportionment in the upper house favorable to the east. Manhood suffrage was included in the new constitution, thus enabling the westerners, at a later date, to elect one governor.

What especially irritated the westerners was the tax concession the easterners bestowed on themselves, by fixing property assessment at actual value with the exception of slaves; this threw an unequal portion of the tax bill on the slave-scarce west.

Warning of the events in the making came from the lips of Daniel Webster. He told the Virginians that if they became involved in the secession movement then gaining momentum in the South, western Virginia would break away from the east and become a separate State. For this reason, eastern Virginia leaders began to grant some concessions to the western section to create a more 'United Virginia.'

Considering the social elements of population, differing features of territory and contrasting interests, the formation of a new State by separation from the mother State was entirely logical. There had been three previous serious proposals to separate Virginia and the ultimate decision was the inevitable result of a half-century of sectional controversy over the inequalities under the constitution of 1776.

The approach to civil war gained momentum with turmoil in Kansas, the Dred Scott decision, the rise of the Republican party, and the raid by John Brown at Harpers Ferry. Brown had been a militant Free-

Soiler in Kansas and fought pitched battles with the pro-slavery element in the territory. Leaving Kansas after it apparently had become free-soil, he turned his attention to freeing the southern slaves. He planned to establish places along the Alleghenies where escaped slaves could find refuge while on their way to free-soil territory and freedom.

Brown and his followers seized the arsenal at Harpers Ferry on October 16, 1859, an act which was regarded as treasonous by both Virginia and the United States. Marines under Lieutenant-Colonel Robert E. Lee captured the ringleaders, and Brown was tried at Charles Town, sentenced to death, and hanged on December 2, 1859. This event solidified sentiment in Virginia on the question of division and further widened the breach between eastern and western Virginia.

The next year Lincoln was elected. Before his inauguration, seven southern States left the Union and formed themselves into the Confederated States of America. Then came the open breach.

Governor John Letcher of Virginia convened the General Assembly of Virginia in an extraordinary session January 7, 1861. A week later this session of the assembly ordered a convention of delegates to meet in Richmond on February 13. The assembly's action in doing this without first submitting the question of calling it to the people was without precedent.

When the convention met, representatives of three States that had seceded addressed the convention and urged Virginia to join them, but against their appeal the eloquence of Waitman T. Willey and others, including some eastern Virginians, prevailed and on the first vote taken on April 12, the ordinance of secession was defeated by a vote of 89 to 45.

South Carolina fired on Fort Sumter on April 12, and three days later President Lincoln asked for 75,000 volunteers to put down the rebellion. Brought face to face with the issue, Virginia, the strongest champion of States' rights, yielded to the pleas of her sister States of the South. On April 17, the ordinance of secession was passed by a vote of 88 to 55, to be valid when ratified by a vote of the people. Of the 46 members from what is now West Virginia, 9 voted for the ordinance, 7 were absent, 1 was excused, and 29 voted against it.

Twenty-two of the Virginia delegates held a secret meeting in the Powhatan Hotel in Richmond and resolved 'that the retiring delegates would oppose secession to the last, that they would keep Virginia or as much of her as possible loyal to the Union and that they would eventually move for dismemberment.'

At a meeting held in Clarksburg on April 22, 1861, attended by 1,200 citizens, resolutions were passed calling a general convention at Wheeling May 13, 1861. Twenty-six counties sent delegates.

John S. Carlile, just back from Richmond, was the moving spirit of the 'New Virginia Now or Never' fever at the first Wheeling Convention. Carlile wanted immediate steps taken to divorce the west from the east, but cooler heads gained the upper hand. Conservatives led by Waitman T. Willey pointed out that the vote on secession had not yet been taken, and that in any case the proper legal procedure would have to be gone through to create a new State. In the election which followed, the northwestern counties voted overwhelmingly against secession.

A second convention, held in Wheeling June 11, nullified the Virginia ordinance of secession, vacated the offices of the State government at Richmond and formed the 'Restored' government of Virginia. Francis H. Pierpont became governor and a month later, on August 20, provisions were made for a popular vote upon the formation of a new State.

The popular election of October 24, 1861, resulted in a vote of 18,408 to 781 in favor of the creation of a new State. A third convention, in which 47 counties were represented, met at Wheeling on November 26. It completed, on February 18, 1862, a constitution that was ratified early in April by a vote of 18,862 to 514.

President Lincoln on April 20, 1863, caused a proclamation to be issued under which 60 days later West Virginia became the 35th State of the Union.

WEST VIRGINIA AS A STATE

The new State's first governor, Arthur I. Boreman, and other officers were inaugurated on June 20, 1863, when Governor Pierpont turned over to them the government of West Virginia, and retired to Alexandria, the new capital of Virginia. Here he maintained the Restored government of Virginia until the end of the War between the States. He then moved the seat of government to Richmond where he maintained it until Congress took charge under military reconstruction.

Military operations in West Virginia favored the Federal troops from the beginning. The opening clash at Philippi, June 3, 1861, was a surprise attack at dawn that resulted, with few casualties, in the utter rout of the Confederate troops (about 700 men) under Colonel George A. Porterfield. General Robert S. Garnett commanded a force of 6,000 Confederates posted at Beverley in the Tygarts Valley between Cheat

Mountain on the east and Rich and Laurel Mountains on the west. It was a strategic point; the road from Staunton, Virginia, forked here, one road leading to Wheeling and the other to Parkersburg. Garnett divided his forces to protect both roads.

General George B. McClellan advanced against Garnett with a force of 10,000 Union troops. On July 11, part of McClellan's army under General W. S. Rosecrans decisively defeated part of Garnett's army under General John Pegram at the Battle of Rich Mountain.

Garnett with the remainder of his army was defeated on the 13th by the other wing of McClellan's forces commanded by General Thomas A. Morris at Corrick's Ford, near Parsons, in an engagement in which Garnett was killed (*see Tour 8a*).

In the Kanawha Valley, Federal General J. D. Cox moved on Charleston from Ohio, intent on driving out Confederate General Henry A. Wise. In a sharp skirmish, July 17, at Scary Creek, below the mouth of Coal River, the Federals were delayed a few hours. Finding the Federal army too overwhelming, Wise retreated up the valley, considering the region lost to the South because of the attitude of the people, and advised his superiors to this effect.

As a result, Confederate General John B. Floyd marched into the valley with a large army. Federal General W. S. Rosecrans, who succeeded to McClellan's command, moved south over the Weston-Gauley Bridge road to attack the Confederates. His advance guard was badly beaten on August 26 at Cross Lanes in Nicholas County. This Confederate victory was followed by defeat a few days later and the rout of General Wise's army near the mouth of Gauley River. Jealousy between Confederate Generals Floyd and Wise prevented them from joining forces and probably holding the valley for a longer time.

General Rosecrans came up with reinforcements and attacked General Floyd in a strongly fortified position at Carnifex Ferry, September 10. The battle was indecisive. Floyd learned that his position would be open to heavy artillery fire and, for fear Rosecrans would encircle him, retreated to the Greenbrier Valley. In November 1862, he was defeated at Gauley Bridge by General Roscrans, and with this battle the Federals gained control of the lower Kanawha Valley.

General Robert E. Lee made a futile attempt to gain lost ground by moving against Federal forces guarding the mountain passes near Staunton. After a feeble skirmish before a Federal fort on Cheat Mountain, September 12–13, the campaign was abandoned. This was the last serious attempt the Confederates made to recover lost ground west of the Alleghenies.

A small Confederate force did fortify a position on Greenbrier River and successfully hold off a strong Federal force under General Joseph J. Reynolds, on October 3, but they failed to follow up their victory. Retreating to Allegheny Mountain, they entrenched themselves again and repulsed another Federal assault, but failed once more to follow up their advantage. Shortly afterward, they retreated to the Shenandoah Valley, leaving West Virginia free of Confederate control.

From this time on the Confederates confined their operations to criss-crossing the State with lightning-like raids, destroying property, taking prisoners and disrupting Federal lines of communication. The Eastern Panhandle bore the brunt of the fighting, owing to its proximity to the Shenandoah Valley, which served as a place for the Confederate forces to dart in and out on raids into north and northwestern Virginia, which became West Virginia's northern counties.

In this fighting, Romney changed hands at least 56 times and 'Stonewall' Jackson once (September 15, 1862) captured Harpers Ferry with its garrison of 11,000 men.

The Baltimore & Ohio Railroad was subjected to attack continuously. The railroad officials tried to maintain a neutral position, but they changed their tactics after Jackson had corralled a large portion of their rolling stock and run it into the Shenandoah Valley. Their support was thrown to the North and made itself felt in the formation of West Virginia and the later inclusion of the Eastern Panhandle counties in the new State.

With only 550 men, Confederate General A. G. Jenkins entered Monroe County and marched up the Greenbrier River to the Staunton-Parkersburg road and then westward to the Ohio River in Jackson County in August 1862. He crossed into Ohio, circled, and returned to Virginia through the Kanawha Valley after a march of more than 500 miles.

Confederates under General W. W. Loring made a raid into the Kanawha Valley the following month, defeated General Joseph A. J. Lightburn, and captured considerable military supplies. Loring retreated shortly afterwards, fearing he would be surrounded.

Two divisions of 5,000 Confederates crossed the Alleghenies in 1863 and penetrated almost to the Ohio River. General William E. Jones led one division into Preston County and destroyed the railroad bridge across Cheat River. He went on to Morgantown and tried to burn the suspension bridge but it would not burn. Jones joined the main force under General John D. Imboden at Weston and the two divisions raided the oil fields of Wirt County, burning large stores of petroleum. From here they moved into the Kanawha Valley and destroyed what property they were unable to carry away.

Losing patience with the bewildered efforts of the State's Union soldiers to curb the raiders, the Federal Government placed General W. W. Averell in command of the State forces. He mounted the infantry and the chase of Confederates was on. His troops repelled an attack on Beverly. Then, marching in an attempt to reach Gettysburg before fighting began, they met a part of the retreating Confederates forces at Martinsburg and defeated them. In September General Averell drove a raiding party of 2,000 under General Sam Jones out of the Greenbrier Valley after a hard two-day battle from which Jones withdrew, after running out of ammunition and losing one-sixth of his men.

Another effort of the Confederates to penetrate beyond the mountains was frustrated when on November 6, 1863, Averell met General John Echols at the Battle of Droop Mountain in Pocahontas County. It was such a forceful meeting that Echols barely had time to escape from the field.

Averell's turn to reverse the order of things and raid a bit on his own part came with orders to make a lightning dash into enemy territory and cut the railroad leading from Virginia into Tennessee, where the Confederates were besieging General A. E. Burnside's army at Knoxville. Driving south from Keyser in December, he moved through several armies sent out to head him off and reached the railroad at Salem. After driving back an opposing force, he destroyed 16 miles of track.

Heavy rains had swollen the streams by the time Averell was ready to retreat. Perilously, he picked his way through hostile territory, dodging swift-moving forces bent on trapping him. When it looked as though they might succeed, an enemy dispatch rider was captured with information that led Averell to take the one road left open over the mountains of Pocahontas County. Taking it, blanketed with sleet and rain, he managed to escape after beating off forces attacking his rear.

In retaliation, General Jubal A. Early in January 1864 made a destructive raid on Petersburg. This was followed by four raids in the South Branch Valley. Averell struck back and destroyed part of the Virginia Railroad at Dublin. In August he swooped down on General John McCausland at Moorefield, defeated him, and captured hundreds of prisoners.

A Confederate force under Colonel V. A. Witcher attacked Weston, and took many prisoners and much livestock in September 1864. A pitched battle occurred later at Beverly, with the Confederates losing half their force and the Federals one-fourth of theirs.

The most persistent tormentors of the Federal command in the upper Potomac Valley was McNeill's Rangers. In May 1864, Captain J. H. McNeill, with 61 of his Rangers, captured Piedmont and destroyed a great deal of railroad property.

The last military operations of any size in West Virginia were the driving of a force of 800 Federals from Keyser and the taking of some prisoners in November 1864, and the capture of 580 prisoners at Beverly in January 1865 by Confederate General T. L. Rosser.

Confusion reigned throughout the entire war, with conflicting loyalties splitting families and friends, sometimes forever. Only in Hancock County was there a decisive adherence to one side. Southern sympathizers were concentrated in the southern counties and in the double tier of counties next to Virginia up to and including the Eastern Panhandle. They were so strong in some localities as to prevent the functioning of local government under the Restored Virginia regime and later under the new State.

Partisan bands of both sides roved the more divided counties and committed numerous outrages—arson, intimidation, robbery, and murder. This condition continued despite the efforts of the Home Guards, a semimilitary organization whose purpose was expressed in its title.

West Virginia contributed 36,530 soldiers to the Union Army and about 7,000 to the Confederate Army.

After the war, the Virginia legislature tried to patch up the dismemberment of the State in 1866, but the answer of the West Virginia legislature was 'that the people of this State are unalterably opposed to reunion . . . and will not entertain any proposition looking to that end.' Shortly afterward the dispute arose regarding to which State Jefferson and Berkeley Counties belonged. The Supreme Court decided in favor of West Virginia in 1871.

The question of West Virginia's share of the public debt of Virginia prior to January 1, 1861, immediately caused a 'back-fence fuss' between the two States, and the controversy lasted for 45 years. After early halfhearted efforts at settlement, the matter came to a head when

Virginia took the case to the Supreme Court in 1906. Virginia had taken the initiative to remove the debt in 1871 when it arbitrarily assumed two-thirds of the total and issued 'West Virginia Certificates' to the bondholders to cover the other third. In an adjustment with the bondholders in 1894, Virginia secured release from all obligations for a third of the debt, but promised to do everything possible to secure a settlement with West Virginia.

West Virginia had claimed that the debt should be settled by computing the difference between the amount of taxes sent to Richmond from western Virginia before 1861 and the amount spent on public improvements in that part of the State. On this basis, a West Virginia Senate Finance committee in 1873 figured that Virginia owed West Virginia $525,000; at this point the matter rested for several years, while 'West Virginia Certificates' sank lower and lower on the bond market.

Virginia claimed the debt should be settled on the basis of the 'equitable proportion' clause that had found its way into the first West Virginia constitution, apparently unintentionally.

The Supreme Court appointed Charles R. Littlefield, of Maine, to investigate the question. He declared that West Virginia's portion of the debt should be settled on the total valuation of all property in Virginia as of January 1, 1861—excluding slaves. This amounted to $7,182,507.46. But this was immediately scaled down to $4,215,622.28 through the benefits this State should get from the stocks and other securities held by Virginia.

By the time West Virginia got around to paying the debt, it amounted to $14,562,000.28, including interest. A cash payment of $1,062,876.16 was made in 1919 and the balance was taken care of by 23½ per cent bonds. Some money was saved by early judicious buying of the 'certificates' on the open market at their depressed price; others were lost and never presented.

First of West Virginia's public institutions was a lunatic asylum. In 1860, before the dissatisfied counties withdrew to form a separate State, the Virginia government had begun at Weston construction of such an asylum, the only State institution west of the Alleghenies. The new State completed the work in 1866.

Funds obtained by the sale of public lands donated in 1862 by the Federal Government enabled the State to establish the West Virginia Agricultural College at Morgantown, with the aid of donations of the properties of the Monongahela Academy and the Woodburn Female

Seminary in 1866. The name was changed to West Virginia University two years later.

There followed in quick succession the establishment of six normal schools to furnish teachers for the expanding school system. They were Marshall, West Liberty, Fairmont Normal, Glenville, Shepherd, and Concord—all by 1872. A school for the deaf and dumb was also established, at Romney in 1870. Erection of the State Penitentiary at Moundsville shortly after 1866 relieved the growing problem of where to keep State prisoners.

The crying need for State institutions delayed for several years the erection and location of the permanent State capital. After the organization of the State government, the capital remained at Wheeling until 1870, when it was moved to Charleston. Five years later the capital was moved to Wheeling.

An election to decide the permanent site of the capital, between Clarksburg, Martinsburg, and Charleston, was held in 1877, to take effect in 1885. Charleston won, and the capital was moved in 1885 to that city, which became the permanent seat of the State government.

All this was a side issue of a graver problem. The returning Confederate veterans found they were barred from the polls unless they took an oath of allegiance to the United States and to West Virginia. Their bitter reaction to this law led to the passage of a more stringent one—the Test Act of 1865 requiring the voter to swear he had never borne arms against the United States or aided armed hostile forces. More than 15,000 adult males were disfranchised after this law went into effect in 1866. Enforcement varied according to the proportion of Confederate votes; in Greenbrier County, where several Confederate veterans were elected to the legislature, enforcement was lax.

Passage of the Registration Act placed registration in the hands of county boards who appointed local registrars and supervised their work. This put more teeth in the Test Act. On a wave of bitterness created by these acts, the Democratic majority increased in the State. They elected their first governor in 1870 and that year the Test Act was repealed. W. H. H. Flick, a former Union soldier from Pendleton County, obtained the adoption of an amendment repealing the disfranchising amendment in 1866. It was ratified the following year and for a quarter of a century the Democratic party controlled all branches of the State government.

Calling a constitutional convention in 1872, the Democrats set about doing all they could to erase Republican legislation. In the election of delegates, the Democrats garnered 66 out of a total of 78. Stinging partisan feeling motivated the remodeling of the State government as nearly as possible along the lines established by the provisions of the Virginia constitution. There were even objections to flying the Stars and Stripes over the convention hall and to recognizing the United States Constitution as the supreme law of the land.

But liberal Democrats voted with the Republicans to nullify the efforts of the hot-headed anti-Federal extremists. They narrowly defeated return to *viva voce* voting, but a provision giving the voter a choice of open, sealed, or secret ballot was adopted. For many years, voting in the more remote sections took place at convenient crossroads with a representative of each party seated under a tree marking the votes in books, which were sealed and sent to the county seat. As late as 1883 it was two weeks after election before election returns could be obtained from counties such as McDowell, which had only four or five hundred votes at that time.

Drastic changes were made in the government. The terms of elective State officers were changed from two to four years and the office of lieutenant-governor was abolished. The meetings of the legislature became biannual and many persons were barred from qualifying as lawmakers. Local and special legislation was curtailed and the judicial and local government systems were changed.

West Virginia was controlled by the Democrats from 1871 to 1897. Under the governorship of John J. Jacob, the legislature confined itself to bringing the statute laws into conformity with the new constitution. Progress was also made in the administration of newly established State institutions.

The 'Bloody Shirt' campaign of 1876 saw the election of former Confederate soldiers to office. The Democratic governor was Henry M. Mathews, whose administration was characterized as 'an era of good feeling' because he appointed able men outside of the party to office and encouraged outside capital to enter and develop the State's natural resources.

The following Democratic governor, Jacob B. Jackson, made determined efforts to amend the tax laws. Assessment on property had not been increased, although the population had increased 40 per cent in 10 years. The legislature ignored recommendations of a tax commission of experts who studied the question, thereby setting a precedent followed faithfully by succeeding legislatures. But, Jackson, by executive order, increased the value of property on the tax books by $8,000,000.

For several reasons the Democratic majorities of 1884 dropped about 5,000. E. Willis Wilson started attacking the railroads soon after being elected. He made a vigorous effort to raise the assessment of railroad property to the general level of other property, to reduce discriminatory rates charged West Virginians, and to forbid the favor-currying practice of giving free passes to State officials. He warred also on trusts and election laws.

Election corruption was spotlighted by the close election of 1888. Following counter charges of corruption by Nathan Goff (R) and Aretus B. Fleming (D), an investigation revealed there had been illegal voting of Negroes in Mercer and McDowell Counties. On a joint ballot, the legislature declared Fleming the winner. Legislation was passed to prevent a recurrence of the incident.

This election brought to light in the public consciousness the place of the Negro as a citizen, a voter, and possible holder of public office. To a certain extent, the Negro had been instrumental in widening the breach that, before the War between the States, existed between eastern and western Virginia; the land in western Virginia was unsuitable for plantation farming, and few large plantations existed west of the mountains. This imposed a hardship on western Virginia farmers, who could not compete on the market with products grown by slaves on the large eastern Virginia plantations. As early as 1831–2, the trans-Allegheny farmer had backed a movement to free the slaves, and thereby equalize costs of agricultural production in eastern and western Virginia.

In 1860 there were 18,000 slaves and 3,000 free Negroes in the State, but most of them lived in the Eastern Panhandle and were employed as agricultural workers or domestics. Industrial expansion after 1870, however, attracted the Negro by its comparatively high wages, and by 1910, as the railroads opened up the great coal fields, the bulk of the Negro population was found to have shifted to Kanawha, Mingo, Fayette, Raleigh, Mercer, McDowell and Logan Counties, while the total Negro population had increased to 61,000.

Although an act of the legislature of February 3, 1865, abolished slavery, it was not until the Constitutional Convention of 1872 that there was established the Negro's right to vote and to hold public office. For a decade thereafter the Negroes were politically unorganized, but held a certain balance of power because they foreswore allegiance to either of the two parties. West Virginia, however, was spared the Reconstruction evils of carpetbag government, which brought ill-feeling and hatred between Negroes and whites in States farther south, and after 1880 the Negro came into some prominence in public affairs.

This possession of political power has extended to the election of Negroes to the legislative halls, to county and city positions, to membership on county, State, and national Republican executive committees, to appointive positions, to advanced social legislation and civil rights victories.

By slightly less than a 4,000 majority, William A. MacCorkle (D) became governor in 1892, but faced a Republican legislature. Labor troubles, which were met by the governor's calling out the militia, marked the administration. MacCorkle co-operated with the Republican legislature in a futile attempt to remove State institutions from the influence of politics.

The political tide turned in West Virginia in 1896, to continue, almost unbroken, Republican for 36 years, the continuity being broken only by John J. Cornwell (D) in 1916. G. W. Atkinson (R) was elected governor in 1896 by a plurality of 12,070 votes. The State's population was constantly increased by infiltration from Republican States, and the Republicans gained in power with each election. Atkinson advocated many reforms, such as free public libraries, labor legislation, and new election laws. Public hangings at court houses were abolished during his term.

Albert B. White became governor in 1900. His administration was devoted to financial and tax reforms, creation of the office of tax commissioner, and establishment of greater control over local assessments.

Victor over Albert B. White, the next Republican governor was William M. O. Dawson. He continued the policies of his predecessor in tightening the tax system. The administration of State institutions was placed in the hands of a central body, the State Board of Control. Dawson's administration was made noteworthy by the strict enforcement of tax laws.

A split endangered the Republicans in 1908, but two candidates retired and W. E. Glasscock stepped in to take the nomination and election. Labor troubles occurred during his administration.

Henry D. Hatfield (R) became governor by a 8,770 plurality in 1912. The labor controversy subsided during his regime and laws were passed to adjust the government to changing economic and social needs. The legislature of 1913 provided for a workmen's compensation law, a 'blue sky' law, a water-power bill, and the creation of the Public Service Commission to perform necessary regulation of public utilities. The labor strife bore fruit in the creation of the State Bureau of Labor, and the Department of Mines was established for the regulation of mine safety. Other legislation affecting health, prohibition, elections, and 'bucket shops' was enacted.

As a bit of political insurance, Hatfield proposed and secured the enactment of a bill that would make it almost impossible for an incoming governor to remove State officials.

The Republican party looked on for the next four years as Governor John J. Cornwell, Democrat, headed the State government. His administration was one of the most hectic any governor has ever had, with World War emergencies, strikes, and other troubles stirring the State. He called a special session of the legislature to enact needed emergency laws. Levies were increased, idleness became a crime, and speculation in food and fuel was outlawed. Disorders in the southern West Virginia coal fields resulted from the efforts of the operators to prevent unionization, and Federal troops were called in to maintain order until the tension was eased.

Republican Governor Ephraim F. Morgan inherited labor unrest in Logan County, where Federal troops were again used to restore peace.

Other aspects of Morgan's administration were confined to the promotion of legislation and taxation relating to the improvement of roads. Numerous amendments were made to the road laws.

During the regime of Republican Governor Howard M. Gore, much progress was made in the construction of permanent roads. The gasoline tax was increased twice and a $35,000,000 road-bond issue was authorized. The administration of the university was also altered by placing it under the control of an appointive board of governors.

Governor William G. Conley (R) came into office in 1928 in a period of artificial prosperity, but before his term expired, West Virginia had been caught in the grip of a Nation-wide business slump. During his administration, a power company secured concessions from the administration to develop the water power of the Cheat watershed. The State press and other interests fought it on the grounds of questionable honesty of purpose and the conditions it imposed. A bitter fight through the courts ended with the State Supreme Court declaring the concessions void.

Pushed by the West Virginia Farm Bureau for the farmers and favored by real-estate owners all over the State, the Broad Classification Tax Amendment was claimed by both political parties in the gubernatorial campaign of 1932 and became law soon afterward. It placed a limit on taxation of general property and brought to a halt the growing sale of property for taxes. It is estimated that this law saved the farmers of the State 50 per cent of their tax bill.

In 1932 Herman Guy Kump became the first Democratic governor of West Virginia since the World War. During his administration new revenue measures were recommended and passed by the legislature, as well as the county-unit school law requiring extensive consolidation of schools. Funds were stipulated for the improvement and construction of secondary roads under the administration of the State Road Commission. Prohibition was repealed and beer became legal.

Homer A. Holt (D) succeeded Kump in 1937 and pursued the policies of his predecessor, under whom he had served as attorney general. This included co-operation with the Federal Government in public works projects and relief. Social Security legislation to tie in with Federal provisions and other social legislation were passed. The 1937 legislature levied a special one-cent gasoline tax earmarked for work on secondary roads, to expire July 1, 1939, which was renewed by the next legislature to last until July 1, 1941.

Industrially, the State changed most markedly during the 1890's from the self-sufficing economy of the local communities not dependent on railroads to the dependence on labor's wages in the awakening industrial era. Formerly, the isolated communities produced almost everything they needed, all of the extra money they might need for taxes came through sale of surplus crops. Today, the State has no self-sufficient communities; all are united in the modern specialized and differentiated industrial system.

Population and Its Distribution

RANKING twenty-seventh in population among the States, West Virginia has a density of population more than 70 per cent greater than the average for the United States: 72 persons per square mile as compared with 41.3 for the Nation. This is a greater density than exists in two of its bordering States, Kentucky and Virginia, but not nearly so great as that of the other three—Pennsylvania (214.8), Maryland (164.1), and Ohio (163.1). Density within the State varies from 13.8 in Pendleton County, southernmost bulge of the Eastern Panhandle, to 674 in Ohio County in the Northern Panhandle.

Distribution of population coincides with that of the State's coal, oil, and natural-gas fields and of the industries located to take advantage of proximity to them. The Northern Panhandle, the Great Kanawha Valley, and the upper Monongahela are the three most thickly populated parts of the State; and in these areas also are the principal coal fields and the larger industrial enterprises.

West Virginia has 12 cities with populations of more than 10,000, 13 cities with between 5,000 and 10,000, and 20 incorporated towns with between 2,500 and 5,000. Of cities above 10,000 in population, eight are within the three industrial areas and seven are on commercially navigable waters.

The small communities, for the most part, are of two distinctly different types: trade towns and coal-mining towns. The trade towns, serving the needs of limited agricultural and grazing areas, are usually older than the State itself, have changed little in appearance and population over many years, and represent one of the most stable aspects of the State, both socially and economically. Most of the coal towns have originated since 1900 and are almost wholly dependent on the miners for their existence.

More than 90 per cent of the State's population is made up of persons born in the United States, and nearly three-quarters of its

61

1,901,974 residents live on farms or in non-urban communities. The foreign-born population, which in 1930 was 51,865, is concentrated in six industrial cities: Wheeling, Clarksburg, Charleston, Fairmont, Huntington, and Morgantown. In 20 of the 55 counties, native whites form more than 98 per cent of the population, and here the proportion of rural-farm population is high.

The United States Census Bureau classified 45.6 per cent of the population in 1940 as 'rural-nonfarm.' The extensive coal mines of the State supply the explanation for this large percentage: the rural-non-farm group is made up principally of coal miners living either in company houses or on small farms that provide part of their livelihood. The rural-farm group in 1940 formed only 26.3 per cent of the total population, and the urban group only 28.1 per cent.

The agricultural census of 1935 showed that during the depression years following 1930 the rural-farm group had increased by 114,000 persons. This decided gain was attributed to the flight of unemployed industrial workers to the farms and to the continued residence on farms of young people who in good times would have sought work in industry. Consequently, the trend is regarded as impermanent. At the same time the increase in the State's total population slowed. Between 1920 and 1930 the general gain surpassed that of any previous decade; but the rate of increase since 1930 was 10 per cent, more than half that of the decade preceding. Census statisticians have predicted that the State's population will be stationary by 1960.

At the beginning of the American Revolution, western Virginia was peopled by approximately 30,000 German, Scotch-Irish, Welsh, and English immigrants, who had made scattered settlements in the Eastern Panhandle, along the upper Ohio River Valley, and in the Greenbrier and New River areas. The majority were Germans and Scotch-Irish from Pennsylvania, New York, and Maryland, who differed in habits and customs from the English of eastern Virginia. Hessian ex-soldiers also took up lands in the western counties at the close of the war. Land promoters were active in bringing in new settlers; apparently some of them were what a later era would have termed 'high-powered salesmen.' In 1808 a group of New Englanders chose French Creek, in Upshur County, for settlement, in preference to a site on which the city of Chicago now stands.

When West Virginia became a State (1863) its population of 380,000 included about 20,000 Negroes and 17,000 foreign-born. The latter were principally Germans and Swiss, although a considerable number

The Mountain State

otograph by courtesy of Janet M. Taylor

CACAPON STATE PARK

CHAMPE ROCKS, NEAR MOUTH OF SENECA CREEK

MOUNTAIN PANORAMA

SENECA ROCK, NEAR PETERSBURG

Photograph by courtesy of U.S. Forest Serv

ENTRANCE TO SMOKE HOLE SECTION, MONONGAHELA NATIONAL FOREST

MEETING OF THE POTOMAC AND SHENANDOAH RIVERS, HARPERS FERRY

Photograph by courtesy of Baltimore & Ohio Railrc

BLACKWATER FALLS, NEAR DAVIS

MOUNTAIN STREAM, MONONGALIA COUNTY

WINTER ON CHEAT MOUNTAIN

GERMANY VALLEY

BLACK BEAR, IN THE MONONGAHELA FOREST

RHODODENDRON, THE STATE FLOWER

Photograph by courtesy of Janet M. Tayl

were Irish who had come to America after the great potato famine of 1847, worked as construction laborers on the Baltimore & Ohio Railroad, and made numerous settlements along the route.

In 1864 the State legislature created the post of commissioner of immigration, whose function was to encourage further settlement, but the real-estate interests and individual promoters continued to supply the chief stimuli for migration. In 1869 a New York firm induced Swiss emigrants to establish a colony in a mountainous section of Randolph County, which they named Helvetia. Their descendants follow the occupations of their ancestors, retain many of the customs and traditions of the homeland, and speak German and English with equal fluency (*see Tour* 15).

In the decades since 1890 the rate of population growth in West Virginia has exceeded the United States average. This has been owing to the demand for labor created by exploitation of natural resources, and the subsequent expansion of industries. Italians, Germans, Poles, Hungarians, and Irish have flocked to the mining and manufacturing centers. Between 1910 and 1920 the peak of immigration to the State was reached.

Eighty per cent of the foreign-born are from countries of southern and southeastern Europe. Italy leads with 23.3 per cent of the total; Poland is represented by 10.7 per cent; and Hungary by 7.1 per cent. People of other nationalities in order of their numerical importance are English, German, Czech and Slovak, Greek, Yugoslav, Austrian, and Russian. Only in Wheeling and Clarksburg are the foreign sections concentrated enough to be distinguishable. Usually the immigrants are eager to take part in local political and commercial activities and soon abandon most of their native ways. Italians, Poles, Syrians, and Czechs, however, often have their own churches, parish schools, and social organizations.

Fifty-nine per cent of the 114,000 Negroes living in West Virginia in 1930 were migrants from other States. Of these nearly half were from Virginia, and a large proportion of the rest were from Alabama and North Carolina. Distribution of the Negro residents of West Virginia is highly localized; 75 per cent live in the southern counties of Kanawha, Raleigh, and McDowell, while in seven counties in the western part of the State, comprising an area of 2,725 square miles, the combined Negro population in 1930 was only 103. Rural-nonfarm Negro population in 1930 was nearly 80,000; urban, 31,224; rural-farm, only 3,815.

The 1930 census reported 570,459 West Virginians classed as gainful workers, and of this total 122,000 were engaged in manufacturing, 118,000 in agriculture, and 110,000 in coal mining. The peak of employment in coal mining was in 1927, with a total of 125,000. Since that year the farmers have outnumbered the coal miners in each annual report of occupational statistics.

In 1880 the average number of persons in a West Virginia family was almost six. In 1930 the number per family had declined to 4.36, but this figure was still considerably higher than the United States average of 3.4. The rural farm group has the largest families, averaging 4.48, while urban residents have the smallest, 3.47.

West Virginia's illiteracy rate for persons ten years of age and above was 4.8 per cent as compared to the United States average of 4.3 per cent in 1930. Illiteracy among the foreign-born is high, especially in the industrial and mining areas. The regions with the highest ratio of illiteracy are the extreme southern counties in the Big Sandy and Kanawha River basins and some of the eastern counties in the Potomac River basin, where communities are isolated for lack of good roads.

School attendance in the State was slightly under that for the nation in 1930. Only 49.8 per cent of the young people in the 16- to 17-year age group were included. As a general rule children quit school at an early age and go to work at farming, at coal mining, or in one or another industry dependent on, or connected with, the State's natural resources. Of each 100 pupils who enroll in the second grade of school, 67 reach the eighth grade, but only 25 complete their high school education. Of these, eight enter some university or college, but only three continue to the senior year. These percentages, however, are believed to have improved since 1930, because of steadily increasing transportation facilities provided by the State.

Contemporary Government

GOVERNMENT in West Virginia varies little from the traditional form of American commonwealths. The State constitution adopted in 1872 differs from the first constitution of 1863 chiefly in the abolition of test oaths as a qualification for the right to vote and hold office. The later document contains a bill of rights, reserving to the people certain liberties and privileges, including the right to be secure in their houses and persons against searches and seizure without a warrant, freedom of speech and of the press, religious freedom, the right to jury trial, and the provision that private property shall not be taken without due process of law or confiscated for public use without just compensation, which 'shall be ascertained by an impartial jury of freeholders.'

The question of calling a constitutional convention must be decided by a majority vote of the people, upon a demand by a majority of the members elected to both houses of the legislature. If a constitutional convention is held, its proceedings must be ratified by popular vote. A proposed amendment must receive approval by a two-thirds vote in the legislature; then it is submitted to the people at the next general election. Only a majority vote by the people is necessary for ratification.

The powers of the State government are vested in three branches: executive, legislative, and judicial.

The chief executive officer, the governor, is elected for a term of four years, and for a like period after his term of office expires he is ineligible to succeed himself. He is invested with the usual veto and pardoning powers. The other elective executive officers, chosen for four-year terms, are secretary of State, State superintendent of free schools, State treasurer, State auditor, attorney general, and commissioner of agriculture. These elective officers, who may succeed themselves, and the governor compose the board of public works, the duties of which are many and varied: the most important are making up the State

65

budget and presenting it to the legislature, investing the State workmen's compensation fund, and assessing the values of public-service utilities for the purpose of taxation.

The school system is administered by the State board of education composed of the State superintendent of free schools and six members appointed by the governor. The school system is based on the county unit plan, which supplanted the old system of independent rural and urban districts. A constitutional amendment limiting the amount of the direct levy on property was one contributing cause of this change. Another was the growing belief that rural school children should have all the advantages enjoyed by urban school children. Under the new system the county boards of education have taken over the functions and property of the district boards.

The legislature of West Virginia is composed of two houses, the senate and the house of delegates. The State senate is composed of 32 members, two from each of the 16 senatorial districts. Each district is made up of from one to six counties. State senators are elected for a term of four years. The house of delegates has 94 members, each county being represented by at least one delegate, the number ranging from one to eight according to population. Delegates are elected for a term of two years.

Bills may originate in either house, but for passage must be approved by a majority in both and either be signed by the governor or be allowed to become a law after having been before him for five days (Sundays excepted) without his veto. If a bill is vetoed and returned to the legislature, it can be repassed and become a law by a majority vote of both houses. In regular session the legislature convenes biennially for 60 days at Charleston on the second Wednesday in January in the odd-numbered years.

The judicial power of the State government is vested in the supreme court of appeals, circuit courts, courts of limited jurisdiction under special enactments of the legislature, and in justices of the peace.

The supreme court of appeals is composed of 5 judges, elected for a period of 12 years each, and has original jurisdiction in cases of *habeas corpus, mandamus,* and prohibition, and appellate jurisdiction in cases from the various circuit courts and in some instances from the rulings of State boards and commissioners.

The 24 circuit courts of the State are composed of from one to four counties each. Judges are elected for the term of eight years, and a circuit court must be held in every county at least three times in each year. In the majority of circuits the courts have original jurisdiction in all cases, civil (above a certain amount involved both at law and in equity) and criminal, except in more populous counties where they are relieved by other courts created by special acts of the legislature.

The circuit courts have appellate jurisdiction over justices of the peace and inferior courts. The special courts have only the jurisdiction conferred upon them by the legislature. Justices of the peace have a limited jurisdiction in both civil and criminal cases, subject to appeal to the circuit courts.

There are two Federal courts in West Virginia, the State being divided into two judicial districts, northern and southern. The Federal court has jurisdiction in cases involving crimes and offenses against the Federal Government, and in the naturalization of aliens. Its civil jurisdiction is confined almost entirely to cases of diverse citizenship (a suit between a resident of this State and a resident of another State) and to suits involving the constitutionality of State and Federal laws.

West Virginia is represented by six members in the lower house of Congress. The make-up of congressional and of State senatorial districts, and also of the various judicial circuits, as well as the time for holding courts in each circuit, is fixed by the legislature.

The sheriff, the chief financial and peace officer of the county, is elected for a period of four years and cannot succeed himself. A county court is composed of three commissioners, who decide probate matters and govern the fiscal affairs of the county. The prosecution of all major crimes originates with an indictment by the grand jury and is followed by trial in court by a petit jury. The prosecuting attorney, elected for a term of four years, is charged with the prosecution of all crimes. Coroners, overseers of the poor, and road surveyors are appointed by the county courts.

Among the progressive laws that have been enacted in West Virginia are the public-service commission law (enacted in 1913), providing for a commission of three members appointed by the governor to regulate the rates charged by public-service corporations; a workmen's compensation law (enacted in 1913), providing compensation for workmen hurt in the course of their employment and for dependents in case of the death of a worker while discharging his duties; a law establishing the State department of banking (enacted in 1901), which supervises the creation and operation of banking institutions; an insurance-department law, providing for supervision of the licensing and operation of insurance companies and their agents in the State (enacted in 1907); a law providing for the registration of securities before they are offered for sale to the public, and giving the State auditor power to refuse registration to those not entitled to it (enacted in 1913); a State tax-department law (enacted in 1904), which provides for auditing the accounts of the fiscal officers of the counties and cities of the State, and places assessment and collection of taxes under the State tax commissioner; and a public-welfare law (enacted in 1936), which provides assistance to indigent, aged, and blind persons and to dependent children, and physical rehabilitation for physically handicapped adult persons.

Miners profited from a department-of-mines law (enacted in 1905), which provides for inspection of all mining operations in the State and the operation of a rescue division; a department-of-labor law (enacted in 1889), which provides for the protection of working people from unfair practices and adverse working conditions; and a law creating a State board of health (enacted in 1882). More recent legislation includes a law creating a State road commission (enacted in 1909) to have supervision of the construction and upkeep of the roads of the State; a law establishing the department of agriculture (enacted in 1911), which promotes the welfare of farmers and keeps them informed of modern methods; a law creating the State conservation commission (enacted in 1933), which supervises the conservation of forests and the protection of game and fish and has charge of State parks; and a law establishing the department of public safety (enacted in 1921) to patrol the roads and aid in the enforcement of other laws.

Spirituous liquors, in package form for beverage purposes, are sold exclusively by State stores and agencies, and by licensed drug stores for medical use. All sales are under supervision of the State liquor-control commission. The legislature of 1935 enacted a law defining as nonintoxicant ale, beer, and other malt beverages with alcoholic content of not more than 5 per cent. These may be sold either in original packages or for consumption on the premises by those licensed to sell them.

In addition to direct taxes the State has a business and occupation tax based on the amount of income received by persons engaged in gainful occupations; a tax of 5¢ per gallon on gasoline sales; an inheritance tax, a consumers' sales tax; a license tax on corporations based on the amount of their capital stock; and license fees for engaging in certain occupations.

Increased costs of a more complex State government caused such a heavy direct tax on property that the voters ratified a constitutional amendment, which provided that after 1933 the direct tax should not exceed 1¢ on the $100 valuation, except when necessary to pay the principal and interest on then existing bonded indebtedness. This led to the imposition of a consumers' sales tax, by which the purchaser is required to pay a tax of 1¢ on purchases between 6¢ and 50¢ and a tax of 1¢ on each additional purchase of 50¢ or a part thereof. The tax is collected by the retail merchants from the purchaser.

Contemporary government in the State may be said to represent the best achievements of the two major political parties, given power by an unusually large percentage of the population of voting age—85 per cent in the general election of 1936.

The Republican party furnished the first governors of war-born West Virginia—a logical outcome of the inclusion in the first constitution of the provision that no one could vote or hold office who had aided the rebellion against the Union. In 1871, however, the Democratic party swung into power and continued to hold sway until 1897. The Republicans were in power from 1897 until 1933, except from 1917 until 1921 when control was divided between the two major parties. From 1933 until the present year (1941) the Democratic party has again been dominant.

Agriculture

THE most remarkable thing about West Virginia farming is that it is carried on so extensively under such difficult handicaps. The valleys are fertile but narrow and therefore limited in area, and much of the agricultural activity is characterized aptly if facetiously as 'perpendicular farming'—the crops being grown on steep hillsides. Of the State's 15,374,080 acres, less than one-fifth have a slope of less than 12 feet per 100 feet of expanse. Three million acres slope from 12 to 25 per cent, 6,000,000 from 25 to 40 per cent, and 4,000,000 more than 40 per cent. Nevertheless, 61 per cent of West Virginia's total acreage is owned by farmers; the State's agriculture provides a livelihood for more than a quarter of its population, and agricultural commodities rank fourth in value in the annual production total.

Considering rainfall, temperature, and soil, West Virginia is naturally adapted to a diversity of crops. Rainfall in the State averages from 40 to 50 inches annually; and this is sufficient for the production of crops in every farming area of the State. The great range in altitude from 240 to 4,860 feet gives to the several sections of the State differences in temperature that permit the production of a wide variety of crops. Crops that cannot be grown in States farther south because of excessive heat and crops that cannot be grown in northern states because of the early frosts are produced in abundance in West Virginia.

Most of the farms are small, averaging only 90 acres as compared with the United States average of 157. The opposite was true when George Washington, Lord Fairfax, and other colonial leaders held extensive land grants in this territory, and continued true long after. The difficulties of travel and transportation seriously hampered agricultural growth. But as the land was gradually acquired by Scotch-Irish immigrants and other settlers who could not afford slaves for working extensive holdings, small-scale farming began. After coal mining became the State's principal industry, there developed still another type of farming: that of men who divided their time between tilling a few acres and working in near-by mines or industrial plants.

In 1935, 9,423,655 acres, or 61.3 per cent of the State's total area, was classed as farm land, and the value of agricultural products was $79,308,000. The 1930 census reported 118,000 West Virginians gainfully employed in agriculture, which was 8,000 more than the number engaged in coal mining. A 'back-to-the-farm' movement in the depression period of 1930–35 increased the State's farm population by an estimated 114,000, though this increase is not expected to be permanent.

Another feature of the depression years was a tremendous increase in farm gardening, the result of thousands of unemployed persons growing a large part of their own foodstuffs. During 1934 and 1935 the Federal Emergency Relief Administration and other Federal agencies spent $250,000 to promote this activity in the State, but since 1937 the project has been under the State department of public assistance. In 1937 this department spent $15,000 for seeds for 20,495 gardens, and a like amount was spent on approximately 30,000 gardens in 1938. In some localities gardening is stimulated through prize awards offered by civic organizations, service clubs, and merchants. Several coal companies sponsor competition among their employees in growing vegetables and flowers, and one miner was awarded first honors for four consecutive years at the annual dahlia show held in the exclusive Greenbrier Hotel at White Sulphur Springs.

Nearly three-fourths of West Virginia's farms are owner-operated; only 25.8 per cent of them were occupied by tenants in 1935. Of the owner-operated farms 59.7 per cent were free from debt in 1930—a higher percentage than in any other State.

Almost 70 per cent of the total farm income is from livestock and livestock products, milk alone accounting for 29.5 per cent and poultry and eggs for 14 per cent in 1935. Cattle, hogs, sheep, and poultry are produced throughout the State, and 52.5 per cent of the total farm acreage is in pasturage. The principal cattle-raising areas are in the north-central and western parts of the State, embracing the Monongahela, Kanawha, South Branch, and Greenbrier Valleys, in which are luxuriant fields of bluegrass.

In 1930 West Virginia produced 462,000 pounds of butter; in 1935 the figure dropped to 356,000, a decline of 23 per cent. To improve this situation the State department of agriculture started a campaign of modernizing cream stations, raising testing standards, and improving cream quality. The re-establishment of home-owned butter plants was encouraged and promoted. Results were shown by the 1938 production of 3,500,000 pounds—an increase of 883 per cent over that of 1935. West Virginia had 205 licensed cream stations in 1938, representing an increase of 67 per cent in two years; and there were 9 butter-manufacturing concerns within the State.

Most State institutions maintain their own dairy herds and are rapidly developing purebred stock. Probably the most unusual dairy herd in West Virginia is that owned by a coal company at Holden, Logan County, in an area entirely without pasturage. Its 50 cattle have never tasted green grass but, fed entirely on concentrated feeds, ranked second highest in the State in butterfat production in 1938.

Hampshire and Hardy Counties in the northeastern section and the counties bordering the lower Ohio River are the leading poultry-producing areas. The production of both swine and sheep is well distributed over the State's 55 counties.

The high ratio of livestock production accounts for the fact that two feed crops, hay and corn, make up 77.5 per cent of the cultivated crops; winter wheat, oats, potatoes, and buckwheat (a high-altitude crop) follow in order. Only New York and Pennsylvania lead the State in buckwheat production. In 1937 West Virginia produced 350,000 bushels of buckwheat grown in 25 counties. The topography of West Virginia is against extensive wheat-growing, and wheat is regarded as more valuable as a 'nurse-crop' for young grass and clover than as a source of profit. Crops of lesser importance include tobacco, rye, barley, soybeans, and sorghum. The tobacco area, in counties near Huntington, is not large but is highly productive. Farm gardens produce 8 per cent of the total farm income.

The Eastern Panhandle of West Virginia dips into the Shenandoah Valley, one of the country's best apple-producing areas; and nearly 7 per cent of the State's farm income is from this fruit. One of the early horticulturists in this section was George Washington, who in 1774 leased William Bartlett 125 acres of Berkeley County land with the stipulation 'that within seven years, an orchard of winter apple trees and 100 peach trees be planted . . . and that the number thereof be kept up during the term of the lease.' The Northern Panhandle section also is important for apple production, and it was here that a popular variety of yellow apple, the Grimes Golden, originated. Near Wellsburg, Brooke County, where the first Grimes Golden was grown, stands the only monument in the world erected in honor of an apple tree. Another variety of yellow apple, the Golden Delicious, had its origin in Clay County, in central West Virginia.

Apple producers of West Virginia, Virginia, Maryland, and Pennsylvania support and maintain a marketing organization known as Appalachian Apples, Inc., with headquarters at Martinsburg. No part of the fruit is wasted; even the core and seeds are made into stock feed.

At Martinsburg and Inwood in the Eastern Panhandle are large canning and vinegar plants. Peaches, also grown chiefly in the panhandles, are the second important fruit, and during the August-September marketing season special peach trains are run from these production centers to the large eastern cities. Most farmers grow pears, plums, cherries, quinces, grapes, and strawberries for home use and, to a lesser extent than peaches and apples, as market crops. Native wild fruit—pawpaws, persimmons, strawberries, blackberries, dewberries, huckleberries, and cranberries—are marketed locally. There is also a ready local market for black walnuts, hickory nuts, and butternuts.

Although the character of the country does not permit extensive use of tractors and other modern farm machinery, practicable improvements have been adopted on many West Virginia farms. Natural gas is generally used for fuel and lights, and electrification is being extended into many sections. Motor trucks transport commodities to markets over well-built highways, and in the more prosperous farming sections nearly every rural family owns a passenger automobile. Radios, many of the dry-cell battery type, bring the farm family entertainment as well as the informative farm programs sponsored by the State department of agriculture and other agencies. The West Virginia Department of Agriculture began weekly farm information broadcasts in 1937, and a year later the programs had become so popular that broadcasts were made five days a week.

The State department of agriculture, created by the legislature in 1911, provides general agricultural information and, through special divisions, offers assistance in problems concerned with feed, seed and fertilizer control, plant and animal diseases, dairying, livestock care, marketing, crop and livestock reporting, grading products, and bee control. An increasingly important function of the department is the supervision of public markets and the grading of farm products at collecting centers, shipping points, and public markets. The graders, with authority to give Federal inspection certificates, assure both shipper and buyer of protection; and livestock producers who have made use of the public markets in the State have obtained substantially better prices.

The two co-operatives, West Virginia Livestock Association and West Virginia Co-operative Shippers' Association, deal principally in lambs, although some sheep and calves are handled. State-graded lambs sold through the co-operatives in 1938 totaled approximately 125,000 head, as compared with 75,000 in 1937 and 50,000 in 1936. Sheep raisers also participate in a wool-marketing co-operative in which State grading is maintained. The 1938 wool-pool crop totaled 569,028 pounds, valued at $134,427.

In addition to the co-operative markets, 22 commercial livestock markets in 1938 handled all kinds of livestock and, in some instances, vegetables, fruits, and other commodities. Many of these take advantage of the services of the State graders at their sales. Since 1936 numerous truck gardeners have called on the graders for co-operation in marketing small fruits and vegetables.

A fresh-egg law, which became effective in West Virginia in 1937, requires that the quality of eggs purchased for resale must be shown on the invoice and that storage eggs must be so labeled. In carrying out the intent of this legislation, the department works educationally with retail organizations and instructs small producers how to candle eggs.

The department co-operates with the State university at Morgantown, which offers a four-year agricultural course leading to a B.S.A. degree. The U. S. Department of Agriculture maintains an agricultural experiment station on a 1,000-acre farm on the university grounds. This station has general supervision over another experimental farm near Wardensville, Hardy County, on 937 acres donated to the State by the heirs of the late Lawrence Reymann for use in the development of dairy herds. The farm's Ayrshire cattle have won numerous world and national championships in milk production. Branch experimental and demonstration stations are located near Lewisburg for beef-cattle problems, at Lakin for truck-crop problems, and at Inwood for problems pertaining to fruit growing and fruit packing.

A comparatively new activity undertaken by the department is a campaign for more extensive agricultural use of the State's huge lime deposits. A large part of West Virginia's farm land has become unproductive, but could be revitalized through intensive fertilization. In 1937 a new law defined specifications for lime and fertilizer, and the department maintains a laboratory to assist the farmers in obtaining high-grade products. Some communities have co-operative lime-grinding projects and lime-burning kilns.

County farm agents, appointed by the university's extension division with the approval of county farm bureaus and county courts, help co-ordinate these activities and are always on hand at the county seats to aid farmers in solving their problems. There were agents in 51 counties in 1938. They are maintained with funds provided by two or more—in some cases all five—of the following agencies: the farm bureau, the county court, the county board of education, the State government, and the Federal Government. Many counties also have home demonstration agents, appointed and maintained in the same manner; and some have club agents, usually provided through the joint efforts of the extension division and the county board of education.

The West Virginia Farm Bureau, a farmers' co-operative organized in 1916, has units in 51 counties, each with a minimum of 150 members. The farm women's bureau, a similar organization for farm women, has units in 36 counties. Most of the counties have units of the Agricultural Conservation Association, composed of farmers receiving payments under the Agricultural Adjustment Act. The 4-H clubs, with more than 1,000 groups and 20,000 members among the farm boys and girls of West Virginia, offer early training for future farmers and farm women.

The Negro takes an active part in agricultural activities. Under the supervision of West Virginia State College, farm extension workers are located in 11 counties. In 1928 a 4-H Camp for Negroes was located in Cabell County, under the direction of the Negro 4-H Club, Boy Scout and Girl Scout leaders. In 1938 there were 112 Negro 4-H Clubs in West Virginia with a membership of 2,359. In 1937 the legislature approved the establishment of a Negro 4-H Camp; construction of the Camp is underway at the present time. Five Negro high schools have agricultural departments.

The first fair in the State was held at Mecklenburg (Shepherdstown) in 1766. Now many counties have annual fairs, while several others hold them more or less regularly; and the exhibits, demonstrations, and contacts at these events are an important part of the general program to encourage agricultural development. In addition, the producers of apples, potatoes, tomatoes, strawberries, and tobacco conduct annual festivals.

Industry

THE foundation of West Virginia's industrial structure has always been its natural resources, chief of which are coal, oil, gas, and lumber. Out of the exploitation of these have sprung other industries. Ranked in the order of the value of their products in 1940 the leading industries were: coal, natural gas, iron and steel, petroleum, glass, chemicals, cloth and clothing, electric power, lumber, meat packing, and chinaware and porcelain. The number of gainful workers in the State, according to the 1930 census, was 570,452, most of whom were employed in coal mining, chemical and mechanical industries.

West Virginia industry may be characterized by three general assertions: it has been self-generative; it is interdependent to a marked extent; and it has been financed almost wholly by absentee capital, with control vested in nonresidents of the State. An examination of the present industrial pattern reveals an interrelation that proves the second of these statements and suggests the first; a glance at the capital structure discloses the third. The State's social fabric and its political mold have been influenced greatly by the third characteristic.

Since John P. Turner supplied the salt works at Burning Springs with coal from his small mine, the tendency of one industry to produce another and to be dependent upon it has continued to exercise its force in producing the West Virginia industrial pattern. The earliest industry in the State was that of lumber, if home-building by the settlers can be called industry; or perhaps, iron-smelting, for as early as 1790 a furnace was founded on Kings Creek in Hancock County to make cannon balls, some of which helped Perry to win the Battle of Lake Erie. The first large and well-organized industry was salt-making. Both salt and iron demanded a better fuel than wood; as a result the industrial possibilities of coal were recognized 75 years after John Peter Salley first found it on Coal River in 1742. The new fuel proved so efficient that it was adopted for use by the railroads, which were already penetrating the western wilderness in an attempt to head off the canal movement that threatened to deprive Baltimore of its trade. More mines were opened, and more railroads were built to exploit the mines. Wherever the rails were laid, towns grew and people built homes. Increased population demanded more products, and industries were started to satisfy new demands. New factories thus begun sought outlets to world markets. And so the endless chain built itself link by link until the whole became so interlocked that the removal of any link would disturb seriously all the others and, in the case of an important link such as coal or natural gas, destroy the chain.

It is especially notable that coal is the important element throughout, uniting and binding together the other industries. Coal furnishes raw material for many manufactures and fuel for others, and it is mainly because of coal that railroads, without which the sale of other products in the world's mart would not be possible, have been built and maintained. This is the explanation of coal's predominance in any industrial portrait of West Virginia.

When the first iron ore furnace west of the Alleghenies was erected on Kings Creek in 1790, wood was still the fuel. From the days of first settlement, the settlers with broadaxe and whipsaw had laid waste vast areas of the yellow poplar, birch, ash, oak, spruce, hemlock, black walnut, and other varieties of West Virginia timber, to build homes, fences, barns, and boats and for fuel. With the rivers and wagon roads providing the ways of transportation, a gradual development of the lumber industry began, especially after the introduction of the water-powered sawmill, about 1755. The advent of the railroad brought a slow expansion, but not until 1881 when the band mill replaced the water mill did lumber come into its own. The swing of the long-bladed saw of the water mill had been so slow that lumbermen dubbed it the 'up today and down tomorrow' mill. The new mill was steam-powered. Production increased rapidly, and by 1909 West Virginia's output reached a peak of 1,472,942,000 board feet, the largest State production in the Union. Rapidly the virgin forests melted away under unbridled exploitation. No effort at conservation was made. Today, lumber no longer rates first in the State's economy; it ranks ninth in the value of its products. Yet the industry still supplies the State and Nation with hemlock, spruce, white pine, ash, basswood, beech, birch, chestnut, hickory, maple, oak, walnut, and yellow poplar, to a total of 252,974 board feet (1935 figures), and other products including shingles, lath, veneers, staves, clothes pins, pulp, and paper. A program of conservation has shown promise of restoring a part of the lost forests, but the number employed and the amount invested in lumber is so small today that the West Virginia Blue Book lists lumbering among the miscellaneous industries.

Iron and steel is more typical of State industry than lumber. From the first small iron furnace, the industry expanded rapidly to supply the needs of the pioneering hordes, to furnish rails and spikes and locomotives for the railroads, to supply hoes and spades for the farmers, and shovels and picks for the miners, not only for those in the immediate vicinity of the furnaces but for the entire State and later the Nation. This industry centered in the Northern Panhandle, which in an industrial sense is part of the 'Pittsburgh steel area.' Concentrated in four counties are most of West Virginia's 57 plants connected with iron and steel, including the nationally known Wheeling Steel and Weirton (National Steel) mills (*see Tour* 19). Although the first mill at Wheeling was established in 1832, the completion of the Baltimore & Ohio extension in 1852 began the rapid development in the Wheeling district, which could then obtain coal not only from its own fields but from those of the Monongalia area as well. The discovery of the rich beds of ore in the Lake Superior region threatened for a time the State industry, and ended the use of the very poor ore beds of the northern counties; but, supplied with cheap transportation by rail, the mills secured ore from the Lake region, and today West Virginia ranks sixth among the States in the output of iron and steel products. The development of the automobile and other new uses for steel during the early part of the twentieth century caused great expansions, such as that of the Weirton plant from a ten-mill establishment in 1910 to one embracing 42 mills, 14 blast furnaces, and 111 by-product coke ovens in 1938. From the Wheeling center the industry reached out to other parts of the State, to the world's largest axe factory in Charleston, to a car and foundry plant at Huntington, to a huge tin-plate factory at Clarksburg and a shovel plant at Parkersburg. The products have a world market.

When the iron industry was in its infancy, its companion, salt-making, also was beginning to grow. As early as 1770 a village of Delaware Indians on the Little Kanawha were producing a few pounds of salt by crude methods. The white settlers learned to use the natural brine springs, and enterprising entrepreneurs began to exploit those of Burning Springs, Malden, and Mason City at an early date. For over a century the industry prospered and in 1874 23 furnaces in the Mason City and Malden sections alone produced 5,000,000 bushels.

From its limited distribution to the early settlers, West Virginia salt had sought an ever wider scope until all the world used it and the Kanawha became one of the world's great salt-producing centers. Then, after over a century of growth and prosperity, the competition of rock salt (*see Tour* 15*b*) made production from brine uneconomical, and the Kanawha field declined. Salt-making has never regained its lost place in the industrial picture, but the salt brine today furnishes the raw materials for much greater industry.

In the early 1800's the salt manufacturers drilling for brine in the Kanawha Valley often struck gas or traces of oil, frequently abandoning their wells because of these 'nuisances.' William Tompkins, in 1841, conceived the idea of making one of the nuisances into an asset by using it to evaporate the brine; succeeding, he became the first man in the United States to use natural gas for industrial purposes. Gas was tried successfully as fuel for industrial boilers in 1874, and its use increased rapidly in succeeding years, to reach a peak production of 308,717,101,000 cubic feet in 1917. A decline followed, which ended in 1937 when many new 'strikes' were made. Although operators are not required to report the results of their drillings, they voluntarily reported 2,551 new producing wells between January 1, 1938, and September 1, 1938. Surpassed only by Oklahoma, Texas, Louisiana, and California, West Virginia in 1937 produced 156,442,782,000 cubic feet, a large part of which was piped to Baltimore, Pittsburgh, Cleveland, Cincinnati, Akron, and Youngstown for domestic consumption.

Another nuisance that became the basis of a major industry was oil. Not until May 1860 was a well drilled for the purpose of producing crude oil, and once more Burning Springs in Wirt County was the scene. Just nine months earlier the first successful oil well in the United States had been brought in on Oil Creek, Pennsylvania. The boom that began in the Wirt County area terminated quickly when Virginia seceded from the Union. After the War between the States, however, production was resumed and mounted to a total of 16,000,000 barrels in 1900. This had dropped to 3,845,000 barrels by 1937. Over 1,500,000 barrels of gasoline were produced that year, representing approximately one-third of the gasoline consumed within the State. The capital investment of $288,498,000 exceeded even that of the coal industry, and the value of the product was led only by that of iron and steel and coal. Among the States, West Virginia ranks 13th in the petroleum field.

The prosperity of all the State's industry, with the exception of natural gas and oil, is dependent upon the railroads. When the extension of the Baltimore & Ohio reached Wheeling, the iron furnaces were stimulated to great activity; this activity and the railroad's own consumption of fuel coal increased the output of coal and led to greater interest in its exploitation. New sections of timber, hitherto deprived of a cheap way to market, were exploited as well. The amount of outside capital invested in lumbering was small until the railroads came, but with them came the absentee control that largely distinguishes the structure of the State's industry today.

The men who financed the laying of the strips of steel were interested, naturally, in profiting from the stores of resources their roads opened up. Since West Virginians did not possess the capital to exploit the wealth of their State, they relinquished control to the capitalists of the east, who furnished the cash and credit to open the mines, to cut the virgin timber, and build the railroads to transport both coal and lumber to market.

After the pioneering Baltimore & Ohio had proved that the natural topographical barriers were not insurmountable, other groups of capitalists organized companies, started new roads, and penetrated new areas of wealth; while many of these failed through lack of capital or perseverance, many succeeded. The greater measure of success came to the financially powerful out-of-staters. For example, capital control of the Chesapeake and Ohio shifted many times from January 1873, when under the financial god-fathering of Collis P. Huntington the last spike was driven on the line to Huntington, to September 1888, when the firm of Drexel, Morgan & Company gained control by furnishing money needed to extend branches throughout the state. The Norfolk & Western Railway was another example of outside capital taking a powerful grasp on West Virginia industry. The men who owned the road also held leases on enormous coal properties of the now famous and immensely rich Pocahontas field it was to serve. The Virginian Railway, a jerk-water four-mile line, became an important trunk line when Standard Oil interests gained control of it. Today, the economically diverse divisions of the State are united by bands of shining steel, and for the support of this union the State pays huge profits out of a treasure house of natural resources to its absentee owners.

While the first railroads were not built to develop coal areas, later ones were, and today the major reason for their existence is coal. Even the first commercial shipment in 1853 was transported by narrow-gauge railway to the Kanawha River before shipment by flatboat on the Kanawha and the Ohio to Cincinnati. In the ten subsequent years coal mining made such rapid progress that, when the new State was created in 1863, a miner with pick over shoulder was depicted on the Great Seal. Spurred on to greater and greater expansion by the ever extending railroads, production reached 4,983,490 tons in 1888 and in 1900 was 21,153,341. Although in 1913 the capacity of already opened mines exceeded the actual output of 1917, a major year, by 25,000,000 tons, no thought of the threat inherent in over-expansion was permitted to interfere with the development of the coal empire. Railroad owners and mine operators worked hand in hand to develop every new prospect. During the war years 1914–18 the rate of expansion accelerated, and by 1920 there were 6,200 commercial bituminous mines operating; by 1923 there were 9,331. Capacity reached 900,000,000 tons, while only 600,000,000 would supply the Nation's need.

Disparity between profits and wages led to unionization and labor strife. Nevertheless, production continued to rise until in 1927 a peak of 146,088,121 tons was reached. Ten years later coal still could boast a production of 118,956,066 tons, of which McDowell County alone produced 22,852,772 tons—more than the total production of Canada. In the same year, the industry provided employment for 114,685 workers, 40.3 per cent of the 284,368 workers in all industries as reported to the West Virginia Workmen's Compensation Fund. Union strength has assured the miner a high wage per day but so far no definite number of working days a year. He is still a victim of the chaotic conditions of competition. The very fact that the store of coal is almost inexhaustible has tended to produce evil conditions for both producer and worker.

The coal extracted since 1863 if loaded into 50-ton gondola cars would make a solid train encircling the earth at the equator thirteen and a half times. Yet there are billions of tons still to be dug. New mines continue to open despite the fact that present mines can furnish more coal than can be used. Improved energy utilization, cheap hydroelectricity, and the inroads of competitive fuels lessen the demand as expansion increases the possible supply. To meet the situation new methods of operation are tried. Drift-mining, the method chiefly used in West Virginia, has progressed from the pick, wedge, and shovel stage, to the use of explosives and compressed air, to electric power and highly mechanized operation. Until recently mechanization was not believed to be economical and, in the Pocahontas field particularly, machines are few.

But the use of mining machines has grown, along with mechanization in all fields of industry. The early breast cutter was replaced by another that decreased the manual labor required to operate it. That in turn was replaced by the arc cutter, which cut coal faster but was a nuisance to the miner because the coal had to be shot up as well as down after cutting. The air-compressed pile-driver type of cutter on a truck was another improvement. Electricity furnishes the power for modern cutting apparatus that is being improved continually. The use of explosives has improved along with machine methods, and the improvement is of far more value to the worker. From an early use of lime to break the coal by expansion, then black powder and squibbs, the industry has turned to dynamite and now to Cardox that has practically no flame and therefore is more safely used in gaseous mines. Drills, too, have improved. From the old type for which the entire power was furnished by the legs and arms of the miner, the drill has been mechanized until the physical effort required of the miner is slight. In the same way, the new conveyer-belt machines decrease manual toil by lowering the height to which the coal must be raised for loading from 50 to 20 inches.

The one deterrent to adoption of the conveyer and mechanical loader has been its tendency to increase the number of minor accidents and, consequently, of man-hours lost. The vibration of the mechanical apparatus precipitates slate falls and prevents the laborers from hearing the warning cracking sound, which under the older system enabled them to escape the fall of slate. Fatalities have not increased, however.

In a few mines, such as that at Carbon in the Cabin Creek field, mechanization has proved very successful. With conveyer belts, cutting machines, and the continued use of human loaders, production has been brought to ten tons per man-shift; included in the shift are all employees, clerical as well as manual and supervisory, connected with the work of readying the coal for market. This compares with a seven-ton average loading under the old system. In a small number of mines, mechanical loaders have been tried but with varying success. Some mines after installing machines have later abandoned them and returned to the older method. Increased wage rates and the competition of other fuels are causing the operators to turn to mechanization, and a survey conducted by the Bituminous Coal Commission showed that the use of both conveyers and mechanical loaders is increasing. Several West Virginia operators stated at the Cincinnati coal congress in the spring of 1939 that they were keeping on the pay roll in various capacities the 33 per cent of their employees who otherwise would have been displaced by the introduction of machines. This indicates a general displacement of 40 per cent as given by Percy Tetlow, secretary of the commission, to a Congressional committee; Tetlow also said that, without any change in the total output, mechanization and other improvements in mining have reduced the total number of miners in America from 700,000 to about 500,000.

Of West Virginia's two types of coal, bituminous and semi-bituminous, the latter, known as smokeless or Pocahontas coal, is the established bunker fuel of the world and is used exclusively by the United States Navy because of its excellent steam-producing quality. Because the coal from the New River-Pocahontas field is largely free of impurities, it forms a big part of the coal used in the Nation to produce coke. The 'cannel' coal of the Kanawha Valley is another excellent coking fuel, and is rich in the by-products, coal tar, pitch, creosote, naphtha, phenol, analine, and toluene.

These, and other by-products, as well as coal itself, provide a basis for the newest of West Virginia's major industries, chemicals. From the by-products formed in the coking process and from coal in its natural state, hundreds of products are made. Very little of the coking is done within West Virginia, and while in production of bituminous coal the State ranks first, it ranks eighth in the value of by-products. One reason for this is that West Virginia is plentifully supplied with natural forms of two of coal's chief by-products, oil and gas, making artificial production unnecessary and uneconomical.

The second source of chemical raw materials is the salt brine, which regained a position of major importance when the First World War trade conditions forced this country to re-examine its own resources for the elements it could no longer import. Chlorine and carbon are basic to many chemical products. Brine and coal supply them. Interest in chemicals began in earnest in 1910 when a coal by-products plant was established at Benwood, and the cessation of importation from Germany in 1914 started the chemical industry on a progressive expansion. The plants at Charleston, Wheeling, Huntington, Clarksburg, and Parkersburg produce hundreds of compounds and many finished products. Products from the Kanawha region include bromine, magnesium, sodium, barium, ammonia, and many of the intermediate compounds used in the manufacture of rubber, plastic, and rayon. In

1937, 12 concerns were operating in the State with a production valued at $58,267,326, and the Great Kanawha Valley from Nitro to Gauley Bridge had become one of the world's chemical centers.

Another industry whose output is almost equal in value to that of chemicals is glass making. With natural gas available and ideal as a fuel—cheap and free from foreign substances—and great deposits of sand running as high as 99.89 per cent in pure silica content, West Virginia possesses the perfect requirements for the glass industry. The first plant in the State was established at Wellsburg in 1815. Expansion came much later, caused principally by the adoption of natural gas as a fuel, by the invention in 1908 of a machine for turning out sheet glass by the web, and by the invention of a bottle-making machine by Michael J. Owens, a West Virginian; this machine produces as many bottles in a day as 200 men could turn out under the old method of blowing. The sheet glass and bottle plants at Charleston are among the largest in the world; other plants are located in Huntington, Clarksburg, Fairmont, and Moundsville. The value of glass products reached $52,954,985 in 1937, and 48 plants were employing 12,763 workers.

Early in the nineteenth century the first mills of the cloth and clothing industry were built in Wheeling and Wellsburg. These plants carded and rolled the wool that was then made into finished products by the housewives with looms and spinning wheels. The eastern counties, especially Berkeley and Jefferson, have long led in this industry; hosiery mills are located at both Martinsburg and Berkeley Springs. However, the industry is not concentrated and there are plants making wool blankets in Charleston, and overalls and work clothes in Huntington and Wheeling. The American Viscose Corporation operates a plant at Nitro, which converts raw cotton stock into pulp form suitable for making rayon yarn, and another at Parkersburg, employing about 5,000 people. This corporation was formed to utilize the viscose process in the manufacture of artificial silk. Although patented in 1892, the process was neglected until C. F. Topham, 1900, invented a mechanical spinning apparatus that made its use practical and profitable. In brief, the process takes cotton and wood pulp cellulose, mercerizes it with caustic soda, presses the caustic out, and grinds the cellulose into small particles. The alkali cellulose is treated with carbon bisulphide to form cellulose xanthate which in turn dissolves in water to form viscose. The cellulose is then regenerated into filaments and threads by forcing the alkaline viscose through spinnerettes into an acid which neutralizes the caustic and converts the cellulose into rayon yarn.

Nylon, a new fabric belonging to three industries—chemicals, coal, and clothing—has been developed by the Du Pont chemists from carbon and nitrogen; it resembles silk but is stronger and more durable. A plant to produce and process the material will be completed at Belle in 1941. A hosiery mill at Eleanor, employing persons from the Rehabilitation Homestead (*see Tour* 14), plans to use the new material. The value of cloth and clothing products ranks the industry seventh in the State, its 1937 total amounting to $44,346,976. With the utilization of nylon the prospects are bright for future expansion.

Out of the mushroom growth of industry with its attendant railroad development came West Virginia's eighth ranking industry, electric power. The first plant was built at Wheeling in 1882. In keeping with the interlocking pattern of State industry, most of the present power is produced in coal-burning plants; only 13 per cent of the 1937 total was hydroelectric. The plants are located at vantage points throughout the State and are connected by great transmission lines, which permit a constant supply of power at any point of need. More and more, today, the interest in cheaper production turns the industry to water power. As yet there are but two large hydroelectric plants, at Lake Lynn and Hawk's Nest.

The chief obstacle to utilization of the power of the State's many rivers, the Great Kanawha, the New, the Elk, the Greenbrier, the Gauley, the Little Kanawha, the Buckhannon, the Monongahela, the Cheat, and the Potomac and its tributaries, has been their uneven flow. The construction of dams, one of which has been completed near Grafton on the Tygart River, will solve this problem, and part of the 1,000,000 horsepower of potential energy in these rivers (according to expert opinion) may be used in a new and larger industrial development. Hydroelectric power production at present employs only 2,500 persons.

Ranking lowest, and yet a very important item in the list of major State industries, is the manufacture of pottery, porcelain, and chinaware. Since 1785 when the first pottery was established at Morgantown, this industry has retained its importance. Today, the Homer Laughlin China Company plant at Newell is one of the largest in the world. From Cornwall and Canada, Missouri and Maine, Colorado and Alaska come the ingredients that are here made into the finest earthenware available; even the chalk cliffs of Dover in England supply kaolin and whiting. The industry is largely centered in the rich clay beds of Hancock and two neighboring counties.

The combined products of 49 small meat-packing plants are sufficiently valuable to place that industry ahead of pottery in the table of values. Located in 16 cities, these plants pack hogs, sheep, and cattle. Armour & Company maintains plants in eight localities; Swift & Company in six. The total output in 1937 was valued at $20,073,470. The number employed is small.

Service industries and the production of things incidental to modern business and living form a very large part of the industrial pattern, although individually they seem unimportant. The businesses and trades connected with the automobile industry alone provide an industry valued at $45,451,079, and employ 3,948 persons. Railroad shops, beer and carbonated beverages, dairy products, flour and grain products, foundry and machine shops, leather goods and tanneries, oil well supplies, pulp and paper, printing, telephone and telegraph, and tobacco products employ nearly 20,000 persons and have a total output valued at approximately $86,500,000.

West Virginia has been made by industry. There can be little doubt that the historic separation from the mother State was motivated partly by the difference of opinion natural to an industrial west and an agrarian east. Although the west was largely undeveloped at the time, the people of the western counties felt that they were more closely allied to Pennsylvania than to Tidewater Virginia. Perhaps, they felt a premonition that time would find their land industrial to an extent no actual situation then indicated. The rugged mountains that repelled even the Indians were no attractive havens to lure the farmer. True, the land in the Kanawha Valley and along the Ohio, and perhaps in the South Branch, was farming land, but the valleys elsewhere were small and narrow. It was first the lumber and salt industries, then iron and coal, that brought men to the Mountain State. The railroads attracted hordes of immigrants, Irish chiefly, who settled the raw country of the north. The mines brought other hordes, Slav and Italian, Swede and Pole. From the south came the released slaves in search of unskilled paying jobs; they found the mines. From other States came many types and breeds seeking economic gain in the swift-growing empire of hills.

The State became aware of its industrial future and made laws to protect it. Labor fought for rights that in the early turmoil had been ignored. Reforms came slowly, and industry continued to expand.

Coal, in spite of the inroads made by new fuels, by hydroelectric power, and by the increased energy utilization of coal itself, finds strength in new markets and new uses. The chemicals industry is creating new products and improving the old. Gas is now sold for fuel consumption, for the most part unrefined and unprocessed; the use of present day refining processes would increase its value several times. Oil, the extraction of which is decreasing, can be processed to increase its value by millions of dollars. The almost undeveloped resource of limestone promises a large and important new field. The present number of cement plants trebled would barely supply the needs of the State. The insulating industry is still in the early stages, but all the requirements for development are present in the State. Mineral springs are plentiful and may form a basis for tourist trade that will rank them among the important natural resources of West Virginia.

Labor

THE workmen's struggle in West Virginia for better working conditions and the right to organize has been a long one and, in the mining industry particularly, one marked by bitter conflict, violence, and tragic incident. The problems of adjustment in this State, for both employer and employee, have been peculiarly difficult to solve. The rapid rate of industrialization of a previously rural area, the nature of the major industries, the uneven growth and distribution of population, and—of great significance—the individualistic traditions of both owner and mine worker, all these factors must be considered in any study of the labor movement in West Virginia. It is necessary to know something of the background in order to understand why, after prolonged and strenuous effort, relations between employer and employee have shown noticeable improvement only within recent years. Today, many progressive labor laws are in effect, more and more disputes are settled at the conference table, and comparative quiet prevails in most industrial areas.

Shortly after West Virginia became a State in 1863, the coal miners made several attempts to organize and to present a united demand for improved working conditions, but these efforts were always defeated by the powerful opposition of the mining companies. In the next decade, the State took a prominent place in the labor movement, when the first serious incident in the first Nation-wide strike in the United States occurred at Martinsburg. Following the panic of 1873, the wages of all railroad workers were reduced year by year, and in June 1877 the Eastern roads ordered a further 10 per cent reduction. The general strike, which came to be known as the Great Railroad Strike of 1877, was called, and, on July 17, freight trains passing through Martinsburg, an important Baltimore & Ohio railhead, were stopped by striking railroad workers. Sympathy strikes broke out in many other railroad towns. In Martinsburg, attempts to resume service resulted in street fighting and acts of violence, and the strike was broken only when President Hayes sent in 200 infantrymen, at the request of Governor Mathews—probably the first time Federal troops were used for this purpose (*see Tour* 1). Wages were further reduced when the railroad men returned to their jobs.

The industrial depression of 1893 brought unemployment and hard times to millions of workers, and the subsequent wage cutting and strong antiunion movement among employers led to defensive action on the part of labor throughout the country. The strike in 1894 in the coal fields of West Virginia was part of a Nation-wide suspension that ended in a compromise wage-rate agreement. West Virginia miners participated in another Nation-wide strike in 1897; conditions in industry were generally improving, but, while coal prices rose, wages remained at a low level. Under the leadership of John Mitchell, president of the United Mine Workers of America, coal diggers in several States struck on July 4. In September the operators agreed to a temporary increase in wages, pending the outcome of a joint conference for western Pennsylvania, Ohio, Indiana, and Illinois. The workers in West Virginia gained nothing.

In 1901 a more vigorous effort to organize the miners of West Virginia succeeded in the forming of 80 locals, with approximately 5,000 members. In 1902 a State miners' convention was held at Huntington, which was attended by representatives of 'mountain whites' and Negro workers. In the strike that followed, 16,000 miners quit work in Kanawha, New River, and Norfolk and western districts in the down-State area. Injunctions were issued as fast as new strikes were called, so that the strikers, blocked by the courts and militiamen, finally agreed to a compromise settlement. Only in a small area in the Kanawha field did the union gain recognition.

Efforts of the national union to organize the rest of West Virginia were unsuccessful. The operators, in order to compete with Northern fields for Northern coal markets, reduced their production costs, the chief item of which was the wages of the miners; and the drive against unions was intensified. By a decision based on an old common-law provision, the miners were deprived of the right to organize, and the worker who wanted a job had to sign away his right to join a union. Private armed guards were employed by the operators in increasing numbers; deputy sheriffs, commissioned by the county officers, were paid by the companies.

In the face of all opposition, labor representatives met in Huntington in February 1903 and organized the West Virginia Federation of

Labor, representing 57 different crafts, among them the United Mine Workers of America. By 1906, the Federation had 65 locals and a total membership of 6,000.

By 1907, protests against private guards were so numerous that Governor Dawson referred to them in his message to the legislature: 'They are used at some of the collieries to protect the property of owners, to prevent trespassing, and especially to prevent labor agitators and organizers of a miners' union from gaining access to the miners . . . Many outrages have been committed by these guards, many of whom appear to be vicious and dare-devil men who seem to add to their viciousness by bull-dozing and terrorizing people.'

Paint Creek miners struck in April 1912, when the operators withdrew from the Kanawha agreement and attempted to enforce working conditions such as existed in adjacent nonunion areas. Cabin Creek Valley and New River miners who joined the strike were evicted from their homes and had to live in tent colonies. Martial law was declared on three occasions.

In this strike, the miners were aided by 'Mother' Jones, heroine of many American labor struggles. The United Mine Workers rallied around her, as she led marches of angry miners and faced machine guns at Paint Creek. Mother Jones was jailed many times at Logan and finally, in 1913, was court-martialed and sentenced to 20 years. A tireless worker for unionism, Mother Jones would not be termed a 'radical' today. Opposed to 'the I.W.W. and Bolshevism,' she advocated industrial peace based on reconciled differences between capital and labor.

Three thousand miners petitioned Governor Glasscock to recall guards patrolling the Kanawha Valley region and Paint Creek, but no action was taken. After 16 months a climax was reached, when a volley fired from an armored train into the tent shelters of the miners at Holly Grove killed a man and a woman and wounded 16 other persons. An armed force of miners marching toward Mucklow were met by a posse led by mine guards; in the battle that followed, 12 miners and 4 guards were killed. Governor Glasscock then sent two companies of militia to restore quiet.

When reports of the mine wars were spread across the front pages of the Nation's newspapers, Senator Kern of Indiana sponsored a resolution in the United States Senate to investigate the situation. Among other abuses, the investigating committee condemned acts of the military tribunals and the use of armed guards.

Governor Henry D. Hatfield, a year later, proposed that the operators concede to the miners the following points: right to organize, a 9-hour work day, right to trade in other than company stores, semi-monthly pay days, and no discrimination against union men. Both the miners and the operators agreed to these terms, and the strike ended April 28, 1913.

For several years, especially during the first World War, quiet prevailed, as the industry strained to meet increasing demands for fuel. Many new mines were opened, but, although half of the State's coal mines were organized by the end of the war, the new fields stubbornly remained nonunion. In spite of intimidation, the miners were organizing the fields around Logan and Williamson, and in September 1919 union miners assembled in large force near the Logan County line to march on Logan, in an attempt to organize the miners there. They were turned back by Governor Cornwell's promise to investigate the miners' grievances in Logan County.

A lockout that had important repercussions took place in May 1920, at Matewan in Mingo County. Operators imported Baldwin-Felts detectives and evicted union miners from company houses, whereupon open warfare broke out in the streets of the town. In a battle between miners and mine guards, the Baldwin-Felts men were routed by the blazing six-shooter of Matewan's late chief of police, Syd Hatfield, an officer of the Old-West type.

In a three-hour battle between guards and strikers in Mingo County, on the morning of August 21, 1920, six men were killed and a score wounded. Governor Cornwell requested the aid of Federal troops, declaring that the State militia was unable to cope with the situation. President Harding dispatched 500 regulars of the United States Army, but District President Keeney, of the United Mine Workers (District 17), threatened a general strike in the State unless the Federal soldiers discontinued 'strike-breaking activities.' Governor Cornwell consented to their withdrawal, but fresh outbreaks brought them back, and martial law was declared. Several thousand miners and their families spent the winter of 1920-21 in tent colonies, and in May 1921 armed conflict was resumed. Again martial law was declared, this time by Governor Morgan. Union miners of the Paint Creek and Cabin Creek fields mobilized to go over to Logan and organize the miners there and, if necessary, to fight force with force. Don Chafin, sheriff of Logan County, gathered an army of 500 deputies. The governor appealed to the War Department for troops to avert a clash, and an officer was sent to observe the situation. A battle seemed imminent, until District President Keeney persuaded the miners to turn back. They had started to disperse, when news came that, on the night of August 28, armed deputies had killed five miners. Immediately, the men took up their march again; automobiles were commandeered, and several thousand miners advanced.

Meanwhile the operators had collected their forces; machine guns and airplanes were brought in, and steel vests issued to the deputies. The miners entrenched themselves along a mountain ridge, not far from Blair, and withstood successive attacks during a four-day battle. At the governor's appeal for aid, President Harding ordered the miners to disperse, but they refused. Their ranks were daily enlarged by miners from Kentucky, Ohio, and northern West Virginia fields. After the arrival of 2,100 soldiers of the regular United States Army and a squadron of Government planes, the miners gradually retreated. Finally 600 men surrendered to the Federal troops; they were dismissed and sent home.

As a result of these efforts to win the right to organize, a Logan County grand jury indicted 325 miners for treason and 200 for conspiracy and bearing arms; all were acquitted. The miners' defeat in Logan and Mingo Counties was felt by the unions throughout the State, and, whereas in 1920 the UMWA had approximately 45,000 paid-up members in West Virginia, by 1929 there were barely a thousand in the union.

The labor situation in northern West Virginia has never been as critical as in the southern part of the State. From 1913 to 1925, joint wage-scale contracts were made between miners and operators in the Fairmont field. However, in 1925, market conditions were so unstable that many operators broke their contracts with the United Mine Workers. A strike followed, but, because the miners were not in financial condition to hold out, they were forced to accept the terms of the operator. From then until the Roosevelt Administration, labor in the northern fields was powerless. The establishment of the NRA gave encouragement to the workers, and they rushed back to the union. Wages were raised, hours of labor shortened, and conditions of employment improved generally.

Causes of industrial strife in West Virginia are deep-rooted, but perhaps the notorious 'mine guard' system, under which guards were deputized by county sheriffs and their salaries paid by the operators, precipitated most of the violence. An emphatic indictment of the system in West Virginia was made in a report in 1922 to the United States

History

History

Senate Committee on Education and Labor by Senator William Kenyon of Iowa: 'The system of paying deputy sheriffs out of funds contributed by operators, and not out of the public treasury, is a vicious and un-American policy and a practice that should cease.'

Mine guards in the coal fields of West Virginia and adjoining States were employed through the Baldwin-Felts Detective Agency, headed by Thomas L. Felts, with headquarters in Bluefield. In the days of railroad building and mine development, Felts supplied operatives mainly to protect property, to guard pay rolls, and to run down robbers. Later, he gave less attention to crime and specialized in providing armed guards, strikebreakers, and labor spies to industrialists. In 1935, the legislature amended the law under which the mine-guard system was permitted to operate. The Baldwin-Felts Agency went out of business after the death of Felts in 1937.

Another serious cause of friction was the 'company union,' which was brought to national attention by the Weirton controversy in the late 1930's. In 1937, the CIO, fresh from victories in 'Big Steel' and 'Little Steel,' undertook to organize the employees of the Weirton Steel Company at Weirton, known as the largest company town in America, and to win the right to represent them as bargaining agency. These efforts, made by the Steel Workers Organizing Committee, affiliate of the CIO, were unsuccessful, chiefly because of the existence of the Employees Security League. The League, formed in 1933 by E. T. Weir and modeled after employee-representation plans in Eastern mills, had previously been investigated in 1933. A strike called in that year by the American Federation of Labor, under NRA provisions, led to a series of National Labor Board hearings, but after invalidation of the NRA, the hearings were suspended. The SWOC, in 1937, charged that the Security League was a company union, not free to bargain independently, and requested the National Labor Relations Board to investigate the league's status. After an investigation, the board charged the corporation with unfair practices under the Wagner Labor Relations Act. The company denied the charge at a hearing begun in August 1937. A NLRB ruling in July 1940 held the company guilty of Wagner Act violations, but the case is still (1941) pending board decision.

Industrial relations in the last decade have been comparatively peaceful. Only once, in the Appalachian shutdown of 1939, was there danger that armed conflict and violence would again occur. Nearly 100,000 miners in the State were out of work, while a conference on a new two-year collective-bargaining agreement was being held. Governor Homer

A. Holt offered to reopen the mines with the aid of troops if the workers wished to return to the pits without a renewal of their contract. The miners refused the offer; but the potentially explosive situation was shortly relieved by the conclusion of a two-year wage-and-hour agreement.

Union membership in West Virginia in coal, steel, and allied industries increased rapidly after the inauguration of the New Deal Administration. In 1937, the United Mine Workers of America, sponsor of the Committee for Industrial Organization, was expelled from the American Federation of Labor. Following this rift in labor's ranks, the West Virginia Industrial Union Council was founded in 1938, with John B. Easton as president. Soon afterward, the West Virginia State Federation of Labor was reorganized, with Thomas Cairns as president, and membership limited to unions affiliated with the A.F. of L. Substantial gains have been made by both groups in the lumbering, chemical, and manufacturing areas, in service industries, such as laundering, cleaning and pressing, restaurants, retail trade, bus, truck and transfers, and in the teaching profession. Latest approximate membership statistics issued by the two State bodies are: The West Virginia Industrial Union Council (CIO), 200,000; West Virginia Federation of Labor (AFL), 90,000. At the beginning of 1941, increased activity was being shown by the CIO, which had undertaken to organize miners at Gary, one of the few nonunion mines in the State, chemical workers of the Kanawha Valley, and transport workers in Charleston, Huntington, and other cities.

Organized labor is now recognized by the State administration as an important factor in government affairs; active trade unionists have been placed on administrative boards and are appointed to conference commissions and to important positions in State departments. Labor is represented on the advisory board of the Department of Public Assistance by a trade unionist, and in the Department of Unemployment by two union members. Each year, the governor commissions two trade unionists to represent the State at the National Conference on Labor Legislation, held in Washington, D. C.

The West Virginia Department of Labor, created by an act of the legislature in 1889, is the enforcing agency of laws pertaining to the health, safety, and welfare of the workers in mills, workshops, mercantile establishments, and all other places of employment except mines. It is charged with the enforcement of laws governing the employment of women, child-labor laws, the steam-boiler inspection law, supervision over fee-charging public employment offices, the enforcement of the weights and measures law, and gathering and compiling statistical data relating to financial, social, educational, and sanitary conditions of working people. The department also bears much of the responsibility for the enforcement of several provisions of the Federal Fair Labor Standards Act of 1938.

The 1935 session of the legislature gave labor and social-security legislation more favorable consideration than had been accorded at previous sessions. Among the chief enactments were amendments to the workmen's compensation law, passage of a prevailing wage-rate law, and abolition of the mine-guard system.

A law providing compensation for workmen suffering disability or death as a result of silicosis was also passed at this session. This was in response to the public outcry that arose, after it was learned that an undetermined number of men had died of silicosis, contracted in the building of the Hawks Nest Tunnel. A labor subcommittee of the United States House of Representatives investigated the affair, and in April 1936 Congressman Glen Griswold of Indiana, committee chairman, submitted a report charging that 'the whole driving of the tunnel was begun, continued, and completed with grave and inhuman disregard of all consideration for the health, lives and future of the employees.' The committee concluded with the statement that, 'if by their suffering and death they will have made life safer in the future for men who go beneath the earth to work, if they will have been able to establish a new and greater regard for human life in industry, their suffering may not have been in vain.' The amended workmen's compensation act provides for a separate workmen's compensation silicosis fund and for a silicosis medical board.

A law preventing employment of children under 16 and 18 years of age in certain hazardous occupations was enacted by the Legislature of 1939. Employment of child labor is strictly regulated in West Virginia, and the laws pertaining thereto are rigidly enforced by labor inspectors, who confer with county superintendents of schools—in regard to the issuance of age certificates, work permits, vacation and special-work permits—and co-operate with juvenile courts in matters of child welfare in industry. Care is also exercised to safeguard the life and health of women workers engaged in industry. Other legislation beneficial to labor passed by the 1939 lawmakers included regulation of industrial homework; laborers' priority lien for wages, whereby the State labor commissioner was authorized to collect wage claims from employers at no cost to the workers; simplification of the unemployment compensation law; and clarification and broadening of the workmen's compensation law.

A State labor-relations measure, patterned after the Federal Act (and apparently approved by the voters, when they elected its advocate, Senator Matthew M. Neely as governor of West Virginia in 1940), was defeated by a close margin in the Legislature of 1941, under pressure of a powerful business lobby. A miners certificate law, requiring six months apprenticeship in West Virginia mines before certification for work, was enacted at this session.

The United Mine Workers are interested at present in the passage of a Federal mine-inspection bill, introduced by Senator Neely and passed by the Senate. This bill provides for supplementing the State inspection system, in order to cut down the number of fatalities resulting from explosions—more than 100 miners have lost their lives in blasts at Bartley, Beckley, and Carswell since January 1940.

West Virginia's recent labor history, in contrast with violent eras of the past, thus gives solid ground for hope that relations between employers and employees will find a harmonious balance, and that the industrial structure of the State will grow stronger and more stable.

Transportation and Communication

D ESPITE the barriers of the Blue Ridge and Allegheny Mountains and the rugged hills of the interior, which confined even the mighty buffalo and the tireless Indian to a few difficult trails, the State with the highest mean altitude east of the Rockies boasts spectacular achievements in transportation.

After having disembarked at Jamestown in 1607 to establish a colony in Virginia, the first settlers explored the rivers, hoping to find a way to the South Sea and imagined gold. Later settlers penetrated the vast wilderness that is now West Virginia along Indian trails and bison paths, the only routes to the interior. Now the Mountain State has 34,350 miles of state roads of which 13,068 miles are surfaced. These roads are among the best that traverse the Appalachian Mountains.

Over a steel network of 7,147 miles of railway, modern steam and electric locomotives haul the products of an industrial empire still in its infancy to Tidewater and the Great Lakes, and palatial air-conditioned passenger trains streak their way from the Atlantic to the West across the State's borders. The State has more than 600 miles of navigable rivers. Through many miles of pipe line oil and gas are pumped to supply fuel to cities near and far.

Buffalo trails and Indian trails sometimes were identical but more often they diverged. The Indian generally followed the rivers and, when a water route was obstructed, took to the land, carrying his light canoe until he reached a point where his journey could be resumed by water. Where the ground was rough the Indian turned to a smoother way, while the buffalo followed a straight course between two points, despite precipices, swamps, and rivers.

Although difficult country had to be traversed, there were many of these trails in West Virginia. The Little Warrior Trail, crossing the Ohio River near New Martinsville, passed along Fish and Dunkard

Creeks into the Monongahela and Cheat River Valleys. The trail was used by the raiding Shawnee from Ohio into Virginia.

The Kanawha, or Buffalo Trail, crossed the Allegheny Mountains into the Greenbrier Valley east of Marlinton, passed branches of the Meadow River, crossed Gauley Mountain, and followed the Great Kanawha Valley to Charleston. Here the trail divided, one branch roughly following the course of the Great Kanawha River to the Ohio at Point Pleasant, the other crossing the Kanawha into Teays Valley to Huntington and across the Big Sandy River into western Kentucky.

The Seneca Trail followed the South Branch of the Potomac River from its mouth to the point where the North Fork flowed into it, ascended the North Fork to the mouth of Seneca Creek, and up Seneca Creek; then it crossed the Spruce, Rich, Middle, and Shavers Mountains of the Allegheny Range near the headwaters of the two forks of Cheat River and followed Shavers Fork of Cheat River to Elkins. Here it became a part of the historic Warriors Road, which extended from the St. Lawrence River to Georgia, entering West Virginia from Maryland ten miles north of Thomas and running south through Elkins, Huttonsville, Marlinton, Lewisburg, and Princeton to leave the State near Bluefield and pass through Virginia to North Carolina. A branch of the Seneca Trail turned west from Mingo Flats and followed the waters of the Little Kanawha River to Parkersburg on the Ohio. Another branch, known as the Dunmore, or Pocahontas Trail, turned from the main trail near Seneca Rocks to run along the course of the North Fork of the South Branch of the Potomac to Dry Run and thence over Snowy Mountain across the present Virginia-West Virginia Line to Crabbottom.

Another much used path was the McCullough traders' trail that extended from Winchester by way of Wardensville, Moorefield, and Greenland Gap, over Patterson Creek Mountain of the Allegheny Range, across the North Branch of the Potomac River to the headwaters of Youghiogheny River west of Oakland, Maryland; thence through Bruceton Mills to the waters of Cheat River near the Pennsylvania Line.

In spite of these numerous trails, which were followed by the early hunters, fur traders, and settlers, it is plain that the natural barriers and difficult mountain terrain discouraged even the buffalo and the Indian for a long trek, for both Nemacolin's Path and the Virginia Warriors' Path, the greatest Indian trails from the eastern seaboard to the western country, bypassed all but the borders of the present

State. The inevitable result was to retard the settlement and development of western Virginia for many years.

Along these two great trails pioneers crossed over the mountain barrier of the Appalachians to settle the new West. Nemacolin's Path left the Potomac River at Cumberland, Maryland, turned northward into Pennsylvania before reaching the West Virginia-Maryland Line, then followed the Youghiogheny River to the headwaters of the Ohio at Pittsburgh. It was along this path General Edward Braddock marched toward Fort Duquesne where he met defeat and death, and it was here the youthful George Washington began his military career. The same path was followed roughly by the National Road, until it cut across 15 miles of West Virginia's Northern Panhandle to Wheeling on the Ohio.

The Virginia Warriors' Path ascended the Shenandoah Valley to the head of Clinch and went through Cumberland Gap into Kentucky, passing south of what is now West Virginia; but a branch turned north from the eastern part of the present border of Virginia into the Great Kanawha Valley and followed it to the Ohio. This road became Daniel Boone's Wilderness Road and the gateway from the shores of Virginia into the wilds of Kentucky.

It was along one of the early Indian and buffalo trails that the State's first established road—from Winchester, Virginia, to the home of Colonel Morgan Morgan at what is now Bunker Hill, Berkeley County —was authorized in 1743 and built soon thereafter under Colonel Morgan's supervision. But this mountainous country offered so many obstacles that the early settlers depended on pack horses and canoes or rude boats for transportation facilities, and but few passable roads had been built before 1800.

Rivalry between colonies, and later between States, played an important role in the location of the early turnpike routes; and even George Washington, although an ardent supporter of improved means of transportation, was influenced by a desire to have Virginia reap the benefits of such improvement. Washington expressed the belief that the mountains might form a barrier between two great sections of the country that would cause them to drift apart and become separate and independent countries, as had happened in Europe. To prevent this, he wished to bind the two sections together by roads and canals, and after visiting his western lands, extending to the Ohio River, he urged the Virginia assembly to begin their construction. As a result the Potomac Company was incorporated in December 1784, for the purpose of con-

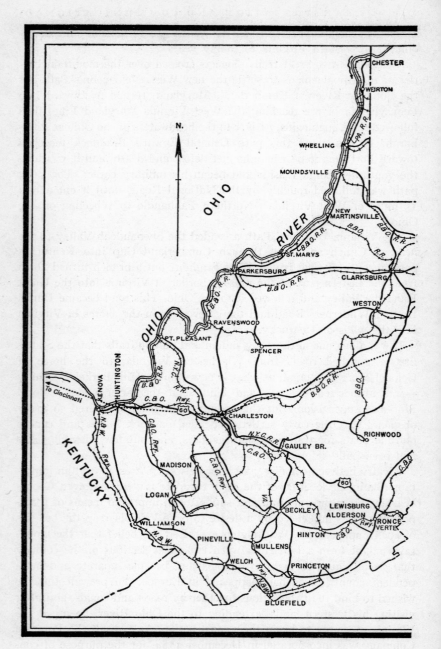

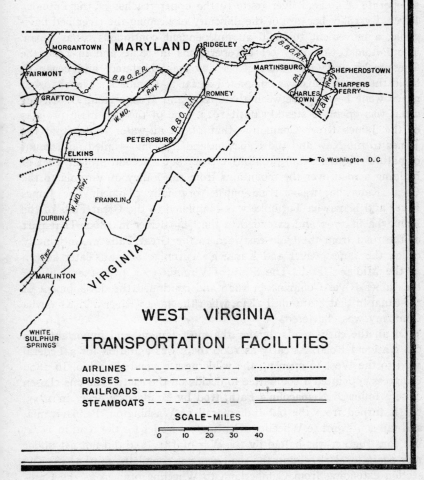

PENNSYLVANIA

MARYLAND

MORGANTOWN

FAIRMONT

GRAFTON

B. & O. R.R.

W. MD. Rwy.

RIDGELEY

ROMNEY

B. & O. R.R.

MARTINSBURG

SHEPHERDSTOWN

PA Rwy.

HARPERS FERRY

CHARLES TOWN

N. & W. Rwy.

B. & O. R.R.

PETERSBURG

ELKINS

→ To Washington D.C

FRANKLIN

W. MD. Rwy.

DURBIN

Rwy.

MARLINTON

VIRGINIA

WHITE
SULPHUR
SPRINGS

WEST VIRGINIA
TRANSPORTATION FACILITIES

AIRLINES -------------- ....
BUSSES --------------- ━━━━━━━━
RAILROADS ----------- ┣┿┿┿┿┿┫
STEAMBOATS ---------

SCALE-MILES

0   10   20   30   40

necting the Potomac River with other waters to tap Ohio River trade. In 1785 the James River Company was incorporated for the purpose of connecting the James River with New River and the Great Kanawha, and also to construct a road over the Allegheny Mountains to the Falls of the Great Kanawha River. Washington was made president of both companies.

The Potomac Company, planning to use the river beds and canalize only the naturally impassable points, began construction of a detour around Little Falls and Great Falls in August 1785, and in 1800 began to operate this canal-river route to the upper reaches of the Potomac River. By 1820, because of the difficulty of keeping the river bed navigable, a movement to build an independent continuous canal began. The Potomac Company ceased operations in 1826, and in 1828 the Chesapeake and Ohio Canal Company was chartered, and began to build the canal. This was completed as far as Cumberland in 1850 but never went beyond. Between that place and Washington, D. C., the canal was operated steadily until 1924. One of the two main projects of the James River Company—that of an all-water route from the James to the New and the Kanawha and the Ohio—failed on account of natural obstacles and prohibitive cost; but a second project, that of building a road over the mountains from the Valley of Virginia to the Great Kanawha, was carried out as originally planned. The James River and Kanawha Turnpike was completed to the Great Falls of the Kanawha in 1790 and extended to the Ohio River in 1800. That part of the road from the Ohio eastward to the Great Falls was originally called the James River and Kanawha Turnpike and was later known as the Midland Trail. The State of Virginia took over the rights of the James River Company in 1820 and continued the development of the canal in that State until 1832, when the James River and Kanawha Company was chartered.

Of all the early roads, by far the most famous and important was the National Road. As early as 1800 there was agitation for a Federal road to the West to open up the wilderness beyond the Ohio. In 1806 Congress appointed a committee to decide on the route. The one chosen closely followed Nemacolin's Path, trod by Braddock's army in 1755, but it turned from the old Indian trail at Washington, Pennsylvania, and ran southwest to Wheeling. Contracts were let for the road in 1811, but construction was halted by the War of 1812 and did not get under way again until 1815, and the road was not completed until 1818. The section extending from Cumberland to Wheeling, known as the Cumberland Road, became a link in the great National Road, which pushed through to Columbus, and Vandalia, Ohio, and eventually to the Mississippi opposite St. Louis. By that time railways had considerably lessened the importance of the highway.

The building of this road stimulated immigration to the Northwest Territory, but it crossed only a narrow strip of Virginia. While the road increased trade and settlement in the Wheeling area, most of those who traveled it were bound for the territory west of the Ohio and it did not advance the interest of Virginia as a whole or help settle or develop the western part of it.

The demand for an all-Virginia highway led to the building of the Northwestern Turnpike from Winchester, Virginia, to Parkersburg, by way of Romney and Clarksburg. The route was suggested by Washington for a wagon road in 1784, when he found that the adoption of the Mason-Dixon Line as the boundary between Pennsylvania and Virginia gave to Pennsylvania a large strip of territory (containing lands owned by him), which he along with many other Virginians had believed a part of Virginia. The construction of this road was begun in 1827 and completed in 1838. The highway had an immediate and far-reaching effect on the development of that part of the country through which it ran (*see Tour* 4).

In 1823, the Virginia General Assembly ordered surveys to be made for a highway to extend from Staunton, Virginia, over the Alleghenies and across western Virginia to the mouth of the Little Kanawha River where it joins the Ohio. This road, authorized in 1824, was known as the Staunton and Parkersburg Turnpike. It crossed the present Virginia-West Virginia Line 15 miles northwest of Monterey, Virginia, and extended through the central part of West Virginia to Parkersburg. Completed in 1847, the road was a great stimulus to the development of the section of the country it traversed.

These four roads were the nucleus for the present highway system, but its development came slowly. Until 1908, when State aid for public highways was provided for the first time, each county was charged with building and keeping in repair its own roads. The initial State-aid plan lasted only until 1911, when the legislature decided it had been 'usurping the rights of the people' and tossed the road problem back into the lap of the counties, retaining a State road bureau for advisory purposes only. Conditions then became so bad that when the bureau made a survey in 1914 it reported that West Virginia had 'the worst roads in the United States.' Two years later Congress passed a

Federal-aid plan, and in 1920 the electorate of West Virginia approved a $50,000,000 bond issue for road building; since that time West Virginia has gradually constructed a system of improved highways. An additional $35,000,000 bond issue was approved for road building in 1928.

West Virginia's extensive utilization of natural resources and subsequent rapid industrial development are a tribute to the determination and skill of the planners and builders who, accepting the challenge of the rugged country, gave the State a web of highways and railroads to augment the natural waterways. How well the engineers and constructors succeeded in surmounting the natural barriers is exemplified in the undisputed claim that West Virginia has faced and solved more diversified road-building problems than any other State east of the Rocky Mountains.

In the mountainous or extremely hilly regions the engineers have overcome countless obstacles by the use of huge through-cuts with diversion ditches, benched slopes, and roadside development as protection against slips and erosion; massive retaining walls; intricate bridges and viaducts over numerous streams and gaping ravines; high fills covering long culverts; stream-channel changes and systems of ditches for subdrainage.

Other mountainous States have some of these difficulties, but they have the advantage that their roads, once built, usually stay put. Many of West Virginia's do not; for about two-thirds of the State (along with comparatively small areas of Pennsylvania, Ohio, and Kentucky) lies in a geosyncline principally made up of tilted shale, siliceous sandstones, and porous clays—strata which, when wet, are particularly conducive to slides.

West Virginia's 45-mile speed limit is considered by highway engineers in planning the alignment of a road. They seek to attain moderate curves and gradients with ample sight-distance to permit traffic to move at the highest speed consonant with safety. Curves are straightened or widened to provide a safe minimum non-passing sight-distance of 450 feet, and considerable extra cutting and filling is often needed to meet this standard. Super-elevation, or 'banking' of curves, is used to counteract the centrifugal force developed by vehicles. Full protection is provided in this manner on curves up to and including a 6° curve for the legal rate of speed. A super-elevation of 1½ inch per foot is considered the safe maximum for heavy and slow-moving trucks, as they tend to slide off the super-elevated section. Except in a few instances where the character of the terrain makes the requirement impossible to meet, the gradient of all Federal-aid highways in the State is set at 7 per cent and on all other State primary routes at 9 per cent.

Reaching all but 3 of the 55 counties, the railroads of West Virginia have grown with the commerce and industry of the State. Their branch lines and spurs reach out to connect with all the important coal and oil fields and the manufacturing centers. In several instances the branch lines were built by coal companies and later taken over by the railroads. Out of a total trackage of 7,147 miles, 6,475 are maintained by the following six roads: Baltimore & Ohio, 2,229; Chesapeake and Ohio, 1,807; Norfolk and Western, 1,116; Western Maryland, 508; Virginian, 468; and New York Central, 347.

As with the first highways, the routes of the early railroads were determined in a large degree by sectional rivalries. Baltimore capitalists, fearing that construction of the Erie Canal would interfere with the commercial supremacy of their city, planned the Baltimore & Ohio Railroad to tap the Ohio River trade. The tracks were completed to Wagner's Bridge, opposite Harpers Ferry, in 1834, when construction came to an abrupt halt. The original plan was to go through the Shenandoah Valley, across the mountains to the headwaters of the Great Kanawha, and along this stream to the Ohio; but Norfolk people, jealous of Baltimore, together with backers of the James River and Kanawha Turnpike fought the proposed railroad. Aided by the protests of settlers, who claimed the trains would frighten their wives and children and kill their hogs and cattle, they succeeded in getting the State to stipulate that the route must cross at a point north of the Little Kanawha River.

This meant that the promoters would have to construct 200 miles of track over the Alleghenies, through the roughest region ever traversed by pioneer railroad builders. Construction was resumed in 1840; the road reached Cumberland, Maryland, in 1842, and work to extend it to Wheeling began in 1848. The last spike was driven to connect east-west construction at Rosbys Rock, 18 miles east of Wheeling, on December 24, 1852; and on New Year's Day, 1853, the first train from the Atlantic seaboard to the Ohio reached Wheeling. From Cumberland to Wheeling construction required 11 tunnels and 113 bridges. The railroad, used for transporting troops and supplies, was an important factor in the War between the States, and later in the industrial development of the new State. Between 1881 and 1910 the Baltimore & Ohio constructed nine important branch lines in West Virginia.

Norfolk's determination to divert trade from Baltimore to itself was responsible for the beginning of the Chesapeake and Ohio Railway, whose Norfolk backers planned a route through central Virginia to the Ohio River. Originally called the Louisa Railroad and later the Virginia Central, the line had reached a point 10 miles east of Covington, Virginia, when construction was interrupted by the War between the States. Meantime the State of Virginia had undertaken the building of the Covington and Ohio Railroad from Covington to the Ohio River. After the war Virginia and West Virginia co-operated in merging the Virginia Central and the Covington and Ohio under the name of the Chesapeake and Ohio Railroad Company. Construction was resumed, financed by Collis P. Huntington, the California 'empire builder,' and completed to Huntington in 1873, the last spike being driven at Hawks Nest, Fayette County, on January 2, 1873. The name of the road was changed to the Chesapeake and Ohio Railway Company in 1878, after a reorganization following a receivership. Subsidiary lines of the Chesapeake and Ohio branch out to the richest coal and lumber regions of the State.

The Norfolk and Western Railway was the first to project a trunk line through West Virginia for the express purpose of reaching rich deposits of coal and transporting it to Tidewater and the Great Lakes. It reached the Pocahontas coal fields in 1883 and was extended to the Ohio River in 1892.

Financed by Henry Gassaway Davis and associates, another railroad constructed primarily for hauling coal, the Potomac and Piedmont, was begun in 1880, comprising the foundation of the line that was later taken over by the Western Maryland.

Unlike other coal-carrying roads, the Virginian Railway had as its objective the most direct line from the rich coal fields of southern West Virginia to Tidewater. It did not seek a winding course that would touch the larger towns along its route. Instead, it bridged streams and tunneled mountains to obtain a direct route and permit gravity to help haul its coal trains over a large part of the way; and Roanoke, Virginia, is the only sizable town between its terminal points. Its main line extends from Sewalls Point on Hampton Roads, Norfolk, Virginia, to Deepwater on the Kanawha River in Fayette County, West Virginia, where, crossing a railroad bridge over the Kanawha, it connects with the New York Central System for a through route from Tidewater to the Great Lakes. Between Mullens, West Virginia, and Roanoke, Virginia, the Virginian is electrified, and over it are operated some of the largest locomotives and heaviest freight trains in the world.

In 1902 Henry H. Rogers and associates acquired the Deepwater Railway Company, which then owned only four miles of track, used chiefly to haul timber from Deepwater to Robson, West Virginia; and plans were made at once to extend it through the heart of the coal fields of southern West Virginia to Tidewater, Virginia. These plans were executed with such dispatch that the two other coal-carrying roads whose territory would be invaded, Chesapeake and Ohio and Norfolk & Western, did not realize that the immense Standard Oil fortune of Rogers was behind the enterprise, nor were they aware of the magnitude of the undertaking until engineers for the Deepwater, which later became the Virginian, appeared in Jennys Gap in August to begin a preliminary survey. Alive to its danger at last, the Chesapeake and Ohio had engineers working in the gap the same day; but the Deepwater projected a survey, completed its location, filed maps, secured right-of-way deeds, and laid rails with such speed that it had the law of possession on its side. The Chesapeake and Ohio claimed the right-of-way through Jennys Gap under a survey made in 1899 and filed a bill for an injunction in the Circuit Court of Raleigh County, which rendered a decision in its favor. The Deepwater appealed the case to the Supreme Court of Appeals of West Virginia, which reversed the lower court and gave the Deepwater control of this strategic gap. The road was completed and in operation from the West Virginia coal fields to Tidewater in 1909.

Financiers who projected the first railroads through West Virginia reaped immense profits by giving rebates and by charging favored shippers on long hauls rates lower than those charged less favored customers for shorter hauls; in many cases the favored shippers were companies they themselves controlled. Railroad magnates also used their immense influence to add laws favorable to themselves to the statutes of the State and Nation. The practice of charging a lower rate for a long haul than for a short one was abolished in 1887, but the rebate evil was not eliminated until the passage of the Hepburn rate bill to take the rate-making power for freight transportation from the railroads and vest it in the Interstate Commerce Commission.

From the time pioneers reached the Ohio River at Pittsburgh, that broad stream played an important part in the development of the territory which it drains. Before the railroads came it was the principal thoroughfare into the Middle West, and over it moved much of the commerce of the newly opened region. As industries started and expanded along its banks and those of its tributaries, greater stream depths to take care of larger vessels were found indispensable. In 1793 the Virginia legislature passed an act to clear the Monongahela River for canoes and flatboats. Steamboats ascended it to Morgantown in 1826 and to Fairmont in 1850. The first attempt at canalization of the Great Kanawha River was represented by sluice-ways built along the Great Kanawha River in 1825, and the present system of locks and dams was begun on the same stream in 1873.

With government aid, the canalization was extended to other streams, and it was gradually built up until five rivers—the Ohio, the Monongahela, the Little Kanawha, the Great Kanawha, and the Big Sandy— had a total of 81 locks and dams under government operation in 1938. Four new units were completed early in 1938 at a total cost of nearly $25,000,000. One of these, the $10,000,000 unit on the Ohio at the mouth of the Great Kanawha at Gallipolis, Ohio, largest dam of the roller-gate type in the world, can handle twelve 175-foot barges at one time.

Locks and dams on the Ohio provide a navigation depth of 9 feet from Pittsburgh to the mouth of the river. From a point 4 miles above Fairmont, 15 locks and dams give the Monongahela a navigable depth of 11 feet for 100 miles and a 7-foot depth for the remaining 30 miles to Pittsburgh. A new system of 4 high-lift locks and dams, including the Gallipolis unit on the Ohio, gives the Great Kanawha a 9-foot navigable depth from its mouth to Deepwater, a distance of 90 miles. Three locks and dams on the main stream and one each on the Tug Fork and Levisa Fork assure the Big Sandy and these tributaries of 58 miles of 6-foot navigation depth. The Little Kanawha has 5 locks and dams, providing a 4-foot navigable depth for 48 miles, from Creston to the river's mouth at Parkersburg.

During the 10 year period of 1924–33 these five West Virginia rivers had a total freight traffic of 40,962,000 tons. More than half this total, or 21,800,000 tons, was moved on the Monongahela, whose freight tonnage during that decade was among the highest in the world. The greater part of this was in coal shipments to the Pittsburgh steel area, coal comprising between 80 and 90 per cent of the traffic on the Monongahela, Ohio, and Great Kanawha, while gasoline and fuel oil made up approximately 90 per cent of shipments on the Little Kanawha and Big Sandy. The early flatbottomed boats have been supplanted by high-powered steam and gasoline boats that push fleets of barges containing coal, steel, lumber, oil, and gasoline along the deep channels.

Although exact statistics have not been compiled since 1933, it is known that river shipping has steadily declined since then. The Great Kanawha's annual tonnage was expected to show a substantial gain following completion of the new system of locks and dams, which increased that stream's navigable depth from six feet to nine feet. Total coal shipments by river decreased from 3,270,674 tons in 1936 to 2,874,111 tons in 1937, a drop of 12.12 per cent as compared to a gain of 3.3 per cent in truck shipping and a 0.73 per cent increase in railroad shipment.

Before the advent of railroads and improved highways the rivers provided a popular and profitable method of passenger transportation, but this business is now negligible except for ferry traffic, although several steam and oil packets still carry passengers on the Ohio. They obtain a large part of their annual trade by providing excursion trips.

In 1938 transportation by air was little advanced in West Virginia, and extensive development was expected to be slow, largely because of topographic conditions that make the construction of adequate landing fields both difficult and expensive. Only one major line—American Airlines—passed through the State, stopping at Elkins, Charleston, and Huntington on its route between Washington and Cincinnati, with daily service of one plane each way. Airports considered of sufficient size and in condition to accommodate commercial aviation in some measure were located at or near 21 cities: Charleston, Huntington (field across the Ohio River in Ohio), Wheeling, Parkersburg, Clarksburg (at Bridgeport), Elkins, Morgantown (two fields), White Sulphur Springs, Moundsville (at Glendale), Martinsburg, Logan (at Chapmanville), Beckley, Princeton, Hinton (at Pence Springs), Marlinton, Logan, Petersburg, Ravenswood, Sutton, Weston, and Spencer. Those at Charleston, Huntington, Clarksburg, and Elkins are soon to be equipped with night-landing facilities, while the Sutton and Petersburg airports have complete equipment for night landing.

In the late eighteenth and early nineteenth centuries communication between settlements and towns and the dissemination of news in western Virginia were largely dependent on the willingness of itinerant traders and other travelers, although Wheeling had a river mail service to Cincinnati before the first post roads, from Pittsburgh to Wheeling and Morgantown, were opened in 1794. The river mail boats, operated in four relays, required six days downstream and twelve days upstream on the Cincinnati-Wheeling route.

The Pittsburgh-Morgantown post road followed a route established by the *Pittsburgh Gazette,* an enterprising pioneer newspaper that obtained part of its advertising business in Morgantown and Clarksburg until Morgantown's first newspaper began publication in 1804.

Numerous post road routes were established to other points in the State during the early 1800's, and keen competition developed among stage-line operators. One of the outstanding contests, the outcome of which sometimes determined which line should receive mail contracts, hinged on the rapidity with which the President's message to Congress was distributed. On such occasions the fastest horses obtainable were used—and the drivers did not spare them. A National Road driver, Dan Noble, boasted that he made the run from Hagerstown, Maryland, to Wheeling in 15½ hours, and another driver on the same road, Dan Gordon, claimed a record when he covered 32 miles in 2 hours and 20 minutes. Some of the early mail routes were over such rough trails that the mail was carried on horseback.

Carrying the mail was greatly expedited with the coming of the railroads, and at about the same time there was developing a new means of communication—the telegraph. The first use of this invention in the State was in 1847 at Wheeling, where a tap wire was run to a main line on the western side of the Ohio River. Western Virginia had several telegraph lines when the War between the States began, and these were taken over by the Union Army for military use for the duration of the war. Among the greatest obstacles to early telegraph and telephone line construction were the mountaineers; not understanding the purpose of the wire, they would cut it and take it for their own use.

Wheeling also had the distinction of having the first telephone line in the State—a line installed by the Behrens brothers in 1879 for use between their two grocery stores. In 1880, four years after Alexander Graham Bell had invented the telephone, an exchange was established in Wheeling to serve 52 subscribers. The first toll line was constructed in 1883, connecting Wheeling with Pittsburgh; between 1882 and 1895 exchanges were installed in ten other cities, and by 1900 the State had a fairly extensive telephone system. On September 1, 1938, the Chesapeake and Potomac Telephone Company (a Bell System affiliate) had a capital investment of $26,000,000 in the State, with 100 central offices, 400,000 miles of telephone wire, and 127,500 telephones in service. In addition, there were about 75 small companies, with about 22,000 subscribers; most of these give service to rural communities, operating party lines on which as many as 25 or 30 persons may listen in on a conversation.

Radio broadcasting, like the telegraph and telephone, had its earliest West Virginia trial in Wheeling, where station WWVA first went on the air on December 13, 1926. The State now has nine stations: WWVA, Wheeling, WSAZ, Huntington; WMMN, Fairmont; WHIS, Bluefield; WCHS and WGKV Charleston; WPAR, Parkersburg; WJLS Beckley; and WBLK, Clarksburg. WWVA, WMMN, WCHS, WSAZ and WPAR are affiliated with the Columbia Broadcasting System.

Transportation by means of electric railway has shown a marked decline in the past decade. In 1929, there were 376 miles of city and interurban railway lines operated in the State, but by 1939 the track mileage was only a little in excess of 200 miles. During this period some electric railway companies entirely abandoned their lines; others replaced them wholly or in part by busses. Three companies operate over 80 per cent of the remaining lines. The Charleston Transit Company has abandoned all of its city lines and installed busses, and it operates interurban bus lines to St. Albans, Marmet, and Dunbar. The Monongahela West Penn Public Service Company operates interurban cars from Fairmont to Clarksburg, Weston, Bridgeport, and Wilsonburg; and from Parkersburg to South Parkersburg and to Marietta, Ohio. The Co-operative Transit Company operates lines in the Wheeling area.

With improved roads came motor bus transportation. In 1923 the legislature authorized the operation of motor vehicles transporting passengers for hire over regular routes between fixed points. Now 55 bus companies operate 650 motor coaches over highways of the State.

Newspapers

O F the 31 daily newspapers, 121 weeklies, 2 biweeklies, and 12 monthlies or quarterlies that were being printed in West Virginia in 1939, not one can boast of a century of continuous publication.

The *Potomak Guardian and Berkeley Advertiser,* established at Shepherdstown in November 1790, was the first newspaper published in western Virginia. Its publisher was Nathaniel Willis, father of Nathaniel Willis who founded the *Youth's Companion,* and grandfather of Nathaniel Parker Willis, well-known poet, author, and journalist of Poe's day. Printed on a sheet 9 by 15 inches, the paper hardly had room for its full name. When Willis moved his shop to Martinsburg in 1795 he shortened the name to *Potomak Guardian.* Files of his paper have been collected and preserved in the State department of archives and history.

The original name of the *Potomak Guardian* was outspanned by that of the second newspaper published in what was to become West Virginia. This was the *Impartial Observer: or Shepherd's-Town, Charles-Town & County Advertiser,* which was founded at Shepherdstown in 1797. The *Berkeley Intelligencer* appeared at Martinsburg in 1799, but the paper was soon given a more straggling title, the *Berkeley and Jefferson County Intelligencer and Northern Neck Advertiser*—thus beating the Shepherdstown paper's 60-letter name by four letters.

The first newspaper west of the Allegheny Mountains was the *Monongalia Gazette and Morgantown Advertiser,* which started publication at Morgantown in 1803. In 1807 the *Repository* was published at Wheeling, and in 1808 the *Farmer's Repository,* the first agricultural paper in the State, appeared at Charles Town. The *Bye-Stander* was established at Clarksburg in 1810, and was followed by a long line of publications carrying such picturesque names as the *Rattlesnake,* the *Countryman,* the *Compiler, Scion of Democracy,* and the *Log Cabin.* The *Kenawha Spectator* was published at Charleston in 1820 and was followed shortly by the *Western Courier,* which in turn was succeeded in 1826 by the *Western Virginian and Kanawha County Gazette.* The name was later shortened to the *Western Virginian.*

The first religious publication in the State was the *Christian Baptist,* published in 1823 by Alexander Campbell, who operated a small press in his home at Bethany (*see Religion*). In 1824 John S. Gallaher published at Harpers Ferry the *Ladies' Garland,* one of the first papers in the country devoted mainly to the interests of women. It contained poetry, stories, and household hints.

In content and make-up these early papers were much the same. The small type, often script, was set solid below single-line heads in capital letters only a few points larger. They carried little advertising, and what did appear consisted of announcements of property for sale, candidacies for local offices, and rewards for runaway slaves. These rewards ranged from 1¢ to $3.

Reminiscent articles by ex-soldiers or local personages and letters to the editor gave almost the only breath of life to the early papers. Columns on the front page were devoted to detailed accounts of the proceedings of Congress, or letters from United States ministers in foreign countries, printed under such headings as 'Foreign Intelligence' or 'The Latest from Europe.' Only during heated political campaigns or when major scandals or crimes occurred did local happenings take precedence over national or foreign affairs.

The editorial page dominated the early newspapers. Long, ponderous, and often florid comment was written by editors who were adept in invective and epithet. Their freedom in personal criticism often provoked physical combats or led contemporary writers and editors to air violent opinions of each other, and these exchanges made entertaining reading for the public and increased the circulation of the papers. How far in vituperation an editor could go is illustrated by Editor Mason Campbell, publisher of the *Western Virginian* in Charleston, who resented Anne Newport Royall's 'passing notice of Kanawha County' in her book, *Sketches of History, Life and Manners in the United States.* In the issue of September 20, 1826, Campbell offered his criticism of the book, referring to Mrs. Royall as 'a woman whose manners exhibit as little refinement and good breeding as her past life has modesty and virtue.' Mrs. Royall had gained wide attention as a writer, but in the opinion of the Charleston editor her writings 'serve the detestable purpose of a woman, whose brazen-faced affrontery is without parallel, and whose old age and the decay of personal beauty have unfitted her for employment, which at an earlier period of life, yielded her a comfortable, though infamous, support.' Mrs. Royall's reply, if any, is not a matter of record.

Almost every issue of these papers contained one or two columns of poetry, usually written by local versifiers and published under such headings as 'Seat of the Muses.' Fiction, literary essays, and book reviews clipped from Richmond, Philadelphia, and New York papers filled several columns and gave many of the earlier papers something of the tone of magazines.

Newspapers in western Virginia changed ownership frequently and were largely one-man publications, the publisher being the editor, reporter, typesetter, printer, and distributor. The day after printing—the press run was usually on Wednesday—the editor filled his saddlebags with papers, mounted his horse, and set out to deliver them to his scattered subscribers. At each stop he sounded a tin horn to announce the paper's arrival.

After 1830 the creation of new counties required publication of more legal and official notices, the advertising revenue of the press became more profitable, and papers were established in almost every county. By 1850 three dailies and 21 weeklies were being published in western Virginia.

Between 1850 and 1860 newspaper publishing developed rapidly. The number of publications, 24 in 1850, increased to 43 in 1860: 3 dailies, 2 tri-weeklies, 36 weeklies, and 3 monthlies, published in 19 counties.

Not every newspaper of this period was dependent upon courthouse favor. The *Kanawha Republican,* founded at Charleston in 1842, and the *Intelligencer,* established at Wheeling in 1852, assumed the appearance and size of metropolitan dailies. The *Intelligencer,* under the leadership of A. W. Campbell, became a leading daily and the only one strongly to support the new State movement. The *Intelligencer* is the only West Virginia daily newspaper established before the War between the States that has continued publication. Two weeklies established before 1860, the *Spirit of Jefferson,* founded at Charles Town in 1844, and the *Herald,* founded at Wellsburg in 1846, are still published. The *Virginia Free Press,* started at Harpers Ferry in 1821, the State's oldest newspaper to survive into the twentieth century, ceased publication in 1916.

The 31 dailies in existence in 1939 were published in 21 towns and cities; but only two places, Charleston and Moundsville, had competing papers under separate ownership. In other towns where more than one paper was issued, the same owners controlled all the publications, and in most instances all were printed in the same plant. Chain ownership has reached West Virginia, and 13 of the 31 dailies are controlled by Herschel C. Ogden, of Wheeling. Of the 121 weeklies, 13 are owned by Woodyard Publishers and 6 by the West Virginia Newspapers Publishing Company.

Of the dailies, 17 are Republican papers, 12 Democratic, and 2 profess to be nonpartisan in politics. Of the 135 weeklies and periodicals, 61 are Republican, 55 Democratic, 16 nonpartisan, 2 claim to be independent, and 1 is not listed politically. As a general rule, the daily and weekly newspapers in each county of the State are almost equally divided politically. Wood County lacks a weekly newspaper, though Parkersburg, the county seat, has two dailies. Circulations of the dailies range from 2,147 to 62,000; some of the weeklies circulate to only 350 readers.

West Virginia has no foreign-language publications, and only one paper, a small weekly published in McDowell County, is devoted exclusively to the interests of Negro readers.

The largest collections of the files of West Virginia newspapers from the earliest times are in the State department of archives and history, Charleston, and the West Virginia University Library, Morgantown. Other sizable collections are owned by publishers who keep complete files of their publications. Scattered numbers of the earliest newspapers in the State can be found in the Library of Congress, Washington, D. C., and the Virginia State Library, Richmond. Berkeley County Courthouse has the most complete collection of early papers published in Martinsburg.

Education

WEST VIRGINIA'S free school system, with plants representing a property investment of more than $72,000,000 (in 1938) and an annual enrollment of nearly 500,000 pupils, evolved from log structures built by early settlers to serve as both schools and churches.

One of the first of these buildings was that erected at Old Fields in what is now Hardy County, where a party that included George Washington began a land survey in August 1748. Another was built at Pearsall's Fort, now Romney, in 1752. Services of the teacher in such pioneer schools were secured by subscription: a paper was passed around the community and each parent indicated how many children he would send and whether the teacher could expect cash remuneration, produce, or 'bed and board.' The teachers were often wandering pedagogues, settling wherever they could obtain enough signers to assure a living. The buildings were usually situated on hard-scrabble or worn-out lands and were called 'old field schools.'

With the exception of a few maintained by the churches, schools were supported entirely by subscription until 1796, when the Virginia assembly passed a law authorizing a State subsidy to provide each white child with three years of instruction in reading, writing, and arithmetic. Parents had to pay if they wanted their children to attend longer than three years. At the suggestion of Thomas Jefferson, the assembly in 1810 created a 'literary fund' of $20,000, to be raised by the sale of public lands, to provide additional schooling for children whose parents were unable to pay. The plan met with little success, as such schools had the stigma of pauperism, and the pioneers were usually too proud to allow their children to attend them.

Eastern Virginians had control of the assembly, and the western members were unable to obtain what they considered adequate school legislation for their part of the State. This added to the dissatisfaction of western Virginians that resulted later in the separation of West

Virginia from the mother State. The act of 1845 was an example of unsatisfactory legislation. It called for county elections to establish schools to be maintained by public taxation, and contained so many detailed provisions that most counties found it impossible to carry them out. By 1860 only four counties in western Virginia had established free schools under this act.

These early schools were roughly built of logs, with clapboarded roofs and huge fireplaces, for which the boys chopped and carried wood. The split-log seats had no backs and were so high that only the taller pupils could touch the floor with their feet. Before the coming of sawmills, the writing desks were long slabs fastened to the walls with wooden pins driven into augur holes. Pens were made from the wing feathers of geese, turkeys, or eagles, and ink from the juices of pokeberries and barks. A water bucket and a common dipping gourd or cup completed the physical equipment. Textbooks in general use were primers, Webster's *Spelling Book,* and the New Testament; pupils of all ages used *Gulliver's Travels* and *Pilgrim's Progress* as readers until McGuffey's readers displaced them in the 1840's.

With the advent of sovereignty for the new State, the legislature passed an act setting up a free school system in 1863, and by 1865, notwithstanding the war in progress, public education had grown until schools were in operation in 22 counties, with 16,000 pupils in attendance. By 1868 there were 1,756 schools in operation, employing 1,810 teachers, and the first free public schools for the Negro in the South had been established at Parkersburg and Clarksburg.

Mindful of the demand for better educational facilities, the drafters of the new State's constitution in 1872 wrote into its provisions for a system of free public schools, to be supported by an irreducible school fund, by direct taxation, and by proceeds of fines and forfeitures. The first legislature adopted an enabling act to establish the system and also approved funds for teacher training in normal schools. Frame structures then began to displace the crude log schoolhouses, although there were still about 1,000 of the latter in use as late as 1890.

Educators generally recognize Alexander L. Wade as West Virginia's outstanding contributor to modern educational methods. While serving as superintendent of schools for Monongalia County from 1875 to 1879, Wade devised a grade system for country schools. In 1890 the legislature passed an act making the Wade plan an integral part of the State school system. Other States, led by Massachusetts and New Jersey, began adopting this plan about the same time, and today it is used in most rural public school systems throughout the United States.

West Virginia had only one high school in 1870 and 25 in 1900. Not until 1911 did this class of schools begin to receive State aid. In the nineteenth century the function of the high school was performed after a fashion by private academies (at one time numbering as high as 65), which in several instances developed into institutions for higher education. Among the earliest were the Lewisburg Seminary, founded in 1812, now Greenbrier College for Women (junior); the Romney Academy, opened in 1820 by the Virginia Literary Society, now the West Virginia School for the Deaf and Blind; and the private academy opened at Huntington in 1837, which became Marshall College. This institution and Bethany College, started in 1840 by Alexander Campbell, founder of the Disciples of Christ Church, were the only schools of college rank and name in West Virginia when it became a State.

In 1938 there were 328 high schools with a total enrollment of 92,416, and 106 junior high schools with 28,223 pupils. Of the high schools 247 (19 of them for Negroes), with a total enrollment of 90,730, were rated as first class; 137 were members of the North Central Association of Colleges and Secondary Schools. This organization rates schools in 20 States, using as basic criteria the adequacy of school plant and instructional equipment, administration policies, and training of teachers. West Virginia educators are proud of the fact that more than half of the State's schools are eligible for membership, that more are added each year, and that the State's standards for teacher qualifications are higher than those of the North Central Association.

The most far-reaching change in West Virginia's school system since the advent of public schools was effected by legislation in 1933 substituting county units for district units. Under the old plan, schools were financed by direct taxes on personal property and real estate in each magisterial and independent district, but when property values declined during the depression it was found that the tax income of many rural districts was insufficient to support their schools during a full nine-months term. To provide equality of opportunity between children attending urban and rural schools, the new law reduced the administrative units from 397 to 55, or one for each county, and provided a guarantee of State financial aid to each county in proportion to the total amount of money necessary to keep its schools open during a full term each year.

The county now pays a part of the cost, the percentage depending upon its revenue-raising ability, and the State makes up the remainder. In 1937–8 this State aid varied from 30 per cent in Ohio County to 92 per cent in Pendleton County, with an average of 55 per cent for all counties. State school financing totaled $13,996,595.

Consolidation of schools and the employment of more adequately trained teachers are among the principal objectives in the administration of the new school law. Improved roads are a valuable contribution to consolidation, and poorly located one-room elementary schools, as well as the smaller and less well-equipped junior high and high schools, are steadily being abandoned. In the school year of 1932–3, 45 counties used 362 busses and transported 45,000 pupils. In 1937–8, all 55 counties provided such transportation, using 1,057 busses, and transporting 105,220 pupils.

West Virginia maintains separate schools for white and Negro pupils in institutions for higher education as well as in the elementary and secondary grades. According to Horace Mann Bond, *The Education of the Negro in the American Social Order*, 'West Virginia was the first state in the South to provide for a separate system of public schools for Negroes.' Provisions for Negro schooling were first made in 1863, when agitation began for a system of separate schools of equal rank in curricula and academic standing with those for white children. An advisory council on Negro education was set up in 1923 to assist the State board of education, but this council was supplanted in 1933 by a State board of Negro education, which has joint control with the State board of education over Negro schools.

School attendance of children from 7 to 16 years of age is compulsory. Counties are authorized by law to establish kindergartens wherever it is considered necessary for children between 4 and 6 years of age, but enrollment in the three public kindergartens, all in Wheeling, totaled only 529 in 1937–8. Pupils in elementary, junior high, and high schools buy their own textbooks if financially able; the law provides that county boards of education must supply textbooks when the parents are unable to do so.

West Virginia elementary schools have pioneered in teaching two comparatively new subjects—safety and conservation. A State-wide program was started in 1936–7 whereby all elementary schools are expected to teach three phases of safety as outlined in the manual for the course: safety on highways and streets, safety at school, and safety in the home. This training is integrated with art, music, arithmetic, and other subjects. In co-operation with the State conservation commission, the department of education experimented with conservation studies in a limited number of schools during 1936–7 and found the work so successful that a course of study was initiated in all 12 grades of the public schools in 1937–8. This instruction, also interwoven with other studies, is principally concerned with the natural resources of the State that can be conserved or replaced.

A club system sponsored for the fifth to eighth grades, inclusive, does much to encourage study in the standard courses; the pupil who enters competition attendant upon club membership becomes a 'Discoverer' in the fifth grade, an 'Explorer' in the sixth, a 'Pioneer' in the seventh, and a 'Junior Citizen' in the eighth, if all examination requirements are passed. Junior Citizens are eligible to compete for the Golden Horseshoe, a pin made in the same design as that awarded by Governor Spotswood to the men who accompanied him across the Alleghenies in 1716 and bearing the Latin phrase *Sic jurat transcendere montes*—'Thus he swears to cross the mountains.' This coveted honor may be awarded to only four members (three whites and one Negro) in each county each year. With it goes a trip to Charleston and participation in a public presentation ceremony in the State Capitol. The examination is so difficult that it would baffle most adult West Virginians, but 167 boys and girls won the badges in 1938. There were 110,902 club members in 1937–8, an increase of 6,072 over the previous year.

Under the general supervision of Dr. W. W. Trent, Superintendent of Free Schools, a wide program of vocational education has been carried on, chiefly in the high schools, in three fields of instruction: trades and industries, homemaking, and agriculture. Federal financial aid for vocational education must be matched on a fifty-fifty basis with State or local funds; the total allotment in 1937–8 was in excess of $120,000. Special training courses for vocational teachers are provided at West Virginia University, New River State College, and West Virginia State College, a Negro institution.

Classes in agricultural education are of three types: all-day classes for pupils of high school age who can spend full time in school; part-time classes for persons 14 years of age or older who have entered employment but are able to spend part of their time in school; and evening classes for adults. In 1937–8 the all-day classes had an enrollment of 3,490, the part-time classes 340, and the evening classes 1,803.

Vocational education in trades and industries covers a wide range of subjects, including phases of mining work, the electrical industry, automobile mechanics, wood and metal-working, and other arts and crafts. In addition to high school vocational courses, special vocational classes in 1935–6 had an enrollment of 1,868 in the evening schools, 854 in the part-time day schools, and 309 in all-day schools. Special evening classes are sometimes established to meet the local needs in a particular industry, such as the class for moldmakers and decorators in bottlemaking set up at Fairmont in 1934. West Virginia University conducts extension part-time classes in mining work, including studies in mine ventilation, fires, and explosions, and shorter extension courses in the technical phases of mining, accident prevention, and rescue methods.

One division of the State department of education co-operates with the Federal Board of Vocational Education in carrying out a rehabilitation program for physically handicapped persons. Commercial courses are given in business schools, instructors are furnished in industrial and commercial establishments, tutoring is provided in some cases where no other form of instruction is available, and training is sometimes augmented by correspondence courses. In 1937–8 there were 434 persons receiving training, while 610 who had finished their training were provided with employment in 107 occupations and received an average weekly wage of $18.85. The average rehabilitation cost was $330 per person.

Educational facilities are provided in each of the State's charitable and correctional institutions for minors. Vocational instruction is given those capable of rehabilitation in the West Virginia Training School (for mentally defective cases) at Spring Run, while the children in the West Virginia Children's Home, Elkins, and the West Virginia Colored Children's Home, Huntington, attend the public schools. Special State training institutions are the West Virginia School for the Deaf and Blind, founded in 1870 in the buildings of the old Romney Academy, and the West Virginia School for the Colored Deaf and Blind at Institute. The department of education furnishes teachers for the correctional schools: the Industrial School for Boys at Pruntytown, the Industrial Home for Girls at Industrial, the Industrial School for Colored Boys at Lakin, and the Industrial Home for Colored Girls at Huntington. A first-class high school is maintained in the home at Industrial, and some high school work is provided in the Pruntytown institution.

West Virginia University was established at Morgantown in 1867 as the Agricultural College of West Virginia, the name being changed to the present one in the following year. It ranks today as a standard State university, and in 1937-8 had an enrollment of 2,780. Other institutions of higher education are Marshall College at Huntington, New River State College at Montgomery, and seven teachers' colleges. This group comprises Concord State at Athens, founded in 1872; Fairmont State, founded in 1852 as Fairmont Academy and acquired by the State in 1868; Glenville State, 1872; Shepherd State, formerly an academy, acquired by the State in 1867; West Liberty State, founded in 1853 and acquired by the State in 1867; and Bluefield State (for Negroes) founded in 1895.

Institutions for Negroes include the State-supported West Virginia State College at Institute, founded in 1891 and headed by President John W. Davis, one of the Nation's foremost Negro educators; and Storer College (junior college rank) at Harpers Ferry, supported by both State and private funds.

Chief among the denominational and private colleges are Alderson-Broaddus (Baptist), at Philippi, 1901; Bethany (Disciples of Christ), 1840; Davis and Elkins (Presbyterian), at Elkins, 1904; Morris-Harvey (Methodist), at Charleston, 1888; West Virginia Wesleyan (Methodist), at Buckhannon, 1890; and the one junior college, Greenbrier College for Women at Lewisburg.

West Virginia University is accredited by the Association of American Universities, and Marshall and West Virginia State are accredited by the North Central Association of Colleges and Secondary Schools. The teachers' colleges, with the exception of Bluefield, are accredited by the American Association of Teachers Colleges.

A long list of outstanding private schools includes the two degree-granting institutions, Mason College of Music and Fine Arts at Charleston and Linsly Institute of Technology at Wheeling. The latter, a school of engineering founded in 1814 as a military school, still gives military training, but Greenbrier Military School at Lewisburg, an approved college preparatory school, is rated as an honor school by the United States Government. Chief among the Catholic schools is the De Sales Heights Visitation Academy (a boarding school for girls), Parkersburg, founded in 1864, and Mount de Chantal (a preparatory school for girls), Wheeling, founded in 1848, which gives courses in music, dramatics, and art.

Religion

THE search for religious liberty was one of the principal factors that led pioneer settlers, especially the Scotch-Irish and German, to West Virginia. Meetings for purposes of free worship were centers of social life in early settlements even before communities were large enough to warrant construction of church buildings. Early services were held in private homes or, in favorable weather, outdoors. They were usually prayer meetings, except on occasions when itinerant preachers or circuit riders appeared in the community, perhaps to preach a single sermon and then move on to the next settlement, perhaps to stay awhile and conduct a series of meetings. The circuit rider, traveling rough trails in all kinds of weather, fording streams or swimming his horse across them, suffered his share of frontier hardships and, since the Indians had no respect for his calling, braved considerable danger.

There is no authoritative record of when the first church building was erected. The German Quakers, or Friends, had an organized congregation at Mecklenburg (Shepherdstown) in 1738, but it is doubtful whether they had a building before a Protestant Episcopal group, headed by Morgan Morgan, built the Mill Creek church (1740) at Bunker Hill, in the Eastern Panhandle. Congregations of these two faiths, as well as Presbyterians, Lutherans, Moravians, and Baptists, erected numerous churches between 1740 and the Revolutionary War. In many cases the building served as both church and school.

Of the religious sects prominent in the early history of West Virginia, Quakers, Dunkards, Mennonites, and Moravians have since left the State or dwindled to very small numbers. All of these groups except the Moravians opposed taking oaths and bearing arms, and the Dunkards refused to take Indian lands without purchasing them. During the Indian campaigns, Colonel George Washington reported to Lieutenant Governor Robert Dinwiddie his difficulties with the Quakers, 'who will neither bear arms, work, receive provisions or pay, or do anything that tends in any respect, to self-defense.' Ordered by Dinwiddie to 'confine them with a short allowance of bread and water till you bring them to reason,' Washington reported some weeks later that he had been unable to accomplish this, but added 'there is no denomination among us who are more exemplary and useful citizens.'

The Lutherans, the Dunkards, and most of the Quakers were Germans. The Moravians, followers of John Huss, came from Moravia, a province of Bohemia. Moravian missionaries entered western Virginia as early as 1749 and preached to all who would listen, but did not attempt to organize congregations. The beliefs and form of worship of the Mennonites were very similiar to those of the Quakers; the chief difference was in respect to the marriage ceremony—with the Mennonites this was a simple affair in which the principals merely made public confession of their love.

During the years before and immediately after the Revolution, the Baptists and Presbyterians probably outnumbered the members of any other denominations in western Virginia. Among their remaining early churches is the Presbyterian Old Stone Church at Lewisburg, built in 1796 to replace a log structure erected in 1783. The Baptist Forks-of-Cheat Church at Stewartstown, east of Morgantown, organized in 1775, has had four successive buildings on the same site and has the longest continuous history of any church in the State. Although they had a few congregations, the Methodist and Roman Catholic denominations attained no prominence until after the Revolution.

Prior to 1785, when (largely owing to the urging of Thomas Jefferson) the Virginia assembly established religious liberty, the Protestant Episcopal denomination (Church of England) was the State church, supported by taxes. Baptists, Presbyterians, Methodists, and other dissenters could worship as they pleased, though they were not excused from contributing taxes for support of the established church.

Methodist circuit riders became active in western Virginia about 1775. The first Methodist church building in the territory, Rehoboth Church, erected in 1786 near Union in Monroe County, is said to be the oldest Methodist church west of the Alleghenies. By 1805 Francis Asbury and his fellow circuit riders had established nine regularly traveled circuits, embracing practically all of western Virginia. They originated the camp meeting, a series of outdoor services lasting from a few days to a few weeks, and other denominations soon adopted the practice. When the Methodist Episcopal branch of Methodism was organized in 1784, Asbury was made its first bishop in western Vir-

Photograph by Highton; courtesy of Work Projects Administration

OLD MARKET BUILDING, SHEPHERDSTOWN

HOME OF GENERAL CHARLES LEE, LEETOWN

HAREWOOD (1770), THE WASHINGTON HOME, NEAR CHARLES TOWN

PORTRAIT OF COLONEL SAMUEL WASHINGTON, AND FIREPLACE, HAREWOOD

OLD STONE CHURCH (1796), LEWISBURG

Photographs by Highton; courtesy of Work Projects Administration

RICHARD MORGAN HOUSE, SHEPHERDSTOWN

HOME OF HORATIO GATES, NEAR CHARLES TOWN

THE LEE BARN, LEETOWN

HOME OF ALEXANDER CAMPBELL, FOUNDER OF DISCIPLES OF CHRIST CHURCH, BETHANY

BIRTHPLACE OF PEARL BUCK, HILLSBORO

THE PRESIDENT'S COTTAGE, WHITE SULPHUR SPRINGS

HARPERS FERRY ARSENAL, CAPTURED BY JOHN BROWN, OCT. 16, 1859

FIRE ENGINE HOUSE USED AS FORT BY JOHN BROWN AT HARPERS FERRY

John Brown's Fort,
Harpers Ferry, W. Va.

ginia. The Methodist Protestant Church, another division, was formed
in 1828; one of its first congregations, the Hackers Creek or Harmony Church, was organized in 1829 near Jane Lew, in Lewis County.

Schism in the Baptist denomination gave rise to the Seventh Day
Baptists, who observed Saturday rather than Sunday as a day of rest
and worship. Originating in Rhode Island in 1671, this sect grew
steadily in western Virginia, establishing a church at Salem in 1792.
The Non-Missionary Baptists, more commonly known as Primitive or
Hardshell Baptists, were once fairly numerous in the State, but now
have only a few scattered congregations. A feature of this sect's service
is foot washing, with communion. Men line up on one side of the
church, women on the other, and each person washes and dries in
turn the feet of the person next to him.

Although founded across the border in Pennsylvania, the religious
body known as the Disciples of Christ, or Christian Church, had much
of its early growth in West Virginia. The sect was initiated in 1809
by Thomas Campbell, a Presbyterian clergyman who had joined the
Baptists and later left that denomination because its leaders would
not listen to his plan for a union of all churches. Campbell and his
followers organized a new church at Brush Run, Pennsylvania, in
1811, with his son Alexander Campbell as the first preacher. Alexander Campbell moved the church to Bethany in 1827, and it was
from this point that its doctrines spread throughout the country. Its
followers were originally called Campbellites. This is one of the denominations that hold public baptisms, in which new converts are
immersed in shallow rivers or creeks. These ceremonies are usually
announced well in advance and attract large crowds. Weather makes
no difference, and at times the baptisms take place in water of icy
coldness.

Roman Catholic immigrants were barred from Virginia, and Catholic residents were subjected to more persecution than any other sect,
prior to the establishment of religious liberty. The few who did enter
had no spiritual contacts except infrequent visits from Maryland
priests, whose difficulties have been mentioned by John Gilmer Shae,
a Catholic historian: 'Father Fambrack from Frederick, Maryland,
visited it [the Virginia side] only by night and slept by his horse,
ready to mount and put him at full speed at the slightest warning.'
There is a record of masses being held in private homes in the Eastern
Panhandle in 1810, but the first Roman Catholic church in the State
was not built until 1821 or 1822. This was at Wheeling on a lot do-

nated by Noah Zane. When the Wheeling diocese was established in 1850 it had only four churches, those at Wheeling, Parkersburg, Weston, and near Kingwood. The remarkable growth of the Roman Catholic Church in later years is largely attributable to the expansion of industries and public works in the late nineteenth century, which brought to America many Irish and other immigrants of the Roman Catholic faith.

Throughout most of the period between the Revolution and the War between the States the churches were active in furthering secondary and higher education, founding numerous academies and seminaries. Some of these, and others founded later, attained such repute as educational institutions that they became State-approved colleges.

The slavery controversy before the war involved the churches, particularly the Methodist Episcopal, which forbade its ministers to own slaves. The State law made emancipation almost impossible, and a minister of this denomination who had acquired slaves, as sometimes happened by inheritance, was obliged to violate either state or church law no matter which course he chose. The Methodist Episcopal conference's decision against a slave-owning Georgia minister in a test case in 1845 led to a division of the church into northern and southern bodies; the line of division partially followed the eastern and southern boundaries of West Virginia. Other denominations, notably the Baptist and Presbyterian, were similarly split.

As the differences that caused these schisms have been settled or reduced to minor importance since the War between the States, a steady growth of sentiment for unification has been perceptible in all branches of Protestantism in recent years. The first actual merger in West Virginia, however, was that of Methodist churches at Clendenin on October 2, 1938, when Wood Memorial Methodist Episcopal Church and Elizabeth Methodist Episcopal Church, South, united to become Clendenin Methodist Church. These churches are believed to be the first to act on the consolidation plans adopted by State conferences. All Methodist churches were united at a convention of delegates from the Methodist Episcopal Church, the Methodist Protestant Church, and the Methodist Episcopal Church, South, held at Kansas City, Missouri, in May 1939. The Presbyterians are still divided into the Presbyterian Church in the U.S.A., the northern branch, and the Presbyterian Church in the U.S., the southern branch.

New classes of settlers in the post-war period introduced new religious sects into the State, among them the Jewish, Greek Orthodox,

Russian Orthodox, Christian Science, and others. The Mennonites moved westward, while the earlier Dunkard Church became the present Church of the Brethren.

According to United States Census figures (*Religious Bodies:* 1926) total church membership in West Virginia is 531,983. The Methodist church is the strongest numerically with 184,723 members; the Baptists come next, with 113,157 members; followed by Catholics, with 71,265 members. There are 4,286 church edifices, collectively valued at $41,058,000.

The first Negro sect to hold gatherings in the State was the Baptist. A congregation was formed as early as 1852 in Kanawha County and meetings were held at the homes of members until 1865, when a building was erected. Other Baptist groups were organized throughout the State, and in 1866 Methodist churches for Negroes were established. At first these churches were under the supervision of the white church organizations, but by 1900 the African Methodists and African Baptists maintained separate organizations with Negro officials. Previous to 1852 Negroes, if they attended church at all, worshiped in their master's church from balconies especially built for this purpose. Today, the church is perhaps the greatest social force in the life of a Negro community. Ministers are molders of public opinion; controversial subjects involving politics, labor, and prohibition are often discussed from the pulpit. All day 'sings,' box suppers, chicken dinners, lectures, and occasional political rallies are held in the churches, which are used as social centers as well as places of worship. Protracted meetings, generally held during the winter season, are anticipated not only as a time for spiritual regeneration, but as important social events. In larger communities church basements are equipped with recreational facilities and are open to the public.

Total Negro church membership is 32,754, of which 24,285 are Baptists. Methodist Negro groups come next, numerically, with 7,594 members, and the small remainder of church membership is found in the Presbyterian ranks and in minor sects. The number of church organizations in denominations wholly or in part Negro is 1,954; and the value of Negro church buildings is $2,434,526.

Fourteen of the 42 Protestant denominations affiliated with the International Council of Religious Education are represented by churches in West Virginia and work co-operatively in the West Virginia Council of Religious Education, which has headquarters in Charleston. The State Council was incorporated in 1924 as successor to the West Virginia Sunday School Association, formed in 1880. Its principal activities are Sunday-school work, furtherance of Bible teaching in the public schools, sponsorship of vacation church schools and weekday church schools, leadership training, and co-operation with lay organizations in religious worship, dramatics, and the use of leisure time. The council maintains a circulating religious library, sending books all over the State at no cost to members except for postage. The assistance provided by the council is particularly helpful to the smaller churches in isolated communities, where as in pioneer days the church is still the principal social center. The village and rural churches usually raise most of their funds by holding 'socials,' and these with various other entertainments are notable events in the community.

Camp meetings are still an important adjunct to West Virginia religious life, especially in the Northern Panhandle, where they are held annually in several communities. Visiting evangelists and singers, often of national note, are usually in charge of the services. The meetings are attended by thousands of persons, and many converts are made.

Medicine and Public Health

THE State Department of Health of West Virginia is the product of 65 years' progress since the State Medical Society in 1875 adopted Dr. S. L. Jepson's resolution that every influence be brought to bear on the legislature to the end that such an organ of government be created. In March 1881, a law was enacted that established a Board of Health of eight members (later raised to ten and then twelve) whose action was limited to the examination of physicians seeking to practice in the State. The appropriation of a meagre $2,500 permitted little attention to the public health in general, and not until 1913, through the efforts of Dr. H. D. Hatfield, then governor-elect, and Dr. F. F. Farnsworth of the legislature, was a new law passed that raised the appropriation to $15,000, made the secretary of the board a full-time official, and provided for a hygienic laboratory and instruction to the people in matters of hygiene and sanitation. Dr. Hatfield was again instrumental in obtaining a further improvement in 1915 when the board of twelve was replaced by a Public Health Council of seven members, and the Department of Health was divided into the Division of Communicable Diseases and the Division of Sanitary Engineering.

The duties of the Public Health Council are to promulgate rules and pass regulations for the promotion of public health, to hold examinations for physicians applying for license to practice medicine in this State, and to pass on the credentials of those applying for reciprocity. The Public Health Council also takes evidence on appeals, holds hearings, and regulates the practice of medicine in the State, as well as approves appointments of physicians nominated by county courts as health officers.

The Health Commissioner, who is a licensed physician and who is required to have had five years' experience in the practice of medicine, is appointed by the governor for a period of four years. He acts as an ex-officio member of the Public Health Council, serves as its secretary, and performs all executive and other duties incident to his office.

For the purpose of administration, the legislature has created the following divisions and bureaus: Division of Communicable Diseases, Division of Maternal and Child Hygiene, Division of Vital Statistics, State Hygiene Laboratory and Bureau of Barbers and Beauticians. The Public Health Council has created the Bureau of Venereal Diseases, the Bureau of Public Health Education, Bureau of County Health Work, Bureau of Industrial Hygiene.

The function of the Division of Maternal and Child Hygiene is the promotion and protection of the health and welfare of mothers and children of the State and the program is carried on mainly in co-operation with local health departments. This division is also charged with the licensing and supervision of midwives.

The Division of Communicable Diseases, for the purpose of determining the trend of communicable diseases and evaluating the program that is being carried on, and for control and guidance in change of program, collects and analyzes morbidity data from all the counties. This division, from time to time, makes certain recommendations to the Public Health Council for changes in the regulations governing communicable diseases. Control work is carried out through the field units. The Division also co-operates with the United States Public Health Service by supplying morbidity reports from the individual counties of the State each week.

The Division of Vital Statistics is charged with the collection of data concerning births, deaths, and marriages in the State. The Division also supervises local registrars in the collection of data and co-operates with the United States Bureau of Census in Washington in supplying copies of birth and death records.

The State Hygienic Laboratory with county health departments fosters and participates in laboratory work essential to the diagnosis, treatment and control of communicable diseases. Laboratory service is also furnished private physicians when the patient is unable to pay for it. Biologicals are produced and distributed through this division to county health units and practicing physicians where indicated.

The duty of the Bureau of Venereal Diseases is to conduct a program aimed at control of venereal diseases by educating the public to their danger and the necessity for treatment of those diseased, and through the establishment of venereal disease clinics where all indigent cases can be treated. Drugs are supplied through this bureau to all clinics and to practicing physicians upon request. There are, at the present time, 50 clinics in the State in which persons infected with venereal diseases may receive treatment if unable to pay a private physician. Most of these clinics are conducted in co-operation with county health departments, but in some instances they operate in co-operation with the Department of Public Assistance, particularly in counties where no full-time health service exists.

The Bureau of Industrial Hygiene co-operates with mining and manufacturing industries in preventing industrial diseases, assists the medical profession in the diagnosis of occupational diseases, advises the Compensation Commission about hazards attached to different types of industry, makes surveys in the industrial health field, and works with county and district health departments on industrial health problems.

By preparing news stories for all State newspapers, by writing monthly articles for the 4-H papers and School Journal, by conducting a loan department where books, films, and other material of a health educational nature may be obtained by interested agencies, by preparing exhibits for State meetings, by assembling material, including programs, talks and plays for May Day, and Child Health Day, and by holding an Annual State Health Conference, the Bureau of Public Health Education stimulates and maintains the public interest in and awareness of the health conditions of the State.

The Bureau of Barbers and Beauticians supervises sanitation and hygiene in barber shops and beauty shops and issues licenses to practice barbering and beauty culture to persons who have passed a qualifying State test.

The Bureau of County Health Work promotes a full-time health service in the counties and supervises the work carried on by individual health officers. It is also charged with the duty of securing financial aid and preparing budgets for full-time county health departments. At the present time there are 16 counties in the State receiving the services of a full-time county health department. These departments have a minimum personnel of one physician, one sanitary engineer and at least two nurses. Twenty of the counties are grouped into districts, each county in a district having a full-time nurse and the necessary secretarial help. Over the district and in charge of the activities of all health personnel is a full-time health officer. There is also a sanitary engineer attached to the district office. There are six counties which have only a nursing service, operating under a part-time health officer. The remaining 13 counties have no service other than that rendered by a practicing physician, who acts as part-time health officer.

Private medicine has inspired and promoted public health work in West Virginia. From the experience of urban specialist and rural practitioner has come the plans and programs of the Health Department. Independently and through State agencies 79 hospitals have been established in the State. Sixty-two general hospitals with bed capacities ranging from 10 to 225 are located in 38 communities. Of these four serve special groupings of the population, two are for Negroes only. Tuberculosis sanitariums number six, with a total capacity of 1,041; all are either public or non-profit institutions. Five mental hospitals, all State controlled, accommodate 3,911 patients. There are four specialized institutions, one orthopedic, one eye, ear, nose, and throat, and two for crippled children. A total of 10,082 adult patients could be accommodated by State hospital facilities at one time; special provision for infants and children would raise this total by 568.

These facilities barely indicate the immense task of West Virginia's medical profession. In order to reach groups of the population whose income is not sufficient to meet heavy hospital costs, several hospital service associations have been organized in the State. These services are based on a low monthly assessment that varies from 50¢ to $1 for an individual and from $1.50 to $2 for a family. This entitles the insured person or family to all ordinary hospital services for a limited number of days in any 12 month period, with a discount on days in excess of the period. 'Ordinary services' include board, general nursing care, routine dressings, such medications as are ordinarily dispensed in a hospital (but not serums, vaccines, or orthopedic appliances), use of operating room, anesthesis, and all diagnostic X-ray and clinical examinations (whether the patient is admitted to hospital or not). A private room is included on request of the physician.

Because West Virginia is dependent upon surface water for the greater part of its public water supply, the Division of Sanitary Engineering has attempted to prevent the stream pollution that has bred epidemics, made the water unfit for recreational purposes, and caused great monetary loss to industry. The pollution comes from two sources: untreated raw domestic sewage and industrial waste. Major efforts have been directed toward encouraging safer water systems through frequent inspection of water specimens. The Division encourages the extension of municipal sewage systems and aids in abating dangerous nuisance conditions resulting from sewage defects and the discharge of raw sewage without dilution. In rural sections the departmental efforts are directed toward securing approved sanitary privies or septic-tank systems at every home, school, and place of business. This work was greatly facilitated by the Sanitation Program of the Work Projects Administration under which 187,157 sanitary privies have been built in West Virginia. The labor for this work was provided by Federal funds appropriated to the Work Projects Administration, and the materials were contributed locally.

In conjunction with the State Water Commission, the Health Department has encouraged the construction of sewage disposal plants. As yet only three of West Virginia's towns have complete disposal facilities—Bluefield, Hurricane, and Martinsburg. Ten others have partial disposal plants and five additional towns have plants under construction. Disposal systems are contemplated by 10 other cities and towns. In 1939 all but 3 of the 150 large municipalities of the State emptied the untreated waste from a population of 600,000 into rivers and creeks, creating a constant health menace. Coupled with acid drainage from the mines and industrial wastes from manufacturing establishments, this situation becomes perilous during a period of unusually dry weather; such was the case at Charleston and at Weston in 1930, when water supplies became so foul and devoid of oxygen that even the most extreme measures of filtration and chlorination failed to prevent a widespread outbreak of intestinal disorders affecting 10,000 people. The Division of Sanitary Engineering is constantly on guard to see that the sewage is properly diluted and that streams are kept as free from stagnant pools as possible. It has encouraged municipalities to take advantage of Federal aid in constructing new sewage systems and extending those already in use. Many interceptor sewers have been constructed and several hundred miles of new sewers and extensions have been completed. Five of the twelve disposal plants now in use were constructed with Federal grants, two by the Work Projects Administration with relief labor. One of these, the Bluefield plant, is a model for other communities desiring complete sewage disposal.

The industrial waste problem has been solved partially by the action of several of the larger industries, which have installed waste reclaiming plants of their own accord. These either reclaim the waste or remove the harmful elements in them. In the Ohio Valley the West Virginia Health Department co-operates with the health department of four other States in a program to prevent pollution of their rivers by either industrial or domestic waste. Inside the State the largest single effort is the mine sealing program of the Work Projects Administration.

The mine sealing program, begun in 1933, employing miners who could find no jobs in private industry, has greatly decreased the acid evil. Of the 1,698 abandoned mines in the State, 720, or 42.4 per cent, have been sealed completely. Some of the openings of many more mines in the counties in which the program has operated have been closed. The result has been a reduction of 71 per cent in the daily acid load of the State's streams. The health benefits of such a change are many. The cost of neutralizing acid water has prevented many towns from having a pure, safe water supply. The economic loss from acid corrosion has also been a factor in preventing the establishment of better water and sewage systems. In addition, the acid content of the rivers delays the decay of waste matter by slowing the process of oxidation. In a State where dilution is almost the sole method of handling sewage, this creates a grave problem. The mine-sealing work has affected great savings in equipment and in purification costs for the public water systems. The saving in purification costs is evidenced by the report from the Ten Mile Creek division of the B. & O. Railroad that prior to 1933 it has been necessary to use 546 pounds of soda and 290 pounds of lime to each 80,000 gallons of water, but that after 66 of the 136 abandoned mines in Harrison County had been sealed only 90 pounds of soda and 68 pounds of lime neutralized 100,000 gallons of water. Equipment savings have been reported as equally great.

Already emergency conditions have arisen that have proved the value of the sealing program as a health agency. When the Cheat River was called upon unexpectedly to furnish the water supply for Kingwood, Preston County, in the 1936 drouth, only the sealing of 26 former commercial mines in the preceding three years permitted the use of its waters. The acid content in that period has been reduced from a prohibitive 60,093 pounds daily to a moderate 15,425, a reduction of 74 per cent or 22 tons daily.

Large sections of the State in which coal and lumber in commercial quantities are no longer available find that recreational assets are their sole base for further development. To these sections mine sealing means a restoration of many streams to their former recreational value. On Roaring Creek in Randolph County no fish had been observed below Alton Dam in 25 years; today fish are plentiful. On Beaver Creek in Tucker County in 1936 trout were able to spawn for the first time in many years. Mine sealing had affected an 80 per cent reduction in the acid content of this stream. The cost of the entire program has been $1,403,309.

The 1939 Sanitation Act provided the Department of Health with wider powers over State sanitation than it had possessed before. It authorized the Public Health Council to adopt and enforce all needed regulations concerning public water systems, sewage treatment plants, sewerage systems, swimming pools, and excreta disposal. In addition, it also gave the State Health Commissioner or his representative power to issue orders to correct improper conditions in 'any system of plumbing, drainage, water supply, excreta disposal, or garbage refuse disposal, whether publicly or privately owned,' where such endangers the public health. Thus empowered to extend its control over all sanitation facilities of the State, and possessed already of regulatory powers over milk supplies, tourist camp facilities, railroad facilities, theaters, stores, laundries, bakeries, and other phases of activity that involve dangers to public health, the State Department of Health is in a position to eliminate many of the remaining health hazards. The private physician joins with the public servant in the endeavor to make West Virginia a healthier place in which to live.

Folklore

I N the mountain fastnesses of West Virginia a wealth of traditional
song, story, and belief has grown up or been preserved from early
times. With antic gestures mountain storytellers illustrate their
tales, told simply and directly in the homely and archaic speech of
the backwoods. The hunters' campfire is the favorite place for relating
heroic and legendary exploits with bears and other big game. One of
these fabled hunters, old 'Rimfire' Hamrick, of Webster Springs, Webster County, the model for Bush Brown's statue of the West Virginia
Mountaineer on the State Capitol lawn, thus relates how he was given
his name by Colonel John T. McGraw. 'The colonel, he kinder liked
my style an' we went on lots o' huntin' trips together. I used to carry
a .25 calibre rifle that fired on the rim instead of in the center of the
cartridge. Now the colonel, he just couldn't hit nothin' without my
rifle, an' he tuk to callin' me "Rimfire," an' purty soon all the folks
around the big hotel heerd him an' tuk it up.'

Returning late one evening from a not too successful day's hunt,
Rimfire came upon the roosting place of a flock of wild turkeys. 'At
first I thought of shootin' one off and tryin' to fergit about the tothers
for I had only one bullet left,' he said, 'but than I noticed the whole
thirteen of 'em was perched on a limb no bigger 'n a man's wrist. That
gives me an idear. Loadin' my bar'l about a quarter way full o' powder and rammin' th' last bullet down on hit, I tuk aim at the limb of
th' tree an' fired. The bullet split the limb and let them thar turkeys'
toes drop down in the crack. Before they had time to fly off, the split
closed up an' ketched their toes. I clumb up the tree, cut off the limb
with my pocket knife and packed the whole dang flock home just as
I'd ketched 'em.'

Hillside cultivation is no easy matter, and hilltop farming is not
much better. The natural difficulties that beset the West Virginia hill
farmer are the source of much humor and exaggeration; however, the
story of the clifftop farm in Wayne County, where the fields are

reached by ladders and the mule and plow are hoisted by block and tackle up the cliff, is no myth (*see Tour* 18*b*). Slightly exaggerated is the story of the motorist on a narrow valley road who, perceiving a great commotion and a cloud of dust ahead, pulled to one side and stopped his car. As the cloud settled and a gnarled figure emerged rubbing his elbow and beating the dust from his denim jeans with a tattered hat, the startled traveler inquired:

'What in the world happened?'

In a tone of plaintive disgust the dusty one replied:

'That's the third time I've fell outen that danged cornfield this mornin', and I've still got seven rows to grub.'

Witch tales and ghost stories, usually attached to some particular place or personality, are frequently told and widely accepted. Sometimes a local legend gains such currency that even incredulous cynics who scoff at the idea of ghosts and witches acknowledge it as 'one of those happenings that no one can explain.' Indian legends, black-cat stories, the headless horseman, and the inevitable haunted house all have their place.

Of the English and Scottish ballads collected by Francis James Child, whose monumental work is the Bible of American ballad scholars, 45 have been recovered in West Virginia. In the lumber camps, about the mines, and on railroad construction jobs, work songs and ballads of folk origin grow and live. No folk character is so exclusively the property of West Virginia as John Henry. The titanic contest of the Negro steel driver with a steam-driven rock drill during the construction of the Big Bend Tunnel (*see Tour* 16*a*) in 1872 was the basis of the ballad that bears his name. The vigor of the John Henry tradition has carried it around the world, and versions of the ballad have been gathered in every quarter of the globe. But despite its wide dissemination, it is pure West Virginia folklore, and John Henry is unquestionably the outstanding native folk character of the State. Free of the gross exaggeration that borders on the ridiculous, the story of his contest with the steam drill lends this steel-driving Negro an epic quality and a dignity that set him apart as a folk figure. Vital as the men who sing as they labor, the song survives as a great industrial ballad. Of the hundreds of variant stanzas the following are representative:

> John Henry was just a baby
> When he fell on his mammy's knee;
> He picked up a hammer and a little piece of steel,

Said, 'This hammer'll be the death of me, Lawd, Lawd,
This hammer'll be the death of me.'

John Henry was a very small boy
Sitting on his daddy's knee,
Said, 'The Big Bend Tunnel on the C. & O. road
Is gonna be the death of me, Lawd, Lawd,
Is gonna be the death of me.'

John Henry went upon a mountain
And came down on the side;
The mountain was so tall, John Henry was so small,
That he laid down his hammer and he cried, 'Lawd, Lawd,'
That he laid down his hammer and he cried.

John Henry told his captain,
'Captain, go to town
And bring me back two twenty-pound hammers,
And I'll sure beat your steam drill down, Lawd, Lawd,
And I'll sure beat your steam drill down.'

John Henry told the people,
'You know that I'm a man.
I can beat all the traps that have ever been made,
Or I'll die with a hammer in my hand, Lawd, Lawd,
Or I'll die with a hammer in my hand.'

The steam drill set on the right hand side,
John Henry was on the left.
He said, 'I will beat that steam drill down
Or hammer my fool self to death, Lawd, Lawd,
Or hammer my fool self to death.'

John Henry dropped the ten-pound hammer
And picked up the twenty-pound sledge;
Every time his hammer went down
You could see that steel going through, Lawd, Lawd,
You could see that steel going through.

John Henry was just getting started,
Steam drill was halfway down;
John Henry said, 'You're ahead right now,
But I'll beat you on the last go-round, Lawd, Lawd,
But I'll beat you on the last go-round.'

John Henry told his shaker,
'Big boy, you better pray
For if I miss this six-foot steel
To-morrow will be your burying day, Lawd, Lawd,
To-morrow will be your burying day.'

The men that made that steam drill
Thought it was mighty fine;
John Henry drove his fourteen feet
While the steam drill only made nine, Lawd, Lawd,
While the steam drill only made nine.

John Henry went home to his good little woman,
Said, 'Polly Ann, fix my bed,
I want to lay down and get some rest,

I've an awful roaring in my head, Lawd, Lawd,
I've an awful roaring in my head.'

John Henry told his woman,
'Never wear black, wear blue.'
She said, 'John, don't never look back,
For, honey, I've been good to you, Lawd, Lawd,
For, honey, I've been good to you.'

John Henry he was a steel-driving man,
He drove in many a crew;
He has now gone back to the head of the line
For to drive the heading on through, Lawd, Lawd,
For to drive the heading on through.

John Henry had a little boy,
This is all the children he had.
John Henry is now at rest,
But his boy is driving steel like his dad, Lawd, Lawd,
But his boy is driving steel like his dad.

A significant chapter in the controversy over John Henry's origin is Dr. L. W. Chappell's *John Henry, A Folk-Lore Study* (1933). The West Virginia University folklorist followed the trail of John Henry from the Great Lakes to the West Indies and was the first to discover the immediate region of his activity, as revealed by tradition.

A good deal of West Virginia folk song has found its way into print, but much of it still remains unpublished. Professor Chappell has collected more than 1,000 texts and made phonographic recordings of over 300 tunes. Dr. J. H. Cox, of West Virginia University, author of studies of 'John Hardy' and 'The Yew Pine Mountains,' has edited *Folk-Songs of the South* (1925). Many West Virginia songs are included in Josiah H. Combs' dissertation *Folk-Songs du Midi des États-Unis* (1925).

Because of poor roads, which once rendered many sparsely settled localities inaccessible during a great part of the year, and lack of ready money to pay for licensed medical practitioners had they been available, the mountain people developed and still retain an unusual degree of ingenuity and self-reliance in time of illness. Although many common-sense cures are sought through the use of herbs and roots, which are also prescribed by the medical profession, superstition and sorcery constitute a large part of the remedial lore of the mountains.

Remedies are generally considered more efficacious if administered during the time of waning moon, on the theory that the illness will likewise wane; and the seventh child of the seventh child is thought to possess extraordinary healing powers. Teas made from herbs and roots are regarded in high favor: horehound tea for coughs and colds;

catnip tea for colds and colic; sassafras tea as a spring tonic and blood purifier; mullein leaf tea for asthma; Shawnee berry tea for kidney trouble; slippery elm tea for intestinal disorders; wild cherry bark tea as a laxative; tea made from the inner bark of post oaks as a laxative; sage tea and honey for pneumonia; smartweed tea for. blood poisoning; tansy tea for worms; peach-tree leaf tea for dysentery, blackberry root tea for dysentery; Jerusalem oak tea for worms; pennyroyal tea for stomach disorders; willow bark tea for women's ills; cherry bark tea for yellow jaundice; and swamproot tea for kidney trouble.

Of things to be worn about the neck the following are considered by some to have healing power: gold beads as a remedy for sore throat; amber beads for goiter; red beads for nose bleed; a black silk cord for croup; rattlesnake bones as a protection against fever; and a flat leather band to prevent whooping cough and other diseases of childhood.

Bear's-paw root tea is considered good to cure a cold or a fever, although the remark is made that 'it takes a good nerve' to drink it because of its 'dark bitterness.' Water dipped out of an open stream before sunrise on Ash Wednesday is said to cure rheumatism. The same ailment may be 'warded off' by wearing a buzzard's feather in one's hatband or by carrying a buckeye in the pocket. A fragment of the entrails of a sheep sewed up in the seams of a child's garment is considered a preventive of children's diseases. Washing in rain water from a shower on the first day of June will remove freckles. The same efficacy is accredited water in which a blacksmith has cooled his irons.

To cure cramps in the feet, turn the shoes bottom side up before going to bed. To heal chapped lips, kiss the middle rail of a five-rail fence. In order to insure a luxuriant growth of hair, cut the hair during the new moon. Washing the irritated surface of skin rashes with dew or with a blend of honey and buttermilk is considered beneficial. A hog's tooth carried in the right pants pocket is said to ward off toothache. Freshly chewed tobacco is 'reckoned' to withdraw the poison from bee sting. Tobacco juice, or ambeer as it is called, is considered excellent for earache. Red percoon is good for distemper. The sap of wild grapevines is used extensively as a hair tonic. To cure fits, tear off the victim's shirt and burn it. Burfine root is excellent for coughs and for the flu. A cough medicine is made from pine needles. The proven worth of many of these remedies can easily be accounted for. The active agent in oak stump water that makes it effective in removal of warts is tannic acid, and the therapeutic qualities of many barks and herbs are fully recognized by the medical profession.

European customs and manners introduced by the first settlers survive in some sections. Swiss folk dancing and cheese making still persist in the Swiss community of Helvetia (*see Tour* 9). At Capon Bridge the custom, of German origin, called *Peltzer* has been in vogue since the first settlers came in the eighteenth century. On Christmas Eve the young folk go masked and costumed from house to house to entertain and be served refreshments.

Possibly the oldest, and certainly the most picturesque custom in West Virginia is the South Branch Valley sport of riding 'tournament' (*see Tour* 5a). For more than a century and a half, succeeding generations of young men of this area, one of the first settled in the State, have kept alive this pastime, which is a direct lineal descendant of the feudal tournament or joust. A similar sport is practiced by the Lancers of the British army, but whereas the Britons tilt at a 6-inch board, the Knights of the South Branch tilt with needle-pointed lances, 7 to 9 feet long, at suspended rings, a half inch in diameter. Some of the lances are 60 to 100 years old. The tournament course consists of 3 arches, 60 feet apart, beneath which the horseman rides at a dead run. A ring is suspended in each arch, and the object is to get all three rings on the tip of the lance.

The tournament is attended by great ceremony and a fixed ritual that has never changed. The 'Knights,' who usually acquire their titles early in life, receive the 'Address' delivered in the presence of the assembled audience, after which the conduct of the tournament is turned over to the 'Grand Marshal,' who calls the knights to post.

The Marshal calls the first rider: 'Knight of Silver Bend—Ride!' and 'Knight of Hampshire, get ready!'

The Knight of Silver Bend mounts his horse and with lance at rest rides slowly through the arches and in each arch suspends a ring. When the third ring has been hung, the Marshal calls in measured tones, as the contestant rides slowly to the extremity of the course: 'Knight of Silver Bend — — — — — Sir Kni—i—ight!' Then, timed to a nicety, at the moment the rider reaches the end of the course: 'CHARGE!'

At the command, the horseman wheels like a flash and, as he rides at full gallop, rises in the stirrups, sets his lance, and in a split second of time impales the tiny circlets on its point. Jabbing hard with a pencil at a one-inch curtain ring may give some idea of the keen eye, the steady nerve, and the perfect horsemanship this exacting sport demands.

The first three courses are run at 1½-inch rings. All 9-ring men, or the leading five, qualify for the course at ¾-inch rings. The final course is run at rings ½-inch in diameter (about the size of a little-finger ring). To the winner goes the privilege of naming the queen of the tournament; and to the next four, the right to select her maids in waiting.

Out of the exigencies of frontier life, necessity developed customs that have in some cases survived the original conditions. Such is the gradually disappearing practice of holding a funeral service for one long dead. This 'second' funeral, sometimes held years after the death of the person honored, includes the sermon, the procession to the grave, the reading of the burial office, the singing of the favorite hymn, the mourning, and the floral offerings. This custom, rapidly disappearing, has come down from the time when there were no ordained ministers to bury the dead and when a circuit rider on an infrequent visit might find himself called upon to preach a belated funeral for a woman three years' dead and then perform a marriage ceremony for the widower and his new wife.

Because West Virginia's 6 per cent Negro population is largely migratory and of recent acquisition, most of the Negro folklore has come from States farther south; and because 95 per cent of this group is engaged in industry, the Negro and the mountain-folk materials of the State have remained separate and distinct. The spiritual has become so much an integral part of the musical literature of America that it scarcely needs treatment here. Among many others, the sweetly solemn 'Go Down Moses,' 'Nobody Knows the Trouble I've Seen,' 'Deep River,' 'Swing Low, Sweet Chariot,' and the more spirited 'Joshua Fit de Battle of Jericho,' 'It's Me, O Lord,' 'Git on Board, Little Chillen,' and 'Little David, Play on Your Harp' are widely sung.

The Negroes of West Virginia and the South have elaborated many superstitions common to other groups, but in the case of an evil omen the elaboration is usually intended to break the sinister spell. For example: If a black cat crosses your path and you keep going, you will have bad luck; but if you walk backward across the cat's path the spell is broken. If you break a mirror you will have seven years of trouble; but if you place the fragments of the broken mirror in running water the trouble will pass away in seven hours. If you sneeze with food in your mouth, it is a sure sign of death; but if you spit out the food and rinse the mouth thoroughly with water, death will be avoided.

To be touched with the business end of a broom is a sure sign of going to jail. If you bite the head of a butterfly you will get a suit the color of the butterfly. If a bird gets into your home it is a sure sign of death in the family. If you tear a dress the first time you wear it, someone will lie about you before night. To bring peanuts to a gambling hall is a sure sign that the place will be raided. The rainmaker gives this advice: 'Go kill a snake and hang him high and turn his belly to the sky and it will surely rain.'

Each year at White Top Festival, on the summit of White Top Mountain in southwest Virginia, West Virginia folk musicians distinguish themselves with their folk song variants and improvisations. Thus, while the scholars and learned groups collect and preserve West Virginia folklore, festivals and radio programs diffuse and popularize tradition.

The Arts

LITERATURE and the other arts first appeared in West Virginia in the homely folk ballads and hearthside legends, work chanteys, wood carvings, clay moldings, and needlework of the settlers who ventured beyond the mountain passes and settled in the 'Ohio country.' In the early settlements there was time to cultivate only those arts that were of direct service to the pioneers in their arduous lives. Myths and Biblical tales repeated orally formed part of moral education; songs were sung to divert the mind during wearisome labor; the beauty of a handmade tool was the mark, too, of its efficiency and durability.

LITERATURE

The literature of West Virginia begins with a considerable body of writings produced by travelers who published journals, sketches, and impressions of western Virginia as early as 1671. In that year Colonel Abraham Wood published his *Journal* giving an account of his exploration into western Virginia under the authority of Virginia's Governor Berkeley. For more than a century thereafter western Virginia writings, whether by residents or by outsiders coming into the region, consisted almost entirely of travel narratives. The *Journal* of John Peter Salley, published in 1742, recorded the author's impressions during a descent of the Coal and Great Kanawha Rivers; and in 1750 Christopher Gist described in his *Journal* the Ohio Valley. In 1748 young George Washington gave an account of his surveying trip through this area in his *Journal of My Journey Over the Mountains while Surveying for Lord Thomas Fairfax, Baron of Cameron*, 1747–1748, describing the settlement of the Eastern Panhandle counties; and in a later journal (1770) he described his visit to the Ohio country.

These writers came west over the mountains, but two early journalists, Lewis Summers and Patrick Gass, were residents of western Virginia. Summers, while on a trip to locate lands, traveled down the

Greenbrier and Great Kanawha Valleys, then up the Ohio River to Wheeling, and across the State to his home near Alexandria, publishing in 1808 an account of the journey. Gass, who lived in Wellsburg, was a member of the Lewis and Clark expedition, and published a diary of the expedition in 1806. Anne Royall, who later achieved notoriety as a newspaperwoman in the national capital, lived in Monroe and Kanawha Counties for many years, and portrayed the lives and customs of western Virginia residents in her *Sketches of History, Life and Manners in the United States* (1826).

The first book published in West Virginia was *The Christian Panoply* (1797) by Richard Watson, Bishop of Llandaff, a collection of letters and polemics directed against Thomas Paine's *The Age of Reason*. An early volume that received much notice was *Notes on the Settlement and Indian Wars of the Western Parts of Virginia and Pennsylvania* (1824) by Joseph Doddridge, printed at Wellsburg. Seven years later came the first native work to attract national attention, Alexander Scott Withers's *Chronicles of Border Warfare*, a volume of tales of Indian conflict based on materials collected by Judge Edwin S. Duncan of Barbour County and others interested in frontier lore.

Among the earliest literary works are 'Saint Helena' (1821), a poem by J. K. Mitchell of Shepherdstown; *Logan* (1823), a dramatic piece by Dr. Joseph Doddridge; *Widow of the Rock and Other Poems* (1824), attributed to Margaret Blennerhassett of Blennerhassett Island; and *The Musings of Carol* (1831), a volume of poetry by Thomas Lees of Wheeling.

The first novel dealing with the region was *Young Kate* (1845), reissued ten years later as *New Hope, or the Rescue—A Tale of the Great Kanawha* and credited to John Lewis. Shortly afterward, in the work of Rebecca Harding Davis, (1831-1910), mother of Richard Harding Davis, came some of the first writings in this country to deal in a significant manner with labor and the beginnings of modern industrial life. While a resident of Wheeling, Mrs. Davis wrote 'Life in the Iron Mills,' a realistic story infused with high moral passion of a Welsh miner's struggle against poverty; this story was published in the *Atlantic Monthly* in 1861 and reprinted in 1866 in a collection entitled *Atlantic Tales*. In *Margaret Howth* (1862) Mrs. Davis dramatized certain ethical and social problems brought into being by the rise of industry in a rural community, and in *David Gaunt* (1862) she portrayed hardships of the West Virginia small farmer.

The distinguished essayist, D. H. Strother, was born at Martinsburg, in 1816. In the 'fifties and 'sixties Strother wrote Irving-like sketches for *Harpers* under the pen name of 'Porte Crayon' and accompanied these with original drawings. He was the author of *Virginia Illustrated* (1857) and other travel works. *The Blackwater Chronicle, a narrative of an expedition into the land of Canaan, in Randolph County Virginia* (1853) is frequently attributed to Strother or to John P. Kennedy, famous Maryland novelist of the nineteenth century. Actually it was written by John's brother Philip Pendleton Kennedy (1808–64), a cousin of Strother, and illustrated by Strother's drawings. During the War between the States, Strother served with the Union Army, earning a general's rank, and each night took notes on the day's events. These he assembled after the war and published in a series in *Harpers* under the title *Personal Recollections of the War* (1871–4).

Frank Stockton, author of *Rudder Grange* (1879), spent his last years in Jefferson County, where he wrote *The Captain's Toll-Gate* (1903), the short story 'Kate Bonnet,' (1902), and many letters concerning his story 'The Lady or the Tiger' (1884). Thomas Dunn English (1819–1902), poet, anthologist, and children's writer, was the first mayor of Logan. While a resident of that city he wrote poems about the Guyan and Gauley Rivers. James Lane Allen held a professorship at Bethany for several years, and the father of N. P. Willis, prominent author of the nineteenth century, lived at Martinsburg, while the parents of Mark Twain resided for a time in Mason County.

The first years of the new State found war reactions depicted in *Nine Months in the Quartermaster's Department, or, The Chances of Making a Million* (1862), written by Charles Leib, a Union soldier, and *Four Years a Soldier* (1887), by David E. Johnston, a Confederate, of Monroe County; while the same topic was treated in a spirit of humorous whimsey from a Union point of view in *The Flying Gray-Haired Yank* (1888), by Michael Egan of Parkersburg. Soldier poets of the Allegheny region combined their writings to publish *The Sunny Land* (1868), highlighted by several poems by Colonel Buehring Jones of Lewisburg; while William Leighton, long a resident of Wheeling, wrote the historical poems 'Sons of Goodwin' (1876) and 'At the Court of King Edwin' (1877), crowning his works with a long ode read at the dedication of a soldiers' monument in Wheeling, 'The Price of the Present Paid by the Past' (1881).

John Brown's raid at Harpers Ferry has been the inspiration of an extensive literature, from the 1860's to the present day. Shortly after his execution, 'Osawatomie' Brown entered American song in the war-time ballad, 'John Brown's Body.' James Redpath's *Echoes from Harpers Ferry* (1860) and Osborn P. Anderson's *A Voice from Harpers Ferry* (1861) show close familiarity with the raid and its participants. The attack has been interestingly described by Joseph Barry in *The Annals of Harpers Ferry* (1872), which contains an eyewitness account, and later in *The Strange Story of Harpers Ferry* (1903). In the numerous biographies of the antislaver, 'friends and enemies,' says Gamaliel Bradford, 'have torn his memory to pieces in the effort to make him out devil or saint.' *The Life and Letters of John Brown* (1885), by F. B. Sanborn, an abolitionist and friend of Thoreau, and Richard J. Hinton's *John Brown and His Men* (1894) are sympathetic biographies by writers who knew Brown personally and respected his aims and motives. W. E. B. Du Bois's 'John Brown' (1909) is the tribute of a Negro scholar to one whom his race worships as a hero. *John Brown: Soldier of Fortune* (1913) is a violent anti-Brown study; and Robert Penn Warren's *John Brown: The Making of a Martyr* (1929) is a scholarly work of detraction, written from the neo-Confederate point of view. Oswald Garrison Villard's *John Brown: A Biography Fifty Years After* (1910) still continues to be considered the most comprehensive and authoritative study. In poetry John Brown has been celebrated by Edmund Clarence Stedman, Carl Sandburg, and by Stephen Benet's Pulitzer Prize winner, *John Brown's Body* (1928). Leonard Ehrlich's *God's Angry Man* (1933) re-creates Brown's life, character, and times in a fine historical novel.

Probably the most important poet born in West Virginia is Daniel Bedinger Lucas, 'the poet of the Shenandoah Valley,' who was born in 1836 near Charles Town. Judge Lucas's poems, much praised in his day, show the influence of Keats, Tennyson, and Poe. They were collected in a posthumous volume, *The Land Where We Were Dreaming* (1913). Several verse plays, 'The Maid of Northumberland,' 'Hildebrand,' and 'Kate McDonald' also were collected in a posthumous volume, *Dramatic Works of Daniel Bedinger Lucas* (1913).

Post-war industrial development and economic turmoil saw the rise to prominence of William Hope 'Coin' Harvey, famous free-silver agitator and author of the 'Coin' series on finance, born in Buffalo, West Virginia (*see Tour* 14). Harvey wrote a novel, *Tale of Two Nations* (1895); but he is best known for his *Financial School* (1894)—said to have been in its time the only book in the English language as widely read as the Bible—and *Coin on Money, Trusts and Imperialism* (1899).

Melville Davisson Post (1871–1930), born at Romines Mill, near Clarksburg, has contributed much to American fiction. In the writing of detective stories, Post's work stands second in importance to that of Poe, in the opinion of Blanche Colton Williams, historian of the American short story. 'Before the age of fifty,' she writes, 'he had established himself among the immortals.' Edward O'Brien, in *The Advance of the American Short Story* (1923), says that in plot construction, Post's work equals that of the masters. In his 14 volumes Post offers detective stories of many types, but the most original are those included in *The Strange Schemes of Randolph Mason* (1896); here Post, who was a lawyer as well as an author, created a character who by his knowledge of the law was able to defeat the ends of the law. Among his best stories are those dealing with Uncle Abner, a sort of rural Sherlock Holmes, and 'The Doomdorf Mystery,' the most widely read, is included in the anthology *The World's Best 100 Short Stories*. West Virginians especially enjoy Post's stories because in them they can so often recognize familiar scenes. *Dwellers in the Hills* (1901), for instance, deals with cattle buyers in the State and with the hill region and its folks and ways.

Among the most important West Virginia writings after those of Lucas, Strother, and Post, are the novels, *Daughter of the Elm* (1899) and *The Rending of Virginia* (1902), by Granville Davisson Hall; *Up from Slavery* (1901), the autobiography of the great Negro educator, Booker T. Washington (*see Tour 15b*); and the poems and critical writings of Waitman T. Barbe, one of the State's leading literary figures whose book of poems, *Ashes and Incense* (1891), has been highly praised by critics both in this country and abroad.

The growth of West Virginia's literature has been impeded by the State's comparative youth as a separate entity, by the heterogeneity of the population, by a rugged terrain that made intrastate communication difficult until recent years, and, lastly, by the State's tremendous mineral wealth, in the development of which the people tended to neglect their cultural needs. Of late years, however, the growth of local literature has been rapid and, with the mounting interest of American writers in native folk study and regional backgrounds, ever increasing numbers have sought out the mountain fastnesses where dwell the earthy people now considered to be uniquely representative of America's indigenous past.

The mountaineer life of West Virginia has provided much material for local-color literature. Margaret Prescott Montague, of White Sulphur Springs, has for some time been writing stories dealing with mountain folk. Among her best known are the *Sowing of Alderson Cree* (1907) and *Uncle Sam of Freedom Ridge* (1928). Miss Montague's stories have been widely published, and in 1919 she was the winner of the O. Henry Memorial Award. In *Up Eel River* (1928) she told a story of West Virginia lumbermen. Fanny Kemble Johnson, of Charleston, is the author of the novel *The Beloved Son* (1916) and of many short stories. Hubert Skidmore, who was born on Laurel Mountain and has lived at Webster Springs and Gassaway, is 'one of the few authors who present a picture of the mountain folk with genuine verisimilitude,' according to the *Christian Science Monitor*. His book, *I Will Lift Up Mine Eyes,* won the Avery Hopwood and Jule Hopwood Prize in 1936, and he has since written *Heaven Came So Near* (1938). Roy Bird Cook's *Family and Life of Stonewall Jackson* (1924–5) is recognized as one of the most authoritative biographies of West Virginia's greatest soldier. Alberta Pierson Hannum, of Ohio, came to live at Moundsville in order better to deal with southern highland life. Her best books are *Thursday April* (1931) and *The Hills Step Lightly* (1934). Eleanor Carroll Chilton, born at Charleston, is the author of *Shadows Waiting* (1927) and *Follow the Furies* (1935). Readers of agricultural journals are familiar with the articles of Mary Meek Atkeson, author of *The Woman on the Farm* (1924), *The Shining Hours* (1927), and *Pioneering in Agriculture* (1937).

An outstanding contemporary author born in West Virginia is John Peale Bishop, of Charles Town, who has written about his native city and the Shenandoah Valley. The best of his stories are included in the volume *Many Thousands Gone* (1931). His *Act of Darkness* (1935) based on his early boyhood in Jefferson County, touches upon the question of West Virginia's debt. The most recent contributor to West Virginia fiction is Stella Morgan, of Fairmont, whose *Again the River* (1939) has received wide praise. The novel portrays the indomitable struggle of an Ohio Valley farmer against the ruinous floods of the bottomlands. Pare Lorentz, born in West Virginia in 1905, produced for government agencies the documentary films, *The River* and *The Plow That Broke the Plains,* in which a speaker's voice accompanies the continuity with a stirring recital. *The River* was issued in book form in 1938.

Historical, biographical, and theoretical works of importance have been produced by native West Virginians on the staffs of the State colleges and the university. One of America's great scholars in the field of English literature, Charles Frederick Tucker Brooke was born at Morgantown (1883); he is author of *The Shakespeare Apocrypha* (1908), *The Works of Christopher Marlowe* (1910), *Tudor Drama* (1911), *Shakespeare of Stratford* (1926), and *Shakespeare's Sonnets* (1936). Readers of educational journals see frequently the writings of Walter Barnes, author of several textbooks, whose most recent works are *English for American High Schools* (1931) and *The Photoplay as Literary Art* (1936). Charles Henry Ambler has contributed many valuable works, notably the thorough and intensive study *A History of Transportation in the Ohio Valley* (1932), *George Washington and the West* (1936), and a life of *Francis H. Pierpont* (1937); and in 1937 Festus P. Summers published a life of *Johnson Newlon Camden*, followed by the *Baltimore and Ohio Railroad in the Civil War* in 1939.

ART

Among the pioneers, creative work in art was limited to the making and decoration of useful objects—furniture, baskets, implements, pottery, utensils, and textiles. The crafts were handed down from generation to generation, sons and daughters learning from their elders how to handle tools and materials and how to achieve beauty and durability in the finished product. Within the traditional styles and methods, individual craftsmen distinguished themselves for their skill and imagination and even embarked upon specialization: a woodworker for his carved gun stocks, another for his slat furniture, a housewife for her patchwork quilts or cloth fabrics. The patterns of these objects often reached such intricacy and charm that they are eagerly copied today by craftsmen and designers.

Coverlets, counterpanes, and quilts were much cherished by the mountain women. Today in isolated sections mothers and daughters still spend the long winter months piecing, weaving, and needling, and then stack away their handiwork in cupboards or on shelves until the time when a son or daughter marries. With perhaps dozens on hand, they would not consider selling one of the 'kivers' even when in great need.

The oldest dated quilt in the country was made in 1795 at Clear Fork, Virginia (now West Virginia). It is decorated with lavender, purple, blue, pink, and green flowers and designs of piecework appliquéd in buttonhole stitch. The quilt, well preserved and often exhibited, belongs to a descendant of the family.

Old designs for coverlets and quilts have been designated for generations by such picturesque names as *Maid of Orleans, Kentucky Snowflakes, Wonder of the Forest, Sunrise on the Walls of Troy, Tennessee Trouble, The Drunkard's Path, Napoleon's Wreath, Bird in a Tree, Bear's Paw,* and *Noah's Dove.* The weaver of the coverlet follows a pattern or 'draft' marked on strips of paper; some of these are very old and extremely difficult to decipher.

The quilting bee, generally for the purpose of making an 'autograph quilt' for the preacher or a bride, is still an important event in the social life of mountain communities. On each square of the quilt is embroidered the name of the donor.

Early mountain furniture was very simple to design, with little effort expended toward decoration. The old-style furniture has for the most part been supplanted by modern types, for which machinery is used in the preliminary stages and hand work in finishing. Chairs, tables, bedsteads, benches, and other pieces of furniture are still made, however, with old-fashioned tools in open-air shops. It is customary to join this furniture without screws, nails, or glue; a careful shrinking process fastens the joints so securely they will last 'forever.'

Basket weaving, one of the oldest of the crafts, is practiced in several communities in the State. Flower, fruit, and work baskets and a variety of other receptacles are made from native honeysuckle, broom sedge, corn husks and stalks, wheat and rye straws, and willow and hickory splints.

A glass factory in Milton employs about 20 highly skilled craftsmen in the manufacture of sheet glass used in stained-glass windows. Workmen trained in Europe supervise the young men, brought from various parts of the United States, who undergo long years of apprenticeship in order to master the intricate and difficult trade. Glass from this plant has been used in the restoration of Williamsburg, Virginia, in the Washington Cathedral, the Cathedral of St. John the Divine, and other notable buildings throughout the world (*see Tour 15c*).

In a small shop at Blacksville a group of craftsmen, headed by Charles Tennant, produces pottery with native clays on handmade kick-wheels. Products from this plant are considered among the most beautiful in the country. Pewter candlesticks, made in Preston County, were selected by the American Federation of Arts for display at the 1937 Paris Exhibition as representative of American craftsmanship.

In the last decade much support has been given to the encouragement of production and marketing of handmade products. In 1932 the Mountaineer Craftsmen's Co-operative Association was organized in the coal-mining area at Morgantown by the American Friends Service Committee of Philadelphia as part of its relief program for destitute mine families. The Association, a member of the Southern Highland Handicraft Guild, quickly developed a program comprising furniture making, weaving, quilting, basketry, and iron and other metal work. With the aid of trained instructors, many unemployed miners and their families have produced home furnishings and clothing for themselves as well as articles for sale in both pioneer and modern styles. Bud Godlove, of Morgantown, introduced the miners to the methods of making the Godlove chair in the traditional mountain style. Since 1937, home-industries classes have been operated by the Trade and Industrial Service of the Vocational Division, State Department of Education. Classes in pottery, weaving, needlecraft, and woodcarving are conducted in Monongalia, Greenbrier, Monroe, and Preston Counties. The Associated Craftsmen of West Virginia was organized in 1938 to assist craftsmen in marketing products. Numerous sales outlets have been set up in State parks and other tourist centers.

West Virginia's fine arts progressed slowly prior to the War between the States, perhaps owing to the fact that the States had no wealthy or aristocratic class to patronize artists or purchase their work. Elliot Daingerfield (1859–1932), West Virginia's foremost artist, was born at Harpers Ferry, but spent most of his life in North Carolina as head of the art school at Blowing Rock. He came early under the influence of his friend, the great George Inness. His figure studies and landscapes are well known both in this country and abroad, especially his *My Lady Rhododendron, Planting, The Lost Sheep,* and *The Tanagra.* Eleazer Hutchinson Miller (1831–1921), born at Shepherdstown, won wide fame as an etcher and illustrator of books such as *Tam O'Shanter* and Mrs. Springer's *Songs of the Sea.*

Joseph H. Diss Debar (1820–1905) of Doddridge County, designer of West Virginia's State seal and coat-of-arms, was a gifted artist who made many sketches of prominent people and places in the early days of West Virginia. He also compiled and published the first *Handbook of West Virginia.*

Frank Holme, artist and newspaper cartoonist, born near Terra Alta, Preston County, in 1868, is often referred to as 'a shorthand writer in art' because he was one of the most rapid and pointed illustrators of his day. At various times he was a staff artist for the *Chicago Daily News,* San Francisco *Chronicle,* New York *World,* and

Chicago *Evening Post,* doing for the last-named a series titled *Picturesque Street Types,* which attracted wide and favorable attention. He sketched William Jennings Bryan in hundreds of dramatic attitudes, and drew thrilling pictures of the Homestead Riots and the Johnstown Flood for the Pittsburgh *Press* and the New York *Graphic.* Newspaper artists look upon Frank Holme as one of the foremost illustrators produced by the Fourth Estate.

A transplanted West Virginian, William Robinson Leigh, now a resident of New York but born in Berkeley County, has won numerous prizes for his oils, notably silver and bronze medals in competition at Munich. His *The Poisoned Pool, The Maya Historian,* and *The Stampede* are especially well known.

The *Statue of Stonewall Jackson,* by Moses Ezekiel, cut in Italy in 1910 and now mounted on the west lawn of the State Capitol, and *Mountaineer Soldier,* by H. K. Bush-Brown, carved in 1912 and also on the Capitol lawn, are outstanding among the State's sculptures.

Today the leading stimuli for art in West Virginia are the Allied Artists' Association, the Art Club of Wheeling, the Marshall College Museum of Fine Arts, and the Old White Colony (*see Tour 15a*). The Artists' Association, organized in 1928 and incorporated in 1936, annually sponsors two free art exhibits in the State Capitol, and seeks to promote among its members an interest in local landscapes, portrait, and still life. Prizes are awarded for meritorious canvases. The Marshall Art Museum contains a group of oils, by members of the Federal Art Project of the Work Projects Administration, and exhibits the canvases of students and local artists as well as loan collections of camera studies, watercolors, wood block prints, and children's art.

William C. Estler, of Huntington, is prominent among younger West Virginia artists. His recent work shows much interest in scenes from local life. In 1938 his *Le Grande Jatte, Fountainebleau, Temperance Suitable for a Sunday Supplement,* and *Notre Dame de Paris, Rive Gauche* received the Allied Artists' first prize for the best three paintings by a West Virginia artist. Miss Randolph Venable won first prize in landscape watercolor for her *Perce Rock from North Beach,* while Mrs. Nell Hayden, of Huntington, took first place in figure composition in oils with her *Composition for a Dream.*

Two West Virginia artists have been elected by the Studio Guild, national art organization of New York City, to participate in its enlarged exhibition program. They are Annie Campbell, of Charleston, whose paintings have been exhibited at the Dayton Art Institute, and Virginia B. Evans, painter and lecturer, of Moundsville.

Other artists whose work has attracted favorable attention at exhibits are Naomi S. Hosterman, of Charleston, the State's ranking still-life and flower-composition artist; Thomas W. Moore of Charleston, landscapist; Clara E. Wiltse, of Huntington, whose etching *West Virginia Capitol from Kanawha River* is widely exhibited; Stewart Reuschlein, now of New York, formerly of Huntington, internationally known authority on Italian Renaissance art; Joseph S. Jablonski of Huntington, now director of Marshall College's art department, whose watercolors are well known throughout the eastern seaboard States; Alice Kershaw, portrait artist of Huntington; Arthur Hurton Rhead, craftsman in ceramics and architectural decorations of Newell; Irving Dugan and Kendall Vintroux, cartoonists; Blanche Lazzell, block painter and muralist of Morgantown; Patty Willis, muralist of Charles Town; Mary Jane McLean and Lois Cochran Rogers of Parkersburg; Dorothy Dyer Barnes, Mrs. Carl F. Bauman, Grace Martin Frame, Joseph Hugo, Lucina Keane, and Sara Gravatt, all of Charleston.

Courses in art have become an increasingly important part of the curriculums at West Virginia University and the State colleges; the University and Marshall College have especially well-developed art departments. The Marshall College art department was headed for more than 30 years by the late Edwin Emmett Myers; he was dean of West Virginia landscape artists, and maintained a summer art colony at Monterey, Virginia, where he painted mountain scenes distinguished by an individual use of blue to achieve an effect of distance. The Mason College of Music and Fine Arts of Charleston, long under the direction of the late Professor W. S. Mason, is the leading private art school in the State and offers courses embracing all phases of art.

MUSIC

Since the era of the homemade fiddle and buckskin banjo, the mountain ridges and steep-walled valleys of West Virginia have echoed to ballads and jigs, set to scores as simple and direct as the hill folk who originated them. Scotch-Irish and German pioneers brought with them ballads of their homeland, and later a native folk music gradually developed. Mountain bards sang first of battle and of border hazards, then of events of community interest; but they never neglected the simple everyday happenings around the hearth. Jingles lightened the

Industry

'STILL COLUMNS'—GAS PURIFICATION TOWERS, BELLE

Photograph by Highton; courtesy of Work Projects Administrati

CHEMICAL PLANT, BLAINE ISLAND, NEAR CHARLESTON

'HYPERS'—GAS COMPRESSORS IN BELLE PLANT,
USED IN MANUFACTURE OF AMMONIA AND ALCOHOL

Photograph by courtesy of duPont Compa

Photograph by courtesy of *Bollinger*

OIL WELL DERRICK

STEEL MILL, WHEELING

COLD REDUCING MILL, USED IN MODERN TINPLATE MANUFACTURE, WHEELING

otograph by courtesy of *Elk Refining Company*

OIL REFINERY, FALLING ROCK

RAILROAD YARDS, BLUEFIELD

Photograph by courtesy of Bluefield Chamber of Commer

COKE OVENS, LONGACRE

Photograph by courtesy of Farm Security Administrati

PICKING TABLES IN A COLLIERY

LOADING BOOMS, MINE TIPPLE, BARTLEY

TRANSPORTING TIMBER

Photograph by courtesy of U.S. Forest Servic

RIVER CARGOES OF WHEELING PIPE FOR SOUTHERN MARKET, BENWOOD

Photograph by courtesy of Wheeling Steel Corporatio

day's toil; short verses to a simple melody were sung by the pioneer wife as she cooked, spun, or sewed, or as she rocked the baby to sleep. Many Indian songs, especially those of the love-lorn brave and the happy squaw, were quickly adapted by the colonists.

After the Revolution, the land west of the Alleghenies was settled rapidly and cities began to develop; with industrialization, the cities came to dominate the regions commercially. The War between the States interrupted this development and brought a train of bitter feelings, but out of the tumult of civil war came the beginnings of a closer relation among the inhabitants of western Virginia and, finally, State independence. A host of folk tales and legends grew from this nearness to strife, and many soldiers' ballads and songs; a southern camp-meeting hymn was given words at Martinsburg and became nationally famous as 'John Brown's Body Lies A'mouldering in the Grave.'

Internal development during the reconstruction period inspired some famous ballads, such as 'The Wreck of the Old 97' and many variations of the story of 'John Henry,' all set to simple melodies. The John Henry hammer song, some authorities hold, originated in 'The Big Bend Tunnel on the C & O Road' in southern West Virginia (*see Folklore*). Although the cities grew, they remained small as compared to urban centers elsewhere, and only in recent years have they become culturally conscious; thus, while music in its simpler forms remains an integral part of community life in the mountain region, the development of formal music in the cities has been slow.

Outstanding among the State's musical events today are the Charleston May Festival, the Ohio Valley Festival Chorus at Wheeling, and the concerts of the Wheeling Symphony Orchestra. The Annual May Festival, inaugurated in 1934, brings together musical talent of the Kanawha Valley, guest soloists, organizations, and distinguished directors, for the enjoyment of music lovers. The Wheeling Symphony, founded in 1929, is the leading orchestra of the State, with a personnel numbering 73 under the direction of Antonio Modarelli, former conductor of the Pittsburgh Symphony.

The Federal Music Project maintains concert orchestras at Huntington, Parkersburg, and Wheeling, and music schools at the Federal resettlement projects at Red House and Arthurdale. The Huntington unit, organized in February 1936, was enthusiastically received; in April 1937 it obtained civic backing and was transformed into the Huntington Little Symphony of 45 pieces under the baton of Raymond Schoewe. Quarterly concerts since that time have achieved outstanding success, drawing audiences from the entire tri-State area. The Wheeling unit, conducted by Albert Albinger, and the Parkersburg unit, conducted by George Secrist, have adhered to the project's policy of presenting various kinds of music in an endeavor to promote appreciation of the finest.

Outstanding among composers in the State was the late C. E. Haworth (1860–1929) of Huntington, whose *Te Deum* and *Jubilate* are universally known in Episcopal church services. Harry E. Mueller, professor of music education at Marshall College, has written an *Overture in D,* a *Fantasy for Piano and Orchestra,* and other orchestral and instrumental pieces.

Susanne Fisher of Sutton, soprano in the Metropolitan Opera Company, is the ranking West Virginia vocalist. Other musicians whose work has won favorable comment include George F. Gillespie, instructor at the Mason College of Music and Fine Arts at Charleston, composer of a ballet and the *Scherzo* for piano, which won the 1939 State Composition Contest sponsored by the Federation of Music Clubs; Paul Mason of Moundsville, talented clarinetist and arranger now engaged at Radio City; Ralph Federer of Morgantown, pianist and composer; and Eleanor Steber, of Wheeling, who made her debut at the Metropolitan in 1940.

The West Virginia Federation of Music Clubs was organized at Clarksburg in 1917 to stimulate interest in good music and encourage education of native talent. There are now 88 local clubs in the State with a membership of 2,500. State contests in piano, voice, violin, in high school orchestra, band, and church choir work, and in composition are sponsored regularly.

THE THEATER

The theater came to western Virginia in 1824, when the introduction of steam navigation on the Ohio provided an inducement for traveling companies to leave the three circuits then established around New York, Philadelphia, and Richmond. Troupes of actors, generally all in the same family, would cross the mountains to Pittsburgh, then work their way down the Ohio Valley, stopping at each town for a one-night stand.

Traveling theater companies were at their height in the decades following 1860, and the commercial theater was introduced ten years later. During this period, the first theaters in the State were erected in Wheeling and Charleston. Many noted actors and actresses appeared in West Virginia in the best comedy, drama, and melodrama of the time; Sara Bernhardt, Maude Adams, Raymond Hitchcock, Frank Bacon, Guy Bates Post, and a host of others became familiar figures to audiences in the larger cities.

These early theaters gave place to the Burlew Opera House in Charleston, erected in 1892, the Camden Theater in Parkersburg, and the Third Avenue Theater in Huntington, both products of the same decade, in which crowded galleries roared applause at performances of *Chanticleer, Lightnin', Turn to the Right,* and *The Old Soak.*

Contemporary with the road show and touring companies was the fleet of picturesque showboats that annually entertained residents along the Ohio, Monongahela, and Kanawha. On the *Cotton Blossom, Valley Belle, River Queen,* Markle's *Floating Palace,* and other boats, the mustachioed villain quailed nightly before the jeers of audiences who palpitated in sympathy with the handsome hero and his fair sweetheart.

Last of these floating opera houses is *Billy Bryant's Showboat,* which still visits the Ohio and Kanawha Valley towns annually with a repertoire of heartbreakers like *East Lynne, Ten Nights in a Barroom, Nellie the Switchman's Daughter,* and *Over the Hill to the Poor House.* Complete with rough-and-ready cast, gaudy trimmings, and standard props such as the sawmill blade and the railroad tracks to which the villain ties the heroine, the *Showboat* presents these tear jerkers in an atmosphere of *bonhomie,* in which the audience as well as the actors contribute burlesqued emotion.

With the passing of the professional theater came the little theaters, composed of amateur and semiprofessional talent, and now concentrated in Charleston, Wheeling, Huntington, Bluefield, Fairmont, and Martinsburg. The oldest of these, the Kanawha Players of Charleston, was founded in 1922. This organization, with a membership of 1,500, produces six plays each year, its more successful presentations including such dramas as *Elizabeth the Queen, Winterset,* and *Night Must Fall,* each of which played to audiences of more than 2,000 persons. The Wheeling Little Theater won praise for its productions of *Accent on Youth* and *Petrified Forest* and for its open-air performances at Oglebay Park of *A Midsummer Night's Dream* and *Tristan and Isolde.* The Bluefield Little Theater, founded in 1937, was received enthusiastically and has already become entrenched in the cultural life of the city.

The Children's Theater of Charleston, founded in 1932 by Miss Sara Spencer, is designed to give children practical training in acting before formal audiences. The organization gives five productions each year, using only plays based on children's tales. Recently, it presented *Cinderella, Tom Sawyer,* and *Rip Van Winkle* with much success.

Institutions of higher education in the State have theater groups that produce one-act and three-act plays; an annual contest is held at which awards are voted to the best collegiate actor, actress, and one-act play troupe.

Two West Virginians well known in the theater world are the famous actress, Henrietta Crosman, who was born at Wheeling, and Pare Lorentz of Upshur County, who recently achieved great success in motion pictures with his documentary films *The Plow That Broke the Plains* (1935), *The River* (1938), and *The Fight for Life* (1940).

Architecture

THE original settlers of the area that now comprises West Virginia were English and Scotch-Irish from the Atlantic seaboard and Germans from Pennsylvania. Irish immigration was marked between 1830 and 1850, and German immigration after 1850. Following the War between the States, industry again attracted many from the neighboring States, and, within recent years, some 50,000 foreign-born came to live in the State.

The early settlers brought with them notions of architecture they had known elsewhere, but before they could proceed to the building of adequate habitations, they had to subdue the country, bring the land under cultivation, and erect defenses against the Indians. Thus for a time only the roughest habitations were possible and these not far from the stockade forts and other strongholds that the pioneers constructed for protection.

Architectural trends in West Virginia have paralleled in general the history of building upon the Atlantic seaboard, except that here the successive changes were somewhat belatedly reflected. Even though the western part of the commonwealth was not explored until long after considerable settlement had been effected in the east, it is possible to establish a chronology which, in the main, holds good throughout the State. Naturally, changes in style became apparent first in the Great Valley region, to be passed on later to the Allegheny Plateau of the west.

During the Colonial period (1726–98) three pioneer types of building appeared and, after 1755, houses in the Georgian style. The first phase of the pioneer was represented by the rough log cabin and fort; later the logs were hewn and carefully joined; and in the third phase came the stone house of rubble masonry, which was to give place to the symmetrical and finely proportioned Georgian types. The early Federal Style, marked by delicacy of detail and refinement of proportion, was dominant from 1798 until about 1820, when the influence of the Greek Revival (1825-70) began to be noticeable in pillared porch and portico. Between 1835 and 1870, the Gothic Revival affected church architecture particularly. The War and Reconstruction years (1860-70) produced little architecture of note, but between 1870 and the present year examples of many styles appeared: French Renaissance, Richardsonian Romanesque, Neo-Classic, Neo-Gothic, Neo-Colonial, and Modern.

West Virginia is amply endowed with materials suitable for building purposes. Well timbered, the area presented to the settler the following excellent woods that today form the basis of the State's extensive lumber industry: white oak, chestnut, black walnut, maple, yellow poplar, and cherry, to mention only a few found on the Plateau. To these, of course, should be added the spruce and white pine resources of the Panhandle.

The State possesses an almost inexhaustible supply of limestone. In fact, on the "barrens," as they were called by the pioneers, stone was more plentiful than wood. Thus stone figured as an architectural material almost from the beginning of settlement and has continued popular to this day. With abundant and valuable clay deposits to draw on— the raw material of the State's thriving ceramic industry—brick-making early influenced architecture in this area, and brick continues to be a popular structural material.

The development of an iron and steel industry, the production of tin and terneplate, the rise of an important glass industry—all predicated upon abundant coal, gas, oil, iron, and other mineral resources—have had their influence upon architecture.

The first cabins in West Virginia were built as early as 1719, but the first of record are about 1726, by Morgan Morgan on Mile Creek in what is now Berkeley County, and by Germans from Pennsylvania near Shepherdstown. A few years later other settlers from Pennsylvania and Maryland settled on various creeks flowing into the Potomac as far west as the South Branch. When George Washington surveyed this land for Lord Fairfax in 1748-51, he recorded many squatters largely of German origin in the region.

By the middle of the eighteenth century frontiersmen were crossing the Allegheny divide into the Greenbrier and other valleys, the waters of which discharge into the Ohio. The French and Indian War of 1754-63 forced back many of them, and in 1763 George III, desirous of preventing future conflicts with the Indians, forbade further settlements. But, in spite of these discouragements and the continued hostility of the Indians, it is estimated that by 1775 there were 30,000 settlers in what is now West Virginia. Most of these were living in log cabins built of horizontal logs adjacent to log forts, which themselves usually consisted of a cluster of such cabins placed so as to form a hollow rectangle. The palisaded walls between these cabins were constructed of vertical logs set firmly into the ground. Fort Seybert in Pendleton County (1758) and Fort Henry at Wheeling (c. 1776) were of such construction.

These temporary shelters of unhewn logs were provided with a chimney of rough stones, topped with a crib of sticks set in clay mud. Chinks between the logs were closed with pieces of wood and clay, while the roof was covered with shakes. Floors, at first of earth, were soon replaced by puncheons, and the only openings in these early houses were the chimney and the door.

As soon as possible these temporary cabins were replaced by more secure structures of neatly hewn logs, squared and notched carefully so as to leave only small cracks between them. Lime mortar was now used for chinking, and the chimneys were constructed of carefully selected squared stones, placed inside the structure as a defense measure. These houses, sometimes of two stories, had a spacious central hall flanked by two or more rooms; the upper story was arranged in a similar manner. Windows now appeared, at first filled with greased paper, and ponderous doors, hung on hinges of wood or iron, continued to be the rule. Good examples of this type are the old log church at Smoke Hole and 'Fort' Ashby near Romney. After sawmills were set up, many of these interesting and well-built cabins were covered with clapboards (siding). Numerous examples of this type of construction still may be seen in the older towns, as witness the so-called 'oldest house in Shepherdstown' and the Mytinger House at Romney.

Except in the towns, sawn lumber and bricks were not used for house construction until well after 1800. Some of the better dwellings were of stone, however. In some localities, as in Shepherdstown, limestone was the most convenient structural material and on the 'barrens' it was more plentiful than wood. In such places, the second or 'permanent' house was often constructed of this stone. Many massive stone barns, with their overshot lofts, recall the sturdy farm buildings of Pennsylvania. Outstanding among the excellent old stone houses are the home of General Charles Lee at Leetown in Jefferson County, Travelers Rest, the home of General Horatio Gates near Leetown, and the Whitemore-Lemen house in Martinsburg.

These houses, built in the Colonial style, do not exhibit the refinements of proportion or the classic details that were eventually to be brought into West Virginia from the seaboard towns and plantations. However, Travelers Rest, with its story-and-a-half mass, its carefully joined masonry, its neatly formed shutters and doors, its simple but well-membered stairway, interior cornices, paneling, and wainscots, certainly anticipates the full-bloom Georgian manner.

In 'Harewood' (c. 1769–70), the home of Samuel Washington, near Charles Town, the two-story rectangular stone mass of true Georgian plan, with neat exterior cornice and low hip roof, made its appearance. The north first-story room is beautifully paneled to the ceiling, and the walls broken into well-proportioned bays by fluted Doric pilasters, finely modeled and handsomely disposed. The central feature of the north wall of this room is a simple but splendidly proportioned mantel in dark green marble. Tradition has it that in this room the 'charming widow, Dolly Todd, plighted her troth to the stout little bookworm, James Madison.' The stairhall and the south room (present living room) are likewise paneled, but in a simpler style. The balustrade of the stairs is delicately turned.

Notable among the many fine old Georgian houses that grace the West Virginia countryside are 'Cedar Lawn' at Charles Town, 'Piedmont,' near by, built by Dr. John Briscoe about 1780, 'Altona' in the same neighborhood (c. 1792–4), Maidstone-on-the-Potomac, or the Episcopal rectory at Shepherdstown.

Another structure of excellent Georgian lines is the old stone Presbyterian church at Lewisburg built in 1796. Of simple rectangular mass about 45 by 72 feet, this structure is crowned by a hip roof bearing an open wooden cupola. The principal charm of the edifice attaches to the exterior, however, as the interior, somewhat stark and bare, is unprepossessing. The surrounding churchyard with its gnarled trees gives the church a perfect setting.

After the achievement of American independence, an architecture influenced by that new and delicately chaste variety of classicism known in England as the Adam Style appeared along the seaboard. Many houses in West Virginia were designed in this 'Federal' mode. 'Monument Place' (1798) built on the site of Fort Shepherd in Elm Grove, Wheeling, is a fine old house, which in general mass recalls certain of the late Georgian types in the vicinity of Philadelphia, yet exhibits a certain delicacy of detail too late for Georgian origins. The ballroom particularly, with its delicately carved interior trim, recalls in its detail the work of Samuel McIntire of Salem.

'Claymont Court' near Charles Town overlooking the Shenandoah Valley and the Blue Ridge, built about 1820 by Bushrod Corbin Washington and rebuilt in 1838 after a fire, is one of the finest of the old homes of West Virginia. The main house, formed of a central pavilion fronted by a two-story veranda and flanked by lower wings, is joined by brick corridors enclosing courts to outlying slave quarters and service rooms at either side. The house with its dependencies has a frontage of some 250 feet. The staunch stone walls and massive end chimneys contrast markedly with the delicate woodwork of the verandas and interiors.

Among other West Virginia buildings in the Federal style are 'Willow Wall' (1815) a few miles north of Moorefield, 'President's Cottage' in the middle of 'Louisiana Row' at White Sulphur Springs, and the old Wirgman Building at Romney built about 1825 to house the newly established branch of the Bank of the Valley of Virginia.

But the Federal style was short lived in West Virginia because the Classical Revival, championed by Jefferson and Latrobe, presently became popular. While Roman forms were promoted by Jefferson in the Piedmont, it was Greek classicism that found greatest favor in what is now West Virginia. Appearing first in the Panhandle, Greek details were soon applied to buildings that were otherwise quite typically Federal or late Georgian. 'Belleview' near Shepherdstown (c. 1820), a stone house characteristically Georgian, is fronted by a tetrastyle Ionic portico of slender columns, bearing a fine window-pierced pediment. Another somewhat Georgian mass, this time in brick, fronted by a Doric portico is found in the Willey House, 128 Wagner Road, Morgantown. Here, however, the windows, filled with 12-paned sashes, exhibit a characteristic trend of the Greek Revival. A curious feature of the portico is its use of five columns instead of the usual even number encountered in most classic architecture. This arrangement seems to have been enforced by the presence of two doors. An outstanding Greek Revival house is 'Oglebay Park' in Wheeling, which presents a typical Greek mass in brick flanked by a two-story tetrastyle Ionic portico and accompanying lower porches. Houses of this character were popular during the period from 1825–60.

In West Virginia the Greek Revival Style was also frequently adapted to public buildings. The old courthouse at Romney, built in 1833 and demolished in 1922, was a good example of such civil structures, while the Presbyterian church in Charles Town illustrates the characteristic handling of an ecclesiastical structure of the period. McMurrin Hall in Shepherdstown, built in the 'seventies, represents the lingering twilight of the Greek Revival, which projected itself beyond the War between the States.

Tendencies toward Gothic design appeared in the 1830's in the old Episcopal church in Shepherdstown (now used by a Negro congregation), which had pointed door and windows. The Gothic Revival Style (1835–60) was employed principally in the design of churches and chapels, but during the 1850's and 1860's a good many houses of wooden and even masonry construction showed in their wooden brackets, in the lace-like jig-saw ornamentation of their porches, and in their barge boards a certain relation to the Gothic. The Alexander Campbell homestead near Bethany is such a house. Campbell's little cupola-lighted study on the same estate has the octagonal plan of the Greek Revival, but its pointed arches and corner buttresses are Gothic.

The War and the Reconstruction Period were discouraging eras for American architecture generally. In West Virginia the separation from Virginia, accomplished in 1863, made necessary the construction of certain civil buildings for the use of the new government, but architectural design remained at a low ebb. Nor did it recover anything of its old luster until, under the expansive industrial era that followed Reconstruction, building again received the attention of the people.

By this time architectural design began to be markedly influenced by the architects who, trained in Paris, were returning home to practice the eclecticism they had studied abroad. Richard Morris Hunt, who returned to this country around 1863, championed the French Renaissance. Lesser men following his brilliant lead flooded America with mansard-roofed structures of French extraction. Excellent public examples of this vogue are to be found in Martin and Woodburn Halls on the campus of West Virginia University at Morgantown and in the West Virginia School for the Deaf at Romney. Houses in many cities also reflect this movement.

While Hunt espoused the French Renaissance, Henry Hobson Richardson, another American architect trained in Paris, returned at the end of the War to promote the Romanesque of the south of France and the north of Spain. So successful were his designs for structures like Trinity Church, Boston, and the libraries, schools, college buildings, and residences that he erected in many places in America that a movement in architecture—called the Richardsonian Romanesque—

was founded. West Virginia, like many eastern States, has good examples of this style, particularly the Administration Building at the University.

Once eclecticism had set in, however, the architects felt free to examine any past style and to adopt that which seemed appropriate to the task in hand. So West Virginia, like America as a whole, has been exposed to a succession of architectural fads now French, now English, now Italian, now Spanish, now Modern. Thus it was that the Gothic (Neo-Gothic) was again invoked as an inspiration for church design, while the Classic provided suggestions for civil architecture. Certainly in the State Capitol, designed by Cass Gilbert, Neo-Classic architecture demonstrates its superiority for this purpose, and in such buildings as the new courthouse at Romney it reveals its adaptability to smaller civil structures. Gothic tradition has been perpetuated admirably in Trinity Episcopal Church in Shepherdstown.

Meanwhile architects were also reviving American architectural precedent for whatever suggestion it might offer for residential types. So the Neo-Colonial was promoted as a logical and beautiful style in which to design such structures as the Governor's Mansion at Charleston, Elizabeth Moore Hall at the University, Greenbrier College at Lewisburg, and the Greenbrier Hotel at White Sulphur Springs. The style was used for residences throughout the State.

Nor has the modern non-traditional style left West Virginia untouched. The skylines of Wheeling, Charleston, Clarksburg, and other cities reveal the progress that modernism is making in the architecture of a State that, down to the present, has been rather conservatively traditional. But the tall steel or concrete framed building calls for an aesthetic treatment adapted to its needs and expressive of its purpose. The taller structures in the cities exhibit the various solutions architects have developed in the treatment of this problem. Certainly as modern a structure as has yet been erected in West Virginia is the Harrison County Courthouse at Clarksburg.

PART II
Cities

Berkeley Springs

Bus Station: Baltimore & Ohio R.R. station, N. end of Washington St., for West Virginia Transportation Co. busses; connect at Hancock, Md., 6 m. N. with Baltimore & Ohio R.R.
Traffic Regulations: Unlimited parking; no one-way streets or stop lights.

Accommodations: 2 hotels; boarding houses; accommodations in private homes.

Information Service: Fairfax Restaurant, Washington St. between Fairfax and Congress Sts.

Motion Picture Houses: 2.
Swimming: State Park Swimming Pool; Potomac River, 4 m. W. on State 9, 25¢; Cacapon State Park, 10 m. S. on State 38, no charge.
Baths: State Hot Bath and State Sanitarium, Berkeley Springs State Park, on W. edge of town.
Tennis: Pennsylvania Glass Sand Corporation Court, N. end Wilkes St.; no charge, reservations at company offices.
Riding: 0.5 m. E. on State 9, horses $1 per hr.

Annual Events: Band Concerts in State Park every Sun. from late June to early Sept.; Tomato Festival, first week of Sept.

BERKELEY SPRINGS (Bath) (612 alt., 1,039 pop.), one of the oldest spas in the South, spreads its serene and shady streets along Warm Springs Run, in a narrow hollow between the steep wooded side of Warm Springs Ridge and the more sloping spurs of Hogback Ridge, in the northwestern part of the Eastern Panhandle. At the western edge of town is the State park and sanitarium, its baths supplied by warm springs that gush from the Oriskany sandstone at the foot of Warm Springs Ridge. Century-old elms, maples, and sycamores shelter the park and bathhouses and line the tranquil streets. In June flowering catalpa trees scent the air and drop white blossoms upon the sidewalks. An air of peace and unconcern pervades the old resort.

The life of the town centers around the State park and springs. Although Berkeley Springs is no longer the 'smart' place to take the cure, its summer hotels and boarding houses are filled with health seekers who, between steamings, baths, massages, and treatments, rock placidly on wide verandas or walk along shady paths of the park discussing their symptoms. The waters of the springs, which are piped for all purposes throughout the town, lack the medicinal taste usually associated with mineral springs, but are fresh and slightly sweet. They are reputed to be beneficial in treatment of rheumatism, stomach disorders, skin troubles, and infantile paralysis. A few inhabitants not directly dependent on the springs for livelihood are employed in a glass-sand plant, a hosiery mill, and a ginger-ale plant. The slow tempo of life in 'Berkeley,' as the inhabitants call the town, quickens on summertime Saturdays when farmers with produce to sell and week-end parties from Washington crowd the streets. In September the town celebrates with three days of festivities in honor of the tomato, chief crop of surrounding farms. The owner of the choicest bushel is made king of Morgan County tomato growers and, with the queen, presides over festivities, including a parade, a pageant, a mountain-music contest, a candlelight vesper and choral service, a baby show, a drum-corps drill, a fireworks display, and the queen's ball.

Berkeley Springs' greatest excitement occurs in spring when an occasional cloudburst in the mountains south of town sends tiny streams spilling over their banks. For a few hours water swirls through the streets two and three feet deep, only to ebb as swiftly as it came, leaving little damage in its wake.

Before white men came, the Indians regarded the warm springs as a gift of the Great Spirit and observed the valley as a neutral area. Tuscarora, Shawnee, Delaware, Iroquois, Catawba, and Huron, some of them bitter enemies, came from widely separated regions, camped side by side on the ridges around the springs, and bathed together without animosity. About 1740 a few white families staked out tomahawk claims around the springs. These, however, were invalidated in 1745, when the boundaries of Lord Fairfax's estate were determined and the springs included in the estate.

It was owing to George Washington's enthusiasm for the waters that Berkeley Springs first became known as a resort. While surveying for Lord Fairfax, Washington, on March 18, 1748, wrote, 'this day call'd to see y Fam'd Warm Springs.' Washington was so impressed with the springs that he returned again and again, sometimes bringing his family. It was probably at his prompting that Lord Fairfax in 1756 granted the land around the springs to the colony of Virginia with the stipulation that the springs were 'to be forever free to the publick for the welfare of suffering humanity.'

In October 1776 the Virginia assembly passed 'An act for establishing a town at the Warm Springs in the county of Berkeley.' The town was called Bath for the spa in England, and although better known by its post-office name, Berkeley Springs, the town legally is still Bath. It was platted in 1777, and among the purchasers by proxy at the first sale of lots are listed many of the noted soldiers, statesmen, and businessmen of the day—General George Washington, General Horatio Gates, Colonel Warner Washington, Robert Throckmorton, Charles Carroll of Carrollton, Colonel Mynn Thruston, and Samuel Washington.

During the Revolution the springs were thronged with a strange mixture of guests—refugees from the war-torn coast, wives and families of Revolutionary officers, sick and wounded soldiers, paroled Hessian officers, land barons taking the cure, and fashionable women. Dozens of makeshift cottages and shelters along the hillsides above the new-born town made it resemble an army encampment.

Following the Revolution, Bath was at the height of its popularity. Among the younger men, drinking, gambling at cards, betting on horse races, and dancing were the chief amusements. Bishop Francis Asbury who visited Bath at this time wrote in his journal, 'My spirit is grieved at so much vanity as is seen here at Bath, by the many poor careless sinners around me. The living is expensive, four dollars per week.' On subsequent visits the bishop further lamented 'this place of wickedness' where 'everything that is good is in low estimation' and 'the people showed little affection for the Word.'

Among the numerous taverns was 'a very commodious boarding house' opened by Robert Throckmorton and James Rumsey in 1784. Rumsey, however, gave little time to the business; for that year he built five bathhouses and other buildings on the State property and worked on the model of his 'mechanical boat,' with which he experimented at the mouth of Sir Johns Run on the Potomac River, three miles from town. In September he demonstrated his boat for George Washington and a few witnesses who were pledged to secrecy. Washington, much impressed, gave Rumsey a certificate of confidence in his invention and commissioned him to build a dwelling house on Washington's lots in Bath. Rumsey's first boat was not impelled by steam but by mechanical means. However, he began immediately to experiment with steam. Through Washington's influence, Rumsey obtained a ten-year patent on his invention from the Virginia assembly. His first sizable steamboat was destroyed by fire before completion, but he persisted, and in December 1785 the improved steamboat was launched from the mouth of Sir Johns Run and navigated down the Potomac to Harpers Ferry, where experiments were continued until the successful public demonstration at Shepherdstown in 1786 (*see Shepherdstown*). Rumsey's boat operated on much the same principle as the modern toy 'pop-pop' boat; a stream of water taken in at the bow by a steam pump was forcibly expelled through a pipe at the stern, thus propelling the boat forward. The principle, used in many of the earlier experimental steamboats, did not prove commercially successful.

With the rise of newer resorts—White Sulphur Springs, Rawley's Spring, Lee's White Sulphur Spring and others—the popularity of Bath waned in the 1830's, but many old southern families continued their annual pilgrimages. 'As the circle of visitors at Berkeley Springs decreased its society became more and more mellow until its frequenters reckoned it "the cream of cream," and showed themselves more and more jealous of its reputation.' This tide, however, turned again when the Baltimore & Ohio Railroad was completed to Hancock, Maryland, six miles north, in 1843.

Even destruction by fire of several of the better boarding houses and hotels in 1844 could not stem the influx of visitors. The new Berkeley Springs Hotel, erected by Colonel John Strother, accommodated 500 guests and at the height of the season turned away as many more. During hot weather the exodus from the national Capital to the springs was nearly complete; many cabinet meetings were held and matters of State were decided in the comfortable coolness of the resort.

This prosperity ceased suddenly in 1861 with the outbreak of the War between the States. Berkeley Springs underwent a succession of captures and recaptures, bloodshed, fires, and wholesale destruction of property. Numerous clashes occurred between northern and southern sympathizers.

Popularity was difficult to regain after the war. Many families of the Old South were too impoverished to return, and others would not patronize a resort now in a 'northern' State. In 1885 David Hunter Strother, widely known as author and illustrator under the name of Porte Crayon, purchased from his father a half interest in the Berkeley Springs Hotel and revived the vogue for Berkeley Springs by making it a gathering place for writers and artists. In their wake followed Washington society and many summer homes were erected on surrounding hills.

The Berkeley Springs Hotel was burned in 1897 and was not rebuilt; but during the first two decades of the twentieth century the town experienced a short-lived awakening with the opening of five sand mines near by, employing 400 persons. The mines were consolidated in 1919 and employment was reduced to 15 men, leaving the town again to depend on the few faithful frequenters of the newer hotels.

POINTS OF INTEREST

BERKELEY SPRINGS STATE PARK AND SANITARIUM is a tree-shaded area on the western edge of town, its boundaries extending upward along Warm Springs Ridge. Included in the State-operated park are the three principal warm springs and the State bathhouses built around them. All buildings are of brick, painted a cream yellow and trimmed with green.

The park centers around the long one-story building, erected in 1887, containing the SWIMMING POOLS (*open 6–6 daily, Apr. 1 to Oct. 1; adm. 25¢*). The main room, lighted by skylights, has two swimming pools, one 30 by 85 feet and the other 30 by 60 feet. The larger was originally the men's pool and was separated from the women's by a partition. Now there is only a tile curbing between. Dressing booths are along one side of the pools, and spectators' benches are along the other. Showers and small private steam baths occupy the rear of the building. A small adjoining unit contains the rest rooms. In front of the swimming-pool building is a wide, grassy area interlaced by gravel walks and equipped with benches, swings, picnic tables, and a sand pile for children. Here Warm Springs Run winds between stone-lined banks. In the center of this area is a small octagonal BANDSTAND, painted yellow and green, where band concerts are presented every Sunday afternoon throughout the summer.

Near by, at the NW. corner of Washington and Liberty Sts., stands the WASHINGTON ELM, a huge white elm with a tablet imbedded in its trunk bearing the inscription, 'Elm planted by George Washington.' The date and occasion of the planting are uncertain, and it is not known when the tablet was placed, but tradition recounts that the tree was planted with ceremony during Washington's last visit to Bath in 1794. Near the tree is the RUMSEY MARKER, a millstone said to have been taken from Rumsey's gristmill, set on a concrete base. The waters of the springs are conducted in open cement channels along the foot of the hill into a small open wading pool and to the CITY WATER WORKS at the northern edge of the park. From this yellow-painted brick building the 2,000-gallon-a-minute flow from the springs is distributed to the bathhouses and throughout the town.

Adjoining the water works is a two-story building, the OLD HOT BATHHOUSE (*open* 9–5 *daily*), reputed to be nearly a century old but remodeled about the time the swimming pools were built. It contains 10 sunken Roman baths in which the water, normally at a temperature of 74.3° F., is regulated to any desired temperature ($1 *a bath,* 10 *for* $7.50). The DRINKING SPRING, adjacent to the Old Hot Baths, is enclosed in a colonnaded pavilion. The water is free and a penny cup-vending machine provides containers. Yellow brick columns support a frame-and-plaster second story in which is the MORGAN COUNTY LIBRARY (*open irregular hours Tues. and Thurs.*). The FAIRFAX BATH-TUB, south of the drinking spring, is a rectangular hollow in the ground, about the size of an ordinary bathtub, lined with rock and sand. Spring water seeps up through the bottom. Lord Fairfax had this tub constructed when he built his summer house and in it took his baths, a little apart from the pool in which the rest of the health-seekers bathed. The WADING POOL, near the bathtub, is roughly triangular and is enclosed by a cement curbing. Originally deeper than it is now, this was the first pool used for bathing. It was surrounded by a screen of boughs, and in early days of the resort a horn was sounded at established times to announce the different bathing periods for men and women. Occasionally some newcomer would appear at the wrong time to the great confusion of the bathers. The NEW HOT BATHHOUSE (*open* 9–5 *daily*), at the southern end of the park, was built in 1930 and accommodate 10 persons. It is a long, low, one-story brick building, which contains showers, Turkish baths, and electric cabinets (*treatments* $1.50 *and* $2).

The CASTLE (*private*), which looms above the State park from the dense foliage on Warm Springs Ridge, is a gray stone structure modeled after a Norman castle, with a round ivy-covered battlemented parapet and tower at one corner. The coping of the porch is also battlemented. The Castle was built in 1887–8 by Judge S. T. Soult for his wife and daughter, who had come to Bath for the daughter's health. The two were in the habit of picnicking on the mountainside above the park and became so fond of the spot that the judge promised to build them a 'castle in the air,' if he could buy the ground. At dinner one evening he told a group of Washington visitors of his idea, and A. D. Mullett, designer of the State, War and Navy Building, sketched a plan on the back of a menu and tossed it across the table with the remark, 'There's your castle, my friend.' The design was used. Snowden Ashford, government architect, built the Castle. At one time a secret passage led through a sliding panel in the ballroom underground to the 'keep,' a round stone tower that guarded the entrance to the driveway. The road up the mountain, however, now cuts between the Castle and the keep, destroying the passage.

The SITE OF THE FAIRFAX INN, Fairfax St. facing the park, is occupied by a lunch room. In 1814 Robert Bailey operated the Old Coffee House here, and about 1840 John O'Farrell established the O'Farrell House, which under successive proprietors was called the Florence House, the St. Charles, and finally the Fairfax Inn. The O'Farrell House welcomed distinguished guests with music by a local band. On one occasion, Henry Clay arrived and was greeted and escorted to the hotel by the usual band. At the door of the tavern he paused and made a speech to the musicians, inviting their political support. The speech finished, he inquired how many belonged to his party. Only two stepped forward. During the War between the States the tavern was operated by John O'Farrell's widow, an attractive woman with southern sympathies who encouraged the attention of the colonel in command of Union troops stationed near by in order to gather information to send to the Confederates. Her son, Charles, rose to the rank of brigadier general in the Confederate army. The inn was destroyed by fire in 1902.

The ALLEN HOUSE (*private*), SW. corner Wilkes and Congress Sts., is a large three-story weatherboarded-over-log house, with a two-story addition at the rear and a two-story gallery running across the front. The house was built prior to 1800 and, as the Blue House, the Buckhorn Inn, and Hunter's Ordinary, served as a tavern for half a century. The original imperfect glass is in the windows, and the interior, with its heavy walnut doors, wide board flooring, and hand-hewn beams, remains much as when the house was built. No modern improvements have been made, although the building is in use as an apartment house.

The SITE OF THE FLAGG HOUSE, NE. corner Wilkes and Congress Sts., is occupied by a red brick hotel erected in 1938. As early as 1783 an inn, the Sign of General Washington, was operated here by John Hunter, an Irish immigrant. The building, which was erected even earlier, was of logs covered with plaster. It was built on a stone foundation over a spring, which furnished a private water supply. It is a tradition in the Hunter family that George Washington stayed at this inn during his last visit to Bath in 1794. In 1814 the inn was rented for a time by Robert Bailey, proprietor of the Old Coffee House, who advertised in the *Martinsburg Gazette* that he would 'accommodate those that chuse to call on him . . . Good wishes for parties and every attention paid by the public's humble servant, Robert Bailey.' Upon Hunter's death the inn was inherited by his daughters, Rosanna and Delilah, and passed from them to John Flagg, Rosanna's husband. Flagg enlarged and weatherboarded the house, which stood until the spring of 1938, when all but the rear wing was torn down to make room for the new hotel.

The WASHINGTON PROPERTY, SE. corner Fairfax and Mercer Sts., is marked by a stone with a bronze plaque indicating the two lots that were purchased by George Washington in 1776 at the first sale of lots in the town. Washington commissioned James Rumsey to build him a dwelling house, kitchen, and stable, which were finished in 1784. The first President did not at any time live in the house, and when he and his heirs failed to pay the taxes on the property it reverted to the town trustees, who sold it in 1823 to Robert Gustin. The present rambling gray frame house was built in 1869 by William P. Dole, Commissioner of Indian Affairs under President Lincoln, and is now (1941) a tourist home.

The CATHOLIC RECTORY (*private*), Washington St. between Liberty and Fairfax Sts., is a square three-story brick-over-log house, built about 1779 by Philip Pendleton, one of the first trustees of Bath. Cement columns, banded at wide intervals by bulging cement rings and topped by Corinthian capitals, support the roofs of first-and-second-story balconies that run along the front and one side of the house. Few changes have been made inside; the wide board flooring, white-plastered walls, and hand-hewn foundation beams remain. The stairway, however, was taken from the Washington house when it was torn down.

The STROTHER HOUSE (*private*), SE. corner Washington and Warren Sts., built by William Duckwell in 1850, is a rectangular, two-story, white-painted brick house trimmed in brown. A wide porch runs across the front, and a single dormer window rises at each end of the hipped roof. A bay window, added later, juts from the south side of the house, and a wing with white plastered walls has been added to the back. General David Hunter Strother (Porte Crayon) bought this house in 1861 and to it brought his second wife. During the War between the States, Union troops occupied the house, and the second floor was used for meetings of the Union League. A small study formerly stood in one corner of the yard on a site now occupied by a filling station. Here Strother did much of his writing.

The PINES, a quarter-mile E. of Bath on Pendle Hill, is an institution for the care and rehabilitation of children crippled by infantile paralysis. The main building is an old residence built by Judge Josiah Dent in 1851 and taken over in 1934 by the West Virginia Foundation for Crippled Children. The house is of red brick, two stories high, with a gabled slate roof. A small steepled cupola rises from the center of the roof. Two smaller bungalows on the 16-acre grounds are used for schoolrooms and treatment rooms. In 1938 the capacity of the institution was increased from 25 children to 75 by the addition of wards, a treatment room, an office, schoolrooms, a recreational room, and a swimming pool. Water from the warm springs is piped to The Pines for use in treatments. The institution is partially supported by the State.

PORT JAMES RUMSEY, 3 m. NW. on State 9 and left on an unnumbered gravel road, is the secluded inlet at the mouth of Sir Johns Run where James Rumsey in 1784 conducted experiments with his 'mechanical boat' and the use of steam in navigation. The spot, cleared of underbrush and developed as a small park, was dedicated as a shrine to James Rumsey in 1939 by the West Virginia Rumseyan Society.

POINTS OF INTEREST IN ENVIRONS

Cacapon State Park, 10 m. S. on State 38 (*see Tour 1*).

Charleston

Railroad Stations: S. end of South Side Bridge for Chesapeake and Ohio Ry.; Broad and Smith Sts. for Baltimore & Ohio R.R., New York Central System, and Virginian Ry.

Interurban Busses: To Cabin Creek 40¢; St. Albans 30¢; Dunbar 18¢.

Bus Station: 155 Summers St. For Atlantic Greyhound Lines, West Virginia Transportation Co., and Logan-Williamson Bus Co.

Airport: 9.2 m. W. on US 35 for American Airlines; taxi 75¢.

Taxis: 20¢ and upward according to distance and number of passengers.

Busses: Local: north of Great Kanawha River 7¢, Kanawha City and South Hills 10¢.

Traffic Regulations: Chief one-way streets, Capitol (north) between Kanawha and Washington Sts., Quarrier (west) between Broad and Capitol Sts., Hale (south) between Lee and Virginia Sts.

Street Order and Numbering: Numbers run east and west from Elk River; north and south from Great Kanawha River.

Accommodations: 15 hotels; tourist homes.

Information Service: Southern West Virginia Automobile Club, Ruffner Hotel, Kanawha and Hale Sts.; Chamber of Commerce, 807 Kanawha St.

Radio Stations: WCHS (580 kc.); WGKV (1490 kc.).

Theaters and Motion Picture Houses: Shrine Mosque, Capitol St. between Washington and Lewis Sts., for Kanawha Players, a little-theater group giving 6 plays annually, and other local organizations; Children's Theater group, giving 5 plays annually at High School and other places; 12 motion picture houses, including 1 for Negroes.

Swimming: Y.M.C.A., Capitol St. between Washington and Lee Sts.; Y.W.C.A., 1114 Quarrier St.

Golf: Capitol View Golf Course, 35th St. between Staunton and MacCorkle Aves., Kanawha City, 9 holes, greens fee 35¢ weekdays, 50¢ Sat., Sun., and holidays; Kanawha Country Club, South Charleston, 5.7 m. W. on US 60, on side road (L), 18 holes, greens fee, those residing within 40 miles $3, others $1; Meadow Brook Golf Club, 2 m. N. on Ruffner Hollow Rd., 18 holes, greens fee $1 weekdays, $1.50 Sat., Sun., and holidays; Edgewood Country Club.

Tennis: Laidley Field, Elizabeth St., Piedmont Rd., and Hansford St., 5 courts, 15¢ per hour, reservations made at High School; Charleston Tennis Club, 19th St. between S. Kanawha St. and MacCorkle Ave., 15¢ per hour.

Boating and Canoeing: City Levee, S. side of Kanawha St. between Summers and Capitol Sts., speedboats $5 per hour, outboard boats $1.50 per hour; Kanawha and Bradford Sts., canoes 50¢ first hour, 25¢ each additional hour.

Riding: NW. corner MacCorkle Ave. and 16th St.; MacCorkle Ave. and Mission Hollow Rd., horses $1 per hour.

Skating: S. end of Kanawha City Bridge, rink open during winter, adults 40¢, children 20¢.

Baseball: Kanawha Baseball Park, SW. corner MacCorkle Ave. and 35th St., Middle Atlantic League (Class C).

Seaplane: City Levee, S. side of Kanawha St. between Summers and Capitol Sts.; short hop $1, hourly rate $7.50.

Annual Events: Rose Show, State Capitol, spring; May Music Festival, vocal and instrumental concerts, 3 days, Shrine Mosque; Dahlia Show, State Capitol, late summer; Washington and Lee-West Virginia University football game, Laidley Field.

Crowded into narrow valleys where the Elk River joins the Great Kanawha in the western foothills of the Appalachian Mountains, CHARLESTON (598 alt., 60,408 pop.), with its Italian Renaissance State Capitol and its elmshaded residential sections, is the center of State government and of an industrial area that fringes the city.

Three representative views of the city are afforded from the three highway bridges across the Great Kanawha River.

From the South Side Bridge the main part of Charleston appears to be a broad mass of elms, maples, and sycamores, pierced by the gold-leafed Capitol dome, church steeples, and a score of tall office buildings, hotels, and apartment houses. Prominent among these are the narrow 13-story Union Building, its back to the water front, and the modern 20-story buff brick Kanawha Valley Building, topped with two airplane beacons, one revolving, the other stationary and pointing to the municipal airport. West of the bridge is Charleston's small but busy water front. A little red seaplane operates from the wharf, landing and taking off from under the tall bridge, rising several hundred feet before it can clear the steep wooded hills on either side of the river. On week ends and summer evenings the river is dotted with varicolored canoes, rowboats, shiny motor launches, an occasional sailboat, and now and then a bicycle-pedaled pontoon contrivance. Businesslike tugs push long black rectangles of coal barges between sand and gravel dredges at work in the stream, and diminutive stern-wheel river boats, built in the exact proportions of larger craft, nose into the landing. Billy Bryant's showboat, popular up and down the Ohio and Mississippi River systems, visits Charleston in early spring, and its tooting calliope announces the show's in town. Lily Pons, coloratura soprano, when appearing for a concert at Charleston, stopped over an extra day for her first visit to a showboat performance. Southward, across the river, are the Chesapeake and Ohio tracks and depot, a highway, and the steep-sloped South Hills, where a few of the finer residences look out through their columns across the city.

From the Kanawha City Bridge, at the eastern end of the city, is a view of recreational Charleston, particularly busy after five in the evening and on week ends. Partly under the bridge, on the west side, is a boathouse, its neat craft as carefully stalled and blanketed as horses in a racing stable. In times of leisure the boats shining and brightly painted, string out up and down the river. The tall lamp standards of the baseball field mark a hollow square to the south of the bridge; golfers may be seen among the trees on the riverflat course; smartly outfitted equestrians posting the bridle paths, and white-clad tennis players making their way to the tennis courts. An ice-skating rink just south of the bridge is well patronized in winter, and a local hockey team competes with teams from other cities. To the east are the modern homes of Kanawha City, spread out on flat lowland, and westward rises the dome of the Capitol.

From the Patrick Street Bridge, at the western end of the city, there is a representative view of industrial Charleston. The glass and chemical plants, like all those in the Charleston area, are outside the city limits and closed to visitors, owing to secret processes and the danger of accident. The Carbide and Carbon Chemicals Corporation plant of the Union Carbide Corporation, with its shining aluminum-painted tanks and towers, occupies the whole of Blaine Island, just west of the bridge. Tall smokestacks loom above the blackened roofs of two- and three-story red and gray brick factories, and large storage tanks behind high wire fences line the landscaped riverbanks.

Charleston is a rapidly growing trade center for the Great Kanawha Valley, whose resources of coal, oil, gas, and brine rank it high among the Nation's chemical and glass centers. Each important plant has its own small town, some adjoining Charleston, others a few miles away (*see Tour* 15).

Within the narrow Kanawha Valley, where trains come and go at all hours, Charleston is unusually train-conscious. Particular attention is paid those on the Chesapeake and Ohio road on the south side of the river, within seeing and hearing distance of the city's river front. People check the trains in and out almost automatically, identifying them by name or number—'The *George Washington's* four minutes late tonight,' or 'Number Three is right on the dot.'

Industrial activity is reflected in the busy downtown district where buildings ranging from 3 to 20 stories are crowded along the crooked one-way streets, and very narrow sidewalks accommodate large crowds of shoppers who come from the southern half of the State to do their principal buying. In the summer, women peddlers offer bright-colored bunches of garden or wild blossoms and, in fall and winter, men and small boys sell bittersweet, holly branches, and other shrubs and plants from the near-by hillsides.

The low-lying east bank of Elk River (which divides the city into east and west sections), with a number of small houseboats tied up at the river's edge, presents an unkempt appearance in marked contrast to the orderly banks of the Kanawha. When the river rises, occasionally a houseboat breaks loose and a floating home moves on to a new location.

Kanawha Boulevard, a projected five-lane thoroughfare with landscaped water front, is now (1941) nearing completion; when completed, it will skirt the north bank of the Great Kanawha from the Kanawha City Bridge to the Patrick Street Bridge. The earliest settlements of Charleston were made along the eastern section of Kanawha Street near its intersection with Brooks Street, the main part of the old town being along Kanawha and Virginia Streets west to the confluence of the Kanawha and the Elk. The section extending east from Broad Street on the north side of Kanawha Boulevard has many fine examples of modern architecture and a few imposing old Georgian Colonial houses with white-columned porticos. Most of these are surrounded by broad lawns, with tall trees, shrubbery, evergreen plants and hedges, and, here and there, holly trees notable for their size.

Charleston has two degree-granting colleges, Morris-Harvey and Mason College of Music and Fine Arts. Community organizations include the Open Forum, which sponsors discussions and addresses by recognized authorities on current topics; the Civic Music Association, which sponsors several concerts each season by artists of national repute; and the Kanawha Players, a little-theater organization.

The first white persons known to have reached the site of Charleston were Mary Ingles and Betty Draper, who had been captured by Indians during the Ingles-Draper massacre at Draper Meadows (Blacksburg), Virginia, in 1755, and were being taken to the Shawnee village at Chillicothe, Ohio. Eighteen years later Colonel Thomas Bullitt and a party of surveyors stopped briefly at the mouth of the Elk River while on their way to Kentucky. Bullitt returned in 1775 and staked a claim of 1,040 acres, which included most of the area that is East Charleston. Upon his death the claim went to his brother, Cuthbert Bullitt, who obtained a patent signed by Governor Thomas Jefferson.

Bullitt held the tract until 1787, when he met Colonel George Clendenin at Richmond. Clendenin, who had been elected to the assembly from Greenbrier County and who had camped on the site with General Andrew Lewis's army in 1774, bought the claim for five shillings (about 87¢). A few weeks later he was designated by Governor Edmund Randolph to organize a company of rangers for the protection of the Great Kanawha Valley, and in 1788 he erected Fort Lee, named for Governor Henry Lee of Virginia, on his land along the Great Kanawha River at the foot of present Brooks Street. Some historians refer to it as Fort Clendenin, but it was never called that in official records.

The completion of the fort marked the beginning of Charleston; Scotch-Irish and German settlers emigrated from the Shenandoah Valley, and in 1789 Kanawha County was organized, with Fort Lee as the meeting place of the county commissioners until a courthouse was erected.

'The town at the mouth of the Elk' and 'Clendenin's Settlement,' as Fort Lee was most frequently called by Richmond officials and travelers, lost much of its military character when the Virginia assembly, in 1794, authorized the establishment of a town on 40 acres of the Clendenin tract. It was named Charles Town for Clendenin's father; later, common usage shortened the name to Charleston. Fort Lee's connection with the military system of Virginia ended in 1795 when Wayne's treaty with the Indians was consummated (*see History*).

Two vivid personalities—Daniel Boone and 'Mad Ann' Bailey—were among the small group of pioneers at and near 'Clendenin's Settlement' from the time Fort Lee was erected until Charles Town was established.

Boone lived with his family in a two-room log cabin at what is now the Kanawha City section of Charleston, within sight of the present Capitol grounds, and alternated his hunting and Indian scouting with brief attempts at being a merchant, surveyor, and politician. The abundance of game and the thrill of an Indian fight, not the security of a military garrison, attracted Boone to the Great Kanawha Valley, and even though he was appointed a lieutenant-colonel in the county militia in 1789, and was elected to the Virginia assembly at Kanawha County's first election in the fall of the same year, he returned to Kentucky in 1795, when it became apparent that he was no longer needed as a defender and that the growing number of settlers was making game less abundant.

As a legislator, Boone served on the assembly's committee on religion, and on the committee on 'propositions and licenses.' Frontier defense was one of the much discussed questions, and the Assembly Journal for December 12, 1789, shows that Boone handed in the following memorandum and report:

> For Kanawha County 68 privates; Lenard Cuper Capt. at Pint Plesent 17 men; Joell Dane, Insine at Bellevelle 17 men, John Young, Scout at Elke 17 men. Two spyes or Scutes will be nesery at the pint to sarch the Banks of the River at Crosing places. More will be wanting if the could be alloude. Those Spyes must be compousde of the inhabitance who Well know the woods and waters. From the pint to Belleville, 60 miles, no inhabitence; also from the pint to Elke no inhabitence, from Elke to the Bote yards 20 miles all inhabited.
> This from your most Obedient
> D. BOONE

During the same session it was voted to send ammunition for the militia on the Monongahela and the Great Kanawha, who were to be called out for the defense of the frontier. Boone, somewhat an opportunist, wrote to the governor as follows:

> Monday 13th Decr 1791
> Sir—as sum person Must Carry out the armanstion [ammunition] to Red Stone [Brownsville, Pennsylvania] if your Exclency should have thought me a proper parson I would undertake it on conditions I have the apintment to vitel the company at Kanhowway so I could take Down the flowre as I paste that place.
> I am your Exclenceys most obedent omble servant,
> DANL BOONE

Boone was awarded the appointment, but later records show that he was apparently sometimes remiss in fulfilling the terms of the contract. Various militia leaders complained of his failure to bring supplies as needed, and at one time his fellow legislator, Clendenin, reported to the governor that there had been 'a total noncompliance' on the part of Boone.

In his seven years in the Kanawha Valley, Boone acquired little property; records show that he owned only two horses, a Negro, and

500 acres of land. Nevertheless he was a power in the community. When he left Charleston, almost the entire village attended a farewell feast prepared of his favorite game, and then loaded his few personal possessions on a flatboat at the foot of what is now Morris Street.

Ann Bailey, a cockney-speaking Englishwoman, was a hard-riding, fearless pioneer who changed her feminine apparel for the buckskin garb of an Indian scout and set out to avenge the death of her first husband, Richard Trotter, at the Battle of Point Pleasant. When she came to Fort Lee with her second husband in 1788 she already was known to the Indians, who believed her to be invested with an 'evil spirit,' as the 'Great White Squaw,' and to the frontier settlements as one who 'halways carried a hax, a hauger, and could chop as well as hany man.' She was an expert rifle shot and had the reputation of being able to shoot, from the back of her horse, a 'howl from a helm tree on the Helk River.'

Whether the story of her perilous ride to save Fort Lee is fact or legend is still a question. Certain it is, however, that the midnight ride of Paul Revere does not exceed in interest the purported exploits of Ann Bailey, which were first told 72 years later (1861) in the poem, 'A Legend of the Kanawha,' written by a soldier-poet, Charles Robb. Prior to that, historians and contemporary writers had made no mention of the ride—in fact, later historians have not been able to find any record of such an attack on Fort Lee. But Robb, exercising poetic license, told a dramatic tale that many since have accepted as fact. According to his story, Fort Lee was besieged by Indians in 1789. When it was discovered that the powder supply was not sufficient to withstand the attack, Colonel Clendenin called the garrison together. To get additional powder would require a 100-mile trip to Fort Savannah (Lewisburg). Who would risk his life to save the garrison from slaughter? A silence fell. Then from the back of the room was heard the coarse-voiced declaration 'I will go.' Every member of the company recognized the voice of Ann Bailey.

The fleetest horse of the stockade was brought. At an opportune moment the gate was opened, and Ann dashed out on the long journey up the valley and across the mountains to Fort Savannah. She arrived late the next day and, after resting briefly, set out on the return trip with the powder loaded on a second horse. Late in the third night a tapping was heard at the stockade gate. 'Mad Ann' had returned!

As a reward for her heroic feat the garrison voted to give her the horse that had served her so well. After that, so the popular story goes, she continued her exploits, carrying information and supplies from fort to fort, always riding her prized mount, which she called Liverpool for the place of her birth in England. However, some historians say there is evidence to show that Liverpool was in her possession long before and that he would have been more than 20 years old when she was supposed to have made the famous ride.

Charleston proper did not grow so rapidly as the surrounding area, but in 1801 a post office known as Kanawha Court House was established, and mail was brought fortnightly from Lewisburg. Three years later the Lewisburg-Warm Springs Road, or Kanawha Turnpike (US 60), was extended to the Great Kanawha Valley, making Charleston a point of transfer for east-west travelers who came by wagon or horseback, and then boarded flatboats made in local boatyards to continue their journey. The growth of the salt industry at Kanawha Salines (*see Tour 15b*) aided Charleston, for in 1805 a salt-tub mill was opened here. Ten years later a pottery, which made whisky jugs and milk crocks, was opened. The first school, Mercer Academy, was started in 1818, and the first newspaper, the *Spectator*, was published in the following year.

The opening of steam navigation in 1824 and the use of steam engines to operate brine pumps stimulated the salt business and increased the importance of the Charleston area. Long trains of Conestoga wagons brought supplies from the east and went back laden with salt.

By 1856 Charleston had a population of 1,500, but in that year the near-by salt industry reached its peak and began to decline. As a result, attention was turned more and more to the county seat, which became the center of coal, oil, and gas developments of the valley. During most of the War between the States, which retarded the town's growth, Charleston was held by Federal troops and sentiment was preponderantly for the Union. In September 1862, General W. W. Loring's Confederate army engaged the Federal forces of General Joseph Jackson Lightburn, known as the Fighting Parson, in the only battle fought in the Charleston area.

The town grew more rapidly following the war and by 1870 had a population of 4,000. In that year political control of the State government changed from Republican to Democratic, and Charleston made a successful bid for the Capitol. The State officers and records were brought to Charleston from Wheeling on the steamboat *Mountain Boy*, but because the Capitol was not completed, offices were established in churches and bank buildings until December.

The Chesapeake and Ohio Railway was completed to the Ohio River in 1873, but Charleston had the disadvantage of being situated across the unbridged Kanawha River, which, according to the *Wheeling Intelligencer*, had the 'poorest excuse of a ferry that was ever allowed to cross a stream. The capital city's facilities for modern travel are restricted to a "John boat" controlled by a lazy oarsboy impervious to the appeals and signals of beckoning passengers.' The paper further predicted that Charleston would soon become another Switchville along the line. Instead, however, the railroad and improved navigation on the Great Kanawha opened coal mining on a large scale, and the town grew more rapidly than ever before.

The northern city's agitation against Charleston continued and became more intense until 1875, when the legislature ordered the Capitol removed to Wheeling. The personnel and records had been returned to Wheeling only a short time when the question of a permanent seat of government arose. The legislature adopted a resolution calling upon the people to make the choice at a special election in May 1877, providing that the decision would become effective in 1885. Critics already were talking about the Capitol on wheels, but Charleston, Martinsburg, and Clarksburg made bids and sent spokesmen over the State to drum up votes. Charleston's representatives, Romeo H. Freer and John E. Kenna, who later served two terms in the United States Senate and whose statue stands in the Hall of Fame at Washington, were particularly unsuccessful during the early campaign—they had not even been able to attract listeners for their speeches.

Only ten days remained before the election, and Kenna and Freer arrived in Huntington, fatigued and discouraged, but determined to make one last effort. They were attracted by the shrill whistling of a steam calliope—a circus parade was approaching. 'And,' said Kenna, 'this is to be our competition for today.' Their last hope had faded, and they returned to the hotel bar, where a stranger invited them to have a drink. In the conversation that followed Kenna and Freer complained of their dilemma and lamented their failure to attract audiences. Their host said he was connected with the circus and added, 'There ought to be some way to help you fellows. Come to the entrance of the show today and ask for John Lowlow.'

So Lowlow, the noted clown, took up his task of helping Charleston in its fight for the Capitol. He arranged for the two to travel with the circus and they were allotted five minutes during each performance to speak for their cause. For a week they traveled the territory they had failed to arouse, speaking to as many as 5,000 circus fans at one time. In the election Charleston was selected by a vote greater than the total vote cast for its rivals.

Years later, when Kenna had attained high standing among his associates in Washington and was a trusted adviser of President Grover Cleveland, John Robinson's Circus showed in the national Capital. Recalling old days, Kenna organized a senatorial party and all went as his guests to the circus. During the evening's performance a white-faced clown stood on a barrelhead and waved for silence. 'Is there in the audience a man by the name of Kenna—Senator John E. Kenna of West Virginia? He used to travel with this circus.' That night John Lowlow was the guest of a party given by Senator Kenna and the clown's part in locating West Virginia's Capital was made known to the group.

When in 1885, the capital was removed from Wheeling to Charleston, the original statehouse, set in a square formed by Washington, Capitol, Lee, and Dickinson Streets, was enlarged at a cost of $390,000, and in 1902 an annex was completed. These two buildings housed the various departments of the State government until January 3 1921, when the old Capitol was destroyed by fire. At the 1921 session of the legislature

Governor Ephraim F. Morgan appointed a commission to build a new Capitol, which was completed in 1932. During the interim the State government functioned in temporary quarters.

Regular sessions of the legislature are held biennially beginning on the second Wednesday of January. A few of the wealthier members of the legislature in sessions held between 1870 and 1875, when the Capitol was at Charleston for the first time, lived at the Saint Albert Hotel, on the north side of lower Kanawha Street, then considered the last word in hotel luxury in this section of the State.

The railroads and other corporations, many charged, had gained control of the legislature by this time, and legislators in the good graces of the railroads traveled on passes and lived at the hotels, besieged by an ever-increasing group of lobbyists, well-dressed suave, smiling gentlemen, with unlimited expense accounts, many of them lawyers picked not for their ability before court and jury, but for their influence in delivering votes for the interests they represented. They flourished in spite of the blasts of fiery Governor E. Willis (Windy) Wilson, elected in 1884.

Between 1885 and 1912 Charleston and the surrounding area continued to grow slowly but steadily as a center of the coal, oil, and gas industries. Several small manufactories were established here because of the proximity of an abundant fuel supply and rail and water transportation facilities. A new era of industrial development was started in 1913 and 1914, when two small plants were established in the western part of the city to manufacture tetrachloride, liquid chlorine, dyes, caustic acid, and other chemicals. This was followed soon by the erection of two glass plants at Kanawha City and the Federal Government's establishment of a high explosive plant at Nitro, 16 miles west of Charleston.

From 1885 until the burning of the old State Capitol, legislative sessions caused a bustle of excitement that increased the tempo of Charleston's political, business, and social life. But the scene began to change with America's entry into the First World War. Increased demand for coal and the beginning of chemical development in the Kanawha Valley brought an influx of foreign capital and new residents. More hotels sprang up. The erection of the new Capitol moved the political scene to Duffy Street, nearly two miles east. Edgewood, South Hills, Fort Hill, Kanawha City, and new residential areas on the west side grew to make room for the expansion. While a session of the legislature stimulates activity in the city nowadays, the legislators and lobbyists find themselves jostled by busy executives, professional men, statehouse and Federal employees, thousands of workers of store, shop, and factory—a citizenry that little resembles the old population of the State's capital city.

Of the several definite changes made in the character of the city by the industrial expansion of the war years, one of the most noticeable was the shifting of population percentages caused by an influx of migrant labor. While the northern West Virginia cities attracted to their heavy industry men and women of strong foreign stock or first-generation Americans, Charleston drew heavily from the Negroes of the Deep South, eager to leave their exhausted farms and shareholds for steady work at high wages. Although there had always been a small percentage of Negroes in Charleston, only after the frantic expansion of the war years lapsed into steady economic progress was there noticeable a marked increase in the number of settled Negro residents in the city. From this group there has come a Negro population exceeding 7,000, the largest group of urban Negro residents in the State.

Charleston's Negroes quickly established a community life almost exclusively their own. They now operate their own retail establishments, restaurants, cleaning and dyeing shops, laundries, taxicabs and night clubs. Their proximity to West Virginia State College for Negroes has enabled them to penetrate the skilled trades and professions. Their community numbers doctors and lawyers, educators and clergymen of recognized standing, architects and real-estate operators.

Since 1920 the industrial expansion in Charleston proper has been slight, but up and down the Great Kanawha Valley many chemical plants, some of which are the largest of their kind in the country, have been constructed to utilize the natural resources of the section. The erection of each new factory and the expansion of each old one within a radius of 15 miles added to Charleston's population, for many of the executives and salaried employees established residences in the city rather than in the small communities that adjoin the plants.

Less noticeable than its industrial growth, but as great and as rapid, has been Charleston's development as a distributing and commercial center. Wholesale houses here serve virtually every type of retail establishment in the southern half of the State. Most State associations have headquarters here.

POINTS OF INTEREST

1. The KANAWHA COUNTY PUBLIC LIBRARY (*open* 10–9 *weekdays;* 2–5 *Sun.*), SE. corner Lee and Hale Sts., is a vine-covered three-story stone structure of classic design, surmounted by a low metal dome. The librarian's desk is directly inside the doorway, and reading rooms open on either hand. The children's room is on the second floor. The administration offices of Morris-Harvey College are on the second and third floors, respectively. The WEST VIRGINIA MEDICAL LIBRARY (*open* 9–5 *Mon.-Fri.,* 9–12 *Sat.*), in the basement, has about 1,000 volumes, including current medical literature.

The building was erected in 1902 as an annex to the old Capitol, which was burned in 1921. In 1925, when offices were moved to the completed unit of the present State House, the annex was purchased by the Charleston Library Committee. It was organized as the Charleston Public Library in 1909. When the State's county-unit school law went into effect in 1933, it became the Kanawha County Public Library, maintained by the county board of education. It has approximately 40,000 volumes and serves the county with two bookmobiles, specially built trucks with bookshelves and checking equipment. The GARNETT LIBRARY (*open same hours*), 905 Lewis St., opened in 1927 for Negroes, is a branch of the Kanawha County Public Library.

2. The MUNICIPAL AUDITORIUM, NW. corner Truslow and Virginia Sts., is a fan-shaped modern structure with a center tower that faces the street intersection. The auditorium, designed by W. F. Wysong and completed in 1939, has a seating capacity of 5,000.

3. The STALNAKER DRUGSTORE (*open 8 a.m.–11 p.m. weekdays, 10 a.m.–1 p.m., 6–11 p.m. Sun.*), 612 E. Kanawha Blvd., believed to be the oldest pharmacy in West Virginia, has been in operation continuously since 1824 under the ownership of two families. It was founded by Dr. Henry Rogers, who came to Charleston in 1818 and shortly thereafter put on the market a chest of family remedies. With the exception of one brief period, the store has operated on the same site, although in different buildings. The interior of the present green-fronted, three-story structure, built in 1840, resembles a museum almost as much as a drugstore. Indian relics, old ledgers, and countless items associated with local men and affairs are displayed in glass cases and on shelves. A silver inlaid rifle that once belonged to Robert E. Lee and a pair of shears once the property of Daniel Boone are prize items. The store was owned by the Rogers family until 1909, when it was sold to Dr. T. B. Stalnaker. During its early days it was a gathering place for men who could recall the founding of Charleston and recount the Indian fights and exploits of Daniel Boone. Its customers have included such men as Henry Clay, Sam Houston, and, tradition says, Edgar Allan Poe.

4. The SITE OF FORT LEE, in front of 1202 E. Kanawha Blvd., is marked by two bronze plaques on the north and south exposures of a blackened boulder. One commemorates the fort site, the other the historic rides of Ann Bailey and Fleming Cobb. Cobb, historians record,

---

KEY FOR CHARLESTON MAP

1. The KANAWHA COUNTY PUBLIC LIBRARY, SE. corner Lee and Hale Sts. 2. The MUNICIPAL AUDITORIUM, NW. corner Truslow and Virginia Sts. 3. The STALNAKER DRUGSTORE, 612 Kanawha St. 4. The SITE OF FORT LEE, in front of 1202 Kanawha St. 5. KANAWHA RIFLEMEN'S MEMORIAL PARK, between 1578 and 1596 Kanawha S. 6. HOLLY GROVE, 1710 Kanawha St. 7. The GOVERNOR'S MANSION, 1718 Kanawha St. 8. The STATE CAPITOL, Kanawha St. between Duffy St. and California Ave. and extending to Washington St. 9. LIBBEY-OWENS-FORD GLASS COMPANY PLANT, just outside the eastern limits of the Kanawha City section of Charleston on the S. side of US 119. 10. OWENS-ILLINOIS GLASS COMPANY PLANT Number Six, opposite the Libbey-Owens-Ford plant, on the N. side of US 119, beginning just outside the limits of Kanawha City. 11. The PATRICK STREET MARKET, on each side of Patrick St., from W. Washington St. to Seventh Ave.

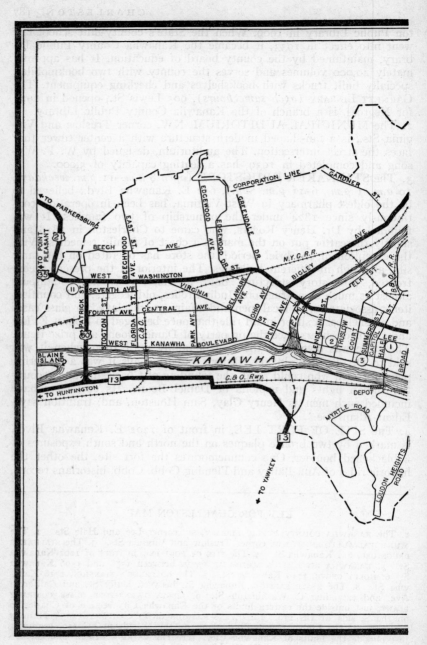

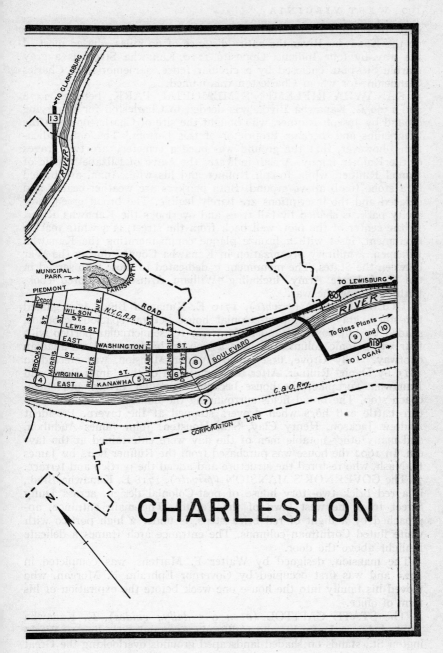

CHARLESTON

went to Point Pleasant for powder and on his return poled a canoe up the Kanawha River the entire distance of 60 miles, chased most of the way by four Indians. Opposite 1210 Kanawha Street is a gray marble SUNDIAL enclosed by a circular fence, a memorial to Charles Clendenin, for whom Charleston was named.

5. KANAWHA RIFLEMEN'S MEMORIAL PARK, between 1578 and 1596 E. Kanawha Blvd., was deeded to Charleston for a burying ground by Joseph Ruffner, who bought the site of Charleston from the Clendenins and 'became Proprietor of this bottom.' The only indications, however, that the ground was once a cemetery are two graves of the Ruffner family. A slab indicates the grave of Elizabeth, wife of Daniel Ruffner, while Joseph Ruffner and his wife, Anna, are buried in a stone tomb above ground. Both markers are weather-beaten and defaced and the inscriptions are barely legible. The broad green, now a city park, is shaded by tall trees and overlooks the Kanawha River. In the center of the plot, well back from the street, is a white marble monument, inset with a bronze plaque commemorating the Kanawha Riflemen, a military organization in Kanawha County during the War between the States. The monument is dedicated to those who served in the Confederate Army, including 'William Armstead, colored cook, faithful during the war.'

6. HOLLY GROVE (*private*), 1710 E. Kanawha Blvd., is a gabled two-story, gray brick, post-colonial house set on spacious grounds, shaded by tall boxwood and holly trees. Its semicircular portico with four white Ionic columns shelters a wooden balcony and a Palladian doorway. Holly Grove, first called Ruffner Mansion, was erected in 1815 by Daniel Ruffner. After the completion of the James River and Kanawha Turnpike, the house became a popular tavern and stagecoach stop. The broad fields surrounding the house were used to pasture cattle and hogs when drovers stopped at the tavern. President Andrew Jackson, Henry Clay, Sam Houston, John James Audubon, and many other notable men of the day were entertained at the tavern. In 1902 the house was purchased from the Ruffner heirs by James H. Nash, who restored the structure and added the portico and terrace.

7. The GOVERNOR'S MANSION (*private*), 1718 E. Kanawha Blvd., is a red brick two-story house of post-Colonial design, across Duffy Street from the west lawn of the Capitol. The main entrance, approached by a flight of red brick steps, is under a high portico with white fluted Corinthian columns. The entrance arch frames a delicate fanlight above the door.

The mansion, designed by Walter F. Martens, was completed in 1925 and was first occupied by Governor Ephraim F. Morgan, who moved his family into the house one week before the expiration of his term of office.

8. The STATE CAPITOL (*open 9–5 daily; guides*), E. Kanawha Blvd., between Duffy St. and California Ave. and extending to Washington St., stands on shaded landscaped grounds overlooking the Great

Kanawha River. Designed in the Italian Renaissance style by Cass Gilbert and completed in 1932 at a cost of $10,000,000, the symmetrical U-shaped structure, of limestone and marble, has a porticoed central section and two four-story wings; its flat roof is enclosed by a balustraded parapet. A dome 300 feet high, embossed with gold leaf, crowns the central unit, which measures 120 by 558 feet. Atop the crowning lantern is a bronze staff upon which is poised a golden eagle. Including the basement, the Capitol has 14 acres of floor space. The outer walls are adorned with pairs of Doric pilasters, two stories in height, which rise in support of the main cornice.

The main entrance on Kanawha Street, protected by a monumental Corinthian portico, is approached by a broad flight of steps. The colonnade of the portico rises in support of a plain classic pediment under a copper-colored gable roof. The south portal is protected by sliding storm doors of Roman design, cast in solid bronze. The paneled doors are decorated with rosette-shaped clusters of foliage representing trees native to the State.

The main south entrance opens into the rotunda on the principal floor, a circular-arched hall directly beneath the dome. Its pilastered walls of Vermont marble, pierced with four massive arches, rise to a carved frieze at the base of the drum. The north and south arches open upon the two entrance porticoes, while the two others give access to the east and west foyers. These foyers lead to the house and senate chambers, in the east and west wings respectively of the central unit. The arches extend to the base of the dome and are adorned with lunette panels of deep-blue plaster. The floor of the rotunda, circular in plan around an open well, is inlaid with Italian travertine and white Vermont marble. A balustrade encircles the well in the rotunda floor, through which can be seen a colonnaded hall on the floor below. Gold-leaf bands decorate the walls of the circular drum and ceiling of the dome, which are in shades of blue, gray, and old rose. A row of slender windows covered with gold-leaf grilles encircles the dome at the base of the bell.

The walls and floors of the foyers are of the same marble as that of the rotunda, but the ceilings are embellished with square coffered panels, each decorated with a bronze cluster of leaves against a background of rose. Light comes softly through translucent Italian alabaster urns, supported on standards of black and gold Belgian marble. Benches of breeched violet marble are on both sides of the foyers.

Designed with strict classic proportions, the SENATE CHAMBER, at the west end of the main unit, has an air of quiet dignity and beauty. Public galleries framed by massive arches open on three sides of the room, and a fourth arch, set with a blue panel, is a background for the dais. The walls are divided by rose-colored panels of acoustic plaster. Behind the galleries are small arched windows covered with ornamental bronze grilles. The domical ceiling, topped with a small cupola, is in the form of a paneled skylight with stained glass. In the center, hung on a brass chain, is a chandelier of imported hand-cut glass. Behind the dais is a gold-trimmed wall clock. The desks and chairs are of West Virginia black walnut, and the president's desk and chair of natural unvarnished walnut. A heavy rose-colored carpet covers the floor.

The decorations and furnishings of the HOUSE CHAMBER, at the east end of the main unit, are similar to those in the senate. The house of delegates uses the electric voting system, which was installed in 1935. On each desk is a cluster of buttons, released for voting by the delegate's individual key. Pressing one button flashes on a green light for 'aye' opposite the legislator's name on the wall behind the speaker's desk. Another button flashes a red light for 'nay.' Provision is made for the legislator to change his mind, for he may press a center button, erase his vote, and start all over again. A fourth button summons a page. Votes are totaled mechanically on the speaker's desk, and after that a vote cannot be changed except by unanimous consent. The vote of the 94 delegates is recorded in 2 minutes, whereas by roll call it usually required from 15 to 30 minutes.

Double flanking stairways of white marble, leading off the hallway on the south side of the rotunda, descend to the DORIC HALL, under the rotunda on the ground floor. This hall has fluted Doric columns and six crystal lights suspended on bronze chains. In the center of the hall is a circular colonnade of 16 square Doric piers, enclosing the well in the rotunda floor. Bronze light stands are arranged in pairs inside the colonnade. High above the well is the blue vaulted ceiling of the dome. A crystal chandelier, 8 feet in diameter, containing more than 3,300 pieces of hand-cut crystal and weighing more than 2 tons, is suspended from the dome ceiling. A circular design on the floor has the same diameter as the chandelier far above. The chandelier is lowered by a hand windlass from within the shell of the dome for cleaning and the replacement of bulbs. The operation of lowering and raising requires more than three hours.

The OUTER RECEPTION ROOM of the governor's suite, on the ground floor in the extreme west end of the main unit, is regarded as the show room of the Capitol. It is of Georgian Colonial design with ivory-colored walls, embellished with fluted Corinthian pilasters. The parquet floors, of herringbone design, have a border of quarter-sawed oak, black walnut, and maple. The floor is covered with a tan rug, 26 by 60 feet and weighing 1,800 pounds, made especially for the room and said to have been the largest seamless rug in the United States at the time the Capitol was constructed. Two large crystal chandeliers and many crystal wall brackets light the room; a fireplace of black and gold Belgian marble is at the eastern end. The windows are draped in satin.

In the basement, directly under the executive suite, is the STATE MUSEUM. A number of collections illustrate the history, science, and social conditions of the pioneers. There are several industrial exhibits, including one containing relics of mine disasters. Implements used by the Indians and Mound Builders are displayed in several glass cases. There are mounted specimens of native birds and animals and a number of native fossils. A beaver trap said to have belonged to Daniel Boone reveals how little basic change there has been in the design of the steel trap. Boone's rifle, Lewis Wetzel's rifle, Aaron Burr's spectacles, a model of James Rumsey's steamboat, and a model of the Blennerhassett mansion are among other prized items in the museum.

On the third floor of the east wing is the SUPREME COURT OF APPEALS CHAMBER. Opening on three sides of the room are Ionic colonnades with bronze-colored capitals and bases of black Belgian marble. Flanking these are aisles, screened from the room by dark red draperies. The ceiling, opened by a paneled skylight, is coffered in bronze. The floor is insulated with compressed cork, and the furnishings are all of American walnut.

The STATE LAW LIBRARY (*open 9–5 Mon.—Fri., 9–12 Sat.*), at the north end of the hallway, has about 85,000 volumes of textbooks on legal subjects, legal philosophy, State reports, and decisions of courts of record of the United States, Canada, and England. The collection was started soon after West Virginia was created in 1863, but until 1892, when the legislature made the first appropriation for reference books, it was supported by contributions from lawyers of the State.

On the fourth floor of the east wing is the STATE DEPARTMENT OF ARCHIVES AND HISTORY (*open 9–5 Mon.—Fri., 9–12 Sat.*). The department has charge of all documents relating to the settlement of the State, the period of the reorganized government of Virginia, the formation of West Virginia from the territory of Virginia, and biographical matter pertaining to important men, public records, state papers, documents of the legislative, executive, and judicial departments and all state officials from June 20, 1863, to the present time. The library has more than 100,000 volumes. All books and papers are for use in the room, but none may be borrowed.

Tours into the DOME are made only with guides (*tours 11:30 and 2:30 daily*). A flight of stairs on the north leads to an inside and outside balcony at the base of the dome. From the interior balcony there is a good view of the rotunda below and of the huge chandelier that hangs on a 45-foot bronze chain.

A door on the north opens to an exterior balcony at the base of the drum, the highest point to which visitors are usually permitted. From the deck of this balcony there is a comprehensive view of the low rugged hills, the city, and the winding river. Encircling the outer drum is a peripteral colonnade of 36 slender Corinthian columns, which rise to a second balcony around the clerestory of the drum, surrounded by a carved balustrade. Below is a sculptured band of festoons. Above the clerestory is the gold-plated cap of the dome, surmounted by a lantern cupola. At the base of the lantern is another balcony surrounded by a metal railing covered with gold leaf. From this balcony may be had an even better view of the city and surrounding country.

On the west lawn of the Capitol are TWO MONUMENTS standing side by side. One, a statue of Stonewall Jackson by Sir Moses Ezekial, was 'erected as a memorial to the Confederate soldiers.' The other, the symbolic figure of a mountaineer, posed by Rimfire Hamrick, is dedicated to 'the brave men and devoted women who saved West Virginia to the Union.' In the southwest corner of the grounds is the figure of a Union soldier; the base of the statue bears an inscription 'to the 32,000 soldiers, sailors and marines contributed by West Virginia to the Union.'

9. Just outside the eastern limits of the Kanawha City section of Charleston on the S. side of US 119 is the LIBBEY-OWENS-FORD GLASS COMPANY PLANT (*private*), the world's largest flat-glass plant under one roof.

The plant, consisting of one large brick building and several smaller ones, extends along the highway for a third of a mile. Here window glass and blanks for plate glass are manufactured. The blanks for plate glass are shipped to other plants of the company for grinding and polishing. The plant employs 1,800 men at capacity.

Glass is produced by fusing sand, soda ash, lime, and certain other ingredients. In the early years of American history, panes for windows were obtained by blowing glass in spherical shapes and whirling these rapidly until they became disks, but the pane was always marred by a defect in the center called a bull's-eye. The substitution of compressed air for lung power was the first step in improving the manufacturing process, but defects in window glass were not eliminated until Michael J. Owens and Edward D. Libbey perfected a more economical machine for its manufacture. Owens was a poor boy who came out of the West Virginia hills to become a glass blower. His ability and aggressiveness earned for him the post of superintendent in the Libbey glass plant at Toledo.

10. Opposite the Libbey-Owens-Ford plant, on the N. side of US 119, beginning just outside the limits of Kanawha City, is the OWENS-ILLINOIS GLASS COMPANY PLANT Number Six, one of the largest bottle factories in the world. It extends along US 119 for a third of a mile and is similar in appearance to the Libbey-Owens-Ford plant. The Owens-Illinois plant and many others use a bottle machine, also invented by Michael J. Owens, which did away with the old process of blowing bottles by lung power. A single machine of this kind does work that formerly required a great many men.

11. The PATRICK STREET MARKET is a row of one-story buildings on each side of Patrick St., from W. Washington St. to Seventh Ave. Seasonal fresh vegetables and dairy products are on sale in open- and glass-front shops, and one section of the market is devoted entirely to poultry. Cider and buttermilk in gallon jugs, honey, fruits in season—including quinces and pawpaws—old-fashioned pumpkins

and squashes in fall, and many locally produced foods are on sale at the market. Handmade chairs, rough brown pottery, and a few other objects of pioneer simplicity can also be found in the various shops.

POINTS OF INTEREST IN ENVIRONS

Kelly Axe and Tool Works, 1.8 *m.;* Carbide and Carbon Chemicals Corporation Plant, 3.9 *m.;* Indian Burial Mound, 3.9 *m.;* U. S. Naval Ordnance Plant, 3.9 *m.* (*see Tour 15c*).

Charles Town

Railroad Stations: North St. at Mildred St. for Baltimore & Ohio R.R.; Harewood Ave. beyond corporation limits for Norfolk and Western Ry.
Bus Station: Thomas Jefferson Hotel, 109 E. Washington St., for Brenner Motor Lines.
Taxis: 25¢ in city.
Street Order and Numbering: Dividing line for east and west, north and south numbering, Jefferson County Courthouse.

Accommodations: 1 hotel; tourist homes and boarding houses.

Information Service: Thomas Jefferson Hotel, 109 E. Washington St.

Motion Picture House: 1.
Swimming: B. & E. Beach, Shenandoah River, 4 m. E. on State 9.
Golf: McDonald Golf Course, 3 m. N. on Shepherdstown Road, 9 holes, greens fee 25¢.

Annual Events: Charles Town Jockey Club Meets, spring and fall; Charles Town Horse Show, first week in Aug.; Fall Flower Show, no fixed date.

CHARLES TOWN (530 alt., 2,434 pop.), seat of Jefferson County and scene of two treason trials, is a tranquil southern town, steeped in tradition and proudly conscious of an aristocratic lineage. Situated in the midst of the fertile, rolling agricultural section of the Eastern Panhandle, it is an orderly pattern of tree-shaded streets and old homes, many of which were built in the late eighteenth century. The mellowness of well-preserved age marks buildings and streets, and an inherent southern leisureliness is evident in the small and quiet business section that surrounds the Jefferson County Courthouse.

In an effort to preserve the traditions and social life brought from Tidewater Virginia by the Washingtons and their contemporaries, Charles Town has always discouraged the establishment of industrial plants and the influx of a laboring class and a foreign-born population. It remains aloof from the soot of industry and is a purely residential community. In the contiguous town of Ranson, however, are industrial plants in which Charles Town residents find employment. In Ranson, too, are the comparative newcomers, industrial workers employed in the brass and iron foundry, the apple-products plants, and the saddlery. There are few retail stores in Ranson, so its residents come to Charles Town to do their shopping and to see the movies.

Charles Town stirs from its easygoing serenity seven times a year—four times when the circuit court sessions create unwonted activity in the courthouse square and business district, and three times when racing meets enliven the whole town. For a month each spring and fall and for four days in August the town assumes a gala air to welcome the several thousand racing fans, most of whom come from Washington and Baltimore. Temporary businesses blossom on nearly every street; the hotel and boarding houses are filled, and many private homekeepers earn a little extra money by taking in roomers; the ordinarily quiet streets are congested with automobiles from many States, and the jargon of race track and stable becomes the idiom of the day.

Although there were settlers in the vicinity of Charles Town possibly as early as Braddock's march through this section in 1755, history does not record their names. About 1770 Colonel Charles Washington, youngest brother of George, acquired a large tract, including the site of the town, and in 1786 had 80 acres surveyed and laid out in streets for a town, which was established by the Virginia Assembly the same year. The place was named Charles Town for its founder, the principal street was named Washington for his family, and other streets were given the Christian names of members of the family.

Most of the first settlers were of English descent, members of the old families of Tidewater Virginia and a few tavern keepers, blacksmiths, tailors, coachmakers, weavers, merchants, and hairdressers who came to serve them. They were followed by Germans, Scots, and Irish who were attracted by the fertile soil. Life in early Charles Town followed much the same serene pattern as today. Industrial activity was confined to one or two gristmills.

The town became an educational and social center. The Charles Town Academy for Boys was founded in 1787 and a few years later a female academy was established across the street from the boys' school. Numerous taverns sprang up, for the wealthy landowners who left the actual work of farming to their many slaves and overseers had much time to spend in genial companionship over wine and cards or in traveling from one home to another for social calls. Among the

---

KEY FOR CHARLES TOWN MAP

1. The JEFFERSON COUNTY COURTHOUSE, NE. corner George and Washington Sts. 2. The SITE OF THE OLD JAIL, SW. corner George and Washington Sts. 3. CHARLES WASHINGTON HALL, NW. corner George and Washington Sts. 4. The INDEPENDENT FIRE COMPANY, 110 N. George St. 5. The TIFFIN HOUSE, Liberty St. between Charles and Lawrence Sts. 6. OLD EPISCOPAL LECTURE ROOM, NE. corner Lawrence and Liberty Sts. 7. CHARLES WASHINGTON'S OFFICE, Lawrence St. between W. Liberty and W. Washington Sts. 8. The CITIZENS FIRE COMPANY, NW. corner W. Washington and West Sts. 9. MORDINGTON, Mordington Lane at the southern end of town. 10. The SITE OF THE JOHN BROWN GALLOWS, Samuel St. between Mc-Curdy St. and Beckwith Alley. 11. The WILSON HOUSE, SE. corner Mildred and E. Avis Sts. 12. ZION EPISCOPAL CHURCH, E. Congress St. between Mildred and Church Sts. 13. The PRESBYTERIAN CHURCH, Washington St. between Samuel and Mildred Sts. 14. The CRANE HOUSE, SE. corner W. Washington and Samuel Sts. 15. The CHARLES TOWN RACE TRACK.

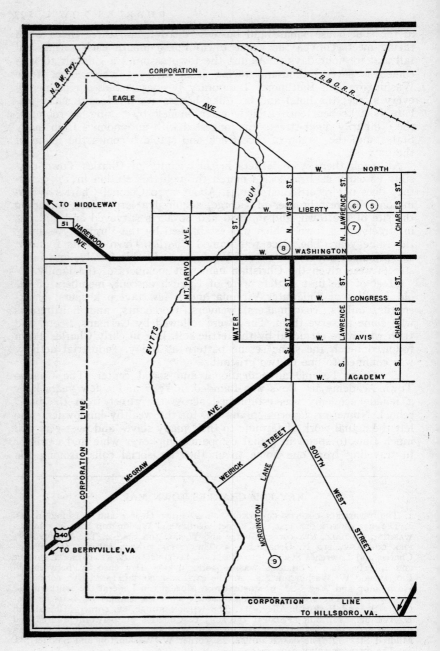

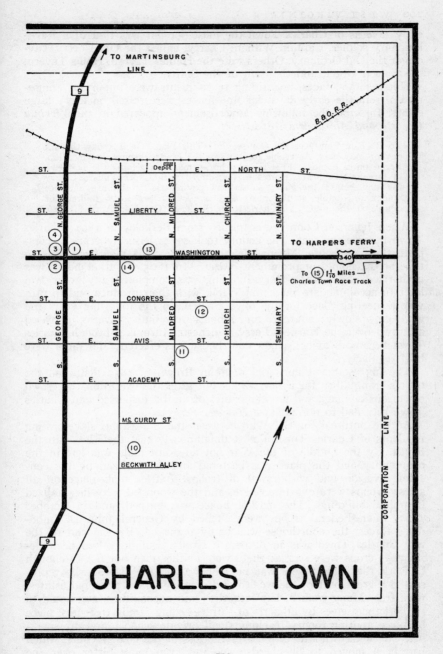

TO MARTINSBURG
LINE

9

B.&O.R.R.

St. Depot E. NORTH ST.

N. GEORGE ST.

N. SAMUEL ST.

N. MILDRED ST.

N. CHURCH ST.

N. SEMINARY ST.

ST. E. LIBERTY ST.

4
3 1 E. 13 WASHINGTON ST.
2

TO HARPERS FERRY

340

To 15 1 1/10 Miles
Charles Town Race Track

14

GEORGE ST.

SAMUEL ST.

MILDRED ST.

CHURCH ST.

SEMINARY ST.

ST. E. CONGRESS ST.

12

ST. E. AVIS ST.

11

S. GEORGE ST.

S. SAMUEL ST.

S. MILDRED ST.

S. CHURCH ST.

S. SEMINARY ST.

ST. E. ACADEMY ST.

MC CURDY ST.

N

10

BECKWITH ALLEY

9

CORPORATION LINE

CHARLES TOWN

early taverns of Charles Town the most popular was that of a Revolutionary soldier, Captain William Cherry, called the Old Cherry Tavern or the Old Ordinary. Others were the Haines Tavern, Holl's Tavern, the Fulton Hotel, and the Sign of the Shift.

Horse shows, races, and riding tournaments were important amusements from the early days, for fine horses were raised on every large estate. In 1786 the following advertisement appeared in the *Virginia Gazette and Alexandria Advertiser:*

> To Be Run For Over the Course Near This Place, On Tuesday the 9th day of May next, Agreeable to Rules of the Fredericksburg Jockey Club. For a purse of 40 £. Free for any horse, mare, or gelding the best two in three 3-mile heats. Horses to be entered with Capt. William Cherry the day before the race; subscribers paying thirty shillings entrance money or double at the post; and non-subscribers forty shillings or double at the post. . . . Charlestown, Berkeley Co., Va., April 8, 1786.

When Jefferson County was formed from Berkeley in 1801, Charles Town became the seat. The county took seven leisurely years to complete the courthouse. Meanwhile, the county court met from time to time at the homes of prominent citizens. In 1805 a market house was authorized and a three-story building was completed a year or two later to accommodate the country folk with their produce and to provide a meeting place for the town council. In the following years the town grew slowly; churches and schools were built; taverns increased as travel over the Harpers Ferry-Winchester turnpike through Charles Town became heavier; a new courthouse was erected; and races were held regularly.

The imprisonment and trial of John Brown in 1859 disturbed the town's tranquillity for a few weeks, but after the execution the crowd of curious civilians and the companies of militia dispersed and Charles Town returned to normal (*see Harpers Ferry*).

At the outbreak of the War between the States the slave-owning residents of Charles Town almost unanimously cast their lot with the South. By the middle of the War not an adult male was left in the community and the place was battered and demoralized by the constant invasion and withdrawal of troops. Battles took place on all sides. Troops were quartered here, and the wounded were hospitalized in public buildings. The market house was burned, and in October 1863, when Federal troops were shelled by General John D. Imboden's forces, the courthouse was badly damaged. By the end of the war Charles Town was in desperate straits. Buildings had been destroyed; crops were scarce; there were neither men nor horses enough to work the fields; there was no money; and the slaves, who represented a great part of the wealth and security of the principal estates, were free. Many women, left fatherless and husbandless, attempted to support themselves by all sorts of shifts—selling family treasures, piece by piece, renting rooms, teaching small private schools, and dressmaking. Charles Town was bitter over the loss of the county court, which had been moved to Shepherdstown, and even more bitter over the annexation of Jefferson County by the new State of West Virginia, for, through enforcement of test oaths, most of the town's population had been disfranchised and had no voice in the decision. Many refused to acknowledge the new State and continued to subscribe themselves as from 'Jefferson County, Virginia.'

Faced with the mighty task of reconstruction, the survivors returned to the normal occupation, farming. Horse shows and races were resumed in 1867, but the new State forbade betting. With the discovery that the soil and climate of the Panhandle were ideal for apple culture, large orchards were planted, and canning and by-products plants were established in the adjoining community of Ranson, which soon became a packing center. The county seat was returned to Charles Town in the fall of 1871 amid great rejoicing.

Pari-mutuel betting was legalized by the State in 1933, and Charles Town returned to an old love—horseracing. Periodic racing meets now bring back the old excitement and a measure of prosperity.

POINTS OF INTEREST

1. The JEFFERSON COUNTY COURTHOUSE, NE. corner N. George and E. Washington Sts., was twice the scene of treason trials— John Brown in 1859 and the leaders of the miners' armed march on Logan County in 1921. It is a red brick Georgian Colonial building set on a high stone foundation and separated from the street by a tiny yard. Extending across the front is a tall portico with four Doric columns, their fluted metal bases supporting an angular pediment, the design of which is repeated in pediments over the windows of the first floor and above the four faces of the clock in the square-domed tower. A small iron balcony juts above the front door, and ornamental brackets follow the lines of the eaves. A metal tablet on one corner of the building honors the memory of Colonel Charles Washington. The old candle-burning chandelier, now wired for electricity, survives in the courtroom.

The first county courthouse in Charles Town, a small brick building erected in 1808 on the lot donated by Washington, was replaced about 1836 by a larger structure, nucleus of the present courthouse. During the War between the States the court records were removed by wagon to Lexington, Virginia, and the courthouse was damaged by shellfire. The building was then neglected until 1871–2, when it was extensively remodeled and the records reinstalled. A wing was added at the rear in 1916.

The miners' trial, in 1922, was in sharp contrast to the tense atmosphere that prevailed in the first floor room (now used by the county commissioners) when John Brown was tried and found guilty of treason, conspiracy to commit treason, and murder, in connection with his seizure of Harpers Ferry.

Brown was arraigned one week after his capture for preliminary examination. Cannon were trained on the courthouse, a threat against any who had ideas of either rescue or lynching, and the prisoner walked from the jail to the courthouse between files of militia. Asked by the court if he had counsel, Brown took the opportunity to make a defiant speech, beginning with these words:

> Virginians, I did not ask for quarter at the time I was taken . . . If you seek my blood, you can have it at any moment, without this mockery of a trial . . . I am ready for my fate . . . I have now little further to ask, other than that I may not be foolishly insulted only as cowardly barbarians insult those who fall into their power.

Counsel was assigned by the court.

On the following day, after the grand jury had returned a true bill embodying all three counts named in the indictment, Brown changed his attitude. Wounded during the raid, he had to be carried to the courthouse on a cot. He made another speech, this time requesting that the trial be postponed because, he contended, he was incapacitated from having been beaten about the head with the blunt end of a sword wielded by one of his captors. The jail physician testified that Brown was perfectly able to stand trial and the plea for delay was denied. Throughout most of the trial he lay on the cot, seldom rousing except to answer questions.

Brown reassumed his defiance, however, when his counsel sought to introduce evidence that insanity was hereditary in the Brown family. Such a defense would have meant repudiation of his avowed aims, and Brown arose from his cot to berate his attorneys:

> . . . I look upon it as a miserable artifice and pretext of those who ought to take a different course in regard to me, if they took any at all, and I view it with contempt more than otherwise . . .

Counsel was obliged to abandon the idea of defense on these grounds.

In his final address to the jury, Prosecutor Andrew Hunter declared Brown's real purpose went much further than a mere plot to aid slaves in reaching Canada. He asserted Brown had established residence in Maryland, just over the Virginia Line, 'for the nefarious and hellish purpose of rallying forces into this Commonwealth, and establishing himself at Harpers Ferry, as the starting point for a new government. Whatever it was, whether tragical, or farcical and ridiculous, as Brown's counsel has presented it, his conduct showed . . . that it was not alone for the purpose of carrying off slaves . . . His "Provisional Government" was a real thing, and no debating society, as his counsel would have us believe . . .'

The jury required less than two hours to reach its verdict of guilty on all three counts as charged. There was no demonstration; only a slight rustle in the crowded courtroom as the tension relaxed. Brown did not raise his head or show any emotion.

On the following day, Brown sat at counsel's table, and when asked if he had anything to say before sentence was pronounced, he arose and, hands resting on the table, addressed the court:

> I deny everything but what I have all along admitted; of a desire on my part to free slaves . . . I never did intend murder, or treason, or the destruction of property, or to excite slaves to rebellion . . . it is unjust that I should suffer such a penalty . . . Had I acted in behalf of the rich, the powerful, the intelligent, the so-called great . . . every man in this court would have deemed it an act worthy of reward . . . I say I am too young yet to understand that God is any respecter of persons . . .

When Brown resumed his seat Judge Richard Parker promptly pronounced sentence; that Brown be publicly hanged on December 2— just one month from the day of sentence. A man who began to clap his hands was taken into custody, and townsmen hastened to explain to northern visitors that he was not a resident of the neighborhood.

During the month's interim Brown adopted the role of martyr for himself, declaring 'I am worth now infinitely more to die than to live.' Some southern leaders expressed the fear that Brown's execution would serve to forward his cause more than anything he could do if permitted to live, and this belief was given credence by the statements of some of the more fervent abolitionists. Henry Ward Beecher said:

> Let no man pray that Brown be spared. Let Virginia make him a martyr. Now he has only blundered. His cause was noble; his work miserable. But a cord and a gibbet would redeem all that, and round up Brown's failure with a heroic success.

On December 2 Henry Wadsworth Longfellow wrote in his diary:

> This will be a great day in our history. The date of a new Revolution— quite as much needed as the old one. Even now as I write they are leading old John Brown to execution in Virginia for attempting to rescue slaves. They are sowing the wind to reap the whirlwind, which will come soon.

Abraham Lincoln's appraisal of the *cause célèbre,* made public on the same date, was more dispassionate and objective:

> Old John Brown has been executed for treason against a State. We cannot object, even though he agreed with us in thinking slavery wrong. That cannot excuse violence, bloodshed and treason. It could avail him nothing that he might think himself right.

Sixty-three years after John Brown was sent to the gallows, more than 200 miners and union leaders, indicted in Logan County on charges ranging from misdemeanor to treason, were brought to Charles Town for trial on change of venue as an aftermath of the miners' armed march of 1921. Three men, Walter Allen, William Blizzard, and Cal McCoy, were tried on treason charges. Allen was convicted and sentenced to ten years' imprisonment. Blizzard and McCoy were acquitted. Others were acquitted or found guilty of minor offenses.

2. The SITE OF THE OLD JAIL, SW. corner S. George and W. Washington Sts., in which John Brown was confined in 1859, is occupied by a modern, red brick, one-story post office. The old jail, built of brick and stone, stood on this site from about 1803 until 1922, when it was razed to make way for the present building.

3. CHARLES WASHINGTON HALL, NW. corner N. George and W. Washington St., sometimes called the Market Building, a two-story brick structure painted gray, with a wide gable at the center of each façade, stands on the site of the public market, erected about 1805. Engaged brick pilasters divide the façades into three sections with the largest in the center. The first floor is occupied by shops. The second floor, used for offices, has arched windows surmounted by brick pediments. The original three-story market house was destroyed in 1862 when Federal soldiers set fire to it to prevent ammunition they had stored there from falling into the hands of advancing Confederate forces. It was rebuilt in 1872 with part of the original materials. At one time the Charles Town post office was in this building, and the first rural free delivery mail route in the country was inaugurated from this post office, while William L. Wilson of Charles Town was Post-master General under President Grover Cleveland. Although three routes, starting from Charles Town, Halltown, and Uvilla, had been designated for simultaneous openings on October 1, 1896, Harry C. Gibson, the Charles Town carrier, started over his route a few days before the official time. A marker on the present post-office grounds commemorates the event.

4. The INDEPENDENT FIRE COMPANY, 110 N. George St., one of two independent fire companies in Charles Town, occupies a three-story, gray-painted brick structure, erected in 1895, with square towers at the front corners. A garland of black crepe often hangs over the entrance, for the fire company honors the memory of deceased members by hanging crepe for 60 days. The company was organized in 1884 under Captain Julius C. Holmes. Upon organization of the group there was a heated contest between Holmes and J. W. Russell for captaincy of the company, and when Holmes won, Russell seceded with his supporters and formed the Citizens Fire Company. For a number of years the two companies were bitter rivals and when both answered a fire alarm the members spent as much time fighting each other for the honor of putting out the fire as they did in fighting the fire. The company that succeeded in attaching its hose first had to patrol the line to prevent members of the other group from cutting it. The rivalry gradually died out, but the town still has two companies.

5. The TIFFIN HOUSE (*private*), W. Liberty St. between N. Charles and Lawrence Sts., is a red brick two-story house with wide end chimneys, gable roof, and a small four-columned portico. The flat deck roof of the portico forms a second-story balcony with an iron railing. The house was owned by Edward Tiffin, who practiced medicine in Charles Town from 1789 to 1796 and afterwards became the first governor of Ohio.

6. The OLD EPISCOPAL LECTURE ROOM (*private*), NE. corner N. Lawrence and W. Liberty Sts., is a two-story building of light-gray native limestone converted into a residence by the addition of a frame porch and a frame wing at one side. Stone quoins are used at the cor-

ners and over the windows. Over the shuttered side windows of the second story large hewn stones are arranged in pointed arched headings. The building was erected prior to 1801 and used until 1844 for Sunday school and mid-week meetings by the Episcopal congregation of Saint George's Chapel and later by the congregation of the Old Grove Church in Charles Town.

7. CHARLES WASHINGTON'S OFFICE, N. Lawrence St. between W. Liberty and W. Washington Sts., is a small one-room brick building painted yellow and used for storage. Charles Washington built this office about the time of the founding of Charles Town and rode into town several times a week to conduct business and meet with the town trustees here.

8. The CITIZENS FIRE COMPANY, NW. corner W. Washington and N. West Sts., occupies a two-story brick gable-roofed building that was operated as a tavern about 1840 by Henry Haines. The tavern was well known as a stop on the turnpike that passed through Charles Town, and during the War between the States was used as a barracks by Union troops. Later it was used for stores, and for a short time was occupied by a girls' school. The fire company bought the building in 1899 and built over the pavement a cornerwise marquee on which was erected a high, square frame tower. Part of the building is occupied by apartments.

9. MORDINGTON (*private*), S. end of Mordington Lane at the southern end of town, was originally Happy Retreat, the home of Charles Washington; he died there in 1797. Between two-story brick wings is a wide two-and-a-half-story central unit with a fanlight in the center of the gable end, which forms the front of the house. The Georgian Colonial building is painted yellow, with green shutters. The 12-paned sash windows are trimmed in white; door and window sills are of native limestone. The massive hand-carved door, with transom and sidelights, is sheltered by a flat-roofed Doric portico. The two wings were built by Charles Washington after 1774 and originally were connected by a covered passage. The house was sold by his daughter to Judge Isaac R. Douglas, who renamed the estate Mordington and in 1833 built the central unit. Behind the east wing is a one-room brick building to which is joined a one-room stone wing; this was originally the kitchen and contains a huge fireplace with a brick oven. A brick slave house stands at the rear of the kitchen, and scattered flagstones and bits of brick paving mark the site of other slave quarters. In the grove east of the house a limestone tablet marks the place where Charles and Mildred Washington and two of their grandchildren are believed to be buried.

10. The SITE OF THE JOHN BROWN GALLOWS, S. Samuel St. between McCurdy St. and Beckwith Alley, is marked by a pyramid of three stones, said to have been taken from Brown's cell in the Charles Town jail.

Early in the morning of the date set for his execution John Brown was awake and reading his Bible. He wrote a brief note to his wife, enclosing a codicil to his will and the epitaphs of his dead sons and himself, which he wished chiseled on the old tombstone of his grandfather, for whom he was named. Guards came and led him to the cells of five men who had been with him in the Harpers Ferry raid, all under indictment for their participation. Brown gave four his blessing as he said good-bye to them, but to John E. Cook, who had given damaging testimony against him, the condemned man said: 'You have made false statements that I sent you to Harpers Ferry.' As Brown left the jail he handed a piece of paper to one of the attendants. It read:

Charlestown, Va. 2nd December, 1859.

I, John Brown, am now quite certain that the crimes of this guilty land: will never be purged away; but with blood. I had as I now think; vainly flattered myself that without very much bloodshed it might be done.

Beside the jail porch was a wagon upon which rested a coffin. In front of the wagon stood three companies of infantrymen, their rifles gleaming in the sunlight. Additional companies were swinging into formation a short distance away. 'I had no idea Governor Wise considered my execution so important,' Brown commented. He climbed into the wagon, seated himself atop his coffin, the driver spoke to the team of white horses, and the procession to the gallows began.

Cannon were trained on the scaffold, which sat on a low rounded knoll, and 1,500 troops were massed around it. Behind the scaffold could be seen the red and gray uniforms of the Virginia Military Institute cadets. The infantry battalion was commanded by Major William Graham, and the howitzer section of 21 men was commanded by Major Thomas J. Jackson, who later achieved distinction as General 'Stonewall' Jackson. In the ranks of Company F of Richmond stood a militiaman who was later shot to death for his own crime—John Wilkes Booth.

'This is a beautiful country,' John Brown remarked as the wagon drew into the square of troops, 'I never had the pleasure of seeing it before.' He mounted the scaffold ahead of the attendants, lifted his loosely bound hands, took off his hat and dropped it to the floor. The hood was slipped over his head and the rope adjusted to his neck. 'I can't see, gentlemen, you will have to lead me,' Brown said through the hood. The sheriff asked him if he wished a private signal just before the end. 'It doesn't matter,' he answered in a composed, deliberate voice. 'If only they would not keep me waiting so long.' A short time later a wagon, drawn by a team of white horses, bore his body away.

11. The WILSON HOUSE, SE. corner S. Mildred and E. Avis Sts., is a two-story clapboarded house painted yellow, with a one-story portico. Set back from the street in a shaded lawn, it is surrounded by trees and shrubs. From 1876 until his death in 1900, this was the home of William L. Wilson, soldier, lawyer, and educator, who moved

to Charles Town with his widowed mother in 1847 when he was four years old. He was educated in Charles Town Academy, Columbian College at Washington, and the University of Virginia. During the War between the States he served with the Virginia cavalry and afterwards, when the test oath was annulled in 1871, began the practice of law in Charles Town. He served as president of West Virginia University in 1882, as a member of the U. S. House of Representatives from 1893 to 1895, and as Postmaster General under President Grover Cleveland. While a member of Congress, he was chairman of the ways and means committee and drafted the tariff bill that, with modifications, passed under the name of the Wilson-Gorman bill. It included the first proposals for an income tax. From 1897 until his death he served as president of Washington and Lee University.

12. ZION EPISCOPAL CHURCH, E. Congress St. between S. Mildred and S. Church Sts., is a red brick, ivy-covered church with a high steeple and Gothic stained-glass windows. In the vestry is a walnut communion table, the only surviving piece of furniture from St. George's Chapel (*see Tour 1A*). Surrounding the church and separating it from the street is a cemetery in which are the graves of about 75 members of the Washington family and of many Revolutionary and Confederate soldiers. West of the church in the Rooker burial plot, partly hidden by a sassafras tree, is a tombstone erected in 1788 by LaFayette in memory of 'Master Tallifero Brooks,' the child of his friend, Commander Walter Brooks. Originally placed in the family burial plot at 'Retirement,' near Alexandria, Virginia, the stone was brought to Charles Town in 1880 by Miss Harriet Rooker, granddaughter of the commander. The first church on this site was built in 1819 to succeed St. George's Chapel, and was known as the Grove Church. It was furnished with the imported pews and other equipment from the chapel. The Grove Church was replaced in 1849 by another building, which was destroyed by fire a few weeks after completion. The present church was built in 1852.

13. The PRESBYTERIAN CHURCH, E. Washington St. between N. Samuel and N. Mildred Sts., is a plain brick structure of Greek Revival design fronted by a high Ionic portico and surmounted by a steepled belfry adorned with coupled fluted pilasters. In the vestibule hangs a deed signed by Charles and Mildred Washington, dated 1787, conveying to the Presbyterian congregation a lot at the corner of Congress and West Streets, upon which the first church was built. The present building, erected in 1853, is the third to serve the congregation. The first church, a small stone structure, was built in 1787 and torn down in 1830 to make way for a large stone building. The second church was razed in 1851 and rebuilt in its original form on Liberty Street by Major Wells J. Hawks who used it for many years as a coach factory. It is now a garage. On the original site of the church nothing remains but a few tumbled weather-beaten tombstones of

the old graveyard and numerous holes from which bodies have been removed for reinterment in other cemeteries.

14. The CRANE HOUSE (*private*), SE. corner E. Washington and S. Samuel Sts., is a two-story, cream-painted brick residence, partly covered with Virginia creeper. A wing extends along Samuel Street. The house was built prior to 1800 and was the home of Battaile Muse, Washington's man of business. In 1804 it was leased by Ferdinando Fairfax who inherited the title of Lord Fairfax but renounced it because he considered 'the honor of being an American citizen quite sufficient in this free land.' Fairfax was prominent in the early governmental affairs of the town, and manufactured whisky in partnership with Robert Worthington. He speculated in land, and became so involved that he was declared bankrupt.

15. The CHARLES TOWN RACE TRACK, 1.1 m. E. on US 340, is a three-quarter mile course with a grandstand seating nearly 4,000 persons, and stables for 700 horses. Racing meets are held here each spring and fall by the Charles Town Jockey Club, and a four-day horse show and racing meet is held every August by the Charles Town Horse Show Association. Except for the years during the War between the States, races and shows have been held in or near Charles Town annually since 1786. Following the war the new State prohibited betting, but after 1867 horse shows and races were held by various associations; prizes were given for winners in various classes. The Charles Town Horse Show Association, previous owner of the track, was organized in 1914, and still has annual shows and races. In 1933 pari-mutuel betting was legalized by the State and a year later the present Jockey Club purchased the track.

POINTS OF INTEREST IN ENVIRONS

St. George's Chapel, 1.8 *m.;* Claymont Court, 2.6 *m.;* Harewood, 3.3 *m.;* Middleway, 6.9 *m.;* Prato Rio, 10.9 *m.;* Traveler's Rest, 14.6 *m.* (*see Tour 1A*). George Washington's Cave, 2.9 *m.;* Blakeley, 3.4 *m.;* Beall Air, 4.7 *m.* (*see Tour 2*).

Clarksburg

Railroad Station: Baltimore St. at N. end of 5th St. for Baltimore & Ohio R.R.
Interurban Trolley: Terminal Building, S. end of N. 4th St. Bridge for interurban cars to Fairmont, fare 77¢; Weston, 70¢; Wolf Summit, 21¢; Bridgeport, 14¢.
Bus Stations: 117 N. 4th St. for West Virginia Transportation Co.; Terminal Building, S. end of N. 4th St. Bridge for Capitol and Atlantic Greyhound Lines, Blue Ridge Lines, and Reynolds Transportation Co.
Airport: Tri-County Airport, 6 m. E. on US 50; taxi, $1.75; no scheduled service.
Taxis: 1 to 4 passengers, 25¢ and up according to distance.
Streetcars and Busses: 7¢ local.
Traffic Regulations: Parking meters, 5¢ per hour; chief one-way streets: W. Main (east) and W. Pike (west).
Street Order and Numbering: Dividing lines, Elk Creek for E. and W. numbering; Pike St. for N. and S.

Accommodations: 9 hotels; tourist homes and boarding houses.

Information Service: A.A.A., Waldo Hotel, N. 4th St. between W. Pike St. and Hewes Ave.; Chamber of Commerce, 214 Court St.

Radio Station: WBLK (1400 kc.).
Motion Picture Houses: 3.
Golf: Clarksburg Country Club, 4 m. W. on US 19, and 2 m. on Country Club Rd., 9 holes, greens fee $1; Sunnycroft Club, 3 m. W. on US 19, 9 holes, greens fee 50¢.
Tennis: Broadway St., 25¢ per hr.
Skating: Rollerdrome, 2 m. S. on State 20 at Nutters Fort, ladies 20¢, men 30¢.

Annual Events: Washington Irving and Victory High School football game, fall.

CLARKSBURG (1,007 alt., 28,866 pop.), in the north-central part of the State at the confluence of Elk Creek and the West Fork of the Monongahela River, is a busy industrial city—the trading center for an area of coal mines, oil and gas fields, and grazing land. The winding streams and the crowding low hills divide Clarksburg into five sections, which, loosely connected by a maze of bridges, bear little relation to each other in street planning or numbering.

Clarksburg always appears to be busy, but on Saturdays the streets are jammed by a steady stream of traffic that enters from all sides over a network of State and Federal highways. The sidewalks are so crowded with cattlemen, farmers, miners, and their families that there is hardly room for movement. The shopping section, between W. Main and W. Pike Streets and Second and Sixth Streets, is particularly congested. The area around the courthouse, however, is always lined with people in from the country to attend to legal matters, prospective jurors when court is in session, people from town and country seeing each other after long intervals, and chronic talkers about weather, crops, religion, and politics.

The city has five glass plants producing flat glass, tumblers and containers, glass tubing, and more than half of the world's toy marbles. Other manufactories produce cinder building blocks, carbon electrodes, tinplate, pottery, and beer. Several coal, oil, and gas companies maintain headquarters in the city.

The first white settler on the site of Clarksburg was John Simpson, a trapper from the South Branch Valley, who in 1764 erected a hunting camp on the West Fork River opposite the mouth of Elk Creek. By 1772, other pioneers had settled near by and erected Nutters Fort on the site now occupied by a small industrial town of the same name. Simpson moved farther west.

In 1773 Daniel Davisson took up a claim of 400 acres on the site of the present business district, and he was soon followed by others. At the first public meeting of the settlers in 1781, a Mr. Shinn suggested that the place be called Clarksburg in honor of George Rogers Clark. The new name was evidently put into use immediately, since it appears on deeds for land recorded in 1782. By 1784 Clarksburg, platted by Daniel Davisson and Joseph Hastings, consisted of a double row of cabins, about three blocks long, on both sides of Elk Creek. At the first meeting of the Harrison County Court in that year the village became the county seat, and a year later it was established as a town by the Virginia assembly. In 1788 a branch road was opened to Morgantown to connect with Winchester, and three years later one was completed to the Ohio River opposite Marietta. Travelers to and from the Ohio settlement often came by way of Clarksburg, stopping here because the town was on the very fringe of settled territory. Cattle were collected here for driving westward, and furs and skins were packed for shipment eastward.

By 1798 Clarksburg had more than 50 houses, a post office, and an academy. In the next decade boatyards and wagon shops were established. In 1810 the first newspaper, the *By-Stander*, was established. Whisky and some flour and meal were transported to Pittsburgh, floated on flatboats down the West Fork and Monongahela Rivers or taken across the mountains on pack horses, but generally, as the shipment of breadstuff was too expensive, the grain was fed to cattle, horses, and hogs, which could transport themselves 'on the hoof' to eastern markets.

Clarksburg's central position, which made it a convenient point for collection of goods to be shipped down-river to Brownsville, Pennsylvania, and thence eastward, led to partially successful attempts in 1830 to improve the Monongahela and West Fork Rivers for navigation. In the same year a line of stages was established connecting Clarksburg with the National Road at Brownsville, and six years later the Northwestern Turnpike was completed.

By 1846 the town had two academies and 1,100 citizens, whom J. H. Diss Debar, State commissioner of immigration, described as a 'somewhat exclusive conservative set.'

The coming of the Baltimore & Ohio Railroad in 1856 quickened the industrial life of the town and made it an important military and supply base for Federal forces during the War between the States. No actual fighting occurred here, though Federal troops built earthworks, the remains of which are visible, on Lowndes Hill to the south and mounted guns on the summit of Pinnickinnick Hill to the north.

While there was civil commotion at the outbreak of the war, the town was largely Union in sympathy. The new-State movement of 1861 had its inception at a mass meeting in Clarksburg. The Clarksburg convention condemned the Secession Ordinance and laid plans for the First Wheeling Convention, to be composed of the 'wisest, best and discreetest men' of Virginia (see History).

A narrow-gauge railroad from Clarksburg to Weston, authorized in 1866 and completed in 1879, was the beginning of a system of short lines converging at Clarksburg and Grafton. The opening of the Fairmont coal fields in 1870 brought prosperity to Clarksburg, for the Pittsburgh coal seam extends southward through Harrison County.

Clarksburg boomed with the opening of oil fields west and south of the city about 1889. Railroad lines were built to transport supplies to the mines and oil fields and to ship out coal and manufactured products. Grass-carpeted hillsides were dotted with oil and gas derricks. Municipal improvements were inaugurated; a waterworks was established; an electric light plant was opened; a street railway was built in 1900; and gas was piped in to light and heat the city. Fields of corn and wheat gave way to smoking factories; streets were paved; tall office buildings were erected; and the city grew with little thought of plan. Between 1900 and 1920 the population increased from 4,050 to 27,869, and the glass industry, a direct outgrowth of an abundant supply of natural gas, became the main support of the city. Many chemical plants had been established in the vicinity of Clarksburg prior to the First World War. When the war began and the chemicals hitherto imported from Germany were cut off, the country looked to the Clarksburg area for its supply of many items, such as brine for making chlorine gas and by-products of coal, gas, and oil.

POINTS OF INTEREST

The DAVISSON CEMETERY, W. Main St. between Summer and S. Chestnut Sts., is a grassy tract of land high above the street level, enclosed by an iron picket fence. Only a few headstones with illegible inscriptions remain. Daniel Davisson, founder of the town, and his contemporaries are buried here in unmarked graves. Davisson deeded the cemetery in 1790 to the Hopewell Baptist congregation. A few years later the first church in Clarksburg, no longer standing, was built on the lot. The graveyard was used until after the War between the States. In 1930 it was cleared of underbrush by the D.A.R. and the few remaining headstones were straightened.

The EPISCOPAL CHURCH, N.W. corner S. 6th and W. Main Sts., built in 1853 by the Reverend Robert A. Castleman, is a one-story structure of gray-painted brick with Gothic arched windows and a square tower at the front. Over the door is the inscription, '1853 The Lord is in His Holy Temple.' The church is furnished with old-fashioned walnut box pews.

The DUNCAN HOUSE (*private*), 521 W. Main St., is the oldest dwelling in Clarksburg. The original house is a plain two-story brick structure, painted brown. A wing, projecting in an ell toward the street, and a porch have been added; the original small-paned windows set high in the walls have been altered to full length, arched, sash windows. The interior contains the original wideboard flooring and hand-carved woodwork and mantels. The house, probably built sometime before 1800, was bought by Judge Edwin S. Duncan in 1826 from heirs of Daniel Davisson and is still owned by the Duncan family.

The NATHAN GOFF HOUSE (*private*), 463 W. Main St., is a large three-story red brick structure with a mansard roof, set in a narrow yard enclosed by an iron picket fence. The windows are tall and narrow with brown inside shutters. The roof is broken by many small dormers. The house was built in 1840 by Nathan Goff, who served as an officer in the Union Army during the War between the States and was Secretary of the Navy under President Rutherford B. Hayes. Later he was a member of the House of Representatives and the United States Senate. In 1876 and in 1888, Goff was Republican candidate for governor. An unofficial count of the vote of 1888 gave Goff a small plurality, but his opponent, A. B. Fleming of Fairmont, contested the count and the matter was referred to the State legislature. Four persons claimed the governorship. Goff took the oath of office and demanded the position. Fleming also claimed the office, and Robert S. Carr, president of the senate, maintained it was vacant and under the constitution he was entitled to the seat. Governor Emanuel Willis Wilson refused to yield to their claims and continued to hold office for nearly 12 months after his term had expired. After a year of investigation, which revealed that 12,000 more votes had been cast than there were qualified voters, the legislature declared Fleming the winner by a plurality of 237 votes. He was inaugurated February 5, 1890. Nathan Goff's son, Guy Despard Goff, born in Clarksburg in 1863, also served in the United States Senate.

The SITE OF THE BIRTHPLACE OF STONEWALL JACKSON, 328 W. Main St., is marked by a bronze tablet on the wall of a ten-cent store. Here stood the small brick house where Thomas Jonathan Jackson, Confederate military hero, was born January 21, 1824. In 1830 he went to live on his grandfather's farm, now Jackson's Mill. He walked the three miles to Weston to attend brief sessions of school there and at 18 entered the United States Military Academy, where, tradition says, he was so engrossed in his studies he did not speak to a girl during his entire cadetship. In 1846 he was graduated 17th in a class of 59. In the Mexican War, Jackson was brevetted captain and major for heroic conduct, but resigned from the army in 1852 to become professor of artillery tactics and natural philosophy at Virginia Military Institute, Lexington, Virginia, a post he held for ten years. With the outbreak of the War between the States, Jackson, who deplored the idea of a war over slavery but hated abolitionists, resigned his professorship to become a colonel of the Virginia Volunteers. By October 1862 he had risen to the rank of lieutenant general, second in command to General Robert E. Lee, and his command, noted for heroic conduct, became famous as the Jackson Brigade. During the First Battle of Bull Run, their firm stand caused General Barnard E. Bee to exclaim, 'There is Jackson standing like a stone wall.' From this remark came the nickname 'Stonewall,' which Jackson always insisted was meant for his brigade, not for himself. On Sundays, whenever possible, he avoided fighting and held religious services. Before important engagements or after a campaign, he would call his troops together for devotions. Ordinarily a reserved and modest man, he occasionally lost his temper. When the Confederate Secretary of War had frustrated his plan for holding the town of Romney, Jackson indignantly wrote to him offering his resignation, and to Governor Letcher of Virginia:

This morning I received an order from the secretary of war to General Loring and his command to fall back from Romney to Winchester. The order was promptly complied with, but as the order was given without consulting me, and is abandoning to the enemy what has cost me much preparation, expense and exposure to secure, and is in direct conflict with military plans, and implies a want of confidence in my capacity to judge when General Loring's troops should fall back, and is an attempt to control military operations in detail from the secretary's desk, at a distance I have . . . requested to be ordered back to the institute . . . If I have ever acquired, through the blessings of Providence, any influence over troops, this undoing of my work by the secretary may greatly diminish my influence . . . I take it for granted that he had done what he believed to be best, but I regard such policy ruinous.

The matter was smoothed over and Jackson remained in command. After the Battle of Chancellorsville he was wounded by his own men, who mistook him and several other officers for Federal cavalry. Weakened by the wound, Jackson died of pneumonia May 10, 1863.

The HARRISON COUNTY COURTHOUSE, W. Main and S. 3rd Sts., is a six-story modern structure of buff limestone and black granite, erected in 1931. A terrace wall of polished black granite with an inside boxwood border encloses the courthouse yard. Trees shade the terrace and the entrance walk, which is paved with pearl-gray granite. A metal flagpole surmounts the main façade of the building, and below it, in the parapet wall, is the town clock. On either side of the clock, panels sculptured in low relief represent the *Scales of Justice*.

Decorative eagles with outspread wings, of white Benedict metal, designed by Henry Hering, surmount long modern lanterns on each side of the doorway. At the head of the short flight of steps leading to the first floor, a block of black granite supports an open book of metal, on which are inscribed the Roman numerals from i to x, symbolizing the Ten Commandments of Mosaic law. The main entrance is through sliding doors that open into a corridor with gray Tennessee marble floor, low wainscoting, and white plaster walls. The ceiling is of cast aluminum, the staircase of marble, and the floors of mosaic rubber tile in shades of brown. The walls of the offices and courtrooms are of black and gold marble. On the fourth floor is the HARRISON COUNTY LAW LIBRARY (*open 9–5 weekdays*), which contains about 3,554 volumes. The present building is the fifth to house the courts of Harrison County. The first, built in 1787 and replaced in 1813, was a small one-room frame structure at the northeast corner of Main and Second Streets.

The JACKSON CEMETERY, E. Pike St. between Cherry St. and Charleston Ave., is a public cemetery, part of which has been converted into a playground, and is the burial place of members of Stonewall Jackson's family. In the Jackson family plot, enclosed by an iron picket fence, are the graves of John Jackson and wife, Elizabeth Cummins, great-grandparents of Stonewall Jackson; Mrs. Mary Payne Jackson and Mrs. Mary Coles Payne, sister and mother of Dorothy (Dolly) Madison; Jonathan Jackson and Elizabeth Jackson, father and sister of Stonewall Jackson. The plot was granted by the Jackson family as a public cemetery in 1808.

The CLARKSBURG PUBLIC LIBRARY (*open 1:30–9 Mon.— Fri.*, *10:30–9 Sat.*), W. Pike St. at S. 4th St., occupies a two-story Georgian Colonial mansion, known as the Lowndes House, at the back of a block-deep lawn shaded by tall maple trees. The green-shuttered, gray-brick building, fronted by a tall Ionic portico, was erected in 1840 by Waldo Percy Goff, father of Nathan Goff. In 1930 the house was bequeathed to the city by Mrs. Richard T. Lowndes to be used for a library. Over the oaken door, with its lion-head knocker, is a graceful fanlight surrounded by a classic pediment. The interior of the building, although remodeled to accommodate the library, retains its original broad fireplaces, mirrors, and mantelpieces of classic design and mahogany and white staircase with hand-carved balustrade. The library contains 16,083 volumes.

The LEE HOUSE (*private*), Lee Ave. between Boring Lane and S. 5th St., was built in 1835 by Judge George H. Lee, a judge of the circuit court and later of the Virginia Court of Appeals. The wide two-story cream-colored frame house, with green shutters and one-story wings, suggests the generous hospitality for which Judge Lee was known. It stands back from, and above, the street on a broad lawn shaded by tall old pines and dotted with clumps of rhododendron and other native shrubs. A flat-roofed portico with four Doric columns shelters the paneled double doorway, which is framed by half-length sidelights and surmounted by a wide fanlight. A wide gable with a Palladian window breaks the line of the slate roof in the center.

The BIRTHPLACE OF JOHN W. DAVIS (*private*), 303 Lee Ave., a two-and-a-half-story yellow brick house of Georgian Colonial design, overlooks from an eminence the business district of Clarksburg. Davis, lawyer and statesman, was born here April 13, 1873. He began the practice of law in Clarksburg in 1895, served in the State legislature and Congress, and was appointed solicitor general of the United States in 1913. From 1918 to 1921 he was ambassador to Great Britain. In 1924 he was Democratic candidate for President of the United States.

LOWNDES MUNICIPAL PARK, entrance S. end of S. 2nd St., a ten-acre tract on Lowndes Hill, was given the city in 1930 by the late Richard T. Lowndes. A winding road ascends the steep hillside to a narrow flat on top, from which there is a good view of the city. Evidence of old trenches, dug when Union troops fortified Lowndes Hill in the War between the States, can be seen.

The AKRO AGATE COMPANY (*open to out-of-State adults upon application at office*), W. end of Harvey St., occupies a low rambling building on the bank of the West Fork River. Founded in 1915, the plant produces approximately 60 per cent of the toy marbles used in the world, glass balls for use in signs, lithographic balls, toy dishes, florists' ware, and other glass novelties. When running at capacity the plant employs 125 persons and produces 120 marbles a minute.

POINTS OF INTEREST IN ENVIRONS

Jackson's Mill, State 4-H Camp, 22.2 *m*. (*see Tour* 10a).

Fairmont

Railroad Stations: Cleveland Ave. at foot of Madison St. for Baltimore & Ohio R.R.; Merchant St. at E. end Million Dollar Bridge for Monongahela Ry.
Interurban Trolley: Jefferson St. between Meredith and Adams St. for Clarksburg interurban; Adams St. at Madison St. for Rivesville interurban.
Bus Station: Jefferson St. between Meredith and Adams St. for Blue Ridge Lines and West Virginia Transportation Co., Millersville and Meadowdale local busses.
Taxis: 25¢ and upward according to distance and number of passengers.
Streetcars and City Busses: Fare 7¢.
Traffic Regulations: Parking meters downtown. Chief one-way street, Monroe going east.
Street Order and Numbering: Numbers run north and south from Monongahela River; east and west from Coal Run.

Accommodations: 3 hotels; boarding houses; tourist homes.

Information Service: Fairmont Hotel, NE. corner Washington and Jefferson St.; Board of Commerce, Home Savings Bank Bldg., 207 Adams St.

Radio Station: WMMN (920 kc.).
Motion Picture Houses: 3.
Swimming: Municipal Pool in South Side Park, 12th St. and Minor Ave., 25¢.
Golf: White Day Golf Course, 7 m. N. on State 73, 9 holes, greens fee 25¢, Sat., Sun. and holidays, 35¢; bus 20¢.
Tennis: Rosier Field, Fairmont State Teachers College, Locust Ave. at city limits, 6 courts, reservations; West High School, Oakwood Rd. at Park Dr., 2 courts, reservations; East Side High School, Morgantown Ave. at Alta Vista Ave., 2 courts, reservations; South Side Park, 12th St. at Virginia Ave., 2 courts, reservations; Reservoir Park, 2 m. SW. on Pleasant Valley Rd., 2 courts, no fee.

Annual Events: Dahlia Show, Fairmont Hotel, late summer; Safety Week and parade, Nov.

FAIRMONT (883 alt., 23,159 pop.), seat of Marion County and commercial center of a rich coal-mining area, is built on a series of steep, rugged hills in the north-central part of the State, near the point where the Tygarts Valley and West Fork Rivers unite to form the Monongahela River; the Monongahela divides the city into East and West Fairmont. Streets slope steeply up and down hills, and at intersections, and sidewalks often terminate in flights of steps up or down to the next street level. Houses, built upon lots pitched at angles of 45 degrees, or even greater, are tall and narrow, with their front entrances often a story above their back yards, and back porches frequently upon a level with the chimneys of the houses a block behind them.

Agriculture

YOUNG FARMER, TYGARTS VALLEY

FARM ON A MOUNTAIN TOP

Photograph by courtesy of Soil Conservation Serv.

FARMSTEAD

Photograph by Post; courtesy of Farm Security Administrat.

otograph by Highton; courtesy of Work Projects Administration

FODDER IN THE SHOCK

PASTURE

otograph by courtesy of U.S. Forest Service

Photograph by Post; courtesy of Farm Security Administrat.

IN THE CO-OPERATIVE, TYGARTS VALLEY

AN ARTHURDALE RESETTLEMENT PROJECT DWELLING

Photograph by courtesy of Farm Security Administrat.

ELK RIVER FARMING SECTION

TYGARTS VALLEY HOMESTEADS

Photograph by courtesy of A. Aubrey Bodine

APPLE PICKER

APPLE HARVEST

Photograph by courtesy of State Road Commission

THE COUNTY AGENT VISITS

WOOL GRADING AT FARMER'S POOL

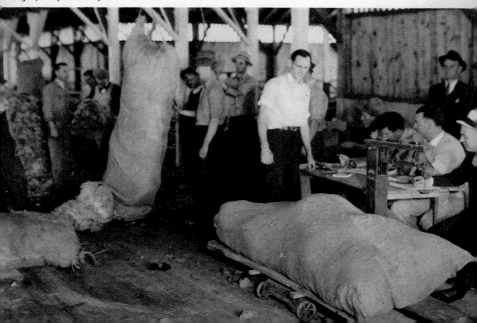

THRESHING

WASHING PRIZE BULL, RED HOUSE RESETTLEMENT PROJECT

The business district, occupying the comparatively level crest of a rise and sloping steeply downhill in three directions, bears much the same crowded up-and-down appearance as the rest of the town. Below the business section on a narrow strip of land between the river and steep hillside are railroad tracks, warehouses, and freight stations. Westward along Fairmont Avenue are elaborate mansions in landscaped grounds, built by coal barons in the prosperous days between 1870 and 1900, when the Fairmont coal fields were opened. At the western edge of town is Fairmont State Teachers College, too isolated to lend a collegiate atmosphere to the town.

There are no coal mines within the city limits, but Fairmont's existence depends upon the mining industry. Lines of coal cars move continually along the railroad tracks on both sides of the river, carrying 9,000,000 tons of bituminous coal from this region annually; soot and coal dust sift upon buildings and streets; a few miners live in Fairmont and commute to the mines.

In spite of industrial and commercial developments, Fairmont retains some of the pleasant characteristics of a country town. On Saturday its streets teem with country folk and miners' families. Groups gather on street corners or stand idly twirling the handles of parking meters as they discuss the state of crops or county politics. Miners in the Fairmont area are the sons and grandsons of farmers, and nearly every home in the middleclass residential districts has a small garden patch.

In the late 1770's several families settled in the vicinity, but the land on which Fairmont stands remained an impenetrable laurel thicket until 1793, when Jacob Paulsley built his home on the east side of the river. After a State road was opened between Clarksburg and Morgantown in 1819, a half-way stopping point between the two cities was needed. Land owned by Boaz Fleming on the west bank of the river, too rough and poor for cultivation, was selected for a town, which was incorporated as Middletown. Three ferries and a hotel operated by Frederick Ice were the first business establishments, and by 1831 fulling and carding mills were turning out woolen products. In the meantime a post office known as Paulsley was established on the east side of the river, where a settlement had grown up around a copper factory and machine works, and in 1838 this village was incorporated as Palatine.

In 1843 the two towns were incorporated as Fairmont. At this time Middletown had 70 dwellings, 5 stores, and several hotels and taverns, but most of the industries were across the river in Palatine.

About 1849 the approach of the Baltimore & Ohio Railroad stimulated other activities in the vicinity. Three turnpikes were opened, connecting Fairmont with eastern and western settlements, and the arrival of the first steamboat, the *Globe*, inaugurated navigation of the Monongahela during high water and led to numerous plans for slackwater navigation, none of which were completed before the War between the States. The town prospered as a supply base for railroad construction crews, all of whom were Irish 'fresh from the bogs of Connaught and the lakes of Killarney, who carried with them all their local feuds and prejudices which induced them to transfer their sectional fighting from the old sod to the land of greater freedom and opportunity.' On one occasion 200 Connaughters from Bentons Ferry attacked Fardowners at Ice's Mill. Taken by surprise, the Fardowners fled to Fairmont for protection, the Connaughters pursuing with shouts and gunshots. County officers, aided by citizens, quelled the riot, arrested 88 'accessible assailants,' and placed them in the local jail, 'where they had an opportunity to study their first lesson in Americanization.'

In January 1852 the railroad reached Fairmont, and a few months later a suspension bridge linked the east and west sides of the river. A year later the arrival of the first passenger train between Baltimore and Wheeling was celebrated. The train with 400 passengers, including company officials and members of the Virginia and Maryland legislatures, arrived in Fairmont in the afternoon, and by contemporary accounts 'brought to Fairmont its first touch of real high life, in which champagne and other costly liquors added flame to the fires of good fellowship. It is the general impression that the most regrettable feature of the affair was the early departure of the train westbound carrying with it its cargo of "wet goods." '

The town began to boom, for the coal underlying the surrounding region could now be shipped profitably. A State bank was established in 1853 and a year later the first coal mine in the area was opened by Francis H. Pierpont and James Otis Watson.

This dawning prosperity was halted by the War between the States. Although Fairmont was an important supply center for Union troops, only one raid took place. On April 29, 1863, Confederate General William Ezra Jones's cavalry division swept through the town, took 260 prisoners, destroyed the half-million dollar railroad bridge across the Monongahela River and raided the home of Governor Pierpont.

By 1870 the region had sufficiently recovered from the war to resume the development of its resources. Outside capital stimulated the opening of several mines, and such prominent West Virginians as A. Brooks Fleming and James Otis Watson (often referred to as the 'father of the West Virginia coal industry') acquired and developed large tracts of coal lands. After the fire of 1876, which destroyed the business district, Fairmont rebuilt with better buildings and wider streets.

Development of the coal industry was retarded for a time by high railroad freight rates, but the operators met this problem by building their own lines. Watson and his associates completed a railroad between Morgantown and Fairmont in 1866 and then opened the Montana Mines, where they installed the first battery of beehive coke ovens used in the State. In 1890 a railroad, controlled by Senator Johnson

N. Camden, was built between Fairmont and Clarksburg. Seven years later it became a part of the Baltimore & Ohio Railroad.

Meanwhile, Fairmont was developing as an educational center. With the close of the War between the States, a private normal school was opened in the basement of the Methodist Protestant Church. In 1868 it was made a branch of the State normal school and after a period of struggle began to grow. Since that time the school has expanded and moved twice, the last time, in 1917, to its present site on Locust Avenue.

The coal-mining industry underwent numerous booms and setbacks following 1900, and Fairmont's fortunes vacillated with each fluctuation in coal. In 1907 the city suffered with the Nation in a panic that depressed the coal industry, and in the same year the Monongah mine disaster occurred near by (*see Tour 10a*). Later, with the war-time demand for coal, Fairmont's fortunes soared, only to fall again following 1930. Although the town's largest industrial plant is that of the Owens-Illinois Glass Company, it is still dependent upon the mines for the larger part of its business.

Fairmont is the home of Matthew M. Neely, lawyer, soldier, United States senator from 1922 to 1940, and present Governor of the State.

POINTS OF INTEREST

The MARION COUNTY COURTHOUSE, NW. corner Adams St. and Jefferson St., when erected in 1897–1900 was the cause of a controversy that nearly split the county. It is a three-story Corinthian structure of gray Cleveland sandstone, with an octagonal, green-domed clock tower surmounted by a copper statue of *Justice*. Its three entrances are reached through elevated porticoes with fluted Corinthian columns and elaborately ornamented pediments. A two-story brick courthouse with a cupola, erected in 1842, stood on this site before the present courthouse was built. Residents considered it a very fine building, and when in 1897 the county court ordered it razed as crowded and unsafe, there was much indignation among the taxpayers in the northern part of the county. Fairmonters, however, were delighted at the prospect of a new building and voluntarily set to work wrecking the old structure. The northern objectors assembled at Mannington to protest the court order and more than 200 men boarded the evening train intending to get to Fairmont in time to prevent the razing of the building. The train was derailed en route, and by the time the protest committee reached Fairmont the courthouse was half gone. Feeling ran so high that delegates were sent to Charleston to petition the formation of a new county from the northern part of Marion County, and a subscription was begun to build a courthouse at Mannington. The petition failed after it was discovered that subscribers to the plan possessed more enthusiasm than money.

The SITE OF GOVERNOR FRANCIS H. PIERPONT'S HOUSE,

NE. corner Pierpont Ave. and Quincy St., is occupied by a filling station. The house stood here from about 1843 until it was razed in 1934. When Confederates raided Fairmont in 1863, they planned to burn Pierpont's house, but out of pity for the widowed Mrs. Boydston, whose house adjoined it so closely that it also would have burned, they refrained and contented themselves with making a bonfire of Pierpont's large law library, papers, and other personal property. Pierpont was in Wheeling at the time serving as Governor of the Restored Government of Virginia.

Pierpont, often called the 'father of West Virginia,' was born at Pierponts, Monongalia County, in 1814. When he was a year old his family moved to a farm near the site of Fairmont, where his father operated a tannery. At the age of 21 Francis walked 180 miles to attend Allegheny College at Meadville, Pennsylvania, where he worked his way through and was graduated with honors in 1839. Following a short period of teaching in Mississippi, during which he also read law, he was admitted to the bar in his home county. At the beginning of the War between the States he opposed secession and was active in planning the Wheeling conventions (*see History*). At the Second Wheeling Convention he was elected governor of the Restored Government of Virginia and governed from Wheeling until admission of the new State, after which he moved the government to Alexandria, Virginia, and remained there until the end of the war. His middle-course policies displeased both radicals and conservatives, and when Congress took over the work of reconstruction he was removed from the governorship by order of General John M. Schofield in 1868. Pierpont returned to West Virginia and took part in State politics with varying affiliations and fortunes, finally retiring from public life to make the church his chief interest. He died in 1899, and was buried in Woodlawn Cemetery, Fairmont. In recognition of his services to the State, his statue was placed in the Hall of Fame at Washington, D. C.

The GOVERNOR FLEMING HOUSE, NE. corner Jefferson and Washington Sts., is a two-story, white-painted brick house, erected in 1842 on the site of the first house in Middletown. A porch extends across the width of the house, its roof carried out over the driveway at the side to form a carriage porch. A. Brooks Fleming, lawyer, coal operator, and eighth governor of West Virginia, bought the house in 1871 and occupied it until his death in 1923. In 1933 the Red Cross took over the property.

The MILLION DOLLAR BRIDGE, the construction of which cost nearly that amount, is a quarter-of-a-mile concrete span linking East Fairmont and West Fairmont. Completed in 1921, it accommodates five lanes of traffic and has two six-foot pedestrian lanes.

SONNENCROFT (*private*), Morgantown Ave. between Mason St. and Alta Vista Ave., is a two-story stucco-finish, stone and steel house modeled after Inverness Castle in Scotland. Three-story towers, battlemented at the top, rise from three corners of the building. The house, which contains 50 rooms and has a large swimming pool in the basement, stands in landscaped grounds. Sonnencroft (Ger., home of sons) was built in 1914 by Mr. and Mrs. C. E. Hutchinson. Holmboe and Lafferty, of Clarksburg, the architects, drew the plans from photographs of Inverness Castle. It has been unoccupied since 1934.

The OWENS-ILLINOIS GLASS COMPANY PLANT (*open on application at office*), Plant No. 3, Morgantown Ave. at Cochran St., is the largest single industrial plant in Fairmont, employing 1,500 persons at peak capacity. Its principal product is beverage bottles.

ST. JOSEPH'S VILLA (*private*), Fairmont Ave. between 8th and 9th Sts., is a rest home and school for the Sisters of St. Joseph. The house, designed by Horace Trumbauer of Philadelphia and built in 1910 for James Edwin Watson, Sr., coal operator, is of Elizabethan half-timbered design. The walls for the first story, are veneered with blue-green native rubble stone and, above the first floor, are stuccoed between six-inch strips of stained chestnut. The red tile roof is broken into numerous gables, and all of the 500 windows of the building are composed of many small panes. Indiana limestone trim is used around windows and doors, and for the carved porch entablatures. Scrolled verge boards of chestnut ornament the gable eaves. The entrance vestibule is paved with white Vermont marble and trimmed with pink Tennessee marble. The floors are of parquetry design with mosaics of oak and mahogany; the interior walls are paneled in oak; handrails of the stairway and moldings are hand-carved; mantelpieces on the first floor are of elaborately carved Italian marble; a butler's pantry contains a sink of German silver; ceilings are ornamented in relief with plaster designs of oak leaves and acorns. The coach house also of half-timbered design, is almost as elaborately finished as the house. The grounds of the estate are terraced and formally landscaped with shrubbery, boxwood hedges, scattered flower beds, and magnolia, white birch, and catalpa trees. Left of the driveway is a sunken garden and beyond it a lily pond and rose garden. The estate, built at a cost of nearly $300,000, was known as Higate until it was purchased by the Sisters of St. Joseph in 1929.

FAIRMONT FARMS (*grounds open*), Fairmont Ave. between 9th and 12th St., is a large property, most of it within the city limits, owned by former Senator C. W. Watson. The area is bordered on Fairmont Avenue by an iron picket fence covered with rambler roses and approached from Ninth Street by a winding gravel drive. The grounds around the Watson homestead, a large 20-room stucco house of modified Spanish Mission design built in 1868, are landscaped with rhododendron and evergreens and shaded by groves of large maples and elms. Along the winding drive rhododendrons grow in profusion. West of the main house is a two-story log house with a stone chimney, built prior to 1849 and still in use as a dwelling. On the farm is a greenhouse and a large vegetable garden, where experiments in hybridization are conducted. The estate was founded in 1849 by James Otis Watson, who was prominently identified with coal development in the region. One of the first telephone lines in the section, a private line connecting the estate with the A. B. Fleming house, was used by Watson and Fleming to discuss coal deals. During the War between the States, Watson did a good business at Fairmont Farms in selling horses to the Federal Government. At one time Confederates raided the farm and confiscated a number of horses. After the war the Watsons raised prize show horses such as Lord Baltimore, Kitty Grey, and My Maryland, which they exhibited in America and Europe.

FAIRMONT STATE TEACHERS COLLEGE (*buildings open during school hours unless otherwise noted*), Locust Ave. at city limits, occupies the summit of a hill at the western edge of Fairmont. The MAIN BUILDING (1917), which overlooks Locust Avenue from the crest of the hill, is a long three-story structure of buff brick trimmed with limestone, with two-story wings at each end. Four pairs of fluted Ionic columns support the flat roof of a shallow portico that rises the full height of the façade. The main unit contains administrative offices and classrooms; in the east wing is the auditorium, in the west wing the cafeteria and library. Behind the main building and at right angles to it is the three-story, buff brick SCIENCE HALL, constructed in 1931. North of Science Hall is MORROW HALL (*not open*), the women's dormitory, also of buff brick. A two-story portico with four Ionic columns fronts the building. The plain rectangular doorway is surmounted by a flat stone lintel supported by scrolled brackets of stone. To the north on the other side of the hill, reached by a gravel drive, is ROSIER FIELD and STADIUM. A stone FIELD HOUSE, built by WPA in 1934–5, stands near the field. The TRIAL GARDEN of the West Virginia Dahlia Society (*open upon application at the college*), in which only new varieties of dahlias are grown, is at the northeastern end of the campus. New varieties are brought in each year from all parts of the country for trial.

Founded by J. N. Boyd in 1865 as the first private normal school in the State, it was granted State support in 1867 and in 1868 became a State normal school. A grant of $1,500 was obtained from the Peabody Fund in 1867, the first allotment made to a normal school from the fund established by George Peabody in that year for the aid of southern schools. Classes were first held in the basement of the Methodist Protestant Church, 418 Quincy Street (still standing). In 1872 the school moved into a building of its own in the center of town, became known as Fairmont State Normal School, and held its first graduating exercises. During the next ten years the State legislature refused to appropriate sufficient funds and the existence of State normal schools was in jeopardy. In 1879 the teachers served voluntarily without pay. After 1881, however, the normal school was firmly established and appropriations were made annually. A new building on Fairmont Avenue was erected in 1892 and the school moved to that location, operating there until 1917, when the present site was chosen and the present main building erected. In 1923 the institution was authorized to grant degrees and in 1930 the name was changed to Fairmont State Teachers College. The college is coeducational.

COLLEGE PARK DAHLIA PATCH (*open by telephoned appointment*), 1264 Bryant St., is a dahlia garden owned by Professor Oliver Shurtleff. The garden contains at least 600 plants and is in bloom from late August until frost.

RESERVOIR PARK, 2 m. SW on Pleasant Valley Rd., is a 90-acre municipal park on a high hill overlooking Fairmont and the surrounding countryside. Driveways shaded by beech, maple, oak, walnut, poplar and persimmon trees wind through the park, which centers around the filtration plant and oval reservoir of the Fairmont water system. It is equipped with fireplaces and picnic tables, tennis courts, a bandstand and pavilion, rest rooms, drinking fountains, and a children's playground.

POINTS OF INTEREST IN ENVIRONS

Monongah Mines, 4.9 *m.* (*see Tour* 10a).

Harpers Ferry

❯

Railroad Station: Potomac St. one block W. of Shenandoah St. for Baltimore & Ohio R.R.
Bus Station: Shenandoah and Potomac Sts. for Potomac Motor Lines.
Taxis: 25¢ and up, according to distance and number of passengers.

Accommodations: Tourist homes; boarding houses; no seasonal rates.

Riding: Hill Top House, Ridge St. between York and Columbia Sts., $1 per hour.

HARPERS FERRY (275 alt., 705 pop.), site of the brief but violent episode of John Brown's raid, occupies a narrow, ridged tongue of land at the confluence of the Shenandoah and Potomac Rivers. At this point three States converge; across the Potomac rise the hills of Maryland, across the Shenandoah those of Virginia, with the sentinel-like structure of Chimney Rock in the foreground. Around the base of the Maryland cliffs winds the disused channel of the Chesapeake and Ohio Canal. A combined railroad and traffic bridge spans the Potomac to the Maryland side, carrying the main line of the Baltimore & Ohio Railroad, which disappears into the Maryland cliff through a tunnel mouth. For nearly a mile, separated only by the hump of land on which Harpers Ferry stands, the Potomac and Shenandoah flow nearly parallel between sheer cliffs until, united, they rush in a series of rapids through a deep-rived gap in the Blue Ridge Mountains. Beyond the gap on clear days a stretch of level, green, and placid countryside is visible. In winter, with the forbidding outlines of the cliffs exposed and the wind whistling coldly across the heights and through the gorges, Harpers Ferry wears a harsh and desolate aspect. Summer softens the hard rock outlines with foliage and brings to the meeting place of the two rivers the wild and lovely appearance that Thomas Jefferson considered 'worth a trip across the Atlantic.'

Along the narrow shelf at the base of the precipitous rocky bluff stretch Shenandoah Street and Potomac Street, the two oldest thoroughfares. Later-built streets extend up the steep hill and along its crown where they join with those of Bolivar, a separate town politically.

Harpers Ferry, war-battered and flood-damaged, is but a relic of the thriving village that before the War between the States centered about the Government armory and Hall's Rifle Works and seemed destined to become an important industrial town. Its population has declined more than two-thirds since that prosperous era, and only the memory of the early industrial activity remains. Residents find employment in the Baltimore & Ohio Railroad shops at Brunswick, Maryland, four miles away, in near-by quarries, and in the small retail shops of the town. About a fourth of the population of Harpers Ferry and Bolivar is Negro.

In summer, tourist-service enterprises blossom along the main thoroughfares; tourist homes, closed during winter months, reopen; and post card and souvenir venders are busy. Nearly every citizen considers himself a volunteer guide, and a few charge small fees for conducting the sightseer up the natural stone steps, past the Harper House to Jefferson's Rock and John Brown's Fort. During winter months the townsfolk return to their quiet round of church suppers, bingo parties, knitting circles, and occasional trips to the movies at Charles Town or Martinsburg.

In 1734 Robert Harper, taking a little-explored short cut through the Hole, as this gap in the Blue Ridge was called, became so enthralled with the wild beauty of the place that he bought a small cabin, a canoe, and a corn patch for 13 guineas (about $65) from Peter Stephen, a German squatter, and his Indian companion Gutterman Tom, and the following year purchased the land from Lord Fairfax for 60 guineas ($300). He established a ferry across the Potomac River, and around it grew a village called Shenandoah Falls. The town suffered from floods, notably the Pumpkin Flood of 1753, so called because it washed down so many pumpkins from Indian fields upstream. The town was named Harpers Ferry when established by the Virginia assembly in 1763.

In 1796, possibly at the suggestion of George Washington, Congress ordered an arsenal established at Harpers Ferry because of the abundant water power. The arsenal and the later addition of Hall's Rifle Works changed the placid village into a busy community of 3,000 persons and one of the most important towns in Virginia.

Thomas Jefferson, when he visited Harpers Ferry in 1801 and made his statement about the notable view, took a keen interest in some eagles that nested in a great oak tree across the Shenandoah from Jefferson Rock. After he was elected President, Jefferson wrote Colonel Perkins, superintendent of the arsenal, and asked for some young eagles. Perkins's sons captured three eaglets and sent them to Washington. Jefferson sent one as a present to the king of Spain and received in return a fine Andalusian ram. For this he 'was accused of receiving presents from a foreign potentate.'

An interesting character in the early history of Harpers Ferry was the Scottish Dr. Brown, who came here about 1810, after serving as a surgeon in the Revolution. He charged only for actual services, never for medical advice. The doctor, an eccentric bachelor, had 50 dogs and 50 cats, whose barking and yowling kept the townspeople awake nights. The dogs accompanied him on professional calls. Under the persuasion that he would return to life in nine days, Dr. Brown had a windowed coffin built to be placed upright in a brick vault. When he died in 1824, he was buried according to his wishes.

With the coming of the Baltimore & Ohio Railroad and the Chesapeake and Ohio Canal, the main flow of east and west commerce was brought through the town. The railroad was completed as far as Wager's Bridge, across the river from Harpers Ferry, in 1834. In 1836 a Y-shaped covered bridge, 900 feet long and carrying the railroad and highway, was completed. During the next four years, however, the Virginia assembly and financial troubles prevented the railroad from extending farther westward, while the canal forged ahead to Hancock, Maryland. By the time further extension of the railroad was started in 1840, the mule-drawn barges of the canal already were passing through Harpers Ferry. The railroad reached Cumberland in 1842, eight years before the ·canal, and captured the coal traffic upon which the canal promoters had counted. The canal, with diminishing profit, continued to carry freight and occasional passengers through Harpers Ferry until 1924, when floods damaged the waterway so greatly that it was not restored.

In the summer of 1859 a party of men, led by an austere old man who called himself Isaac Smith, appeared in the vicinity, established headquarters at the Kennedy Farm on the Maryland side of the Potomac River, and under the pretense of prospecting for minerals in the near-by hills perfected plans for an attack on the slavery system. On the night of October 16, 1859, Isaac Smith revealed himself as John Brown, already widely known as Osawatomie Brown of the sanguinary antislavery warfare in Kansas. According to his biographer, W. E. B. DuBois, John Brown chose Harpers Ferry for many reasons, his love of beauty among them. DuBois writes:

> He chose Harper's Ferry because a United States arsenal was there and the capture of this would give that dramatic climax to the inception of his plan which was so necessary to its success. But both these were minor reasons. The foremost and decisive reason was that Harper's Ferry was the safest natural entrance to the Great Black Way—One has but to glance at the mountains and swamps of the South to see the Great Black Way. Here, amid the mighty protection of overwhelming numbers, lay a path from slavery to freedom, and along that path were fastnesses and hiding-places easily capable of becoming permanent fortified refuges for organized bands of determined armed men.

Brown, who claimed he was an 'instrument of God sent to liberate all slaves,' was a terror to pro-slavery settlers in the west, and during his active career as an abolitionist many believed he was insane. Thoreau, on the contrary, rejoiced that he was Brown's contemporary. Vernon Parrington gives Thoreau's judgment in these words:

> He had talked with John Brown in Concord and recognized him as a primitive idealist of rugged mold, a stern moralist who set justice above the law. That this man should be so grossly misunderstood by lesser men, so foully slandered, filled him with sorrow and with wrath also.

After a short speech to his 22 followers, 6 or 7 of whom were Negroes, John Brown marched upon Harpers Ferry while the town slept, captured and imprisoned two watchmen, and took possession of the Government armory. The raiders also seized as hostages several prominent citizens, among them Colonel Lewis Washington of Beall Air. The first man killed was a free Negro, Heywood Shepherd, a railroad porter who was shot by Brown's men when he failed to obey an order to halt. With the raiders in possession of the large stock of arms, the town was at their mercy, and Brown confidently awaited the arrival of the arms and ammunition train, which according to his plan were to follow him. The Baltimore & Ohio westbound train was stopped and delayed until early morning; then, being allowed to proceed, it spread the alarm.

Wild rumors spread through the countryside the next morning, and by noon companies of militia from Charles Town, Martinsburg, Shepherdstown, Winchester, and other communities converged upon the town. Citizens with squirrel rifles and other assorted firearms were already exchanging shots with the raiders. By evening all avenues of escape were cut off, and Brown, with his men and prisoners, took refuge in the engine house of the armory, still hopeful that reinforcements would arrive. Late that night Brevet Colonel Robert E. Lee and Lieutenant J. E. B. Stuart arrived from Washington with 90 marines. At daybreak, when Brown refused to surrender, the marines stormed the fort, using a battering ram to break down the door. In the raid, 10 of Brown's command were killed, including 2 of his sons, 4 townsmen, and 1 marine; and 12 were wounded. Five of the insurrectionists escaped, but Brown and 6 others were captured and lodged in the county jail at Charles Town. Brown was indicted for treason against Virginia, tried, and hanged at Charles Town (*see Charles Town*). The seizure of Harpers Ferry and the attempt to encourage slave rebellion were recognized by fervent abolitionists as the beginning of the conflict soon to come. Even southern leaders feared its effects and expressed the belief that the sympathy Brown gained in his role as martyr to the cause would serve to forward it. The John Brown raid, the cause behind

---

KEY FOR HARPERS FERRY MAP

1. The SITE OF THE ARMORY, near river E. of Baltimore & Ohio depot. 2. The JOHN BROWN MONUMENT, Potomac and Shenandoah Sts. 3. The NATURAL STONE STEPS, High St. between Shenandoah and Church Sts. 4. The HARPER HOUSE, Stone Steps at E. end of Public Walk. 5. ST. PETER'S ROMAN CATHOLIC CHURCH, on the hill above the stone steps. 6. The RUINS OF ST. JOHN'S EPISCOPAL CHURCH, Church and Cliff Sts. 7. JEFFERSON'S ROCK, Cliff St., one block W. of Stone Steps. 8. The HARPER CEMETERY, E. end of Fillmore Ave. 9. The ODD FELLOWS HALL, McDowell St. between Washington St. and Fillmore Ave. 10. STORER COLLEGE, Fillmore Ave. between Jackson and McDowell Sts. 11. LAUREL LODGE, Ridge St. between Taylor and Jackson Sts. 12. The LUTHERAN CHURCH, Washington St. between Taylor and Union Sts. 13. The WILSON HOME, Washington St. between Union and Downing Sts. 14. HERRS ISLAND is a desolate, deserted 13-acre island in the Shenandoah River.

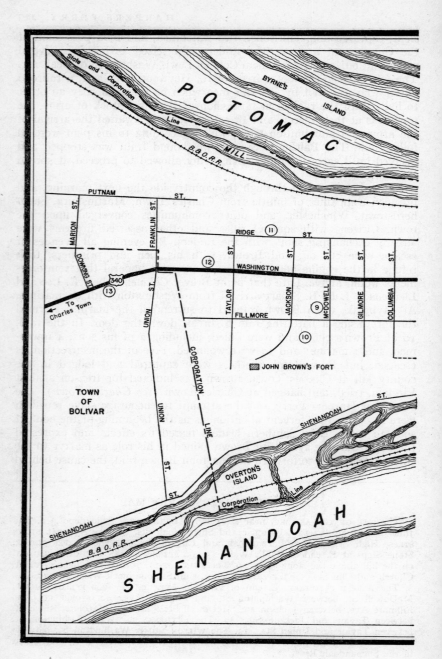

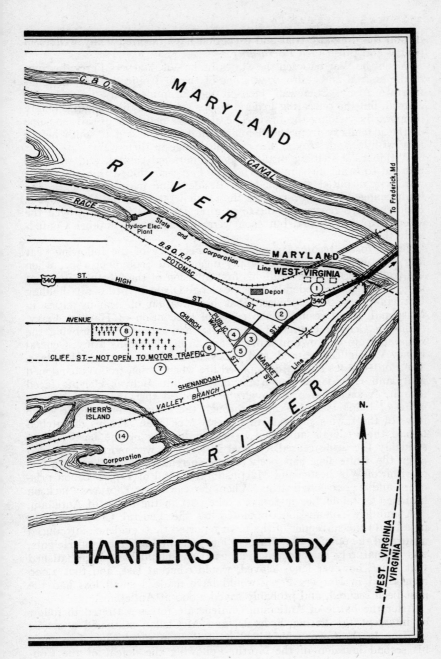

HARPERS FERRY

it, and the dramatic trial and execution have inspired many writers in poetry and prose (see Literature).

When the War between the States broke out, Harpers Ferry, because of the arsenal and railroad, was one of the first objectives of the Confederate Army. Stonewall Jackson moved immediately to seize the arsenal, but the retreating Federal troops set fire to the buildings before temporarily yielding the town. The attackers managed to salvage some of the machinery from the flaming buildings and sent it south before they withdrew, destroying the railroad bridge in their wake.

Within easy striking distance of the national capital, and with the railroad to bring up supplies, Harpers Ferry continued throughout the war as a disputed strategic base. Besides nine major exchanges, the town changed hands every time the Confederates crossed the Potomac. Federal troops reoccupied the town after Jackson's force destroyed the arsenal April 18, 1861, but soon were driven out by another Confederate thrust.

Union forces regained possession in February of the following year and occupied the town as a supply depot until September 1862, when General Robert E. Lee made his first invasion of the North. A force of more than 10,000 Federals under Colonel Dixon S. Miles was holding Harpers Ferry. Lee surmised that his invasion of near-by cities in Maryland would result in the peaceful evacuation of Harpers Ferry. Although General George B. McClellan had advised withdrawing the Federals from the town in order to add to his defending army, General Henry W. Halleck refused, and Jackson was sent to capture the place. The Confederates had hardly opened fire when Union troops abandoned Maryland Heights, an important outpost, and Bolivar Heights faced assault. A small force of cavalrymen muffled their horses' feet with strips of blankets and escaped through the enemy's line to carry the news of the town's situation to General McClellan. Troops dispatched to aid the Federals advanced to within hearing of the battle, when suddenly the firing ceased. Colonel Miles, who was mortally wounded after the white flag had been raised, surrendered, together with the garrison of Winchester and Martinsburg, a total of 12,520 Union prisoners and 13,000 small arms. When the town was captured, Jackson hastened to rejoin Lee in time to take part in the battle of Antietam.

A military commission appointed by the Federal Government to investigate the surrender of the town reported that 'evidence introduced confirmed the opinion that Harpers Ferry, as well as Maryland Heights, was prematurely surrendered. The garrison should have been satisfied that relief, however long delayed, would come at last, and that 1,000 men killed in Harpers Ferry would have made a small loss had the post been secured, and probably saved 2,000 at Antietam.'

After the battle of Antietam, Confederate forces scattered to follow or intercept the fleeing Federals, and McClellan stationed a strong garrison in the town, which held it until June 1863, when Lee made his second invasion of the North. Following the defeat of the Confederates at Gettysburg, Harpers Ferry changed hands again; Federals reoccupied the town on July 4, but held it only five days until Confederates, attempting to reach the national Capital, again effected a capture. Failing in their attempt on Washington, the Confederate troops retreated and Harpers Ferry remained in the hands of Union soldiers until the close of the war. The railroad bridge was destroyed and rebuilt nine times, and by the end of the war the town was in ruins. 'A place more thoroughly gutted could not be imagined,' wrote General David Hunter Strother (Porte Crayon) in his diary.

Many of the inhabitants straggled back when peace returned, but the Government did not reopen the arsenal. The property was sold at public auction in 1869. In September 1870, a flood in the Shenandoah River submerged the streets at the foot of the bluff and wrecked the buildings on Herr's Island. Later floods several times have swept away bridges.

With the realization that the armory would not reopen, Harpers Ferry turned to other expedients for the difficult period of reconstruction, the most profitable of which was the resort trade. The town became a fashionable gathering place for those attracted by the beauty of the setting and for the curious who wished to visit the scene of John Brown's raid. For a time the Y-bridge across the Potomac was a favorite place for eloping couples to get married, for the tollgate keeper on the bridge was a retired parson, and honeymooners swelled the tide of visitors. Today Harpers Ferry is wholly a residential and resort town. The water power once used to turn the wheels of the arsenal is utilized by a power company that generates electricity for use in Bolivar and Harpers Ferry and feeds its surplus current to Brunswick, Maryland.

POINTS OF INTEREST

1. The SITE OF THE ARMORY, near river, E. of Baltimore & Ohio depot, is marked by white-painted flagstones on the green lawn, to show the outlines of Government buildings that once stood here.

2. The JOHN BROWN MONUMENT, Potomac and Shenandoah Sts., is a simple white obelisk erected in 1895 by the Baltimore & Ohio Railroad on the site of the engine house in which John Brown and his raiders made their last stand. To the right of the monument a row of five bronze tablets carries an account of the capture of Harpers Ferry by Stonewall Jackson, September 15, 1862.

3. The NATURAL STONE STEPS, High St. between Shenandoah and Church Sts., lead from the street up the steep hillside to the Public Walk and a path to the Catholic Church. The 44 steps were carved in the solid rock cliff under the supervision of Mrs. Laura Wager about 1810.

4. The HARPER HOUSE (*private*), Stone Steps at E. end of Public Walk, is a massive two-and-a-half-story stone house built against the side of the hill. Robert Harper built the house about 1780 but never lived in it. The first occupant was Mrs. Laura Wager, his niece, who

inherited the property. Behind the house a steep flagstone street, known since 1830 as the Public Walk, cuts between it and the perpendicular hillside in which are a number of cave-like rooms that serve as cellars for the Harper House and adjoining dwellings. From an upper story a wooden bridge spans the walk to gardens on the hill. This walk was originally a private path belonging to the Harper property, but in 1830 Mrs. Wager granted communicants of the Catholic Church the right to use the path to save them the tedious climb up the stone steps.

5. ST. PETER'S ROMAN CATHOLIC CHURCH, on the hill above the stone steps, was built in 1830 and extensively remodeled in 1896. The church, of Gothic design, is constructed of rough native stone, with a steeple at one corner. During the War between the States this was the only church in Harpers Ferry that conducted regular services undisturbed by both armies.

6. The RUINS OF ST. JOHN'S EPISCOPAL CHURCH, Church and Cliff Sts., occupy the slope above and to one side of the Catholic Church. Only the four ivy-covered stone walls and the frames of its 24 windows remain. The church, unused since 1893, was built early in the nineteenth century and was used as a guardhouse and hospital during the War between the States.

7. JEFFERSON'S ROCK, Cliff St., one block W. of Stone Steps, is a natural rock bench from which Thomas Jefferson in 1801 viewed the confluence of the Potomac and Shenandoah Rivers, which he later described in his *Notes on Virginia* as 'one of the most stupendous scenes in nature.' The view is essentially unchanged.

8. The HARPER CEMETERY, E. end of Fillmore Ave., occupies land set aside by Robert Harper for a graveyard. The older part is overgrown by underbrush and brambles. In this section is the GRAVE OF ROBERT HARPER (1713–82), surrounded by a moss-covered stone wall and marked by a tombstone. Here also are ten other graves, unmarked or marked by stones with illegible inscriptions. In a newer and well-kept part are the more recent graves.

9. The ODD FELLOWS HALL, McDowell St. between Washington St. and Fillmore Ave., is a rectangular brick building with a plain wooden porch over which is a frame addition. Abraham Lincoln lodged in this house in 1862 when he came to Harpers Ferry to confer with General George B. McClellan. The Odd Fellows Lodge that uses the building was founded in 1833 and is said to be the oldest lodge of the I.O.O.F. in the State.

10. STORER COLLEGE, Fillmore Ave. between Jackson and McDowell Sts., is a Negro coeducational school founded by John Storer in 1869. The school is partially State-supported and offers secondary and a few junior college courses. At its inception the college had only four large brick houses, donated by the United States Government after the armory was closed, but it now owns 15 buildings and 40 acres of ground. ANTHONY MEMORIAL HALL, the main building, which was burned in 1928 and rebuilt in 1928–9, is a two-story gray-painted brick structure

with two wings. A square cupola rises from the roof of the central unit. In this unit are the offices, chapel, laboratory, and classrooms. CURTIS MEMORIAL CHURCH is a comparatively modern building of pressed brick with stained glass memorial windows.

JOHN BROWN'S FORT (*open on application at college*), the engine house in which John Brown made his stand against the marines, occupies the cliff top overlooking the Shenandoah River. The square brick building, with its arched windows and doors and its small wooden bell cupola, is used as the college museum, and contains a collection of old guns, helmets, money, and other curiosities. When the armory was burned during the War between the States this was the only building left standing, and after the war it was an attraction for sightseers. In 1892 it was dismantled and shipped to the World's Columbian Exposition at Chicago. After the exposition it was sold and would have been used for a stable if the Negroes of the country, led by Miss Kate Field, an actress, had not raised funds to buy it and have it shipped back to Harpers Ferry. It was rebuilt two miles from town and stood on an obscure site until 1910 when it was moved to the campus of Storer College. Although 'bricks from John Brown's Fort' have been sold to tourists ever since the War between the States, the structure is believed to contain the greater part of its original brickwork.

11. LAUREL LODGE, Ridge St. between Taylor and Jackson Sts., a tourist home, is a two-story house of rough stone built in 1914 by an ex-mayor of Harpers Ferry. Locally, it is called the Crazy House. Imbedded in the concrete pavement are bullets, small guns, bayonets and sabers arranged in fanciful designs. In the concrete columns of the porch and the inside plaster walls of the house are bottles, keys, plates, jugs, coins, spoons, and war relics of all sorts collected by the builder. Iron chains of various sizes are stretched between the columns, and window sills and cornices are studded with small pebbles. Printed in pavements, porch floors and steps are such inscriptions as 'Be a Booster,' 'Don't Worry—Grunt,' 'Do you say your prayers?,' 'I'm from Missouri,' 'Step easy,' 'Hell Will Freeze Over When You Get There.' A small stone summer house on the lawn is named the Wanderlust.

12. The LUTHERAN CHURCH, Washington St. between Taylor and Union Sts., is a plain brick structure on a rough stone foundation. Built in 1850, it was used as a Federal hospital and stable during the War between the States. After the war it was believed haunted by a huge black dog and other specters that uttered moaning sounds.

13. The WILSON HOME (*open 9–5 weekdays*), Washington St. between Union and Downing Sts., is a two-story red brick house, of post-Colonial design, the original part of which was built in 1828 by James F. Wilson, father of Emanuel Willis Wilson, governor of West Virginia from 1885 to 1890. Governor Wilson, born in this house in 1864, lived in Harpers Ferry until the armory, where his father was employed, was burned during the War between the States. Wilson, after the close and bitter election of 1888, retained the office of governor nearly a year

after his term had expired while the legislature was investigating charges of election fraud and deciding whether Nathan Goff or A. B. Fleming was entitled to the office (*see Clarksburg*).

14. HERRS ISLAND, once the site of an industrial village called Virginius, is a desolate, deserted 13-acre island in the Shenandoah River containing flood- and war-battered ruins of an earlier era. Virginius, which then included a sawmill, tannery, oil mill, and 12 dwellings, was established by the Virginia assembly in 1827, but remained essentially a part of Harpers Ferry. Hall's Rifle Works, a part of the Government armory, also stood here, and the place thrived through the War between the States until the flood of 1870, which washed away or wrecked most of the buildings. The flour mill of Abraham Herr, for whom the island was named, escaped damage in this flood and operated until 1887, but subsequent floods destroyed it and the few remaining buildings.

丿丿丿

Huntington

Railroad Stations: 7th Ave. between 9th and 10th Sts. for Chesapeake and Ohio Ry.; 2nd Ave. and 11th St. for Baltimore & Ohio R.R.
Bus Stations: Union Bus Terminal, 836 4th Ave., for Atlantic Greyhound Lines, Southeastern Greyhound Lines, Logan-Williamson Bus Co. and Cackley Bus Co.; Ohio River Bus Station, 1142 4th Ave., for Ohio River Bus Co.
Wharf: N. end of 10th St. for steamboat service to Cincinnati in summer.
Airport: Municipal, 3 m. NW. across the Ohio River, for American Airlines; taxi 75¢ plus bridge toll, minimum 15¢.
Bridge: Huntington-Chesapeake, 2nd Ave. and 6th St., US 52; toll 15¢, car and 1-6 passengers, extra passengers 5¢ each; trucks 15¢ to $1.20.
Taxis: Zone system, 25¢ first zone, 50¢ to city limits; no charge for extra passengers.
Street Order and Numbering: First St., running south from Ohio River, divides city into east and west sections.

Accommodations: 8 hotels; tourist camps and boarding houses.

Information Service: Chamber of Commerce, First Huntington National Bank Bldg., SW. corner 4th Ave. and 10th St.; A.A.A. of West Virginia, Frederick Hotel, NW. corner 4th Ave. and 10th St.

Radio Station: WSAZ (930 kc.).
Theaters and Motion Picture Houses: Little Theater plays and Marshall College Theater plays in College auditorium, E. 16th St. and 4th Ave.; 11 motion picture houses.
Swimming: Y.M.C.A., 6th Ave. and 11th St.; Second Presbyterian Church, 9th St. W. and Jefferson Ave.; Camden Park, 8 m. W. on US 60; Dreamland Pool, 10.4 m. W. on US 60.
Golf: Spring Valley Golf Club, on side road (L) from US 60 at 7.1 m. W., 18 holes, greens fee 50¢, week ends and holidays 75¢; Wayside, municipal course, 6 m. W. on US 60, 9 holes, greens fee 50¢.
Tennis: Descriptive list available at office of park commission, City Hall, 5th Ave. and 8th St.
Riding: Spring Valley Drive, 1 block (L) from US 60 at 7.1 m. W., horses $1 per hr., holidays $1.25 per hr.
Skating: Ice skating, 7th Ave. and 1st St. W., open Nov. to Mar., adults 35¢, children 30¢, spectators 10¢. Roller skating, Camden Park, 8 m. W. on US 60.
Baseball: League Park, Ohio Ave. and 8th St. W., for Mountain State League games.
Football: Fairfield Stadium, Charleston Ave. and Shelton Lane, for high school and college games.

Annual Events: Band Music Festival, West Virginia high school bands, spring; Junior League Horse Show, June; Marshall College Homecoming and Dad's Day Celebration, fall; Bible Pageant, Oct.; Tobacco Festival, Nov.

HUNTINGTON (564 alt., 75,572 pop.), West Virginia's largest city, lies in a semicircle between a barrier of broad, low-lying hills and the

Ohio River, in the southwestern section of the State. The valley of the Ohio broadens at Huntington, the point of confluence with the Guyandot (locally called Guyan) River, and to the south the hills recede in gentle undulations for about three miles beyond the business district. A comparatively new city, Huntington has expanded according to a plan based on the original survey made in 1870, with wide level boulevards, tree-lined residential avenues, and a geometrically perfect street layout in the downtown section.

From a center at Government Square, a spacious plaza between the post office and city auditorium, the city radiates to the cardinal compass points in four quite different sections: east toward a residential area of individual homes, the campus of Marshall College, and a shopping center at Twentieth Street; north toward the central concentration of business houses and office buildings; west toward a roomy area of middle-class homes; south along apartment-lined avenues to a group of estates and country homes on the hills overlooking the city. An initial impression of roominess is borne out in the arrangement of buildings, for the city has widely spaced individual dwellings and few tenements.

The downtown business center covers 25 city squares, situated between Seventh and Twelfth Streets on the west and east, and First and Sixth Avenues on the north and south. A nine-mile water front is almost completely filled with freight yards, warehouses, and industrial plants, while the remaining industries stand at the city's eastern and western edges. Monel metal, made from nickel in the huge plant of the International Nickel Company, and stoves, glassware, shoes, steel rails, thermos bottles, and commercial dyes are products of these plants; but the financial life-blood of the city is provided largely by commercial investments, which serve to make Huntington the base for a wholesale trade that supplies the great coal and lumber regions of southern West Virginia and the tobacco, grain, and dairy products areas of southeastern Ohio, northeastern Kentucky, and southwestern West Virginia.

A commercial rather than an industrial city, Huntington lacks the ethnic groupings common in other urban areas of the State, and except for a relatively small group of Negroes, most of whom live in the southeastern section of the city, the population is racially homogeneous— 95 per cent white and native born. The West Virginia Industrial School for Colored Girls and Barnett Hospital for Negroes are in Huntington.

Huntingtonians show an active interest in all things pertaining to their city, and there is an absence of social cliques and small sectionalism. They are great joiners, however, and are for or against everything, apathetic to nothing. Parades, pageants, tableaux, and community and organization drives constantly break the routine of the city's life. Clubs, guilds, fraternal orders, and the American Legion take a proprietary interest in all local affairs. Especially do they take a great pride in the college.

The concerts, recitals, plays, and lectures sponsored by the college set the city's cultural tone, as its athletic teams supply a common diversion, and all are enthusiastically supported. The townspeople gaily celebrate an outstanding athletic triumph, and generously co-operate when college-sponsored gatherings create a demand for living facilities. Crowds good-naturedly jostle through Fairfield Stadium—Huntingtonians and other West Virginians from small adjoining towns, as well as enthusiastic visitors from Southern Ohio and Kentucky. If an out-of-town game is crucial, Huntington crowds pile into automobiles and carry the Green and White into enemy territory; one notable exodus took 2,000 townspeople on a 300-mile drive in the face of a wintry gale to witness a conference championship game.

Huntington is a city of many churches and frequent revivals. Common enough in the State, revivals are notable here for the many visiting evangelists and for the huge attendances they draw in an urban area. They are held in frame sheds or tents and in the city's largest theaters. A Bible parade and pageant is sponsored each October by the Huntington Ministerial Association, with about 20 churches of all denominations participating. The parade is made up of floats depicting scenes from the Bible, and usually includes bands from Marshall College and the Huntington and Ceredo-Kenova high schools. After the parade a Bible pageant is presented in the Ritter Park Amphitheater.

A tobacco festival is held each November in Huntington, center of the principal tobacco-growing area of the State. Growers of choice burley tobacco exhibit their wares for six days before the prizes are given.

Captain Céleron de Bienville and a party of explorers, sent by the French Government in 1749 to reaffirm claims to the Ohio region first made by La Salle in 1669, were the first white people on the site of Huntington. In 1772, a large tract lying between the Big Sandy and Ohio Rivers was granted to a number of soldiers for services in the French and Indian War. The largest tract was given Captain John Savage and was known as the Savage Grant. The original owners sold their lands, and no settlement was made until 1796, when Thomas and Jonathan Buffington came to establish homes on land left by their father, William Buffington, purchaser of part of the Savage holdings.

Thomas erected a house on the south bank of the Guyandot River on a high knoll overlooking the Ohio. Jonathan built nearer the mouth

---

KEY FOR HUNTINGTON MAP

1. GOVERNMENT SQUARE is a broadening of 5th Ave. between E. 8th and E. 9th Sts. 2. CABELL COUNTY PUBLIC LIBRARY, E. 9th St. and 5th Ave. 3. MEMORIAL PARK, a two-lane parkway extending along the edge of Kiwanis Park from 7th St. W. to 21st St. W. 4. RITTER PARK, 13th Ave. between E. 8th and E. 12th Sts. 5. MARSHALL COLLEGE, in the east central section of Huntington, has its main entrance at E. 16th St. and 4th Ave. 6. CHESAPEAKE AND OHIO SHOPS, between 5th and 8th Aves. and 23rd and 28th Sts. in the east end of the city. 7. INTERNATIONAL NICKEL COMPANY PLANT, along the Guyandot River at Main St. and Riverside Dr. on the eastern corporation line of the city.

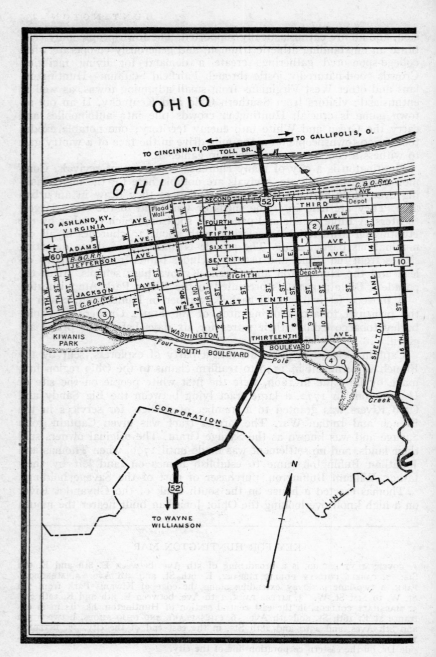

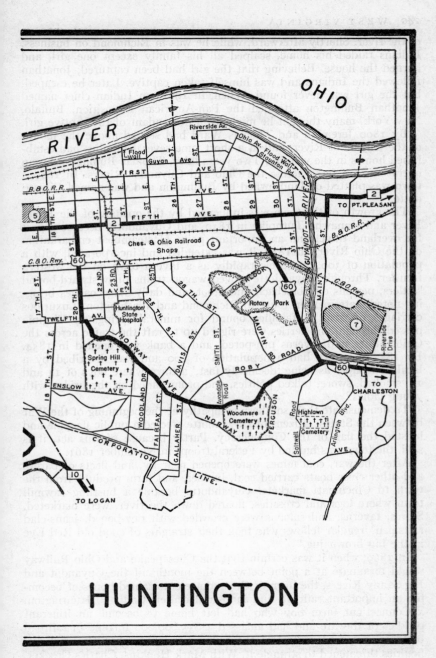

HUNTINGTON

of the river. Shortly afterward, while he was in Richmond on business, Indians raided his home, scalped all his family except one girl, and burned the house. Believing that the girl had been captured, Jonathan followed the Indians and was himself taken captive. Later he escaped, but the girl was never found. When, in 1901, an Indian chief named Jonathan Buffington attended the Pan-American Exposition, Buffalo, New York, many thought he might be a descendant of the captive girl.

By 1800 Jeremiah and Thomas Ward had settled above the mouth of the Guyandot River, and in a short time several families had established homes in the vicinity. Two years later, Thomas Buffington began operation of a ferry across the Ohio and Guyandot Rivers. In 1810 a town was platted on land owned by Buffington and was named Guyandotte.

The growth of the town was influenced by the opening of the James River and Kanawha Turnpike in 1830, and Guyandotte became a post for overland travel and an important point of steamboat embarkation on the Ohio River. In 1849, it was extended and incorporated, with a population of 300, and grew rapidly as a tavern town on the western frontier. Through Guyandotte moved wagon trains of westward-bound settlers, persons on horseback and afoot, and daily stagecoaches bringing noted statesmen en route to Richmond and Washington. Luxurious carriages of wealthy families bound for mineral springs in Virginia passed through, and ferries were rigged up to raft the traffic across the Ohio. Stores and taverns prospered, and a bank was opened in 1854. By 1857 the town had a population of 600 and was described by a local newspaper as being 'decidedly fast,' a town where boys of 14 and 15 'smoked, swore, talked politics, and promenaded on the bridge with young ladies.'

To demonstrate their southern sympathy at the beginning of the War between the States, citizens of Guyandotte erected a public flagpole and hoisted the flag of the Confederacy. Partly because of this act, it is said, the town was burned by Federal troops in November 1861.

After the war, coal mines were opened near by, and fleets of barges and other river boats carried coal, lumber, and farm produce from the town to Cincinnati markets. Guyandotte became a bustling sawmill town where logs and crossties, floated down the river, were marketed. Stores, taverns, and saloons were crowded with raw-boned, jeans-clad raftsmen, 'regular fellows who took their straights of good old Red Eye in the big brown jug.'

In 1869, when it was certain that the Chesapeake and Ohio Railway would terminate at a point between the mouths of the Guyandot and Big Sandy Rivers, the town of Guyandotte entertained hopes of becoming an important railroad and industrial center. Collis P. Huntington, a Connecticut farm boy who had left home to become an itinerant peddler of tinware and had amassed a $35,000,000 fortune in railroad building, acquired control of the railroad in 1869 when financial difficulties threatened to strangle it. With Mark Hopkins, Charles Crocker, and Leland Stanford, Huntington had just completed the Central Pacific, a transcontinental road fulfilling the dreams of all railroad men of the time, and he was known as one of the largest real-estate owners in the country.

Huntington was dissatisfied with Guyandotte as a railhead, however, and set about looking for a site upon which to build his own city. Upon the advice of Delos W. Emmons, brother-in-law of Mr. Huntington, a site was considered at the mouth of the Big Sandy River. Options were obtained on land extending two miles west along the Ohio from the west bank of the Guyandot River. Originally called Holderby's Landing, this was a fertile stretch of level land owned by well-to-do farmers. The post office was Maple Grove and the only buildings were scattered farm houses and a frame structure occupied by Marshall College. Citizens of Guyandotte were indignant at the selection, perhaps even more so because the proposed city was on their western doorstep. The local newspaper published a long list of 'advantages,' explaining why Guyandotte was the point where the railroad should end. To this a resident of Maple Grove replied, conceding that Guyandotte had some advantages, but declaring it would 'take a search warrant to find them in the annual crop of dog fennel, popcorn, and empty pint bottles.'

After right-of-way and space for the railroad yards and shops had been reserved, the land for the city was conveyed to the Central Land Company, and a real-estate boom was well under way even before the city was mapped. In 1871 the city was chartered and named for Huntington. The charter provided a mayor and council form of government, and the marshal was instructed to find or build a 'comfortable and safe place to confine prisoners.' Later he reported the fulfillment of these instructions at a cost of $8.10. Almost overnight stores, hotels, frame houses, and a generous number of saloons were built. Work on the Chesapeake and Ohio shops was started and a woodburning engine, the *Greenbrier,* was transported down the Ohio River to begin work on the western end of the railroad. For two years the town hugged the Ohio River front, but with the opening of the railroad in 1873, it gradually built farther back from the river and nearer the railroad shops and yard.

It was a wintry day in January 1873 when the first Chesapeake and Ohio train, carrying officials and distinguished guests, drew into Huntington from Covington, Virginia. Celebration followed, and with elaborate ceremony a barrel of James River water was poured into the Ohio, signifying the union of the two rivers. A tour through the town was hampered by a 'sea of mud' that covered the streets.

The town was scarcely two years old when Sandy Little, an easterner, en route to Cincinnati, wrote:

It is a right big little town, not as big as Cincinnati but has gained on it about two thousand five hundred population in the last two years. It has numberless streets, avenues, etc., many of which are not entirely built up. In fact, there are almost as many Chesapeake & Ohio Railroad cars as there are houses, and the employees of said railroad make the majority of the population . . . Just now the Ohio is rather low—like many New York stocks—considerable 'below par!' After a heavy dew, however, steamers from Cincinnati get up this far and discharge immense quantities of freight for eastern markets . . . Bourbon seems to be abundant. There are eight churches and four hotels, a college, etc. The town extends along the river front a long distance, and I should judge that mosquitoes do a good business here in their 'busy season.'

In September 1875, Huntington had its first real taste of outlawry when a band of horsemen rode into town and robbed the Huntington Bank. The people of the town never knew who the robbers were, and always referred to the event as the 'Jesse James Robbery.' There was a Methodist conference going on and those who saw the robbers riding into town thought they were visiting preachers, though some commented on 'what good horses they were riding.' Sheriff D. L. Smith formed a posse and set out in pursuit. He related afterward that when he was about to close in and capture the robbers, some of his men had to tighten their saddle girths. By the time they got started again the robbers were out of sight.

For a decade the town had a flourishing growth. Factories were established to produce soap, mine supplies, freight cars, and railroad car wheels. A land boom followed.

The city council, early annoyed with besetting issues such as preventing milch cows, hogs, horses, and geese from roaming the public common, control of liquor sales, and informal bathing in the Ohio and Guyandot Rivers, directed their attention to industrial and cultural developments. The presence of a college added to the cultural tone of the city; literary societies were organized; and in 1886 Mr. Huntington presented plans for a public park to the city council. The plan, however, was defeated by a vote of the council.

In 1887 the county seat was moved from Barboursville to Huntington. By 1890 the Chesapeake and Ohio acquired lines that gave direct connections with Louisville, Cincinnati, and Chicago. In addition to these, numerous branch lines that penetrated rich coal and timber regions east and south of the city terminated in Huntington.

The Cleveland panic in 1893 temporarily halted the growth of the city. By 1903, however, it had recovered and began another boom. In 1910 the greater Huntington charter was granted, taking in numerous small independent suburbs, the largest of these being Guyandotte on the east and Central City on the west, and set the present boundaries of the city.

Floods in 1913 and 1935 caused some damage but served chiefly as an omen of worse disaster. The great Ohio River flood of 1937 poured billions of gallons of muddy water through the city, reaching 69.1 feet at the crest, exceeding by 20 feet the depth at which the Ohio leaves its banks. The flood inundated four-fifths of the inhabited area of the city.

Construction of a flood wall and reservoir project designed to protect the city from a flood stage of 72.2 feet was begun in 1938 under the supervision of the United States Army Engineers.

POINTS OF INTEREST

1. GOVERNMENT SQUARE is a broadening of 5th Ave. between 8th St. E. and 9th St. E., and was so named because three sides of it are occupied by Federal, county, and city buildings. On the south the two-story gray stone GOVERNMENT BUILDING covers more than half the block; west is the stone-block green-domed CABELL COUNTY COURTHOUSE, three stories in height with a four-faced clock tower rising above the tops of the trees that shade its block-square lawn; north is the two-story cut stone and buff brick CITY BUILDING, adorned with pilastered walls and a high balcony portico over each of its two entrances. The square is used for parade formations, band concerts, and civic and municipal exhibits.

2. CABELL COUNTY PUBLIC LIBRARY (*open 9–9 weekdays; children's room open 2–5:30 Mon.-Fri., 9–12 Sat.*), 9th St. E. and 5th Ave., is a two-story buff stone building with a high Ionic portico and ornate pediment. Over the doorway and the double windows are heavy pediments, and engraved in the frieze are the names of men famous in the history of literature. The reading room is on the first floor; offices of the Cabell County Board of Education occupy the second floor. The building was erected in 1903, and the library, which has 40,373 volumes, maintains a circulating service for the county.

3. MEMORIAL PARK, a two-lane parkway extending along the edge of Kiwanis Park from 7th St. W. to 13th St. W., is dedicated to the memory of the Huntington and Cabell county men who died in the First World War. Memorial trees with metal markers commemorating the dead are placed at intervals along the boulevard. At the east entrance to the park stands MEMORIAL ARCH, a reproduction of the Arc de Triomphe in Paris, erected by the Cabell County War Memorial Association in 1924. The decorative motif of the arch centers around the service insignia of the A.E.F., with holly wreaths and coils of leaves carved in the stone. Field artillery pieces from World War battlefields stand in a grass-covered plaza directly in front of the arch.

4. RITTER PARK, 13th Ave. between 8th St. E. and 12th St. E., directly south of the business section, is a 70-acre tract of level and rolling land lying on both sides of Four Pole Creek. North of the creek the land is level but toward the south the park covers tree-shaded hills cut here and there by shallow ravines. Opposite the south end of Tenth Street are six tennis courts, and foot and bridle paths wind around the hill slopes. On a high knob is CALDWELL MEMORIAL, a circular pavilion of gleaming white granite with eight Doric columns, honoring James Lewis Caldwell, who served in the War between the States and was one of the first settlers in Huntington. Across Four Pole Creek at the south end of Eighth Street is the arched stone entrance to the ROSE

GARDEN, a half-acre oval-shaped plot, enclosed by a low wall of native stone. The ground, landscaped to conform with the general slope of the hill, is in three terraces separated by stone walls, with steps leading from terrace to terrace. Brick walks separate the circular rosebeds at the front of the garden and lead to a lily pool near the south wall. Over the stone walls and a brown-stained arbor at the west end clamber red, yellow, white, and pink rambler roses. Sixty varieties are represented in the 2,500 bushes, and in midsummer the whole plot is a varicolored carpet of fragrant roses. Lying along the slopes of a small ravine, east of the Rose Garden is the AMPHITHEATER, with wooden seats to accommodate 1,000 spectators, built along two slopes overlooking a stage and bandstand.

5. MARSHALL COLLEGE (*all buildings open during school hours*), in the east central section of Huntington, has its main entrance at 16th St. E. and 4th Ave. It has an average enrollment of 1,750 students, about half of them women. The 25-acre campus is oblong in shape, with most of the buildings placed along the outer edges. Inside this hollow rectangle are spacious lawns, an athletic practice field, and fields for intramural sports.

Established in 1837 and named Marshall Academy in honor of Chief Justice John Marshall of the United States Supreme Court, who had died two years previously, the college is the second largest seat of higher education in the State. The Virginia General Assembly in 1838 authorized the incorporation of the academy and the appointment of a board of trustees. Three months later the board purchased a one-acre tract for $40, and arranged for the construction of a four-room frame school building to replace the log cabin then in use. Two teachers comprised the first faculty.

A Presbyterian chapel occupied one of the rooms in the new building, and the academy became a center of church activity. The Presbyterians and later the Methodists were closely identified with the growth of the academy during the next decade, when increased enrollment reflected the growing population of the surrounding area. After progressing slowly and with varying degrees of success, the academy passed under the control of the Methodist Episcopal Church, South, in 1850. In 1858 the Virginia assembly raised the academy to college standing, but financial stringency made it increasingly difficult to keep the institution open. In 1863 the property was sold under deed of trust to Mrs. Salina C. Mason for $1,200, and during the unsettled period of the War between the States the work of teaching was carried on by unpaid volunteers, with the one building serving alternately as a school and as an infirmary for wounded soldiers.

In 1867 the West Virginia Legislature appropriated $30,000 for the establishment of a State normal school, to be augmented by $10,000 raised by local subscription. The regents purchased an additional 12 acres of land and added another story to a brick building that had replaced the frame structure. Through construction or purchase the college has since shown a steady growth in physical plant, and in enrollment and faculty membership. In 1920 the Teachers College was given the power to grant degrees, and four years later the College of Arts and Sciences was organized, with courses leading to the A.B. degree. In 1937 the college celebrated the 100th anniversary of its founding with an extensive program including addresses by prominent educators, symposia on education, a historic pageant, and the dedication of numerous art gifts and three new buildings erected at a cost of $600,000.

Entering the college grounds through the pillared west entrance, a serpentine drive passes in front of the Administration Building and College Hall Dormitory, located on the south at College Avenue. Just inside this west entrance stands the marble BUST OF JOHN MARSHALL, unveiled during the final ceremonies of the college's centennial celebration.

OLD MAIN, facing 4th Ave., is the oldest and largest building and houses the administration offices, bookstore, cafeteria, auditorium, and classrooms. Three stories high and built in four sections at different periods, the present structure is of red brick with carved stone cornices. The center section was finished in 1874.

COLLEGE HALL, a three-story red brick dormitory for women, is attached to the rear of Old Main. It overlooks 3rd Ave. from a shaded knoll and broad lawn, with a grove of trees intervening between the hall and the avenue. The original structure was erected in 1874, but was remodeled in 1895, and added to in 1936.

The remaining buildings conform to the Georgian Colonial style of architecture, and, with the exception of the Shawkey Student Union Building, are constructed of red brick. NORTHCOTT SCIENCE HALL, on the corner of 16th St. E. and College Ave., which runs east and west between 4th and 5th Aves., is an oblong, three-story structure, finished in 1915, housing classrooms, kitchens, and practice and research laboratories. One block east, at E. 17th St., is the PHYSICAL EDUCATION BUILDING, opened in 1921, a three-story structure flanked by tennis courts and housing classrooms, athletic offices, gymnasium, and two swimming pools. On the northeast corner at this intersection stands the ALBERT GALLATIN JENKINS TRAINING SCHOOL, completed and opened in 1938, a three-story laboratory school for teacher training, boasting the finest of modern educational equipment.

HODGES HALL for men and LAIDLEY HALL for women, dormitories completed in 1937 and each housing 150 students, stand on the eastern boundary of the campus at E. 18th St., the first on the corner of College Ave., the second on the corner of 3rd Ave. A row of tennis courts fills the area between the dormitories. MUSIC HALL, adjoining Laidley Hall on 3rd Ave., is a two-story structure purchased by the college and remodeled to provide practice rooms for piano and voice students, recital halls, classrooms, and facilities for band practice. MORROW LIBRARY, on 3rd Ave. east of College Hall, was opened in 1930 and named for James E. Morrow, former President of the college and father of the statesman Dwight W. Morrow, who was born in a house that formerly stood on the college grounds. The three-story building of red brick, with wide hewn-stone steps and Colonial dormers, is set off by an entrance portico supported by four Corinthian columns rising the height of the building. The library contains 34,000 volumes. The reading room on the second floor is vaulted and soundproofed, and has indirect lighting and a maximum of wall space given over to windows. Three murals adorn the wall over the librarian's desk, a gift of Mrs. Marion Vest Fors, West Virginia artist, during the centennial celebration of 1937. From left to right, they depict American literature, the growth of the college, and West Virginia literature. Classrooms and an art gallery containing a small permanent collection of paintings occupy the remaining space in the building.

The SHAWKEY STUDENT UNION BUILDING, a low, rambling structure of brick and frame construction painted white, stands at College Ave. and Elm St. where the serpentine driveway leaves the campus. The center of campus social life, it contains a dance floor and recreational facilities. Finished in 1932, the building was named for Dr. Morris P. Shawkey, former president of the college. EVERETT HALL, 5th Ave. and Elm St., a three-story brick residence owned by the college, provides room and board for 25 men. The TRAINING SCHOOL ANNEX and the COLLEGE CLINIC are frame buildings on 5th Ave. at E. 17th St. The former houses the overflow from the Jenkins Training School and certain special classes, while the latter serves the college physician and houses a dispensary. The PRESIDENT'S HOME, just west of Elm St. on 5th Ave. is a three-story brick and stucco building, gabled and chimneyed in the Colonial manner.

6. CHESAPEAKE AND OHIO SHOPS (*open upon application at office*), between 5th and 8th Aves. and 23rd and 28th Sts. in the east end of the city, are the largest locomotive and passenger-car repair shops on the C. and O. line. The shops include 74 frame and metal supplementary structures scattered between the larger red brick locomotive and car repair buildings, brass foundry, blacksmith shops, and roundhouse. Most of the buildings were erected over a period of years prior to 1926, but the main locomotive shops were built in 1929–30. Their maximum output of heavy repairs is 50 locomotives in 25 working days, or two locomotives received and two discharged every eight hours. Locomotives dispatched from road service for repairs have their fires dumped, ash pans cleaned, and boilers blown down and drained before the main shop forces take charge. Then the tender is removed, and a storage-battery locomotive hauls the engine to the stripping shed. An inspection determines the materials needed for repairs, then a stripping gang removes all pipes, gauges, and mountings, while the tender is stripped in another section of the shop. Next, all main and side rods and motive apparatus are removed from the locomotive, as are the lagging, air pumps, and power reverse gear; firedoor and feedwater-

heater pumps are stripped and the stoker is loosened. The wheels and binders are dropped and a 250-ton crane lifts the locomotive atop a pit for repairs. There all parts not taken off in preliminary stripping are removed, and boiler, machine, and erecting shop crews make inspection and repairs covering every detail of the engine's construction. The locomotive is then reassembled and released for service after a final inspection.

7. INTERNATIONAL NICKEL COMPANY PLANT (*open workdays upon application at office; guides*), along the Guyandot River at Main St. and Riverside Drive on the eastern corporation line of the city, is the largest plant in the world devoted exclusively to the production of nickel and nickel alloys. Opened in 1923, the plant occupies a 90-acre tract, and its 60 red-brick and steel buildings are enclosed by a high cyclone fence. Employing 1,200 men, the plant produces rolled nickel, monel metal, and inconel, metals silvery white in color and highly resistant to rust and corrosion; the two latter are alloys developed by the company's metallurgists for specific uses to which pure nickel is not applicable.

Nickel sheet is made from matte, an ore from which all impurities, except sulphur, have been removed, and which is brought to Huntington from mines in Ontario, Canada, to be baked in huge dehydrating ovens called calciners at a temperature of 2,300°. Monel oxide is formed by this process. The oxide is mixed with charcoal, then sent to the refinery, where, in furnaces developing 2,750°, more charcoal is added, burning out the oxygen and bringing the residue to almost pure metal. Final purification takes place in electric furnaces at 2,800°. The molten metal is poured into ingot molds to cool, and when cooled the ingots go to a chipping department where rough surfaces are removed by chipping machines. Next, huge steam hammers forge the ingots into smaller sizes, called blooms, after which they are returned to have surface defects removed by pneumatic chisels. The blooms are then heated and changed in size and shape under the rolls of a 24-inch mill. From this point, the ultimate product dictates the operations through which the metal will pass; sheet is either hot- or cold-rolled in a sheet mill; strip is both hot- and cold-rolled; rods, bars, and wire are fabricated in the rod and wire mill. Final treatment of all products includes pickling or cleaning in acid baths and polishing, before they are sent to the warehouse to be shipped to all parts of the world. Nickel sheet is used for metal coinage, domestic utensils, bridge construction forms, and other structural shapes; alloys are used in the manufacture of ordnance steels, case-hardened parts, armor-piercing shells, electrodes, and other materials requiring extraordinary hardness in metal.

The FLOOD WALL, a construction project of the Department of War, financed with Department funds, is designed to protect the city from a flood crest of 72.6 feet of water, three feet more than the peak figure reached during the disastrous flood of 1937. Of the three units of construction planned, two were under way in 1940. The Guyan unit is along the western bank of the Guyandot River from the hills behind the city to high ground below 3rd Ave., on the Ohio River, a total length of 3,600 feet; the business unit is 20,000 feet long, running along the Ohio from high ground in the eastern residential section to 3rd St. W. The western unit as planned will proceed from that point to the western limits of the city.

With an overall length of 11 miles, the project will cost $11,000,000. The wall will utilize natural ground elevation as far as possible, being 20 feet in height at its highest point. Seven pumping stations will provide for sewage disposal in flood time, and huge sliding traps will fit into slotted pillars at openings in the wall where roads and railroad tracks enter and leave the city.

POINTS OF INTEREST IN ENVIRONS

Camden Park, 7.9 *m.;* Dreamland Pool, 11.5 *m.* (*see Tour* 15c).

↑↑

Morgantown

Railroad Stations: Moore and Garrett Sts., for Baltimore & Ohio R.R.; Long St. at Monongahela River, Westover, for Monongahela R.R.
Bus Station: 1058 University Ave. for Blue Ridge, White Star, and Mountain Lake Bus Lines.
Airport: 2.5 m. E. on US 119; no scheduled service.
Taxis: Zone system, fares 25¢, 35¢, and 50¢.
Busses: City fares, 10¢.
Traffic Regulations: Parking limitations marked; free parking lot on Forest Ave.; principal one-way streets in business district are High, Spruce, Chestnut, Fayette, Walnut and Pleasant Sts.
Street Order and Numbering: Streets numbered east from Monongahela River and north and south from Deckers Creek.

Accommodations: 1 hotel; tourist homes and boarding houses.

Information Service: Chamber of Commerce, City Hall, Fayette and Spruce Sts.

Motion Picture Houses: 3.
Swimming: Riverside Park, 9 m. N. on Bobtown Rd.; Sunset Beach on Lake Lynn, 5 m. NE. on Cheat Rd.
Golf: Morgantown Country Club, 1 m. N. on Star City Rd., 18 holes, greens fee 75¢ weekdays, $1 Sun.
Tennis: First Ward School, Madigan Ave. at Leonard St.; Suncrest Park, 2 m. N. on Star City Road.
Riding: Lake Lynn, 5 m. NE. on Cheat Rd., horses $1 per hr.
Boating: Whip-poor-will Camp and Sunset Beach, Lake Lynn; canoes, foot of Pleasant St., 50¢ first hr., 25¢ each additional hr.

Annual Events: Spring Music Festival, folk music and dances; Commencement at West Virginia University, June; Lantern Parade, playgrounds' display of colored lanterns, late summer; Fall Music Festival, folk fiddlers, dancers, and instrumental music; West Virginia Fox Hunters' Association Bench and Field Show, 8 days, late Oct.

MORGANTOWN (892 alt., 16,186 pop.) spreads over the narrow valley at the confluence of Deckers Creek and the Monongahela River (Ind., river of sliding banks) and upward over the hills that rise north, east, and south of the valley in a natural amphitheater. The hill to the west, across the river, is occupied by the suburban town of Westover. Dorsey Knob (1,438 alt.), a cone-shaped, rock-crested hill southwest of town, is a landmark of the section and a vantage point, accessible by car and foot trail, from which to view the curving river, the city, and the surrounding hills. Imaginative old-timers have been heard to say that they 'knew Morgantown when Dorsey Knob was a frog pond.' Much of the residential area overlooks the rest of the town, and night views from residential hilltops and highway approaches are impressive and beautiful, with twinkling lights in chains and clusters. The campus of West Virginia University, roughly triangular in shape, occupies a series of terraces that climb from the willow-bordered river toward the summit of Observatory Hill, northeast of the business section. High Street, the main thoroughfare, which boasts a brilliant 'white way' fully lighted only on special occasions, descends abruptly to the base of Observatory Hill, then gradually slopes to Deckers Creek and climbs into a residential section on the south side. At the base of the hill begins the business section, occupying several blocks south on High Street to the Deckers Creek Bridge and westward to University Avenue. Westward along the Monongahela River are railroad tracks, warehouses, glass factories and crowded streets, where there is a small community of foreign-born industrial workers.

Morgantown has a few industries, chiefly glass manufactories, and lies between the small industrial towns of Sabraton and Star City. West, north, and south are rich and active coal fields. In spite of industrial interests and the presence of the university, Morgantown retains much of the atmosphere of an old-fashioned county seat. For five days of the week the university dominates the scene; students crowd downtown streets and gather on sidewalks to converse while townsfolk try to pass. Freshmen, wearing old-gold 'pancake' caps with blue visors and following the campus rule of speaking to all upperclassmen, add to the appearance of sociability on the streets. Co-eds trip along in groups or pairs, or stroll laughing with men students. Sweatered, broad-shouldered football men form a nucleus for many impromptu gatherings on campus and street. Saturday, however, the streets seethe with an influx of farmers, coal miners, and industrial workers. In the public square, hawkers, vagrant folksingers, and traveling evangelists attract large crowds. If the show is good the coin cup is well filled; if not, the crowd turns away grinning, only to gather again when another performer takes the stand. Students add their touch to the scene later in the evening as they pass along the crowded streets, usually in formal dress, on their way to some social event, while the countryfolk wind up their day at a square dance.

In the fall of 1758 Thomas Decker led a party of settlers to the mouth of Deckers Creek near the present site of Morgantown and established a village, but the following spring raiding Delaware and Mingo Indians destroyed the settlement and killed or captured all the settlers except one, who escaped to Fort Pitt. In 1767 Zackquill Morgan, son of Morgan Morgan, and others reached the mouth of Deckers Creek, made a clearing, and erected log houses and two forts. Indian raids were frequent, but, with the protection of Fort Kern and Fort Morgan, the village grew, and in 1781 a 400-acre tract belonging to Morgan was laid off in lots for a town. In 1783 the seat of Monongalia (variant of Monongahela) County was moved here; the following year the village contained several log houses, a frame courthouse, jail, store, and gristmill. That year George Washington came to the community to confer with Colonel Morgan on the possibilities of an inland waterway or a land route to the west through Virginia territory. The following year the town was incorporated by the Virginia assembly and named for its founder. By 1793 Morgantown was the southern terminus of a road opened by the *Pittsburgh Gazette,* which distributed its papers by private riders. A year later a post office was established and post roads were opened to Hagerstown, Maryland, and Brownsville, Pennsylvania. Because it was the nearest point at which immigrants from the east could reach the navigable western waters, Morgantown felt a stimulating influence from the tide of westward immigration. By the close of the eighteenth century it was one of three post towns in western Virginia, had stores, taverns, potteries, wagon shops, boatyards, two tanneries, and a distillery owned by Hugh Neeley turning out 'Old Monongahela Rye.' A lively flatboat traffic supplied western settlements with whisky and crockery, products for which early Morgantown was well known. An iron industry started in 1790 took on importance, with more than 1,200 persons employed at one furnace. The town was the trading center for numerous settlements in Monongalia County, which, by 1810, had a population of 12,783.

Morgantown early realized the need of education and supported a number of frontier subscription schools. In 1814 Monongalia Academy was incorporated as a boys' school, and in 1839 Morgantown Female Collegiate Institute was established.

In 1825, as Morgantown began to need better transportation, numerous improvements were made for slackwater navigation on the Monongahela River. The first steamboat, the *Reindeer,* arrived on the rainy Sunday morning of April 29, 1826, and tied up in a bend about a mile below the town. When word arrived that the boat was there church congregations unanimously arose, left ministers in the midst of their sermons, and hurried down to the river in the rain to view the wonder. Several State roads were constructed into adjoining counties, connecting with the Ohio River, but in 1827, when one of the earliest proposed routes of the Baltimore & Ohio Railroad was surveyed by way of Deckers Creek through Morgantown to the Ohio River, citizens of the town and county joined in opposing the line. They contended that the 'soulless corporation with their screeching locomotives would affect wagon traffic, reduce the price of horse feed, set our haystacks on fire, and frighten to death our hogs and wives,' and at mass meetings demanded that the railroad be made to stop at Cumberland, so that 'all the goods will be wagoned through our country, all the hogs fed with our corn, and all the horses with our oats.'

For a score of years, although the construction of the Northwestern Turnpike diverted some trade, Morgantown had no reason to regret its fight against the railroad. The town's activity was stimulated by a cross-country wagon trade, furnishing supplies to construction camps and whisky to the laborers, whose drunkenness and rioting often taxed the law officers of near-by counties. The brisk whisky trade was followed by a strong prohibition period led by the churches, but in 1860 someone facetiously remarked 'that in spite of W. T. Wiley's [later one of the first United States senators from West Virginia] orations on temperance and politics far too many citizens of Monongalia County continue to drink whisky and vote the Democratic ticket as they did under Jackson.'

When the railroad was completed from Baltimore to Fairmont in 1852 and trade began to slump, Morgantown realized its early mistake and tried as hard to obtain a railroad as it had previously done to keep one away. During the War between the States, however, the lack of railway lines was an advantage, for most cities so situated were the targets of many attacks. Morgantown's only war experience came in the spring of 1863, when Brigadier General William Ezra Jones with 2,000 Confederate troops, assigned to destroy railroads and collect supplies, bivouacked in the town for two days. The raiders took all the horses, hats, boots, drugs, and whisky they could find, but they did not altogether forget their southern gallantry, for one of the officers apologized to a town lady, explaining that the local whisky was far superior to brands found in the South.

Morgantown's interest in education was reflected in the growth of Monongalia Academy and Female Collegiate Institute and the establishment of Woodburn Female Seminary in 1858. This educational foundation made Morgantown the logical choice for a State institution of higher learning, and in 1866 the State accepted an offer of the property of Monongalia Academy and Woodburn Seminary for the establishment of the Agricultural College of West Virginia. The school opened in 1867 and a year later, with an enlarged and revised program, was renamed West Virginia University. While providing for higher education, town officials did not neglect elementary educational facilities, for in 1866 they established the first public school, with 100 students enrolled, and the first school for Negroes, with 40 students.

For two decades following the War between the States persistent efforts were made to obtain railway connections, and in 1886 a branch line of the Baltimore & Ohio Railroad was extended from Fairmont. The impetus given by the railroad was reflected in new enterprises, increased real-estate values, and civic improvements, although a majority of the townspeople continued to put custom and sentiment before material progress and to resist what seemed to them radical changes. Only after a struggle did the town council succeed in having hitching racks removed from the main streets, and there was considerable opposition to the erection of a new courthouse.

Near-by oil fields were opened in 1889, pipe lines were laid through the town, and a pumping station was established in 1890. In 1896 the availability of natural gas brought a number of glass plants; the first was the Seneca Glass Plant, which was moved from Fostoria, Ohio. By 1910 there were nine glass plants and the population of Morgantown reached 9,000, exclusive of the suburban residential towns of Westover, Riverside, Granville, and Sturgiss City, which looked to Morgantown for their trade. Between 1910 and 1920 the glass industry reached a peak employment of 1,500 persons with an annual pay roll of $1,500,000. In 1929 and 1930, however, this industry experienced severe setbacks and more than half of the plants were closed. Of the city's former industries, only three glass plants and a shirt factory remain.

POINTS OF INTEREST

The McCLEERY HOUSE, SW. corner High and Pleasant Sts., is probably the oldest building in Morgantown. Erected in 1790, the two-story frame Georgian Colonial structure with its sagging gable roof is reinforced by brick walls on the first story and is occupied by a drugstore and photographer's shop. Colonel William McCleery, who built and lived in this house, was an Irish immigrant. He took an active part in the settlement and government of this section and in defending it against Indian attacks. His wife was Isabella Stockton, who was captured by Indians at Fort Neally when she was a girl.

The MONONGALIA COUNTY COURTHOUSE (*open 9–5 week-days*), High St. between Walnut and Court Sts., a brick and stone structure of Gothic architecture with a tower at one corner, is set at the back of a broad tree-shaded concrete square. At the base of the tower is the entrance to the building and at its top is the town clock. In the summer farmers and retired townspeople gather here early in the morning and while away the day lounging on well-worn benches beneath the elms and maples that shade what local residents call the 'concrete green.' The women set up small stands for the sale of eggs, jelly, and handiwork. On the square is a deep-well drinking fountain.

The first courts of Monongalia County were held in Zackquill Morgan's house. In 1802 a two-story brick building was erected on the present site and served the county until 1846, when it was replaced by a larger two-story building with a small dome, topped with a hand-carved wooden statue of Patrick Henry. The statue is preserved in the Morgantown High School auditorium. In 1884 this building was pronounced dangerous and the county court hired an architect from Pittsburgh to draw plans and estimate costs for a new building. Strenuous objections were made by citizens, who claimed that the county could not afford a new building and proposed that temporary repairs be made on the old one. In 1890, however, the court, influenced by leading citizens, awarded the contract for a new building, but bond issues to raise money for its construction were voted down. When citizens for the second time voted against the proposed bond issue, the court resorted to strategy. After authorizing the removal of the old building, which was to begin at midnight, September 13, 1890, the circuit judge and other court officials absented themselves from town to forestall injunction proceedings. At an early hour the following morning persons who opposed the new building saw the old one being demolished, and when they attempted to stop it they discovered that officials were away. To meet the emergency need for a new building, county orders were used to pay for the construction. The opposition attempted to bring court proceedings to secure an annulment but could not find a lawyer who would present the case. The present building was dedicated in 1891, but for many years citizens of the county lamented the great waste of money spent for such a large building.

The OLD STONE HOUSE, Chestnut St. between Walnut and Fayette Sts., now an antique shop, was built sometime prior to 1813. It is a two-story native sandstone building with green shutters and a gable roof. On one side is a small one-story frame wing. The earliest record of the building was set down in 1813 when John W. Thompson moved into it. There is a local tradition that the first rug in town was placed on the floor of this house, and that visitors who came to view the new household refinement were careful to step over it.

WEST VIRGINIA UNIVERSITY (*all buildings open during school hours unless otherwise noted*), entrance Willey St. at University Ave., occupies a series of terraces that rises steeply from the Monongahela River; the campus proper, covering 66 acres, is roughly triangular in shape. It has an annual enrollment of about 2,700 students, a third of them women.

In addition to the curriculum of the College of Arts and Sciences, the university offers courses in law leading to the degree of Bachelor of Law. The *West Virginia Law Quarterly,* official organ of the West Virginia Bar Association, is published by the College of Law.

The College of Engineering offers courses in chemical, civil, electrical, and mechanical engineering. It maintains an engineering experiment station specializing in studies on coal, oil, gas, clays, stone, sand, timber, water power, sewerage, sanitation, and road building. Findings are published in bulletin form. The School of Mines, offering courses in coal mining and geology and oil and gas engineering, operates a department of mining and industrial extension that is of great importance to the State. A six-weeks' short course in coal mining is offered in June and July of each summer for mine operators, officials, and employees of mines in the State. The curriculum includes methods of operation, mine gases, safety lamps and their use, mine fires and explosions, and safety organization and administration. Following the short course, the State department of mines conducts an examination for mine foremen and fire bosses. Vocational courses are offered in numerous towns within the State, an extension instructor traveling from town to town to hold weekly classes until a four-year course is completed. The School of Mines also holds an annual water purification conference and conducts an annual training school for firemen. A road school is held each year in co-operation with the State road commission, and problems of highway construction and maintenance are given practical consideration.

The College of Agriculture operates an experiment station; offers the usual courses in home economics and agriculture; has a four-year course in forestry, including management, utilization and protection of forests, with field study on forest lands in the Monongahela National Forest; and carries on a widespread program of agricultural extension through county agents, the 4-H Club Camp at Jackson's Mill (*see Tour* 10*a*), a recreation and rural-urban relations program at Oglebay Park (*see Wheeling*), and a demonstration community apple-packing plant at Inwood. The college owns and operates eight farms, five of them near Morgantown, for experimental and demonstration purposes.

The university was established as a land-grant college by the State legislature in 1867. At first the school amounted to little more than a classical secondary school, but with the recovery of the State from post-war conditions, the institution grew. To the original Arts and Science College other colleges and schools were added. After a long controversy women were admitted to the classical departments of the university in 1889 and to other departments in 1897. Since 1928 the institution has worked toward the ideal of 'building the university into the life of the State.'

The oldest part of the campus is THE CIRCLE, a level terrace on University Ave. just north of its intersection with College Ave.

MARTIN HALL, south side of the Circle, the oldest of the college buildings, erected in 1870, is an ivy-covered, two-story red brick structure with a mansard roof surmounted by a white cupola. Stone quoins decorate the corners of the building and the arched entrances.

WOODBURN HALL, west side of the Circle, was erected in 1874–6 on the site of the old Woodburn Seminary building, which burned in 1873. Traditionally the symbol of the university, Woodburn is the shrine of returning alumni. The three-story red brick structure, with mansard roof and towers at the wing ends and over the west entrance, is crowned with a domed clock tower. The crowning achievement of undergraduate pranksters occurred in 1902, when a cow was successfully led into the bell tower. Having docilely ascended four flights of steps, she would not be led down again and was finally lowered by means of an improvised derrick. Woodburn now houses the College of Pharmacy and the Department of Journalism, which publishes the *Daily Athenaeum,* a student-edited campus newspaper.

SCIENCE HALL, north side of the Circle, a three-story building of red brick erected in 1893, completes the open quad that encloses the Circle. On the second floor is the BIOLOGY MUSEUM, containing mounted specimens of animals and plants native to the State.

North of Woodburn Hall and overlooked by its classroom windows is the great horseshoe of MOUNTAINEER FIELD STADIUM. Built in 1924 with a seating capacity of 40,000, the stadium occupies what was formerly the bed of Falling Run, a small stream that now flows through a conduit far beneath the playing field. At home football games and field and track meets the stadium is lined with flags and pennants of the university and visiting teams. The stands crackle with yells led by white-sweatered cheer leaders, the cadet band swings into 'It's West Virginia, it's West Virginia,' and the symbolic mountaineer, garbed in buckskin and wearing a coonskin cap, leans quietly on his long rifle throughout pre-game and 'tween-halves demonstrations. The Fi Batar Cappers, members of the university's fun fraternity, dressed in top hats and tails and carrying canes, solemnly remove their hats as they sing the indecorous 'Lydia Pinkham.' South stands and bowl seats are reached from the Circle and the campus end of University Bridge, while north stand seats are reached from Campus Driveway. Southeast of the Circle and downhill from it are ELIZABETH MOORE HALL, recreation and physical education building for women, a red brick structure of modified Georgian Colonial design; the PRESIDENT'S HOME, a two-story house with a two-story Corinthian portico and colonnaded porch; the INFIRMARY; the MUSIC SCHOOL; and the MEDICAL BUILDING, where a two-year course of medical training is given.

The LAW BUILDING, University Ave. south of the President's Home, was completed in 1923. It is a three-story building of red brick, trimmed with Indiana limestone and fronted by a pedimented portico with four Doric columns. Over the arched end windows of the building is a raised stone representation of the State seal of West Virginia, and a frieze bears the names of eminent jurists, including Coke, Blackstone, and Story. The building houses classrooms, the law library, a practice court room, and the University Bookstore in the basement.

The FIELD HOUSE, Beechurst Ave., contains, in addition to locker rooms and showers, a sectional wooden basketball floor, which is removed for indoor track meets. The building is the center of men's activities in physical education.

East of the Circle are three other groups of buildings. In a triangular area bounded on two sides by University Avenue and College Avenue are the EXPERIMENT STATION, a rambling two-story red brick building begun in 1869 and added to from time to time; OGLEBAY HALL, a four-story red brick and limestone building with a colonnaded entrance back of the Experiment Station, and OGLEBAY HALL ANNEX. All are used by students of the College of Agriculture. On the east side of College Avenue, extending from Commencement Hall to Oglebay Hall, is the steam-heated sidewalk. Because heating conduits run beneath, it dries rapidly in wet weather and rids itself quickly of snow in winter. In the basement of Oglebay Hall is a student-operated store where dairy products from the university farm are sold.

East of the agriculture buildings and slightly above the rest of the campus on the hillside is WOMAN'S HALL, a long red brick and Indiana limestone dormitory, fronted by an elevated portico with Corinthian columns. The central part of this building was erected in 1917–19, and the wings were added later. Below Woman's Hall are COMMENCE-

MENT HALL, a three-story red brick building begun in 1869 and completed in 1892, and the OLD LIBRARY, built in 1902, a gray stone structure of Gothic design with a colonnaded tower at one end. This building, looking very much like a church, now houses administrative offices. Back of the Old Library and flanked by Commencement Hall, the CAFETERIA, the rambling red brick MECHANICAL HALL, and the two-story castle-like red brick ARMORY, is the OLD ATHLETIC FIELD, used for university baseball games, football practice, and R.O.T.C. military drill and parades. Mechanical Hall houses the College of Engineering, the School of Mines, and the laboratory of the State Road Commission, where materials used in West Virginia roads are scientifically tested.

West of this group, across Prospect Street, are the four-story CHEMISTRY BUILDING, completed in 1926, and the LIBRARY (*open 7:45 a.m.– 10 p.m. weekdays; 2–5 Sun.*), a red brick and Indiana limestone building of Georgian Colonial architecture completed in 1931. The present building is two stories high with a basement, but architect's plans call for a central section to contain stack rooms, rising as high again as the present building. Around the entrance the building is faced with Indiana limestone, with a raised seal of the State over the door. The library contains 175,000 books, including a number of rare volumes, among them a Latin Bible printed in 1491, a Breeches Bible printed in 1610, and a Hebrew manuscript with the Book of Ruth printed on a parchment scroll. Among the first editions are *Poems of Samuel Drayton* (1640), Milton's *Paradise Lost, East and West* by Bret Harte, *Chronicles of Border Warfare* by Alexander S. Withers, *Butterflies of North America* by William H. Edwards, and *Christian Panoply* by Bishop Richard Watson, the first book published in West Virginia (Shepherdstown, 1791).

Southwest of the Library is the FACULTY CLUB HOUSE, formerly the I. C. White House. It is a rambling two-story frame structure painted brown and yellow, with a jigsaw woodwork around the eaves and the top of the porch. A small turret rises at the back of the house, and at the front a round tower is crowned by a steeple. I. C. White (1848–1927) was professor of geology at the university from 1877 to 1892, assistant geologist of the United States Geological Survey from 1884 to 1888, and West Virginia State geologist (the first occupant of this position) from 1897 until his death. In 1882 he gained international recognition for his anticlinal theory of oil and gas deposits, which led to the opening of oil and gas fields in West Virginia. For two years, 1904–6, he was in Brazil at the invitation of the Brazilian Government studying the coal deposits of that country. He served as treasurer and president of the Geological Society of America, vice president of the American Society for the Advancement of Science, and president of the American Association of Petroleum Geologists; and he represented America at the International Geological Conference held in St. Petersburg, Russia, in 1897 and at the meeting held in Paris in 1900. A few years before his death he deeded to the university and the city of Morgantown a 1,900-acre tract of coal land, the income to be used for development of the geological department of the school and the maintenance of parks and hospitals in the city.

The MEN'S DORMITORY, a four-story, M-shaped, red brick building, stands across North High Street from the campus.

The UNIVERSITY DEMONSTRATION HIGH SCHOOL, N. High St., completed in 1933, occupies the crest of the hill, high above the university grounds and separated from them by residential streets. In this air-conditioned three-story building of red brick and Indiana limestone, students in the department of education do their practice teaching. The Dalton plan, in which each student completes his work in installments, or contracts, at his own speed, is used in the school, but revised to include group recitation periods.

LYONDEL (*open by telephoned appointment*), 836 Price St., is a semicommercial informal flower garden owned by Leon H. Leonian, assistant professor of biology at the university. Back of a tree-shaded lawn, landscaped with evergreens, a fish pool and a stone summer house, are long beds of Oriental poppies flanked by beds of delphiniums, and border beds of iris, day lilies, and columbines. Mr. Leonian experiments with hybridizing delphiniums and many experimental varieties are produced in this garden as well as on a tract of land he maintains at Terra Alta. The garden, in blooming season, is a favorite gathering place for humming birds.

The SENECA GLASS PLANT (*open on application at office*), Beechurst Ave. and 7th St., is the oldest glass plant operating in Morgantown, having been moved from Fostoria, Ohio, in 1896. The factory is a long, low, rambling series of connected buildings, some of brick, some of corrugated steel and frame construction, with a two-story frame office building. The plant manufactures table and stemware and during peak production employs 250 workers.

The ALEXANDER WADE HOUSE (*private*), 256 Prairie Ave., is a two-story red brick house with a mansard roof. The house was built by Judge Bunker about 1860 and in 1872 was purchased by Alexander Wade, who made it his home until his death in 1904. Wade, as a teacher in the schools of West Virginia and superintendent of the schools of Monongalia County, developed a system of graduation in country schools that was adopted nationally. He suggested that more work would be accomplished in country schools if a definite amount of work was assigned to be accomplished in a given time, and in 1874 introduced his system of graduation and promotional examinations in the Monongalia County schools. The plan attracted national attention in 1879, after Wade had read a paper before the National Education Association at Philadelphia, and the association adopted a resolution urging 'that the attention of State Superintendents of Public Instruction through the United States be called to the propriety of adopting a Graduating System for Country Schools.' In 1881 Wade published *A Graduating System for Country Schools*. West Virginia legalized the system in its public schools in 1890, and other States adopted similar graduating systems.

The WAITMAN T. WILLEY HOUSE (*private*), 128 Wagner Rd., is a two-story brick dwelling covered with Virginia creeper. Five fluted Doric columns support the triangular pediment of the portico. Paired chimneys rise at the gable ends of the main unit. The house was built in 1838 by Waitman T. Willey (1811–1900), lawyer, orator, and statesman. Born near Farmington, Willey gained his education by the hard 'hit-or-miss' method of the frontier. At 16 he walked 45 miles to enroll in Madison College at Uniontown, Pennsylvania. He worked his way through the school and later studied law. During his early political career in Monongalia County he was known as the wheel horse of the Whig party in northwestern Virginia. He served as clerk of the county court, as presidential elector in 1840, and as a member of the Reform Convention of 1850. When the break between the North and South came, Willey took his stand against secession, and in the first Wheeling Convention stood with the conservatives in influencing the group's vote to delay the new-State movement until Virginia's position was clear. The Restored Government of Virginia elected him to the United States Senate to fill the vacancy created by the withdrawal of James M. Mason. Later he was one of the first two senators elected from the new State.

The BERGY GARDEN (*open by telephoned appointment*), 317 Dormont St., is an informal rock garden owned by Professor G. A. Bergy of the College of Pharmacy of West Virginia University. It includes more than 100 varieties of vines and flowering plants, including native wild flowers and a few rare varieties from Europe and Asia.

POINTS OF INTEREST IN ENVIRONS

Cheat Lake, 7.2 *m.*; Coopers Rock State Forest, 9 *m.*; Arthurdale, 17.1 *m* (*see Tour 21a*).

Parkersburg

Railroad Stations: 6th St. at Avery St. for Baltimore & Ohio R.R. (Main Line);
Ann St. at 2nd St. for Baltimore & Ohio R.R. (Ohio River Division).
Airport: Parkersburg Airport, 3 m. N. on US 21; taxi 50¢, interurban 7¢; charter
planes only; day and night service.
Bus Station: 414 7th St. for Atlantic and Capitol Greyhound Lines and West
Virginia Transportation Co.
Taxis: 1-4 persons, 25¢ in city.
Streetcars: 7¢ in city; interurban to Williamstown 28¢, to Marietta, Ohio, 35¢.
Traffic Regulations: Market St. one-way for south bound traffic.

Accommodations: 6 hotels; tourist homes and boarding houses.

Information Service: Board of Commerce, City Building, NW corner Market and
5th Sts.

Radio Station: WPAR (1450 kc.).
Theater and Motion Picture Houses: Coliseum auditorium, NE. corner 7th and
Green Sts. for local stage productions; 5 motion picture houses.
Riding: 1 m. S. on US 21, horses $1 per hour.
Swimming: City Park, Park Ave. and 19th St., open May 29—Sept. 5, adults 25¢,
children 10¢; Y.M.C.A. pool, 8th St. between Market and Juliana Sts., non-
members 35¢.
Golf: Nicely-Villa Field Club, 4 m. S. on Gihon Road, 18 holes 60¢, 9 holes 35¢.

Annual Events: Spring and Fall Flower Shows, May and Sept.; School Children's
Field Day, May; Horse Show, no fixed date; Dahlia Show, fall.

PARKERSBURG (615 alt., 29,625 pop.), seat of Wood County, is
an industrial and shipping center at the confluence of the Little Kanawha and Ohio Rivers in the northwestern part of the State. The triangular business district, few buildings of which are more than four
stories high, and the loosely connected residential areas are a result
of several periods of rapid and haphazard expansion. These periods
followed the coming of highways, discovery of oil and gas near by,
the coming of railroads, and finally the city's industrial development.

Although it is one of the five major centers of population and manufacturing in West Virginia, the city proper is spared the usual congestion, smoke, and disorder of an industrial city, for most of the plants
are grouped along the Little Kanawha River in an unincorporated
section at the southern approach to the city. A few of the plants extend northward along the Ohio River front. In the 30 principal manufactories are produced equipment for oil and gas wells, shovels and
garden tools, office furniture, fence and roofing supplies, glass table-

ware and novelties, milk bottles, shoes, corrugated fiber boxes, iron and steel products, silk yarn, rayon yarn, vitrolite, and porcelain and tile products.

Three major highways US 50, US 21, and State 2, bring a heavy tourist business to Parkersburg each summer and a large volume of rural trade throughout the year. It is the junction of the east-west and north-south lines of the Baltimore & Ohio Railroad in West Virginia and the shipping point for an Ohio Valley farmers co-operative association. The main line of the railroad is carried across the principal business district on a viaduct.

The site where Parkersburg stands was once an Indian hunting ground. The first white people to come to this region were possibly French trappers and traders; the first Englishman of whom there is any record was Christopher Gist, who passed through here on his expedition to Ohio in 1751. Captain William Crawford and a group of explorers came to the Ohio River in the vicinity of the Little Kanawha River in 1769.

The following year George Washington came here to locate lands awarded him by Governor Robert Dinwiddie of Virginia for military service. In his journal Washington tells of leaving the canoes at the mouth of the Little Kanawha River, 'intending to meet them at the mouth of the Muskingum River, about 12 miles above the point,' and then notes the lay of the land, streams, fertility of the soil, and the abundance of game in the region.

In 1773 Robert Thornton made a claim for a part of the site of Parkersburg by tomahawk entry, a method of claiming land by notching trees bounding the area with a tomahawk or ax. In 1783 Thornton sold his 1,350 acres to Alexander Parker of Pittsburgh for $50. The land, which is on the north side of the Little Kanawha River and includes the 'Point,' was not settled immediately by Parker, but in 1785 Captain James Neal, who had surveyed the Parker tract, led a small party of settlers to a site on the south bank about a mile above the mouth of the river. They called the settlement, which included a stockade fort, Neal's Station. Meanwhile, John Stokely built a cabin on the Point and, because of the confused land records of Virginia,

---

KEY FOR PARKERSBURG MAP

1. The POINT, confluence of Ohio and Little Kanawha Rivers. 2. NEMESIS PARK, on the summit of a hill just south of the mouth of the Little Kanawha River. 3. The STRATFORD HOTEL, NW. corner Court Square and 3rd St. 4. PARKERSBURG RIG AND REEL COMPANY PLANT, 620 Depot St. 5. OAKLAND, 1131 7th St. 6. CITY PARK, Park Ave. and 19th St. 7. In the CENTRAL JUNIOR-SENIOR HIGH SCHOOL, Dudley Ave. between Stadium Dr. and 19th St. is the STAHL RELIC COLLECTION. 8. The TAVENNER HOUSE, Central Ave. between George and East Sts. 9. The AMES BALDWIN WYOMING COMPANY PLANT, Camden Ave. between Myrtle St. and Broadway. 10. The W. H. BICKLE ESTATE, 2.5 m. sw. at the junction of the Marrtown and Lubeck Rds. 11. BLENNERHASSETT ISLAND is 2 m. s. of Parkersburg in the Ohio River.

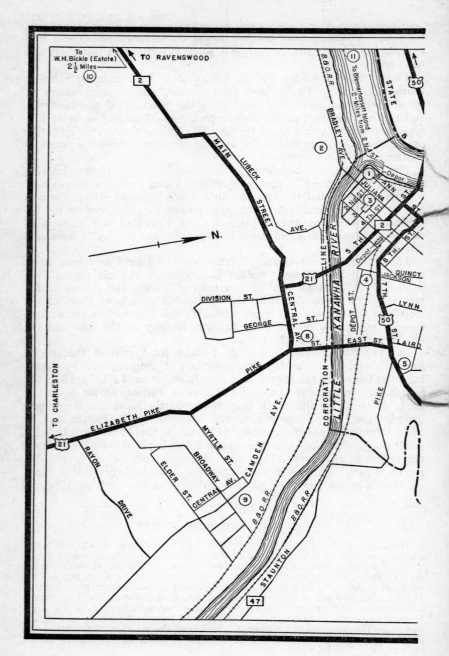

TO W. H. Bickle (Estate)
2½ Miles
⑩

➤ TO RAVENSWOOD

B.&O.R.R.

⑪

To Blennerhassett Island
2 Miles from 2 N. ST.

STATE

50

②

MAIN STREET

LUBECK AVE.

BRADLEY AVE.

Depot

①

ANN ST.

JULIANA
2 N. ST.
③
3 N. ST.
4 TH ST.

②

B.TH. ST.

N.

LINE

LITTLE KANAWHA RIVER

5 TH

Depot

QUINCY
JACKSON

21

CENTRAL AV.

DIVISION ST.

④

7 TH

50

GEORGE ST.

DEPOT ST.

LYNN

CORPORATION

LAIRD ST.

PIKE

⑧ ST.

EAST ST.

TO CHARLESTON

ELIZABETH PIKE

21

RAYON DRIVE

ELDER ST.

BROADWAY

MYRTLE ST.

CAMDEN AV.

CENTRAL AV.

⑨

B.&O.R.R.

B.&O.R.R.

PIKE

⑤

STAUNTON

47

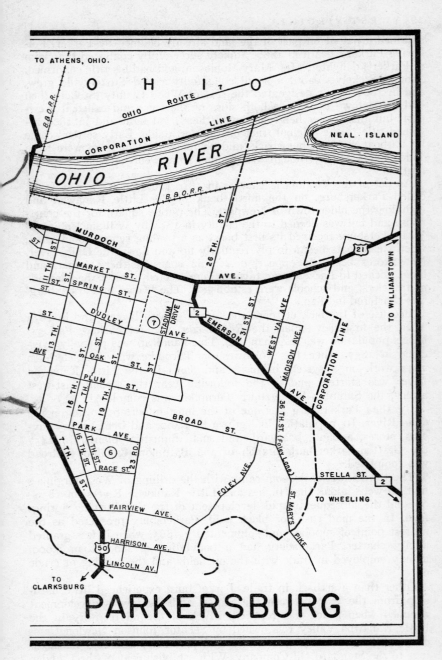

PARKERSBURG

obtained a patent on part of the land already claimed by Parker. Following Parker's death in 1880, Stokely successfully contested the claim of Parker's daughter, Mrs. Mary Robinson, and had his title confirmed. Around Stokely's cabin a small community called Stokelyville grew, and in 1801 it was designated the seat of Wood County. Stokely then laid out a town to include both sides of the river and called it Newport, but the Parker heirs continued their legal fight and in 1809 regained title to the original tract on the north side. Early settlers came by flatboat, raft, on horseback, and on foot. Most of them were from Tidewater Virginia, though many came from Pennsylvania and Connecticut.

An act of the Virginia legislature in 1810 provided for a new town, called Parkersburg, on the north bank of the Little Kanawha and including the older town of Newport. The public square for the courthouse and jail was deeded to the county in 1811 by William Robinson, Jr. Parkersburg received its first boost as a trading center about 1818, when steamboats began to ply regularly up and down the Ohio River. New stores began to appear, dealers in shoes, leather, timber, and hides flocked to Parkersburg, taverns were erected to meet the demands of travelers, and schools were established. The 'Town of Parkersburg' was chartered in 1820.

Because of the lack of roads the town's growth lagged, and in 1833 when the first newspaper, the *Republican,* was established, Parkersburg's population was less than 400. This handicap was partially overcome in 1837, when the Northwestern Turnpike was completed. In 1842 work on a system of locks and dams in the Little Kanawha River was started, and in the following year the second east-west artery, the Staunton-Parkersburg Turnpike, was completed.

By 1844 Parkersburg was one of the most important towns on the Ohio River. Its population had grown to 1,400, and it had many taverns, stores, a bank, boatyard, and small industrial plants. In 1857 the Grafton-Parkersburg branch of the Baltimore & Ohio Railroad was completed.

The town's first real boom came with the drilling of West Virginia's first oil wells, along the Hughes and Little Kanawha Rivers, in 1859–60, and the subsequent rapid development of the rich Burning Springs field. In the mad rush for black gold, Parkersburg prospered as the nearest point of supplies and shipment. By 1863, when it was granted a city charter, Parkersburg had a population of more than 3,000, mainly employed in trade with the oil fields and the refining of crude oil.

Other than a setback in trade, Parkersburg experienced little hardship from the War between the States, and the town's development resumed when peace was restored. Much of the oil territory in the Little Kanawha Valley was owned by Senator Johnson Newlon Camden, politician, financier, and industrial promoter, who sold his holdings to the Standard Oil Company. With establishment of the Camden

Refinery, Standard Oil, and other refineries, the city became the chief source of kerosene for much of the South and West.

Parkersburg's development as an industrial city greatly increased after the 1880's, when the rich gas fields east of the city were tapped and industrial plants began using natural gas instead of coal as a manufacturing fuel. After 1900 the oil fever abated, and by 1937 the last oil refinery in Parkersburg had closed, although the manufacture of oil-well equipment continued.

POINTS OF INTEREST

1. The POINT, at the confluence of the Ohio and Little Kanawha Rivers, now occupied by Murphy Park, a tiny strip of green with a walk and benches, was the scene of the first settlement and activities on the site of Parkersburg. Washington stopped here on his trip down the Ohio in 1770. Prior to 1800 the first cabins of Stokelyville were built near here. The public landing for packets and flatboats was on the Point, a scene of lively activity during the early days of westward migration on the Ohio River.

2. NEMESIS PARK, on the summit of a hill, originally known as Mount Logan, just south of the mouth of the Little Kanawha River, occupies the site of Fort Boreman, erected in 1863 to protect the city from Confederate invasion. The park, landscaped and developed as a picnic area, is owned by the Shriners but is open to the public during summer months. From the winding drive that encircles the hill there is an excellent view of Parkersburg, Blennerhassett Island, and the surrounding country. After the war the fort was converted into a private residence and stood until 1916 when it was destroyed by fire. The last public hangings in Wood County, those of two murderers, Grogan and Boice, were held on this hill in 1866. A large white oak tree used for the hangings is on the south slope of the hill.

3. The STRATFORD HOTEL, NW. corner Court Square and 3rd St., built in 1812, is the oldest business building in Parkersburg. The three-story hotel is built of brick, stuccoed over, painted yellow, and modernized until there is little resemblance to the original brick structure. Atop the original building in a brick tower was a large bell, which rang vigorously to summon guests at meal times. The place, originally called the Bell Tavern, later was known as the United States Hotel, Hill's Central, and the Commercial Hotel. In 1924 it was remodeled and renamed the Stratford Hotel.

4. PARKERSBURG RIG AND REEL COMPANY PLANT (*open on application at the office*), 620 Depot St., is the largest local plant manufacturing oil-well equipment and one of the largest in the country. The long, low rambling, many-windowed plant extends for nearly two blocks beside the Baltimore & Ohio Railroad tracks. Six hundred persons are employed in the manufacture of derricks, drills, and pumps for oil fields in the south and southwest of the United States, South America, and India.

5. OAKLAND (*house private; garden open*), 1131 7th St., the Stephenson homestead, is a square red brick Georgian Colonial house set on a knoll in the midst of a ten-acre landscaped lawn. South of the house is a rock garden in a small ravine, shaded by a grove of oak trees. The flower garden, in which iris, daffodils, dahlias, and poppies are the predominating blooms, borders the ravine. Construction of the house, originally part of a large estate, was started by James McNeil Stephenson in 1833 but not finished until ten years later, largely because much of the work was done by slave labor of materials made on the estate. Early attempts to make brick without expert direction failed and the first walls erected fell of their own weight. Finally a skilled German foreman was put in charge. The ornamental woodwork was hand-carved by one of the slaves.

6. CITY PARK, Park Ave. and 19th St., is a 50-acre public recreation area, shaded by elms, maples, and oaks. Facilities include a swimming pool, baseball diamond and bleachers, dance pavilion, band shell, refreshment stand, picnic areas, and lily and lotus ponds.

The CENTENNIAL CABIN MUSEUM (*open Thurs. afternoon*) occupies a two-story log cabin built in 1804 by Henry Cooper on a site about nine miles east of Parkersburg. The cabin was purchased by the city in 1910 and removed to the park to be preserved as a museum of the life of the pioneers. In it are relics and documents of the frontier days of the area. The LILY POND, said to be one of the largest in the country, is a circular three-and-a-half-acre lake fed by a fountain in the center. From May until the first frost it is a mass of pink and white blooms. The LOTUS POND, half the size of the lily pond, contains Egyptian and Japanese lotus, which as the summer advances grow into a waving jungle of large green leaves and huge pink and yellow blossoms that almost conceal the water. The park area, purchased by the city in 1896, was originally owned by the estate of Eugene Levassor—father-in-law of Joseph H. Diss Debar, designer of the State seal,—John S. Camden and others.

7. In the CENTRAL JUNIOR-SENIOR HIGH SCHOOL, Dudley Ave. between Stadium Drive and 19th St., may be seen the STAHL RELIC COLLECTION (*open during school hours*), many items of which were found on Blennerhassett Island. The collection includes mounted fish and birds, stone hammers and axes, arrow points, prehistoric ornaments, pottery, primitive musical instruments, coins, idols, cloth fossils, and other articles. The collection was made by the late Professor Henry Stahl, immigrant from Alsace-Lorraine, who lived in Parkersburg from 1864 until his death in 1923. It was purchased by the Parkersburg Board of Education in 1923.

8. The TAVENNER HOUSE (*private*), Central Ave. between George and Pike Sts., was erected in 1800 and is the oldest house in the vicinity. It is a two-story rectangular structure of crumbling red brick with inside brick chimneys, a massive, square, paneled doorway, and square sash windows. Before the house, which stands 100 yards from the

street, is a stone outbuilding, crumbling with age, and two frame outbuildings. The building was erected by Colonel Hugh Phelps, who operated a tavern and ferry. As a militia officer in 1806 he was ordered to arrest Aaron Burr and Harman Blennerhassett, but found that they had escaped down the Ohio River. In 1823 he sold the house to Colonel Thomas Tavenner, also an officer of the militia, and it is still in the possession of the Tavenner family. For many years this section of the town was known as Tavennerville. In the TAVENNER CEMETERY, Central Ave., a small fenced-in area across from the Tavenner House, the oldest marked grave is that of Alexander Tavenner (1768–1848).

9. The AMES BALDWIN WYOMING COMPANY PLANT (*open to groups by telephone appointment*), Camden Ave. between Myrtle St. and Broadway, manufactures 'the shovel that built America.' The advertising slogan is based on the claim that Ames shovels were first manufactured at North Easton, Massachusetts, in 1774, and were used to dig trenches at Bunker Hill and on the battlefields of every war in which the United States has engaged. The Parkersburg plant was erected in 1931 and employs, during peak production, about 600 men.

10. The W. H. BICKLE ESTATE, 2.5 *m.* SW. at the junction of the Marrtown and Lubeck Roads, is a private property of 358 acres. The stone house, which occupies the summit of a knoll, is surrounded by a broad landscaped lawn. West of the house are the STABLES and a PARK (*both open upon application at the house*). In the stables are several head of race and show horses including four white Arabians. The park is equipped with picnic facilities, a playground for children, and an artificial lake for boating. Northeast of the park is a small MENAGERIE, containing bison, elk, deer, Texas burros, zebus or sacred cows, swans, geese, ducks, guinea hens, peacocks, and turkeys. South of the menagerie is a half-mile RACE TRACK and grandstand seating 1,200 persons. Harness races and horse shows are sponsored by the owner each spring and fall.

11. BLENNERHASSETT ISLAND (*open to sightseers; picnicking, camping, and swimming prohibited*) is 2 *m.* S. of Parkersburg in the Ohio River (*can be reached only by motor launch from the foot of 2nd St.; 50¢ per person, minimum charge $2 per trip; 1 hr. for round trip*). The 507-acre island was a wilderness paradise in 1805 when Harman Blennerhassett and Aaron Burr laid their plans for setting up an empire in the Southwest. Hidden in the overgrowth of willow trees are three private dwellings, small garden patches, and a heap of foundation stones—all that remains of the once magnificent $60,000 Blennerhassett mansion, a model of which is in the State Museum at Charleston.

George Washington referred to the island in his diary in 1770, when he journeyed down the Ohio, as a 'cluster of islands.' In 1797 Blennerhassett, a wealthy and eccentric Irishman who had come to America with his young bride in search of a refuge where he could live quietly and luxuriously and carry on his experiments in the natural sciences free from the critical tongues of his family, acquired 170 acres at the head of the island. Three years later he completed the long, semicircular stone mansion, which was the show place of the Ohio Valley. In it the Blennerhassetts entertained the wealthier and better educated families of the neighboring villages.

Stories of their wealth and influence reached Aaron Burr, who, embittered and disappointed by the public's reaction to his fatal wounding of Alexander Hamilton in a duel, was seeking financial and moral support for a plan to conquer and set up an empire in the Southwest. Although his visit to the mansion at first was resented, Burr pictured for his host a Utopia where Blennerhassett would be surrounded by wealth and the intelligentsia—exactly what he had dreamed for his island estate—and Blennerhassett put his wealth and ability into the plot. With a small fleet of river boats and a company of young adventurers from the vicinity Blennerhassett started down the Ohio River under cover of darkness December 10, 1806, planning to meet Burr at Natchez. Rumors of a treason plot already had spread over Virginia and had reached President Jefferson at Washington, and the next morning a body of Virginia militia came to the island to arrest the two conspirators. Both had gone but the mansion and island were confiscated and many of the beautiful furnishings were damaged or destroyed. Mrs. Blennerhassett and the children fled. Burr and Blennerhassett were arrested by militia near Natchez, Mississippi. After the case against Burr was dismissed by a Mississippi court, he was taken to Richmond, Virginia, and there charged with treason, but he was acquitted after government witnesses failed to connect him definitely with an overt act against the Federal Government in Virginia. Blennerhassett was freed without being brought to trial, but both were held in custody to answer any indictment that might be brought against them for treason committed in Ohio. The government refused to press for indictments in Ohio and both were released. Creditors already had seized Blennerhassett's estate, and in 1811 the mansion was destroyed by fire.

For a time he attempted to recoup his fortune on a cotton plantation in the South, but meeting with only moderate success he went to New York to practice law. He failed miserably at this, and after family and former friends in Ireland refused to help him, he went to Canada and then to the Isle of Guernsey, where he died in 1831. Mrs. Blennerhassett returned to the United States in 1842 and attempted to recover from the Government for damage done to their island home while it was occupied by Federal officers and militia. She died while Congress was considering the claim, introduced by Henry Clay.

///

Shepherdstown

Railroad Station: Mill St. between German and High Sts. for Norfolk & Western Ry.
Bus Station: In front of McMurran Hall, German St. between Princess and King Sts., for Emory Bus Line, local, connecting with Blue Ridge Lines at Martinsburg.
Ferry: Across Potomac River, State 48, N. Princess St., 24-hour service; fare 25¢ car and 2 passengers, 5¢ each additional passenger.
Traffic Regulations: Parallel parking; no U turn at German and King Sts.

Accommodations: Tourist homes.

Motion Picture House: 1.
Annual Events: Confederate Memorial Day, first Saturday in June; Commencement at Shepherd State Teachers College, June; Homecoming at college, fall.

Biennial Event: May Day by public school and training department of Shepherd State Teachers College, odd years.

SHEPHERDSTOWN (405 alt., 888 pop.), which claims the distinction of being the oldest continuously settled community in the State, occupies about a square mile of rolling land above the Potomac River in the Eastern Panhandle. Lacking the stimulus of industry, Shepherdstown remains a compact community that has expanded little beyond the orderly plat made by Thomas Shepherd in 1762, when it was established under the name of Mecklenburg. Rows of gable-roofed old houses, many of them remodeled log structures set flush with the street, give the town a Dutch Colonial appearance. Through the center of the village flows Town Run, a small stream along which, in the early days of the settlement, there were half a dozen small mills. All but one of these have vanished, and Town Run is noted chiefly for the fine trout taken from its cool depths by villagers, who scarcely need to stir from established loafing places to cast their lines.

There is little in the placid life of present-day Shepherdstown to recall the bustling village of Mecklenburg where James Rumsey in 1787 gave the first successful demonstration of his steamboat, and where George Washington in 1790 considered locating the National Capital. Periodically Shepherdstown comes to life—during the apple season, from September to late November, when young and old work in the apple packing sheds; at Shepherd State Teachers College homecomings and commencements; on Confederate Memorial Day; and at election time, when, although 95 per cent of the people vote the Democratic ticket and there is usually only one local ticket, every street corner supports a group of argumentative amateur statesmen. Crowds of countryfolk throng the one main street on Saturday night, while the townspeople celebrate at Martinsburg, or at Hagerstown, Maryland.

Socially Shepherdstown expresses itself in 'Soups,' a form of celebration peculiar to the neighborhood and probably a heritage from thrifty German forbears. 'Soups,' like the church suppers and bazaars common in other communities, are given by civic and church organizations for pure sociability and to raise money. When the latter is the case the ingredients are collected—a few potatoes here, a dozen onions there—from members of the organization and put into a common pot. The resulting brew is sold by the bowl or by the quart and delivered to the buyer by volunteer messengers. Each organization tries to outshine the others in the quality of its soup specialty. In summer, soup is the main dish at lawn fetes, accompanied by ice cream and cake.

About 1730 and perhaps much earlier a group of Germans from Pennsylvania crossed the Potomac at Pack Horse Ford about three miles downstream and, without establishing title to the land, formed a small community called Mecklenburg for their former home in Germany. About the same time Richard ap Morgan obtained a legal grant to a large tract of land including the site of Shepherdstown. From him some of the settlers bought their farms. Thomas Shepherd, who arrived in 1732, bought a large part of Morgan's holdings, laid out lots and streets, and the town of Mecklenburg was chartered in 1762. It was evidently a neat little town, with its 96 'good dwellings 20 feet long and 17 feet wide with . . . stone or brick chimneys,' each on a roomy lot 103 feet wide. In the next 50 years the town grew to nearly its present size. Pack Horse Ford was a principal crossing of the Potomac River, and Mecklenburg, a frontier town on a main line of travel between the North and East and the Valley of

---

KEY FOR SHEPHERDSTOWN MAP

1. SHEPHERD STATE TEACHERS COLLEGE occupies a block in the business district on German St. between Princess and King Sts., extending to High St. 2. The SHEPHERDSTOWN FLOUR MILL, High St. between Mill and Princess Sts. 3. The 'OLDEST HOUSE IN THE STATE,' High St. between Mill and Princess Sts. 4. RUMSEY STATE PARK, N. end Mill St. 5. The LUTHERAN GRAVEYARD, German St., between Mill St. and the corporation line. 6. CHRIST REFORMED CHURCH, SE. corner German and Mill Sts. 7. The BILLMEYER HOUSE, German St. between Mill and Princess Sts. 8. The OLD MARKET HOUSE, in the middle of King St. at German St. 9. The SHEETZ HOUSE, NW. corner German and King Sts. 10. The OLD EPISCOPAL CHURCH, SE. corner Church and High Sts. 11. The PRESBYTERIAN MANSE, NW. corner Church and German Sts. 12. TRINITY EPISCOPAL CHURCH, SW. corner Church and German Sts. 13. The HARRINGTON HOUSE, German St. between Church and Duke Sts. 14. The SHEPHERD GRAVEYARD, New St. between Church and King Sts. 15. The GROVE HOUSE, SW. corner King and New Sts. 16. The COMMUNITY BUILDING, SE. corner King and New Sts. 17. The PRESBYTERIAN CHURCH, SW. corner King and Washington Sts. 18. WILD GOOSE, 3 m. N. on the Shepherd Pike. 19. MAPLE SHADE, 4 m. N. on the Shepherd Pike. 20. BELLEVUE, 0.5 m. N. of Shepherdstown on the Shepherd Pike (extension of Duke St.).

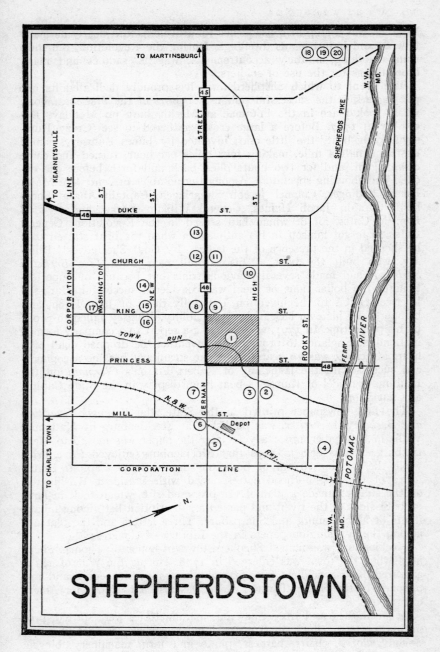

TO MARTINSBURG

18 19 20

W. VA.
MD.

45

STREET

SHEPHERDS PIKE

TO KEARNEYSVILLE

LINE

48   DUKE   ST.

ST.   ST.   ST.

CORPORATION

13

CHURCH   ST.

12   11

WASHINGTON

10

14   48   HIGH

15   NEW   8   9   ST.

17

KING   ST.

16   ROCKY ST.

TOWN   RUN

1

PRINCESS   ST.   48   FERRY

RIVER

N. & W.

GERMAN

7   3   2

TO CHARLES TOWN

MILL   ST.   Depot

6

5   Rwy.

4

POTOMAC

CORPORATION   LINE

W. VA.
MD.

N.

SHEPHERDSTOWN

Virginia, was a stop of consequence for travelers, with nearly as many taverns and industries as dwellings. During the Revolution, the town made 'clothing, military accoutrements, wagons, saddles and many other things for the use of soldiers.'

The event to which Shepherdstown has proudly dedicated its one public park is the successful public launching of the first steamboat, which took place in the Potomac at Mecklenburg on Monday, December 3, 1787. Before a large crowd gathered to see 'Crazy Rumsey's flying boat,' the little craft invented by James Rumsey steamed upstream half a mile, making four miles per hour, turned and came down again, and for two hours plied back and forth before the excited and shouting spectators. Among the notables present were Major Henry Bedinger, Colonel Joseph Swearingen, Captain Abram Shepherd, Captain Jacob Haines, General William Darke, and General Horatio Gates, all of whom had served in the Revolution. General Gates so forgot himself in his enthusiasm when the boat started that he shouted in the presence of the ladies, 'By God! She moves!' Rumsey, who built the boat at his sawmill near Bath (see Berkeley Springs), had made several previous trials but because of imperfections of the boiler none of them was considered successful. Harassed by rival claims to the invention, especially those of John Fitch, and hampered by his own lack of business ability, Rumsey failed to profit by his pioneering. In 1791, while making a report to a company formed in London, England, to promote his invention, he dropped dead of a heart attack. It was 20 years before the steamboat became a commercial success with the launching of Robert Fulton's Clermont on the Hudson. A model of Rumsey's boat is on display in the State Capitol at Charleston.

The first newspaper printed in the State, the Potomak Guardian and Berkeley Advertiser, was published at Mecklenburg by Nathaniel Willis in November 1790; a year later the paper was moved to Martinsburg. It was also in 1790 that Mecklenburg enjoyed for a brief while the exciting dream of becoming the National Capital. Dignitaries of the neighborhood corresponded with President Washington on the subject, made a plat of the proposed site, which took in land on both sides of the river, and passed a subscription list among inhabitants of Mecklenburg and Sharpsburg. Three letters and the plat are among the Washington papers in the Library of Congress.

Mecklenburg was named Shepherdstown in honor of Thomas Shepherd when the town was enlarged in 1798. During the War of 1812, captured British soldiers were brought here for safekeeping and imprisoned in the Entler Tavern, which was also a barracks for American troops.

Between 1825 and 1925, numerous manufactories were started, producing pottery, shuck mattresses, liquor, woolens, leather, lumber, wagons, clocks, chairs, harness, plows and farm machinery, bicycle chains, paper, limestone, cement, and flour. Of these products, only the last two were produced in sufficient quantities to supply more than local markets.

The completion of the Chesapeake and Ohio Canal to Hancock, Maryland, about 1840 and to Cumberland in 1850 boomed these industries. Flour and cement were shipped east to Washington on mule-drawn barges, and much of the coal supplied to Shepherdstown was floated in from Cumberland by barge. Standard supplies for the Cumberland-Washington trip were 2 gallons of whisky, 4 tin cups, 4 boatmen, 20 feet of rope and 30 pounds of bacon. The water front, now almost ignored in the life of Shepherdstown, was the scene of bustling activity.

During the War between the States, although battles were fought on all sides—Antietam was but seven miles away in Maryland—Shepherdstown escaped the severities of the conflict. Local men served in regiments of both sides; but the stay-at-homes were confined to exchanging shots with Federal soldiers stationed at Sharpsburg, and to nursing the wounded brought here from neighboring battlefields.

After the war, Shepherdstown was the county seat until 1871, when the government was returned to Charles Town. Late in 1871 a group of citizens headed by Joseph McMurran founded a classical and scientific school called Shepherd College. The school used the old courthouse and offered its lease to the State upon condition that it take over the school. In 1872 Shepherd State Teachers College was founded. In the last three decades of the nineteenth century, commerce on the Chesapeake and Ohio Canal declined; the Baltimore & Ohio Railroad, which did not pass through Shepherdstown, diverted traffic to other cities, and, with the rise of industrial Martinsburg (*see Tour* 1), Shepherdstown ceased to be anything but the quiet country and college town it is today.

POINTS OF INTEREST

1. SHEPHERD STATE TEACHERS COLLEGE (*all buildings open during school hours*) occupies a block in the business district on German St., between Princess St. and King St., extending to High St. A low stone wall bounds the campus, and Town Run cuts across one corner. Buildings are set back from the street with an expanse of tree-shaded, landscaped lawn before them.

McMurran Hall, a two-story, buff-painted brick structure, now used as an auditorium, classroom, and laboratory building, was erected in 1859 for a town hall. From 1865 to 1871 it was used as the courthouse of Jefferson County. The central part of the building is the original structure; the wings were added to accommodate county offices. The imposing Greek Revival portico, which rises the height of the façade, has a triangular pediment and fluted Corinthian columns. Door frames and the heavy bracketed lintels over the first-story windows are ornamented with scroll and acanthus-leaf designs. Triangular pediments cap the four faces of the clock tower and the main doorway, while the tower is surmounted by a lantern with a colonnade of eight Corinthian columns. The clock was donated to the town in 1842 by R. D. Shepherd, and first housed in the tower of the Episcopal church. Now infirm with age, it has lost the hands from two of its four faces, and has been known to strike more than 100 times before stopping.

REYNOLD HALL, adjoining McMurran Hall on King St., is of buff-painted brick and houses the college theater. The building was erected by the town in 1889 as second town hall and later placed at the disposal of the growing college.

KNUTTI HALL, SE. corner King and High Sts., the college administration building, is a modern (1904) two-story buff-painted brick building, fronted by Corinthian columns in harmony with the other college buildings. The corners are decorated with stone quoins. Knutti Hall contains the college library of 16,000 volumes.

The HOME ECONOMICS COTTAGE, High St. between King and Princess Sts., a small story-and-a-half log house, covered with weatherboards, is used for home economics classes and as a meeting place for school organizations. The cottage occupies the site of Fort Shepherd, erected by Thomas Shepherd during the French and Indian War. According to tradition, this house was formerly haunted by the ghost of a murdered cobbler, George Yontz, who lived here with his black cat, Ham. Yontz was found dead December 4, 1910, and was believed to have been murdered, although no one was ever accused of the crime. After his death Miss Net Entler moved into the cottage and adopted the cat, Ham. Every year on the anniversary of Yontz's death, Ham grew restless and would finally scratch wildly on the attic door, meowing to be let up the stairs to the second floor, where terrifying sounds of battle could be heard. The sounds, heard only on the anniversary of the murder, would cease in about an hour, after which Ham would return downstairs and resume a normal cat life. When the college acquired the property in 1917, however, the ghostly noises ceased, some say because Yontz's wraith despaired of competing with fraternity initiations.

The MINIATURE FARM PROJECT, Princess St. between German and High Sts., is a model farm constructed on a small scale and conducted by the teachers' training school, for demonstration purposes. A child-size limestone cottage, complete in every detail, with dormer windows and a recessed doorway topped by a fanlight, stands near the street. Behind it is a miniature dairy barn. The grounds are laid out in tiny gardens and fields, and rustic bridges span Town Run, which flows past the house.

RUMSEY HALL, NW. corner German and Princess Sts., is a rambling, unadorned three-story red brick building with a two-story wing, used as a men's dormitory. The building was the Entler Hotel operated by Joseph and Daniel Entler until 1808, when Joseph opened a rival tavern, known as the Entler Tavern, in the present Harrington House. The hotel remained in the family until several years after the War between the States. Among the numerous taverns of early Shepherdstown the Entler Hotel had the longest life, operating until 1922, when it was bought by the college.

2. The SHEPHERDSTOWN FLOUR MILL (*open 7-6 weekdays*), High St. between Mill and Princess Sts., occupies a site upon which a mill has been in continuous operation since before the founding of the town. It was built in the 1880's upon the foundation of a mill erected by Thomas Shepherd between 1734 and 1762, and at present it employs two millers, producing flour and 'old-fashioned water and burr-ground corn meal.' The 40-foot water wheel, reputed to be the second largest of its kind in operation in the world, is turned by the Town Run, which is dammed a short distance above the mill and piped to a tank above the wheel. In earlier days the water was carried down a long chute to the wheel, which hung between high stone piers; these are still standing, several hundred yards north of the mill.

3. The 'OLDEST HOUSE IN THE STATE' (*unoccupied*), High St. between Mill and Princess Sts., is a small ramshackle frame structure, reputedly built in 1727 by Richard ap Morgan. Records, however, indicate that this property was a vacant lot when Thomas Shepherd sold it to Henry Bedinger in 1764.

4. RUMSEY STATE PARK, N. end of Mill St., occupies two acres of rocky bluff overlooking the Potomac River, where James Rumsey in 1787 conducted his successful experiment with a steam-propelled boat. The RUMSEY MONUMENT was erected in 1915 on a concrete platform on the highest point of the bluff. It consists simply of an Ionic column of granite, 75 feet high, resting on a pyramidal base and topped with carved capital and plinth. A bronze tablet on the base records the story of Rumsey's invention.

5. The LUTHERAN GRAVEYARD, German St. between Mill St. and the corporation line, antedates the establishment of the town. Many of the graves are marked by thin sandstone slabs, rounded at the top, or are covered with stone slabs on which wind and rain have rendered the inscriptions illegible. Many are inscribed in German. West of the cemetery is a stone foundation and a few scattered bricks, which are all that remains of the first Lutheran church, built in 1795.

6. CHRIST REFORMED CHURCH, SE. corner German and Mill Sts., built in 1876, stands on the site used by the German Reformed congregation since its organization about 1780. It is a plain, gable-roofed, red brick building with stained-glass windows. Ornamental brackets support the cornice. A square tower of native stone, part of an earlier stone church, rises at the back of the building, surmounted by a steepled belfry, which contains three bells imported from Germany by Michael Yeasley, a Revolutionary soldier, a few years after the Revolution. The bells are French, and according to a Shepherdstown tradition, which ignores the discrepancy in dates, they were taken

to Germany by Napoleon. Engraved on the largest bell is the date 1732, a cross, and the word 'Rouen.' Before the bells were placed in the tower, the largest was filled with wine and passed around the congregation. Prior to the split between the Lutheran and Reformed congregations in 1782 the two denominations worshipped together in a small log building on this spot. East of the church is the old Reformed burying ground. Most of the older tombstones are too time-worn to be legible, but two, those of 'Harina Schel, begraben 1728, War alt 85' and 'George Kuckus, 1725,' indicate the age of the cemetery.

7. The BILLMEYER HOUSE (*private*), German St. between Mill and Princess Sts., was formerly the Wyncoop Tavern, most fashionable hostelry of early nineteenth-century Shepherdstown. A tavern stood on this site as early as 1769 when Martin Entler owned the property. In 1781 Cornelius Wyncoop acquired the lot and the log tavern that stood on it. John Fitch stayed here in 1789, and James Rumsey's friends accused him of spying upon Rumsey's experiments with the steamboat. In 1791 or 1792 Wyncoop erected the present red brick two-story house with its gable roof and paired and joined end chimneys. The west wing and two flat-roofed porticoes with fluted Doric columns are later additions, as is the ivy now covering the taverns.

8. The OLD MARKET HOUSE, in the middle of King St. at German St., is a narrow, part-brick, part-frame building, with a corbie-stepped front gable. Over the door in a semicircular niche is the Odd Fellows' symbol of the Seeing Eye. The Market House was authorized in 1800 with the specifications that it 'be 57 feet in length and 20 feet high; be raised upon good stone or brick pillars and covered with a good shingle roof,' and for 45 years, until the Odd Fellows added the frame second story, it was an open pavilion in which the country people kept their stalls on Wednesdays and Saturdays. For a time the first floor was used as a fire engine house. The building houses a PUBLIC LIBRARY (*open 7–9 p.m. Wed. and Sat.*), maintained by the Women's Club, a courtroom, and a lodge hall used jointly by the D.A.R. and the I.O.O.F. The town jail occupies a small wing at the back. As early as 1765 this intersection was the center of village activities; the town whipping post stood here. In that year the town council passed the resolution:

> Ordered that Jacob Eoff is authorized to procure a sufficient number of cats to destroy the rats that infest this town and to procure as soon as possible, and that the money expended in procuring the same to be levied for him on the tenth day of June next.

The next market day the square was the scene of a lively cat sale, as the country people flocked to town with bags and baskets full of cats and kittens. The town council failed to record whether their 'Pied Piper' succeeded in destroying the rats.

9. The SHEETZ HOUSE (*private*), NW. corner German and King Sts., is a plain red brick house with green shutters and a gable roof. A shoe shop and the deputy sheriff's office, a favorite gathering place

for Shepherdstown's old soldiers, occupy the first floor. From 1810 to
1821 this was the Jacob Sheetz Tavern, where occasional town elections were held. Later, William Sheetz manufactured gun stocks here
for use in the government armory at Harpers Ferry. When the armory
was destroyed during the War between the States, Sheetz used his
left-over supply of gun stocks to build a picket fence that was a local
curiosity for years. It no longer stands.

10. The OLD EPISCOPAL CHURCH, SE. corner Church and High
Sts., has been used by the African Methodist Episcopal Church since
1867. The building is a shabby rectangular structure of stone, coated
with a peeling layer of cement and surmounted in front by a square
wooden tower. An Episcopal church built of logs stood on this site in
1775, and the present building is believed to have been erected a few
years later around the log structure. The stone front and tower were
erected in 1842 to hold the town clock. Because the Episcopal congregation, when first organized before the Revolutionary War, could get
no minister of its own denomination, a Lutheran minister, the Reverend Peter Muhlenburg, was sent to England to be ordained by the
Church of England. Upon his return, Muhlenberg served as minister
for the Lutheran and Episcopal churches until 1776, when he joined
the Continental Army.

11. The PRESBYTERIAN MANSE (*private*), NW. corner Church
and German Sts., a red brick, L-shaped building with white trim and
ornamental sidelights around the front door, was long considered one
of the finest houses in the town. It was built in 1798 by John Kears-
ley, Revolutionary soldier and second president (mayor) of Shepherdstown.

12. TRINITY EPISCOPAL CHURCH, SW. corner Church and German Sts., raises its gray stone spire high above the other buildings in
town. The church, a Gothic Revival structure of native stone surrounded by evergreens, was built in 1859, and the spire was constructed
to hold the town clock, which the congregation intended to remove
from the old church. However, the town council decided that McMurran Hall was a more appropriate place for the clock. A chapel, similar
in design to the church, stands unused in the churchyard.

13. The HARRINGTON HOUSE (*private*), German St. between
Church and Duke Sts., is a rambling two-story stucco building, once
the Entler Tavern or Great Western Hotel. The nucleus of the present
structure, a large log tavern, was built during the Revolutionary War
and was a rendezvous for American forces in the neighborhood. The
yard behind it was a drill ground for troops. Joseph Entler bought
the building in 1808 and added to it. After the War of 1812, during
which it was used as a barracks for United States soldiers, the Entler
Tavern was popular with wagoners, teamsters, and traveling circuses
because of its large barn with space for 25 horses, and the vacant lot
next to it on which circuses pitched their tents. During the War between the States the hotel was occupied by first one army, then the

other. Soldiers tore out the woodwork for firewood and destroyed the stable. The tavern was closed in 1866. Later, the building was weatherboarded and made a residence.

14. The SHEPHERD GRAVEYARD, New St. between Church and King Sts., enclosed by a high stone fence, is the private burial ground of the Shepherd family. It contains the unmarked grave of Thomas Shepherd, founder of the town, the grave of his son Abram, first mayor of Shepherdstown, and that of his grandson Thomas Thornborough, both of whom served in the Revolutionary War.

15. The GROVE HOUSE (*private*), SW. corner King and New Sts., is a red brick house on a high foundation, used as a boarding house. The main part of the building is a weatherboarded log structure, which from 1810 to 1821 was the Thomas James Tavern. This was a favorite meeting place for the town trustees and the court of hustings, and occasionally elections were held here. In 1801 the trustees decried 'the continual breach of the Sabbath, especially by the young children, apprentices, servants, and slaves of the in habitants being suffered to collect in the streets . . . to follow their games, pastimes, plays and diversions upon said Day. . . .' Town records show numerous bills from Thomas James for use of room and liquor; the liquor bill for one trustees' meeting was $6.25.

16. The COMMUNITY BUILDING, SE. corner King and New Sts., a red brick building of Gothic design with arched windows and a square steepled tower at one corner, was constructed in 1912. It houses the motorized fire engine and the hand-pulled fire engine of the volunteer fire department, the council room, and an auditorium in which church suppers, bazaars, entertainments by various civic groups, and 'soups' are held. The long narrow kitchen on the first floor, which was originally designed to serve as the town jail, is equipped with a special 30-gallon soup kettle built into the mammoth stove.

17. The PRESBYTERIAN CHURCH, SW. corner King and Washington Sts., resembles a schoolhouse. Above the front gable of the plain red brick building is a belfry. Two rows of many-paned windows give the impression of a two-story structure. The upper row of windows was built to light a wide gallery, which originally ran around three sides of the auditorium but now extends only across the back. In 1780 the congregation, formed a number of years earlier, built a log church on the corner opposite the present site, and shortly after 1787, when the first resident pastor was appointed, replaced it with a frame building. Abram Shepherd sold the Presbyterians the lot with the added stipulation that they pay him or his heirs annually an ear of corn in ground rent. The church was partly paid for by lottery. When the present church was built in 1836, George Feaman, who owned the site, persuaded the congregation to exchange lots with him. His lot, also purchased from the Shepherds, carried an annual ground rent of $1.11. The exaction of annual ground rents from purchasers of land was a common law custom practiced by a number of the large landowners of

In the Cities and Towns

Photograph by courtesy of Bollinger

THE CAPITOL, CHARLESTON

GOVERNOR'S MANSION, CHARLESTON

COUNTY COURT HOUSE, CLARKSBURG

Photograph by Highton; courtesy of Work Projects Administration

GREENBRIER COLLEGE FOR WOMEN, LEWISBURG

WOMAN'S HALL, WEST VIRGINIA UNIVERSITY, MORGANTOWN

MANSION HOUSE, OGLEBAY PARK, WHEELING

AIRVIEW, HUNTINGTON

Photograph by courtesy of American Airlines, I

CHARLESTON'S NEW KANAWHA BOULEVARD

Photograph by courtesy of Bolling

COUNTY COURT HOUSE, BECKLEY

McMURRAN HALL, STATE TEACHER'S COLLEGE, SHEPHERDSTOWN

Virginia in the early days. The Shepherd heirs abandoned the collection of the annual ear of corn but continued to exact the cash until about 1880, when the town persuaded them to terminate ground rents.

18. BELLEVUE (*private*) 0.5 m. N. of Shepherdstown on the Shepherd Pike (extension of Duke St.), a large, square, two-story, white-painted stone house with an imposing portico, is on the summit of a knoll overlooking a bend in the Potomac River. Other native stone buildings, some of them dating from the late eighteenth century, are scattered about the grounds. The main house has been enlarged at different times since it was built, sometime before 1800. A low native stone wall surrounds the estate. Thomas Swearingen, who operated a ferry across the Potomac River above Shepherdstown in 1755, founded the estate, which was sold by his family before the War between the States. Beside Swearingen's Spring, which issues from the hill below the house, a band of Catawba Indians came upon one of their enemies, a Delaware chief, and, according to legend, buried him alive. The water issues from the spring in spurts supposedly impelled by the beating heart of the buried chief. In earlier days Bellevue was said to be haunted. Colonel Joseph Van Swearingen, a veteran of the Revolution, went for a walk in his garden one August night in 1820. When he returned to the house he found a beautiful dark-haired girl asleep. She awoke, foretold that he would die in one year, and vanished. The colonel went for another walk and when he returned the second time he found a blonde young woman asleep. She, too, awoke, foretold his death within a year, and vanished. Colonel Van Swearingen did die in 1821, just one year later.

19. WILD GOOSE (*private*), 3 m. N. on the Shepherd Pike, was built by Rezin Davis Shepherd before the War between the States. The quadrangular frame house has been enlarged by the addition of two wings and large porches. The name, Wild Goose, recalling the flocks of wild geese that paused along the Potomac in their migrations, is wrought into the iron gates of the drive, and a weathervane shaped like a goose tops the barn. When Rezin Shepherd died in 1865 the estate was inherited by Henry Shepherd II, about whose great wealth stories are still told. Shepherd built the four-mile Shepherd Pike and is said to have had it swept clean every day, the stones in his fields painted green, and every inch of soil replaced that washed from his farm during rains.

20. MAPLE SHADE (*private*), 4 m. N. on the Shepherd Pike, originally belonged to Captain Abram Shepherd, son of the town's founder. The white-painted stone house was built by Henry Shepherd before the War between the States, and inherited by Henry Shepherd II and Henry Shepherd III. Henry III was even more wealthy and prodigal of his wealth than Henry II. While his father was content with harness trimmed in silver, Henry III had his trimmed in gold. He built a race track at the farm and dissipated much of his fortune by entertaining. The estate was bought in 1914 by William H. Martin, who,

noticing three springs that bubble from the ground close together, placed above the strongest spring the sign 'Republican Party.' The next strongest he labeled 'Democratic Party' and the weakest of all, 'Prohibition.' Visitors were expected to drink from the spring of their party affiliation. The signs remain.

POINTS OF INTEREST IN ENVIRONS

Antietam Battlefield, 5 *m.* E. (*see Maryland Guide*).

Wheeling

Railroad Stations: 1700 Market St. for Baltimore & Ohio R.R.; 11th and Water Sts. for Pennsylvania R.R. and Wheeling and Lake Erie Ry.
Bus Stations: Union Bus Terminal, 16th and Market Sts., for Atlantic Greyhound Lines, Pennsylvania Greyhound Lines, Red Star Way Lines, Blue Ridge Lines, Penn-Ohio Coach Lines, West Virginia Transportation Co., Co-operative Bus Co., Wheeling Public Service Co., Eastern Ohio Transport Co.; Consolidated Bus Depot, 11th and Chapline Sts., for Arcodel System; 1619 Market St. for Lincoln Trailways.
Airport: 3 m. NW. of city across Ohio River on Ohio 7; no scheduled service.
Taxis: 1-4 persons 25¢ in urban district.
Streetcars and Busses: Fare 5¢ and 10¢ within city limits, 5¢ to Island, 10¢ to Oglebay Park.
Traffic Regulations: One-way streets, N. on Market and S. on Main between 10th and 16th Sts.
Street Order and Numbering: E. and W. streets numbered from 1st to 48th, N. and S. streets named.

Accommodations: 7 hotels; tourist homes and boarding houses.

Information Service: Chamber of Commerce, Market Auditorium, Market St. between 10th and 11th Sts.; Wheeling Automobile Club 81 12th St.

Radio Station: WWVA (1160 kc.).
Theaters and Motion Picture Houses: Little Theater plays in St. Michael's church auditorium, 129 Edgington Lane, or Market Auditorium, Market St. between 10th and 11th Sts.; 12 motion picture houses.
Swimming: Oglebay Park, 5.4 m. N. on State 88, open May 30 to Sept. 15, 15¢; Wheeling Park, 4.7 m. E. on US 40, open June, July, Aug., 15¢.
Golf: Oglebay Park, 5.4 m. N. on State 88, 18 holes, greens fee, 25¢; Wheeling Park, 4.7 m. E. on US 40, 9 holes, greens fee, 25¢.
Tennis: Oglebay Park, 5.4 m. N. on State 88, and Wheeling Park, 4.7 m. E. on US 40, 40¢ per hour.
Riding: Oglebay Park, 5.4 m. N. on State 88, horses $1 per hour.
Skating: Ice skating, Wheeling Park, 4.7 m. E. on US 40, during winter; roller skating, State Fair Park, S. end Wheeling Island, adults, 35¢, children 10¢.

Annual Events: Easter sunrise service, Oglebay Park; Dog Show, Apr., Market Auditorium; Ohio Valley Arbor Day, May, Oglebay Park; racing, spring and fall, Wheeling Downs; regional 4-H Club and Panhandle Autumn Festival, Oglebay Park.

WHEELING (678 alt., 61,659 pop.), manufacturing and commercial center of the Northern Panhandle, sprawls T-shaped along the narrow valleys of the Ohio River and Wheeling Creek, between and over a series of sharp-rising hills and across Wheeling Island in the Ohio River. North and south of the business section on the banks of the Ohio are the long sheds of steel mills, iron works, and metal manufactories. From their stacks rolls a constant cloud of smoke that settles heavily in soot over straight-fronted tenement houses that crowd up steep streets back of them, and blackens even the most recently constructed office buildings in the downtown area. Around the mouth of Wheeling Creek, which winds sluggishly beneath numerous bridges into the Ohio south of the commercial area, cluster a myriad of block-shaped, brick factory buildings producing stogies, china, mattresses, glassware, matches, sausages, macaroni, textiles, and paper boxes. In the suburb of Fulton are meat packing houses, and throughout the city are other smaller enterprises. Across the river are the small mining and manufacturing towns of Bridgeport and Martins Ferry, set amid the low green hills of Ohio.

Eastward, along the valley of Wheeling Creek, is the Out-the-Pike section, a string of residential suburbs along the winding course of the National Road. Here are the finer homes of the city and the recreational areas, the parks, and playgrounds.

Incessant activity in the business district marks Wheeling as more akin to its neighbor cities of Ohio and Pennsylvania than to the more leisurely-paced cities of West Virginia. Architecturally, old and new mingle in a motley companionship. Close to the river front, century-old cobbled streets rise steeply from the water's edge, passing between buildings whose straight fronts and simple trim, doorways opening directly on brick sidewalks, identify them as among the earliest buildings of the city. On the main streets, however, the massive pretentiousness of the Victorian era and the square, simple lines of modern architecture, predominate.

Wheeling, with its throngs of shoppers, its traffic-filled streets, and the variety and abundance of its cultural and recreational facilities, appears to be a larger city than its population figures indicate. With its mature business and industrial life, Wheeling, more than any other West Virginia city, has developed the civic consciousness characteristic of a long-settled metropolitan area. Throughout the city are many playgrounds, and in its two large municipal parks are elaborate recreational facilities. Civic interest in music is expressed in the support of one large symphony orchestra and a number of smaller ones, as well as numerous choral and instrumental groups. Art exhibits, lectures, and city-sponsored courses of study at Oglebay Park provide for participation in other cultural activities.

Wheeling's industrial development has attracted foreign-born groups, among which the Germans, Italians, Poles, Russians, Assyrians, and Greeks have their own churches and fraternal societies. In religious observances they preserve many of the customs of their native lands, such as the services held at St. Ladislaus Polish Roman Catholic Church on the Feast of Our Lady of the Flowers (August 15) and the blessing of foods at the same church on Holy Saturday, the day preceding Easter.

The first known white visitor to the mouth of Wheeling Creek was

Captain Céleron de Bienville, who, with a party of French explorers, paused in August 1749 at the mouth of the creek they called Kanououara and buried a leaden plate bearing the royal seal of France and an inscription claiming, in the name of their king, the territory drained by the stream.

The earliest authentic record of the name Wheeling, which by many years antedates the settlement of this site, is in an old map of the interior of America, published in London in 1755, on which appear the names of Wheeling Island and Wheeling Creek in their locations. The most probable explanation of the name is that given by John Brittle, a Pennsylvania pioneer who was captured in 1791 by Delaware Indians near Wheeling and lived with the tribe for five years. He related that Chief Hainguypooshies (Big Cat) told him that the first white settlers venturing down the Ohio were captured and beheaded by a band of Delawares, and the heads placed on poles near the mouth of the stream as a warning to other invading whites. The spot was known thereafter to the Indians as *Weeling* (place of the skull), and the 'h' was added later when white men corrupted the pronunciation.

Settlement was first made on this site in 1769, when the three Zane brothers, Colonel Ebenezer, Jonathan, and Silas, emigrated from the South Branch Valley and followed an old Indian hunting trail to the mouth of Wheeling Creek. Impressed by the beauty and fertility of the valley, they made a clearing, built a cabin, and planted a crop. They divided Wheeling Island into three tracts and laid off large tracts on the mainland, covering most of the area where Wheeling now stands. Silas, the youngest, was left to guard the place while his brothers returned for their families. 'It is like a vision of Paradise,' Ebenezer told his friends, and several families accompanied him to the new settlement.

When the murder of Chief Logan's family in 1774 precipitated a general Indian uprising, Lord Dunmore ordered a strong fort built on the bluff north of the mouth of Wheeling Creek. Fort Fincastle, as it was first called, constructed by Captain William Crawford and soldiers from Fort Pitt, consisted of a log barracks, officers' house, storeroom, well, and cabins, enclosed by a strong stockade of heavy logs. In 1776 the outpost was renamed Fort Henry in honor of Patrick Henry, first governor of Virginia. Garrisoned by the Zanes and other pioneers, Fort Henry was an important military outpost during the American Revolution. In 1777, the bloody year of the three 7's, the fort withstood an onslaught by a band of Wyandot, Delaware, and Shawnee. Again, in September 1782, although peace between the British and Americans had been consummated, Fort Henry was attacked by nearly 300 British and Indians in what has been called the last battle of the Revolution. After a two-day siege the attackers withdrew, defeated.

In spite of the war and Indian menace the settlement continued to grow, and the return of peace accelerated its growth. In 1793 Ebenezer Zane platted the town, and a post office called Zanesburg was established here in 1794. In 1795 the town was established by an act of the legislature and two years later the seat of Ohio County was moved to Zanesburg from West Liberty. The village became an important commercial center for other western settlements and a point of embarkation for westward-bound settlers. Pioneer speculators and traders along the borders of Kentucky and Ohio made the village their headquarters. In 1806 the town was chartered under the name of Wheeling, and a year later the first newspaper, the *Repository*, was published.

The National Road, first wagon route between the east and the Ohio River, was opened to Wheeling in 1818, and the future of the town was assured, for it was a point through which the bulk of the travel and commerce between the East and West must pass. A year before, the *Washington*, one of the first successful steamboats on the Ohio, had been built in Wheeling, and now the boat-building industry boomed. Iron manufacturing began; glass factories were opened; dozens of taverns, blacksmith shops, and provision stores sprang up. Hundreds of wagonloads of merchandise, flocks of sheep, herds of cattle, droves of hogs, and bands of slaves were transferred at Wheeling from road to boat, and the streets were constantly thronged with eastward-bound statesmen or westward-bound pioneers. Packets, flatboats, and watercraft of all kinds arrived and departed daily, and the river landing became the busiest part of the town. In 1831 the flow of imports through Wheeling was so heavy that the town was made a port of entry by act of Congress.

In 1836 it was an incorporated city, and during the next ten years waterworks were built and the city was lighted by gas. Soon after, the first telegraph line in the state was used at Wheeling. A free school system was established in 1849, and about this time Wheeling became known as the Nail City, because of its iron works, and expressed an ambition to become the leading manufacturing center of the west. Its rival was Pittsburgh and their bitterest fight was waged over the suspension bridge.

In 1836 a wooden bridge was built across the west channel of the river from Wheeling Island to the Ohio shore, leaving the east channel open to navigation. When a bill in Congress, supported by representatives of Virginia and Ohio, urged the erection of a bridge from Wheeling to Wheeling Island to facilitate trade and travel on the National Road, Pittsburgh contended successfully before the Supreme Court of the United States that the bridge interfered with navigation because its clearance was not great enough to permit high-stacked packets to pass under it. More probably, Pittsburgh feared that Wheeling would become the head of navigation on the Ohio River, making useless its extensive facilities for river transportation between the two cities. Of 230 boats on the river between Cincinnati and Pittsburgh, the seven large boats of the Pittsburgh packet line carried half of the goods and three-fourths of the passengers along the route. The bridge was finished in 1849, in spite of a restraining order. Wheeling again carried its case to Congress, which established bridges as military and post roads and ordered that the height of the steamboat chimneys be governed by the clearance of bridges. When the bridge was blown down by a severe wind storm in 1854, Pittsburgh newspapers rejoiced and the packet *Pennsylvania* continued in derision to lower her chimneys when passing between the abutments of the bridge.

As soon as replacement of the destroyed bridge was started, Pittsburgh again appealed to the Supreme Court, but this time Wheeling won, and the new 1,010-foot span was completed in 1856. At that time it was the longest suspension bridge in the country. It still is in use, with huge cables supporting a wooden floor safe for six-ton vehicles.

Meanwhile railroads pushed westward to connect the rival cities with the East. Wheeling again won over Pittsburgh. The last spike completing the Baltimore & Ohio Railroad into Wheeling was driven 18 miles east of the city on Christmas Eve 1852, and two weeks later a colorful celebration and elaborate banquet was held in Washington Hall for nearly 1,000 guests, including men of national note. 'Edibles disappeared as if swallowed by a maelstrom, after which champagne corks resounded through the halls like the prompt report of a miniature artillery.' Speeches were made, and toasts were drunk; but even champagne could not drown the bitterness of Wheeling citizens for Pittsburgh, and a toast was proposed:

> Poor Pittsburgh is flung—for her steamboats no more
> Can whistle in scorn, as they pass Wheeling's shore,
> No chimneys to lower, no action to bring,
> For a flatboat, she'll find, will soon be the thing;
> She may war on all bridges—save one for herself,
> But her trade on the river is laid on the shelf.

The town continued to grow as an industrial city and as a center for western culture. Public and private schools were promoted, and in 1852 a public library was opened. Civic and social organizations were active. Jenny Lind, the Swedish singer, was brought to Wheeling for a concert; Mark Twain lectured; Presidents and statesmen were honored with elaborate banquets when they passed through the city.

This prosperous and happy period was interrupted by the War between the States, when western Virginia turned to the support of a movement for a new State west of the mountains. Two conventions of delegates from the western and northern counties of Virginia were held at Wheeling in 1861 (*see History*), and out of these grew, first, the Restored Government of Virginia and then the new State of West Virginia, both of which made Wheeling their first capitals (*see Charleston*). The city also was an important point on the Underground Railroad before the new State was established, and hundreds of slaves were brought here for crossing into the free State of Ohio. Wheeling has at present (1930) a Negro population of 2,192. No actual fighting occurred at Wheeling, although it was alarmed once when General Benjamin F. Kelley wired Governor Pierpont that 'the rebels are coming through Cheat Mountain pass in considerable forces.'

After the war, Wheeling resumed its industrial and commercial prominence, and at the close of the nineteenth century railroads had displaced river traffic. After 1900 the steel industry increased in importance, and the city also became a major center of manufacture of tobacco, glass, clay, and textile products.

Wheeling's greatest disaster was the flood of March 1936, when the swirling, muddy torrents of the Ohio River rose 19.5 feet above flood stage and remained at that height for 15 hours before ebbing slowly to leave the city fighting against disease, hunger, and enormous property loss. Wheeling Island was entirely covered; only the tops of the tallest buildings were above water. The waters of Wheeling Creek flowed through the four main streets of the city and for two days boats were the only means of travel. Communications were limited, electricity failed in flooded areas, and the city's water supply in sections was polluted. The final toll was 8 dead, more than 100 injured, and property damage amounting to $5,000,000.

As the city rebuilt, factories, some of which had been closed five or six years, opened with full forces, and within a few months the city was its normal busy self.

POINTS OF INTEREST

1. The CITY-COUNTY BUILDING, Chapline St. between 15th and 16th Sts., is a massive three-story red brick building of Romanesque design, trimmed with gray limestone. Above the central unit rises a square three-story bell and clock tower. The four corners of the north and south wings are surmounted by squat, domed towers. The building, designed by J. S. Fairfax, was erected in 1876 by citizens of Wheeling and donated to the State as a capitol, but it reverted to the city in 1885 when the capital was moved to Charleston. A granite MONUMENT TO SOLDIERS AND SAILORS OF THE CIVIL WAR stands on the southwest corner of the grounds. On opposite sides of the shaft are the figures of a soldier and a sailor; at the top is the draped figure of a woman holding a sword and shield. On the northeast corner is the TRADES AND LABOR MONUMENT, erected by employees of the Pollack Tobacco Company in honor of Augustus Pollack, one of the first tobacco manufacturers in Wheeling and a supporter of organized labor. The figures of a workman and an employer clasp hands in front of a slender fluted Corinthian column, atop which stands an eagle with outstretched wings. The PAXTON FOUNTAIN, in front of the main entrance, was given to the city by James W. Paxton in 1878. From the center of a large octagonal pool rise two elaborate groups of figures, one supporting and the other surmounting a basin. Beneath the basin rim are four pairs of half-draped female figures in contemplative attitude, chin on hand, and between each pair are the figures of two small boys astride a large red-mouthed fish. Above the basin are figures of cherubs playing about the feet of a standing woman. From the mouths of the fish and from

pipes held by the cherubs and women gush tiny streams of water. The fountain and the curbing around the pool are painted silver.

2. The CUSTOMHOUSE (*open 9–5 weekdays*), 1526–8 Market St., is a four-story building of smooth-faced gray stone, owned by the Conservative Life Insurance Company. Constructed about 1854 to serve as a post office and customhouse, the building is of modified Classical Revival architecture, having many narrow deep-set windows and an arcaded portico with red granite Corinthian columns across the principal façade, which is approached by a well-worn flight of stone steps. A highly decorative cornice encircles the top of the building. During the War between the States the building rivaled the courthouse as a public center, and its steps were constantly crowded with men discussing war, politics, and the new-State movement. In the Federal courtrooms on the second floor the Constitutional Convention was held, which formed the first organic laws of West Virginia. In these same rooms citizens were later required to swear anew their allegiance to the Union. The building served as headquarters for Governor Pierpont until his offices were removed to Alexandria, Virginia, in 1863, and nearly all of the sessions of the legislature of the Restored Government of Virginia met here. Ammunition and arms were stored here for Federal troops during the entire war, and to the duties of the port surveyor were added those of custodian of the arsenal.

3. ST. JOSEPH'S CATHEDRAL (*open at all times*), SE. corner 13th and Eoff Sts., is the seat of the Wheeling Diocese of the Roman Catholic Church. Of Lombard Romanesque architecture, the massive Indiana limestone structure was designed and executed by Frank Aretz of Pittsburgh. Interior decorations are by Felix B. Lieftuchter of Cincinnati. The austere round-arched style of the exterior is relieved by the richness of carved details, while the interior is elaborately ornamented with carved and painted representations of sacred scenes and symbols. The round-arched door is flanked by two octagonal turrets with peaked roofs topped by stone crosses. The roof is finished in rust-brown and red tile. Over the door is a rose window. The cathedral is built on the traditional cruciform plan, with a high dome over the arms of the cross. An open turret containing three bells rises at the back of the building. Within the entrance of the cathedral is a marble font with a lid of bronze and copper. Stone arches supported by monolithic columns separate the nave from the aisles, while the triple-arched openings of the triforium over the nave arches are carried on slender colonnettes with carved capitals and molded bases. The vault of the dome is frescoed with a representation of the nine choirs of angels, and the triple-arched stained-glass windows of the dome depict the four archangels, Michael, Gabriel, Raphael, and Urial. Other stained-glass windows, designed by George Sotter, of Holicong, Pennsylvania, portray the life of Saint Joseph, the four cardinal virtues, and the life of Christ. The five altars of the church are of imported marbles from Italy, Greece, and France. Over the high altar is an elaborate ciborium, the vault of which is of

cerulean blue glass mosaic inlaid with gold stars. Statues are of Caen stone, and furniture of richly carved oak. Altar fittings and vessels are of solid lacquered brass.

4. WASHINGTON HALL, NE. corner 12th and Market Sts., is a six-story office building of smooth yellow-gray stone, its first floor occupied by Western Union offices and a drugstore. When erected in 1853, the building was a sturdy three-story, brick and stone structure, with tall double windows ornamented with curved lintels. Above the main entrance rose a high Gothic spire. It was here that the First and Second Wheeling conventions were held (see History). In 1877 the building was extensively remodeled and since that time has been used as a theater, motion picture house, bank, and office building.

5. The SITE OF THE GOODING INN, NW. corner 12th and Main Sts., is occupied by the Hotel Windsor, a ten-story brick and stone structure. About 1810 Jacob Gooding built a small brick inn facing the river near the landing. About 1815 the inn was sold to Zachariah Sprigg, who erected on the site a rambling wooden structure, two stories high, with a long colonnaded porch across the front. A tunnel led from Main Street to the ground floor and beyond to the hotel grounds, where as many as 50 stagecoaches often stopped at one time. By 1825 the Sprigg House, which had come to be known as the St. James Hotel, was torn down and in its place was built the larger United States Hotel; the latter was razed in 1914 to make way for the present structure.

6. WHEELING WHARF, foot of 12th St., for a century and a half has been a public landing. Cobblestones, laid early in the nineteenth century, later supplemented by bricks, extend from the river's edge to Water Street. Although the wharf is not the center of activity that it once was, it is still used by occasional excursion steamers and small craft. It was here on May 24, 1825, that the steamboat *Herald* docked, and Lafayette, his son, George Washington Lafayette, and a party of statesmen were received by Wheeling citizens.

7. The SITE OF FORT HENRY, Main St. between 11th and Ohio Sts., is marked by a bronze plaque imbedded in a small stone. Erected in 1774 the stockade withstood two sieges, in 1777 and 1782. An incident of the latter, the last battle of the Revolution, has grown into the Betty Zane legend. The garrison ran short of powder, and a number of young men volunteered to go for more from a supply stored in the strongly fortified home of Colonel Ebenezer Zane, about 150 yards away. Betty Zane, sister of the town's founders, however, insisted that she be allowed to go instead, remarking, " 'Tis better a maid than a man should die.' The gates were unbarred, and she ran for the house. The Indians, amused at her frantic dash, withheld their fire, crying, 'A squaw, a squaw!" But when she emerged from the storehouse carrying a load of powder in her apron, they realized her intention and fired at her. Shots pierced her skirts, but Betty, unhurt, reached the fort with the powder. The incident was not recorded in Colonel Zane's terse

report of the battle. Elizabeth Zane McLaughlin Clarke died in 1823 and was buried near her home in Martins Ferry, Ohio, across the river.

8. The UPPER MARKET HOUSE (*open weekdays*), Market St. between 10th and Ohio Sts., is a gray brick structure a block long, erected in 1911. Its chief architectural characteristics are high arched windows and finely denticulated cornices that encircle the building at the top of each story. The two-story north and south wings are joined by a central unit that rises several feet above the wings and overhangs the sidewalk on both sides. It houses the large Municipal Auditorium and a spacious balcony. A wide passage extends from Market to Main Street, providing the main entrance to the markets on the first floor. Here on each side of a long hall are neat arrays of fruit and vegetables, flowers, and dairy and poultry products. The second floor of the building is used for headquarters of various civic organizations, the chamber of commerce, and two smaller auditoriums. All activities of the markets are regulated by city ordinance.

9. The M. MARSH AND SONS PLANT (*open on application*), 919 Market St., founded in 1840, is the oldest stogie manufacturing company in Wheeling. The company operates in two box-shaped brick buildings, the main plant on Market Street and the other at 18th Street. The company employs 600 persons and produces between one and three million stogies a week. In the Market Street plant three brands are produced by machine. In the 18th Street plant the original Old Kentuck, now the Old Reliable brand, with which the company began

---

KEY FOR WHEELING MAP

1. The CITY-COUNTY BUILDING, Chapline St. between 15th and 16th Sts. 2. The CUSTOMHOUSE, 1526-8 Market St. 3. ST. JOSEPH'S CATHEDRAL, SE. corner 13th and Eoff Sts. 4. WASHINGTON HALL, NE. corner 12th and Market Sts. 5. The SITE OF THE GOODING INN, NW. corner 12th and Main Sts. 6. WHEELING WHARF, foot of 12th St. 7. The SITE OF FORT HENRY, Main St. between 11th and Ohio Sts. 8. The UPPER MARKET HOUSE, Market St. between 10th and Ohio Sts. 9. The M. MARSH AND SONS PLANT, 919 Market St. 10. The WHEELING PUBLIC LIBRARY, SE. corner Market and 21st Sts. 11. The LOWER MARKET, center of Market St. at 22nd St. 12. The BLOCH BROTHERS TOBACCO PLANT, Water St. between 39th and 41st Sts. 13. MOUNT WOOD CEMETERY, Mount Wood Rd., on the steep slopes of Wheeling Hill. 14. WETZEL'S CAVE, 100 yards s. of the Baltimore & Ohio Railroad tunnel on the Peninsula. 15. LINSLY INSTITUTE OF TECHNOLOGY, Theda Pl. on the Peninsula. 16. MOUNT DE CHANTAL ACADEMY, Valley View Rd. and Mount de Chantal Rd., situated high on Mount de Chantal Hill overlooking the valley of Wheeling Creek. 17. The J. D. MERRIMAN GARDEN, Stamm Lane. 18. The PINES, Stamm Lane. 19. The WEISS GARDEN, at Elmcrest, Elmwood St. 20. JOHN DIECKMANN AND SONS GREENHOUSES, Floral Ave. in Elm Grove. 21. The OLD STONE PRESBYTERIAN CHURCH CEMETERY, Stone Church Rd. which leads off US 40 (L) one block w. of Forbes Ave., on the slope of a steep hillside overlooking Elm Grove. 22. The FRANK HOFFMAN GARDEN, on Park Rd. near Woodsdale Park. 23. The JOHN C. TUCKER GARDEN, on Hawthorne Court. 24. WASHINGTON FARMS, reached by a private road off the Greggsville, Clinton and Potomac Rd. 25. OGLEBAY PARK, 5 *m.* N. on State 88. 26. SITE OF FORT VAN METER, northwest of Oglebay Park on the Consolidated School Grounds, Greggsville, Clinton and Potomac Rd.

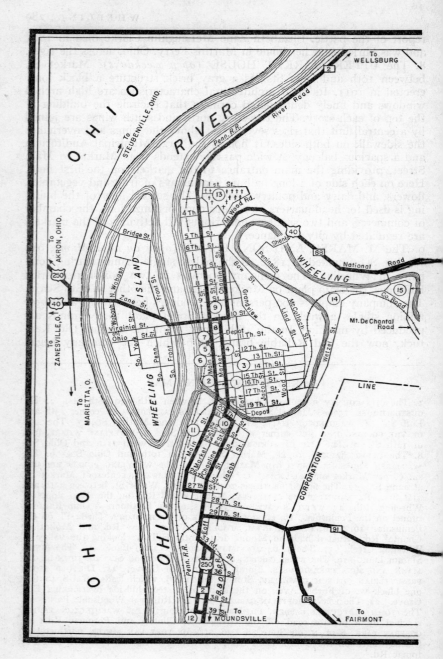

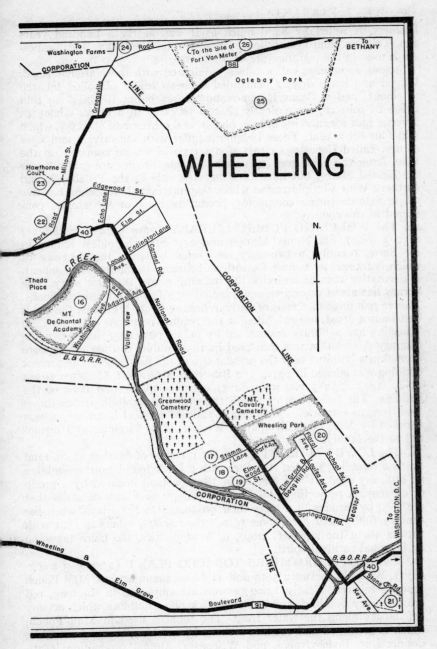

WHEELING

To Washington Farms
CORPORATION
24 Road
To the Site of Fort Van Meter
88
26
To BETHANY

Greagsville
LINE
Oglebay Park
25

Milton St.
Hawthorne Court
23
Edgewood St.
Echo Lane
Elm St.
Eddington Lane
Carmel Rd.
N.

22
Park Road
40
Locust Ave.
Ave.
Adams Ave.
CREEK
Theda Place
16
MT. De Chantal Academy
Washington Ave.
Valley View
National Road
B.&O.R.R.
CORPORATION
LINE

Greenwood Cemetery
MT. Cavalry Cemetery
Wheeling Park
20
Floral Ave.
School Av.
17 Stamm Lane
Park Av.
18
19
Elmwood St.
CORPORATION
Elm Grove & Bogg Hill Rd.
Louisa Ave.
Decator St.
Springdale Rd.
To WASHINGTON, D.C.

Wheeling
a
LINE
B.&O.R.R.
40
Stone Ch. Rd.
Elm Grove
Boulevard
91
Key Ave.
21

business, is rolled by hand much as it was nearly a hundred years ago. Tobacco from Connecticut, Pennsylvania, Kentucky, and Tennessee is used in the manufacture of Marsh stogies.

Stogies, sometimes called tobies, originated with the National Road. Wagon and stage drivers demanded a cheap brand of rolled tobacco to smoke, and a Pennsylvania manufacturer began to roll long thin twists of tobacco, conveniently shaped to carry in a driver's boot (a favorite spot for carrying knives, pistols, and other small objects), which sold four for a cent. These became popular with the drivers and were at first called Conestoga cigars, for a type of wagon common on the Pike. Later the name was corrupted to stogie. Stogies are sold all over the United States, but have their heaviest sale in the Pittsburgh and northern West Virginia region where they originated. Wheeling has five stogie manufacturing companies, producing most of the stogies consumed in the country.

10. The WHEELING PUBLIC LIBRARY (*open* 9:30–9 *weekdays;* 2:30–5 *Sun.*), SE. corner Market and 21st Sts., the oldest library in the State, occupies a two-story, red brick building, the doorway of which is framed by marble Corinthian columns and a classic pediment. A decorative cornice encircles the building above the first story. The library has about 60,000 volumes, including a few rare historical books. Twelve paintings of scenes of early Wheeling by J. J. Owens, the city's best-known artist, are exhibited in the reading room. As early as 1809 Wheeling had a library maintained by public patronage, and when the Literary Association was chartered in 1859, public reading rooms were opened in a building near the present site of the post office. The present building was opened in 1910. The BENNETT MEMORIAL MUSEUM (*open* 10–12 A.M., 1:30–5 P.M. *weekdays*) occupies the second floor of the building. The collection, of which the principal exhibits are costumes from foreign countries, old firearms, and old musical instruments, was donated by Mrs. Louis Bennett of Weston, West Virginia, as a memorial to the family.

11. The LOWER MARKET (*open Sat.*), center of Market St. at 22nd St., is a rambling wooden structure with a brick foundation, resembling an ordinary shed. It was erected in 1855 on land donated by a group of citizens. A projecting roof forms a canopy over outside stalls that are used by farmers to display their products. On Saturdays, when the country folk gather here, some to sell their wares, others to chat with friends about the weather, crops, or local politics, the place takes on an informal carnival spirit.

12. The BLOCH BROTHERS TOBACCO PLANT (*open* 9–3 *weekdays*), Water St. between 39th and 41st Sts., manufactures Mail Pouch chewing tobacco. Nearly 1,000 persons are employed in the long, red brick factory buildings and modern, brick office building which occupy two blocks along the water front. The tobacco used in Mail Pouch, which is processed and cut into ribbons by machine, comes from Ohio, Connecticut, Pennsylvania, and Wisconsin. Annual production is ap-

proximately 100,000,000 packages. The company, originator of the ribbon-cut type of tobacco, was formed in 1879 by S. S. and Aaron Bloch and was the first to buy leaf tobacco for the express purpose of manufacturing cut chewing tobacco.

Mail Pouch, especially during the development of oil and gas in West Virginia, was generally used by drillers and their helpers. It is said that when the Kansas and Oklahoma oil fields opened later, and experienced workmen went West, a package of Mail Pouch—indicating a West Virginian—was as good as a letter of introduction in getting a job.

13. MOUNT WOOD CEMETERY, Mount Wood Rd., is on the steep slopes of Wheeling Hill near the spot where Major Samuel McCulloch leaped over the precipice (*see Tour 23*), and where tradition says Ebenezer Zane halted on his first westward trip to view the Ohio River and valley. From the cemetery there is an excellent view of the city, surrounding hills and valleys, and distant towns in Ohio. Many of the old-fashioned slabs covering the tops of graves are so weather-beaten that their inscriptions are illegible. Sepulchres that open into the steep hillsides are sealed with heavy stone or wooden doors fastened by rusty padlocks. Hundreds of flags indicate graves of war veterans, and massive monuments the graves of prominent citizens. A marble monument marks the grave of Dr. Simon P. Hullihen (1810–57), often called the 'Father of Oral Surgery.' Dr. Hullihen was the first doctor to confine his practice to surgery dealing with the mouth, nose, and throat. Much of the modern technique in dealing with hare-lip, cleft palate, and fractured jaw has developed from his discoveries. He invented several dental and surgical instruments and made improvements in others. From 1835 to 1857 he was a resident of Wheeling and was instrumental in having a hospital organized in the city, the first given a charter in what is now West Virginia.

14. WETZEL'S CAVE (*open*), 100 yards S. of the Baltimore & Ohio Railroad tunnel on the Peninsula, was a hideout for Lewis Wetzel, probably the most noted Indian killer in the history of West Virginia. The entrance to the cave is through a low round hole in the ground; a passage leads downward to two large rooms where an Indian once hid to lure unwary pioneers to their deaths. When a hunter passed by on his way to or from the fort, the Indian gave a perfect imitation of a wild turkey's call. Hunters that stalked the bird were never seen again. Wetzel heard of the sudden disappearance of several men and investigated. Hearing the turkey call, he took a roundabout approach to the cave. The Indian emerged to call again; Wetzel fired and later added another notch to the barrel of his flintlock.

Wetzel was only 14 years old when a band of Indians came upon the family cabin south of Wheeling, scalped his German parents, and took young Wetzel and his brother prisoners. When they escaped shortly afterwards, Lewis swore vengeance against all Indians and spent his lifetime carrying it out. It is said that 'he would suffer any hardship or danger for an Indian scalp.' The Indians regarded him as their most dreaded foe, yet on many occasions they spared his life because of their admiration for him. They were awed by his ability to reload his rifle while running and often said that the white warrior's gun was always loaded.

15. LINSLY INSTITUTE OF TECHNOLOGY, Theda Place on the Peninsula, is a private degree-granting school of engineering for men, with emphasis on military training. The plain brick buildings of the school stand in the midst of wide grounds and drill fields. Near the main entrance stands the *Aviator,* a statue by Augustus Lukeman. It was erected in 1924 by Mrs. Louis A. Bennett in memory of her son, Louis A. Bennett, Jr., a lieutenant in the Fortieth Squadron British Royal Air Force, who was killed in action during the First World War. The school was founded in 1793 by Noah Linsly, a leading citizen and philanthropist of Wheeling. For more than a century it occupied the old Linsly Institute building at the corner of 15th and Eoff Streets, which was used as the first Capitol of West Virginia. In 1925 the institute was moved to the present site. Courses are given in structural, chemical, and electrical engineering.

16. MOUNT DE CHANTAL ACADEMY, entrance Washington and Adams Aves., situated high on Mount de Chantal Hill overlooking the valley of Wheeling Creek, is a Catholic boarding school for girls. The three-story, rambling structure is of modified Norman design. The central building is flanked by identical wings connected by two-story units. Above the main building rises the dome-shaped belfry, in which is the Angelus bell. Smaller belfries similar in shape rise above the connecting units. Established in 1848, the school is in charge of the Sisters of the Visitation, Blessed Virgin Mary. Preparatory courses and postgraduate work in English, history, and language are offered.

17. The J. D. MERRIMAN GARDEN (*open by telephone appointment*), Stamm Lane, is a large formal garden, laid out in 12 beds, centered around a lily pool, and surrounded by a hedge of shrubs and flowering plants.

18. THE PINES (*open by telephone appointment*), Stamm Lane, is the estate of A. C. Stifel. Attractive features are the sunken lily pool edged with iris and other annuals, the rose garden, an informal garden of perennial plants, and the hedge of pines for which the estate is named.

19. THE WEISS GARDEN (*open Sat.*), at Elmcrest, Elmwood St., contains a large oval lily pond and, behind it, a rock garden in which are junipers, sedum, ivy, and showy annuals.

20. JOHN DIECKMANN AND SONS GREENHOUSES (*open 9–5 weekdays*), Floral Ave. in Elm Grove, is the largest florist establishment in the state. Behind a two-story office and shipping building of concrete and brick, designed in Spanish style, are nearly five acres of greenhouses. Twenty acres of open beds surround the greenhouses, and a farm of 70 acres is maintained farther out the Pike.

21. The OLD STONE PRESBYTERIAN CHURCH CEMETERY on Stone Church Rd., which leads off US 40, (L) one block W. of Forbes Ave., on the slope of a steep hillside overlooking Elm Grove, was the earliest burying ground in Wheeling, and many prominent names are on the weather-beaten markers. A tablet marks the Site of the Old Stone Presbyterian Church, built in 1807 under a large oak tree that is still standing. The congregation of this Presbyterian church, organized in 1787, held its first meetings under this same tree; later the oak sheltered the first crude, tent-like structure with raised platform, erected in 1790. The old church was torn down in 1913 and replaced the following year by a larger stone structure of Gothic architecture, built at the foot of the hill.

22. The FRANK HOFFMAN GARDEN (*open by telephone appointment*), on Park Rd. near Woodsdale Park (*inquire locally*), is bordered by pink-flowering dogwood, elms, and Japanese cherry trees. Flower beds are informally arranged.

23. The JOHN C. TUCKER GARDEN (*open by telephone appointment*), on Hawthorne Court (*inquire locally*), is a rock garden with creeping plants, interspersed with Japanese honeysuckle and rambler roses.

24. WASHINGTON FARMS (*open*), reached by a private road off the Greggsville, Clinton and Potomac Rd., is a large estate on a hill overlooking the valley of Wheeling Creek. A driveway circles the hill, following closely the course of a small stream. The ravine is landscaped, with small pools and rock gardens. Near the top of the hill is a large modern brick house, and near by a modest two-story frame house. The smaller house was erected by Lawrence Augustine Washington, son of Samuel Washington and nephew of George Washington, who came to Wheeling in 1817 from the Kanawha Valley, to buy a farm. On the slope of the hill across the drive from the old house are the graves of Lawrence Augustine Washington, his wife, Mary Dorcas, and his daughter, Emma Tell Washington.

25. OGLEBAY PARK, 5 m. N. on State 88, occupies a 750-acre tract of high, rolling, and partly forested land. It is a municipal park with extensive recreational and educational facilities, including a large greenhouse, an arts and history museum, camp buildings, nature museum, auditorium, game rooms, tennis courts, golf course, hiking trails, bridle paths, 60 picnic sites, swimming pool, and flower gardens.

The main buildings of the park center around the MANSION HOUSE, now used as an arts and history museum (*open 2–5 daily June 1 to Aug. 31, 2–5 Sun. May 7 to May 30*). The large yellow-painted brick mansion, situated on the crest of a hill, was built in 1801 and remodeled by Earl W. Oglebay early in the twentieth century. A two-story, white-trimmed portico with fluted Ionic columns and heavy angular pediment fronts the main entrance. Flanking the central part of the building are white-columned open galleries topped with wooden balustrades. The residence, camp buildings, and office buildings are painted yellow and white in harmony with the mansion. North of these, and separated from them by part of the golf course, is a swimming pool, 67 by 175 feet, and a stone and stucco recreation building and locker room. East of the main building, on a winding motor road, are a restaurant and camp sites.

Through the Wheeling Park Commission and Oglebay Institute, which jointly administer and finance the park, a year-round program of education-recreational activities is conducted. These include clubs for enthusiasts in astronomy, botany, and ornithology; Sunday morning nature study hikes under the direction of Dr. A. B. Brooks, park naturalist; concerts, lectures, exhibitions, plays, Friday night dances and athletic tournaments. Symphonette concerts by local orchestras are presented Sunday afternoons; community sings with occasional guest choirs are held Saturday nights. Each summer, under the auspices of the Agricultural Extension Division of West Virginia University, a two-weeks' training course for nature leaders is given. Daily field classes are held in ornithology, botany, herpetology, geology, astronomy, and nature handicraft, with occasionally an added two weeks of field study in some other part of the State.

Prior to 1928 the park was Waddington Farms, the estate of Earl W. Oglebay, who bequeathed it to the people of Wheeling for so long as they 'shall operate it for purposes of public recreation and education.' Soon after the park was established, Oglebay Institute was organized to help administer the activities initiated by a volunteer committee and the Agricultural Extension Division of West Virginia University.

26. Northwest of Oglebay Park on the Consolidated School Grounds, Greggsville, Clinton and Potomac Rd., is the SITE OF FORT VAN METER, erected in 1774 and commanded by Major Samuel McCulloch, noted Indian fighter. Men from this fort reinforced Wheeling settlers when Indians attacked Fort Henry in 1777. After a lifetime devoted to scouting and development of the frontier, McCulloch was killed by a raiding party of Mingo and Wyandot, while on a hunting trip with his brother John, on July 30, 1782. Fearing him for his cunning and yet respecting him for his courage—especially after his bold escape from them in 1777, when he rode his horse over a 300-foot precipice to avoid capture—the Indians had tried many times to take the major alive but had always been foiled by his daring and resourcefulness. After waiting in ambush a short distance from the fort, they killed him but allowed his brother to escape unharmed. When soldiers found his body the next day, he had been scalped and his heart cut out. According to tradition, the Indians divided the heart, each eating a small piece, and chanted, 'We be bold like Major McCulloch.' McCulloch's grave is a short distance from the fort site.

POINTS OF INTEREST IN ENVIRONS

The Narrows, 7 *m.;* Grave Creek Mound at Moundsville, 12.9 *m.* (*see Tour* 22c). Wheeling Island, 0.4 *m.;* McCulloch's Leap, 0.7 *m.;* Wheeling Municipal Park and Madonna of the Trail Monument, 3.7 *m.;* Old Stone Mill, 5.4 *m.;* Monument Place, 5.7 *m.* (*see Tour* 23).

PART III
Tours

Tour 1

(Leesburg, Va.)—Charles Town—Martinsburg—Berkeley Springs—
Paw Paw—(Cumberland, Md.); State 9.
Virginia Line to Maryland Line, 73 *m*.

Stone and macadam surface.
Baltimore & Ohio R.R. roughly parallels route between Charles Town and Hedgesville.
Accommodations at short intervals.

State 9 traverses the Eastern Panhandle and the valley of the Cacapon River, two strikingly different areas. Separated from the remainder of the State by the Allegheny Mountains, the Eastern Panhandle is closely related to the Old Dominion economically and socially. In this typically Virginian part of West Virginia the people have retained the Tidewater philosophy, the soft Virginian accent, the easygoing Southern manner, and an interest in racing and apple orchards. In the wilder and more rugged country west of Cacapon Mountain there is a noticeable change in the life, manners, and occupations of the people. Farms are smaller; life is more arduous; the slow-spoken, leisurely gentleman farmer gives way to the hard-working, blunt-spoken mountaineer.

State 9 crosses the VIRGINIA LINE 0 *m*., 16 miles northeast of Leesburg, Virginia.

Descending BLUE RIDGE MOUNTAIN, 0.5 *m*. (987 alt.), part of the great range that bounds Shenandoah Valley on the east, the highway overlooks the blue-green waters of the SHENANDOAH RIVER (R) now placid, now tumbling over rapids, as it winds along low wooded ridges.

The St. Andrews Mountain Mission (*open*), 2.8 *m.*, established by the Episcopal Church in 1889 to serve both the spiritual and physical needs of isolated mountaineers, consists of a chapel, a stone parish hall, and a residence for attendants. In addition to the school and church, the mission conducts a dispensary, a nursing service, an employment service, and a circulating library. It distributes textbooks to school children, writes letters for the illiterate, gives advice on everything from the feeding of babies to the settling of a boundary line dispute, harbors ill-used wives when their husbands get drunk, receives and sends telephone messages, and, in general, ministers to almost every human need.

BLOOMERY, 4.3 *m*. (352 alt., 60 pop.), on the bank of the Shenandoah River, was named for the iron furnaces and blooming mill built about two miles upstream in 1742 by Thomas Mayberry and visited by Washington in 1760. These furnaces produced the first iron made west of the Blue Ridge. The river at Bloomery provides excellent fishing and swimming.

CHARLES TOWN, 8.1 *m.* (530 alt., 2,434 pop.) (*see Charles Town*).

Charles Town is at the junction with US 340 (*see Tour 2*) and State 51 (*see Tour 1A*).

In BARDANE, 12.8 *m.* (564 alt., 71 pop.), is the junction with a dirt road.

Right on this road 0.5 *m.*, to the BURR HOUSE, built in 1751 by Peter Burr, as a chiseled stone in the chimney attests. On land purchased from Lord Fairfax, Burr constructed his house of hand-hewn clapboards so stoutly that it has been occupied continuously for almost two centuries, with only a few repairs to the roof.

KEARNEYSVILLE, 15.4 *m.* (548 alt., 412 pop.), is at the junction (L) with an unnumbered hard-surfaced road (*see Tour 1A*).

Right from Kearneysville on State 48, paved, to MORGAN'S GROVE (R), 4.3 *m.*, a deserted fairgrounds, its pavilions and picnic shelters falling to ruin. On July 17, 1775, the Berkeley Riflemen, a company of 100 Virginia Volunteers under the leadership of Captain Hugh Stephenson, met at Morgan's Spring and began their march to join General Washington's troops. Taking a beeline course, they arrived at Boston, 600 miles away, in 26 days. Each of the riflemen had embroidered on his hunting shirt, 'Liberty or Death.' The company agreed to meet again at the spring in 50 years. In 1825 Major Henry Bedinger and Major George Michael Bedinger, the only two survivors of the company, kept the pledge.

At 4.4 *m.* is the junction with an improved dirt road. Right here 0.6 *m.* to FALLING SPRINGS, also known as Crawford Hall, a stately white-painted brick house with paired end chimneys and a high two-story, four-columned portico. A small balcony with an iron balustrade projects above the front door. Falling Springs was built about 1830 by Jacob Morgan, a Revolutionary War veteran, whose grandfather, Richard Morgan, owned the land on which Shepherdstown stands. Near the springs, for which the estate was named, is a two-story house of field stone, built about 1732 by Richard Morgan. One of the oldest in the State, the house is occupied and in good repair. Both Falling Springs and the Morgan house were in the thick of several battles in the War between the States, and the former was damaged slightly by shellfire.

A stone MONUMENT TO THE BERKELEY RIFLEMEN (*see above*), 4.7 *m.*, has a bronze plaque inscribed, 'The Spirit of 1775,' under which appears the story of the riflemen and their march.

At 4.9 *m.* is SHEPHERDSTOWN, (405 alt., 888 pop.) (*see Shepherdstown*).

At 5.4 *m.* is the Maryland Line, at the southern end of a bridge spanning the Potomac River, 11 miles southwest of Boonsboro, Md. (*see Maryland Guide*).

The WEST VIRGINIA UNIVERSITY EXPERIMENT FARM (R), 16.5 *m.*, is maintained for research in the culture of fruits. Its experimental planting of apple root stocks, which include 2,000 European and American varieties, is the most extensive in the United States. Cherry, grape, plum, and nut stocks are also studied and experiments carried on in methods of pruning, soil management, planting of cover crops, root development with relation to soil types, control of insects, and plant diseases. A part of the farm is devoted to such field crops as corn, wheat, barley, alfalfa, and potatoes.

MARTINSBURG, 22.3 m. (457 alt., 14,857 pop.), seat of Berkeley County and the only industrial city in the Eastern Panhandle, produces woolen goods, ladies' garments, socks, apple jelly, vinegar, cement, paper boxes, brick and tile, furniture, limestone, and road-surfacing material. Wide, clean, and uncrowded, its streets run from the banks of Tuscarora Creek into open rolling country.

Three-quarters of a century of industrial development have invested Martinsburg with a livelier air than other towns in the Eastern Panhandle. On Saturday nights its streets are crowded with shoppers. Over a Virginian inheritance of leisurely living has been laid a thin veneer of business briskness, reflected in the hurry of traffic and crowds during working hours. With the five o'clock whistle, however, Martinsburg adopts the easy-going manner of the South.

The surrounding district was settled between 1732 and 1776 by English and German colonists. In 1772 the Berkeley County court was ordered to meet at the house of Edward Beeson here in Martinsburg, then a small settlement of 20 or 30 houses. General Adam Stephen, first sheriff of the county and a Revolutionary War soldier, laid out the town on land bought from the Fairfax estate, and named it for his friend, Colonel T. B. Martin, nephew of Lord Fairfax; the town was chartered by the Virginia assembly in 1778.

Martinsburg began to boom in 1837 when a right-of-way for the Baltimore & Ohio tracks was surveyed through the town; for six years it grew rapidly, prospering from the stores established by the railroad contractors and the camps of Irish and German workers who laid the road. In 1842 the first steam engine passed through, its whistle shrieking wildly. The local militia was at drill, but broke ranks to join the jubilant crowd of shopkeepers and citizens in their rush to the tracks to view the 'miracle.' By 1859 Martinsburg was an incorporated city of 3,000, an important railroad center, and the terminus of a new turnpike from Winchester.

Prosperity ended abruptly at the beginning of the War between the States. The railroad, vital to the transportation of Union troops and supplies, was the target of repeated Confederate attacks. In June 1861, General Stonewall Jackson's troops and General J. E. B. Stuart's cavalry raided the town, burned the newly constructed railroad bridge, tore up miles of tracks, and put 35 engines out of commission. Later the Confederates regretted their destruction, for when they decided to make use of the engines they had to put them on broad-tired wheels and haul them—32 horses to an engine—over muddy roads to Winchester.

More evenly divided in sentiment during the war than most of the Panhandle, Martinsburg was occupied first by one side, then by the other. Horses and prisoners were quartered in the Catholic church; the Lutheran church served the Union Army as a hospital. A number of citizens, uncertain whether to join the Confederate or the Union forces, organized the Home Guard. 'They kept their headquarters at the courthouse, sat up nights, arrested each other and everybody else they found prowling about,' wrote Porte Crayon (*see below*) in his *Personal Recollections of the War*. 'It was shrewdly suggested that the peace of the lonely village might have been better preserved if everybody went quietly to bed and minded their own business.' The Home Guard disbanded quickly when a member was shot through the head while attempting to arrest a stranger. Martinsburg recovered more quickly after the war than other towns in the Panhandle. Reconstruction of the railroad restored its importance as a shipping point. Limestone quarries were opened near by; between 1868 and 1878 the farmers discovered how profitable orchards could be, and Martinsburg became a packing and distributing center for apples, now the principal crop of the area. Woolen and knitting mills were built in the 1890's.

During the depression that followed 1873 trouble developed between the railroads of the country and their workers. Wage cut followed wage cut, and when another of 10 per cent was announced for all workers receiving more than $1 a day, a general strike on all lines was called. The first serious incident occurred at Martinsburg on July 16 when some 30 firemen on the Baltimore & Ohio struck; supported by other railroad workers, they halted all freight trains passing through the town, which was an important division point on the main line. When the company attempted to man the engines with strikebreakers, a large crowd collected at the station. The mayor marshaled all the police at his command, arrested a few of the strikers' leaders, dispersed the crowd, and attempted to speed the trains on their way; but the attempt failed, for the firemen, according to a contemporary newspaper report, 'were reinforced by a large body of citizens, swelling the crowd till it reached the proportions of a large mob.' As many of the police had been railroad men and showed no desire to club their neighbors, they were suspect, and the company telegraphed Governor H. M. Mathews for protection, asserting that 'the town authorities were powerless to suppress the riot.' The Wheeling Light Infantry was ordered in, but after a skirmish in which a militiaman was wounded and a striker killed, the military began to show sympathy with the strikers, and was withdrawn. Governor Mathews then appealed to President Hayes for troops; the arrival of 200 infantrymen broke the strike, and the firemen and other workers returned to the shops and trains at reduced wages.

The BERKELEY COUNTY COURTHOUSE, NW. corner King and Queen Sts., a Romanesque structure of light brick trimmed with limestone, was built in 1856. In its record room is a Book of Commissions containing documents bearing the signatures of all the governors of Virginia from Lord Dunmore to Henry A. Wise, Civil War governor, and also the signatures of George Washington, Patrick Henry, Thomas Jefferson, John Tyler, and James Monroe. In the basement vault are files of

Berkeley County newspapers from 1811 to 1893. Many county records were destroyed when Union soldiers invaded the courthouse during the War between the States. Belle Boyd, a Confederate spy whose exploits were more spectacular than important, was imprisoned in the courthouse on several occasions and amused herself by writing these and other inscriptions on the margins of Chancery Book No. 1: 'Isobel Boyd. Confederate Spy, April 7, 1863,' and 'I wonder if I will be shot tomorrow. B. Boyd. April 1863.'

The EVERETT HOUSE, SW. corner Burke and Queen Sts., is a three-story, L-shaped building. The front and original part of the building, constructed of logs now covered with rough-cast plaster, was built as a dwelling between 1784 and 1796 by Edward Beeson. About 1833 the house was converted into a hotel, the Everett House. The frame wings were added shortly before the War between the States. In 1861 Stonewall Jackson made his headquarters here and reviewed his troops from the long veranda, as did General Phil Sheridan later when Union forces occupied the town.

The ST. JOHN'S LUTHERAN CHURCH, SW. corner Martin and Queen Sts., continues to serve a congregation organized about 1775. The congregation first worshipped with a German Reformed congregation in a log building erected as a tavern. St. John's is a Gothic structure of gray-painted brick; built in 1829–32, it was remodeled in 1854 and again in 1868, after being damaged by Union soldiers who used it as a hospital. A set of chimes with a range of two octaves was installed in 1927 to play before and after church services, and on religious holidays; in the chime tower is a 30-pound cast-iron bell, said to have been the first church bell in the section. The archives contain the original church record book dating from 1779 and written in German.

The FLICK HOUSE, SW. corner King and Queen Sts., a rambling white-painted brick building with a stepped gable and an elaborate two-story portico, was built in 1803. During the War between the States a Federal officer, searching the house for Confederate spies, rode his horse through the wide hall, up the fine circular staircase, and over all the polished floors, in defiance of the Confederate sympathizer who owned it.

The WHITMORE LEMEN HOUSE (*open*), SW. corner King and Spring Sts., is a rectangular limestone structure incorporating walls erected in 1774 as part of a fort never completed. The line of demarcation between the older wall and the added structure can be clearly seen about seven feet above the ground.

The BURKHART HOUSE, NE. corner Spring and John Sts., originally a Methodist Episcopal church, was built about 1774. When outgrown by the congregation about 1830, the little stone building was transformed into a dwelling by adding a mansard roof and partitioning the high-ceilinged auditorium into rooms.

The MARTIN HOUSE (*open by appointment*), NE. corner John and Water Sts., built between 1779 and 1803, is a two-story red brick house with a small portico and gable roof. Although the high small windows have been enlarged to full-length casements, the remainder of the house is much as it was when originally constructed. The woodwork and the elaborate oak paneling in the living room, and the iron strap hinges on the massive oak doors remain as they were. In the entrance hall is a full length portrait of Henry Clay, unsigned, but said to have been painted by Porte Crayon (*see below*).

The PARKS HOUSE, SE. corner Queen and Stephen Sts., one of the oldest houses in Martinsburg, was originally a square stone building with a hipped roof. The house is now covered with cement plaster, and a brick wing has been added. A two-story square bay was added to the front about 1878 so that an invalid member of the family could have a better view of the goings-on in town.

BOYDVILLE, Queen St. between South and Buxton Sts., is one of the most beautiful of the old estates of the Eastern Panhandle. The large white-painted brick and stone mansion sits back from the street at the end of a long shady drive. General Elisa Boyd, statesman and soldier in the War of 1812, erected the house in 1812 on land bought from General Adam Stephen. Hand-wrought brass door knobs and locks, hand-carved mantels and woodwork, and even the brick for the walls were imported from England. In the wide entrance hall hangs the original imported wallpaper, with a panel design in mahogany and green. Very little of the spacious interior has been changed. The original small portico that framed the paneled doorway has been enlarged to make a wide veranda. Small square wings are connected with the main building by covered passage ways. On the lawn stands a small stone building into which the master of the plantation used to retire for privacy. On the southeast corner of the lawn is a MONUMENT TO GENERAL ADAM STEPHEN (*see above*), a square pillar of stone rising from a pyramidal base and capped with a pyramid of cannon balls.

Upon the death of General Boyd in 1841 the estate was inherited by his daughter, the wife of Charles James Faulkner, Minister to France (1859–61), a member of Stonewall Jackson's staff during the War between the States and a delegate to the State Constitutional Convention of 1872. Still owned by the Faulkner family, Boydville was noted for its hospitality; many distinguished guests were entertained here.

NORBOURNE HALL, West Race St., is a large double house of red brick, part of which was erected early in the nineteenth century as a poor house. It is widely known for having been the home in 1851 of David Hunter Strother (1816–88), artist, author, and soldier. Under the name of Porte Crayon, Strother illustrated *Blackwater Chronicles* and wrote articles for *Harper's New Monthly Magazine*. During the War between the States he rose to the rank of brigadier general in the Union Army and became chief of staff to his cousin, General David Hunter. After the war he wrote other articles for *Harper's*, among them his *Personal Recollections of the War*; in 1879 he was appointed consul general in Mexico, remaining there seven years.

Martinsburg is at the junction with US 11 (*see Tour 3*), with which State 9 unites for 1.9 miles (*see Tour 3*).

Left from Martinsburg on Tuscorora Road to the TUSCORORA PRESBYTERIAN CHURCH, 3 *m.*, the congregation of which was organized between 1740 and 1745. Parts of the original building are preserved in the walls of the present stone structure; in the entry are the wooden pegs on which the pioneer worshippers hung their guns during services. Many of the graves in the old cemetery are unmarked; many others have thin sandstone slabs from which the inscriptions have been effaced by time and weather.

HEDGESVILLE, 28.9 *m.* (600 alt., 361 pop.), subsists on trade with neighboring farms and orchards. In the center of town, shaded by century-old oaks, stands (R) the MOUNT ZION EPISCOPAL CHURCH, built in 1817 on ground donated by Josiah Hedges, for whose family the village was named. The red brick structure, the second on the site, has mellowed to a deep pink.

FOOSE'S LAWN (*open*), 31.1 *m.*, an old tavern, was erected by Robert Snodgrass on land patented by William Snodgrass in 1732. The east end of the inn was built about 1740; the west unit of stone and the connecting section of hand-hewn logs, covered with weatherboarding, date from 1800, according to local historians; the upper stories were added later. The original paneled door, with its iron strap hinges and huge lock, is still in place.

In 1769, while on his way to Warm Springs (*see Berkeley Springs*) with Patsy, his little stepdaughter, George Washington stopped at the inn, recording in his diary: '. . . bated at one Snodgrasses and dined there, 7s. 6d. Lodgings cost 11s.' A story has been handed down in the Snodgrass family that a servant dropped Washington's trunk while carrying it across Back Creek from the coach to the inn, soaking the fine clothes it contained. Washington, a fastidious man, refused to come to the dining room without a change of apparel and ordered his dinner served in his room while the careless servant dried his clothes by the kitchen fire.

The highway passes through HEMLOCK FOREST, 39.5 *m.*, also called Spruce Pine Hollow, in which dense growths of hemlock, cedar, and pine darken the road even on the brightest day.

At 47.4 *m.* is the junction with US 522 (formerly State 38).

Left on US 522 is (R) the entrance to CACAPON STATE PARK, 10 *m.*, a 5,400-acre recreation tract (*cabins, picnic facilities, trails, motor roads*). In the park the headwaters of Indian Run have been dammed to form a 6-acre lake (*trout fishing, boating*). On Cacapon Mountain is PROSPECT ROCK, which offers a view embracing parts of four States—West Virginia, Virginia, Maryland, and Pennsylvania. The view was renowned as early as 1769 when George Washington, stopping at Bath with his family, 'rid with Mrs. Washington and others to the Cacapehon Mountain, to see the prospect from thence.' Lawrence Augustine Washington, a nephew, accompanied the party and wrote in his journal, 'We approached to enjoy the beautiful prospect, for beautiful it is. The lofty towering mountains which rise in proud and successive elevations over each other, until their blue and fading summits, which seemed to touch the very heavens, were lost in the azure of the distant retiring horizon—the lovely valley at an immeasurable distance below our feet—the solitary hamlets, with their circling columns of dense smoke, winding slowly up the mountain's top—the two beautiful rivers coursing their romantic passages through this enchanting vale—the passing white fantastic clouds of heaven, whirling over our heads whilst their fleeting shadows glided nimbly over the delightful scene before us—beheld with rapture.'

BERKELEY SPRINGS, 47.9 *m.* (612 alt., 1,039 pop.) (*see Berkeley Springs*).

The highway crosses SIR JOHNS RUN, 49.8 *m.*, named for Sir John Sinclair, quartermaster of General Braddock's ill-fated expedition against Fort Duquesne in 1755. At the mouth of Sir Johns Run, James Rumsey conducted experiments with steam-propelled boats in 1784 (*see Shepherdstown*).

A view from the northern end of CACAPON MOUNTAIN (2,196 alt.), 51.7 *m.*, reveals the Potomac River, railroad tracks, and the Chesapeake and Ohio Canal twisting in parallel courses across the farm-checkered valley. In the middle distance the Cacapon River flows into the Potomac. Beyond the valley looms SIDELING HILL (2,008 alt.), with a fire tower standing guard upon the highest point.

GREAT CACAPON, 53.6 *m.* (500 alt., 363 pop.), has glass sand quarries, opened in 1904 and sporadically active since that time. During the War between the States the village was threatened with destruction when a Confederate force mounted cannons on top of Cacapon Mountain and aimed at the post office where Union troops were stationed. A few shots were fired but struck nothing but intervening trees.

The highway crosses the CACAPON RIVER, 61.2 *m.*, and follows a serpentine course through a region of dense woods and swift streams. Occasional glimpses of distant mountain walls and the smooth flowing river are framed by towering slender trees.

At 69.8 *m.* is the junction with State 29.

Left on State 29 to FORKS OF CACAPON, 6.6 *m.* (718 alt., 63 pop.), which is at the junction with State 45.

1. Left on State 45 to the junction with a dirt road, 0.7 *m.*; R. here to the junction with another dirt road, 1.0 *m.*; L. on this road to CAUDY'S CASTLE, 1.5 *m.*, a jagged rock formation towering 600 feet above the Cacapon River, named for James Caudy who settled near by in 1747. Up the rear of the rock a winding footpath and natural stair (*inquire locally*) lead to the top of the formation. During Indian raids early settlers, led by Caudy, would race up the rock and lie in wait near the top ready to push Indians over the edge of the precipice into the gorge below as they struggled up in single file.

2. Right 12.5 *m.* on State 45 through a country of billowing knolls, dotted with small farms, to the junction with US 50 (*see Tour 5a*).

PAW PAW, 73.8 *m.* (620 alt., 781 pop.), a shipping point for a fruit-growing district, also has a tannery established about 1875 because of the abundant local supply of oak bark. Paw Paw was an important concentration point for Union troops during the War between the States; as many as 16,000 were encamped here at one time in barracks and a blockhouse along the tracks of the Baltimore & Ohio Railroad.

State 9 connects with Md. 51 at the MARYLAND LINE, 73 *m.*, on a bridge spanning the Potomac River, 26 miles east of Cumberland, Maryland (*see Maryland Guide*).

ↆↆ

Tour 1A

Charles Town—Middleway—Kearneysville; 14.8 *m.* State 51 and un-numbered road.

Bituminous macadam surface.
Limited accommodations.

This route loops through a peaceful countryside of open rolling fields and vast apple orchards, fragrant in May with pink and white blossoms and brilliant in autumn with heavy red fruit. In this wide and fertile section of the Valley of Virginia members of the Washington family settled and built large houses, which, like many others in the district, are unoccupied and slowly falling into ruin.

CHARLES TOWN, 0 *m.* (530 alt., 2,434 pop.) (*see Charles Town*).
Charles Town is at the junction with State 9 (*see Tour* 1) and US 340 (*see Tour* 2).

Left from Charles Town on Summit Point Road, improved, is BRADDOCK'S WELL (R), 2 *m.*, which looks much like any farmhouse pump. The well was dug in 1755 by soldiers of General Braddock's command while encamped here. Although Braddock had been informed that there were springs near by, he stubbornly insisted upon having a well dug. A wooden platform now covers the shaft, and an iron pump draws pure water.

CLAYMONT COURT (R), 2.6 *m.*, stands almost a mile from the road, at the end of a driveway bordered with large old oak trees. Built in 1820 by Bushrod Corbin Washington, grandnephew of George Washington, it is the largest and most costly of the Washington homes in the Eastern Panhandle. The original structure was almost destroyed by fire about 1838 but was rebuilt within a few years. The red brick Georgian Colonial mansion has two wings; six dormers break the line of the gable roof, front and back, and four huge chimneys rise at the ends of the main unit and the wings. A small railed observation plat-form surmounts the roof of the center unit. The plainness of the front is relieved by a small flat-roofed portico, with Ionic columns at the entrance. Wide galleries extend the length of the first and second stories in the rear of the main part of the house, and a glass sun porch adjoins the north wing. Two smaller brick buildings, with hipped roofs pierced by square central chimneys, are joined to the main house by small walled courts. The spacious lawn is planted with shrubs and trees. Two terraces are all that remain of the former seven-terraced garden. During the War between the States many members of the Washington family gathered here for refuge and, in spite of the war, carried on the luxurious living of pre-war days. In 1899 Claymont Court was purchased by Frank Stockton, author of *The Lady or the Tiger* (1900).

The WHITE HOUSE TAVERN (L), 5.9 *m.*, is a low, story-and-a-half, whitewashed stone building. A visible line down the middle indicates that its two sections were built at different times. The eastern end, erected in 1742 by Dr. John McCormick, an Irish immigrant, has the thick walls and small windows characteristic of the period when Indian attacks were frequent. The window sills slide back, uncovering secret spaces within the walls in which valuables could be stored if the house had to be abandoned hastily. The western half was added about 1800 by an innkeeper, named Whitehouse, who converted the building into a tavern. He was succeeded by George Locke whose family operated the inn for many years. The old stone barn in front of the house is perhaps as old as the western half of the building.

At SUMMIT POINT, 6.7 *m.* (620 alt., 310 pop.), occurred one of the many skirmishes fought in this section during the War between the States.

Left from Summit Point on a hard-surfaced road, 4.8 *m.*, is RIPPON (537 alt., 250 pop.) (*see Tour 2*), at the junction with US 340 (*see Tour 2*).

ALTONA FARM (R), 1.2 *m.*, known locally as the Davenport Farm, was owned originally by Lawrence Washington, who willed it to Charles Washington. In 1793 Colonel Abram Davenport bought the farm, and around the small house which then stood on the property built the present white-painted brick mansion. Paired chimneys rise in front and back, and tall peaked dormers break the lines of the shingled hip roof; the front and side entrances, above which are fanlights, are sheltered by flat-roofed one-story porticoes, with paired Doric columns. The house was damaged by cannon fire during the War between the States but was restored soon afterward. Parts of the stone fence enclosing the estate were built by Davenport's slaves before the war. The farm, which belonged to the Davenport family for more than 100 years, was sold in 1906; after several changes in ownership, it is again in the possession of the Davenport family.

A short distance from the road, 1.8 *m.*, are (R) the RUINS OF ST. GEORGE'S CHAPEL, a small Episcopal church in which members of the Washington family, and occasionally George Washington himself, worshipped. The church, erected in 1769 by wealthy landowners of this section, is said to have been one of the most beautiful small churches in the Valley of Virginia. The window frames were of cedar, and the carved woodwork and high-backed pews were imported from England. The chapel was abandoned in 1819 when a larger church was built in Charles Town. The furnishings of St. George's Chapel were removed to the new church. During the War between the States the sheet lead roof was appropriated for bullets. Treasure hunters later removed the flooring and dug around the foundations in search of legendary buried wealth.

Near the ruins, and almost half a mile from State 51, is PIEDMONT (R), on an estate that was part of a crown grant of 3,000 acres made in 1730 to Robert Worthington, a Quaker. He erected the massive limestone house that forms the rear wing of the present mansion, and named the estate Quarry Banks New Stile for his old home, Quarry Banks, in England. Worthington's son, Colonel Robert Worthington, forsook his father's religion and was one of the principal subscribers to the erection of St. George's Chapel. The main part of the present house, built in 1780 by Dr. John Briscoe, is of the conventional Georgian Colonial rectangular pattern, with gable roof, wide end chimneys, and a portico. The white trim of the small-paned windows and portico contrasts with the red brick walls, laid in Flemish bond. Unlike those of most southern homes, Piedmont's windows are not shuttered. In the wide entrance hall hang portraits of General William Darke (*see Tour* 2) and his wife, the grandparents of Mrs. Briscoe. The walls of the drawing room are covered with French tapestry wallpaper, imported from Paris in 1802. The paper, designed by Joseph Defour, depicts the adventures of Telemaque.

HAREWOOD (L), 3.3 *m.*, erected about 1770, is perhaps the most widely known of the Washington homes in this section. It was designed by George Washington for his brother, Colonel Samuel Washington. Although the exterior of the rectangular limestone building is plain, the interior is elaborately finished with wainscoting and moldings. The panels of the drawing room and other rooms are joined upon fluted pilasters crowned with capitals. In the drawing room above the porphyry mantel, said to have been the gift of Lafayette, hangs a portrait of Colonel Samuel Washington. Southwest of the house is a small low-walled family burying ground, in which Samuel and two of his five wives are buried in unmarked graves.

Prince Louis Philippe and his two brothers, according to tradition, were entertained at Harewood at the time of their exile from France. Here, in the paneled drawing room, Dolly Payne Todd and James Madison were married September 15, 1794. George Steptoe Washington, who had inherited the estate, had married Dolly Todd's sister, Lucy Payne, and it was at her urging that the wedding was celebrated at Harewood. After the ceremony the young ladies robbed Madison of his lace ruffles, cutting them into pieces for souvenirs. Dolly and Lucy were Quakers, and both were 'disowned' by the Society of Friends a few months after Dolly's marriage, because they had married outsiders.

State 51 forks (L), 6.3 *m.*, to MIDDLEWAY, 6.9 *m.* (500 alt., 226 pop.), a quiet village with aging gable-roofed buildings of white-washed stone, faded brick, or logs, covered with weatherboard or rough-cast plaster. First called Smithfield, the village grew up around SMITH TAVERN (L), built about 1740 on what was then the main line of east-west travel in this section. The sagging yellow log house, now weatherboarded, has a crumbling stone chimney at one end, but is still occupied.

According to local stories, strange happenings took place in Middleway in 1790. Adam Livingston, a settler, gave shelter to a traveler, who fell desperately ill during the night and begged Livingston to call a priest. He refused, saying that there was no priest in the neighborhood, and if there were, he would not have one in his house. The traveler died; no wake was held, for candles brought into the room were mysteriously blown out; and the nameless stranger was hastily buried.

Shortly afterward horses were heard galloping around the house at night; flaming logs jumped from the fireplace and danced about the kitchen; the heads of Livingston's horses, cows, pigs, and chickens mysteriously fell off; his barn burned to the ground; his money disappeared. Clothes, linens, and rugs, locked in chests and closets, were found cut to shreds or with tiny holes snipped in them. The snipping sound of shears could be heard night and day. Curious neighbors who called at the Livingston house went away with their clothes full of holes. Livingston appealed to his minister, but the clergyman was as mystified as the others. Finally, in a dream, Livingston saw a man in flowing robes who offered to help him. Convinced that he was a priest, Livingston went to Shepherdstown to consult Father Dennis Cahill, who returned with him to Middleway, and said Mass in the house. The manifestations stopped immediately. In gratitude Livingston deeded to the Roman Catholic Church 34 acres of ground, and specified that a chapel was to be erected thereon. Trustees were appointed; years passed but no chapel was built. Livingston later sold all his property, except the broad field on the banks of the Opequon Creek, known as Priest's Field, and moved to Pennsylvania. After his death the field was claimed by his heirs; to hold the property, the Catholic Church erected about 1925 a small gable-roofed gray frame building, known as PRIEST'S FIELD CHAPEL. Only one Mass yearly, conducted in September, is held in the church.

In Middleway is the junction (R) with an unnumbered hard-surfaced road, along which the route continues.

In LEETOWN, 10.9 m. (503 alt., 200 pop.), is PRATO RIO (open), a story-and-a-half limestone house with small-paned windows, set high in the walls, and outside end chimneys. To this house, which he had bought in 1775 at the urging of General Horatio Gates, General Charles Lee retired after his retreat at the Battle of Monmouth in 1778 had resulted in a defeat for the Americans. Lee, whose fine record as a soldier in the British Army had made him a rival of Washington for the command of the American Army at the beginning of the Revolution, deeply resented his commander's reprimand after the battle and displayed high temper. Suspended from his command, he secluded himself at Prato Rio with his Italian bodyguard, his slaves, and his pack of hounds, and soon gained a reputation for eccentricity.

The ground floor of Prato Rio had no partitions; Lee marked off the space into four quarters with chalk lines drawn on the floor; in one space he kept his books, in the second his bed, in the third his saddles and guns, and in the fourth the kitchen equipment. Several years later Washington wrote him a note saying that he would call the next day, and that he hoped they could meet as old friends and comrades-in-arms, with all past contention and bitterness forgotten. Lee, however, was not ready to forget. When Washington rode up to the house, he found it deserted and locked, with a sign on the door, 'No meat cook'd here today.' In his years at Prato Rio, Lee had few friends except General

Horatio Gates and General Adam Stephen, both of whom had likewise been suspended from the Continental Army. The three, so it is said, would meet frequently at Prato Rio, and under the influence of wine would propose in quick succession three toasts to one another; the first usually was 'to Major General Charles Lee, who was cashiered from the Continental Army because, when he should have advanced, he retreated'; the second, 'to Maj. Gen. Horatio Gates, who was cashiered because, when he should have retreated, he advanced'; and the third, 'to Maj. Gen. Adam Stephen, who was cashiered because, when he might have advanced or retreated, he did neither.'

Lee's will, on record in the Berkeley County Courthouse, reflects the cynical and embittered mood of his last years. He requested that he might not 'be buried in any church or churchyard, or within a mile of any Presbyterian or a Baptist meeting house. For since I have resided in this country I have kept so much bad company when living that I do not choose to continue it when dead.' Lee died in Philadelphia in 1782 and, in spite of the wish expressed in his will, was buried with full military honors in the Christ Church graveyard in that city.

A U. S. FISH HATCHERY (L), 11.3 *m.*, occupies land that was once part of the Lee estate. In addition to the propagation of fish, studies of fish diseases are carried on here.

At 14.2 *m.* is the junction with a graveled road.

Left on this road is the entrance (R) to a driveway, 0.4 *m.*, which leads to TRAVELER'S REST (*open*), the home of General Horatio Gates (1729–1806), English-born soldier of the French and Indian War and a major general under Washington during the Revolution. The two-and-a-half-story limestone house, which has end chimneys and a porch, was bought by General Gates in 1763. The heavy wooden shutters and many of the original window panes, one with Gates's initials scratched on it, remain. One pane, with the Gates's crest scratched on it, has been removed from the window, and is on display in the house. The front door is fastened with iron strap hinges, and has a huge lock. Gates, like Lee, had been a candidate for the command of the American forces at the beginning of the Revolution; he was suspended from his command when he charged instead of retreating at the Battle of Camden, S. C., and was badly defeated. After his retirement he returned to Traveler's Rest and lived here until 1790, when he removed to New York and became active in politics, dying there in 1806.

KEARNEYSVILLE, 14.8 *m.* (548 alt., 412 pop.) (*see Tour* 1), is at the junction with State 9 (*see Tour* 1).

Tour 2

(Frederick, Md.)—Harpers Ferry—Charles Town—Rippon—(Winchester, Va.); US 340.
Maryland Line to Virginia Line, 15.3 m.

Concrete-paved throughout.
Norfolk & Western Ry. parallels route between Charles Town and Virginia Line.
Accommodations at Harpers Ferry and Charles Town.

US 340 traverses the southeastern section of the Eastern Panhandle. During the War between the States it was the scene of many battles because of its strategic importance. Today it is peacefully agricultural, noted for its large apple orchards. Fine old houses—some abandoned and falling to ruin, others well-preserved—are numerous. Many were built and occupied by members of the Washington family.

US 340 crosses the MARYLAND LINE, 0 m., on the outskirts of HARPERS FERRY (275 alt., 705 pop.) (see Harpers Ferry), 20 miles west of Frederick, Maryland.

BOLIVAR, 1.2 m. (600 alt., 616 pop.), is an incorporated town occupying craggy Bolivar Heights, and is usually regarded as a part of Harpers Ferry.

At 2 m. is the junction with a graveled road.

Right on this road is SCOTTISH CASTLE, 0.3 m., a large stone building with battlements and a square tower at the eastern end. It was erected in 1887 by Colonel R. E. Whitman, a retired British soldier, who was governed by military principles of defense in selecting its site and type of construction. It occupies a strategic position high above the surrounding countryside, and the observation room in the tower commands a view of several miles in all directions.

In HALLTOWN, 4 m. (411 alt., 317 pop.), is (L) the HALLTOWN PAPER BOARD COMPANY PLANT (open).

At 4.1 m. is the junction with a graveled road.

Right on this road 1 m. to BEALL AIR, a rambling brick structure, painted gray, formerly the home of Colonel Lewis Washington, great-grandnephew of the first President. Colonel Washington added the front part of the house, with its stepped gables, to a much older structure built by his grandfather, Thomas Beall, for whom the estate was named. From this house John Brown and his band kidnapped Colonel Washington and held him as hostage on October 16, 1859, the night of the raid on Harpers Ferry. Washington had in his possession the sword that Frederick the Great of Prussia had given to George Washington, with this compliment, 'The oldest general in the world to the greatest.' Brown asked Colonel Washington for this sword, saying that he required it to continue the fight for liberty which the 'Father of his Country' had begun, and on his capture was found wearing it.

At 4.7 *m.* is the junction with a graveled road.

Right on this road, which closely parallels the Baltimore & Ohio Railroad, is the SITE OF THE GENERAL WILLIAM DARKE HOUSE, 1.4 *m.*, marked by a depression in the ground and a few tumbled foundation stones. A long stone house near by, once used for slave quarters, is now a private residence. Behind the house is the grave of General Darke's daughter, Mary. An Indian fighter, an officer in the American Revolution, and a delegate to the Constitutional Convention of 1788, Darke was a huge, blunt-mannered, courageous man— a typical frontier soldier. On one occasion he quarreled with Captain James Stephenson of Martinsburg and challenged him to a duel. Stephenson, a small sprightly man, appeared on the field of honor with a slender rapier; Darke came armed with a long broad sword. The contrast between the two men and their weapons caused their seconds to burst into laughter. After a moment Darke and Stephenson joined in, decided not to fight, and remained good friends to the end of their lives.

DARKE (Duffields Station), 1.8 *m.* (493 alt., 261 pop.), is a crossroads village named for General Darke. In the graveyard (R) of the Ronemus family are the graves of Darke and his wife.

RION HALL (L), 4.9 *m.*, reached by a private driveway, is a large structure of yellow brick, built about 1836, as the home of Judge Daniel Bedinger Lucas (1836–1909), lawyer, orator, and poet. It has been unoccupied since 1930, when Lucas's daughter was killed in an automobile accident at the entrance to the estate. Lucas served for a short time on the staff of Confederate General Henry A. Wise, and in January 1865 ran the blockade to defend his former classmate, Captain John Yeats Beall, under arrest in New York on a charge of espionage. Unable to return home, Lucas spent the remainder of the war years in Canada, and there wrote the poem, 'The Land Where We Were Dreaming.' Between 1890 and 1893 he served on the bench of the Supreme Court of Appeals of West Virginia.

CHARLES TOWN, 7.8 *m.* (530 alt., 2,434 pop.) (*see Charles Town*).

Charles Town is at the junction with State 9 (*see Tour 1*) and State 51 (*see Tour 1A*).

Southwest of Charles Town the route traverses a peaceful countryside of open rolling fields and extensive apple orchards; in May the trees are fragrant with pink and white blossoms, and in autumn the branches are laden with the red fruit.

CASSILIS (L), 8.7 *m.*, a large square house of yellow brick, stands in a grove of huge oak trees some distance from the highway. It was built about 1835 by Andrew Kennedy, and before the War between the States was noted for its hospitality. Andrew's brother, John P. Kennedy, who was Secretary of the Navy under President Filmore, brought many of his friends to visit Cassilis—among others, Washington Irving and William Makepeace Thackeray. These visits, it is said, influenced Thackeray to write *The Virginians* instead of a proposed book on California.

At 9.5 *m.* is the junction with a graveled road.

Left on this road is the GEORGE WASHINGTON CAVE (*adm.* 50¢), 1.2 *m.* The main room is called the Lodge Room because of meetings held there. As a boy of 17, Washington, while on a surveying trip for Lord Fairfax, is said to have carved his name on the wall of his room. In 1754, according to tradition, he revisited the cave with Masonic soldiers under his command. Commemorative exercises were conducted here by local Masons in 1844 and 1927. The walls of the cave bear innumerable carvings, some believed to have been made by Indians long before Washington's time.

At 9.6 *m.* is the junction with another graveled road.

Right on this road is BLAKELY, 1.6 *m.*, built in 1820 by John Augustine Washington, grandnephew of George Washington and one-time owner of Mount Vernon. The plain rectangular structure of brick, now faded to a pinkish hue, is two-and-a-half-stories high, with a two-story wing at the west end, and wide gable end chimneys. A small square brick outbuilding, connected with the wing by a covered passageway, once served as a summer kitchen. The house was partly burned during the War between the States, but later restored. Braddock's men camped near the site on the ill-fated expedition against Fort Duquesne in 1755.

WHEATLANDS (R), 12.3 *m.*, typical of the older Georgian Colonial farmhouses of this section, is a long two-story structure of white-painted brick, with a red gable roof. A wide portico shades the arched front entrance, over which is a sunburst transom; in the pediment of the portico is a semicircular window. Green shutters flank the many-paned windows. Near the house are several small brick outbuildings, also of white-painted brick, some of which were slave quarters.

In 1798 Wheatlands was owned by Henry Smith Turner, whose son, George, was killed in John Brown's raid on Harpers Ferry in 1859. During the War between the States the house was occupied alternately by Union and Confederate forces, and became known as Castle Thunder.

Across the road from Wheatlands, in a hollow, are the stone RUINS OF McBANEY'S MILL, which for more than a half century ground corn and wheat for neighboring farmers.

RIPPON, 13.5 *m.* (537 alt., 214 pop.), a scattered village inhabited largely by Negroes, has two churches, a school, a few stores, and a blacksmith shop.

US 340 crosses the VIRGINIA LINE, 15.3 *m.*, 17 miles east of Winchester, Virginia (*see Virginia Guide*).

Tour 3

(Williamsport, Md.)—Falling Waters—Martinsburg—Bunker Hill—
(Winchester, Va.); US 11.
Maryland Line to Virginia Line, 27 m.

Concrete-paved and bituminous macadam surface.
Pennsylvania R.R. parallels route.
Accommodations at short intervals.

US 11, a heavily traveled route, traverses the rich orchard and farm
country of the Eastern Panhandle. During its settlement early in the
eighteenth century the region was frequently raided by Indians and
during the War between the States was swept continually by advancing and retreating armies.

US 11 crosses the MARYLAND LINE, 0 m., on a modern steel
bridge (*passenger cars, 25¢; trucks 20¢ minimum*) spanning the Potomac River from Williamsport, Maryland.

MAIDSTONE-ON-THE-POTOMAC (R), 0.1 m., a white-painted brick
house, was built in 1744 by Evan Watkins, who for many years operated a ferry 'from ye mouth of Canagochego Creek, in Maryland, across
the Potomac to ye Evan Watkins Landing,' a fact commemorated by
a marker on the river bank. The house has a plain paneled door, recessed within a quoined frame, which is surmounted with a cyma pediment and an oblong transom. Windows on the first floor have white,
solid-panel shutters; those on the second floor, green shutters. A gallery
extends the length of the frame right wing, a later addition.

In the POTOMAC PARK CAMP MEETING GROUNDS (L), 0.7 m., is
held each August the annual camp meeting of the Assemblies of God,
Inc.

FALLING WATERS, 4.2 m. (349 alt., 300 pop.), at a bend in the
Potomac River, was named for a small spring-fed stream that cascades
into the river here. During the War between the States this now
peaceful agricultural village saw much fighting, including the Battle
of Falling Waters in July 1863, when General Robert E. Lee's army,
retreating from Gettysburg, was attacked by Union forces under General George G. Meade, but succeeded in crossing the Potomac here,
which destroyed Meade's hope of shattering 'the matchless Army of
Northern Virginia.'

As the Confederates fell back from Gettysburg, they found that the
Potomac was swollen with heavy rains and that the bridges both here
and at Williamsport had been destroyed by Union troops. The forward

detachments of Lee's army reached the river on July 5, 1863, and for days there were cavalry skirmishes between the contending forces. On July 6 a Union corps launched a heavy attack, and on July 9 Lee arrived with the bulk of his army. Impatient at the slow progress being made in rebuilding the bridges, he ordered the warehouses along the Chesapeake and Ohio Canal to be torn down and their timbers used to construct pontoon bridges. Meade timidly delayed his attack from day to day, but finally advanced in force on July 14, only to find that under cover of night Lee and his forces had crossed here at Falling Waters and at fords along the river, and were retreating south to safety.

The HAUCK HOUSE (R), 5.8 m., a two-and-one-half-story house, with a rough cast plaster finish and a frame rear wing, was built early in the nineteenth century; its wide board floors rest on hand-hewn joists. During the War between the States several rafters were almost severed by cannon fire; plaster patches in the walls and ceiling indicate where heavy shot lodged in the walls.

A MARKER, 6.3 m., commemorates the fact that on July 12, 1861, while seated under an oak tree here giving orders, General 'Stonewall' Jackson was fired on by Federal troops. A cannonball brought down a limb of the tree, and 'Jackson, unhurt, rode calmly away.'

The highway passes extensive WATER-CRESS PONDS, 7.5 m., one of few enterprises of the kind in the country. Water from two springs is diverted by a series of dams and sluices over 35 acres, on which the cress is planted in spring in one inch of running water. As the plants grow, the water level is raised slightly. From May to November the ponds are covered with a thick green carpet of cress, which is harvested continually during the growing season by crews of men in hip boots; they cut the plants with sharp knives, tie them into small bunches, pack and ice them in wooden containers for shipment to market. During the winter the ponds are drained to await spring plowing, re-flooding, and planting.

At 10.7 m. is the junction with State 9 (see Tour 1), which unites with US 11 for 1.9 miles.

A marker, 10.9 m., stands on the SITE OF FORT NEALLY, captured in 1756 by Indians, who killed the garrison and took many women and children as captives.

At 11.4 m. is the junction with a graveled road.

Right on this road is RED HOUSE, 0.1 m., a dilapidated rambling structure in which the first county court of Berkeley County met in 1772. Originally a one-story log building erected in 1766 by John Hunter and sold in 1771 to Edward Beeson, one of the first justices of the court, the house was later enlarged with the addition of a second story. A double gallery extends along the front of the building; another, the length of the rear wing.

MARTINSBURG, 12.6 m. (457 alt., 14,857 pop.) (see Tour 1), is at the junction with State 9 (see Tour 1).

BIG SPRING (L), 15.2 *m.*, occupies the SITE OF FORT EVANS, built
by John Evans in 1755. The next year Indians attacked the fort in
the absence of the men; Polly, Evans's wife, rallied the women, and
in her deepest voice shouted orders as if to a large force. After the
exchange of a few shots the Indians withdrew.

On the outskirts of PIKESIDE, 16.2 *m.* (535 alt., 50 pop.), is
SHEPHERD FIELD, a regular stop on the Tri-State Aviation lines (*day
service*).

DARKESVILLE, 19.9 *m.* (560 alt., 236 pop.), originally known as
Bucklesville, was renamed for General William Darke, frontier hero
(*see Tour 2*), at the time of its incorporation in 1797 by the Virginia
assembly. His boyhood home here, a log cabin built by his father in
1741, is incorporated in the ADAM LINK HOUSE. On October 9, 1862,
Darkesville was the rendezvous for 1,800 Confederate soldiers, assembled by General J. E. B. Stuart for a raid on Chambersburg, Pennsylvania. During the following week they traversed 160 miles of enemy
territory, captured Chambersburg, destroyed $250,000 worth of Fed-
eral property, and captured some 30 men and 1,200 horses, losing
only one man and two horses.

INWOOD, 20.9 *m.* (569 alt., 135 pop.), contains the STATE APPLE
PACKING PLANT (*open*), established on a co-operative non-profit basis
in 1920 to demonstrate the best methods of sorting, grading, and packing fruit, the principal product of the section.

BUNKER HILL, 22.7 *m.* (565 alt., 228 pop.), a crossroads village
on Mill Creek in the midst of fertile orchard and farming land, established some time between 1726 and 1732 by Morgan Morgan, was
the first recorded settlement in the State. White frame houses with
trim yards and vegetable gardens skirt the roadside. A filling station
and well-stocked general store add a touch of modernity to the village,
which otherwise has changed little in two centuries. Its inhabitants
move in the old jog-trot way, content to grow choice apples and till
their fertile meadows.

Morgan, originally from Wales, came to Virginia from Delaware,
and soon secured 1,000 acres on Mill Creek. Here he erected a rude
cabin to which he brought his family. Soon others came, including
the Hite and Briscoe families, and the settlement grew. Morgan became a leader in the life of his community and Virginia; he served as
a justice and as captain of militia, and built roads. An imposing granite (L), on the highway in the eastern edge of the village, erected by
the State in 1924, marks the exact SITE OF THE MORGAN MORGAN
CABIN. The story of Morgan's life is briefly told on a bronze plaque
set in the south face of the monument.

Right from Bunker Hill on an unimproved road is CHRIST CHURCH (R), 0.2
m., which stands on the site of Morgan's Chapel, erected in 1740 by Morgan
Morgan, Joist Hite, and Dr. John Briscoe. The original chapel of unhewn logs
was the first Episcopal church established in what is now West Virginia.
The present structure, an exceedingly plain dark brick building with a gable
roof, was erected in 1853, the third to stand on the site. The foundation stones

are from the second church, a stone building erected in 1818. In the churchyard is the GRAVE OF MORGAN MORGAN, with rudely inscribed sandstone markers at the head and foot.

South of Bunker Hill the highway passes many orchards and skirts APPLE PIE RIDGE (R), known as such since the eighteenth century when Quaker women of the vicinity gained wide renown for the apple pies they brought to all-day meetings.

The PETTIGREW MONUMENT (R), 23 m., a granite column with an Ionic capital on which rest four stacked cannonballs, commemorates the fact that in the Boyd House, 200 yards to the west, died Brigadier-General James Johnston Pettigrew of North Carolina, a Confederate leader in the assault on Cemetery Ridge during the battle of Gettysburg. In the retreat southward General Pettigrew was fatally wounded in the Battle of Falling Waters (see above) on July 14, 1863; a bronze plaque on the monument is inscribed with the tribute paid him by his superior, General Robert E. Lee.

RIDGEWAY, 26.3 m. (590 alt., 115 pop.) a small trading center of the surrounding apple-growing country, has scattered white frame houses set amid broad orchards, enclosed within whitewashed, zigzag rail fences. Here and there along the road are rough plank shelters with rows of shelves, on which apples, peaches, and other fruits are displayed for sale in season.

US 11 crosses the VIRGINIA LINE, 27 m., 9 miles north of Winchester, Virginia (see Virginia Guide).

Tour 4

(Winchester, Va.)—Romney—Clarksburg—Salem—Parkersburg—Belpre, Ohio); US 50.
Virginia Line to Ohio Line, 217.8 m.

Alternate stretches of concrete and macadam.
Baltimore & Ohio R.R. roughly parallels route between Bridgeport and Ellenboro.
Accommodations at short intervals.

US 50, a main transcontinental highway, cuts across northern West Virginia, joining the mountainous country along the Virginia Line with the bottom lands along the Ohio River at Parkersburg. As early as 1784 George Washington had suggested a wagon road to the 'new West' along this approximate route, originally a buffalo trail followed by Indians, traders, and trappers. Desiring an all-Virginia trade route to the western waterways, the Virginia assembly authorized in 1786 the construction of a wagon road from Winchester to Morgantown, by way of Romney; by 1790 its course had been marked as far as Parkersburg, at the mouth of the Little Kanawha, but construction did not start until 1827, when the North-Western Road Company was incorporated. The company encountered difficulty in raising capital through the sale of stock because of public skepticism about the possibility of building a road through such rough and mountainous territory.

In 1831 the State intervened and empowered the company to borrow $125,000 on State credit 'to provide for the construction of a turnpike road from Winchester to some point on the Ohio River.' The routing of the Northwestern Turnpike was placed in the hands of Colonel Claudius Crozet, one of Napoleon's officers, who had become an engineering instructor in the U. S. Military Academy at West Point. By 1838 the turnpike had been extended to Parkersburg, and immediately Conestoga wagons were crowding along it to the rapidly growing West. Taverns sprang up along the highway, providing food for the hungry and floors for tired and weary travelers to sleep on; a hot meal cost 25¢; a cold lunch, 12½¢; both included a jigger of whisky thrown in for good measure. In 1840 stagecoach lines were operating on regular daily schedules; the fare for the 230 miles between Winchester and Parkersburg was $10. Rivalry among stagecoach drivers was keen, and more or less official records were kept of the speed with which they delivered the President's annual message to Congress at points along the way; mail contracts were awarded on the basis of these records.

Freight and passenger traffic along the old highway rapidly declined after the Baltimore & Ohio laid tracks along much the same route, opening service to Grafton in 1852 and to Parkersburg in 1857. With the advent of the automobile the highway has again become a main artery of traffic between the Atlantic seaboard and the Ohio valley.

Section a. VIRGINIA LINE to RED HOUSE, MD., 77 m. US 50.

This section of US 50 follows a roller-coaster course over the Allegheny Mountains through narrow valleys and across wide level plateaus. The wild and rugged mountainous stretches are broken only by occasional farms clinging to heavily timbered hillsides or tucked away in narrow crooked valleys. The only evidence of industrial activity appears where the highway leaves the State for a short distance and cuts across the southwestern tip of Maryland.

US 50 crosses the VIRGINIA LINE, 0 *m.*, 17 miles west of Winchester, Virginia, on the crest of TIMBER RIDGE (1,127 alt.).

CAPON BRIDGE, 3 *m.* (819 alt., 192 pop.), on the bank of the Cacapon River, was settled in the late 1740's. Fort Edwards was erected near by about 1750, after George Washington had surveyed three tracts of land for David, Joseph, and Thomas Edwards. In a bloody battle here in 1756, Indians killed and scalped almost 100 men in a regiment under the command of George Washington, who wrote officials at Williamsburg:

> I am too little acquainted, Sir, with pathetic language to attempt a description of the people's distresses—I see inevitable destruction in so clear a light, that, unless vigorous measures are taken by the Assembly, and speedy assistance sent from below, the poor inhabitants that are now in the fort must unavoidably fall, while the remainder are flying before the barbarous foe—if I know my own mind, I could offer myself a willing sacrifice to the butchering enemy, provided that would contribute to the people's ease.

The highway crosses SCHAFFENAKER MOUNTAIN (1,265 alt.), 4.6 m., and COOPER MOUNTAIN (1,607 alt.), 7.6 m. Crossing the NORTH RIVER, 11.1 m., it begins the gradual ascent of BRUSHY RIDGE (1,129 alt.). West of AUGUSTA, 16.9 m. (1,299 alt., 104 pop.), a hamlet on the brow of a hill, the highway climbs up and over several ridges, and descends to the South Branch of the Potomac.

ROMNEY, 25.6 m. (828 alt., 1,441 pop.), the seat and principal town of Hampshire County, was founded in 1762, being one of the two oldest incorporated towns in the State. It is the trading center of a large area of well-kept farms and orchards. The quiet of the town is not disturbed by the hum of industry; its activities center largely on its educational institutions.

The district was first visited by traders and hunters in 1725, and in 1738 Job and John Pearsall built houses near by. Pearsall's Flats, as the settlement was called, had 200 residents by 1748, which attracted the attention of Lord Fairfax, who saw here an opportunity to recoup his somewhat depleted fortune; he sent a party to make what is believed to have been the first official survey of the region; in the party was George Washington, then 16 years old.

Pearsall's Flats continued to grow steadily until 1753, when the Shawnee and other Indian tribes along the Ohio, led by Chief Killbuck, declared a 'death claim' on every foot of ground between the Blue Ridge Mountains and the Ohio. The villagers erected Fort Pearsall to protect the settlement; in a letter written April 24, 1756, George Washington, commander in chief of the armies protecting the border settlement, reported to Governor Dinwiddie: 'The inhabitants are removing daily, and in a short time will leave this country as desolate as Hampshire where scarce a family lives.'

Killbuck and his followers gradually abandoned the struggle after 1761, and the settlers turned eagerly to rebuilding their homes. Lord Fairfax selected Pearsall's Flats as a townsite, had a ten-acre plat surveyed and laid off into half-acre lots, and named the town Romney for one of the ports on the English Channel. Home-seekers poured in until the outbreak of Dunmore's War in 1774, and that troublesome era was closely followed by the American Revolution. Hampshire County was torn by internal strife; the Tories, led by John Claypole, refused to pay taxes or to contribute to the county's quota of men, pledging themselves to 'drink a health to George the III and damnation to Congress.' They formed a company and were preparing to join the British forces when General Daniel Morgan led 400 militiamen against the insurgents, captured Claypole and other leaders, shot a few, and so thoroughly convinced others of the error of their ways that many volunteered to serve in the Continental Army.

After the war the State of Virginia confiscated the lands of Lord Fairfax because he was a Tory, and the gigantic estate was thrown open to settlement. By 1786 State roads had been built connecting Romney with Winchester and Cumberland, and 10 years later a post office was established. In 1827 an act was approved for the construction of the Northwestern Turnpike from Winchester to Parkersburg. The road reached Romney in 1830, and Parkersburg in 1838. By legislative act in 1846 the Literary Society of Romney, organized in 1819, was authorized to run a $20,000 lottery, the proceeds of which were to be used 'to establish at or near the town . . . a Seminary of Learning, for the instruction of youth in the various branches of science and literature.'

Hampshire County had long favored the formation of a new State west of the Alleghenies, but when the break with Virginia came during the War between the States, Hampshiremen refused to fight against the mother State. In April 1861, citizens of Romney held a meeting and appointed a committee of safety to raise funds for equipping volunteers, and a month later the Hampshire Guards and the Frontier Riflemen left to join other gray-clad Virginia regiments at Harpers Ferry. On June 11, 1861, General Lew Wallace's Union troops attacked and dispersed the Confederate forces stationed at Romney, but a few hours later Colonel McDonald's militia recaptured the town, which during the next few years changed hands 56 times.

By the end of hostilities there was scarcely a family in the county that had not lost one man or more. Gunfire of both armies had destroyed almost all the bridges and damaged long stretches of highway. Citizens proceeded to repair them without waiting for State aid, and at the same time set to work restoring public buildings and reestablishing public institutions. The literary society again took the lead, offering the Classical Institute building to the state in 1870 in a successful bid to have the State's Schools for the Deaf and Blind established here.

The HAMPSHIRE COUNTY COURTHOUSE, High and Main Sts., a three-story brick structure, classical in design, was built in 1922 to replace a structure that had served since 1833. The county court records date back to 1755.

The SITE OF THE KELLER HOUSE, corner Main and Grafton Sts., is occupied by the New Century Hotel, built in 1914, the latest of a series of hostelries on the site. In 1848 Thomas A. Keller and James Poland bonded themselves 'to find and provide in their said ordinary good, wholesome and cleanly lodging and diet for travelers, and stablage, fodder and provender, or pasturage and provender, as the season shall require, for their horses, . . . and shall not suffer and permit any unlawful gaming in this house or suffer any person to tipple and drink more than is necessary . . .' During the War between the States it was military headquarters for both armies, and was occupied successively by General Lew Wallace and General 'Stonewall' Jackson.

The BRADY HOUSE (*open*), corner Main and Grafton Sts., a log structure built about 1800, now covered with weatherboards, was occupied in 1938 by the Hampshire County Department of Public Assistance. This agency's methods of dealing with indigent members of the community would no doubt have startled county officials of 150 years ago. How relief problems were met at that time is pictured in this letter sent by the Court of Frederick County to the Court of Hampshire County, dated August 4, 1794:

> GREETING:—The court of Frederick beg leave to inform the court of Hampshire that we have just received a visit from one Simon Pelman, a pauper, who informs us that he was sent to us by the court of Hampshire. The court of Frederick beg leave to inquire to what we may attribute the honor of this visit from Mr. Pelman, late of your county? The court were not aware that they had merited the distinction of thus being waited upon by your envoy extraordinary. But, not withstanding, this court was taken by surprise, they find themselves in a position to return the honor by returning Mr. Pelman to Hampshire, by the road which he came; with the suggestion that when it again shall please you to accredit to us an ambassador of Mr. Pelman's rank, you will so far observe the rules of diplomacy as to inform us of your purpose, that we may not again be taken by surprise, but may be prepared to meet your envoy on our frontiers and receive him in a manner becoming his rank and the dignity of the court which sent him.

The MYTINGER HOUSE, Main St. one block E. of New Century Hotel, believed to have been built soon after 1770, is the oldest building in Romney. It stands in Gravell Lane, the oldest street in the town—and perhaps in the Northern Neck. Long before any settlement was made on the site, this was an old Indian trail that wound its way through an open meadow, and when the town was laid out the lane became the main street.

The STATE SCHOOLS FOR THE DEAF AND BLIND (R), E. Main St., have a total enrollment of more than 400 white children. The SCHOOL FOR THE DEAF (*open during school hours 9–5*), built around the old red brick Classical Institute (*see above*), includes the administration building, dormitories, shop, and farm buildings. In addition to standard elementary and high school courses, students are given vocational training and lessons in lip reading and speech. Boys are taught printing and linotyping, carpentry and cabinet work, shoe repairing and leather work, baking, and typewriting; girls receive instruction in domestic science, typewriting, and dressmaking.

The SCHOOL FOR THE BLIND (*open during school hours 9–5*) occupies the building that from 1850 to 1916 housed the Potomac Seminary, a rival of the Classical Institute. Vocational courses provide instruction in broom, brush, and mop making, basketry, reed work, chair caning, weaving, sewing, handicraft work, mattress renovating and making, piano tuning and repairing, music, typewriting, and domestic sciences. Reading by the Braille method is supplemented by talking books.

LITERARY HALL, on the campus of the schools, was built in 1870 when the Literary Society gave its Institute building to the State. Now a library, it contains more than 400 volumes of the original library and records of the society, founded in 1819 for 'the advancement of Literature and Science, the purchase of a Library by and for the use of its members; and their further improvement by discussing before the Society such questions as shall be selected under its directors.' These discussions, in the form of debates, attracted widespread interest during Romney's early history.

Romney is at the junction with State 28 (*see Tour 6a*), which unites with US 50 for 7 miles.

The TAYLOR HOMESTEAD (R), 26.9 *m.*, a landmark on the Northwestern Turnpike for more than a century, was widely known during the early days of the pike as a hotel and wagon stand. The highway passes Mill Creek Mountain through MECHANICSBURG GAP, 27 *m.*, so narrow that there is scarcely room for both road and creek between its walls.

At 32.4 *m.* is a junction (L) with US 220 (*see Tour 5a*).

In BURLINGTON, 36.4 *m.* (739 alt., 112 pop.), is (R) the OLD HOMESTEAD TAVERN, a large brick structure, early Colonial in style, built about 1785 and rebuilt in 1925. The town is a recreation center of the Knights of Pythias. Their five-acre CAMPING GROUND, on the eastern edge of town, is equipped with playgrounds, pavilion, three cottages, and a kitchen; many members pitch tents here during the summer. The STAR OF HOPE REFUGE (L), on US 50 on the western edge of town, is a two-story frame building used for a children's home. Organized in 1913 to care for homeless children in the Eastern Panhandle, the home is maintained by donations from people in this section and a small endowment fund.

Right from Burlington on a dirt road to CAMP VAN MYRA, 0.2 *m.*, which has a tabernacle, a pavilion, and 50 cottages; a religious camp meeting is held here annually in August.

The OLD STONE HOUSE (L), 39.9 *m.*, once a tavern on the old Northwestern Turnpike, is a long two-story building, with five brick chimneys rising from the roof gable at regular intervals.

At 40.5 *m.* is the junction with a graveled road.

Left on this road is DOLLS GAP, 4 *m.*, which in 1929 was marked by the State as the site of the reputed BIRTHPLACE OF NANCY HANKS, mother of Abraham Lincoln. The Nancy Hanks Commission, appointed by the State legislature and given $1,500 to investigate facts and erect a proper marker, had scarcely spent the money when documentary evidence proved that at least half a dozen other places could claim the honor with as good authority, and no less than 57 actually did. The commission, however, unveiled the granite monu-

ment with appropriate ceremonies in September 1929, although the Lincoln
National Life Foundation reported that 'as a historical marker designating the
birthplace of Nancy Hanks, it is of no value whatever because there is not one
shred of evidence of documentary nature that implies Nancy Hanks ever lived
within several hundred miles of the spot.'

At 41.5 *m.* is the junction with a dirt road.

> Left on this road is ANTIOCH, 3 *m.* (1,116 alt., 106 pop.), a rural settle-
> ment developed around the ANTIOCH WOOLEN MILL (R); this weather-beaten
> four-story frame building was erected before 1789 with what old-time builders
> called the 'ship-lap splice,' its timbers being joined with handmade locust pegs
> averaging from 6 to 12 inches long. The combination grain and woolen mill
> is powered by a wooden overshot water wheel, its well-worn buckets dipping
> into a mountain stream called Mill Creek Run. The woolen mill section of the
> plant has 3 batting machines, 100 spindles, and 3 looms, while the grain mill
> has equipment for grinding cornmeal and buckwheat flour.
>
> First known as the Old Rodgers Mill, the plant has passed through many
> hands, and is now operated by the owner and his wife. Farmers of the surround-
> ing area bring in wool, either to be purchased outright or to have it worked
> up 'on shares' into blankets, heavy suiting, and woolen thread. Washed, dried,
> and picked by hand, the wool is put through the batting machines, then through
> the spinning machines, where it is spun and twisted and made ready for weav-
> ing into heavy double blankets, natural in color.

On the summit of KNOBLY MOUNTAIN (1,401 alt.), 42.1 *m.*, is
(L) FANEUIL HALL OF WEST VIRGINIA, an abandoned log tavern where
men of the South Branch country met in 1861 and passed resolutions
instructing their delegates in the Virginia assembly to vote against
secession from the Union and to work for the formation of a new State.

NEW CREEK, 44.2 *m.* (990 alt., 150 pop.), has a cluster of tourist
cabins. During the War between the States, Emil Nefflin kept a Union
supply store here, and J. H. Diss DeBar, designer of West Virginia's
State Seal, often visited him, and is believed to have made the original
sketch of the seal here.

New Creek is at the junction (R) with US 220 (*see Tour 5a*).

Emerging from the valley, 46.7 *m.*, the highway starts a long and
gradual ascent to the crest of ALLEGHENY FRONT (2,840 alt.),
52.1 *m.*, and follows a winding course through cut-over land, with small
farms in the occasional clearings that appear in the low second-growth
timber. A marker, 62.3 *m.*, indicates the line beyond which George III
forbade settlement in 1763 in accordance with treaties negotiated with
the powerful Six Nations, who protested white invasion of the western
lands. A second marker, 63.5 *m.*, indicates the SITE OF FORT OGDEN,
one of a chain of forts established about 1755 by George Washington. On DIFFICULT HILL (2,888 alt.), 64.5 *m.*, the highway begins
its descent along the course of Difficult Creek to the North Branch of
the Potomac River.

From GORMANIA, 70 *m.* (2,312 alt., 516 pop.), a small industrial
center with a tannery and a mill, the highway crosses the MARY-
LAND LINE, 66.6 *m.*, on a steeply sloping bridge spanning the North
Branch of the Potomac.

From the summit of BACKBONE MOUNTAIN (3,073 alt.), 71.1 *m.*, is a sweeping view of rolling knolls carpeted with cultivated fields, a crazy-quilt pattern in all shades of green, yellow, and brown.

REDHOUSE, 77 *m.* (2,557 alt., 25 pop.), a crossroads hamlet settled about 1830 when the old Northwestern Turnpike was being constructed, is at the junction with US 219 (*see Tour 8a*).

Section b. REDHOUSE, MD., to CLARKSBURG, 58 m. US 50.

West of REDHOUSE, 0 *m.*, US 50 passes from mountainous to rolling, hilly country; dense forests give way to grassy slopes and cultivated farmlands. Fewer quiet villages appear as the highway traverses central West Virginia with its bustling towns and industrial cities. US 50 recrosses the MARYLAND LINE, 2.2 *m.*

The YOUGHIOGHENY FOREST COLONY, 3.6 *m.*, founded in 1931 by Frank Reeves, a geologist, is housed in 15 cottages, occupied in summer by painters, sculptors, and writers from eastern cities, which stand in a virgin pine forest so dense that even the highway is shaded by the spreading branches.

YOUGHIOGHENY PARK (*cabins for rent*), 4.1 *m.*, a forested area, is popular with botanists for its wide range of flora. The highway is bordered with native flowers and shrubs.

In BROOKSIDE, 4.9 *m.* (2,460 alt., 10 pop.), is (R) the RED HORSE TAVERN (*open*), built in 1839, a stone structure with a weatherboarded frame addition and an enclosed double porch.

AURORA, 6.3 *m.* (2,648 alt., 162 pop.), on the summit of Cheat Mountain, attracts summer visitors because of its high altitude and clean air. They live in summer cottages or pitch tents back from the highway on the edge of broad buckwheat fields, and spend the hottest days of summer in cool comfort.

The first settlement was made in 1787 by the Reverend John Stough; in 1800 John Wheeler moved here from Lancaster, Pennsylvania, and other families settled near by from time to time. In 1840 a town was laid out and named West Union, being rechristened in 1875. In the eastern edge of town are the ruins of RISING SUN TAVERN, built in 1838 by Major David Stemples, and popular in the days of the turnpike; the tavern burned about 1920; only the huge stones in the chimney mark the site.

From CHEAT MOUNTAIN (2,751 alt.), 8.2 *m.*, on the western edge of the Allegheny Plateau, the highway descends steeply along the side of a narrow gorge and crosses the CHEAT RIVER, 13.8 *m.*, on a modern steel and concrete bridge. The old COVERED BRIDGE (L), built in 1835 by Silas Kidwell for the Northwestern Turnpike, is 500 feet long and cost $18,000. Although no longer used, the bridge is in excellent condition and has recently been braced by the State Road Commission to preserve it. West of LAUREL MOUNTAIN (2,603 alt.), 20.2 *m.*, the highway winds in and out among knolls, through hamlets, and past meager farms, as the hills gradually become lower and the road straighter.

BLUEVILLE, 37.4 *m.* (1,230 alt., 100 pop.), a suburb of Grafton, is the birthplace of Ann Jarvis, who in 1907 asked a small group of friends in Philadelphia, where she had lived for several years, to observe with her the first anniversary of her mother's death, by wearing white carnations. The following year the churches of Philadelphia sponsored city-wide observance of Mothers' Day. Four years later the governor of Texas proclaimed the second Sunday in May as Mothers' Day, and in 1913 the U. S. Senate and House of Representatives passed a resolution calling for a national observance on May 10 of that year. In 1914 President Wilson issued a proclamation urging national observance of Mothers' Day. Since 1925 the governor of the State has been authorized to issue an annual Mothers' Day proclamation. Miss Jarvis was president of the International Mothers' Day Association for many years.

Left from Blueville on US 119 to GRAFTON, 1 *m.* (1,000 alt., 7,737 pop.) (*see Tour 22b*).

In FETTERMAN, 40.1 *m.* (990 alt.), a suburb of Grafton, is (R) a granite monument to Bailey Thornsbury Brown, one of the first soldiers killed in the War between the States, having been shot to death by Confederate sentries on the night of May 22, 1861. The highway crosses the TYGARTS VALLEY RIVER, 40.2 *m.*

At 41.1 *m.* is a junction (L) with US 250 (*see Tour 22b*), which unites with US 50 for 3.6 miles.

In PRUNTYTOWN, 43.1 *m.* (1,180 alt., 420 pop.), is the WEST VIRGINIA INDUSTRIAL SCHOOL FOR BOYS. When the county seat was removed to Grafton in 1889, Pruntytown was left with a courthouse and jail for which it could find no use, and in 1890 donated them to the State as a boys' reformatory. Today the institution consists of 17 buildings and 1,881 acres of land, including 6 completely equipped farms. The school offers boys instruction in 21 vocations.

Right from Pruntytown on an improved dirt road to VALLEY FALLS, 6 *m.*, a series of cascades (*bathing and picnicking*) on the Tygarts Valley River.

At 44.7 *m.* is a junction (R) with US 250 (*see Tour 22b*).

MAPLE LAKE (L) 51 *m.*, a small artificial body of water, is frequented by people from neighboring towns, some of whom have summer cottages along its shores.

BRIDGEPORT, 52 *m.* (979 alt., 1,576 pop.), situated in the fertile bluegrass country, is an important shipping point for cattle. On market days its usually quiet tree-shaded streets are noisy with herds moving on foot or in large vans to stock pens on the outskirts of the town. Often the sales last well into the night, disturbing the sleep of townsfolk.

John Simpson, a trapper and the first white man in this section, camped on the site of Bridgeport in 1764. Later the land was patented by Daniel Davisson. In 1816 a town was chartered and named Bridge-port because at this point the first bridge in the section was built across Simpson Creek. Bridgeport was the home of Joseph Johnson, the only governor of Virginia from west of the Allegheny Mountains, and of Colonel Benjamin Wilson, pioneer leader of this section and the father of 30 children.

The SIMPSON CREEK BAPTIST CHURCH, Philadelphia Ave., is a small brick and tile building erected in 1929 on the site of the first Baptist Church west of the Allegheny Mountains. The original building was constructed of logs about 1774 on land donated by David Davisson. The organization consisted of five members and the Reverend John Sutton, pastor.

Evidence of industrial activity multiplies as the highway approaches the West Fork of the Monongahela River; in DESPARD, 56 m., a suburb of Clarksburg, is (R) a large Weirton Steel Company plant.

CLARKSBURG, 58 m. (1,007 alt., 28,866 pop.) (see Clarksburg).

Clarksburg is at the junction with US 19 (see Tour 10a) and State 20 (see Tour 20b).

Section c. CLARKSBURG to OHIO LINE; 82.8 m. US 50.

This section of US 50 traverses a region of winding streams and rounded grassy knolls between the West Fork of Monongahela and the Ohio Rivers. The opening of oil and gas fields between 1880 and 1900 stimulated sleepy towns to great activity, but the boom is long since over and most of the towns have returned to their former peaceful quiet.

On the outskirts of CLARKSBURG, 0 m., the highway crosses the West Fork of Monongahela River and passes through a district in which a few wells still run a trickle of oil. The shores of LAKE FLOYD (swimming, boating), 9.4 m., are rimmed with summer cottages.

SALEM, 14 m. (1,047 alt., 2,943 pop.), was settled in 1790 by 40 families of Seventh Day Baptists headed by Samuel Fitz Randolph. Securing a charter in 1794, they named the settlement New Salem, for the New Jersey community from which they had migrated. A blockhouse erected during the Indian hostilities prior to 1795 was used as a troop station from which Rangers sallied out to intercept Indian parties traveling the warpath up the Middle Island Creek to the West Fork Settlements.

The Indians soon learned to respect this village of log cabins clustered around a blockhouse and, throughout the hostilities, never attacked the settlement. When on the warpath, they crossed the creek above or below the town to avoid the settlers. The pioneers themselves were a virile hardy lot who pursued their daily tasks with one hand 'in the hand of God,' and grasping a rifle with the other. On the Sabbath, armed outposts took turns at sentry duty outside the log church, which had a gallery and a high box pulpit, with a chimney through the center of the roof. A center fireplace had two openings, and men and women were segregated on either side.

The men's weekday dress was primitive, consisting of skins and homespun cloth, but on the Sabbath they donned tow or linen shirts and pants, new moccasins, and coonskin caps; a woman's Sabbath dress was made of eight yards of calico, pieced and sewed by hand in a single day. Prodigious hunters, they often roamed the woods for days and camped far from home while hunting bear. Often a hunter killed 20 bears in a single autumn to supply his family with fresh meat; the hides were traded for salt, gunpowder, and utensils.

Their diet was largely corn bread and bear meat, supplemented by rye coffee, sassafras, and littany tea. Thirstier spirits concocted a semi-lethal potation called 'root beer,' made by boiling down three barrels of sugar water to one in which was mixed sassafras, burdock root, spice brush, scorched meat, and a gallon of yeast.

The community grew little until the 1890's, when the opening of oil and gas fields in its vicinity brought employment and prosperity. On its incorporation in 1905, its name was shortened to Salem.

SALEM COLLEGE (R), 223 W. Main St., is a liberal arts institution established as an academy in 1888 under Seventh Day Baptist auspices. The standards were raised and collegiate courses added in 1890, when the school was incorporated and chartered as Salem College. Nonsectarian and coeducational, the college confers the bachelor of arts degree and has an average enrollment of 500 students.

The academy was founded on a five-acre plot donated by George F. W. Randolph; later gifts added an acre to the campus; a near-by 46-acre tract owned by the college has an open-air theater, picnic grounds, and facilities for outdoor study. Classes were held in rented rooms until the first building, a three-story frame structure, was completed. In 1910 the first brick building, the ADMINISTRATION BUILDING, a three-story neo-Gothic structure, with stone trim and four octagonal towers rising over a central entrance, was completed and opened to classes; it houses the administration offices and the 14,000-volume library. Fire destroyed the frame building in 1915, which was replaced with HUFFMAN HALL, a three-story red brick structure, neo-Gothic in design, which contains classrooms and laboratories. The square, two-story red brick PHYSICAL EDUCATION BUILDING was built in 1932. The frame house of George F. W. Randolph, left to the college by bequest, was converted into a MUSIC BUILDING in 1935.

The WEST VIRGINIA INDUSTRIAL HOME FOR GIRLS, at the western town limit, was established in 1899 on ground donated by Salem. Six buildings stand on a tract of 72 acres, 20 acres of which are in truck gardens. All girls committed to the institution are given a grade school education and instruction in needlework, dressmaking, and other housewifely arts. A few of the girls care for the vegetable and flower gardens during the summer months. Housework in the buildings is done by the girls, as well as work on the well-equipped dairy and poultry farm.

KIWANIS GORGE PARK, 15.9 *m.*, is an 11-acre park equipped with stone tables and ovens, and grassy playgrounds; nature trails wind through the gorge (*open on application to Salem Kiwanis Club*). West of the park US 50 winds through a narrow wooded valley; a tiny stream trickles musically over jumbled rocks into deep pools.

WEST UNION, 29 *m.* (836 alt., 984 pop.), originally known as Lewisport, was incorporated in 1850 under its present name. Once an important oil, gas, and glass center, it is the seat of Doddridge County, a prosperous agricultural region. The courthouse on the hill (L) dominates the town. An old wooden covered bridge (L) is still used, although the highway now crosses Middle Island Creek on a new concrete bridge.

At the foot of JACKO HILL (1,205 alt.), 30.2 *m.*, is the SITE OF JACKO INN, (L), named for Jacko (pronounced jake-o), the innkeeper, who had a cave in the hillside (R), about 150 feet from the road. The cave is believed to have been a station of the Underground Railroad. The inn was a notorious rendezvous of men whose coming and going mystified the neighborhood. Wealthy guests at the inn are said to have disappeared, and many skeletons were later found in the cave.

At 30.4 *m.* is the junction with a dirt road.

Right on this road is CENTRAL STATION, 2.7 *m.* (815 alt., 217 pop.), the scene of one of the most sensational robberies in the history of the State. On October 8, 1915, Baltimore & Ohio train No. 1, westbound, was boarded by two masked men, armed with rifles. They forced the engine crew to cut the engine and mail car from the train, and drive on a few miles, where the crew was ordered off. The bandits rifled the mail car and obtained $100,000 in unsigned bank notes. The bandits were trailed, caught and convicted.

The RULEY HOUSE (R), 30.5 *m.*, a curious four-story frame structure, built in 1881 by Jacob Ruley and now painted red, has narrow inset porches on each of the lower three stories; the scrollwork on the porches and under the eaves is most elaborate.

GREENWOOD HILL (1,167 alt.), 33.8 *m.*, rises above the surrounding knolls, and oil derricks raise their blackened heads among the trees on the hillsides and along the creek.

GREENWOOD, 38 *m.* (850 alt., 211 pop.), is the trading center of farmers and oil workers in the vicinity.

In TOLL GATE, 38.8 *m.* (794 alt., 110 pop.), is a large COMPRESSOR STATION (L), its aluminum-painted buildings set in smooth green lawns. The hamlet was named for the Northwestern Turnpike tollgate that once stood here. Large trees lock branches over the road, and reddish sandstone cliffs line the highway, which crosses the North Fork of the Hughes River on a long concrete viaduct.

PENNSBORO, 44 *m.* (852 alt., 1,616 pop.), is a market and trade town for the surrounding agricultural country, and an important shipping point in an oil and gas producing region. The town, sustained by

oil fields opened in the late 1880's, is built along sloping spurs of timbered ridges at the mouth of Poplarlick Run, known to early settlers
as the 'licks' and frequented by large herds of deer, buffalo, and elk.
Four days each fall the town takes on all the aspects of a city; its
streets seethe with visitors who come to attend the Ritchie County
Fair (*see below*).

John Bunnell, a veteran of the Revolutionary War, settled here in
1800. About 1820 a town was platted by William Penn, a civil engineer of Baltimore, for whom it was named. The coming of the Baltimore & Ohio Railroad, together with the opening of oil fields, stimulated the growth of the town and in 1885 it was incorporated.

The WEBSTER HOUSE (R), on the highway on the western edge of
town, built in 1807 by John Webster, was a popular stagecoach stop,
and is still used as an inn. The rambling two-and-a-half-story house
with walls two feet thick and containing twenty-four rooms was used
as the first post office.

The RITCHIE COUNTY FAIRGROUNDS, 41.9 *m.*, is crowded the first
week of September every year during the Ritchie County Fair, one
of the largest in the State, held regularly since 1887. For days in advance, farmers and their families busy themselves with preparations
for a full week of holidays and a full house of homecoming guests. At
dawn on the opening day lanterns gleam in many farmyards; a 4-H
boy is giving one last grooming to a fine calf or pig, in the hope that
it will take a blue ribbon. All chores are completed before breakfast;
picnic lunches and cakes are carefully wrapped and packed in baskets. Before sun-up the finest cattle, pigs, chickens, corn, and perhaps
choice selections of garden produce, are loaded into a truck, and the
entire family is off for the day.

At the fair the children scatter along the Midway, to spend their
nickels on the ferriswheel, merry-go-round, or perhaps 'that dangerous
octopus that's sure to turn your liver up side down.' Men spend their
time around the stock pens, while the women carefully inspect handiwork, canned fruits, breads, cakes, and potted plants on display. Horse
racing occupies the afternoon, and as the day wanes, one or two members of the family hurry home to do the evening chores and hurry back
again before the big events of the evening. At night the dusty acres
are alive with friendly people; the lights along the Midway sparkle;
above the din comes the cry of 4-H boys selling hot dogs or 'barking'
for entertainment concessions. Near midnight fireworks signify that
closing time is near.

In LAMBERTON, 48 *m.* (792 alt., 30 pop.), is (R) the WASHING-
TON INN (*open*), an elaborate mansion surrounded by tall trees and
wide velvety lawns; on the grounds is a large open-air swimming pool.
The inn was built as a residence by Harry Lambert in 1916, when
he began to experiment with a new type of electric railway. A track
was laid to Ellenboro, but the Electric Undercurrent Company failed,
and the mansion became a hotel.

ELLENBORO, 49 *m.* (784 alt., 330 pop.), is a hamlet lost in dreams of earlier years when it was a bustling trading center for hundreds of fortune-hunters who came to the newly discovered oil fields. Its business activity is confined to a half dozen filling stations and small stores.

Ellenboro is at the junction (L) with State 16 (*see Tour* 12).

In PIKE, 51 *m.* (780 alt., 32 pop.), a crossroads settlement, is the junction (R) with US 50-Alt.

Right on US 50-Alt., which makes a gradual ascent of ALLISON'S HILL and follows the ridge for several miles. On both sides are worn and rounded hilltops, a smooth green in the foreground, shading to a hazy blue in the distance.

SAINT MARYS, 12.5 *m.* (623 alt., 2,182 pop.) (*See Tour* 19*b*), is at the junction with State 2 (*see Tour* 19*b*).

US 50-Alt. crosses the Ohio Line, 12.5 *m.*, at the western end of the bridge (*15¢ car and driver; 5¢ each additional person*), spanning the Ohio River to Newport, Ohio (*see Ohio Guide*).

West of Pike the highway winds through valleys and over occasional ridges. Small farms crown the hills, and many of the valleys are deep ravines. From SAND HILL (1,204 alt.), 62.9 *m.*, wide vistas of choppy hill country extend in all directions.

At 64.4 *m.* is the junction with a dirt road.

Right on this road is BORLAND SPRINGS, 3.6 *m.*, popular among vacationers from Parkersburg and other neighboring communities.

At 65.5 *m.* is a junction with an improved dirt road.

Left on this road is VOLCANO, 3.2 *m.*, now a ghost town. Oil developments in the early 1870's brought a population of almost 3,000 to this boom town. Originally known as White Oak, it was named Volcano because at night many fires and flares made it resemble the crater of an active volcano. The wealthier families lived on the ridge, along what was known as Quality Row. One house, which had an elevator and the first bathtub in town, is still standing, high above the silent skeletons of the dead town. In 1879 Volcano was almost destroyed by fire, and as the boom was waning, was never rebuilt.

The villages of DALLISON, 70.3 *m.* (690 alt., 70 pop.), and MUR-PHYTOWN, 74.5 *m.* (657 alt., 72 pop.), are the trading centers of a farming section.

PARKERSBURG, 82.3 *m.* (615 alt., 29,623 pop.) (*see Parkers-burg*).

Parkersburg is at the junction with State 2 (*see Tour* 19*b*) and US 21 (*see Tour* 13).

US 50 crosses the OHIO LINE, 82.8 *m.*, at the western end of a bridge (*car and driver, 15¢; with passengers, 25¢*), spanning the Ohio River to Belpre, Ohio (*see Ohio Guide*).

Tour 5

(Cumberland, Md.)—Keyser—Moorefield—Petersburg—Franklin—
(Monterey, Va.); US 220.
Maryland Line to Virginia Line, 92.7 m.

Concrete roadbed, with graveled, shale, and bituminous stretches.
Baltimore & Ohio R.R. parallels route between Moorefield and Petersburg.
Hotel accommodations at Keyser, Moorefield, Petersburg, and Franklin; few
tourist camps.

US 220 traverses the valley of South Branch River, which crosses
the State at the neck of the Eastern Panhandle to connect southern
Maryland with western Virginia, where the earliest settlements in the
State were made. The section witnessed much fighting during the Indian wars, the American Revolution, and the War between the States.

The northern section of the route breaks in upon a countryside of
prosperous farms in a broad valley running far back to the green
foothills of the Allegheny Front. To the northwest, range upon range
of spur ridges descends from a blue haze shimmering in the distance
to the valley floor, blending the green of forest with the purple and
brown of ripening fields. South of Moorefield, the highway follows
the South Branch River as far as Petersburg; at Upper Tract the
stream deserts its natural course for a steep-walled channel through
Cave Mountain (*see Tour 5B*). Southward, the route traverses sections of the Monongahela and George Washington national forests
through a rugged region of cascading streams, high mountains, and
deep gorges. Half-explored caverns, unusual rock formations, and fossil remains of plants and animals occur frequently in the limestone
strata of this region. From the mountain peaks the panorama spreads
east to the Blue Ridge Mountains in Virginia and west to the main
divide of the Allegheny Mountains.

Except for small locally owned plants the countryside is untouched
by industry; farming is the chief occupation. Many old houses, their
high-columned porticoes half-hidden from the road by groves of maples
and elms are occupied by descendants of families who settled holdings
of Lord Thomas Fairfax. Weathered tombstones in family cemeteries
bear the names of those who battled Indians and endured hardships to
retain homes in the valley.

Most of the South Branch Valley was included in the huge grant
made in 1649 by Charles II, which later became the 6,000,000-acre
Fairfax estate in the Northern Neck of Virginia, but no survey or set-

tlement was made for almost a century. John Van Meter, a Dutch fur trader from New York, came here in 1715 with Delaware Indians to trade with the Cherokee and Catawba who hunted in the region. Parts of the valley had been cleared by Indians and planted with corn; wells had been dug and walled in. Van Meter told his sons of the rich South Branch Valley, and one of them, Isaac Van Meter, came here in 1736 and made a tomahawk claim to several hundred acres around Indian Old Fields, a part of the extensive holdings of Lord Fairfax, who had inherited the estate from his mother, the only daughter of Lord Thomas Culpepper. In 1745 Fairfax employed George Washington to survey the section and lay it off in lots and estates; Fairfax granted 99-year leases to tenants at $3.33 a 100 acres, or sold the land for a small down payment, called 'composition money,' plus an equal amount of quitrent to be paid each year 'on the feast day of Saint Michael the Archangel.' If the renter settled and improved the land before acquiring title, the annual rent was higher.

During the American Revolution, Virginia enacted laws to prohibit such vast holdings as Lord Fairfax's, and in 1776 the perpetual rent system was abolished, lands being held henceforth in fee simple. The State later confiscated the estates of Tories, including that of Lord Fairfax, then in his ninetieth year, who had not taken sides in the Revolution but was regarded as a British subject; those who held Fairfax leases were given clear titles to their land.

Section a. MARYLAND LINE to PETERSBURG, 48.9 m. US 220.

Through the valley of New Creek, across Knobly and Patterson Mountains, into the South Branch Valley at Moorefield, this section of US 220 passes high forested hills and pleasant valley farms. Numerous fort sites recall struggles between settlers and Indians; many rambling old brick houses with vine-hung porticoes are more than a century old.

US 220 crosses the WEST VIRGINIA LINE, 0 m., at the southern end of a bridge spanning the Potomac River, 22 miles south of Cumberland, Maryland.

KEYSER, 0.2 m. (809 alt., 6,248 pop.), lies among the hills that were strategic strongholds during the War between the States. Here are the shops and yards of the Baltimore & Ohio Railroad and a small woolen mill, the only industrial enterprises in the town. Following the granting of the site to Patrick McCarthy by Abram Inskeep in 1802, the settlement was known as Paddys Town. In 1852 when the B. & O. was built through the village, it acquired a post office and was named New Creek. The present name honors William Keyser, vice president of the railroad at the time the community was incorporated in 1874.

During the War between the States, Keyser was a supply point and battleground for both Union and Confederate forces. Between 1861 and 1865 the town was captured and recaptured 14 times. Both sides made determined fights to hold the railroad, and when Confederates finally lost control they destroyed it. In November 1864, General T. L. Rosser with 2,000 Confederate soldiers surprised the 800 Federals garrisoning Fort Fuller and took the town, capturing large stores of munitions and most of the Union force. Supply houses were burned; most of the business section and miles of railroad track were destroyed. The Confederates were soon routed by General Kelly's army, which remained in the valley to protect the railroad.

The POTOMAC STATE SCHOOL OF WEST VIRGINIA UNIVERSITY, Fuller Street, a coeducational junior college, with an enrollment of 330 students, offers pre-law, pre-medicine, and pre-education instruction, as well as courses in commerce and business administration, home economics, engineering, music, and agriculture. A boys' dormitory, girls' dormitory, science hall, gymnasium, and a red brick, buff-trimmed administration building occupy a 15-acre campus on the crest and slopes of Fort Hill, once the SITE OF FORT FULLER, a strong Federal barricade. Adjoining the campus is the college's 129-acre farm, with hay and dairy barns, poultry house, and training ground for horses. The school was opened in 1902 as the Keyser Preparatory Branch of the University, but in 1919 became an accredited junior college offering a standard two-year college curricula. Its administration is directed by the Board of Governors of West Virginia University.

Between Keyser and the junction with US 50 the highway follows the course of New Creek. Broad and fertile fields extend west to the foothills of the Allegheny Front; to the east heavily timbered New Creek Mountain rises almost sheer from the creek bed.

NEW CREEK, 5.5 m. (990 alt., 150 pop.), is at the junction with US 50 (see Tour 4a), which unites with US 220 for 11.8 miles (see Tour 4a).

At 17.3 m. is the junction (R) with State 28, which unites with US 220 for 31.9 miles.

PURGITSVILLE, 23.6 m. (933 alt., 33 pop.), is a small trading village, near which in 1863 the McNeill Rangers (see below) were ambushed by the Ringgold Cavalry, a Union force, but escaped without a single fatality.

MUD LICK RUN cuts through a ridge of Oriskany sandstone at REYNOLDS GAP, 29.6 m., with sheer 200-foot walls, forming a natural entrance to the valley of the South Branch of the Potomac. The cool shaded pools near the mouth of the Run are stocked with bass; President Grover Cleveland often came here to fish.

OLD FIELDS, 34 m. (808 alt., 41 pop.), known as Indian Old Fields to early settlers who found that Shawnee had plowed and planted corn here, serves a small agricultural area.

Far back from the highway opposite the post office stands (R) FORT PLEASANT, a two-story, 18-room mansion of red brick, classical in style, built in 1832 by Isaac Van Meter (see above) and given the name of the frontier fort that stood near by in 1756. Across the front of the house, which has two wings, runs a two-story porch supported by Corinthian columns. All interior woodwork is hand carved, as are the corner blocks of the doors and windows. The two large drawing rooms to the left of the central hall have mantelpieces, painted black, with double Grecian columns. In the old house are many relics, including an iron kettle which Isaac Van Meter used in the manufacture of gunpowder. The egg-shaped kettle, about 2 feet in diameter and 3 feet deep, is said to have been used by Colonel George Washington in making powder when in this region in 1756.

Left from Old Fields on a dirt road to THE TROUGH, 2 *m.*, a narrow canyon on the South Branch River, visited by George Washington in 1748 and thus described in his journal: 'The Trough is a couple of Ledges of Mountains Impassable, running side and side together for 7 or 8 miles, and ye River running down between them.' At the Battle of the Trough in 1756 a raiding party of 60 or 70 Shawnee braves routed a company of 16 settlers after a long and bloody encounter.

On a farm (R), 31.9 *m.*, is the SITE OF FORT BUTTERMILK, erected in 1756 by Captain Thomas Waggoner.

WILLOW HALL (R), 32.3 *m.*, named for the large willows on the wide lawn about it, stands hidden from the highway behind an ivy-covered stone wall. The three-story brick mansion, with 22 rooms, was built in 1818 by Captain Daniel R. McNeill, and has since remained in the possession of his family. Double chimneys rise at each end of the original unit, to which two wings have been added. During the War between the States the house was the base of operations of the McNeill Rangers, led by Captain Hanson McNeill and his son, Jesse.

With the outbreak of the war, McNeill joined the Confederate army in Missouri as a cavalry captain and took part in the Battle of Springfield. Here he was taken prisoner, but soon escaped and came to Hardy County, Virginia, now West Virginia, where he enlisted a company of less than 200 men for independent service in the South Branch Valley. By their active and daring exploits the Rangers inflicted more damage on Union forces than entire Confederate regiments operating in the area. Every man was familiar with the country, and attacks were planned and swiftly carried out when the Union army least expected them. When Confederates lost control of the B. & O. Railroad to Union troops, the Rangers destroyed miles of the track, blew up bridges, captured train loads of supplies, and burned cars. In their daring incursions into Union territory, they captured hundreds of prisoners, horses, cattle, and quantities of munitions. They operated throughout the Eastern Panhandle, with an occasional raid into nearby Maryland.

In a surprise attack October 3, 1864, Captain McNeill and 60 men captured 100 members of the Eighth Ohio Cavalry stationed near Mount Jackson to guard the bridge across the Shenandoah River. After he had ordered his men to cease firing, McNeill was mortally wounded by George Valentine, a member of the Rangers, whom he had severely reprimanded for stealing chickens from a farmer who lived near a cave used by the Rangers for a hideout; after his death his son Jesse took command.

In February 1865, after a ride of 90 miles through Union-occupied territory, the Rangers arrived in Cumberland shortly after midnight, surprised the brigades stationed in the town, made prisoners of the picket guards, and proceeded to Union headquarters, where they made prisoners of General Kelly, General Crook, and Adjutant General Thayer Melvin. With their prisoners they made a 60-mile dash for the Confederate lines, successfully eluding a force of 2,000 cavalry-men sent from Keyser and Winchester to cut off their retreat.

At 34.2 *m.* is (R) the SITE OF TOWN FORT, built in the 1750's to shelter settlers unable to reach Forts Pleasant and Buttermilk (*see above*) in time of danger.

MOOREFIELD, 39 *m.* (830 alt., 734 pop.), at the junction of the Moorefield and South Branch Rivers, seat of Hardy County and the trading center of the upper South Branch Valley, was chartered in 1777 and named for Conrad Moore, an early settler, on whose farm the town was built. The town has a tannery, a lumber mill, and a cheese factory. The OLD STONE INN (L), a two-story building of rough stone, has the date of its erection, 1788, carved in the lintel over the door. The town is used as a base of operation for hunters, and fishermen, in season.

Moorefield is at the junction with State 55 (formerly State 23) (*see Tour 5A*).

The highway follows the South Branch of the Potomac River to PETERSBURG GAP, 47 *m.*, a rugged gorge with 150-foot walls, at the eastern end of which are carvings of two heads, one of an ox, the other of a fox, believed to have been made by Indians.

PETERSBURG, 48.9 *m.* (937 alt., 1,410 pop.), a trim town of red brick and white frame houses on the broad flood plain of the South Branch, was settled about 1745 by German colonists and named for Jacob Peterson, who opened the first store. In 1833, when it obtained a post office, its name was changed to Lunice Creek because there was already one Petersburg in Virginia. After West Virginia attained state-hood, its original name was restored. The town derives its income from trade with neighboring farmers, and with tourists and sportsmen at-tracted to the region. A tannery is its sole industrial plant. A State trout hatchery is near here.

The RIVERSIDE TANNERY PLANT (*open*), on the eastern edge of town, employs 60 men in the production of sole leather. Flanking the highway (R) are long bark sheds painted brown and white; rows of shelves are stacked with fresh bark to be dried, and the atmosphere has an odor of resin and turpentine.

The TRI-COUNTY FAIRGROUND, reached by a graveled driveway off Virginia Ave., is the scene each September of rodeos, riding tournaments, and similar contests. In the riding tournament, horsemen in uniform bear such titles as 'Knight of the South Branch Valley' and 'Knight of the Middle Mountain,' imparting a medieval air (*see Folklore*) to their contests of skill in racing across the field and tilting with long lances at small rings suspended from a crossbar. The 'Knight' who collects the most rings is privileged to name the Queen of the Fair.

On a knoll in the northeastern part of town is the old MOUNT ZION CEMETERY, adjoining the Mount Zion Presbyterian Church, the congregation of which was the first to be organized in the vicinity. It was assembled in 1825 by the Reverend William N. Scott, a missionary, who is buried in a mausoleum erected in the old cemetery by his congregation. The first church built here on the knoll was destroyed by Federal soldiers during the War between the States.

Petersburg is at the junction with State 28 (*see Tour 6b*).

Section b. *PETERSBURG to VIRGINIA LINE*, 43.8 m. US 220.

This section of the tour traverses the southeastern part of the South Branch Valley through a sparsely settled region of rugged mountains, dark deep-cut ravines, and forest-lined streams that cascade over high cliffs. For many miles it runs along the eastern boundary of the Monongahela National Forest, and the western tip of the George Washington National Forest. Mountain trails and picnic sites make the area a favorite outing spot. Bass and trout abound in the streams; deer, wild turkey, bear, and small game attract sportsmen in season.

On the outskirts of PETERSBURG, 0 m., US 220 crosses the South Branch of the Potomac River.

At 0.7 m. is a junction with a graveled road.

> Right on this road to the ELKHORN ROCK FOREST FIRE TOWER (*open*), 12 m. (3,005 alt.), offering an excellent view of wooded and mountainous country.

Following a tributary of Johnson Run, the highway climbs through a low gap, 3 m., and follows NORTH MILL CREEK. To the south appears (R) CAVE MOUNTAIN (2,825 alt.), its long serrated crest and smooth slopes contrasting sharply with the level crest and ravine-gashed sides of MIDDLE MOUNTAIN (L).

At 16.2 m. is the junction (R) with a dirt road, which leads into a wild region known as the SMOKE HOLE (*see Tour 5B*).

UPPER TRACT, 17.9 m. (1,494 alt., 45 pop.), a scattered mountain settlement, occupies the approximate site of a frontier fort of that name, one of a chain of defenses built during the French and Indian War on the advice of Colonel George Washington, who wrote to the governor of Virginia in 1756: 'We have built some forts and altered others as far north on the Potomac as settlers have been molested, and there only remains one body of inhabitants at a place called Upper Tract, which need a guard. Thither I have ordered a party.' Indians under Chief Killbuck (*see Tour 4a*) captured and burned the fort two years later, killing Captain James Dunlap and the entire garrison of 21 men. South of Upper Tract the road runs along the western edge of the wide valley floor past neat farmsteads and wide grain fields.

In RUDDLE, 23.1 *m.* (1,533 alt., 40 pop.), is the old RUDDLE MILL (L), a gristmill built in 1871 by Edward Ruddle. Driven by an overshot water wheel, it continued to operate until 1936 when floods damaged the plant and changed the course of the stream.

Passing through a narrow gorge, the highway rounds the northern end of WILSON RIDGE, 23.6 *m.* Across the river (L) is an almost perfect stone arch cut by the stream centuries ago. In the arch successive strata of gray Oriskany sandstone, Helderberg limestone, and dark Marcellus shale, one under the other, are clearly marked. South of the ridge the valley widens somewhat as US 220 skirts COLIC MOUNTAIN (2,810 alt.); on an almost vertical cliff, 26.3 *m.*, appears another large stone arch.

At 27.9 *m.* is the junction with US 33 (*see Tour 7a*), with which US 220 unites for 0.9 miles.

FRANKLIN, 29.2 *m.* (1,750 alt., 431 pop.), seat of Pendleton County since 1794, is a farm trade center and a rendezvous for hunting and fishing parties visiting the upper section of the South Branch. A small dam supplies power and water for the village's municipal electric and water systems. Settled in 1769 by Francis (Frank) Evick and named Frankford for him, the name was changed to Franklin when the town was incorporated because there was already one Frankford in the State. Its modern appearance is the result of a fire that in 1924 consumed most of its old buildings.

Among the few old structures remaining is the gabled ANDERSON HOUSE (L), of gray-painted brick, with end chimneys, built in 1850 by William McCoy and now unoccupied. The doorway has narrow sidelights and a rectangular transom; fluted Ionic columns support a one-story portico. In the center of the village stands the red brick courthouse, and adjoining it (L) is a small square building used as a law office, constructed in 1924 of undressed stone of every variety found in the county, arranged in the order in which the stones occur in local strata.

South of Franklin the highway follows a cut in the face of a rock wall (R), exposing fossil beds and the geologic structure of the cliff, an arm of ENTRY MOUNTAIN (2,063 alt.).

At 31.6 *m.* is the junction with a dirt road.

Left on this road to McCoy's MILL, 0.3 *m.*, which has been in operation since 1766 except during its reconstruction in 1850. One of the largest of the old turbine mills in West Virginia, it was built by Ulrich Conrad, who furnished supplies to Colonial troops during Lord Dunmore's War in 1774 and during the Revolutionary War. In addition to flour and meal, Conrad manufactured arms and ammunition in an adjoining foundry. Gunpowder was made from saltpeter taken from a near-by cave on Thorn Creek, the source of power for the mill. General William McCoy acquired the property in 1800, and a

Through the Mining Country

BILLION-DOLLAR INDUSTRY

MODERN COAL TIPPLE, PENMAN

Photograph by courtesy of Norfolk & Western Railw

MINERS' HOUSES

COMMISSARY AT FARADAY

Photograph by Post; courtesy of Farm Security Administration

MAN TRIP TO THE WORKING FACE

CUTTING MACHINE, IN A POCAHONTAS MINE

Photograph by courtesy of Norfolk & Western Railway

LOADING COAL (Old Method) SHOT DOWN BY EXPLOSIVES

MECHANICAL LOADER (New Method)

MOTOR WITH LOADED TRIP, TWO MILES UNDERGROUND

BLUE RHYTHM, AFTER A DAY'S WORK

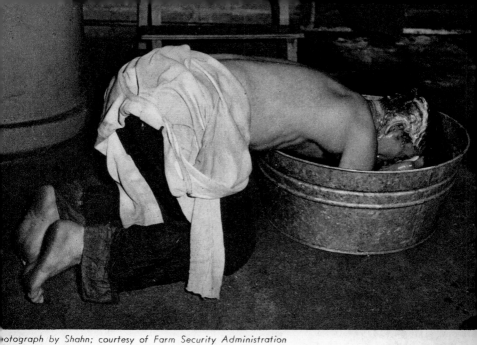

MINER'S BATH

MODERN BATH HOUSE

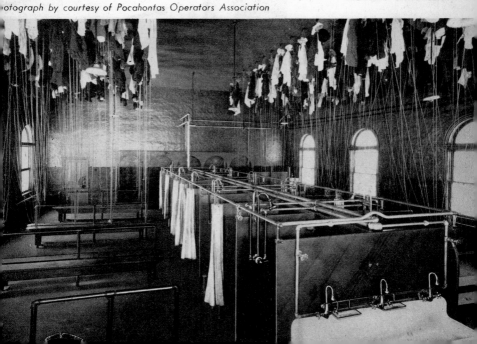

MINER

Photograph by Post; courtesy of Farm Security Administration

Photograph by courtesy of E. E. Jon

NEGRO MINER

half century later his son William, who erected the Anderson House (*see above*), rebuilt the mill, using most of the hand-hewn timbers of the original structure.

THORN SPRING PARK (L), 32.5 *m.*, once known as the Reunion Grounds because soldiers of the Blue and Gray held annual celebrations here, is an attractive picnic spot (*campsites, wading pools, open fireplace*).

South of the park the river and highway wind together between (L) the steep slopes of SANDY RIDGE (3,208 alt.) and (R) those of TROUT ROCK (2,256 alt.). High on the face of the rock is TROUT CAVE, only partially explored (*accessible to experienced climbers*).

South of Trout Rock the valley narrows, as US 220 follows the winding river around many small knolls; on their steeply canted slopes appear the cultivated patches of small mountain farms.

US 220 crosses the VIRGINIA LINE, 43.8 *m.*, 8.1 miles north of Monterey, Virginia (*see Virginia Guide*).

ʅʅ

Tour 5A

Moorefield—Baker—Wardensville—(Winchester, Va.); State 55 and State 259, Moorefield to Virginia Line, 48.1 *m.*

Bituminous-surfaced road.
Accommodations, limited at Moorefield; elsewhere none.

State 55 (formerly State 23) winds through a pleasant region of weather-worn crags, wooded ridges, rocky gorges, and fertile bluegrass valleys; along the way are old covered bridges, once-fashionable watering places with warm and medicinal springs, and the Lost River, which sinks into the ground and reappears miles away as the headwaters of Cacapon River.

State 55 branches east of US 220 (*see Tour 5a*) in MOOREFIELD, 0 *m.*, (820 alt., 734 pop.) (*see Tour 5a*).

At 0.2 *m.* is the junction with South Branch Mountain Road.

Right on this road along the Moorefield River to the crest of SOUTH BRANCH MOUNTAIN (3,266 alt.), 6.5 *m.*
LOST RIVER STATE PARK (*cabins, trails, picnic facilities*), 14 *m.*, is a recreational area developed around the once popular Lee's White Sulphur Springs. Sixteen cabins for vacationists are near the sulphur spring, which is enclosed in an open pavilion. Near by is the LEE CABIN, erected early in the nineteenth century by Henry ('Light Horse Harry') Lee, father of General

Robert E. Lee. The Lees erected a hotel on the property a few years after the tract, a part of the Fairfax grant, had been deeded to 'Light Horse Harry' in 1796 by the Virginia assembly as a reward for his service in the Revolution. It was a two-story log structure, with stone chimneys at each end, and stood until 1910 when it was destroyed by fire.

The highway ascends through a gap, 5.1 *m.*, between (R) SUGARLOAF KNOB (2,160 alt.) and (L) POTATO ROW (2,095 alt.). Crossing the long level ridge of SOUTH BRANCH MOUNTAIN (2,296 alt.), 11.9 *m.*, it passes through NEEDMORE, 15.5 *m.* (1,453 alt., 29 pop.), a cluster of houses, and BAKER, 18.1 *m.* (1,306 alt., 83 pop.), the trading center of the fertile farm country along the Lost River. On the outskirts of the hamlet, in a juniper grove (R), is a picnic ground.

At BAKER State 259 unites with State 55 for 10.7 miles.

HANGING ROCK (L), 21.1 *m.*, juts out over the road from the top of a high cliff, a short distance from McCAULEY, 21.4 *m.* (1,264 alt., 7 pop.), which consists of a store doing a brisk business in selling picture post cards of the rock.

State 55 crosses the dry bed of LOST RIVER, 25.1 *m.*, into the George Washington National Forest.

Right 0.1 *m.* on the footpath from the southern end of the bridge through thickets of willows and alders to a pool, 30 yards in diameter, into which the cascading waters of Lost River pour and disappear for several miles. The old river bed is dry except after heavy storms, when rain water drains off by flowing 'upstream' into the pool.

From the crest of SANDY RIDGE (1,407 alt.), 27 *m.*, under which LOST RIVER flows, appears (R) a deep canyon in which the stream emerges as the CACAPON RIVER. Its point of emergence can be reached only by foot trails from the mouth of the canyon, one mile to the east.

WARDENSVILLE, 28.8 *m.* (1,011 alt., 189 pop.), originally known as Trout Run, occupies the approximate SITE OF FORT WARDEN, a small stockade built by Jacob Warden, one of the first settlers, and burned by Indians in 1758. Chartered in 1832, it is now a placid hamlet, but it hummed with activity from 1830 to 1880, when iron furnaces operated near by. The old WARDENSVILLE JAIL (R), south end of Main St., was built of local stone shortly after the War of 1812.

Left from Wardensville on Main St., which becomes a narrow dirt road, to BLUE SEA GAP (R), 4.9 *m.*, where Trout Run disappears under a high ridge for more than a mile. A half mile beyond the gap, and not visible from the highway, is DEVIL'S GARDEN (R), a cliff towering 500 feet above the stream. The crest can be reached by a stiff climb through dense thickets of rhododendron and laurel around the south face of the crags and a 'tooth-and-toenail' climb for the last 80 feet to the cleft summit (*recommended only for adventurous climbers clad for rough going*).

At 5.2 *m.* is the junction with a dirt road; L. on this road along Trout Run to a COVERED BRIDGE, 1 *m.*, and to the RUINS OF CRACK WHIP FURNACE (L), 3.3 *m.*, once owned by Charles Carter Lee, brother of Robert E. Lee; the furnace continued operations until the late 1870's, being the last in the vicinity to close.

At Wardensville Tour 5A continues north on State 259; State 55 branches east to the Virginia border.

Wedding ceremonies are often performed on the COVERED BRIDGE (L), 30.2 *m.*, a long, single span of 165 feet.

The 931-acre REYMANN MEMORIAL FARMS, 31.3 *m.*, operated as a unit of the State Agricultural Experiment Station, were presented to the State in 1921 by the Reymann family of Wheeling, primarily for the experimental breeding of Ayrshire cattle, but also for studies of the various types of pasturage and the handling of dairy products.

At 35.5 *m.* is the junction with a narrow graveled road.

Right on this road is CAPON SPRINGS, 4 *m.*, discovered by Henry Frye, who moved his family here in 1765. His wife, who suffered from rheumatism, was cured by the use of the waters, and for several years the springs were called Frye's Springs. In 1787 the State of Virginia set aside 20 acres near the spring, laid them out in lots, and placed a Board of Trustees in charge of the resort. The fame of the waters spread and many wealthy families erected summer cottages near the springs.

In 1849 the Mountain House was built, a four-story building with a huge portico supported by ten Doric columns. In front of the hotel was the Bathing Establishment, with hot and cold plunge and shower baths. In the decade before the War between the States the resort reached the height of its popularity and was visited by many distinguished persons. By the outbreak of the war, however, the trustees were $8,000 in debt, and when the State of West Virginia was formed, this sum was included in the Virginia debt that the new State was obliged to assume. The hotel burned in 1911 and was replaced by a smaller structure.

The spring rises from the base of a pile of perpendicular blue rocks and bubbles up with tremendous force. The natural beauty of the spot was described by a writer in the *Baltimore Sun* of July 14, 1851; 'Above (the spring) peaks tower in the most eccentric shapes . . . Sometimes one shoots up perpendicularly, while another leans like an Italian tower. The grouping of the whole bears the most extraordinary resemblance to a ruined castle, such as the Rhine affords . . . When the sun is shining brightly over a blue sky, and its rays fall with full effect upon the peaks, their hues change from their general gray to pure white, and so varied and tossing are their shapes that they seem to be snowy masses of vapor, rising over the trees and relieved against the azure heaven . . . and again, when the sunset throws its hues over the entire scene, these rocks become tinged with the hues of parting day . . . while among the masses of rock that lie scattered around the pavilion, the richest variety of trees and shrubs spring almost with the luxuriance of the tropics and mingle their own bright verdure with the fleeting colors of the sky.'

The highway follows the west bank of the Cacapon River to YELLOW SPRINGS, 41.6 *m.* (901 alt., 67 pop.), in which is (L) an old GRIST MILL, powered by a 30-foot overshot wheel.

At the VIRGINIA LINE, 48.1 *m.*, State 259 joins Va. 259, which branches south from US 50, 17 miles west of Winchester, Virginia (*see Virginia Guide*).

Tour 5B

Junction US 220—Hermit Island—Smoke Hole—Ketterman; 9.4 *m.*, unnumbered road.

Graded dirt road throughout.
Few furnished cabins available; no filling stations or repair shops.

The Smoke Hole country lies isolated in a rugged canyon of the South Branch of the Potomac, which here deserts its broad and ancient valley to pass between the precipitous rock walls into the former bed of its tributary, Briggs Run; for that small stream, the sole proprietor of the Smoke Hole in ages past, 'pirated' the flow of the South Branch River and set it to work in its own narrow defile.

Travel through the 16-mile gorge is not easy; less than 10 miles is accessible by automobile over a narrow winding dirt road carved in the face of a mountain wall 500 feet above the river. Spectacular scenery, virgin forests, abundant game, and a stream well stocked with trout and bass make the Smoke Hole region an ideal vacation spot for those who like to rough it. The Steel family first settled in the Smoke Hole, building a log cabin near the site of the Old Palestine Church (*see below*) sometime before 1760. After the Revolutionary War a number of Hessian soldiers settled in the section; most of its 200 inhabitants today are their descendants, and they have little contact or commerce outside their valley. Barter is still the common practice at the local store; maple sugar, honey, walnut kernels, herbs, and turkeys are exchanged for clothes, salt, sugar, coffee, tobacco, lamp wicks, even iced soft drinks.

Tall, muscular, and bronzed, the typical Smoke Holer leads a simple life, hunting, fishing, and farming just enough to provide him and his family with food. On the rocky farms and hillside pastures a few of the more industrious raise sheep and have a dozen or two lambs and several hundred pounds of wool to offer for sale each spring, almost their sole source of cash income. Extremely hospitable to one another, the Smoke Hole people are shy with strangers and resent 'city airs,' but with patience and tact their reticence can be overcome. Their speech is quaint, containing many archaic forms handed down from the first settlers of the eighteenth century. They use such plural forms as 'postes,' 'beastes,' 'nestes,' 'ghostes,' and analogous verb forms, 'costes' and 'twistes.' They employ 'clumb' for 'climbed,' 'wrop' for 'wrapped,' 'holp' for 'helped,' and such redundancies as 'rifle-gun,' 'rock-clift,' 'ham-meat' and 'tooth-dentist.' Peculiarly free from modern slang, their vocabulary includes such a familiar term as 'budget' to signify a bag, wallet, or bundle. The Smoke Holer is most precise: 'Is that a bushel basket?' he is asked. 'No, I reckon not,' is the reply, 'but hit'll hold nigh onto a bushel.'

Most Smoke Hole families live on the crest of a mountain, or up a hollow from the road, in tiny one- and two-room log houses, with clay-daubed walls, clapboard roofs, and small windows, which are open holes except in winter, when heavy canvas is stretched across them to keep out wind and cold. Floored with splintery whip-sawed boards, the houses have rough walls, occasionally papered neatly with bright pages from seed books, mail order catalogues, and rotogravure sections. Articles of clothing, and often long-barreled rifles, a hunting bag, and fishing tackle, hang from the pole rafters, or from wooden pegs in the wall. Conspicuously placed over the mantel or door is usually a good-luck horseshoe, wrapped in gold- or silver-colored tinfoil. For the most part, the furniture consists of splint-bottom chairs, an unpolished board table with wooden benches, and old-fashioned wooden beds with straw ticks; rusty wood-burning stoves have replaced the 'cat and clay' chimney in most homes. A few families have phonographs, with hillbilly recordings, but many have never heard a radio; two or three of the more prosperous families drive automobiles. Tailored and store-bought clothes are worn only on special occasions and then carefully laid away to be preserved as 'Sunday-go-to-meetin' best.' The women's bonnets, of an ancient vintage, resemble the curiosities in vogue as the *dernier cri* at the present time (1941).

The sole road into the Smoke Hole branches west (R) from US 220 0 *m.* (*see Tour 5b*), at a point 16.2 miles south of Petersburg (*see Tour 5a*).

Deeply shadowed by towering walls, overhanging bluffs, and vaulted archways, the road and river wind their way through a sunless canyon; during one of the frequent summer thunder storms it has a wild and fantastic beauty.

CAVE MOUNTAIN (R), a mass of gray limestone with many explored caverns, frowns through the gloom at the arched walls (L) of BIG MOUNTAIN, which seems to lean toward its neighbor and overhang the narrow trail.

BIG SPRING, 1.1 *m.*, issues from the side of Cave Mountain across the river, and flows noisily to the river at the base of the mountain. During the War between the States huge iron kettles were set up here by the Confederates to extract niter, an ingredient in gunpowder, mined in BIG CAVE (R), 1.6 *m.* Union soldiers, known locally as 'Swamp Dragoons,' raided and captured the works. Big Cave, best known of the many caverns honeycombing the mountain, has been explored for several miles to a sink hole and subterranean river; sawdust thrown into the stream at this point emerges at Indian House Cave 8 miles to the north.

EAGLE ROCK (R) 1.9 *m.*, a perpendicular wall rising abruptly 300 feet above the river, overlooks a narrow strip of valley studded with clumps of virgin timber and thickets of mountain laurel and rhododendron. The rock was named for an early settler, William Eagle, a Revolutionary War soldier, whose grave (L), 2.2 *m.*, was discovered in 1927 and marked with a stone placed by the United States Government.

At CAT PATH ROCKS (L), 2.5 *m.*, the road coils around the face of a steep cliff several hundred feet above the river.

At 2.7 *m.* is the junction with a dirt road.

Left on this narrow and extremely rough road, along the turbulent course of a stream up DRY HOLLOW, to a store, 0.2 *m.*, one of the few in the Smoke Hole region.

In HIGH ROCKS (R), 2.9 *m.*, is revealed a geologic fault line that extends for a mile along the valley. Below the line, strata are tilted at an angle of 75 degrees; above, they lie almost horizontally.

On HERMIT ISLAND, 3.7 *m.*, a heavily wooded and popular picnic spot reached by a low foot bridge (R) from the road, is a double, two-story log house, built in 1928 by Judge H. M. Calhoun as a summer camp. The following summer Judge Calhoun organized a Sunday School, the first in the Smoke Hole section, which met in the lodge or under the tall shade trees near by. The house was also used as a public recreation hall; a phonograph and piano were installed, and to prove that the Smoke Holers were not the lawless lot depicted by prohibition agents who made occasional raids into the section to capture moonshine stills, the house was never locked. Sunday School parties, pie socials, and taffy-pullings were held here, and each Christmas the judge played Santa Claus around a lighted Christmas Tree, bestowing candy and fruit on the children. The Sunday School continued to meet on the island until it consolidated in 1931 with that of Saint George's Episcopal Mission (*see below*). The lodge is now used as headquarters by botany students of West Virginia University on their annual field trips to this region.

At a bridge (R), 4.5 *m.*, is the junction with a foot trail.

Right on this trail, across the river and along a zigzag path around the mountainside and over high cliffs, to SMOKE HOLE CAVERN, 1.7 *m.* Some distance back from the oval-shaped entrance, overhung with large gray boulders, is a circular chamber like an inverted hornet's nest, 14 feet in diameter and 35 feet high. Lacking salt and other preservatives, the Indians and early white settlers, according to legend, brought their meats here to be smoked and cured. Some early families found shelter here while building their cabins; the cavern is now used by sheep and hogs that run free in the woods.

Westward, the valley widens and provides a tiny stretch of level ground converted into a pleasant picnicking and camping site; flagstone walks, tables, benches, and stone chimneys have been built by the Civilian Conservation Corps.

SMOKE HOLE, 5.5 *m.* (1,250 alt., 260 pop.), the market place of the section, centers on the small post office-store, usually crowded with men who come to get their mail and perhaps buy a little salt or tobacco, then linger to swap stories and spin yarns with neighbors, as they sit on the worn benches around the old burnside stove, expertly aiming jets of amber juice at the cinder box.

Social life of the region revolves around the SAINT GEORGE'S EPISCOPAL MISSION; weekly services are held in the chapel, and social functions in the community house. Whole families walk five or six miles to enjoy a few hours of entertainment at pie suppers, peanut socials, square dances, and bingo parties.

> Left from Smoke Hole on a dirt road to NORTH FORK MOUNTAIN, 12 *m.* (3,795 alt.), capped with a 90-foot steel U. S. FOREST SERVICE FIRE TOWER (*open during fire season*), affording a wide vista of blue-green mountain ranges, hazy in the distance.

The OLD PALESTINE CHURCH (L), 5.7 *m.*, is a sturdy little chapel of hand-hewn logs.

FEATHERBED RUN, 7.5 *m.*, is locally associated with the story of an Indian who, learning that white men used feathers to make their beds more comfortable, picked up a feather dropped by a wild turkey, placed it on a large flat rock, and lay down to sleep.

KETTERMAN, 9.4 *m.* (1,175 alt., 49 pop.), the terminus of the road, consists of a combination store-post office from which not a single house can be seen. People come from miles south of the village to trade small surplus crops for necessities.

North of Ketterman is an unbroken wilderness of mountains and forest, for 20 miles impassable except on horse or on foot.

✓✓✓

Tour 6

(Cumberland, Md.)—Ridgeley—Fort Ashby—Romney—Petersburg—Marlinton; State 28.
Maryland Line to Marlinton, 167.8 *m.*

Graveled and shale surface, with stretches of concrete.
Baltimore & Ohio R.R. parallels route between Springfield and Petersburg.
Usual accommodations between Maryland Line and Petersburg; limited between Petersburg and Marlinton.

Through the South Branch Valley with its attractive villages and fertile farmland and thence into the wild and rugged Allegheny Mountains, State 28 roughly follows an old Indian Trail that branched from and paralleled the main Seneca Trail, 30 miles to the west. The area is rich in Indian lore and dotted with sites of long and bitter struggles between the early settlers and Indians. The southern part of the route traverses the Monongahela National Forest over spruce-clad mountain ranges where streams have cut canyon-like valleys through thick folds of Oriskany sandstone. Barefaced anticlines rise from the stream beds, and numerous rock formations are visible through heavy stands of second-growth timber. Trout streams tumble along rock-strewn courses to cascade over a ledge in an unnamed waterfall. Game is plentiful and the route is a favorite with sportsmen.

Section a. MARYLAND LINE to PETERSBURG, 65.4 m. State 28.

This section of State 28 passes through the South Branch Valley, with its quiet, rural towns and fine orchards, vineyards, and stock farms. This fertile valley attracted the earliest settlers to the State, and forts were erected as early as 1754 for protection against Indians. Farming has always been the chief occupation of this section. Broad meadows border the road, and farm houses are set on knolls amid groves of shade trees.

State 28 crosses the MARYLAND LINE, 0 m., at the south end of a bridge spanning the Potomac River, 1 mile southwest of Cumberland, Maryland.

RIDGELEY, 0.8 m. (620 alt., 1,972 pop.), originally named St. Clairsville for Captain Arthur St. Clair, a soldier in Braddock's army, was settled in 1747 as an Indian trading post. Two years later the Ohio Company erected Fort Ohio here, the first of a chain of depots and forts to encourage settlement in the Ohio region. At the opening of Indian hostilities in 1754, Lieutenant Governor Robert Dinwiddie of Virginia ordered a fort built at the Willis Creek settlement on the north bank of the Potomac River, opposite Fort Ohio. As Fort Ohio was less easily defended from Indian attacks, it was abandoned in favor of Fort Cumberland across the river. Ridgeley is largely a residential suburb of the industrial city of Cumberland, Maryland.

South of Ridgeley the highway follows the eastern slope of KNOBLY MOUNTAIN, a series of knobs ranging from 1,500 to 2,000 feet in elevation, and descends to PATTERSONS CREEK.

At 5.7 m. is the junction with a graveled road.

Left on this road to VULCAN FURNACE, 0.1 m., one of the largest and best-preserved relics of the early iron industry in this section. Built in 1840, the engine house and other parts of the furnace have tumbled to the ground, but its flues and massive stack are still standing. John Gamber had visions of making a fortune when he invested $16,000 in 200 acres here and erected the furnace, but his dream faded because of the poor quality of the ore. After a long struggle Gamber was imprisoned for debt and died in the poorhouse. The furnace ceased operations about 1860. Near the furnace is (R) a stucco house, once the iron company's office, now occupied as a residence; behind the house is a barn, formerly the company store.

FORT ASHBY, 12.4 *m.* (610 alt., 325 pop.), a village inhabited by families bearing names associated with the early history of the region, is an agricultural trading center and the home of a number of persons employed in Cumberland, Maryland. Settled about 1735, the community was known as Pattersons Creek until 1755 when the fort was built. In 1787, when the settlement received a charter, it was christened Frankfort, apparently for Frankfort, Germany; the name of Fort Ashby was restored to it in 1932.

The public square, known locally as the Market Place, occupies land donated to the village by Joseph Inskeep, 'for the good of the public.' Owners of buildings on the square cannot acquire title to the ground on which their buildings stand.

On Green Street is Fort Ashby (*open*), the sole survivor of a chain of 23 outposts built under the direction of George Washington. All that remains of the old fortification is a story-and-a-half cabin of hand-hewn logs, secured with dovetail joints at the corners. The half-doors, with original latches and locks, swing on wrought-iron strap hinges extending the full width of the doors. Owned by the Mineral County Court, the fort is being restored (1940) with the assistance of Work Projects Administration funds, under the technical supervision of the National Park Service.

Captain Charles Lewis, its first commander, was succeeded by Colonel John Ashby, for whom the fort was named. Both were instructed by Washington that the stockade was never to be surrendered. In case of attack, they were to 'defend that place to the last extremity, and when bereft of hope, lay a train to blow up the fort, and retire by night to Fort Sellers or Fort Cumberland.' The fort was never surrendered, but in August 1756 Washington wrote to Lieutenant Governor Dinwiddie:

> I have no doubt that you have ere this heard of the defeat of Lieutenant Rutherford of the Rangers, escorting an express to me at Fort Cumberland, and of the dastardly behaviour of the militia, who ran off without one half of them having discharged their pieces, although they were apprised of the ambuscade by one of the flanking parties, before the Indians fired upon them; and ran back to Ashby's Fort, contrary to orders, persuasions, and threats. They are all ordered in, as soon as the people have secured their harvest. Those of King George and Caroline Counties are already here. The rest I expect shortly.

Under Generals Morgan, Matthews, and Page, soldiers of the region were mustered here at Fort Ashby in 1791 when President Washington came to suppress the Whiskey Rebellion.

On the hill opposite the fort is the old FRANKFORT CEMETERY, first used by Indians as a burying ground. Hand-chiseled stones mark the graves of early settlers.

SPRINGFIELD, 18 *m.* (780 alt., 1,200 pop.), is a trading center for near-by farms.

Left from Springfield on a dirt road to PIVOT ROCK (L), 1.5 *m.*, a boulder 40 feet long and 25 feet in diameter, resting on a slender column 15 feet high.

The highway crosses the SOUTH BRANCH of the Potomac River, 20 *m.*, where the river cuts through the hill (L) under a great stone arch.

WAPACOMA, 22.2 *m.* (650 alt., 5 pop.), lies at the eastern end of HANGING ROCK, where the South Branch cuts through Mill Creek Mountain, exposing the curved strata of an almost vertical cliff, half a mile long and more than 300 feet high. The first description of the rock and the community around it was written in 1781 by the Reverend Francis Asbury, then a Methodist circuit rider, later a bishop and leader of the church.

I preached at eleven o'clock to about two hundred people with a degree of freedom. I then rode to R. Williams'. On my way I had a view of a hanging rock that appears like a castle wall, about 300 feet high, and looks as if it has been built with square slate stones; at first glance a traveller would be ready to fear it would fall on him. I had about three hundred people; but there were so many wicked whiskey drinkers, who brought with them so much the power of the devil, I had little satisfaction in preaching.

On the river bank, between the rock and the road, is a row of Indian graves on the spot where a band of Catawba overtook and avenged themselves on a party of Delaware who had raided a Catawba village in South Carolina.

ROMNEY, 26.5 *m.* (830 alt., 1,441 pop.) (*see Tour 4a*), is at the junction with US 50, which unites with State 28 for 7 miles (*see Tour 4a*).

At 33.5 *m.* State 28 branches south (L) from US 50 and unites with US 220 (*see Tour 5a*) as far as PETERSBURG, 65.4 *m.* (937 alt., 1,410 pop.) (*see Tour 5a and b*).

Section b. PETERSBURG to MARLINTON, 102.4 m.   State 28.

This section of State 28 traverses the Monongahela National Forest through thinly populated fishing and hunting country; it was long inaccessible except by Indian trails, later widened into wagon roads by settlers. The highway follows the broad valley of the North Fork of the South Branch of the Potomac River, a bass stream that winds between the high knolls of Allegheny Mountain and the even ridges of North Fork Mountain. Gray masses of tumbled rock, with moss clinging in crevices, and thin growths of scrubby pine cap the ridges. Sharp ragged sandstone formations parallel the river, rising and falling with the contour of the ridges; other exposures of white Medina sandstone take circular forms and from a distance resemble huge monolithic castles. Barren anticlines rise perpendicularly from the river valley. Farther south, the highway follows the wide trough of a series of valleys on the Greenbrier River watershed. Cattle raising has replaced lumbering as the chief occupation of the section.

Germans and a few Scotch-Irish first settled this mountainous region, not long after the Shawnee and Seneca had given it up as a choice hunting ground. Most of the land not in the forest area is still owned by descendants of the first settlers, who grow part of their food on rocky hillside farms, trap game, and earn some cash as hunting guides. The country, abounding in game and fish, is frequented by sportsmen.

PETERSBURG, 0 *m.* (937 alt., 1,410 pop.), is at the junction with US 220 (*see Tour 5b*).

West of Petersburg the highway splits broad meadows on which graze large herds of cattle. In summer, farmhouses are half-hidden by snowball and lilac bushes or rambler roses, and meadows wave with purple clover and timothy grass; in winter, an occasional field, green with young wheat, breaks the monotonous dull brown. From the highway, 2.7 *m.*, the South Branch of the Potomac emerges (L) across the valley from its steep-walled channel through Cave Mountain and the Smoke Hole (*see Tour 5B*), near the confluence with its largest tributary, the North Fork. Southward, a marked difference appears in the contour of the country. Cliffs rise abruptly on both sides of the road, and sandstone strata dip deeply to the water's edge.

A large anticlinal formation, 6.3 *m.*, attains a height of 300 feet; rising from a thicket of mountain laurel, brushwood, and young pines, the lofty mass of rock is tufted with lichens, gray with age. The quiet of the spot is broken by the whispering of the tiny waterfall that trickles over the ledge.

CABINS, 7.4 *m.*, a cluster of white tourist cabins, has a natural swimming pool (*free*) in North Fork River at the base of a cliff. A road (L) crosses the stream on a U. S. Forest Service bridge and leads into the Smoke Hole region.

The road is chiseled in the side of WILDCAT ROCK (R), 8.4 *m.*, a huge gray boulder which rises almost 100 feet and overhangs half the highway. Left is CHIMNEY TOP, a mountain capped with towering rock formations resembling ancient fortresses with lookout towers. The most distinctive outline is that of CASTLE ROCK (R), a series of spire-shaped formations.

At 11 *m.* is the junction with a U. S. Forest Service road.

Right on this road is a beautiful drive through almost unbroken forest along the steep frontal knobs of the Alleghenies. Through stands of second-growth pine, spruce, hemlock, and scattered hardwoods, the trail ascends steep slopes to the DOLLY SODS FOREST LOOKOUT TOWER, 8 *m.*, on the crest of the Alleghenies. From this point is a sweeping view of wooded peaks, deep ravines, and blue-green mountain ranges, rolling away to become a misty blue on the far horizon.

From the highway (L), 17.5 *m.*, appear CHAMPE ROCKS, two lofty chimney-shaped masses across the North Fork. Separated by a deep ravine cut through blue-gray rock by a small stream, they rise 900 feet above the valley floor from thickets of mountain ivy, rhododendron, and young redbud. The rocks were named for Sergeant John Champe, the Revolutionary War soldier who was sent by General George Washington to join the British and kidnap Benedict Arnold. Washington feared that Arnold's desertion and subsequent promotion in the British Army would encourage others to desert. Champe was to pretend to be a deserter, and was promised 'ample reward' and extensive land grants. Under cover of darkness the young sergeant rode his horse from the American camp, but his departure was discovered by a cavalry lieutenant, and troops were dispatched to bring him back. Champe took a short cut to the Hudson River, however, and boarded a British steamer just as his pursuers reached the shore. Champe easily convinced the British that he was a deserter, and was soon sent to join Arnold's command, largely made up of American deserters. Champe kept in close touch with Major Henry ('Light-Horse Harry') Lee while laying the kidnap plans. It was Arnold's custom to walk in the garden of his quarters at night, and Champe planned to capture him during one of these late walks. On the day the plan was to be executed, Arnold's troops embarked for Virginia, and Champe found himself forced to fight against his countrymen. He escaped at Petersburg, Virginia, and rejoined his command under Major Lee. Washington soon gave him an honorable discharge from the Army, but failed to reward him. Champe died in dire circumstances at his home near here in 1804.

South of Champe Rocks the valley widens; here and there appear small hilly farms surrounded by zigzag rail fences.

MOUTH OF SENECA, 23.8 *m.* (1,567 alt., 40 pop.) (*see Tour 7a*), is at a junction with US 33, which unites with State 28 for 11.3 miles (*see Tour 7a*).

At JUDY GAP, (1,850 alt.) 35.1 *m.*, is the junction (L) with US 33 (*see Tour 7a*).

CIRCLEVILLE, 38.3 *m.* (2,054 alt., 65 pop.), a cluster of farmhouses in an isolated valley shadowed by wooded mountains, is a rendezvous for sportsmen, and the social and trade center of a scattered farming section around Upper Timber Ridge. Here families live much as they did in pioneer days. White frame houses with vine-hung porches stand deep in groves of old trees. Most of the cooking is done in iron pots suspended over the blaze in wide stone fireplaces. Kerosene lamps have replaced candles, but the straw-filled bedtick, over which is laid another filled with feathers, is still generally used. The mountaineers here cultivate small gardens, make maple sugar, and pick blackberries, strawberries, raspberries, and huckleberries. In winter, the women spend their time spinning, knitting, and weaving blankets. Social life centers around quilting parties, knitting clubs, and square dances.

The Circleville area was settled about 1820 by Scotch-Irish, whose descendants still practice Scottish folk customs. Between Halloween and New Year's Day grotesque figures wander in groups through the countryside, usually on Saturday evenings, visiting various houses; there is always a welcome and perhaps refreshments; often furniture is moved out of the big kitchen, and many versions of the Virginia Reel are danced to fiddles and banjos.

West of Circleville the highway winds upward through tall forests of second-growth pine, spruce, hemlock, and a few scattered hardwoods. Squirrels jump from tree to tree; rabbits hop across the highway; wild turkeys and ruffed grouse are sometimes seen; an occasional shy deer lingers for one look at the passing motorist before bounding off into the deep woods. Numerous game refuges have been set apart in the Monongahela National Forest. On the SUMMIT OF ALLEGHENY MOUNTAIN (4,017 alt.), 48.3 *m.*, are the headwaters of seven rivers. The Greenbrier, Gauley, and Elk Rivers flow southwest; Jackson River flows east; the south branches of the Potomac, Cheat and Tygart Rivers follow a northerly course. For this reason the section is often referred to as the Birthplace of Rivers.

The highway follows a skyline drive along the crest of the mountain and cuts eastward across a ridge to skirt the Virginia Line for a short distance. The grade down the mountain is steep, and the road winds through dense thickets. Here and there along the slopes, once laid bare by forest fires, are acres of young trees planted by the Monongahela National Forest Service. After the slashing by loggers during the early part of the century, thick stands of blackberry briars sprang up. Then came a heavy growth of hardwoods, but the area was burned so many times that it became barren of all except scrub growth. The forest service has cleared away much of the slashing and litter, and has planted red spruce, Norway spruce, red pine, and a few species of hardwoods adapted to the severe climate and thin soil of the region.

A STAND OF EUROPEAN LARCH, 57.7 *m.*, bordering the highway (L), grew from seeds brought from the Austrian Tyrol and planted in 1907 by Mac Rothkugal, the forester of a local lumber company. Seeds sown on 150 acres along the lower slopes of Fork Mountain failed to sprout.

THORNWOOD, 58.1 *m.* (2,871 alt., 137 pop.), a village of small farmhouses, filling station, and general store in the heart of good fishing and hunting country, is a supply base for sportsmen who come into the region in season.

At 58.3 *m.* is a junction with US 250 (*see Tour 22a*), which unites with State 28 for 2.2 miles.

BOYER, 64.4 *m.* (2,716 alt., 111 pop.), once a busy lumbering town, is now a quiet village of scattered houses.

ARBOVALE, 68.3 *m.* (2,727 alt., 30 pop.), was settled in 1891 by the Arbogast family. During the summer, families from miles around gather at the METHODIST CHURCH (L) for singing school, all day services, and basket dinners.

GREEN BANK, 69.8 *m.* (2,675 alt., 175 pop.), is the cultural center of this isolated district; the GREEN BANK HIGH SCHOOL (R) occupies the site of the old Green Bank Academy, founded in 1842 as a University of Virginia preparatory school. The Mountain Rifles, a company of 100 men more than 6 feet tall, were mustered into the

Confederate Army here in 1861; most of them perished in the 'Bloody Angle' at Spotsylvania, Virginia.

The highway crosses DEER CREEK, 70.8 *m.*, and hills close in as the road turns from the valley of Deer Creek and follows MOOR RUN between (R) PETERS MOUNTAIN and (L) UPPER AND LOWER MOUNTAINS.

DUNMORE, 75.3 *m.* (2,463 alt., 66 pop.), was named for Lord Dunmore (*see Tour* 14) by Major Jacob Warwick, who served under him in Lord Dunmore's War. On the outskirts of the hamlet is (L) the DUNMORE MINERAL SPRING, of alkaline sulphur water, which has been dammed and diverted into a swimming pool. From the meadow about the spring rise the wooded spurs of MICHAEL MOUNTAIN.

Right from Dunmore (straight ahead) on a graveled road is SENECA STATE FOREST, 9 *m.*, 11,049 acres of wooded mountain country, cleared of dead growth, reforested, and opened as a recreational area (*picnic facilities, cabins, hiking trails*). An artificial lake (*swimming, boating*) is fed by cold mountain streams. From MICHAEL MOUNTAIN FIRE TOWER (3,652 alt.), 3.5 *m.*, is a far-reaching view of low pine-covered ridges extending (L) to BACK ALLEGHENY MOUNTAIN and (R) to ALLEGHENY MOUNTAIN, with the misty crests of the Virginia mountains rising beyond. This is an attractive alternate route through the heart of the forest to a junction with State 28 on the outskirts of Huntersville, 20 *m.* (*see below*).

Passing FROST, 82.6 *m.* (2,575 alt., 47 pop.), so named by pioneer farmers confounded by the late spring and early autumn frosts that damaged their crops here, the highway enters the narrow and rugged valley of KNAPPS CREEK, fed by many swift streams that rush down (L) the wrinkled face of Allegheny Mountain.

At 92.7 *m.* is the junction with State 43, an improved dirt road.

Left on State 43 to MINNEHAHA SPRINGS, 0.3 *m.* (2,325 alt., 18 pop.), a deserted summer resort. The rambling, galleried, two-story frame hotel, once filled with vacationers and health-seekers, stands forlornly on a high knoll, at the foot of which is an octagonal swimming pool fed by sulphur springs.

HUNTERSVILLE, 95.2 *m.* (2,271 alt., 100 pop.), laid out in 1821 and from 1822 to 1891 the seat of Pocahontas County, grew up around the cabin of John Bradshaw, which became a rendezvous for trappers and hunters who came here to trade pelts for supplies; from this fact the town derived its name. All that remains of the former county building is the clerk's office (R), a small square structure of brick and weathered board.

In Huntersville is the junction (L) with a graveled road, an alternate route through the forest to WATOGA STATE PARK, 8 *m.*

West of Huntersville the highway follows the broad level valley of Knapps Creek. Willows and young birches fringe the banks of the stream, which ripples over a stony bed and curls in sparkling foam around occasional boulders. The hills are dark with pine, spotted with lighter patches of poplar and ash.

MARLINTON, 102.1 *m.* (2,134 alt., 1,586 pop.), seat of Pocahontas County and the point of origin of many fish and 'b'ar' stories, lies in a small natural bowl at the confluence of Knapps Creek and the Greenbrier River. Hundreds of hunters come to Marlinton every year, for in the surrounding wooded mountain country are deer, black bear, ruffed grouse, wild turkey, wildcats, and, so some say, a few panthers, although there is no record of any being killed for many years.

Stephen Sewell and Jacob Marlin, for whom the town was named, came here in 1749 and lived together in a cabin. After a quarrel over infant baptism, Sewell stormed out of the cabin and established temporary quarters in a hollow tree, which until 1930 stood near the CORNER OAK, left on State 28, about 100 yards east of the C. and O. railroad station. This tree marked the eastern edge of a 470-acre land grant surveyed by General Andrew Lewis (*see Tour* 14) for the Greenbrier Company, and an ax mark made by General Lewis is still visible on the oak stump. The settlement was known as Marlin's Bottom until 1887 when it was made the seat of Pocahontas County, established in 1821 and named for the renowned Indian princess.

A tall four-faced clock tower identifies the POCAHONTAS COUNTY COURTHOUSE, 10th Ave. and Court St., a faded brick building, which stands on the SITE OF GREEN BRYER, a small stockade erected by General Andrew Lewis in 1755. General Lewis was in command of the fort, and it was here that he organized his company for the Battle of Point Pleasant (*see Tour* 14).

At 102.4 *m.*, on the outskirts of Marlinton, is the junction with US 219 (*see Tour* 8*b*).

ʇʇ

Tour 7

(Harrisonburg, Va.)—Elkins—Buckhannon—Weston—Spencer—Ripley—Mason—(Pomeroy, Ohio): US 33.
Virginia Line to Ohio Line, 257.8 *m.*

Bituminous surface from Virginia Line to Franklin, and between Judy Gap and Mouth of Seneca, Spencer and Graham; graveled between Franklin and Judy Gap; elsewhere concrete-paved. Watch for cattle on road between Elkins and Mason.
Baltimore & Ohio R.R. parallels route between Buckhannon and Weston.
Accommodations only in larger towns; picnic and camp sites in Monongahela National Forest. Use extreme care with fire in forests.

Cutting across the central part of the State, US 33 bares a representative cross section of West Virginia's rural life and of the occupations that support its tillers of the soil. Known as the Blue and Gray Trail for the many scenes of struggle between Union and Confederate forces along the route, this highway emerges from the George Washington National Forest, plunges into the mountain fastnesses of the Monongahela National Forest, and then gradually descends to the Ohio Valley flood plain. In its craggy eastern section, where snow lies in rotting ridges along drift fences until late in May, the virgin forest in many places extends as far as the eye can see, with only a crossroads town, a woodsman's cabin, or a hillside charred by fire to dot the green backdrop. In central counties 90 per cent of the land is farmed; grazing, cultivation of small fruits, and the exploitation of natural gas round out the economic scheme. Grazing herds are larger and more numerous, and farmhouses are more substantial, west of Weston.

Section a. VIRGINIA LINE to ELKINS; 81.4 m. US 33.

Emerging from the George Washington National Forest and crossing a recreational area of the Monongahela National Forest, the highway traverses a region in which green mountains alternate with greener valleys, and craggy rock formations rise from forested slopes of steep-walled canyons.

US 33 crosses the VIRGINIA LINE 0 m., on the top of SHENANDOAH MOUNTAIN (3,450 alt.), 22 miles west of Harrisonburg, Virginia.

From the crest of the mountain is a view for miles across the valley to the long range of South Fork Mountain, and beyond to misty peaks and the long blue crest of North Fork Mountain. The road descends to the valley in a straight stretch, passing through the village of BRANDYWINE, 7.1 m. (1,586 alt., 165 pop.), a farm community.

In OAK FLAT, 10.9 m. (1,528 alt., 140 pop.), a marker commemorates the tragic massacre that occurred in 1758 at Fort Seybert, a large stockade erected a few miles to the north during the French and Indian War. While most of the settlers were absent, the fort was attacked by a band of Shawnee under the leadership of Killbuck (see Tour 4a), who offered to spare all who would surrender. Hopelessly outnumbered, the little force opened the gates at the command of Captain Seybert. The Indians immediately lined up half the occupants and tomahawked them; the others were held captive.

Gradually ascending, the highway passes through Hively Gap and Troublesome Valley to the top of LONG RIDGE (3,360 alt.), 13.4 m. The SOUTH BRANCH of the Potomac River is crossed, 18.1 m.; downstream (R) from the bridge, it flows through a high-walled gorge.

At 19.2 m. is a junction with US 220 (see Tour 5b), which unites with US 33 for 0.9 miles.

Following the winding course of FRIENDS RUN in the shadow of Colic Mountain, Cedar Knob (R), and Lankey Mountain and Bible Knob (L), US 33 climbs through a pass in CASTLE MOUNTAIN to the summit of NORTH FORK MOUNTAIN (3,582 ft.), 28.6 *m.* A vantage point, 29.4 *m.*, overlooks (R) Germany Valley (*see below*), settled in the 1760's by German colonists. Beyond the fertile rolling farmlands rise the jagged peaks of the River Knobs, dwarfed by SPRUCE MOUNTAIN in the background. Snake fences zigzag down sloping fields to divide the neatly laid out farms of the valley, with their haystacks enclosed within rail fences. Descending the mountain, the highway follows the course of JUDY RUN, and at JUDY GAP, 33.5 *m.*, passes through the portal cut by the stream in the uplifted sandstone strata.

Judy Gap is at a junction with State 28 (*see Tour 6b*), which unites with US 33 for 11.2 miles.

Between Judy Gap and Mouth of Seneca the road runs through the narrow mountain-shadowed valley of the North Fork River. The Fore Knobs (L), their outlines softened by trees, contrast sharply with the ragged crests (R) of the River Knobs.

At 35 *m.* is the junction with an improved dirt road.

Left on this road, which makes a long twisting ascent of SPRUCE MOUN-TAIN. The muddy trickle of RED LICK RUN crosses the road, 8.8 *m.*, and gaining force and volume as it falls, tumbles almost 3,000 feet down a steep ravine (L) into the North Fork River. A footpath (R) leads 0.5 *m.* to the summit of SPRUCE KNOB (4,860 alt.), the highest point in the State.

Over the extensive flat of broken and jumbled sandstone on the mountain, plays a hard whipping breeze, crisp and chill even in midsummer; vegetation is distinctly northern. The western face of the mountain, which fires have stripped of trees, is thickly covered with bracken, great willow herb, mosses, and grasses. Over the broken rocks on the summit clamber huckleberry, black chokeberry, fetid currant, and wild bleeding heart. Wintergreen, trailing arbutus, mountain cranberry, mountain holly, dwarf cornell, red raspberry, and such wild flowers as painted wakerobin, Canada mayflower, yellow clintonia, pink moccasin flower, and round-leafed orchid, are common. The western slope is more thickly wooded with ground and running pine, mountain ash, mountain maple, red spruce, wild red cherry, mountain laurel, yellow birch, and smaller northern shrubs. Along the course of Red Lick Run and in other moist spots grows the deep-rooted, spiral inflorescence of the bright green American helle-bore, which the natives call 'elleber.'

Below and on all sides is a panorama of the most mountainous section of a mountainous State, a section buckled and folded by prehistoric upheavals of earth, gouged by racing streams for centuries. Eastward and southward the steep crests roll to the horizons in long parallel waves, with North Fork, South Fork, and Shenandoah Mountains billowing above the rest. To the west and north are lower crests, irregularly massed between the long chains of Allegheny, Rich, Cheat, and Shavers Mountains, some covered with unbroken forest, some scarred by fire and erosion.

RIVERTON, 37.3 *m.* (1,782 alt., 85 pop.), is a crossroads hamlet.

Right from Riverton on an improved dirt road, through a gap cut by Stringtown Run, into GERMANY VALLEY, a region of hilly meadows and farms bounded (R) by the long crest of North Fork Mountain. Settled in 1760 by John Justus Hinkle and his four sons, Jacob, Abraham, Isaac, and John, Jr., who were soon joined by the Taters and other German families, the valley took its name from the nationality of its inhabitants, who long spoke their native tongue and retained Old World customs. The SITE OF HINKLE'S FORT, 2 *m.*, is indicated by a stone marker shaped like an arrowhead and enclosed within an iron fence; after the Indians under Killbuck had destroyed Fort Seybert (*see above*) and Fort Upper Tract in 1758, this fort, built by the Hinkles in 1761, was the only place of refuge for residents of the South Branch Valley.

SENECA CAVERNS, 3.5 *m.*, are said to have been used as a retreat by the Seneca Indians. Two series of underground chambers filled with fanciful rock formations are lighted electrically. The deepest cavern is 165 feet below ground; the shallowest, 25 feet. (*Adm.* $1 *for tour through one cavern;* $1.50 *for both; special prices to parties of more than* 15; *children half price.*)

Genetically one of the River Knobs but unique among them for its lack of vegetation, SENECA ROCK (1,000 ft.), 44 *m.*, a mountain of gleaming white Medina sandstone, lifts its crest high above the valley floor. Like the crumbling castle of some mountain giant, it rises starkly from the growth of scrub oak and laurel thicket that climbs its talus slope. The arch of its ragged crest drops away sharply to the south where a little creek has cut a narrow gateway to valley level. Legend has it that Snowbird, daughter of a Seneca chief, grew up in the shadow of the rocks and learned to climb them. Of all the Seneca, she alone could reach the summit. When the time came for her to marry, she agreed to choose from among her seven suitors the one who could follow her to the top of the crag. All essayed the task, but only one survived. The summit is now reached by a footpath (*inquire locally*).

MOUTH OF SENECA, 44.7 *m.* (1,567 alt., 40 pop.), at the confluence of Seneca Creek and North Fork River, lies in the shadow of Seneca Rock.

Here is a junction with State 28 (*see Tour 6b*).

US 33 swings westward through the northern half of MONONGA-HELA NATIONAL FOREST (*camping, picnicking, fishing, swimming, riding, hiking; use extreme caution with fires; permit must be secured from a Ranger before building a campfire*). Comprising 1,673,-652 acres, the forest is bounded roughly by US 50 on the north, US 60 on the south, US 220 on the east, and US 219 on the west. The U. S. Forest Service here protects timberlands and engages in extensive reforestation to maintain the watersheds of the Ohio, James, Potomac, Kanawha, and lesser rivers. Wildlife protection and management, fire protection, and administration of recreation areas constitute the major activities of the Rangers. The recreation areas include tent camping lots, with tables and grates, drinking water, sanitary facilities, and firewood; six forest camps (*open, May 30—Labor Day*) are situated conveniently along the forest's 600 miles of motor road and 500 miles of foot and horse trails. The Alpena Gap, Stuart, and Bickle Knob camps are reached from US 33 (*see below*); Horseshoe camp is reached from US 219 (*see Tour 8a*), Blue Bend from US 60 (*see Tour 15a*), and Smoke Hole from US 220 (*see Tour 5b*).

On Timber Ridge, US 33 parallels the course of Seneca Creek, which tumbles noisily down to join the North Fork River. A backward glance reveals Seneca Rock in white relief against the dark green of North Fork Mountain.

ONEGO (pronounced *wun-go*), 47.8 *m.* (1,761 alt., 63 pop.), is at the confluence of Roaring Creek and Seneca Creek. On the bank of the former (R) is a gristmill, run by a water wheel.

West of Onego the highway winds sharply upward from the narrow valley, ascending Allegheny Mountain in slow spirals to a magnificent view, 51.4 *m.*, of the chasm (L) cut by Seneca Creek, a thread of quicksilver far below. Jumbled mountain ridges, wooded and wild, unfold in succession as the highway reaches the apex of the ALLE-GHENY FRONT (3,293 alt.), 53.3 *m.*

HARMAN, 57.2 *m.* (2,359 alt., 114 pop.), is a neat village, its one residential street lined with frame houses, two restaurants, and several filling stations.

As the road ascends RICH MOUNTAIN, it overlooks (L) the rugged and wooded slopes of LITTLE MIDDLE MOUNTAIN and the northernmost spurs of Spruce Mountain. Between them, far below, winds the shining Dry Fork River. The forest-clad peaks appear green, blue-green, or slate-gray with the movement of light and shadow on cloudy days; the highway tops Rich Mountain (3,368 alt.), 62 *m.*

At 64.2 *m.* is the junction with Middle Mountain Road.

Left on this graveled road, through an almost unbroken forest of spruce, pine, and hardwoods, along the ridge of Middle Mountain; dipping to cross Little River, the road swings upward again on Burner Mountain before it reaches the valley of the East Fork of Greenbrier River. Numerous footpaths lead down the mountainside to fish-stocked streams. In the woods are deer, wild turkeys, and ruffed grouse. The road passes through the BEAVER DAM GAME REFUGE (*open to visitors*), 7 *m.*, a 3,800-acre tract established in 1933 to provide a refuge for deer, turkey, bear, and other wild-life species under the joint management of the U. S. Forest Service and the State Conservation Commission. The LITTLE RIVER GAME BREEDING AREA (*open to visitors*), 20 *m.*, is a 13,000-acre area opened in 1936 to demonstrate the practicability of controlling environment to increase desirable wild-life species. Established primarily as a deer, turkey, and bear refuge, the area was declared closed to all hunting for five years; a program including range surveys, development of feed crops and cover, grazing control, clearing and planting, artificial feeding, and other experimental activities, was begun, resulting in a great increase in all species of wild life. No village or habitation breaks the solitude of the forest.

At 38 *m.* is the junction with State 28 (*see Tour 6b*).

US 33 dips between groves of poplar and pine to cross the sycamore-bordered GLADY FORK of Cheat River, 66.6 *m.;* swinging upward again, it passes through ALPENA GAP, 69 *m.*, on Shavers Mountain.

At 75.4 *m.* is (R) the entrance to STUART MEMORIAL DRIVE, built as a memorial to Major Robert Y. Stuart (1883–1933), former Chief of the U. S. Forest Service, and an authority on reforestation and conservation, under whose guidance the Forest Service rapidly expanded and intensified its activities in the Federal timber preserves.

Right on this one-way macadam road to the junction with two graded roads, 0.4 *m.*

1. Left on the first road 0.5 *m.* to STUART FOREST CAMP, one of the largest of the forest recreational areas. In a meadow embraced by a wide bend

of Shavers Fork is a large graveled parking space and an administration building. Winding flagstone paths lead to secluded campsites and picnic areas, equipped with tables, fireplaces supplied with ready-cut wood, benches, and comfort stations. A sandy beach borders a laurel- and dogwood-shaded pool (*swimming; lifeguard*). On SYLVIAS ISLAND, reached by a suspension bridge, are more secluded picnic spots. Natural woodland beauty has not been disturbed in construction of recreation facilities, and each picnic or campsite is screened by laurel thickets and close-growing trees.

2. Left on the second road 0.2 *m.* to RANDOLPH COUNTY HEALTH CAMP, where underprivileged children between 4 and 12 years old enjoy outdoor vacations. Food and supplies are furnished by the State, and labor by the WPA.

Stuart Drive winds upward 2,000 feet to the summit of BICKLE KNOB (4,008 alt.), 3.5 *m.* Here, overlooking the forest camps below, are more picnic areas; from BICKLE KNOB FIRE TOWER the green mountaintops and valleys are visible for 25 to 30 miles in all directions.

ROOSEVELT FOREST CAMP, 6.9 *m.*, near the exit of the drive, has facilities similar to those of the Stuart Forest Camp.

At 7 *m.* is a junction with US 33.

The highway crosses the western boundary of the Monongahela National Forest, 74.3 *m.* On CHEAT MOUNTAIN (2,586 alt.), 76.1 *m.*, the highway affords (L) a wide vista of forested country.

ELKINS, 81.4 *m.* (1,930 alt., 7,345 pop.) (*see Tour 8a*), is at the junctions with US 250 (*see Tour 22b*) and US 219 (*see Tour 8a and b*).

Section b. ELKINS to WESTON; 47.9 m. US 33.

The country between Elkins and Weston varies from gently rolling to steeply ridged hills. The chief source of wealth in the region is its rich bluegrass pasture land upon which graze prize herds of cattle and large flocks of sheep. Deposits of coal, oil, and gas underlie the area, but the development of these resources is secondary to stock raising.

West of ELKINS, 0 *m.*, US 33 and US 250 are united for 7.6 miles.

NORTON, 8.4 *m.* (1,885 alt., 1,037 pop.), is one of the few active coal camps in the Roaring Creek field. Beside the road is (R) the SCOTT MEMORIAL, a boulder with a bronze plaque inscribed to the memory of Crawford Scott, a Union scout during the War between the States, one of the first to develop the region's coal resources.

A ghostly reminder of the days when this coal field seethed with activity appears (L) in the abandoned coke ovens, 11.5 *m.*, their black mouths outlined against red ash piles. A sharp contrast is offered by a view, across the MIDDLE FORK RIVER (R), 20.6 *m.*, to the bustling lumber town of ELLAMORE, (1,842 alt., 519 pop.), which busily toils in and around a large sawmill. Little steam engines puff at long strings of log-laden cars, worrying them slowly toward the mill's band saws, while donkey engines untangle jams in the thousands of logs piled like spilled matchsticks on the hillside. Burly woodsmen in corduroys and caulked boots leap nimbly from log to log, both in the river and on the railroad cars, and their shouts join with the scream of the saws, and the growling and grinding of the yard engines, while tall stacks of new lumber stand as proof of hard labor well done.

BUCKHANNON, 32.2 m. (1,433 alt., 4,374 pop.), seat of Upshur County, is a college town, with shady streets unblemished by factory soot. Sedate frame and faded brick houses, ornamented with iron and wooden scrollwork, pass their declining years in the shade of stately elms and sycamores. A gentle lavender-and-lace atmosphere pervades the city, reminiscent of the days of octagonal-lensed gas street lights, of tassel-topped buggies with high red wheels, and of children singing.

> You can't holler down my rain barrel,
> 'Cause I don't like you anymore.

Both the city and the river that flows through it were named for a Delaware chief, Buck-on-ge-ha-non, who lived near by. A leader during the border wars, he has been called the 'Washington of the Delaware.' Settled in 1770, the site on which the town stands was not formally claimed until 1806, when it was bought by Elizabeth Cummings Jackson, whose son, Colonel Edward Jackson, platted the town in 1815; 'Stonewall' Jackson was a grandson of the latter. Center of a rich farming and grazing section, Buckhannon has grown steadily; during the War between the States it was pillaged by Confederates and later occupied by Union forces commanded by McClellan. The Male and Female Academy of Buckhannon, which had a brief existence after its founding in 1847, is said to have been the first coeducational school of its kind west of the Alleghenies. The West Virginia Academy, sponsored by the United Brethren in Christ, was incorporated in 1882 and functioned until 1897 when it was moved to Mason (see below); the building is now used as an elementary school.

The WEST VIRGINIA WESLEYAN COLLEGE, College Ave. at Meade St., a coeducational institution sponsored by the Methodist Church, consists of a College of Liberal Arts and a School of Music. Organized in 1890 as the West Virginia Conference Seminary, the institution was primarily a preparatory school until 1902, when it was raised to college standard. In 1905 the first graduating class received degrees. The average enrollment is 450. The ADMINISTRATION BUILDING, a three-story brick structure, stands on a small knoll in the center of the 43-acre landscaped campus. The administration offices, the library, chapel, and classrooms are in this building, which replaced an earlier structure destroyed by fire in 1905. HAYMOND SCIENCE HALL, a square brick building, contains well-equipped laboratories. The GYMNASIUM has been a sports center since 1914 when the State basketball tournament first drew large crowds from all over the State. Later additions and improvements have made Wesleyan's athletic facilities among the finest in the State. The MUSIC HALL is a plain ivy-covered brick building, the smallest on the campus; it contains studios and practice rooms for students of piano, organ, and other instruments. AGNES HOWARD HALL, a four-story brick building with a square central tower, provides rooms for 150 women and is the center of social life on the campus.

Buckhannon is at the junction with State 20 (see Tour 20b).

West of Buckhannon the highway follows the course of FINKS RUN through billowing meadowland that in the 1780's was a hotly contested frontier. The road passes (L) the SITE OF THE SCHOOLCRAFT CABIN, 33.5 *m.*, built about 1773. Within a decade the entire family was killed or taken captive by the Indians. Sixteen-year-old Leonard, captured in 1780, was made to run the gantlet and adopted into the tribe; he later led forays against the whites. Leonard's father, his brothers Austin and Mathias, and Mrs. John Schoolcraft, with eight of her children, were killed in successive raids; five other members of the family were taken prisoners.

BRIDGE RUN, 37.7 *m.*, is the site of a settlement by the Bozarth family, who also suffered from Indian attacks. In 1795, while at work near the settlement, John Bozarth and his son, George, were attacked by Indians. George 'played possum' while the Indians pursued his father; both escaped; on arriving home they found that two small children had been killed, and that two other children had been carried off with their mother; the latter were rescued by General 'Mad Anthony' Wayne during his operations against the Indians in northwest Ohio.

LORENTZ, 40.1 *m.* (1,452 alt., 262 pop.), is a quiet country village founded by Dutch settlers in 1783. Jacob Lorentz, for whom the town was named, established the first store here in 1800. All goods were brought from Richmond by pack train and exchanged for cattle and hogs, which were driven eastward to market on foot; Lorentz once drove 937 hogs to Richmond, a distance of 265 miles.

West of Lorentz the road is crossed at intervals by the Baltimore & Ohio tracks leading to coal mines far back in the hills. The aluminum-painted buildings (L) of the WESTON COMPRESSOR STATION, 45.5 *m.*, glisten in the midst of well-kept lawns.

WESTON, 47.9 *m.* (1,008 alt., 8,646 pop.), the hub of a wide grazing and agricultural area, is a leisurely and shaded city with the atmosphere of a country town and minor political center. The business district displays the varied architecture of a century of steady growth, in keeping with the original plans of the city's surveyor, Colonel Edward Jackson, grandfather of 'Stonewall' Jackson. A few buildings, chiefly homes of retired farmers with fortunes made in oil, manifest the stylistic pretensions and structural oddities of the Victorian era.

Founded in 1818 as the seat of Lewis County, the town was platted on land purchased from Henry Flesher, who had settled here in 1784; it was first named Preston, then Flesherville, and finally Weston. Farming and grazing activities have prospered, and lambs, sheep, and cattle block the roads leading into town each Tuesday, en route to the stock-yards at Deanville. With profits from the land came leisure for political activity, and from 1829 until the turn of the century many county laws were devised here, to the sound of snapping 'galluses' and over excellent chicken dinners at the old Bailey Hotel. Industry grew slowly, and today (1940) 900 persons are employed in glass plants producing table and bar glassware and specialities. The discovery of oil and gas in the vicinity in the late 1890's increased the population, but has done little to change the tenor of community life, strongly influenced by Irish immigrants who came as laborers in 1847 to help build the Staunton-Parkersburg Turnpike, and who remained to farm.

During the War between the States the town was alternately occupied by Union and Confederate forces, but business went on much as usual. During the summer of 1861 Union troops took over publication of the local paper, gave it the name of their regiment, the *Ohio Seventh,* and placed under the masthead the motto, 'We come to protect, not to invade.' The Weston National Bank still possesses a receipt for $5,287-.85, the entire cash resources of the institution in 1864, when it was seized by Captain H. L. Branham for use of the Confederate army.

Weston was chosen in 1859 as the site of the Trans-Allegheny Lunatic Asylum, now the WESTON STATE HOSPITAL (*open* 9–11 *a.m.;* 1:30–4 *p.m.*), which occupies a large landscaped and cultivated tract on the southern edge of town. Authorized by the Virginia assembly in 1858 to care for insane patients west of the mountains, the hospital is the oldest public institution in the State. The three one-story wings, completed in 1864, were almost the only tangible properties West Virginia had to show for its share of the Virginia debt of more than $13,000,000. The huge gray stone main building has nine acres of floor space; completed in 1880, it is said to be the largest hand-cut stone structure in the country. Six wards of the south wing, badly damaged by fire in 1936, have been reconstructed with WPA funds. Surrounding the main building in the spacious well-kept grounds are four brick ward buildings; a two-story building that contains a laundry, tin shop, and plumbing shop; a two-story dining-room-and-kitchen building; and a four-story medical center. On the 350-acre farm, which supplies meat and vegetables for the diet kitchen, are a small coal mine and a gas well. The hospital opened in 1864 with 9 patients; it now (1940) cares for 1,650.

Weston is at the junction with US 19 (*see Tour 10a and b*).

Section c. WESTON to OHIO LINE; 128.5 m. US 33.

West of WESTON, 0 *m.,* US 33 runs through ridge country, in which are long stretches of hilly pasture, scattered oil derricks, and widely separated rural villages; cattle graze on the hillsides, and cornfields slant steeply into narrow valleys.

CAMDEN, 5.8 *m.* (1,095 alt., 72 pop.) was named in honor of Richard P. Camden, uncle of U. S. Senator Johnson N. Camden, for whom the town of Camden in Webster County was later named; it became necessary to add '-on-Gauley' to the name of the second town (*see Tour 9*).

STEWART CREEK HILL, 18.5 *m.* (1,120 alt.), overlooks (R) a narrow valley, bordered with smoothly furrowed hills. Orchard trees appear far below in orderly rows like plants in a cabbage patch.

GLENVILLE, 28 m. (734 alt., 799 pop.), the seat of Gilmer County, is a college town and an agricultural trading center on the banks of the Little Kanawha River. Views from the surrounding hills inspired Mrs. D. H. King in 1885 to write:

> Oh! the West Virginia Hills!
> How majestic and how grand,
> With their summits bathed in glory
> Like our Prince Immanuel's land!
> Is it any wonder then
> That my heart with rapture thrills
> As I stand once more with loved ones
> On those West Virginia Hills?

This and three more verses in a similarly rapturous vein were set to music by H. D. Engle of Braxton County, and are now sung at public gatherings in lieu of an official State song. A minor battle in the War between the States was fought here; on TANK HILL, overlooking the town, are the remains of Union trenches.

The GLENVILLE STATE TEACHERS COLLEGE crowns a hill overlooking the business section. Founded in 1872 to relieve overcrowding at Marshall College (see Huntington), the school, which is coeducational, has grown until its present enrollment exceeds 400 students. The smoothly graded hilltop campus encircles ADMINISTRATION HALL, a two-story brick building erected in 1911, in which are classrooms, laboratories, and the administration offices. KANAWHA HALL and VERONA MAPEL HALL house women students, and contain kitchens, dining rooms, and a laundry. The ROBERT F. KIDD LIBRARY has more than 15,000 volumes. Among other brick structures are the GYMNASIUM, center of physical education work, with a seating capacity of 500; FIRESTONE LODGE, built in 1930, a club-dormitory for men; and a new men's dormitory, completed in 1937. A 122-acre farm, acquired for agricultural demonstration work, furnishes foodstuffs for the dormitory kitchens.

Southwest of Glenville the highway ascends the steep grade of TOWN HILL (1,120 alt.), offering a view of the surrounding country.

NORMANTOWN HILL, 36.5 m. (1,103 alt.), overlooks neighboring ridges separated by narrow fertile valleys, dotted with clusters of trees and the roofs of scattered farmhouses. In NORMANTOWN, 8.5 m. (763 alt., 118 pop.), at the foot of the hill, is a two-story brick high school (L) serving pupils within a radius of seven miles.

LOCKNEY, 39.7 m. (725 alt., 77 pop.), is inhabited by a few retired farmers and the employees of the JONES COMPRESSOR STATION (L).

STUMPTOWN, 43.3 m. (715 alt., 86 pop.), a scattering of frame houses and filling stations, is strung along the road for a mile. Here LITTLE BEAR FORK flows into Steer Creek; the highway follows the course of Little Bear Fork, which swells during heavy rains into a turbulent muddy river and occasionally overflows the road. Each of the neat farmhouses on the other side of the stream is linked to the road by its own homemade suspension bridge or footlog.

From SAND RIDGE, 49.4 *m.* (1,228 alt.), the highway overlooks (R) a deep wooded valley and steeply rising slopes.

MILLSTONE, 51.9 *m.* (803 alt., 39 pop.), consists of a crossroads store and several frame houses, surrounded by oil and gas derricks.

Millstone is a junction with State 16 (*see Tour 12*), which unites with US 33 for 1.7 miles.

ARNOLDSBURG, 53.6 *m.* (712 alt., 197 pop.), a crossroads hamlet, was deprived of its chief cause for existence in 1869 when the seat of Calhoun County was removed to Grantsville, leaving Arnoldsburg with a $15,000 stone foundation for the courthouse, which is still intact. No county in the State had more difficulty than Calhoun in establishing a seat. During the summer of 1857 opposing factions held rival courts in different towns. A frame courthouse was constructed at Brookville but never used. One young lawyer who moved to another county remarked that he had been 'broken up trying to keep up with the county court.' Arnoldsburg seemed to be a final choice, however; the court met here in 1858 and continued to do so for ten years. Work on the stone courthouse began, but only the basement was completed when the county seat was moved to Grantsville.

Arnoldsburg is at a junction with State 16 (*see Tour 12*).

LIBERTY HILL, 56.7 *m.* (1,064 alt.), overlooks grassy pasture slopes; from the summit the road descends between low embankments, now grassy, now wooded.

SPENCER, 68.4 *m.* (726 alt., 2,493 pop.), seat of Roane County is a prosperous small city with hilly, narrow, congested streets. On Fridays the congestion is greatly increased by flocks of sheep and herds of cattle being driven to the livestock market here. The many retired farmers and oil operators, who gather in small groups on street corners to discuss the world and politics, give the town a Saturday-night appearance even on weekdays. Spencer was originally known as Tanners Cross Roads for the first settler, Samuel Tanner, who lived in a cave near by in 1812. Later, Raleigh Butcher left his home on Reedy Creek with the loudly avowed intention of going to California, but he got no farther than the crossroads, which was christened New California in jest and incorporated under that name in 1858. It later assumed the Christian name of Judge Spencer Roane, for whom the county was also named.

The SPENCER STATE HOSPITAL (*open 1–4 p.m., Mon., Tues., Thurs., Sat.*), corner W. 2nd and State Sts., was authorized in 1887 to relieve overcrowded conditions at the Weston State Hospital (*see above*), but was not opened until 1893. Towers and cupolas surmount the four-story main building, which is connected by glass-enclosed bridges with two three-story ward buildings and a three-story dining annex. The solemn red brick buildings strung together in a straight line resemble battlements, pierced by iron-studded embrasures for arquebus and bow, defiantly rearing their bulk across the path of an invader. Other structures on the 184-acre tract, which overlooks the city, are a power house, conservatory, laundry, farm and work buildings, and cottages for the resident doctors and the superintendent. The institution cares for 900 patients.

West of Spencer US 33 circles through close-cropped pasture land, broken here and there by gas wells or compressor stations. Few crops are planted, as each farm has gas wells to provide the farmer a steady income. Fat, red-and-white Hereford beeves are driven along the roads to the livestock markets at Spencer, as are tawny Jerseys and spotted Guernseys, and heavy-flanked Scottish Ayrshires, white as the milk they give. Rich black earth in the creek bottoms is turned by plowshares drawn by magnificent workhorses, broad-shouldered Percherons and heavy-flanked Belgians, some of which weigh almost a ton. Split-rail fences divide the pasture land into even squares. The countryside exudes comfortable well-being and a sense of security based on the little black iron pipe mountings visible in the pasture lands, signs of throttled gas wells.

RIPLEY, 94.1 *m.* (615 alt., 669 pop.), seat of Jackson County, is built around the courthouse square, in the center of which is a gray stone pile, as square and as plain as an arsenal, with solid walls slit by narrow windows set in deep embrasures. From among tall elms rises the three-story courthouse, topped with a four-faced clock tower. A rubbish pile smolders on the lawn behind the courthouse steps, the flames consuming the chaff of the day's official business. Two- and three-story brick business houses, red, yellow, and tan, face the courthouse on three sides, and residences radiate from the square in all directions, up the sides and around the crown of the hill on which the town is built. Automobiles share the streets with droves of kine, heavy farm wagons, and an occasional oxcart. The clean fresh scent of broken earth pervades the town. Settled in 1768 by William John and Lewis Rogers, the village was established in 1832 and named for the Reverend Harry Ripley, who had drowned in Big Mill Creek in 1830.

West of Ripley the highway winds along the valley of Mill Creek, which it crosses several times, and over ridges that afford vistas of rounded wooded hills and small farms.

The EVANS FAIRGROUND (R), 96.6 *m.*, has show pavilions and a race track; the Jackson County Fair is held here annually for five days late in August. Adjoining the grounds is the Otterbein United Brethren Church.

COTTAGEVILLE, 104.6 *m.* (612 alt., 235 pop.), is well named although some of its houses attain two stories. An old gristmill on Mill Creek has been converted into a sawmill and makes use of the curved dam built in pioneer days.

The highway leaves the hills, 111 *m.*, and descends into the valley of the Ohio River. Large barns, herds of sleek cows, and clusters of shiny milk cans appear along the road; fields are dotted with blocks of white chickens, numerous haystacks, cornfields, orchards, and watermelon patches. Many of the farmhouses, usually two-story, bear the ginger-bread ornamentation of the last century. Sand and gravel dredges are frequently seen at work on the Ohio River.

From GRAHAM STATION, 118.8 *m.* (592 alt., 125 pop.), a quiet rural river landing, a ferry (25¢, *car and driver*) crosses the river to Racine, Ohio.

NEW HAVEN, 122.7 *m.* (590 alt., 562 pop.), now an agricultural trading village, was once the active center of the surrounding area of salt wells and coal mines opened about 1850. Mine owners named it for their home in Connecticut.

HARTFORD, 124.4 *m.* (570 alt., 423 pop.), does its washing with distilled water heated by the salt works in the town. After the salt has been extracted from the brine, the hot water is discharged into a metal drum, from which it is taken by townspeople, often in 20-gallon milk cans. The second salt well in the Pomeroy Bend of the Ohio River, or just The Bend as it is locally known, was drilled here in 1854. When incorporated in 1868, the town was named for their home in Connecticut by Morgan Buckley and William Healey, who had investments here. Generations of salt makers have lived here, and townspeople still speak with pride of their 'salty' salt.

The LIVERPOOL SALT WORKS (L), one of the few in operation in the State, operates 5 wells, pumping brine from salt sands ranging in depth from 900 to 1,200 feet. Operations of the SALT FURNACE (*open*) are a study in slow motion, for they are necessarily synchronized to the rate of precipitation of salt from brine. Mud is 'settled out' in settling tanks; bromine and calcium, two important by-products, are removed by the next operation; then the brine is run into seven long, narrow, graining tanks and heated by steam in copper pipes; the best grade of fine salt is produced at a temperature of 180°. Coal for the furnaces is mined near by and hauled here in horse-drawn cars. Crystalline salt, like thin ice, forms on the surface of the steaming brine, then sinks to the bottom. A series of copper cleats on an endless belt propels the precipitated salt along the bottom of the tanks to an incline which leads to a conveyor. The conveyor is steam heated, and the salt is dried as it moves slowly to a bin, from which in turn it is shoveled into barrels. The final product is a salt so strong and concentrated that it is fatal if consumed by beast or man; it is used for glazing tile and brick, and in certain types of road surfacing. Coarse unrefined salt, crystallized into chunks weighing as much as 20 pounds, is sold to farmers of the countryside for their livestock.

MASON, 127.3 *m.* (580 alt., 691 pop.), is the trading center of the apple, tobacco, and dairy area in The Bend; some of its people work in the salt furnaces and coal mines round about Pomeroy, a town of spires and smokestacks etched against a cliff on the Ohio side of the river.

Laid out in 1852 by coal operators, who shipped their products by boat as far as Baton Rouge, Mason was incorporated in 1856, the year in which the first salt well was drilled and the first salt furnace began operations. The town was named for George Mason, a member of the convention that framed the Federal Constitution. After the War between the States a sawmill and a boatyard were established. Although Mason has gradually declined industrially, it remains an agricultural trading center.

US 33 crosses the OHIO LINE, 128.5 *m.*, at the western end of the POMEROY-MASON TOLL BRIDGE (*two-passenger car and driver, 25¢; five- to seven-passenger car and driver, 35¢; additional passengers, 5¢ each*), a graceful structure of gray fabricated steel, which spans the Ohio River to Pomeroy, Ohio (*see Ohio Guide*).

↗↗↗

Tour 8

(Redhouse, Md.)—Elkins—Huttonsville—Lewisburg—Ronceverte—Princeton; US 219.
Maryland Line to Princeton, 217.2 *m.*

Bituminous-macadam surface, with short stretches of concrete.
Western Maryland Ry. parallels route between Parsons and Huttonsville; Chesapeake & Ohio Ry. roughly parallels it between junction with State 28 and Ronceverte.
Tourist accommodations at short intervals, except between Ronceverte and Princeton; hotels in larger towns.

US 219, known in West Virginia as the Seneca Trail, closely follows the section of the Warriors Road that crossed the State. This was the route along which Indians traveled the wilderness from the St. Lawrence River to Georgia, long before the first white man made his way into what is now West Virginia; the formidable Seneca passed this way on their war expeditions against the Cherokee, their southern enemies. The route traversed a region known in the early history of Virginia as West Augusta, which in the dark days of the Revolution is said to have inspired George Washington to say, 'Leave me but a banner to plant upon the mountains of West Augusta, and I will gather around me the men who will lift our bleeding country from the dust and set her free.'

By the treaty negotiated at Albany in 1722 between Queen Anne and the Six Nations of the Iroquois, the highway marked the boundary between the territories of the whites and the Indians. Under the provisions of the treaty the Indians were forbidden to go east of the line under pain of being captured and sold into slavery in the West Indies. George III issued a proclamation in 1763 forbidding settlement west of the line by the adventurous Virginians and demanding the return of those already there, but the early pioneers ignored the proclamation and pushed on toward the Ohio; by so doing they became largely responsible for the long and bloody strife with the Indians. Bred to border conflict, the early settlers of this region filled the ranks of the Virginia militia that combatted the Indians, helped lower the tricolor of France in the Ohio Valley during the French and Indian Wars, and aided the Colonies in their struggle for independence.

The route is sometimes called the Skyline Tour, and is rich in natural beauty and historical associations.

Section a.   MARYLAND LINE to ELKINS, 45.2 m.   US 219.

This section of the Seneca Trail is a lofty route that passes through the northwestern part of the Monongahela National Forest. It crosses Backbone, Pheasant, and Cheat mountains, where on either hand views open across miles of wooded valleys and ridges; in spring, heavy fogs frequently shroud the mountain tops or fill the valleys like a ghostly sea. Along the route are wide buckwheat fields, bare mountains denuded of their timber, grimy coal camps, unspoiled woodlands, rocky gorges, and the city of Elkins, the commercial and railroad center of Tygarts Valley.

Near the close of the nineteenth century few richer stands of virgin timber existed in West Virginia than those that adorned the mountain and valleys now traversed by US 219 from the Maryland Line to Elkins. They had escaped wasteful exploitation by lumber kings and coal barons, in spite of the fact that the area was underlaid with rich deposits of bituminous coal. In 1884, from Piedmont near the Maryland Line to St. George near the present town of Parsons, a distance of 60 miles, there was no town or hamlet, and settlers were not close enough to be neighborly.

It was to tap these vast resources that the West Virginia Central Railroad was built, and untold wealth was reaped by its promoters. Coal is still mined in this area, but the wasteful methods of early lumbering have stripped it of its hardwood forests. Steel rails, log roads, steam engines, band saws, and other machinery marred the grandeur of the region; but the lumberjack, or wood-hick, was the human instrument of this ruthless drive. Physically as strong as the pine knots in the trees he felled, inured to the hardship of the woods, skillful, reckless, and goodhearted, he lived and worked in the lumber camps for months, and let his pay accumulate until he emerged for a brief period, dressed in picturesque garb, to spend his roll in a brief carouse at Cumberland or some other town. He played an important part in that hectic industrial era, but is now as extinct as the beautiful forests in which he worked.

Crossing the MARYLAND LINE, 0 *m.*, 2.2 miles south of Red-house, Maryland (*see Tour 4a*), US 219 enters a prosperous country-side of upland farms. White farmhouses and large red barns with groves of trees and well-kept yards about them stand in the midst of rolling fields of buckwheat. At 1.7 *m.* is (L) artificial SILVER LAKE (*cabins, swimming, canoeing*).

Here the highway gradually ascends BACKBONE MOUNTAIN through groves of oak and sumac to a commanding view of the region, 5.9 *m.* Even on hazy days nine mountain ranges can be seen rolling away to the horizon, like waves of a gigantic sea.

At 7.2 *m.* is the junction with a cindered road.

Left on this road into Maryland, 1 *m.;* R. from the bridge in Kempton on a footpath to the FAIRFAX STONE, 0.6 *m.*, which marks the boundary be-tween West Virginia and Maryland as determined by the U. S. Supreme Court after a dispute between the two states.

The original Fairfax Stone, a pyramid of sandstone bearing the letters 'F X,' stood one mile to the south. Placed in 1747–8, it marked the westernmost corner of Lord Fairfax's 6,000,000-acre grant, a kingdom in itself, one of the largest estates in the world.

THOMAS, 10.4 *m.* (2,986 alt., 1,660 pop.), a coal town and trad-ing center for surrounding mines, was founded in 1884 by U. S. Sen-ator Stephen B. Elkins (*see below*) and U. S. Senator Henry Gassa-way Davis; it was named for Colonel Thomas Davis, their associate in developing the mines of this area. Incorporated in 1892, Thomas was granted a city charter in 1926.

The highway by-passes the center of the city, which lies (L) across a small shallow stream, the North Fork of the Blackwater River. A shaft mine and a drift mine provide employment for a large propor-tion of the city, which has a heterogeneous population drawn from 18 countries—Poland, Hungary, Italy, Greece, Jugoslavia, Lithuania, among others. About 500,000 tons of bituminous coal are mined an-nually in the Thomas area. In the city is a Mine Rescue Station (*see Tour* 18).

Left from Thomas on State 32, which crosses a high flat tableland, thickly carpeted with coarse ferns; once heavily forested, the tableland was completely denuded by fires and timbering operations in the last half of the nineteenth century.

At 2.6 *m.* is the junction with a cindered road; R. on this road to a fork, 3.9 *m.*

1. Left from the fork 0.1 *m.* to a parking space in BLACKWATER FALLS STATE PARK, a leased area of 400 acres. Here the waters of Blackwater River drop over a broken ledge to dash among large boulders 63 feet below, whence they continue their rushing foaming course down Blackwater Canyon. A footpath leads (L) among thickets of laurel and hemlock to a clearing with a fine view of the rugged beauty of the falls and canyon.

2. Right from the fork 1 *m.* along the rim of BLACKWATER CANYON to a parking space (*picnicking facilities*), beside a headland overlooking the gorge. Rising 1,000 feet above the rushing stream, the sheer green-clad walls are crowned with jagged crests of rock and cut by steep ravines down which small streams cascade to join the river. The Blackwater River, named for the

dark hue of its waters acquired in running through coal beds and laurel thickets, winds down the gorge in a series of rapids and cascades, falling 1,350 feet in 10 miles.

DAVIS, 2.8 m. (3,100 alt., 1,656 pop.), the highest town in the State, was founded by U. S. Senator Henry G. Davis, his brother, and other associates in 1883, and named for his family. It had its beginning as a lumber town, but is now the center of large coal operations.

Henry Gassaway Davis represented West Virginia in the United States Senate from 1871 until 1883. In 1904 he was nominated by the Democratic Party as vice president of the United States. Almost entirely self-educated, a brakeman on the Baltimore & Ohio Railroad in 1842 when he was 20 years of age, Davis later became a passenger conductor between Baltimore and Cumberland, Maryland, and was responsible for running the first night train in the United States in 1848, according to railroad records. Davis's superiors had misgivings about the hazardous experiment but gave him authority to try. A curious crowd, mostly skeptics and scoffers, gathered at Cumberland to see the night train start on what they believed would be a disastrous journey. The train moved off in charge of Davis, and although it was necessary to make frequent stops while the brakeman walked ahead to arouse sleeping cows or to remove stones from the track, the trip was completed in safety. After this trip a regular night schedule was maintained.

Davis's appreciation of the industrial and commercial possibilities of the section of West Virginia between Piedmont and Elkins led him to enter the coal and lumber business. He was later associated with his son-in-law, U. S. Senator Stephen B. Elkins (see below), in building railroads and conducting other business enterprises. One of the wealthiest men in the State, he died at the age of 93, and his kindliness and many charities have preserved his name as 'West Virginia's Grand Old Man.'

From the summit of CANAAN MOUNTAIN (3,702 alt.), 6.4 m., the highway overlooks the fertile and beautiful oval basin of CANAAN VALLEY, named for one of the most luxuriant spots described in the Bible. The local valley has been celebrated in the Blackwater Chronicle of Philip Pendleton Kennedy, illustrated by General David Hunter Strother, who wrote under the pen name of Porte Crayon (see Berkeley Springs). Strother, on his exploration of this region in the 1850's, described it as 'so savage and inaccessible that it has rarely been penetrated, even by the most adventurous. The settlers on its borders speak of it with a sort of dread, and regard it as an ill-omened region, filled with bears, panthers, impassable laurel brakes, and dangerous precipices.' Laurel grew so thick that one could walk on it as on a carpet. Not until a forest fire in 1865 cleared out the tangled growth did the settlement of this fertile valley begin.

At 15.4 m. is the junction of State 32 with State 28 (see Tour 6b).

US 219 again ascends Backbone Mountain, and at 19 m. a magnificent panorama of mountain country spreads out before the traveler.

At 20.5 m. is the junction with an improved dirt forest road (open only on Sundays).

Left on this road is the BACKBONE MOUNTAIN FIRE TOWER (3,800 alt.), 1.5 m., affording a 40-mile view in all directions over forested mountaintops.

At 22.9 m. is the junction with a cindered road.

Left on this road 0.2 m. to a U. S. FOREST SERVICE NURSERY, which grows planting stock for the seven national forests in the eastern region: the White Mountain National Forest in New Hampshire and Maine, the Green Mountain in Vermont, the Allegheny in Pennsylvania, the George Washington in Virginia and West Virginia, the Jefferson in Virginia, the Monongahela in West Virginia, and the Cumberland in Kentucky. Some 3,500,000 seedlings are grown here annually for transplantation, a sufficient number to plant from 3,500 to 4,000 acres. Each forest gathers its own seeds of stock adapted to the climatic, soil, and biotic peculiarities of the region, and sends them to the nursery, where they are cleaned, labeled, and stored for sowing in the spring and fall.

The seed is sown in prepared beds, 4 feet wide and 100 feet long; after one year in the seed beds, such hardwood or broadleaf species as red oak, tulip poplar, black cherry, and white ash are ready for transplantation. The coniferous or evergreen trees are carefully cultivated in the seed beds for two years, after which time they are sorted and transplanted in rows about a foot apart and at intervals of two inches, to stimulate fuller root growth and the development of the proper root-top ratio. After another year the young evergreens are transported to the various national forests in the eastern region. The transplanted stock in the national forests is predominantly evergreen; red spruce, Norway spruce, and red pine, for example, account for 95 per cent of the trees planted in the Monongahela National Forest.

PARSONS, 25 *m*. (1,649 alt., 2,012 pop.), seat of Tucker County, boomed as a lumber town in the 1880's; when the boom subsided, tanneries and woolen mills were established, and these remain its chief support.

The BATTLE OF CORRICK'S FORD MONUMENT stands (R) on the courthouse lawn. On July 13, 1861, Union forces overtook Confederates retreating from Laurel Hill (*see Tour* 22) and routed them in a fierce battle fought south of the town. General Robert S. Garnett, Confederate commander, was wounded, and after the battle died in the arms of the Union general, Thomas A. Morris, who had been a classmate at West Point.

Right from Parsons on State 72, concrete-paved, to ST. GEORGE, 6.5 *m*. (1,553 alt., 200 pop.), the site of a fort built in 1772 by John Minear and others. They abandoned it in 1774 because of Indian attacks, but returned two years later to settle permanently. James Parsons, for whom the town of Parsons was named, visited the region in 1763 and patented land here. St. George was the seat of Tucker County until 1893 when it was supplanted by Parsons. The removal was accomplished by an armed guard without bloodshed, although plans had been made by men of St. George to defend the county records with their lives.

PORTERWOOD, 27.5 *m*. (1,687 alt., 30 pop.), an agricultural hamlet, was awakened from its doldrums in 1927 when 'gold' was discovered near by and caused considerable excitement. A gold rush developed but ended abruptly when the State geologist identified the nuggets as iron pyrites, 'fool's gold,' and added that if gold ever was discovered in West Virginia, it would be in such small quantities that its recovery would be unprofitable.

South of Porterwood the highway winds upward among hilly farmlands and pastures on PHEASANT MOUNTAIN (2,239 alt.). A marker (L), 32.6 *m*., indicates where the old Seneca Trail was joined by its eastern branch.

ELKINS, 45.2 *m*. (1,930 alt., 7,345 pop.), seat of Randolph County, lies in a shallow, bowl-shaped valley at a five-mile bend in the Tygarts Valley River. The main part of the town extends from the north bank of the river up the gentle slopes of Cheat Mountain. The business district extends northward from the river and is flanked on the south by the Western Maryland Railway tracks, shops, and yards. Covering a block near the center of the town is a municipal park, shaded by large stands of virgin oak and maple. Solid Victorian houses surrounded by large grounds evidence the timber and railroad fortunes invested in the building of Elkins.

Before 1889 the settlement was a scattered rural community known as Leadsville, having a mill and a country store. Farmers in the upper Tygarts Valley loaded their corn in boats, floated them down to the mill, and then paddled back home. When the main line of the Western Maryland Railway reached Leadsville, yards and shops were established. A town was laid out; in 1890 it was incorporated and renamed for U. S. Senator Stephen Benton Elkins, son-in-law of U. S. Senator Henry Gassaway Davis (*see above*), who together promoted the railroad and other local enterprises.

Strongly built, rugged of feature, aggressive in manner, Elkins played a commanding role in the industrial and political history of West Virginia. Railroad magnate, coal baron, banker, lumber king, astute and powerful politician, he was Secretary of War (1888–92) under President Benjamin Harrison. With an office in the Wall Street district in New York City, an impressive mansion in Washington, and a country house on a high hill here dominating the town named for him, he was the unquestioned boss of the dominant party in the State and stood high in its national councils. To Elkins, as chairman of the powerful Interstate Commerce Committee of the Senate, President Theodore Roosevelt entrusted a bill to increase the authority of the Interstate Commerce Commission in the matter of regulating railroad rates. The bill passed the House, but Elkins refused to sponsor it in the Senate. By articles and speeches Roosevelt so aroused the people about the evil practices of the railroads that Elkins, seeing the handwriting on the wall, made one of his celebrated about-faces, remarking tersely that when the 'political horse is running away,' he preferred to be 'on the seat with the driver, ready to grab the reins.'

The construction of the railroad soon made Elkins a terminus for feeder lines that penetrated the surrounding coal and timber regions; the local lumber industry attracted a tannery and several woodworking plants. The completion in 1905 of the Coal and Coke Railroad between Elkins and Charleston accelerated the city's growth, and it has become an important wholesale and retail center for numerous coal and lumber towns in the region.

Elkins was made the county seat of Randolph County in 1900 after a three-year conflict with Beverly. Pending a decision on the matter by the State Supreme Court, groups of armed men in each town drilled to defend their respective claims by physical force. Breastworks were constructed by the Beverly group, and a special train was drawn up at the Elkins station to make an attack on Beverly, but bloodshed was averted by an address by C. Wood Dailey, chief counsel for the Western Maryland Railway.

Occupying a rolling 60-acre campus of native woodland and land-scaped grounds in the northeastern part of town, once the estates of Senator Davis and Senator Elkins, is DAVIS AND ELKINS COLLEGE, a Presbyterian coeducational institution, with an enrollment of 450 students, granting degrees of bachelor of arts and of science. HALLIHURST, formerly the Elkins home, a women's dormitory, is a gray frame structure designed like an English castle; it stands on the crest of a lofty ridge and overlooks the surrounding countryside, with Rich Mountain (R) and Cheat Mountain (L). The social center of college life, the mansion has large comfortable rooms and a splendid dining service. LIBERAL ARTS HALL, a large brick structure, contains the library, class-rooms, and the offices of the president, treasurer, and registrar. The library on the second floor has a large and well-lighted reading room adjoining the stacks, which contain 17,500 volumes. SCIENCE HALL, of stone and brick, houses laboratories and the Music Department and has an auditorium seating 500. The KELLY OBSERVATORY, built in the spring of 1928 by the Chi Beta Phi Scientific Fraternity of the College, occupies the crest of a hill adjoining the campus. Walls 8 feet high support a revolving dome 5 feet high, with a 3-foot aperture. The telescope is of the Newtonian reflecting type, with a focal length of 90 inches and a 10-inch mirror, and is mounted on a 5-foot pedestal with equatorial mounting; it is clock-driven.

GRACELAND, a pink sandstone structure of Norman design, occupies a spacious maple-shaded lawn adjoining the north edge of the campus; it was erected in 1892 by Senator Davis and named for his daughter, Grace.

The front campus, a grassy carpet of 10 acres overlooking Elkins, is the scene of the Mountain State Forest Festival held annually during the first week of October, which attracts thousands of visitors. The principal events are the crowning of Queen Silvia, the reception of 'forest princesses' representing the congressional districts of the State, the Queen's Ball, and an elaborate parade of floats. The program includes contests in tilting at rings on horseback, in wood-chopping, and in marksmanship with muzzle-loading rifles by mountaineers 60 years of age or over.

Elkins is at the junction with US 33 (*see Tour 7a*).

Section b. ELKINS to LEWISBURG, 107 m. US 219.

US 219 ascends gradually along the course of the Tygarts Valley past the sites of the first settlements in this wooded and mountainous region. It parallels the western boundary of the Monongahela National Forest for a short distance and then enters the forest. Passing over mountainous terrain, it descends to the limestone hills and fertile meadows of the lower Greenbrier Valley, the 'country of the Big Levels.' On the large stock farms here the leisurely life and traditions of the South still persist; life in the valley contrasts sharply with the strenuous struggle for existence on the small rough farms that appear to hang on the mountain sides along other parts of the route.

South of ELKINS, 0 *m.*, US 250 (*see Tour 22a*) is united with US 219 for 17.5 miles.

HARPER FIELD (R), 2 *m.*, is the Elkins municipal airport, a regular stop for American Airlines planes.

A monument (R) indicates the approximate SITE OF WILSON'S FORT, erected in 1774 by Captain Benjamin Wilson, who accompanied Braddock on his disastrous campaign against the French and Indians; after the Revolution, Wilson was given command of all military forces in northwestern Virginia. A cornerstone of the vanished fort tops the monument.

BEVERLY, 5.6 *m.* (1,973 alt., 431 pop.), the oldest town in Tygarts Valley, was settled by Robert Files and his family in 1753. A few months after the family's arrival, the Indians massacred all but one boy, who escaped to Virginia with relatives from the neighboring settlement. After the massacre no settlement was attempted until 1774, when six Westfall brothers constructed a fort at the mouth of Files Creek.

Beverly wears the garment of its past with dignity. Houses built in the last decade of the eighteenth century stand side by side with modern structures along its shady streets. Townfolk point with pride to the old white houses, many of which hide original log structures of pioneer days under a shell of frame siding. Deeply recessed windows indicate the thickness of the walls in the old log buildings.

In the public square a boulder brought from the Rich Mountain Battlefield (*see below*) bears a bronze plaque listing Beverly's historic sites and presenting a brief summary of the Battle of Rich Mountain. On a knoll in MOUNT ISER CEMETERY stands a slender shaft erected by the United Daughters of the Confederacy in memory of the Confederate dead buried here under the grassy remains of Union trenches.

Right from Beverly on an unimproved road, once part of the Staunton-Parkersburg Turnpike, now known as the Crozet Memorial Road, named in honor of Colonel Claudius Crozet, who as chief engineer of Virginia directed its construction (1824–47) and also that of the Northwestern Turnpike, now US 50. An officer under Napoleon, Crozet fled to America after the emperor's downfall, taught in the U. S. Military Academy at West Point, and was one of the founders of the Virginia Military Institute.

The Tygarts Valley River is spanned by a COVERED BRIDGE, 0.1 *m.*, one of many built by Lemuel Chenoweth of Beverly. The present bridge was built in 1873 to replace an earlier Chenoweth structure burned during the War between the States. Although records in Richmond credit Lewis Wernwag with having designed the wooden-arch type of covered bridge, a story current in West Virginia relates that Chenoweth, a cabinet-maker by trade and a student of mathematics, arrived in Richmond in 1850 with a model of his bridge packed in his saddle bags. Before the Board of Public Works of the Commonwealth of Virginia, then considering bids for the construction of bridges on the Staunton-Parkersburg Turnpike, Chenoweth assembled his model, 'made of poplar, and nary a nail in 'er.' He suspended the frail-looking toy between two chairs, stood upon it, and challenged his competitors to put their models to such a test. That he won the contract through this test has been disputed, but he did build many covered bridges in West Virginia between 1851 and his death in 1884. Modern concrete and steel structures have replaced some; rerouting of highways has relegated others to secondary roads; but almost all lasted through three-quarters of a century of constant service, and those still standing remain sound.

RICH MOUNTAIN BATTLEFIELD, 5 m., was the scene of a decisive battle on July 11, 1861, when Union troops under General George B. McClellan made a flank attack on a fortification here and routed the Confederates with heavy losses. General Robert Garnett, who commanded this force and a larger one at Laurel Hill, had been ordered to stop McClellan's advance, but after this defeat he withdrew both forces, leaving the State, as far as the crest of the Alleghenies, open to Federal troops. The battlefield is now a boulder-strewn hillside; an apple orchard surrounds the gray and sagging ruin of the HART HOUSE, built by Joseph Hart, son of a Signer of the Declaration of Independence, and used as an emergency hospital during the battle that raged around it. The weathered walls are bullet-scarred, and the massive hewn timbers of the ruined barn near by have been marked by souvenir hunters digging leaden slugs from the heavy poplar beams. On one of the boulders is a rough and almost obliterated inscription reputedly left by a wounded soldier in memory of a friend: 'Clay Jackson, shot and killed, 1861.'

A small stone marker, 8.3 m., indicates the SITE OF THE DAVID TYGART CABIN, the first in the valley, built in 1753 when Tygart crossed the mountains with Robert Files, a brother-in-law, who settled on the site of Beverly (*see above*). The little clearing about the cabin on the river bank later became a burial ground and is now known as HORNBECK CEMETERY, for Benjamin Hornbeck, Revolutionary War soldier, who is buried here with scores of pioneer settlers.

TYGARTS VALLEY HOMESTEADS (L), 11.4 m. (1,957 alt., 900 pop.), one of the three homestead projects undertaken in West Virginia by the Federal Government, was established in 1933 on a 2,883-acre tract. Shutdowns in the lumber mills had impoverished many families engaged in this and allied industries. The project, designed to give these stranded families the security of homes and employment, provides 195 family dwelling units, each with one to three acres of ground. The houses are grouped on three separate tracts surrounded by farm land. Eight types of frame houses have been built and a few brick houses of four, five, and six rooms. Each house has modern plumbing and electricity and a combination garage, vegetable cellar, poultry house, and feed room. Gas and telephone have been installed in some of the units. Fire protection is provided by a volunteer fire department, two new fire engines, and numerous fire hydrants. The trade center has a general store, a craft shop displaying woven articles, a health center, and playgrounds; a community center has been constructed to serve as a public school. The National Youth Administration operates weaving and woodwork shops, and the Work Projects Administration conducts a nursery school. Homesteaders attend religious services at near-by churches.

At present (1941) the homesteaders occupy their houses under a temporary rental agreement, paying from $11.80 to $13.50 monthly against the final purchase price. They derived their income at first from the construction and development of the project. As the site was settled, homesteaders organized the Tygarts Valley Association, which has charge of all industrial enterprises. Chief among these is the dimension-stock lumber mill, designed to employ 90 men and to cut 10,000,000 feet of timber a year, half the annual output of the Monongahela National Forest and of private sources in the region. Another important enterprise is the co-operative farm, on which livestock, feed crops, potatoes, the principal cash crop, are raised. Other co-operative enterprises include a rock and lime quarry employing 30 men, a large potato warehouse, a general store, filling station and garage, restaurant, beauty shop, and barber shop. Homesteaders grow their own vegetables and fruits in individual gardens.

The homesteaders have formed numerous clubs and social organizations; two of these provide recreation and study for adult women; there are two 4-H clubs for boys and girls between the ages of 10 and 18, health and burial associations, a recreational and music organization, which sent a group to the National Folk Festival, and a Fair association, which sponsored the first annual Tygarts Valley Fair in September 1938.

MILL CREEK, 16.5 *m.* (2,013 alt., 723 pop.), occupies the SITE OF FORT CURRENCE, built in 1774 by William Currence, who operated a gristmill here. The stockade stood a short distance southeast of the present railroad station (R). Currence was killed by Indians at Elkhart (*see below*) in 1790 while on his way to Fort Hadden.

In HUTTONSVILLE, 17 *m.* (2,030 alt., 303 pop.), an agricultural village near the head of Tygarts Valley, a ROADSIDE FIRST AID STATION stands at the junction with US 250 (*see Tour 22a*).

South of Huttonsville, US 219 continues to follow the narrowing Tygarts River Valley.

ELKWATER, 22.8 *m.* (2,150 alt., 305 pop.), occupies the site of a fort erected about 1774 by the Hadden family. Brisk fighting took place here during the War between the States. A Federal trench, which appears at first glance to be an ordinary drainage ditch, intersects the road near the center of the village; near by (R) is a granite MONUMENT TO COLONEL JOHN AUGUSTINE WASHINGTON, aide-de-camp to General Robert E. Lee and grandnephew of George Washington, who was shot from his horse and killed here on September 13, 1861.

At VALLEY HEAD, 31 *m.* R., is a graveled dirt road to Kumbrabow State Forest (2,400 alt., 91 pop.), headquarters for many fishermen and hunters seeking sport in the Monongahela National Forest.

In the hamlet a ROADSIDE FIRST AID STATION marks the junction with State 15 (*see Tour 9*).

MINGO, 35.6 *m.* (2,650 alt., 300 pop.), named for the Mingo Indians who once had a village here, is a widely scattered community with cabins and small houses straggling along the road and back into the hollow between the mountains.

On CHEAT MOUNTAIN (3,478 alt.), 40.8 *m.*, the highway passes through a choppy wilderness of second-growth timber, with the view restricted to brief vistas of deep narrow valleys. On the lower slopes of MIDDLE MOUNTAIN (R), 43.9 *m.*, General Robert E. Lee maintained his headquarters during the summer of 1861 while his army was guarding the road to the south. On VALLEY MOUNTAIN (R) are embankments and trenches constructed by the Confederate soldiers.

The INDIAN MAGIC RING (R), 52.6 *m.*, is a circular space more than 130 feet in diameter, covered with a sort of prairie grass that has not spread from the circle and will not grow in any other place, according to local tradition. The ring appeared when the field was cleared about 1860, at which time it was well defined, but it has since grown so dim that it can be seen only in certain lights. Old-timers report that the circle represented two snakes swallowing each other— the Indian symbol for time—and believe that it marked the site of an old ceremonial ground.

RED LICK MOUNTAIN (3,533 alt.), 57.5 *m.*, overlooks (L) the low rolling hills of the Greenbrier Valley, with higher and more rugged mountains in the distance. Red Lick Spur is locally known as Elk Mountain, possibly because it divides the Greenbrier River's drainage area from that of the Elk River. The blue crests of the Allegheny Mountains (L) form a rampart along the horizon, while (R) Gauley Mountain and wooded Yew Mountain rise near by.

EDRAY (L), 59.8 *m.* (2,409 alt., 125 pop.), occupies the SITE OF FORT DRENNEN, a small stockade named for Thomas Drennen, who settled here in 1774. His cabin was attacked by Indians, his wife killed, and his little son taken captive. Drennen joined General Lewis's expedition against the Indians, fought in the Battle of Point Pleasant (*see Tour* 14), and after the war wandered through the Northwest fighting Indians. Many years later he found his son, who had been ransomed by a trader, and returned with him to the settlement.

At 61.8 *m.* is the junction with a dirt road.

Right on this road to the MARLINTON STATE TROUT HATCHERY, 0.5 *m.*, where 2,500,000 brook trout are hatched annually.

An old TOLL HOUSE (R), 64.4 *m.*, a small frame structure now used as a restaurant, was built in 1852 at the time of the construction of the Huttonsville-Marlinton Turnpike, and tolls were collected here from horsemen and wagons as late as 1896. General Robert E. Lee had temporary headquarters here in 1861.

The toll house is at the junction with State 28 (*see Tour* 6*b*).

MILL POINT, 72.6 *m.* (2,217 alt., 85 pop.), was named for a number of water-driven mills which pioneers erected here. The OLD MCNEEL MILL (R), on the bank of Stamping Creek, was built by Isaac McNeel about 1868 and still operates, driven by an overshot wheel. Stephen Sewell, an early settler, camped near by in a cave in 1750 after his quarrel with Jacob Marlin (*see Tour* 6*b*).

At 73.6 *m.* is the junction with an improved dirt road.

Left on this road to WATOGA STATE PARK, 2 *m.*, reached by a ferry (*free*) across the Greenbrier River. This largest of West Virginia's parks embraces 10,962 acres of forested mountain land. None of its rugged beauty has been spoiled in developing recreational facilities (*picnic grounds; camp sites; hiking and riding trails; furnished cabins $10 a week and up, on application to State Conservation Commission*). The park, a game refuge, shelters deer, grouse, squirrels, and wild turkey. Island Lick Run has been dammed to form a 12-acre lake (*trout, bass, bluegills*).

A large frame house with two-story portico (R), 74.7 *m.*, is the BIRTHPLACE OF PEARL BUCK, author of many novels, including *The Good Earth* and other stories of Chinese life. She was born here in the home of her maternal grandparents, the Stultings, whom her missionary parents were visiting while on leave from China. The Stultings, emigrants from Holland, erected the house in 1858 and took great pains in building 'a goodly twelve-room house of wood, with smooth floors and plastered and papered walls, a city house,' as Pearl Buck has described it. 'The wood they took from their own lands and such of the labor as they could not supply themselves, they exchanged.'

HILLSBORO, 74.8 *m.* (2,302 alt., 220 pop.), was settled in 1765 by John McNeil and Jacob and Charles Kinnison. McNeil had fled to the wilderness under the impression that he had killed a man in a boxing match; on a hunting and exploring expedition the Kinnisons discovered him and assured him that, as his opponent had not been badly hurt, he could safely return home. McNeil had decided to establish a settlement, however, and persuaded the Kinnisons to stay with him. During the War between the States, armies of both sides marched through the village. After raiding Salem, Virginia, General William W. Averell camped here in 1863 before the Battle of Droop Mountain (*see below*).

Right from Hillsboro on graveled road to LOBELIA, 7.8 *m.* (2,505 alt., 64 pop.), a cluster of houses around a dilapidated post office and general store.

1. Right from Lobelia on a dirt road (*impassable for cars beyond 2.3 m.*) to EAGLE FARM, 3.3 *m.*, a half-mile beyond which (*inquire for directions at farm*) is the first of the FALLS OF HILLS CREEK, reached by a stiff climb along a hillside path. Here in a wooded rugged ravine the rushing mountain stream plunges over a ledge in a fall of 60 feet, dropping like a veil across the mouth of a shallow cave; upstream are two more falls, one of 30 and the other of 20 feet. Like others in this limestone region, Hills Creek disappears into the side of Droop Mountain about two miles southeast of Lobelia.

2. Left from Lobelia 1.1 *m.* on a dirt road to the junction with an improved dirt road (*impassable after heavy rains*); L. here to the BRIERY KNOB FIRE TOWER (4,518 alt.), 4.9 *m.*, from which appears a magnificent vista of wooded mountaintops, green cultivated valleys, and distant blue ranges.

South of Hillsboro the highway ascends steadily and reaches the northern entrance to DROOP MOUNTAIN BATTLEFIELD STATE PARK, 79 *m.*, a State recreation area embracing 265 acres of mountaintop (*picnic shelters, overnight cabins*). The park commemorates the battle fought here on November 6, 1863, in which Union forces commanded by General William W. Averell defeated a Confederate army led by General John Echols, crushing the last serious Southern resistance in the State. Footpaths constructed by CCC workers lead to the graves, breastworks, and monuments that dot the battlefield.

Right from the park entrance on an improved dirt road to the DROOP MOUNTAIN OBSERVATION TOWER, 0.1 m., overlooking a wide expanse of mountain and valley. On early spring and fall days the higher peaks are often wreathed with clouds, while the lower slopes are pink and white with redbud and dogwood, or ablaze with autumn foliage.

From the summit of Droop Mountain (3,060 alt.), the highway winds down through fields in which appear outcroppings of blue limestone. In spring, the misty green pastures are thickly sprinkled with gleaming yellow buttercups.

RENICK, 89.8 m. (1,901 alt., 355 pop.), also known as Falling Spring for the streams that issue from the hills near by and flow into the Greenbrier River, was settled by William Renick and Captain Robert McClanahan in 1769. The village is the trading center of an agricultural and cattle-raising section and has a small limestone quarry and crushing plant.

The old RENICK HOUSE (R) was built by William Renick about 1760, near the point where Culberson Creek emerges from a hillside and rushes down a small narrow ravine. A rectangular two-story structure of limestone, the main house contains the original crude handhewn mantels above the fireplace. The brick wing, with two-story portico, was later added at the northern end of the house. Back of the house is an old Negro graveyard in which only one tombstone remains standing; numerous shallow depressions mark the graves of family slaves.

FRANKFORD, 95.5 m. (2,250 alt., 140 pop.), a country village that has outlived a promising youth, was settled in 1769 by companions of Renick and Captain McClanahan (see above), and was named for Frank Ludington, an early settler. In earlier days the village was a trading center and the site of Frankford Academy.

The LUDINGTON HOUSE, erected in the first decade after settlement, stands two doors (L) from the general store. Refinished with a thick coat of stucco and paint, the old log house appears to be the newest in the village.

LEWISBURG, 107 m. (2,084 alt., 1,293 pop.) (see Tour 15a), is at the junction with US 60.

Section c. LEWISBURG to PRINCETON, 65 m. US 219.

South of LEWISBURG, 0 m., the Seneca Trail passes through the southern limestone and bluegrass region, crosses a tip of Virginia along the New River, and traverses a countryside of small farms and dense woodland to the edge of the smokeless coal field.

The GREENBRIER VALLEY FAIRGROUND (L), 2.1 m., is the scene each year during the last week of August of the Greenbrier Valley Fair, one of the largest and best-known fairs of the South. For more than 80 years it has attracted thousands of visitors. In the early days they came to view the wonderful, awe-inspiring Howe sewing machine and the first squeaking Edison phonograph—and still earlier, the prize-winning yearling that grew up to become General Robert E. Lee's war horse, Traveller (*see Tour 15b*). In 1938 it attracted more than 100,000 persons who came to see farm exhibits, purebred horses and cattle, canned goods, needlework in all forms, wood carving, basket weaving, quilting, baking of all kinds, health exhibitions, horseshoe pitching, sack races, croquet matches, trotting races, fireworks, and all the gaudy display and tin-pan whirr of carnival time, to which the magazine *Life* devoted many pages. The fair annually marks the homecoming of hundreds of Greenbrier County's sons and daughters.

RONCEVERTE (Fr., Greenbrier), 5 *m.* (1,663 alt., 2,254 pop.), in the narrow valley of the Greenbrier River, is the trading and railroad center of a small farming and stock-raising section. The development of highways and the growth of neighboring towns checked the growth of Ronceverte, which at one time seemed destined to become the metropolis of this part of the State.

About 1800 Thomas Edgar erected a gristmill on the site now occupied by the largest local industrial plant, the fourth mill to stand on the spot. With the coming of the Chesapeake & Ohio Railway in 1872, the quiet hamlet of a half-dozen farmhouses and a gristmill suddenly expanded into a brisk and noisy railroad town; above the whistling of locomotives came the scream of large bandsaws cutting lumber in a large sawmill. Over the protests of many who saw no need of adopting a foreign name, the town was incorporated in 1882 under its present name.

In the 1890's a large company was formed to build booms and a dam in the Greenbrier River, down which timber was floated at high water from the virgin forest tracts upstream. In the Ronceverte yards more than 20,000,000 feet of lumber were often stacked at one time. In 1908 the last log came down the Greenbrier, the mill was torn down, the dam was destroyed, and the booms and cribs have since fallen to pieces and rotted away.

A ROADSIDE DRINKING FOUNTAIN stands (R) at the south approach of the bridge that spans the GREENBRIER RIVER, 5.1 *m.* The highway ascends from the valley and pursues a winding course among the rolling grassy knolls and sinks of the limestone country.

At 8.9 *m.* is the junction with an improved dirt road.

Left on this road to ORGAN CAVE (*adm.* 50¢), 0.5 *m.*, known for more than a century. More than five miles of caverns and passages have been explored, but they are readily accessible for only a mile. Three-quarters of a mile from the entrance is the white stalactite formation for which the cave was named. The glistening columns resemble organ pipes in appearance and, when struck, produce notes of varying pitch. During the War between the States the cave was known as 'General Lee's Underground Powder Works'; 37 hoppers used at that time remain in one room of the cave.

At 16.2 *m.* is a junction (R) with State 3 (*see Tour* 16a), which unites with US 219 for 4.1 miles.

From the highway, 19.1 *m.*, is an excellent view (R) of SWOOPES KNOBS, a cluster of peaks rising high above the valley. On CALDERS KNOB (3,256 alt.) William Calder, a South Carolinian, built a mansion and a 100-foot tower, from which he optimistically hoped to be able to see his native State. Calder was an enthusiastic Secessionist, and on the night he received news that Fort Sumter had been fired on and captured, he celebrated by burning the tower.

WALNUT GROVE (R), 19.2 *m.*, almost hidden by a dense grove of walnut trees, a fine example of Colonial architecture, was built by Andrew Beirne, Sr., and later enlarged by his son Oliver; many distinguished guests, among them President Martin Van Buren, have been entertained here.

ELMWOOD (L), 19.6 *m.*, a red brick mansion, two stories high, has a white columned portico, with an angular pediment centered by a fanlight; over the arched doorway is a second-story balcony. The house sits among spreading elms well back from the road, at the top of a gentle slope near the northern edge of the little town of Union. Hugh Caperton, prominent in the early history of the Virginias, built Elmwood about 1838, and it was the scene of many brilliant social functions when Washington and old Virginia society sojourned in Monroe County. Upon the death of Hugh Caperton, Elmwood descended to his son, Allen T. Caperton, later a United States senator, who was born here.

UNION, 21 *m.* (2,070 alt., 331 pop.), seat of Monroe County, was settled in 1774 by James Alexander. When the county was formed in 1799, there was not so much as a village within its boundaries. Alexander donated the land for the courthouse and town site; in 1800 a courthouse was erected and a post office and a store were opened. Incorporated in 1868, Union retains much of the Old Dominion atmosphere; most of the houses along its heavily shaded streets date back to antebellum days. In a field (L) is a monument to the Confederate Veterans of Monroe County.

Union is at a junction (L) with State 3 (*see Tour* 16a).

SALT SULPHUR SPRINGS, 22.9 *m.* (1,800 alt., 62 pop.), an unincorporated hamlet, has (R) a stone store and church and (L) two stone dairy buildings, all erected in 1833.

SALT SULPHUR SPRINGS RESORT (L), 23.2 *m.*, a group of buildings on an 11-acre, tree-shaded tract in a shallow ravine cut by Indian Creek, was opened in 1823. The slave quarters and the main building, a two-story Colonial structure with a white-columned portico that extends the entire length of the front, were erected in 1820. In 1830 were added the two-story stone wings, with double porticoes, gable roofs, and triangular-framed, fan-shaped dormer windows. The hotel then contained 98 guest rooms, a spacious ballroom, and a dining room. Board walks, flanked with dense growths of shrubbery, crossed the landscaped lawn to the banks of Indian Creek and the three springs—the Salt Sulphur, the Sweet, and the Iodine. For years wealthy Southern families used to spend part of the summer at Old White (*see Tour 15a*) and the remainder at Old Sweet (*see Tour 16a*) or here at Salt Sulphur. Henry Clay and John C. Calhoun, President Monroe and President Van Buren, were guests at the resort, and Confederate leaders made it their headquarters during campaigns in this valley. After the war the popularity of Salt Sulphur declined. The hotel was closed about 1900 but was reopened in 1927, when the hotel and other buildings, although well preserved, were remodeled and modernized.

An old COVERED BRIDGE spans Indian Creek (R), 25 *m.*, along which the highway runs for eight miles. From the road the bridge appears to run directly into the hillside on the far side of the creek.

At 28.7 *m.* is the junction with an improved dirt road.

At 5.9 *m.* on this road, where it becomes a surfaced highway, is the junction with a dirt road.

Right on this dirt road 0.7 *m.* to LAUREL CREEK CAVE, into which Laurel Creek flows to reappear a half-mile west of Greenville (*see below*). In the cave is a massive stalactite known as 'the Drum,' and a large mound called 'Rocky Mountain.'

Left (straight ahead on the surfaced road) is GREENVILLE, 6 *m.* (1,702 alt., 517 pop.), west of which the surfaced highway again becomes an improved dirt road. Across Indian Creek, reached by a footbridge, is the SITE OF COOK'S FORT, 7 *m.*, erected in 1770 by Captain John Cook. More than an acre in extent, with four blockhouses, it was one of the largest of frontier forts.

At 7.1 *m.* on the improved road is the junction with a dirt road.

Left on this dirt road 0.6 *m.* to SALTPETER CAVE, an important source of saltpeter for Confederate armies during the War between the States. The cave has four entrances and three miles of passages.

Right (straight ahead on the improved road) is RED SULPHUR SPRINGS, 17.4 *m.* (1,532 alt., 60 pop.), which flourished a century ago as one of the popular health and social resorts of western Virginia. In 1832 a large hotel was erected here. In 1844 the license paid was only $35, indicating that fewer people came here than to many of the springs, and that they were, for the most part, people of limited means. During the War between the States the buildings were used as a Confederate hospital, after which the hotel was closed for several years. The property was bought by Levi P. Morton, vice president under President Benjamin Harrison, who in 1906 offered the springs and 10 acres to the State of West Virginia as a site for a tuberculosis sanatorium. The offer was declined and a site selected at Terra Alta (*see Tour 21*). The buildings and the spring pavilion have been torn down, but the springs are open to the public. They lie in a deep hollow at the mouth of a small tributary of Indian Creek; their popularity was based on the belief that the water, which forms a red jelly when acid is added, was helpful in the treatment of pulmonary complaints, especially tuberculosis.

Climbing gradually the highway follows DROPPING LICK CREEK, which cascades gently over many low ledges.

In PETERSTOWN, 44.9 *m.* (1,743 alt., 388 pop.), named for Christian Peters, who settled here in 1784, US 219 crosses Rich Creek, here the Virginia Line, and continues southwest through Virginia for 5.2 miles.

RICH CREEK, 47 *m*. (1,520 alt., 128 pop.), is at the junction with Virginia 8, which unites with US 219 for 3.5 miles.

The towering peak of ANGELS REST (3,600 alt.) looms (L) above a wide horseshoe bend in the New River. Within the bend lies the village of LURICH (1,530 alt., 70 pop.). Below the highway the Virginian Railway tracks cling to a narrow shelf at the base of the cliffs; across the river those of the Norfolk & Western closely follow the sweeping curve of the stream.

EMANUELS HOLLOW PARK (R), 47 *m*., an attractive picnic spot, is in a deep ravine through which a small stream tumbles noisily, with many falls and deep pools.

The highway crosses New River on a modern steel and concrete bridge into GLEN LYN, 49.6 *m*. (1,575 alt., 274 pop.), dominated by a large steam plant generating power for the electrified sections of the Virginian and the Norfolk & Western railways.

US 219 recrosses the Virginia Line, 49.9 *m*., and ascends to HALES GAP (1,787 alt.), 51.1 *m*., where the Virginian Railway emerges (L) from a tunnel under the highway.

OAKVALE, 55.3 *m*. (1,705 alt., 261 pop.), was originally named Frenchville for the first settler, Captain Napoleon French. Through thick woods and a dense growth of rhododendron the road turns (R) abruptly and climbs along Five Mile Creek, which falls noisily over numerous ledges. In a grove of willows (L), 62.5 *m*., is a picnic ground.

At 63.9 *m*. is the junction with State 44.

Right on State 44 to the top of a ridge, 3.6 *m*., from which appears (L) a sweeping view of hills dotted with a brown patchwork of small farms and the deep green of pine and hemlock groves; far beyond is the pale blue bulk of FLATTOP MOUNTAIN (3,566 alt.). At 4.1 *m*. is a view (R) across thickly wooded hills to EAST RIVER MOUNTAIN (3,480 alt.) on the Virginia Line.

ATHENS, 5.3 *m*. (2,596 alt., 628 pop.), was established in 1837 as Concord Church. When application was made for a post office in 1873, the name was changed to Athens. It was the seat of Mercer County from the close of the War between the States until 1869, when, after repeated unsuccessful attempts to have the county government restored to Princeton (*see below*), a group of citizens carried off the records under cover of darkness and returned them to Princeton, where they remain.

CONCORD STATE TEACHERS COLLEGE (L), established in 1872, occupies the top of a rounded knoll overlooking the countryside in all directions. The WOMEN'S DORMITORY is a two-story, red brick structure of modified Georgian Colonial style, as are the ADMINISTRATION BUILDING (L) and the GYMNASIUM (R). The maple-shaded drive, well-kept lawns, and rows of dark evergreens contrast pleasantly with the bright red and white of the halls. The college has on view (*apply at President's office*) a collection of more than 3,000 varieties of native plants, 80 varieties of algae from Lake Shawnee (*see Tour 10c*), and a number of birds and animals.

US 219 passes over the yards of the Virginian Railway, 64.5 *m*., in which stand long lines of cars loaded with coal. In the railway shops (R) are housed the monster steam locomotives that haul mile-long trains of 'black nuggets' eastward.

PRINCETON, 65 *m.* (2,450 alt., 6,955 pop.), seat of Mercer County and trade center of prosperous farming country, spreads over a high plateau surrounded by shelving mountains. Settled in 1826, a village government was organized in 1837. Two years later it became the seat of Mercer County, named for General Hugh Mercer, an officer in the Revolutionary War; the village was named for the battle at Princeton, New Jersey, in which Mercer was killed. By 1860 Princeton had 40 houses. Today it is a bustling section point on the Virginian Railway, which maintains repair shops here.

During the War between the States several engagements were fought near Princeton. In 1862 retreating Confederates under Captain Janifer set fire to the courthouse, which housed large quantities of supplies, and the entire town was burned. Princeton rebuilt itself slowly, and in 1874 a bank was organized by H. W. Straley to serve neighboring farmers. The facilities of the bank were rather primitive; the bank books and paper bills were kept in a hair-covered trunk that served as a safe; the till for coins was a large beaver hat. At night the directors divided the money among them and carried it home for safekeeping. On the day the opening of the bank was announced in the newspapers, together with the fact that it was incorporated for $25,000—a large sum for this section at the time—a well-dressed stranger walked into the crude bank building and introduced himself as a businessman to Judge David Johnson, the vice president. Johnson greeted him affably, offered him a cigar, and finally invited him to his house for dinner. After such hospitality the 'businessman,' Frank James, brother of the renowned Jesse, went back to his gang and reported that the bank was so insignificant that to rob it would be a reflection on their prowess.

In 1865 Judge Nathaniel Harrison of the Seventh Judicial District, generally disliked in Mercer County for his desertion of the Confederate cause during the war, rode into Princeton to hold court; receiving no invitation to alight, he rode on and opened court at Concord Church, later Athens (*see above*). At the close of the term of court 'in the forest,' agitation began for the permanent removal of the county seat to Concord. Five years of conflict followed. Elections were held; special acts of the legislature were secured, first by one party and then by the other; injunctions were obtained; special messengers raced on horseback from Princeton and Concord Church to the State Capital and back again. Finally, in 1869, Princetonians seized the records at Concord Church and returned with them in triumph, a forcible solution legalized in a special election in 1870, which Princeton won.

The MERCER COUNTY COURTHOUSE, Walker and Main Sts., of smooth Indiana limestone in neo-classic style, has interior walls of paneled black walnut. On the north and the south façade are carved stone friezes depicting the various occupations and industries of the county. The building is the fifth on the site. The first small brick structure, erected in 1839 when the county was formed, had to be replaced almost immediately because of faulty construction. The second was burned by Confederates; the third was burned soon after completion, presumably by someone awaiting trial; the fourth was replaced in 1931 with the present structure.

The SOLDIERS AND SAILORS MEMORIAL BUILDING, Main St. north of Courthouse Square, a yellow brick and limestone structure dedicated in 1931, its severe classic design relieved by four fluted Ionic columns supporting a high pediment, houses the Mercer County Library and the local post of the American Legion.

Princeton is at the junction with US 19 (*see Tour 10c*).

Tour 9

Valley Head—Webster Springs—Cowen—Camden-on-Gauley—Junction with US 19; 67 *m.*, State 15.

Baltimore & Ohio R.R. parallels route between Cowen and Camden-on-Gauley. Improved dirt roadbed for 26 miles west of Valley Head, passable only during dry season; bituminous-macadam and shale surfaced.
Accommodations limited.

State 15, literally a 'highway,' follows the lofty ridge of Point Mountain between Valley Head and Webster Springs. Winding through sparsely settled forest and cleared pasture lands, the highway overlooks dark narrow hollows and wooded spurs sloping downward into the deep valleys of Back Fork and Elk River. West of Webster Springs, the highway crosses the highlands of McGuire Mountain, passing occasional level fields and small villages.

State 15 branches west from US 219 (*see Tour 8c*) at VALLEY HEAD, 0 *m.* (2,400 alt., 91 pop.) (*see Tour 8c*).

Crossing the TYGARTS VALLEY RIVER, 0.1 *m.*, and RALSTON RUN, 1 *m.*, the highway begins a winding ascent of Point Mountain. Below (L) are cut-over rocky fields, pitted with the sink holes common in limestone country.

At 6.8 *m.* is the junction with an improved dirt road.

Right on this road to the KUMBRABOW STATE FOREST (cabins, picnic facilities, foot and horse trails), 5.5 *m.*, a 9,425-acre tract purchased in 1934 and under development as a recreational area, game refuge, and reforestation project.

In the forest the PARTING SPRINGS FIRE TOWER, 8.5 *m.* (3,750 alt.), offers a sweeping view of the heavily wooded and almost uninhabited mountain country.

HELVETIA, 17 *m.* (2,100 alt., 290 pop.), scattered over the mountainsides and along the hollows of an isolated district of central West Virginia, has the characteristics of an Alpine village. It was settled in 1869 by a small group of Swiss immigrants, whose descendants retain many of the customs and manners of their forebears. German is spoken more fluently than English by the older generation and by some of the younger. The services at the GERMAN REFORMED CHURCH are conducted in German on alternate Sundays. Community sings and concerts by the Helvetia Red Star Band are held frequently in the COMMUNITY HALL. The great social event of the year is the fair held annually in September, when jellies, preserves, cheese, farm products, and needlecraft are exhibited in the Community Hall and along the village streets. The chief sources of income are farm crops and cheese manufactured at home by the Swiss method for a local market.

On the nearer slopes of wooded mountainsides and deep valleys (L), 8.3 *m.*, the scars left by old logging operations appear in the long perpendicular furrows down which lumbermen once sent felled trees. Where heavy second-growth timber has grown up to the edge of the furrows, the hillsides from a distance appear to have been combed with a giant rake. The highway continues to rise and reaches its highest elevation (3,750 alt.) at 9.6 *m.*; stands of maple, elm, wild cherry, and oak frequently obstruct the view. The curving road follows the contour of the ridge, and for several miles the summits of distant mountains are glimpsed through occasional gaps in the timber. Here and there a one- or two-room house, unpainted and weather beaten, stands isolated in the forest.

At 18.9 *m.* is the junction with an improved dirt road.

Left on this road is INDIAN CAMP, 1 *m.*, an overhanging ledge once used by the Indians as a lookout point.

A sharp curve, 19.1 *m.*, offers another view (R) across the heavily wooded Elk River Valley.

At 19.3 *m.* a path branches from the road.

Right on this path to POINT MOUNTAIN FIRE TOWER (*open*), 0.2 *m.*, a 65-foot tower rising high above the forest on the mountain (3,360 alt.). To the west loom Elk and Hodam Mountains; on the eastern horizon are the ranges of the Alleghenies, dim in the distance.

A small white CHURCH and a SCHOOLHOUSE, 19.9 *m.*, stand isolated in the woods, unexpected reminders of civilization. BERGOO, a coal and lumber town on the Elk River more than 1,000 feet below, appears (L) through a narrow gap in the hills, 22.2 *m.*, and at 23.3 *m.* spreads (R) the valley of the Back Fork of Elk River, with the spurs of Back Fork Mountain rising beyond. Gradually descending, the course of the highway parallels that of Elk River as it flows through Gregory's Bottom far below; at 24.9 *m.* the river is clearly visible. On the far bank of the river, wedged between it and the side of the hill, is a cemetery containing the GRAVE OF COLONEL ISAAC GREGORY, early settler of the valley and soldier in the War of 1812, marked by a stone placed by the Federal Government in 1933. The highway skirts the rocky face of POINT MOUNTAIN (R), 26.1 *m.*, along which the Elk River runs in foaming rapids.

CHERRY FALLS, 28.8 *m.* (1,492 alt., 75 pop.), was named for the wild cherry trees that once grew in profusion here beside a three-foot waterfall in the Elk River.

WEBSTER SPRINGS, 30 *m.* (1,509 alt., 976 pop.), a sportsmen's rendezvous and a trading center for the surrounding agricultural, mining, and lumber region, lies in a narrow triangular valley at the western end of POINT MOUNTAIN, where the Back Fork River joins the Elk. Originally known as Fork Lick because of a saline spring at the forks of the river, the town was incorporated in 1892 as Addison, in honor of Addison McLaughlin, donor of the courthouse site; but it is better known as Webster Springs, its post office name. The spring, or 'lick,' was discovered by Abram Meirs while on a hunting trip in 1785, but the first permanent settler was Polly Arthur, in 1860. Early settlers made salt from the waters of the spring. Later, the medicinal properties of the lick attracted health-seekers, and Webster Springs became widely known as a resort. A 300-room hotel was built by Senator Johnson N. Camden (*see below*); equipped with Russian and Turkish baths, it was crowded throughout the season. The hotel was destroyed by fire in 1926 and has not been rebuilt. A shift in the river's course has choked the lick with sand.

Webster Springs is at the junction with State 20 (*see Tour 20b*).

State 15 crosses the Elk River by way of Bennet Island and twists its way up McGUIRE MOUNTAIN, from which are many wide views of the surrounding country. Woods close in again as the highway dips into THARP HOLLOW to run through narrow glades and across small mountain streams.

The name of BOLAIR, 34.4 *m.*, a shady hamlet, is a corruption of Beau Clair, the title of a song popular with wagoners who once regularly stopped here along the laurel-bordered Gauley River.

CAMP CAESAR, 39.9 *m.*, at the mouth of a long hollow down which a small run flows into the Gauley River, is the Webster County 4-H camp; the county fair is held here each year. The camp contains cabins of various clubs, an assembly hall, a mess hall, the residence of the county agent, sheds for stock, and a swimming pool.

UPPERGLADE, 40.3 *m.* (2,427 alt., 25 pop.), one of the older settlements of the region, consists of a small group of houses in a clearing. Cultivated fields extend on either side as the forest thins out and the highway follows rolling highland.

COWEN, 43 *m.* (2,254 alt., 491 pop.), is the railroad center and shipping point of the surrounding agricultural area.

WELCH GLADE, 45.3 *m.* (2,223 alt., 40 pop.), was the scene of the skirmish in January 1862 in which Perry Connolly, a locally famous guerrilla, was killed by a detachment of Union soldiers.

The highway ascends a hill overlooking the Gauley; on top of COTTLE KNOB a fire tower stands out against the sky.

CAMDEN-ON-GAULEY, 49.3 *m.* (2,034 alt., 435 pop.), was first named Camden for U. S. Senator Johnson N. Camden; the phrase 'on-

Gauley' was added to distinguish it from another town of that name in the State. A marker here commemorates the Stroud Massacre of June 1772. Adam Stroud, a German who had settled west of the town on the creek now bearing his name, returned from a hunting trip and found that his wife and family had been killed and scalped by a marauding band of Indians, believed now to have been Shawnee. In retaliation a party of settlers raided and exterminated a peaceable Delaware village at Bulltown on the Little Kanawha River about 30 miles north (*see Tour* 10*b*).

Johnson Newlon Camden, oil man, owner of vast coal and timber holdings, and politician, represented West Virginia in the United States Senate (1881–7, 1893–5) at a time when the State was suffering from the railroads' practice of granting secret rebates to favored customers and charging less for a long haul to the eastern markets from points west of West Virginia than from points within the State. Camden had promoted several small intrastate railroads and was also interested in the development of the State's oil and natural gas fields. In 1875 he, along with other independent oil men, was being ruined by the competitive practices of Rockefeller's Standard Oil Company, which company was receiving large secret rebates from the Pennsylvania, New York Central, and Erie Railroads. Camden soon traded his oil holdings in West Virginia for stock in Standard Oil, and for some time, Standard Oil received through Camden's companies rebates from its arch foe, the Baltimore & Ohio lines. At Washington, Camden publicly defended the practices of Standard Oil and won a fight to prohibit railroads from charging less for a long haul than for a short one; the victory enabled him to place his coal and timber on eastern markets as cheaply as his western competitors, and also brought relief to his fellow citizens of West Virginia.

BLACK'S CHAPEL (R), 50.1 *m.*, was built about 1857 and named for the Reverend Samuel Black, a Methodist circuit rider, who financed his activities by selling deerskin gloves made by the women of his congregation. In the cemetery by the chapel are the graves of pioneer settlers, many of them Revolutionary soldiers.

West of CALVIN, 57.3 *m.* (2,250 alt., 14 pop.), in the center of a logging region, a narrow-gauge lumber railroad parallels the highway as it winds through the narrow defile of McMILLION CREEK to WORTH, 60.6 *m.* (1,825 alt., 100 pop.). The air is permeated with the pungent odor of fresh-sawed timber, stacks of which line the roadside.

At 67 *m.* is the junction with US 19 (*see Tour* 10*b*), 1.1 miles north of Muddlety (*see Tour* 10*b*).

Tour 10

(Waynesburg, Pa.)—Fairmont—Clarksburg—Weston—Gauley Bridge —Bluefield—(Tazewell, Va.); US 19.
Pennsylvania Line to Virginia Line, 279.9 m.

Concrete roadbed with frequent bituminous-surfaced stretches.
Baltimore & Ohio R.R. roughly parallels route between Rivesville and Roanoke; New York Central R.R. and Chesapeake & Ohio Ry., between Belva and Gauley Bridge.
Usual accommodations, except between Sutton and Summersville.

US 19, known as the Stonewall Jackson Highway, connects the two great bituminous coal fields in the State. South of the Pennsylvania Line the highway winds along the populous Monongahela River Valley, cutting across the northern coal field. US 19 then follows the old Clarksburg, Weston, and Gauley Bridge Turnpike through wooded hills and open pasture lands to Gauley Bridge, where it connects with the route followed by the old Giles, Fayette, and Kanawha Turnpike, completed in 1848, one of the first tributaries of the James River and Kanawha Turnpike. South of Fayetteville the highway traverses the great smokeless coal field for 50 miles, passing many mining towns and small commercial centers. Breasting the mountains south of Beckley, the highway crosses high plateaus and sharp ridges and dips to the industrial area around Bluefield, at the extreme southern tip of the State.

Section a. PENNSYLVANIA LINE to WESTON, 78.9 m. US 19.

US 19 crosses the State Line, here the Mason and Dixon Line, a few miles east of the point on Dunkard Creek where Charles Mason and Jeremiah Dixon, English surveyors, gave up their survey of the boundary between Pennsylvania and Virginia in 1767. They hesitated to proceed farther in fear of Indian attacks, and the survey was not completed until undertaken by John Lukins and Archibald McLean in 1783.

US 19 crosses the PENNSYLVANIA LINE, 0 m., 15 miles south of Waynesburg, Pennsylvania.

The highway passes under a high trestle, 5 m., connecting the gaping black mouths of two mines on opposite sides of the valley. Coal is carried from the mountain (R) across the trestle and through the tunnel of the other mine to reach a tipple on the far side of the hill. A marker, 5.5 m., commemorates Fort Martin, erected by Colonel

Charles Martin one mile east of this point about 1773. Francis Asbury, first bishop of the Methodist Episcopal Church in America (*see Tour 16a*), preached here in 1784.

South of MAIDSVILLE, 6.4 *m*. (900 alt., 50 pop.), a coal community, the Monongahela River (L) flows parallel with the highway for almost four miles.

RANDALL, 7.9 *m*. (920 alt., 165 pop.), a cluster of frame and brick houses on the edge of the Morgantown area, is at the junction (R) with State 7 (*see Tour 21b*), which unites with US 19 for 2.4 miles.

RIVERSIDE, 10.5 *m*. (910 alt., 940 pop.), is a commuters' suburb that sprang up with the growth of the glass industry at Star City, across the Monongahela River, during the first decade of the present century. Incorporated in 1912, the town, like others strung along the Monongahela, depends almost entirely upon the goods and services available in Morgantown (*see Morgantown*). Across the river (L), massed against the hills, appear the buildings of West Virginia University (*see Morgantown*).

WESTOVER, 11 *m*. (950 alt., 1,633 pop.) (*see Tour 21a*), is at the junction (L) with State 7 (*see Tour 21a*).

The highway passes over the tunnels of a shaft mine, 13.9 *m.;* a mine ventilator projects above the ground (L), looking much like the top of a huge meat grinder. The road climbs a high ridge and descends to the village of ARNETTSVILLE, 21.9 *m*. (983 alt., 80 pop.); south of the village it crosses the valley and climbs toward the top of another ridge.

RIVESVILLE, 24.3 *m*. (880 alt., 1,700 pop.), is a typical mining town, with a one-street business district, numerous small frame houses, workmen wearing cap lamps, and, over all, a sifting of coal dust from the mines. The town, laid out in 1837 on the land of Elisha Snodgrass, was known as Milford, because the first gristmill in the region was at a ford in the river here where settlers crossed with their grain. The town later achieved more than local renown for a potent peach brandy distilled here. The large coal-burning MONONGAHELA-WEST PENN POWER PLANT (*open; guides*), a red brick, concrete, and steel building, generates electricity for a large area.

The DAVID MORGAN MONUMENT, on US 19 in the center of town, a rectangular slab of limestone with rounded corners, commemorates the prowess of a son of the first settler in what is now West Virginia. In the spring of 1774 David Morgan arose from a sickbed in his cabin near this spot and discovered two Indians stalking his children, who had gone to perform some farm chores. With his single-shot, flintlock rifle, Morgan killed one Indian as he raised his head above a stump, then retreating in a zigzag course, he drew the shot of the other. The shot missed; Morgan had to dodge the tomahawk of his foe, losing one finger and fracturing another in protecting his head from the flying weapon.

Nevertheless, the ailing frontiersman rushed to grapple with his enemy, and finally plunged the Indian's own knife into his side. According to tradition, Morgan flayed both Indians and made shot pouches and belts of their skins.

FAIRMONT, 27.9 *m.* (883 alt., 23,159 pop.) (*see Fairmont*). Fairmont is at the junction with US 250 (*see Tour 22b and c*).

At 32.4 *m.* is the junction with a paved road.

Left on this road, across a steel bridge spanning the West Fork River, is MONONGAH, 0.4 *m.* (873 alt., 1,909 pop.), a mining town built on the site of a pioneer village called Briartown. In 1768 Captain James Booth came to the West Fork Valley, then the 'lonely wilds of West Augusta,' and was soon followed by other settlers. By 1777 he was able to organize a company of Rangers and lead them for 13 months in the Continental army. He was killed in an Indian ambush, June 16, 1778. The town's growth was slow until the closing decades of the last century, when discovery of coal and the coming of the railroad caused a rapid increase in population. Incorporated in 1891, the town took a shortened form of Monongahela for its name.

Here occurred the worst mine disaster in history on December 6, 1907, when a series of explosions and fires wrecked two large coal mines and killed 361 miners. Rescue crews from West Virginia, Pennsylvania, Maryland, and Ohio worked day and night for six weeks before reaching the last of the entombed dead. The town had a population of almost 6,000 and there was scarcely a family not in mourning. For days houses were deserted as relatives gathered at the mine entrance to claim charred and decomposing bodies. Only four men left the mine alive; they crawled to the surface through an air hole, but died of injuries and exposure a few days later. Sorrow and alarm spread through West Virginia, and labor leaders, politicians, civic leaders, and the man-on-the-street clamored that steps be taken to prevent similar disaster in the future. The legislature appointed an investigating committee, but no legislation immediately resulted. Congress appropriated funds for the study of explosives and accident prevention, however, and in 1910 created the Federal Bureau of Mines, which was charged with the responsibility of promoting safety. The State Bureau of Mines, established in 1907, had already begun to insist on the use of safety lamps and safety powder and had projected the organization of mining schools.

In WORTHINGTON, 35.9 *m.* (899 alt., 405 pop.), is a water mill (L), built in 1852 by Nathaniel and Charles Cochran, and (R) is the faded brick WILLIAM COCHRAN HOUSE, built in 1830 by their father. William Cochran was one of five children of the Indian fighter, Nathaniel Cochran, captured by Indians in the ambush in which Captain James Booth (*see above*) was killed. Cochran was held prisoner by the Indians for 17 years, being traded back and forth among numerous tribes from the old Maumee towns to Canada before he was finally exchanged and found his way home. His grandsons built the dam, water mill, and pier by hand, and operated the plant for more than 70 years, grinding wheat, corn, and buckwheat.

ENTERPRISE, 37.8 *m.* (909 alt., 128 pop.), is a mining town, but has (R) three large greenhouses that supply the surrounding territory. Across the river (L) is the site of the McIntire Blockhouse, built by John McIntire in 1773, but long since destroyed; McIntire's farm included the site of the present town. McIntire and his wife were killed by Indians and are buried on the river bank near the site of their cabin.

SHINNSTON, 40.7 *m.* (910 alt., 2,802 pop.), the trading center of a rich coal field, was settled by Quakers who followed Levi Shinn to the valley of the West Fork River. Shinn established tomahawk rights to 400 acres here in 1773 and brought his family six years later. Shinn's son Jonathan built the first house in 1802. A town was established in 1818, incorporated as Shinn's Town in 1852, and given its present name in 1877. A hotbed of Republican sentiment, the town cast 20 of the 22 votes that Harrison County gave Abraham Lincoln in the election of 1860; it held mass meetings to celebrate his election and loudly demanded the creation of a new State when Virginia seceded from the Union. The opening of mines in the Fairmont field led to discovery of coal near by, and intensive development of mineral resources between 1870 and 1890 determined the lines of the town's development.

At 42.8 *m.* is the junction with State 20 (*see Tour 20a*), which unites with US 19 for 8.7 miles.

In HUGHES, 43.9 *m.* (940 alt., 15 pop.), is a hideous man-made desert, a typical relic of strip mining. A vein of coal was discovered here near the surface, and steam shovels were used to strip away the earth above the seam. Not a blade of grass softens the raw scarred surface.

At 45.9 *m.* is the junction with a paved road.

Left on this road across the West Fork River to MEADOWBROOK, 0.4 *m.* (980 alt., 262 pop.), in which is (L) the GRASSELLI CHEMICAL COMPANY PLANT (*open*), where zinc anodes, zinc dust, and various zinc and brass products are manufactured.

To the south the highway passes through a series of six small coal camps.

CLARKSBURG, 52.9 *m.* (1,007 alt., 28,866 pop.) (*see Clarksburg*). Clarksburg is at the junction with US 50 (*see Tour 4b and c*) and State 20 (*see Tour 20b*).

South of Clarksburg, US 19 crosses rolling farming country and roughly parallels the course of the West Fork River. Herds of cattle graze in bluegrass pastures on the gently rounded hills. A marker, 59.4 *m.*, indicates the approximate SITE OF RICHARDS FORT, erected in 1774 by Arnold Richards. The stockade was also known as Lowther's Fort, for Colonel William Lowther, Indian fighter, Revolutionary War soldier, and a leader of the settlers in this region.

JANE LEW, 69.2 *m.* (1,007 alt., 445 pop.), was named for Jane Lewis, mother of Lewis Maxwell, who laid out the town in 1835. Like other villages of this section, it is steeped in tales of frontier heroism and hardships. In 1770 Edmund West and his two sons erected a stockade, which they called West's Fort; nine years later the fort was attacked and burned by Indians, but the settlers escaped to Buckhannon (*see Tour 7b*). Some of them returned in 1790 and erected Fort Beech; three years later Henry McWhorter, a Revolutionary War soldier, built a gristmill and a log house here; the latter stood on the site until 1927, when it was removed to Jackson's Mill as a historical monument (*see below*).

1. Right from Jane Lew on a paved road is LIGHTBURN, 3.3 *m.* (1,000 alt., 60 pop.), named for General Joseph A. J. Lightburn, a Union general, who became a Baptist minister after the War between the States. He is buried in the graveyard (R) of the BROAD RUN BAPTIST CHURCH, which was organized in 1804.

At 2.5 *m.* is the junction with a paved road; L. here to JACKSON'S MILL (*open*), 5 *m.*, built in 1837 on the farm of Colonel Edward Jackson, grandfather of General Thomas Jonathan ('Stonewall') Jackson. The latter lived here from 1830 to 1842, leaving his birthplace in Clarksburg (*see Clarksburg*) after his widowed mother remarried.

Young Tom came to the farm as a boy of six, bringing with him his sister, Laura. He performed his share of the lighter chores, and as he grew older, joined the slaves and hired men in the forest felling trees for his grandfather's sawmill. Nervous indigestion, which was to trouble him all his life, made him seek eagerly for outdoor activity. He worked under the millers in the gristmill, broke flax with a flail, and tended sheep; he went fishing, coon-hunting, and boating on the West Fork River, attended a country school, and engaged in fisticuffs with his schoolmates. His sketchy schooling aroused in him a desire for greater learning, so he struck a bargain with a slave; the slave was to furnish pine knots to provide light so that Jackson could study at night; in return, the boy promised to teach the slave to read and write. The slave learned well and later escaped by the Underground Railroad to Canada.

In 1837 Jackson was employed in the construction of the Parkersburg and Staunton Turnpike, and in these years he walked three miles each Sunday to hear a sermon. Impressed by his serious character and desire for learning, Colonel Alexander Scott Withers, a justice of the peace, secured an appointment for Jackson as a constable in 1841, a position of dignity and authority in those days. The following year he passed the required examinations and enrolled in the U. S. Military Academy at West Point.

Jackson's boyhood here at the Mills was probably the happiest period of his life, and he often referred to the memories of his youth; a canoe made from a hollowed tree trunk, associated with so many of his boyish escapades, is believed to have been in his mind when speaking these last words as he lay dying: 'Let us cross over the river and rest in the shade of the trees.'

The transplanted McWhorter Cabin (*see above*) stands on the SITE OF THE JACKSON HOUSE, which is also marked by a granite boulder with a plaque. The family farm is now occupied by the State 4-H Camp; facilities include cabins, a dining hall, work shops, bathhouses, barns, a landscaped garden, volleyball and tennis courts, a baseball diamond, and a swimming pool (*open 4 to 6 p.m.; adm. 25¢*). The combined Central West Virginia Country Life Jubilee and 4-H Fair is held here annually the last week in September.

2. Left from Jane Lew on a paved road is the old HARMONY CHURCH, 1 *m.*, built in 1819 by a Methodist Episcopal congregation. The history of the church belies its name, for in 1829 its first pastor, John Mitchell, and Davis Smith disagreed with the policy of the mother church, founded a Methodist Protestant society, and preached their dissenting beliefs in Harmony Church. Mitchell is buried in the churchyard.

On ground once occupied by a Shawnee Indian village, left across an open field at the confluence of Jesse Run and Hackers Creek, is the SITE OF THE JESSE HUGHES CABIN, built in 1771 by the fearless and ferocious Indian fighter who for years carried on a savage one-man campaign against snakes and redskins, drawing no distinction between them. Whether the Indians were friendly or not, he stalked, killed, and scalped them—braves, squaws, and papooses alike. Savage as a wolf, he 'could outrun any Indian that ever prowled the forest'; the Bulltown Massacre (*see below*) was typical of his proceedings. A master scout, he aided the Colonial forces on the western frontier during the Revolutionary War. Hughes subsequently pushed on into Indiana, still hunting Indians, but, like other mountaineers, found the swamps along the Wabash distasteful and unhealthy. Returning, he died in 1829 and was buried at Ravenswood, West Virginia, on the banks of the Ohio.

WESTON, 78.9 *m.* (1,008 alt., 8,646 pop.) (*see Tour 7b*), is at the junction with US 33 (*see Tour 7b and c*).

Section b. WESTON to GAULEY BRIDGE; 113 m. US 19.

This section of US 19 traverses a hilly region in which agriculture and stock raising are the chief occupations. South of Falls Mill the country becomes more rugged; near Gauley Bridge the highway winds through deep narrow valleys so closely hemmed in by high cliffs that the sunlight seldom reaches the road.

South of WESTON, 0 *m.*, US 19 passes through the suburbs of Homewood and Ben Dale and crosses the WEST FORK RIVER, 2.3 *m.*

ROANOKE, 8 *m.* (1,050 alt., 75 pop.), is a shipping point for cattle and agricultural produce of the neighborhood. In earlier days it was a lumbering center, but all timberland in this section has long since been cut over. The old CONRAD HOUSE (*inquire locally*), built of hewn logs in 1845, was an important post on a military courier line established during the War between the States.

WALKERSVILLE, 16.9 *m.* (1,087 alt., 97 pop.), a rural trading center near the headwaters of the West Fork River, was known originally as Bennett's Mill, for William Bennett, the founder, who 'lived 29,780 days without guile and without reproach, the progenitor of 249 living descendants.' In 1868 its name was changed to Walkersville in honor of Samuel T. Walker, of Rockingham County, Virginia, a close friend of Bennett's son.

In IRELAND, 21 *m.* (1,142 alt., 100 pop.), named for the homeland of its first settlers, is a ROADSIDE FIRST AID STATION. South of Ireland the country becomes abruptly more rugged. Black streaks of low-grade coal appear in the roadside bank where the road cuts through a high ridge.

At FALLS MILL, 28.3 *m.* (805 alt., 85 pop.), the Little Kanawha River has cut a deep gap through a rocky ridge (L) and tumbles over a broken ledge in a rushing waterfall; the hamlet was named for a mill that stood near the falls from 1840 to 1925.

BULLTOWN, 31.3 *m.* (777 alt., 35 pop.), was named for Captain Bull, the chief of a small band of Delaware Indians, who had migrated to this section from New York State. Although a roving band of Shawnee was generally suspected of the outrage, Jesse Hughes (*see above*) and four other settlers blamed the Delaware for the murder of the Stroud family near Camden-on-Gauley (*see Tour 9*) in June 1772; in a night attack on the sleeping Delaware village, Hughes and his men killed and scalped every man, woman, and child, and threw their bodies into the river. Although no trace of the operations remains,

Bulltown once had several salt furnaces, set up in 1810 by John Haymond. They supplied salt to a large part of northwest Virginia until the middle of the nineteenth century. During the War between the States a brief but sharp skirmish occurred here, in which the Union forces overcame the attacking Confederates. An old COVERED BRIDGE, painted red, spans (R) the Little Kanawha River.

At 48 *m.* is the junction (R) with State 4 (*see Tour* 11).

SUTTON, 49 *m.* (839 alt., 1,205 pop.), seat of Braxton County and a trading town for an extensive farming section, is recognized as the geographical center of the State. The first permanent settlement was made by John D. Sutton in 1810, although John O'Brien, an adventuring pioneer, had lived here in a hollow sycamore for several years in the previous decade. The town was chartered as Suttonville in 1826, but a new charter granted in 1889 shortened the name to Sutton. In the winter of 1861 Confederate soldiers under Captain Jack Tuning, a guerrilla in this area, burned all of the town with the exception of four houses. Sutton is the home of Susanne Fisher, whose debut as a singer in 1936 marked the rise of another American-born star in the world of opera.

US 19 crosses the ELK RIVER at Sutton and begins a steep ascent of a high ridge, densely forested with evergreens and hardwoods. Descending, the road parallels TWOLICK RUN, which cascades swiftly down a steep grade, churning white foam as it tumbles over rocks and fallen timber. The highway crosses BIRCH MOUNTAIN (1,877 alt.), 58 *m.*, and winds downward along wooded slopes.

At 66.2 *m.* is the junction with a dirt road.

Right on this road is the YOUNG MONUMENT, 2 *m.*, known locally as 'The Lonely Grave.' Henry Young, who is buried here beside his wife, was a Confederate sympathizer who was shot down when he refused to surrender to Union troops. According to one of numerous versions of the story, Young preferred certain death to surrender, and died in a one-man battle with the entire advance guard of General William S. Rosecrans's Union army on September 8, 1861. Enclosed within an iron fence, his grave lies in a lonely but ruggedly beautiful spot, surrounded by groves of pine and oak and thickets of rhododendron.

Climbing POWELL MOUNTAIN (2,232 alt.), 67.5 *m.*, the highway descends a thinly wooded slope, among low hills and level farms, to the widening bottom lands along Muddlety Creek.

At 74 *m.* is the junction (L) with State 15 (*see Tour* 9).

SUMMERSVILLE, 82 *m.* (1,894 alt., 536 pop.), seat of Nicholas County, was founded here on Peters Creek in 1824. Nancy Hart, noted Confederate spy, led a surprise attack on the town in July 1861. The sweetheart of Perry Connolly, a Confederate guerrilla fighter, Nancy (called Peggy by soldiers of both armies) was a tall, lithe, black-eyed beauty, just 20 years of age, when she led the attack in which Captain Starr and a Union force were captured and most of the town burned. Captured, she was charged with espionage and lodged in the Summersville jail, where her striking beauty and bright roving eyes kept her captors in continual turmoil as they vacillated between duty and desire. Connolly was killed at Welch Glade (*see Tour 9*), and Union forces gained control of the country around Summersville, making Nancy's escape impossible and her execution apparently certain. Her guards allowed her to roam the jail at will and to walk in the courtyard with a soldier escort on warm evenings. One evening, it is said, the guard succumbed to her charms and allowed her to examine his pistol; she used it to kill him on the spot and then escaped to Confederate territory. After Lee's surrender she returned to marry Joshua Douglas and live in Nicholas County.

Summersville is at the junction with State 39 (*see Tour 10A*).

US 19 traverses HAUNTED VALLEY, a narrow deep-shadowed section of Peters Creek Valley, which is traveled from twilight until dawn, so it is said, by the ghosts of a soldier and his whimpering dog. The wind must be right, however, or the dog's mournful whine cannot be heard. During the War between the States, according to legend, a band of soldiers, fatigued and hungry, buried alive one of their comrades because they believed his death imminent and they did not wish the body to be found by the enemy. They shot his faithful dog and buried him near by when he refused to leave the fresh grave of his master.

Small villages of scattered one- and two-room cabins and cottages border the road at intervals, and wide level fields alternate with deep V-shaped valleys, where high cliffs shut out the sun.

At 87.3 *m.* is the junction with an improved dirt road.

Left on this road is the CARNIFEX FERRY BATTLEGROUND, 6 *m.*, a 275-acre State park. Here, on September 10, 1861, a force of 5,000 Federal soldiers under General William S. Rosecrans encountered a smaller Confederate force led by General John B. Floyd. After several hours of hard fighting Rosecrans withdrew to await daybreak. Floyd, believing that Rosecrans was preparing to cut off his line of retreat, hastily broke camp and retired with his forces to Gauley Plateau. Trenches and soldiers' graves remain.

DRENNEN, 94.1 *m.* (1,125 alt., 65 pop.), on Peters Creek, consists of unpainted cottages and a few white farmhouses scattered along the flat bottom land between steep hills.

In LOCKWOOD, 97.3 *m.* (1,045 alt., 27 pop.), at the mouth of Otter Creek, is (L) a double grave, in which are buried two little girls, Betsy and Peggy Morris, who were killed and scalped by Indians in 1792. The graves are in a plowed field, marked by a double headstone. Their father, who lived until 1808, is buried beside them.

The road climbs through rugged country up LITTLE ELK MOUNTAIN (1,448 alt.), 98.6 *m.*, then drops rapidly to SWISS, 99.6 *m.* (717 alt., 300 pop.), on the north bank of the swiftly flowing Gauley River. One of the first settlements in the region, the village was settled in 1795 by farmers, who later found the steep mountain fields difficult to till. In 1870 five families of Swiss immigrants settled here, supposedly because the precipitous hills reminded them of their native Alps. They took over abandoned farms and developed them with the skill of a people who for generations have plowed similar terrain, and when lumbering and mining operations stimulated the growth of a village here, it became known as Swiss by common consent.

BELVA, 108 *m.* (724 alt., 162 pop.), is at the junction with State 16 (*see Tour* 12).

GAULEY BRIDGE, 113 *m.* (677 alt., 516 pop.) (*see Tour* 15a), is at the junction with US 60 (*see Tour* 15a and b).

Section c.   GAULEY BRIDGE to VIRGINIA LINE; 88 m.   US 19.

Emerging from the silent wild grandeur of the New River Gorge, US 19 crosses a wide plateau dotted with farms and mines producing smokeless coal, and then descends the broad bare face of Flat Top Mountain to the industrial section about Bluefield.

Southeast of GAULEY BRIDGE, 0 *m.,* US 19 is united with US 60 for 4.5 miles (*see Tour* 15a), following the NEW RIVER GORGE on a ledge far above the river. The OLD MAN OF THE MOUNTAIN (L), 4.9 *m.,* looks out over the road, his stony gaze fixed on the forested slopes across the canyon.

HONEY CREEK FALLS (L), 5 *m.,* tumble over a series of ledges down the steep slope; the highway bridge spans the lower falls. Crossing the NEW RIVER, 6.2 *m.,* here reduced to a mere trickle by the diversion of water at the Hawks Nest Dam (*see Tour* 15a) several miles upstream, the highway ascends the gorge of LAUREL CREEK, which plunges furiously over and around huge boulders on its way to join the river at Cotton Hill. From the highway, 9.8 *m.,* is a wide vista north (L) across rolling hills to GAULEY MOUNTAIN (2,543 alt.), and to SEWELL MOUNTAIN (3,270 alt.), far to the east.

FAYETTEVILLE, 13 *m.* (1,850 alt., 1,143 pop.), seat of Fayette County and the trading center of neighboring farmers and stock raisers, has quiet streets lined with tall elms and old-fashioned houses with elaborate gardens enclosed within wrought-iron fences, embellished occasionally with iron stags and marble statuettes. The town thrives, but without bustle and hurry; its serenity is broken only during sessions of the circuit court, held four times each year. Fayetteville has many weekly newspapers; two or more editors are constantly exhorting the citizenry to keep a watchful eye on officeholders of the opposite party.

Settled in 1818 by Abraham Vandal, the community was first called Vandalia. In 1836 a town was platted on land owned by Edward Vandal, and when made the county seat in 1837, chose its name in honor of the Marquis de Lafayette. The first county courts met in the Vandal home, but $1,500 was levied in 1838 for the purpose of erecting a courthouse 'near a dead chestnut tree in Vandal's rye field.' The present courthouse is the fourth to stand on the site. The town was incorporated in 1883.

During the War between the States, Fayetteville was fortified by both armies, and the breastworks on the low rolling hillsides are still visible. The only action took place on May 19, 1863, when Confederate artillery shelled the Union entrenchments.

Left from Fayetteville on State 85 to the rim of NEW RIVER GORGE, 1.8 *m.*, where the road, heavily shaded by overhanging ledges and dense foliage, begins a steep descent to the level of the river, 4.6 *m.*, here foaming and raging between walls of rock rising sheer 1,000 feet on either side.

South of Fayetteville the highway traverses a section of cultivated fields, orchards, and pastures, with here and there a white church in a small grove of trees.

OAK HILL, 20 *m.* (1,991 alt., 2,076 pop.), on the western edge of a high plateau overlooking rolling wooded hills and lush valleys pasturing many herds, is a merchant's town with well-stocked stores, strong banks, active civic enterprises, and an unusually large number of places of entertainment. The town's business life revolves around the magic phrase, 'pay day at the mines.' Thirteen drab and profitless days may pass, leaving no regrets, but the magic fourteenth brings an influx of miners and their families from Scarbro, Whipple, Carlisle, Summerlee, and other mining towns, bearing pay envelopes to be spent in re-stocking the family larder. The streets are thronged, stores crowded, and movie theaters jammed. Women in shiny rayon 'town' dresses shop with a sharp eye for bargains as they anxiously shepherd numerous children of varying sizes. The bustle subsides as suddenly as it began, and pay day is followed by 13 days of almost rural quiet.

The first settler, William Blake, arrived in 1820, and was followed by other farmers who settled along Arbuckle Creek. In 1848 the Giles, Fayette, and Kanawha Turnpike, a branch of the James River and Kanawha Turnpike, was built across the plateau called Hill Top. Scores of families followed it into the region between 1848 and 1850. A post office was established in 1866 on the Hill Top, a circumstance that gave the town its name when the post office was moved and the town incorporated in 1905.

South of Oak Hill the road runs along a ridge overlooking scattered farms and mining camps.

MOUNT HOPE, 27 *m.* (1,708 alt., 2,361 pop.), situated in a hilltop ravine, is a commercial town serving the surrounding coal field. The entire population is employed either in business houses supplying the wants of miners or in the offices of the two large coal companies that maintain headquarters here. Incorporated in 1897, the young town was almost totally destroyed when 40 business establishments and 150 dwellings burned to the ground on March 24, 1910. With the opening of the New River smokeless field and the consolidation of small independent companies into large operating concerns, Mount Hope became the administrative center of the field. The formation of large operating companies added an all-inclusive word to the miners' vocabulary. Miners, their families, administrative employees, merchants, professional men, and all who live in these coal fields refer to a mining town, a mining camp, or even a mine not by name, but by the blanket term 'operation.' Travelers through the coal fields, inquiring the name of a town, are apt to be informed that it is some company's 'operation,' and learn that the town's name is little known.

Near a ROADSIDE DRINKING FOUNTAIN (L), 27.2 *m.*, are two large blocks of coal, each weighing about 300 pounds, set on a concrete base and placed here in 1932 to test the effects on them of weather and age. Across the road (R) is an outcropping of the New River-Sewell seam, 60 inches thick, faced with gray limestone. Both the coal blocks and the seam are illuminated at night. On the crest of PRICE HILL, 29.6 *m.*, is (R) a RED CROSS FIRST AID STATION.

In SKELTON, 36 *m.*, a coal town, is the junction with US 19-Alt.

Right from Skelton on US 19-Alt. is Beckley, 2 *m.* (2,400 alt., 9,357 pop.) (*see Tour 16a*), at the junction with State 3 (*see Tour 16a and b*).

At 37.4 *m.* is (L) PINECREST SANITARIUM, a tuberculosis hospital, known originally as the Rutherford State Sanitarium, taken over by the State in 1930. On a 300-acre tract donated by the city of Beckley stands a three-story brick main building containing 148 beds, a doctors' and nurses' home, several cottages for employees, and numerous farm buildings. Additions under construction with the aid of Public Works Administration funds will increase the capacity of the hospital to 475 beds.

At 37.5 *m.* is a junction with a dirt road.

Left on this road to GRANDVIEW, 12 *m.*, a rocky ledge 1,300 feet above New River, overlooking a 10-mile horseshoe bend in the stream. Recently acquired by the State for a roadside park, far below, along the river, brown cultivated patches stand out against the green of the forest. The tracks of the Chesapeake & Ohio Railway parallel the turbulent stream, whose muffled roar rises even to the mountaintops. Across the canyon the rounded crest of WAR RIDGE (2,510 alt.) is blanketed with dense green woods, and in the distance rise the pale blue peaks of Sewell Mountain (3,360 alt.). The grandeur of the view compensates for the difficult trip over the narrow rough road.

SHADY SPRING, 45 *m.* (2,675 alt., 367 pop.), a rural community built around a general store and garage serving the farmers of these rolling hills and smooth plateaus, is at the junction (L) with State 3 (*see Tour 16a*).

Through forests of oak and poplar, spotted with bald patches left when extensive stands of chestnut trees were killed by a great blight, the road climbs steadily up Flat Top Mountain.

FLAT TOP, 53.3 *m.* (3,305 alt., 30 pop.), a tiny trade center on the mountain, plays host for two days in mid-August each year to some 75,000 guests who come to attend the Lilly Family Reunion, held annually since 1930. Robert Lilly was one of three sons of an associate of Cecil Calvert, second Lord Baltimore, who came to Maryland in 1640. All three sons migrated, one to Georgia, another to the Kanawha Valley; the third, 'Father' Robert Lilly, married Mary Fanny Moody, and the couple left Maryland with four sons in 1732 to settle at the mouth of the Bluestone River, about 10 miles east of Flat Top. 'Father' Robert died in 1810, aged 114, and his wife in 1807, aged 110. The first of the large families in the Lilly line was that of their grandson, also named Robert, who was the father of 13 children; succeeding generations of large families have rapidly increased the clan.

Within the LILLY FAMILY REUNION GROUNDS (L), on a rolling hillside, are a small grandstand, a stage, and frame booths for sale of souvenirs. During the reunion week end the hillside is as crowded as a summer resort on a hot Sunday. Tourist camps and parking places for miles around are filled. Enormous quantities of fried chicken and sandwiches are consumed by Lillys, Lilly-in-laws, and friends and admirers of the virile line, who gather to exchange news and gossip and become further acquainted with the family. The occasion is usually honored with a speech by the governor of the State. Flat Top is abruptly and strangely quiet again on the following Monday morning, and the reunion grounds, buried under a varicolored snow of debris, await the next high wind to sweep them clean.

In Flat Top is the junction with a dirt road.

> Right on this road is HUFFS KNOB (3,566 alt.), 1 m., the highest of the peaks that constitute Flat Top Mountain. On the knob is a FOREST FIRE LOOKOUT TOWER, with a view of the most beautiful sections of three counties.

Southward the road winds along a wooded ridge, offering glimpses of wooded hills and occasional upland farms, and descends in a series of sweeping curves to reach CAMP CREEK, 61.4 m.

LAKE SHAWNEE (*swimming May 30-Sept. 31; adm. 25¢*), 72.7 m., is a 23-acre artificial lake fed by 12 mountain springs leased by the State as a bass rearing station. On the shore are six frame cottages and eight log cabins, open during the summer. The lake occupies the site of a Shawnee camp ground, on which was made the first important settlement on the Bluestone River. Mitchell Clay, a nephew of Henry Clay, settled on the tract in 1775, and eight years later a band of Shawnee killed his son and daughter; a granite headstone by the lakeside marks the graves of the children.

At 73 m. is the junction (R) with State 10 (*see Tour 17*).

At 76.9 m., on the outskirts of Princeton (*see Tour 8c*), is the junction (L) with US 219 (*see Tour 8c*).

The PRINCETON AIRPORT (*day service only*), 77.4 m., has a 3,500-foot runway.

Passing through a gap on STONY RIDGE (2,413 alt.), 79.9 m., the highway descends into the EAST RIVER VALLEY.

BLUEFIELD, 86.4 m. (2,558 alt., 19,339 pop.) (*see Tour 18a*), is at the junction with US 52 (*see Tour 18a*).

US 19 crosses the VIRGINIA LINE, 88 m., 14 miles northeast of Tazewell, Virginia (*see Virginia Guide*).

Tour 10A

Summersville—Richwood—Cranberry Glades—Mill Point; 66.5 *m.,*
Unnumbered Road.

Asphalt-paved between Junction with US 19 and Richwood; graveled between
Richwood and Cranberry River bridge; elsewhere dirt.
(Road closed for 21.8 miles west of Cranberry River Bridge during fire season
Apr. 1-Nov. 1, except on Memorial Day, Fourth of July, and during Spud and
Splinter Festival. Hunters and fishermen permitted to enter closed area during
open seasons, but must leave cars at gates; no hunting permitted in game
refuge, a small posted area.)
No accommodations, filling stations, or repair shops east of Richwood; fire-
patrol telephones at intervals.

For 25 miles this highway traverses rolling uplands and open plateaus
—fertile potato-growing lands that merge with the industrial Cherry
River bottoms around Richwood. East of Richwood, the highway winds
through 40 miles of wilderness, a primitive and mountainous region,
the habitat of black bear, deer, red fox, wild turkey, wildcat, and small
game. Hundreds of clear mountain streams feed the Gauley, Williams,
Cranberry, and Cherry Rivers, stocked with speckled, brown, and rainbow trout. Near the source of Cranberry River, surrounded by lofty
mountains, are the cranberry glades, notable for their unusual soil formation and their plant and animal life.

The road branches east (L) from US 19 (*see Tour 10b*) in SUM-
MERSVILLE, 0 *m.* (1,894 alt., 536 pop.) (*see Tour 10b*).

The highway crosses GAULEY RIVER, 2.3 *m.*, and starts a steep
and winding ascent of Gauley Mountain. At the top of the mountain
the road widens, and its broad grassy shoulders are bordered with rolling meadows; here and there appear groves of silver maple, beech, and
poplar on the open plateau dotted with farms growing fine potatoes.

From NETTIE, 13 *m.* (2,640 alt., 214 pop.), a rural village with a
church, a community store, and several white farmhouses set far back
in fields enclosed by snake fences, is (L) an extensive view of the surrounding countryside and distant mountain ranges.

Crossing PANTHER CREEK, 14.8 *m.*, the highway follows the
comparatively level ridge of THORNY KNOB to the top of FEN-
WICK MOUNTAIN (2,899 alt.), 19.9 *m.* Almost 1,000 feet below,
at the base of the mountain (R), are BIG LAUREL CREEK and the
coal town of SAXMAN (2,264 alt., 412 pop.), walled in by high ridges.

FENWICK, 21.6 *m.* (2,104 alt., 517 pop.), a scattered community
on the edge of the Monongahela National Forest, was once a thriving
lumber center.

Country Folk and Country Ways

THE WPA'S MILLIONTH PUPIL

A mountaineer, taught in a WPA Adult Education class, reads to his children

THE SCHOOL TRUCK, RED HOUSE RESETTLEMENT PROJECT

SHOPPING TRIP

Photograph by Post; courtesy of Farm Security Administration

MOUNTAIN HOME

Photograph by Shahn; courtesy of Farm Security Administration

Photograph by Post; courtesy of Farm Security Administration

BOILING SORGHUM

QUILTING PARTY

Photograph by Post; courtesy of Farm Security Administration

Photograph by courtesy of the U.S. Forest Servic

DEMONSTRATIONS OF WOODSMAN'S ART, MOUNTAIN STATE FESTIVAL
(Note use of ax for shaving)

TIMBER DRAG

Photograph by courtesy of the U.S. Forest Servic

OLD 'UP AND DOWN' SAWMILL, PENDLETON COUNTY

OLD MILL, MILL POINT

Photograph by Highton; courtesy of Work Projects Administrati

LOG CHURCH, SMOKE HOLE

COVERED BRIDGE, NEAR BEVERLY

AS THE EARTH TURNS . . .

Photograph by Highton; courtesy of Work Projects Administra

RICHWOOD, 25 *m.* (2,193 alt., 5,720 pop.), a lumber town, has concrete sidewalks chipped and broken by the spiked boots of lumberjacks. The city lies along the narrow river bottom of Cherry River, at the confluence of the North and South forks, and spreads up the steep hills that rise on three sides. Along the bottom are railroad tracks and yards, splitting the town in two. Rows of shed-like stacks of drying lumber stand between the tracks and Main Street, which descends a high ridge and skirts the slopes of a hill to the sawmill, always referred to as the Big Mill, beside a mill pond at the forks of the river. On Park Place, east of the business section, are attractive houses set in broad rolling lawns.

Known as Cherry Tree Bottoms until 1900, when the Richwood post office was transferred from Hinkle Mountain, the settlement was chartered in 1901, at the time that the Baltimore & Ohio Railroad built a branch line here. By 1904 the town had a population of 3,000; a sawmill, pulp and paper mill, tannery, clothespin plant, hub factory, and other woodworking plants were established. Timber operations began on the Cranberry and Cherry Rivers. By 1909 Richwood was the leading lumber camp in West Virginia and prospered until 1931, by which time the largest and best tracts of timber along the Cherry, Cranberry, and Williams Rivers had been depleted, leaving only those along the Gauley River. The tannery was dismantled; other woodworking plants were closed, and the brisk tempo of the town's activities slackened. The present annual production of the sawmill is far below its peak of 80,000,000 feet.

Lumbermen and lumbering methods have changed since the days when Richwood was a roaring camp. Tractors and other machinery have made mechanics of the rough-and-ready woodsmen who once vanished into the woods for long periods, only to swagger into town for a week end of carousing and horseplay that taxed the wits of the local police. The average woodsman today is often mistaken for an ordinary countryman, although at festival times, on pay or circus days, an occasional old-timer comes to town to spend in a brief riotous spree the 'stake' he has spent months of hard work earning. In his jaw is a chew of tobacco; the legs of his peg-topped breeches are rolled halfway up his 15-inch calked boots; his blue chambray shirt is open at the neck, with gaudy garters on the sleeves. If the weather is cool, he swings across his shoulders a red-green-and-black plaid mackinaw or a gray 'ritchie' flannel coat, the pockets bulging with a miscellany of belongings. Although changed in other respects, the West Virginia logger has retained his jargon. Cooks are still 'stomick robbers'; their helpers are 'cookees'; coffee is 'jerkwater'; prunes, 'log berries'; biscuits, 'catheads'; and milk is 'cow.'

Annually, in August, Richwood holds a three-day Spud and Splinter Festival—'Spud' for the fine potatoes of the district, 'Splinter' for its woodworking industry. During festivities the Cherry River Navy holds 'maneuvers' in the river, seldom deep enough to float a rowboat and often dry. Its wheeled flagship, *The Clothespin,* is manned by one deckhand and dozens of admirals from the honorary roll of 1,500 names, which includes those of governors, State and local authorities, actors, businessmen, and old-time lumberjacks. Admirals wear cocked hats of black paper, with gold insignia in the shape of crossed clothespins; epaulets of gilded cardboard, with rope fringe; lapel insignia of gold in the shape of clothespins; Sam Browne belts of white clothesline, and sidearms of white maple in the form of giant clothespins. The festival concludes with a parade by the admirals and crew, followed by a banquet and ball.

South of the lumber mill, at the foot of Main Street, are the red brick buildings of the STEELE-WALLACE PLANT (*open 9–5 workdays; guides*), which produces 360,000,000 clothespins annually, in addition to large quantities of paper drinking cups, paper spoons, and wooden butter trays.

On the south bank of the Cherry River is the PULP AND PAPER MILL (*open 9–5 workdays; apply at office for permit and guide*). Spruce and hemlock logs from the sawmill are reduced to paper pulp by an acid process and manufactured into bleached and unbleached specialty paper, of which 30,000 tons are produced annually.

Between Richwood and the head of Stamping Creek on Cranberry Mountain, the highway traverses the Monongahela National Forest, following an old railroad grade along the winding rocky course of Cranberry River, a clear sparkling stream that tumbles over white stones and swirls into deep dark eddies in which lurk numerous trout. Bordering the river are thickets of rhododendron and mountain ivy, patches of tall goldenrod and purple-flowered ironweed. In the spring the air is filled with the sweet fragrance of wild honeysuckle. Nothing breaks the silence but the songs of birds, the roar of waterfalls, or late in the evening the plaintive call of the whippoorwill or the hoot of a mountain owl. Occasional overgrown clearings, foundations of barns, stands of peach and apple trees are the only reminders of the lumber camps and railroad towns that flourished along this route years ago.

At 31.3 *m.* is a junction with a narrow dirt road.

Left on this road to an open field, 0.6 *m.;* here are several abandoned CCC buildings that responsible parties may use for camping purposes (*permit from caretaker*). Skirting the western edge of the field is Cranberry River and the old WOODBINE SWIMMING HOLE, a popular picnicking spot.

At 37.2 *m.* is a junction with Dyer Road.

Right on this road to the junction with a fire trail, 2.3 *m.;* R. here to the RED OAK FOREST FIRE TOWER (*open during fire season*), 4.3 *m.*

East of the gates to the closed area (*see above*), 38.9 *m.*, the narrow dirt road crosses the Cranberry River and follows its north bank, crossing many tributaries.

At the forks of the CRANBERRY RIVER, 51.5 *m.*, is the junction with the Black Mountain Fire Trail.

Left on this road to BLACK MOUNTAIN FOREST FIRE TOWER (*open during fire season*), 7.5 *m.*, affording an extensive view of surrounding mountains.

The CRANBERRY GLADES (3,375 alt.), 57.7 *m.*, embrace 300 acres of damp boggy soil, carpeted in places with blue-green lichens and mosses, overgrown in others with tall rush-like thickets, sedges of alder, and other shrubs. At one time the area was probably a lake, which gradually filled up to form spongy soil; in places the weight of a man is sufficient to sink a slender pole 20 feet into the porous formation. Winding torpid streams are fringed with alders and hollies.

A low timbered ridge called the 'Island' separates the five glades— Big Glade, Flag Glade, Long Glade, Round Glade, and Little Glade, ranging in size from 2 to 56 acres. On the slopes of the surrounding mountains grow red spruce, hemlock, and several varieties of northern hardwoods. Two varieties of cranberries grow in abundance here; the large American cranberry is found along the open borders; the small grows profusely in all parts of the glades; a peculiar 'speckled' form of the latter is found in Round and Flag Glades. Country people come for miles to gather the berries, carrying them across the mountains on pack horses. Other flora include quaking aspen, ground hemlock, northern rattlesnake, plantain, rose pogonia, horned bladderwort, round-leaved sundew, sphagnum, moss, snowberry, buckbean, and several varieties of orchids.

Among the masses of vegetation are runways of small rodents and the trails of larger animals. The yellow-cheeked meadow mouse, masked shrew, smoky shrew, and red-backed mouse, not generally found in this part of the country, have been seen here. Among other birds that frequent the glades are the alder flycatcher, the swamp sparrow, the magnolia warbler, and the barred owl.

The road ascends CRANBERRY MOUNTAIN, 59.4 *m.*, one of the lower ranges, and crosses to the headwaters of Stamping Creek. At STAMPING CREEK GATE, 61 *m.*, the road emerges from the Monongahela National Forest.

MILL POINT, 66.5 *m.* (2,217 alt., 85 pop.) (*see Tour 8b*), is at the junction with US 219 (*see Tour 8b*).

↑↑

Tour 11

Sutton—Gassaway—Clendenin—Charleston—Yawkey; State 4, State 13, 113 *m.*

Baltimore & Ohio R.R. parallels route between Sutton and Charleston. Concrete roadbed except for graveled stretch northeast of Yawkey. Accommodations in larger towns.

State 4 follows the thinly populated valley of the Elk River to its junction with the Kanawha at Charleston, the capital of the State, a busy commercial and industrial center. Southwest of Charleston, State 13 passes through a section of scattered oil derricks, small coal mines, and numerous truck farms to the junction with State 3 at Yawkey.

Section a.   SUTTON to CHARLESTON, 84.8 m.   State 4.

This section of State 4 closely follows the course of the Elk River, lined with sycamores as it winds between ruggedly beautiful hills. Blooming thickets of rhododendron and laurel splash the steep hillsides with pink and white from late May to mid-July, and with yellows, russets, and blazing reds in autumn. In winter the roadside cliffs sparkle in a crystal sheath of ice. The sparsely settled region is a favorite with hunters and bass fishermen, many of whom own cabins along the river banks.

SUTTON, 0 m. (839 alt., 1,205 pop.), is at the junction with US 19 (*see Tour 10b*).

GASSAWAY, 5.7 m. (839 alt., 1,618 pop.), centers about the railroad shops and yards of the Baltimore & Ohio. The town was founded in 1904 as a division point on the railroad between Elkins and Charleston and named for U. S. Senator Henry Gassaway Davis (*see Tour 8*).

STRANGE CREEK, 21.3 m. (807 alt., 60 pop.), has its center across the Elk River at the mouth of a stream of the same name. Originally called Turkey Run, the creek was named for William Strange, who wandered from a surveying party near the headwaters of the Elk in 1795; his companions searched for him in vain. Years later, on the bank of Turkey Run, 40 miles from the spot where he was last seen, his bones were found beneath a great beech tree, against which leaned his rifle, the shot pouch dangling from the ramrod. Carved in the bark was this couplet:

> Strange is my name and I'm on strange ground,
> And strange it is I can't be found.

With the discovery of iron ore here by Jesse S. and William A. Savage in 1874, the village enjoyed a boom. Almost overnight a large hotel, stores, and several taverns were built. An iron furnace was erected and operated for five years, but the grade of ore proved too low for profitable production, and the shipping of pig iron by flatboat down the Elk was both difficult and expensive. The bubble burst, an exodus followed, and the town, which had changed its name to Savagetown, slipped back to its former rural calm and again became known as Strange Creek.

Opposite the mouth of GROVES CREEK, 27.4 m., stands the RUINS OF GROVE'S MILL, abandoned in 1922, the last of the many water-powered gristmills that once lined Elk River. Old-timers well remember when Bill's Mill, the old Duck Mill, another at Frame Town, and the

Sam Fox and Mollohan Mills at Birch were among the most prosperous enterprises in the valley.

Sizable pike are still taken in the Elk, but none compares with the giant hooked by 'Squirrely' Carpenter in the 1880's. It was 'the biggest durn pike I ever seed,' said Squirrely, and there is reason to believe that it was the most elastic too. On one occasion when escorting a party of fishermen who had taken shelter from a torrential rain in the lea of Grove's Mill, he began on his favorite theme and, as he warmed to his story, became more and more excited as he described his titanic struggle. 'And, gentlemen, I hope to die where I stand if that thar fish warn't 69 inches long!' he said, and as he stretched out his arms in a vain effort to demonstrate the length of the monster, his foot slipped on the mossy boards, and Squirrely tumbled backward into the forebay of the mill pond, then running four feet of swift water. Fished out before he struck the mill wheel, he was set dripping and spluttering on his feet. 'Shelt,' his son, who had not stirred from a comfortable seat against the wall, spat out a mouthful of wheat straw and observed: 'Pap! If that durned pike'd been one inch longer, damned if I don't think hit'd drowned ye!'

At 34 m. is the junction (R) with State 16 (see Tour 12), which unites with State 4 for 10.8 miles through the beautiful gorge-like Elk Valley, narrow and sparsely settled.

West of the second junction (L) with State 16 (see Tour 12), State 4 swings away from the river and ascends the Lower Two Run past little one- and two-room cabins to the top of DULLS CREEK MOUNTAIN, 50.1 m. (980 alt.). Across the ELK RIVER, 57.4 m., appears the CORNWELL COMPRESSING STATION, a group of aluminum-painted buildings surrounded by a maze of pipes and tanks. Natural gas from near-by fields is compressed here and piped to Cleveland; gasoline is a by-product of the compression process, which condenses the gasoline vapor present in the natural gas.

QUEEN SHOALS, 62 m. (639 alt., 188 pop.), is a roadside village in an agricultural and oil region.

Left from Queen Shoals on a bridge across the Elk to the MULLENS FARM, 7.6 m., on which stands the ORIGINAL GOLDEN DELICIOUS APPLE TREE. Planted as a seedling, the tree produced a new kind of apple, yellow like the Grimes Golden, but larger and firmer and a longer keeper. A nursery purchased the tree for $5,000 in 1917 and enclosed it in a steel cage with a burglar alarm. As hundreds of grafts have been made from the parent tree, such protection is no longer necessary. The tree, still bearing fruit, is under the care of the Clay County agricultural agent.

CLENDENIN, 66 m. (621 alt., 1,217 pop.), named for the Clendenins who founded Charleston (see Charleston), is a prosperous oil town, the base of operations in the rich Blue Creek oil fields. The town is situated on a narrow strip of land between Elk River and a high hill to the east. The newer residential section lies across the river along US 119.

West of Clendenin the Elk Valley widens, the hills become lower and less rugged, and the region is more densely populated.

Across the river (L), 66.5 *m.*, appears FALLING ROCK, (629 alt., 110 pop.), the site of one of the first cannel coal mines in the State, opened in 1846 when Sutton Mathews discovered the vein here. All that remains of the enterprise is a dilapidated chimney, visible when the trees are bare. Although low in heating power, cannel coal is rich in gas and is used extensively in the production of artificial gas. Its name is a corruption of 'candle' coal, for it burns with a bright flame.

The CHILDREN'S SUMMER CAMP (R), 76.4 *m.*, is maintained by the Davis Child Shelter.

In BIG CHIMNEY, 76.6 *m.* (607 alt., 162 pop.), is (L) the massive stone foundation of an old brick chimney, all that remains of the salt works that made the village a prosperous business center during the days of the salt trust (*see Tour* 15). Carbondale College was opened here in 1884, with an enrollment of 80 students, but closed in 1887 for lack of support.

The KENTON MONUMENT, 77.3 *m.*, commemorates the exploits of Simon Kenton, adventurer, border scout, and spy during Lord Dunmore's War (*see Tour* 14). At the age of 16, he ran away from home in the belief that he had killed a man in a fight over a girl. For a quarter of a century he fought in border wars against the Indians. He is credited with having saved Daniel Boone's life on one occasion, was captured several times, and was twice saved from being burned at the stake, once by Chief Logan, again by Simon Girty. While encamped here on the Elk River in the 1770's, Kenton and two companions were attacked by Indians; a companion was killed, and Kenton seriously wounded, but managed to escape. His last days were spent uneventfully on a farm in Ohio, where he died in 1836 at the age of 81.

CHARLESTON, 84.8 *m.* (598 alt., 60,408 pop.) (*see Charleston*). Charleston is at the junction with US 60 (*see Tour* 15*b and c*), US 21 (*see Tour* 13), and US 35 (*see Tour* 14).

Section b. CHARLESTON to YAWKEY, 28.2 m. State 13.

This section of the route climbs from the industrialized Kanawha Valley about Charleston into a region of small truck farms scattered over rolling hills. Oil derricks reach skyward from tumbling knolls or spindle up in creek bottoms, being the characteristic landmarks of the region.

West of CHARLESTON, 0 *m.*, State 13 unites with US 60 (*see Tour* 15*c*), as far as South Charleston, 3.9 *m.* (600 alt., 5,904 pop.) (*see Tour* 15*c*), where State 13 branches southwest (L) and for several miles traverses a countryside dotted with little houses, each with its garden plot, creating a scene more rural than suburban.

On the crest of a high ridge, 10.3 *m.*, State 13 overlooks (R) the rich DAVIS CREEK VALLEY, known for the size and sweetness of its strawberries. The site of one of the earliest settlements in the Kanawha Valley region, the creek and valley were named for Thomas Davis, pioneer settler, who in 1790 bought for five shillings a 241-acre tract of land at the creek mouth from one Thomas Upton; Davis's deed, filed in 1794, was one of the first recorded in Kanawha County. In the valley pioneers early discovered what they called black band iron ore. Believing the ore to be a mixture of iron with a small amount of coal, they reasoned that, if a furnace were built, the coal in the ore would smelt the iron. Although unsuccessful, the enterprise attracted a railroad to Davis Creek to haul out the 'iron,' which has since become well known as black band coal, a high grade of block fuel.

Climbing to a divide, 13.7 m., State 13 descends past fertile small farms and patches of wood to ALUM CREEK, 16.5 m. (624 alt., 161 pop.), the trading center for neighboring farmers.

The highway crosses the COAL RIVER, 16.5 m., where an old dam and lock (L), built by a mining company in 1856, now serves as a swimming pool for Boy Scouts who vacation at CAMP WALHONDE.

YAWKEY, 28.2 m. (700 alt., 210 pop.), is at the junction with State 3 (see Tour 16b).

↑↑

Tour 12

Ellenboro—Grantsville—Belva; State 16, 104.7 m.

Baltimore & Ohio R.R. parallels route between Ivydale and Hartland.
Hard-surfaced throughout.
Limited accommodations.

State 16 follows a roller-coaster course across thinly populated ridges dotted with oil derricks and patched with occasional grain fields. Hillside meadows, carpeted with daisies in summer, slope steeply into V-shaped valleys. Light and shadow and the changing seasons make subtle contrasts of color on the pastures and fields of grain, and in autumn winding ribbons of red and yellow mark the tree-bordered water courses. South of Millstone, the open ridge country gives way to narrow valleys hemmed in by rugged wooded mountainsides. Between Clay and Belva are several mining and lumbering villages.

ELLENBORO, 0 m. (784 alt., 330 pop.) (see Tour 4c), is at the junction with US 50 (see Tour 4c).

HARRISVILLE, 4.9 m. (870 alt., 1,192 pop.), is a residential town with time to dream of its brief period of activity when speculators and drillers crowded into the surrounding gas and oil fields between 1860 and 1863. Its maple-shaded brick streets, lined with comfortable houses and spacious lawns, bustle with life three times a year when the circuit court is in session. Above the foliage loom the courthouse cupola and three church steeples.

Platted in 1822 on land of Thomas Harris, the community grew slowly until 1843 when, on becoming the seat of Ritchie County, it was named Ritchie Court House. In 1892 it was renamed in honor of General Thomas M. Harris, nephew of the founder and a commissioner in the trial of those accused of plotting President Lincoln's assassination.

South of Harrisville, the highway penetrates a section that was a favorite hunting ground of the Indians, but is now almost deforested and boasts of no game larger than a rabbit. Numerous derricks pump out the 'liquid gold' of the region, while the fertile soil grows large crops of grain and provides bluegrass pastures; cattle-raising is one of the chief occupations of the section.

KING KNOB HILL, 13.3 *m.* (1,151 alt.), affords a fine view of the surrounding farmlands and rounded hills, but numerous sharp curves in the road make it dangerous to park even for a quick survey of the scenery.

SMITHVILLE, 17.3 *m.* (719 alt., 126 pop.), is a village of retired farmers and oil workers. Just north of the town Colonel William Lowther and a party of settlers attacked a band of Indians in 1781, killing five and rescuing several white captives taken during a raid in Tygarts Valley.

Right from Smithville on a graveled road is MACFARLAN, 7 *m.* (668 alt., 150 pop.), where for many years solidified petroleum was mined like coal. The freak formation, a vein of black glossy substance that melts when heated, is the only one of its kind known in the United States. It was discovered by Frederick Lemon in 1852 when waters of a spring freshet washed earth away from the outcropping vein. He concealed his discovery, thinking it was coal, and bought the land. When he tried to burn some, it ran like pitch. The property changed hands several times and was finally developed as a mine by a New York syndicate. A narrow-gauge railroad with wooden rails, nicknamed the 'Calico Railroad' because of its motley equipment, was built to connect the mine with the Baltimore & Ohio Railroad at Cairo. After an explosion had killed several miners in 1874, the superstitious declared that the place was haunted, and few workers would venture into the mine. Although 'grahamite,' as the substance was named, can be refined into an unusually rich oil, the mine was abandoned in 1909 because oil is cheaper to produce; almost every resident of the village has a souvenir specimen of the petroleum.

CAMPBELL HILL (1,128 alt.), 20.9 *m.*, and JACKSON HILL (1,194 alt.), 26.3 *m.*, are excellent vantage points from which to view the surrounding oil fields and farms.

GRANTSVILLE, 30.9 *m.* (726 alt., 1,018 pop.), a quiet rural county seat supported by surrounding stock and dairy farms, lies on the north bank of the Little Kanawha River along a narrow strip ringed by high flat-top knolls covered with bluegrass pasture. In the business district one- and two-story frame buildings line the main street, and in the center of a square of grassy lawn stands (R) the steepled, red brick courthouse. Houses stand back on the hill slopes, usually with small vegetable gardens and pastures. The town's tranquility is broken only during circuit court sessions, and when the high school meets its traditional rival, Harrisville, in an athletic contest.

Grantsville was laid out by Simon P. Stump in 1866 and named for General U. S. Grant. In 1869, after a bitter struggle with Arnoldsburg, the seat of Calhoun County was moved here and soon the town boomed as the center of oil, gas, and lumber operations along the Little Kanawha River. About 1910 a carbon-black plant, said to have been the largest in the country, was established in the town, but operations ceased when gas was found to be more valuable as a fuel.

> Right from Grantsville on State 36, an improved dirt road, is BURNING SPRINGS, 17 m. (635 alt., 250 pop.) the center of the first oil field opened in the State. Up to 1860 the presence of oil was regarded by inhabitants as more or less of a nuisance. An attempt to manufacture salt in 1842 failed because oil collected on the surface of the brine in the wells. Not until 1860, when General Samuel D. Karnes of Pittsburgh purchased the 'old greasy water hole' and tubed it for oil, was its value realized. Seneca Oil, as crude oil was called, sold for about 50¢ a gallon and was used as a remedy for almost all human ailments. More wells were drilled, and then followed a rush almost as frantic as that to the California gold fields a decade earlier. Within eight months the mushroom town contained 6,000 persons, all of whom expected to get rich overnight; tents and shacks served as shelters, while wells were sunk in every available spot. Soon production exceeded the supply of containers, and the oil was pumped into open barges. These frantic operations were halted abruptly in 1863 when Confederates under General William Jones raided the field, destroyed the machinery, fired the oil-laden barges, and sent the flaming craft drifting down the Little Kanawha River. Although operations were resumed, production has never regained the 1860–63 peak.

South of Grantsville the highway rolls across another ridge into a valley studded with oil derricks.

MILLSTONE, 42.8 m. (803 alt., 39 pop.) (see Tour 7c), is at the junction with US 33 (see Tour 7c), which unites with State 16 as far as Arnoldsburg, 44.5 m. (712 alt., 125 pop.) (see Tour 7c).

South of Arnoldsburg the road follows the course of the West Fork of the Little Kanawha River. Settlement of this area was retarded prior to 1843 by a reign of terror established by the 'Hell-Fired Band,' a gang of swashbuckling rowdies who wished to keep the territory unsettled so that they might continue hunting, fishing, and living a wild free life in the forest. For a number of years the group raided pioneer farms and discouraged newcomers by their violence, until four ringleaders were convicted of murder in 1843 and sentenced to 18 years in the penitentiary at Richmond.

ORMA, 49.1 m. (800 alt., 30 pop.), inhabited by retired farmers and stockmen, has a filling station and general store of white frame, which also serves as the post office.

MINNORA, 52.7 m. (774 alt., 33 pop.), consists of a church, a filling station, a general store, and a few houses. The aluminum-painted buildings of the small COMPRESSOR STATION (R), 53.8 *m.*, accentuate the isolation of the spot.

CHLOE, 54.4 *m.* (795 alt., 36 pop.), another tiny country village, differs from other hamlets only in that it was the scene of a skirmish during the War between the States. Most of the farmhouses in this section are large, rambling, two-story buildings with verandas extending along two sides, well painted and prosperous in appearance. Orchards break the monotony of long stretches of pasture and rippling fields of grain on the hillsides.

At 69.3 *m.* is a junction with State 13 (*see Tour* 11), which unites with State 16 for 10.8 miles (*see Tour* 11).

CLAY, 82.1 *m.* (707 alt., 444 pop.), seat of Clay County, was named for Henry Clay; originally called Henry and for a time called Marshall it is more often referred to as Clay Courthouse, or simply as Clay. On a terraced hillside (R) is the yellow brick courthouse. A marker credits the county with being the home of the original Golden Delicious Apple Tree (*see Tour* 11). The three-day Clay County Fair is held here annually during the last week in September.

BRADLY FIELD (L), 83.6 *m.*, is the Clay County 4-H Camp.

HARTLAND, 86.2 *m.* (699 alt., 100 pop.), a mining settlement on the Baltimore & Ohio Railroad, is often the scene on Saturdays of impromptu shooting matches between mountaineers proud of their skill with old-fashioned muzzle-loading rifles.

BICKMORE, 89.8 *m.* (936 alt., 32 pop.), a scattered group of miners' cottages, boomed during the First World War with the rising demand for coal, but almost all activity has now ceased.

South of Bickmore, the country is more rugged. The road dips into a narrow canyon-like valley, where occasional small unpainted farmhouses stand lonesomely on the banks of the creek; patches of corn or other grain cling to steep hillsides, seemingly defying the force of gravity.

LIZEMORES, 96.1 *m.* (988 alt., 521 pop.), BENTREE, 101 *m.* (851 alt., 109 pop.), and DIXIE, 102.8 *m.* (736 alt., 250 pop.), are small lumber villages with unpainted frame buildings.

BELVA, 104.7 *m.* (724 alt., 162 pop.), is at the junction with US 19 (*see Tour* 10*b*).

7 7 7 7 7 7 7 7 7 7 7 7 7 7 7 7 7 7 7 7 7 7 7 7 7 7 7 7 7 7 7 7 7 7 7 7 7 7 7 7 7 7 7 7 7 7 7 7 7 7 7 7 7 7 7 7 7 7 7 7 7 7 7 7 7 7 7 7 7

Tour 13

(Marietta, O.)—Williamstown—Parkersburg—Ripley—Charleston; US
21.
Ohio Line to Charleston, 91.1 m.

Concrete and macadam roadbed, with short graveled stretches.
Baltimore & Ohio R.R. and electric interurban line parallel route between
Williamstown and Parkersburg.
Usual accommodations at short intervals.

US 21, the most direct route between Parkersburg and Charleston,
runs for several miles along the valley of the beautiful Ohio, beloved
of the Indians and important in the early development of the Northwest, and then traverses a rolling countryside of pasture lands and
oil and gas fields.

Agricultural customs of 100 years ago are common in the back country: grain is harvested with horse-powered threshers, and fodder for
livestock is ground in hand mills. Neighbors gather for all-night vigils
at maple-sugar camps; out from the morning mist blanketing the hillsides, men and boys emerge, plodding toward the syrup stills, their
shoulders bent under the weight of buckets of sugar-water suspended
from wooden beams.

US 21 crosses the OHIO LINE, 0 m., at the western end of the
Marietta-Williamstown Bridge (*car and one passenger, 15¢, each additional passenger 5¢*), which spans the Ohio River from Marietta,
Ohio. From the bridge can be seen the wide sweep of the Ohio River
around the bend upstream and (L), BUCKLEYS ISLAND, earlier
known as Kerrs or Meigs Island, near which Washington camped on
his return from the mouth of the Kanawha River in 1770.

WILLIAMSTOWN, 0.4 m. (608 alt., 1,657 pop.), was named for
Isaac Williams, who settled here in 1787, just 17 years after Joseph
Tomlinson and his son Samuel had filed claims for 1,400 acres of land
at this point on the Ohio. A soldier of the Revolution and later a border scout, Williams married Rebecca, sister of Samuel Tomlinson, and
erected a house on a 400-acre site opposite the mouth of the Muskingum River, within the present limits of the town. With the establishment of Marietta across the Ohio in 1788 and the opening of the
Northwest Territory, the river became a main thoroughfare for frontier settlers, and Williamstown grew from a frontier outpost to a staid
farming center, which it has remained. The only large industrial establishment is the FENTON ART GLASS COMPANY PLANT (*open*), which

manufactures ornamental art glass and ceramics for a world-wide market.

The TOMLINSON HOUSE (*private*), 1.3 *m.*, was erected in 1839 by Joseph Tomlinson III, grandson of the first settler, on the site of a log cabin built in 1809 and destroyed by fire. The two-story red brick house, with a wing at the rear forming an ell, has nine rooms and occupies a knoll overlooking the highway, surrounded by lawns and shrubbery and shaded by ancient elms. From 1836 to 1864 Tomlinson was a power in the young community, serving one term in the Virginia assembly and holding numerous minor offices, and the house was a social center until the death of his wife in 1857.

HENDERSONS, 3.5 *m.* (612 alt., 25 pop.), a river village, is dominated by the HENDERSON HOUSE (L), a substantial three-story red brick house on a landscaped terrace overlooking the river. The original wing, now the back of the house, was built in 1831 and called Pohick Hall, for Pohick in Fairfax County, Virginia. The front section was built in 1835, and for many years the mansion was known as Henderson Hall. On the flat roof are a 'widow's walk' and a glassed-in cupola, much like the pilot house on a river packet, which afford a long view of the river and suggest that the family was considerably interested in steamboat traffic during the 1840's and 1850's when freight and passenger service on the river was at its height. Windows of varying sizes are single on the first story, paired on the second, and are placed in groups of three on the third. South of the house, about 100 feet, is a small unexplored Indian mound.

PARKERSBURG COUNTRY CLUB (R), 7.6 *m.*, has a clubhouse, swimming pool, tennis courts, and an 18-hole golf course (*open to members of other golf clubs; greens fees $1.50 on Sat., Sun., and holidays; other days, $1*).

VIENNA, 9 *m.* (608 alt., 2,700 pop.), although not incorporated until 1935, was laid out in 1794 by Dr. Joseph Spencer, who named it for his home, Vienna, in Fairfax County, Virginia. The center of a large truck-gardening section, it is also an industrial town, having the UNIVERSAL GLASS PRODUCTS COMPANY PLANT, manufacturing milk bottles; the PARKERSBURG SILK MILL, spinning thread for hosiery; and the VITROLITE UNIT OF THE LIBBEY-OWENS-FORD COMPANY (*open*), one of two plants in the world manufacturing Vitrolite, a flint-like substance resembling marble, used for store fronts, interior walls and decorations, table tops, and ornamental bric-a-brac.

At 10.6 *m.* is an intersection with a paved road.

1. Left on this road to the MASONIC HOME, 0.5 *m.*, maintained by the Grand Lodge of West Virginia. The group of Georgian Colonial buildings of red brick and white stone crowns a high knoll and overlooks a long reach of the Ohio River and Neal Island.

2. Right on the paved road is the PARKERSBURG AIRPORT, 0.1 *m.*, with a 3,100 foot runway and housing facilities for 20 planes (*day service*).

PARKERSBURG, 13 *m.* (615 alt., 29,623 pop.) (*see Parkersburg*).

The SITE OF FORT NEAL (R), 14.3 *m.*, is marked with a bronze tablet erected by the Daughters of the American Revolution. Captain James Neal, leading a party from Greene County, Pennsylvania, arrived here by flatboat in 1785 and erected a blockhouse. Known as Neals Station, it afforded protection to settlers and travelers alike, withstanding a determined Indian onslaught in 1790 when raiding Delaware burned homesteads in the vicinity and killed all settlers caught outside the stockade.

MINERAL WELLS, 19.4 *m.* (676 alt., 69 pop.), was a fashionable summer resort for more than 40 years. In 1855 a pretentious hotel was erected for the accommodation of visitors to near-by mineral springs. The hotel was abandoned in 1900. A few evergreens remain to mark the landscaped beauty of this former garden spot in the rough surrounding country.

The highway climbs steep grades, dangerous in wet weather, to the summit of LIMESTONE HILL (1,105 alt.), 31.7 *m.*, and then threads its way through a long narrow valley. The hills are worn and scarred by years of cultivation; timber is sparse and scraggly; rock ledges break through the soil here and there; dairy herds graze on the hillsides; but the predominating activity is orchard culture. The production of local oil and gas fields is declining. Soil erosion is plainly evident in this valley; streams cut jagged paths through the fields and after a heavy rain each becomes a raging 'gully-washer.'

A COVERED BRIDGE (L), 46.4 *m.*, is still in use on a secondary road, formerly a part of the main highway.

RIPLEY, 49 *m.* (615 alt., 669 pop.) (*see Tour 7c*), is at the junction with US 33 (*see Tour 7c*).

From SALT HILL (862 alt.), 56.1 *m.*, are views of small farms and pasture land spreading over jumbled knolls. In autumn, farm families gather along the country roads in the narrow hollows of this region to reap green cane, which is boiled down into syrupy ' 'lasses' and used as sweetening in all home cooking during the winter. Entire families toil in the making of sorghum; each member has an assigned task, either at the mill or in the cane patch, even the family mule. The mill itself, usually mounted on a ramshackle wagon frame, consists of cylindrical grinders with vertical grooves, which crush the cane and guide the juice into a pail hung on the wagon frame. The motive power and pace of production are set by the mule; hitched to a long oak pole, he walks in a circle, round and round the mill, and thus sets the cylinders in rotation. One member of the family feeds the mill with fresh cane stalks; a second clears the grinders of crushed pulp; others constantly stir the bubbling seething juice as it simmers in a kettle over a furnace of field stones and clay, while another waves a leafy branch to drive off the myriad insects attracted by the smell. Fresh wagonloads of stripped stalks are unloaded and stacked by the mill, while the children are kept busy gathering wood for the fire under the cooking pot.

It is work willingly performed, and a festive spirit prevails—even the old mule plods around his circle with a bonnet of leaves jauntily over one ear—for everybody is thinking of the gaiety to come when the last day's work is done. The event is celebrated with a ' 'lasses lickin',' attracting neighbors from near and far. The assembled guests are given small wooden paddles to scrape the generous leaving in the boiling pan; games are played; there is group singing; mountain minstrels enliven the gathering with ballads sung to the accompaniment of banjos, fiddles, and guitars. The old folks tell legends to the children while the log fire crackles; young folks wander off in couples, for, as everybody knows and expects, 'they's a sight o' courtin' ben did at 'lasses lickin's.' After a final round of songs, the guests depart with a resolve to meet 'come next harvest moon agin.'

SISSONVILLE, 73 *m.* (624 alt., 140 pop.), a farming community in a section underlaid with oil and gas, began life as a lumbering center, for the Pocatalico River, locally known as the Poca, facilitated logging operations during the middle of the nineteenth century.

CHARLESTON, 91.1 *m.* (598 alt., 60,408 pop.) (*see Charleston*).

Charleston is at the junctions with US 60 (*see Tour 15b and c*), US 35 (*see Tour 14*), and State 4 and State 13 (*see Tour 11a and b*).

Tour 14

Charleston—Red House—Point Pleasant—(Gallipolis, Ohio); US 35. Charleston to Ohio Line, 61.5 *m.*

Concrete and asphalt paved, two lanes wide.
New York Central R.R. parallels the route.
Hotels in Charleston and Point Pleasant; no hotel accommodations and few tourist homes along the route.

US 35 follows an old trail along the Kanawha Valley, connecting Charleston and the coal towns of the upper valley with the small agricultural communities along its lower stretches. A few coal camps appear west of Charleston, but the black seams in the lower valley are few and relatively thin. The hills gradually recede from both banks of the Kanawha River, leaving broad tracts of rich bottom land. Small hillside farms are lost in the distance as the valley broadens to meet the Ohio River; tiny farmhouses on hard-scrabble acres give way to baronial estates with manor-like houses and immense barns.

Down the Kanawha Valley came early visitors to the 'western country,' and they marveled at the possibilities of the region. Daniel Boone more than once followed the old trail. Later came homesteaders to clear farms, wrest salt licks from the Indians, fell the forests, and dig for coal, oil, and gas. The river became part of the great inland waterway system that stemmed from the Mississippi River, the chief artery of travel and commerce as settlers thronged west in mounting waves. The Kanawha still bears cargoes of coal, limestone, and gasoline, loaded in barges towed by stout little tugs. But the days of the gay river steamboats are over, although a traveler in 1936 noted the *Senator Cordill,* plying between Charleston and Pittsburgh. It was scurrying back and forth from one bank of the Kanawha to the other, 'carried no cargo but chickens and eggs, and was reputed to take note of every barnyard cackle.'

CHARLESTON, 0 *m.* (598 alt., 60,408 pop.) (*see Charleston*).

Charleston is at the junction with US 60 (*See Tour 15b and c*), US 21 (*see Tour 13*), State 4 (*see Tour 11a*), and State 13 (*see Tour 11b*).

West of Charleston US 35 unites with US 21 (*see Tour 13*) for 0.2 miles.

At 5 *m.* is the junction (L) with State 25.

Left on State 25 is DUNBAR, 2.2 *m.* (600 alt., 4,189 pop.), which owes its growth to the rapid expansion of the Kanawha Valley chemical industries at the time of the first World War. Established on a site once occupied by mound builders, the city is uniformly middle class in aspect, with many jerry-built frame dwellings, and a few more substantial structures, obviously new. The city has several industrial plants manufacturing glass, enamelware, and agricultural implements.

The KANAWHA COUNTY FAIR GROUNDS (L), 5.7 *m.,* is the scene of 4-H Club competition at a fair held annually during September.

In INSTITUTE, 6.2 *m.* (600 alt., 211 pop.), is (L) the WEST VIRGINIA STATE COLLEGE, offering Negro youth standard courses leading to degrees in the arts, sciences, agriculture, education, business administration, home economics, mechanical arts, and music. Established in 1891, the college has grown steadily to its present average enrollment of 850.

On the 10-acre campus overlooking the Kanawha River are the dormitories and lecture halls of tan brick in quadrangular formation. FLEMING HALL is a dormitory and lecture hall; the A. B. WHITE TRADES BUILDING houses classrooms and laboratories; in GLASSCOCK HALL are the dining hall, storage room, and bakery; PRILLERMAN HALL and HILL HALL are new dormitories for men and women respectively. The ADMINISTRATION BUILDING contains offices, the library, science laboratories, and classrooms. The grounds embrace a 73-acre farm.

The STATE SCHOOL FOR THE COLORED DEAF AND BLIND (L), 6.3 *m.,* opened in 1926, consists of four buildings on a 33-acre campus. The school offers the regular eight-year elementary and four-year high school instruction, with special training in tailoring, shoe repairing, cleaning and pressing, barbering, broom and mop making, cooking, and sewing.

The MUNICIPAL AIRPORT (L), 6.4 *m.,* dominated by a crescent-shaped administration building and control tower, provides Charleston with transcontinental air line connections (*daily service east and west between Washington and Cincinnati*).

At 10.2 *m.* is the approach (L) to a steel bridge spanning the Kanawha River.

Left on the bridge (*car and passengers,* 25¢; *trucks,* 35¢) to the junction with US 60 (*see Tour* 15c) in ST. ALBANS, 0.5 *m.*

NITRO, 12.8 *m.* (600 alt., 5,055 pop.), is the offspring of the lusty community that sprang up around Explosives Plant C, the powder plant erected by the Federal Government in 1918 to supply the American Expeditionary Force and the Allies with smokeless powder. In a flurry the contract for the construction of the plant was awarded to an eastern company on the 'cost-plus' basis. The valley was surveyed; 1,800 acres of farm land were purchased; and 1,000 workers began building the powder plant and a city. Almost over-night the population leaped to 25,000. In addition to the plant itself, the largest in the world, 3,400 buildings were erected, including 2,000 bungalows for workers; a complete water and sewage system was installed; electric light and power lines were brought in; schools, churches, hotels, a 600-bed hospital, stores, and amusement halls were constructed. Speed was emphasized and cost ignored. At the close of the war the plant was almost completed and had cost $70,000,000. Manufacture of powder was abandoned, and in 1919 the entire establishment was sold for $8,500,000 to a syndicate of bankers, who hoped to interest private industry in the factory buildings. The post-war slump upset their plans, and the mushroom city of 1918 slowly shriveled in size and importance. Most of the factory buildings were scrapped; many of the houses were sold to coal companies and shipped down the river on barges without being dismembered. Today, concrete sidewalks lead to crumbling foundations, abandoned concrete kilns, and the remains of 28 huge factory units.

The present city is supported by plants producing pencils, chemicals, and rayon. The State maintains a plant of its own here for the manufacture of automobile license plates.

At 13.3 *m.* State 25 rejoins US 35.

A house of split logs and handhewn slabs on a small rise (R), 6.5 *m.,* is a reminder of frontier days in the Kanawha Valley; the house has clay-smeared walls and hand-riven shingles. Winding around small hillside farms the highway ascends to the top of TYLER MOUN-TAIN (983 alt.), 8.2 *m.*

At 14.9 *m.* is a junction (L) with State 25 (*see above*).

POCA, 16.9 *m.* (595 alt., 300 pop.), is peopled almost entirely by workers who commute to near-by mining and manufacturing towns. The smudged frame dwellings give the impression of having been hastily thrown together by men eager to move on to more remunerative fields. A brick high school building (R), at the western end of town, is the only architectural concession to permanence.

RAYMOND CITY, 17.3 *m.* (590 alt., 100 pop.), is a mining town built around a long dull-silver tipple that crosses the road to convey high-grade coal to strings of gondola cars and barges.

BLACK BETSEY (L), 19 *m.* (590 alt., 150 pop.), is a coal camp of two dozen red frame houses. BANCROFT, 20.3 *m.* (600 alt., 115 pop.), parallels the cinder banks of the railroad track separating the two rows of frame dwellings. In PLYMOUTH, 20.9 *m.* (580 alt., 301 pop.), the last of a string of coal towns, a huge tipple of creosoted timber conveys coal to the railroad and the river.

US 35 becomes a wide asphalt roadway, 22.1 *m.,* on the boundary of a tract of 7,276 acres granted to George Washington for his services during the French and Indian Wars by John Murray, Earl of Dunmore, the last royal governor of Virginia. The grant 'bordered on the

Great Kanawha 12 miles and 227 poles'; in 1773 Washington had 3,953 acres here surveyed and George Muse had the remainder located. Here in the lower Kanawha Valley small coal camps give way to farms with evenly fenced and regularly tilled acres spread around great barns.

At 25.4 *m.* is the junction (L) with State 34.

Left on State 34, under a timber railroad trestle, to an electrically driven ferry, 0.1 *m.*, which crosses the Kanawha River to WINFIELD (570 alt., 294 pop.), county seat of Putnam County, named for General Winfield Scott of Mexican War fame (*ferry operates 6:30 a.m. to 10:30 p.m.; fare, car and driver, 25¢; each additional passenger, 5¢*).

RED HOUSE, 25.5 *m.* (578 alt., 210 pop.), consists of a cluster of houses huddled on a small rise. Shoals in the river here once seriously impeded navigation. In 1819, when the first steamship crossed the Atlantic, the *Robert Thompson* attempted to ascend the river to Charleston, but failed after unsuccessfully bucking the shoals for two days. Authorized by the Virginia General Assembly, wing dams were built and channels dredged to aid navigation. Although the work was not completed until 1828, as early as 1823 the steamboat *Eliza* ascended the river to Charleston and returned with a cargo of salt; in 1830 the *Enterprise*, first steam towboat on the river, dared the shoals with a tow of salt-laden barges, and within a few years coal mining led to rapid growth of water transport.

At 26.6 *m.* is a junction with a graveled road.

Left on this road 0.3 *m.* to U. S. Lock No. 1 (*open to visitors*), which extends across the Great Kanawha River to a point just west of Winfield. It is one of three new roller-type dams built to maintain a 9-foot channel throughout the 91 miles of the river's navigable length. The No. 2 dam is at Marmet; the No. 3, at London; the dams, each of which cost approximately $4,000,000, replaced 11 old dams which maintained a 6-foot channel for almost 40 years.

Completed in 1937, the Winfield dam is composed of six roller crest gates, twin locks, and spillways for generating hydroelectric power. The metal gates, each 100 feet long, are suspended between concrete towers; they can be lowered to concrete sills to cut off all flow of water and in time of flood can be raised as high as 46 feet on slanting notched grooves in the towers. Each gate is operated by an electric motor in the control tower. The spillways drive turbines generating electricity to operate the dam and provide power and light for the adjoining farm area. The twin concrete locks, each 56 by 360 feet, have steel facings to protect the walls from abrasions when barges scrape against them. In the operations building, which rises 95 feet above the low water mark, are the control panels. A steel catwalk connects the top of the building with the tops of the gate towers. Designed to aid navigation and not as a means of flood control, the Winfield dam and others in the series have an over-all length of 1,000 feet. Operated by the U. S. Army Engineer Corps, these dams are the first of the kind in the country, although it is planned to construct others on the inland waterways.

Through low rolling hills, covered with brush and marked with shale ledges and rock outcroppings, US 35 travels north and west past reminders of the valley's pioneers. Clapboard houses, beaten by a hundred summer suns and winter gales, and their predecessors, hand-hewn log barns and outhouses, collapsed and rotting in the fields, are half-hidden beneath moss and ivy. Backwaters of the river intrude upon the lowlands to form small marshes and sluggish pools, while the ever-widening valley reveals roadside communities on each hilltop.

In ELEANOR, 27.5 m. (576 alt., 690 pop.), are the RED HOUSE FARMS (*open* 8:30–4:30 *except Sundays;* 8:30–12:30 *Saturdays*), one of the three Federal Homestead projects in the State, the others being Tygart Farms (*see Tour 8b*) and Arthurdale (*see Tour 21a*). The farms are managed by the Farm Security Administration of the U. S. Department of Agriculture for the West Virginia Rural Rehabilitation Corporation. Situated in a bend of fertile bottom land, the project was designed as a self-sufficient suburban community to provide economical housing and industrial rehabilitation for 150 West Virginia families taken from relief rolls.

The first homesteaders took up residence in April 1935, and soon organized the Red House Association, in which each homesteader has a vote and to which he pays dues. Through the association the homesteaders have a joint interest in the 2,200-acre project, which includes 150 houses, a canning plant, greenhouse, handicraft building, roadside market and restaurant, filling station, garage, pool room, shoe shop, barber shop, a stock barn on the lines of a zeppelin hangar, a dairy barn, a combination grade and high school, and a hosiery mill employing 200 men.

The farms were named for the RED HOUSE, now the Administration building, a stout two-story brick building erected by Joseph Ruffner. Recently discovered records indicate that the house was built prior to 1825 and not in 1840, as was long believed. Georgian Colonial in design, it remains much as it was when built, except for the addition of a tall, square-columned portico. The old slave quarters in the rear of the house have been removed.

Homesteaders live in story-and-a-half fireproof bungalows, built of cinder blocks, each with three-quarters of an acre for gardening, spaced along several red slag roads that curve from the highway toward the hills. The cottages range from two to four rooms, paneled with poplar and chestnut, and each has a garage, a chicken house, and a vegetable cellar. Painted white, the cottages have roofs and shutters of red, tan, and green. Stone for sidewalks and ballast for roads have been taken from the quarry that scars the hillside (R) at the southern end of the project. Rentals run from $9 to $13 per month, depending upon the size of the house; it is planned to allow homesteaders to purchase their bungalows over a 20-year period at prices ranging from $1,500 to $3,000. Communal affairs are governed by an elected council of seven which meets once each month with the community manager.

An asphalt road supersedes the smooth concrete highway through Red House Farms. Thin patches of red cedar appear on the south slopes of the hills; these scattered stands in the lower valley are believed to be the remnants of a once vast cedar forest covering the entire region.

In the center of BUFFALO, 35.1 m. (580 alt., 316 pop.), stands

(R) a grade school, a two-story swaybacked structure with a coat of bilious tan paint; the scarred wooden porch bears the legend 'Buffalo Academy, 1849.' Bullets embedded in the walls and nicks from Minié balls and grape shot evidence the fact that during the War between the States the building was the center of a skirmish. A hospital during the latter part of the war, the building was again used as a school after the peace at Appomattox; many Kanawha Valley leaders received their schooling here.

Adjacent to the school, but unmarked, is the birthplace of William Hope ('Coin') Harvey (1851–1936), a pamphleteer and agitator for the free coinage of silver, the issue on which William Jennings Bryan rose to fame. Harvey attended Buffalo Academy in its heyday and then Marshall College, after which he practiced law in Huntington, Cleveland, and Chicago. In 1884 Harvey gave up his practice and went to Colorado for his health, where he worked as a miner and engaged in real-estate promotion. Concluding that industrial conflict arose because the financial structure of the country was unsound, Harvey returned to Chicago in 1893 and established the Coin Publishing Company to disseminate his views. *Coin's Financial School,* published in 1894, was his most widely read publication; it took the form of a dialogue between one Professor Coin and his pupils, all prominent businessmen. Cartoons and diagrams illustrated the texts, and immediately the public imagination was captured by his unorthodox treatment of economic questions; Harvey was quoted throughout the country as 'Coin.' Other publications in similar vein followed: *A Tale of Two Nations* (1895), *Coin on Money, Trusts, and Imperialism* (1899), *Common Sense, or The Clot on the Brain of the Body Politic* (1920).

When the Democratic Party abandoned its advocacy of the free coinage of silver in 1900, Harvey moved to Arkansas and built Monte Ne, a resort town, where he opened a hotel. Convinced that civilization was doomed, he began construction of a 130-foot 'pyramid of America,' a towering monument of steel and concrete, in the vaults of which were to be sealed the history of American civilization and Harvey's reasons for its downfall for the enlightenment of future historians. The depression of the early 1930's halted work on the pyramid; Harvey emerged from retirement to organize the Liberty Party and in 1932 received 800 votes for the presidency of the United States. At his death in 1936 only the 10-foot thick granite and limestone base of his pyramid had been completed.

WHITE PINES FARM (R), 36.5 *m.,* an experimental dairy farm, is owned and operated by the Red House Association as part of the Red House Farms project; the farm has one of the finest Guernsey herds in the country.

LAWNVALE (R), 37.3 *m.,* a white frame farmhouse (*private*), with green shutters, and a dozen oddly assorted outbuildings are screened by a copse of oak and white pine. Lawnvale was the home of Dr. T. C. Atkeson (1852–1936), agriculturalist and educator, and the birthplace of his daughter, Mary Meek Atkeson, educator, author, and lecturer on country life.

ROBERTSBURG, 38.6 *m.* (570 alt., 135 pop.), and ARBUCKLE, 42.9 *m.* (590 alt., 1,655 pop.), are the trading centers of a rich farming area. In the fields are sleek cattle and hogs; barns are large, and farmhouses manor-like. The highway climbs out of the valley to wind along a high mile-long ledge of red Oriskany sandstone to the northern boundary of a 10,990-acre tract patented by George Washington in 1772, occupied a few years later by the 'Lost Colony' (*see below*).

AMBROSIA, 53.2 *m.* (577 alt., 77 pop.), is so tiny that its cluster of houses is almost shadowed when the sun sinks behind the tall railroad water tower (L).

US 35 swings down a series of curves and under a long black railroad trestle that stretches across the river flats like a basking blacksnake. Here in the Point Pleasant area, where the Great Kanawha joins the Ohio, occurred in 1774 the decisive battle in the conflict known as Lord Dunmore's War. After Great Britain had wrested Canada and the land west of the Alleghenies from France as a result of the French and Indian Wars, the English Government closed the western lands to settlement, against the bitter protests of the colonists along the Atlantic seaboard, who had fought the French in the hope of opening up the rich lands in the Mississippi basin. Hardy settlers had already pushed across the Alleghenies and down the Ohio into the wilds of Kentucky and the Illinois country. The British Government in prohibiting settlement was motivated in part by the desire to pacify the Indians by preventing encroachment on their lands and in part by the desire to preserve the profitable fur trade.

John Murray, Lord Dunmore, was appointed governor of Virginia in 1771, with strict instructions to prevent colonization beyond the mountains, but in 1773 he himself became interested in western lands with the purchase of two large tracts along the Ohio and began to encourage the westward expansion of Virginia. This invasion of their hunting grounds aroused the Indians, and open conflict resulted when a group of drunken whites murdered the family of Chief Tahgahjute, friend of the white man, better known by his English name of Logan (*see Tour 17a and 19a*).

Lord Dunmore ordered the border militia mobilized; Andrew Lewis (*see Tour 15a*), a veteran of the French and Indian Wars, was appointed brigadier general of the Virginia troops. In September 1774, Dunmore signed treaties of peace with the Delaware and the Six Nations of the Iroquois at Pittsburgh and started down the Ohio to give battle to the fierce Shawnee. Meantime, Lewis had marched northwest from Camp Union (*see Tour 15a*) with 1,100 men, camping at the mouth of the Great Kanawha River, at a point known as Point Pleasant. Dunmore found the Shawnee villages along the Ohio deserted, for Chief Cornstalk had marched his braves around behind him through the forest, intending to deal separately with the two parts of Dunmore's army. Early on the morning of October 10, 1774, Cornstalk and his painted warriors crossed the Ohio and approached Lewis's sleeping army; two men hunting deer saw them, and one escaped to arouse the camp. In the fierce battle that followed, Lewis's army decisively defeated Cornstalk's forces, breaking the power of the Indians in the Ohio Valley.

Long recognized as a decisive engagement in the protracted series of Indian wars, the battle of Point Pleasant has become officially known as the 'First Battle of the Revolution,' thanks to the efforts of the local D.A.R. and Livia Simpson Poffenbarger, who conducted a vigorous campaign to support the contention that 'the shot heard round the world' was fired here, and not at Lexington. The Indians, according to their view, had been incited by British agents to trouble the colonists and thus keep their minds off their grievances against the mother country. Success crowned this crusade in 1908 when the U. S. Senate rewrote history by recognizing the claim and passing a bill to aid in the erection of a monument at Point Pleasant, in Tu-Endie-Wei Park (*see below*), 'to commemorate the Battle of the Revolution fought at that point between the Colonial troops and Indians, October tenth, seventeen hundred and seventy-four.'

At 59.9 *m.* is WASHINGTON'S SPRING (R), believed to be the site of Washington's camping ground when he visited the Kanawha Valley in 1770.

POINT PLEASANT, 60.6 *m.* (569 alt., 3,301 pop.), occupies a promontory shaped like an Indian arrowhead, washed on one side (R) by the Ohio, and on the other by the Great Kanawha, which here empties into the larger river. With low hills in the background and wide smooth waters in front, the site of the town justifies the name given it in 1770 by George Washington when he camped here while exploring the vicinity.

For more than 150 years the town has depended on the moods of the rivers for bread and butter, for conversation, for periodic excitement. The day of the sidewheel packet is gone, but the Ohio is still the life force of the town, which profits from its drydocks and the manufacture of steel-hulled watercraft. Although an early traveler described the village as 'above the danger of overflowing,' the rivers invade the lower levels of the town every spring, an occurrence which townspeople accept with equanimity. When word flies about that 'she's risin',' throngs crowd the river banks to exchange reminiscences of past floods and speculations on the size of the imminent one. The flood finds the town in holiday humor; every garage gives birth to a johnboat, and the average householder, having stowed his goods safely on the second floor, spends his time rowing about the streets in conventional flood attire—heavy jacket, hip boots, and derby hat.

The point was visited in 1749 by Captain Peter Joseph Céleron, Chevalier de Bienville, a French explorer. Fort Blair was erected here in 1774, the year in which Chief Cornstalk's force was routed (*see above*). Fort Randolph was built in 1776. During the next few decades the settlement grew very slowly. 'It contains twenty-one indifferent houses, including a court house of square logs, this being the seat of justice of Mason County,' wrote an early visitor. 'The town does not thrive on account of the adjacent country not settling as fast as the opposite side in the state of Ohio, where lands can be bought in small tracts for farms, by real settlers, at a reasonable rate, whereas the Virginia lands, belonging mostly to wealthy and great landowners, are held at four and five times the Ohio price.' In 1810 another visitor here found Goldsmith's Deserted Village 'a paradise in comparison,' and 15 years later Henry Clay described the point as 'a beautiful woman clad in rags.' As settlers began to move west in increasing numbers, travelers built boats here to float themselves and their belongings down the Ohio. Real prosperity came to the town after 1840 when, 'coincidental with the extermination of wolves in the vicinity,' a shipyard was built. When Point Pleasant was incorporated as a town in 1833, horsemen were still using Main Street as a race course.

In TU-ENDIE-WEI PARK (Ind., the point between two waters), an 84-foot granite shaft, erected in 1909, marks the SITE OF THE BATTLE OF POINT PLEASANT (*see above*). Inscribed on its sides are the names of those killed and wounded in the affray; at the foot of the shaft stands the marble figure of a frontiersman, rifle in hand. South of the monument is the GRAVE OF 'MAD ANN' BAILEY (*see Charleston*), intrepid woman soldier and border scout.

In the park, on the river bank, is the MANSION HOUSE (*open*), a log structure erected in 1797 by Walter Newman. The oldest house in the Kanawha Valley, it served as tavern, dance hall, church, and community center. It has been restored as a museum and contains authentic Colonial furniture and collections of early Americana. The CELERON MONUMENT, a headstone on the terrace between the Mansion House and the river bank, commemorates the finding in 1849 of a lead plate buried in 1749 at the mouth of the Kanawha by Captain Peter Joseph Céleron, who thus claimed the Ohio River and its tributaries and all lands drained by them for Louis XV, King of France. Céleron buried four of these plates along the Ohio, but only two have been discovered.

A monument on the river bank, just north of Tu-Endie-Wei Park, marks the SITE OF FORT RANDOLPH, erected in 1776 at the outbreak of the Revolution. The next year Chief Cornstalk and his son came to the fort on an errand of peace; they were seized and killed in retaliation for the scalping of a settler near the fort, presumably by Indians.

The MASON COUNTY COURTHOUSE, a worn two-story brick structure, was built in 1857 to replace a log courthouse dating from the formation of the county in 1804. Incident to the operations of Union General Joseph A. Lightburn, the courthouse received a baptism of fire during several skirmishes in 1862; benches and desks, in the main courtroom, and walls and windowsills are still pocked with marks made by flying lead and iron. The square bell tower, with slatted openings at the top and striped with cement turning green with age, overlooks on the courthouse lawn the GRAVE OF CHIEF CORNSTALK, enclosed within an iron chain suspended on four whitewashed stone posts. Near by, a rough-hewn limestone shaft has been erected to his memory.

Left from Point Pleasant on State 2, which crosses the Great Kanawha on the Shadle Toll Bridge (*car and driver, 35¢; each additional passenger, 5¢*). HENDERSON, 0.8 *m.* (562 alt., 330 pop.), suburb of Point Pleasant, is at the junction with State 17.

Left on State 17, graveled, to TWO MILE CREEK, 2 *m.*, which marks the western boundary of a 10,990-acre tract once owned by George Washington and settled by his 'Lost Colony.' This piece of land, patented in 1772, was the first of several designated by Washington for improvement in 1774, when he sent James Cleveland and William Stevens to clear and plant the area. By December 1775, 14 buildings had been erected, and potatoes, corn, turnips, and peachstones had been planted. The Revolutionary War ended this attempt to colonize the tract; by the end of the Revolution the wilderness had swallowed up all signs of civilization.

At 7.4 *m.* on State 17 is (R) the SHADLE HOUSE (*private*), patterned on Washington's home at Mount Vernon, surrounded with lawns and flower beds, bordered with a picket fence overgrown with rambler roses.

South on State 2 is GALLIPOLIS FERRY, 4.9 *m.* (585 alt., 112 pop.), at one time the home of John Bryan, a farmer, and his wife, grandparents of William Jennings Bryan. A ferry (*25¢, car and driver; 5¢ each additional passenger*) connects the hamlet with Gallipolis, Ohio.

HOGSETT, 12 *m.* (568 alt., 25 pop.), is a rural village at the junction with a graveled road.

Right on this road, 1 *m.*, is the GALLIPOLIS LOCKS AND DAM (*open to visitors; guides*), constructed by the U. S. Government between 1933 and 1937 at a cost of approximately $10,600,000. One of the largest roller-type dams in the world, it replaced three old-type wicket dams on the Ohio and three on the Kanawha; it provides a 9-foot channel for a distance of 48 miles up the Ohio and as far up the Kanawha as U. S. Lock No. 1 at Winfield (*see above*). Its locks, one 110 by 360 feet, the other 110 by 600 feet, are as large as those in the Panama Canal. The dam has an over-all length of 1,116 feet; eight roller crest gates between concrete piers 121 feet high are mounted on concrete sills, from which they can be raised in time of flood to allow free passage of water. Each of the steel rollers is 122 feet long, weighs 360 tons, and can be raised on slanting grooves notched in the towers at the rate of 9 inches a minute by electric motor. The usual river tow can be passed through the locks in 20 minutes; the dam is operated by the U. S. Engineer Corps.

MERCERS BOTTOM, 15.2 *m.* (557 alt., 50 pop.), part of a wide fertile tract of 16,000 acres surveyed in 1770 by order of George Washington, was granted to General Hugh Mercer and others for their services in the Indian wars; Mercer was killed in 1777 in the Battle of Princeton, New Jersey.

GREENBOTTOM, 26 *m.* (585 alt., 57 pop.), part of a tract patented by Colonel Joshua Fry about 1735, was purchased in 1825 by Captain William Jenkins; it was the home of his youngest son, General Albert Gallatin Jenkins, first to carry the Confederate flag into Ohio, who died of wounds received at Cloyds Mountain, 1864. The JENKINS HOUSE (R), a Georgian Colonial structure built of brick made on the estate, has hand-hewn timbers joined with pegs.

The WEST VIRGINIA STATE FOREST NURSERY (R), 26.2 *m.*, occupying 20 acres of river bottomland, produces hardwood and coniferous trees for reforestation purposes throughout the State. Some 4,000,000 forest trees, seedlings, and transplants can be produced annually, including poplar, ash, oak, walnut, and a dozen varieties of evergreens.

LESAGE, 29.1 *m.* (552 alt., 79 pop.), owes its existence to the broken wheel-shaft of an Ohio River packet and the impatience of Jules LeSage, immigrant band-box manufacturer of Paris, France. In 1851, after a short residence in New York, LeSage set out to join a colony founded at Nauvoo, Illinois, on communistic principles evolved by Etienne Cabet. Irked at the delay caused by the broken shaft and tired of travel, LeSage disembarked, purchased 600 acres of land here, and on the hillside (L) built the LESAGE HOUSE, a rambling two-story frame dwelling with a balconied upper story affording a clear view of the river, a characteristic feature of the old valley residences. Carved palings in porch banisters and figured wooden pillars supporting the second-story porch give it the appearance of a steamboat's texas and indicate the influence of steamboat design on the homes of early rivermen.

At 44.4 *m.* is the junction with US 60 (*see Tour 15c*), 0.9 miles east of HUNTINGTON (*see Huntington*).

US 35 crosses the OHIO LINE, 61.5 *m.*, at the western end of a bridge (*car and driver, 25¢ to 35¢; each additional passenger, 5¢*), spanning the Ohio River to the village of Kanauga, 4 miles northeast of Gallipolis, Ohio (*see Ohio Guide*).

✓✓

Tour 15

(Covington, Va.)—White Sulphur Springs—Lewisburg—East Rainelle —Gauley Bridge—Charleston—Huntington—(Ashland, Ky.); US 60. Virginia Line to Kentucky Line, 177.6 *m.*

Bituminous-macadam surface with frequent stretches of concrete.
Chesapeake & Ohio Ry. parallels route between White Sulphur Springs and Caldwell, Falls View and St. Albans, Hurricane and Huntington.
Usual accommodations throughout.

US 60, known as the Midland Trail, crosses the southern half of West Virginia, connecting the open hill country along the Virginia Line with the fertile bottom lands along the Ohio River at the Ken-tucky boundary. Along the way it passes through one of the most fashionable watering places in the country, cuts across the rich blue-grass pastures of the Big Levels in the Greenbrier Valley, follows the winding course of the rich agricultural-industrial Kanawha Valley as far as Charleston, the State capital, which it links with the industrial area around Huntington, West Virginia's largest city. For a few miles farther west this transcontinental highway follows the Ohio River and then crosses the Big Sandy into Kentucky.

Once a meandering buffalo trail, this route was more and more used as the West was opened up and settled, and early in the nineteenth century became the renowned and much traveled James River and Kanawha Turnpike. In 1784 George Washington had urged its development as an all-Virginia road to the West to compete with the profitable routes already established through Pennsylvania and New York, and the next year the Virginia legislature authorized construction of a wagon road along the trail. Known as the Old State Road, or Koontz' New Road, it was completed to present Cedar Grove on the Kanawha in 1790, two months after its authorization, and to the Ohio River during the following decade. By 1804 conveyances with four wheels, called 'shake-guts,' traveled all the way to the Kentucky border. Tolls were charged to keep the road in repair:

Wagon, team, and driver	25¢
Four-wheeled riding carriage	20¢
Cart, or two-wheeled riding carriage	12½¢
Man and horse	6¼¢
Cattle, per head	¼¢
Sheep or hogs, per score	3¢

But the road was soon rutted and almost impassable, for great difficulty was encountered in collecting tolls in spite of the fact that keepers of toll gates were paid 9 per cent of collections to stimulate their zeal in preventing evasions. Private roads were built around the toll houses, some counties financed non-toll roads that paralleled or crisscrossed the State highway, and for a small consideration farmers allowed herds to be driven through their fields to avoid the gates. As the rapidly growing salt works along the Kanawha were clamoring for improved roads to markets in the East, the James River and Kanawha Turnpike was organized in Richmond, and by 1824 an improved highway had been constructed from the Valley of Virginia to Kanawha Falls, and was soon extended through the salt field to Charleston and on into Kentucky. In January 1827, a stage line ran its first coach between Lewisburg and Charleston, and weekly service was soon established to the mouth of the Big Sandy. Within ten years stagecoaches were operating on a regular schedule, carrying passengers and mail between Richmond and Guyandotte (Huntington) in four and a half days.

With the advent of the railroads the importance of the pike declined, but today a mounting stream of passenger cars and heavy trucks flows along the broad modern highway that has supplanted the old narrow wagon road.

Section a. VIRGINIA LINE to GAULEY BRIDGE; 80.8 m. US 60.

This section of US 60 traverses the rolling bluegrass country of the Big Levels in the Greenbrier Valley where stock-breeding gentry live in mellowed old houses much as they did in plantation days. Cutting across the fertile valley, where the earliest settlements west of the

Alleghenies were made, the highway passes leisurely villages, skirts
the State's oldest and most fashionable resort, and worms its course
through high rugged mountain country along the New River Gorge.

Crossing the VIRGINIA LINE, 0 *m.*, 23 miles west of Covington,
Virginia, US 60 descends ALLEGHENY MOUNTAIN (2,450 alt.),
thickly forested with pine and hemlock and hardwoods. This ridge
forms the watershed between streams flowing eastward to the Atlantic
Ocean and westward to the Ohio River and Gulf of Mexico.

The SULPHUR ROADSIDE PARK (*camp and picnic facilities*), 1.4 *m.*,
is maintained by the State Road Commission; in a small grove of pine,
elm, and maple, not far from the road, is a sulphur spring and a drinking fountain.

At 3.7 *m.* is the junction with an improved dirt road.

Right on this road to the SITE OF THE BATTLE OF WHITE SULPHUR SPRINGS
(L) 0.1 *m.*, fought August 26–7, 1863, between a force of 2,000 Confederates
under Major General Sam Jones and 1,300 Union soldiers commanded by
General William W. Averell. General Averell was compelled to retreat, a sixth
of his force having been killed or wounded.

At 2.8 *m.* is (R) the entrance to LA BAR'S RHODODENDRON NURSERY (*open*),
a mass of color during late June and early July when the State flower is in
bloom.

At 4.3 *m.* (R) is WHITE SULPHUR FISH HATCHERY.

WHITE SULPHUR SPRINGS, 4.4 *m.* (1,923 alt., 1,484 pop.),
although chiefly a residential town, has a small business district with
shops and several hotels; it owes its existence to the neighboring
springs that early made the valley a noted spa. The first settler in
the vicinity was Nathaniel Carpenter, who established 'corn rights'
to 950 acres by planting them about 1750, but he and most of his
family were killed by Indians. The springs first attracted attention
in 1772 when the invalid wife of an early settler was carried to the
springs in a litter. Crippled with rheumatism, she was bathed in a
rough trough hollowed in a large tree trunk; into this trough water
was poured and heated by means of hot stones. As she bathed, the
patient 'drank freely of the fountain,' so it is recorded, and 'in a few
weeks she went from her bark [bathing] cabin perfectly restored.'
News of her cure was passed along by word of mouth, and pioneers
and their families began to come to make trial of the springs, living
at first in tents; a few log cabins were later built.

In 1808 a tavern was erected by James Caldwell, grandson-in-law
of Nathaniel Carpenter (*see above*), on the latter's 'corn rights' tract;
Caldwell purchased other land, and to the tavern soon added a dining
hall, a ballroom, and a row of cottages. By the 1830's the resort had
become a center of fashion, a favorite rendezvous of elegant plantation society of the Old South. Other rows of cottages were built—
Paradise Row, Virginia Row, Georgia Row, Alabama Row, Baltimore
Row, Wolf Row—each with its social distinctions. Along Paradise Row
strutted the young newly weds and the charming, eager young belles,
brought by their families 'to the waters' in the hope of arranging a

desirable match. Close by lived the gay young bachelors in Wolf Row, which enjoyed a reputation of its own: 'Unless you be young and foolish, fond of noise and nonsense, frolic and fun, wine and wassail, sleepless nights and days of headache, avoid Wolf Row,' warned a visitor. The resort's greatest charm, added another, was its delightful society of every agreeable variety. 'From the East you have consolidationists, tariffites, and philanthropists; from the Middle, professors, chemical analysts, and letter writers; from the West, orators and gentlemen who can squat lower, jump higher, dive deeper, and come out drier, than all creation besides; and from the South, nullifiers, Union men, political economists, and statesmen; and from all quarters, functionaries of all ranks, ex-candidates for all functions, and the gay, agreeable, and handsome of both sexes, who come to the White Sulphur to see and be seen, to chat, laugh, and dance, and each to throw his pebble on the great heap of general enjoyment.'

A young Philadelphian visited the springs when he set out in 1834 'to see the world and pick up health,' and under the *nom de plume* of Peregrine Prolix left a graphic and amusing picture of the place and time.

> The middle of the valley [he wrote] . . . is cleared of forest, care having been taken to leave a few noble trees for ornament and shade. The buildings consist of a frame dining room about one hundred and twenty feet long, with which is connected a large kitchen and bakery; a frame ball room with lodging rooms over it and at each end; two very large frame stables with eighty stalls in each, of which the exterior rows are open to the air; and many rows of cabins tastefully arranged around the larger edifices, and standing on rising ground. There are several straight and dusty walks laid out with rectangular art; and many artless paths more agreeable to the foot and eye. The cabins are, in general, clean; some suspicion of fleas I confess too, but I detected no bugs, which are perhaps kept away by the nature of the water, for Virgil says in the fifth book of his Georgics:
>
> > Foetidum in aqua non gaudet sulphurea bedbug:
>
> which translated into the Virginia vernacular, means, 'The stinking chinch does not like sulphur water.'

The spring was lined with marble walls in octagonal shape and was covered with a handsome dome resting on white columns, and as for the water, Peregrine noted that it had 'the pleasant flavor of a half-boiled, half-spoiled egg . . . and cures the following diseases, according to popular belief—Yellow Jaundice, White Swelling, Blue Devils, and Black Plague; Scarlet Fever, Yellow Fever, Spotted Fever, and fever of every kind and colour; Hydrocephalus, Hydrothorax, Hydrocele, and Hydrophobia; Hypochondria and Hypocrisy; Dispepsia, Diarrhea, Diabetes, and die-of-anything; Gout, Gormandising, and Grogging; Liver Complaint, Colic, Stone, Gravel, and all other diseases and bad habits, except chewing, smoking, spitting and swearing.' In addition to sulphurated hydrogen and other ingredients, the mineral waters contained 'a very strong infusion of fashion,' he added, and as the latter is 'an animal substance, its quantity cannot be precisely ascertained; it is supposed, however, to be gradually increasing, and no doubt contributes greatly to the efficiency of the water.'

From White Sulphur stage lines ran to other lesser resorts in the region—Red Sulphur, Green Sulphur, Gray Sulphur, Blue Sulphur, Salt Sulphur, Sweetsprings, Warm Springs, and Hot Springs—all of which were often included in a fashionable tour 'of the waters.'

In 1854 the original tavern building gave way to the White Sulphur Springs Hotel, renowned for more than a half century as the Old White. It had a large and resplendent dining room, with crystal chandeliers, and its barroom was known to the élite throughout the country for its mint juleps. During the War between the States the hotel was the local headquarters of the armies of one side and then the other as the battle line moved forward and back again across the valley. After the Battle of White Sulphur Springs (*see above*) it served as a hospital; and the dead and dying were laid in rows in the glittering ballroom and dining room. In 1864 General David Hunter, in command of retreating Union forces, was dissuaded from burning the hotel by his artillery chief, who argued that it could be used as a barracks if their troops should pass this way again. After the war the Old White languished for a time, but many Southern families continued to come to enjoy the season here; they made a brave show of reviving antebellum gaiety and elegance, even though they were impoverished and no better off than the belle who remarked, with a confident toss of her head, that she had been reduced to 'one black silk dress and my grit.' In the 1880's the fashionable, with a sprinkling of the notable, again began to frequent the Old White, which ended its days in 1913 when it was torn down to make way for the present Greenbrier Hotel (*see below*).

At 4.9 *m.* is the junction with Jericho Draft, an improved dirt road.

Right on this road, bordered with grassy meadows, low wooded hills, and landscaped country estates screened from the road by shade trees, to a junction with a dirt road, 2.8 *m.;* R here 0.1 *m.* to OAKHURST (L), the first golf course in West Virginia. In 1884 George Grant, anxious to please his cousin, Lionel Torrin, an ardent golfer who intended to visit America, enlisted the aid of Russell Montague and Alexander and Roderick McLeod, and constructed a nine-hole course on the Montague grounds. These five men formed the Oakhurst Club, and every month for 10 years competed with each other for a medal made for the purpose. Neighboring farmers and visitors at White Sulphur drove out occasionally to watch 'those funny Scotchmen' with amused superiority; when one member imported clubs from Scotland, they were held for three weeks by customs officials who could not believe that any game could be played with 'such elongated blackjacks or implements of murder.'

Jericho Draft crosses the boundary of BLUE BEND PARK, 10 *m.,* a part of the Monongahela National Forest developed by the Federal Government for recreational purposes (*picnic facilities, camp sites*). Blue Bend, known locally as the Blue Hole, is a wide bend in Anthony Creek, where the water is deep blue, changing to green in shallower parts. Flagstone walks wind through the forest among rhododendron, mountain laurel, evergreens, and other mountain trees and shrubs. The large administration building is built of chestnut logs and floored with flagstones, as is the picnic shelter. Swimming (*free*) in the clear cool waters of the creek is supervised by a full-time lifeguard.

At 5.4 *m.*, nestling on a sunlit plateau dotted with lakes and marked by rushing streams, is (R) the 7,200-acre estate of the Greenbrier Hotel and Cottages, familiarly known as White Sulphur Springs. Built on the main line of the Chesapeake & Ohio Railway, 1,925 feet up in the forested Allegheny Mountains, this resort has been nationally famous since colonial days for its facilities for rest, recreation, social life, and curative mineral baths. From the main highway a shaded drive winds to the white-arched portico of the beautiful Georgian Colonial building of white painted brick, which is the NEW GREENBRIER HOTEL, constructed in 1913 and enlarged in 1931.

Behind and east of the main hotel building are eight rows of luxuriously furnished cottages, the oldest of which, those along Paradise Row, were constructed about 1820. Perhaps the best known is the PRESIDENT'S COTTAGE, a colonnaded building erected in 1816 and now a museum of the glories of White Sulphur's past. The cottage was the summer White House during the incumbency of Presidents Van Buren, Tyler, and Fillmore, and President Tyler spent his honeymoon here in 1844. Left of the entrance is the Old White Room, decorated with murals by William C. Grauer depicting scenes of the Old South and of historic events at White Sulphur, and containing a collection of furniture, old papers, letters, and other mementoes. To the right of the entrance is the Lee Room, which contains paintings and memorabilia of Robert E. Lee. In the LEE COTTAGE, No. Balt. C., in Baltimore Row, General Robert E. Lee and his family spent the summers of 1867, 1868, and 1869. Studios of the Old White Art School and Colony, directed each summer by William C. and Natalie R. Grauer, are in the cottages of Alabama and Louisiana Rows.

East of the driveway leading to the hotel is the WHITE SULPHUR SPRINGS, from which the resort takes its name. It is sheltered by a domed pavilion supported by 12 Doric pillars, surmounted with a statue of *Hygeia*. Other springs, including an alum spring and a radiochalybeate spring, are on the grounds. The New Greenbrier accommodates 1,000 guests.

At 5.5 *m.* is a junction with an improved dirt road.

Left on this road is KATE'S MOUNTAIN LODGE (*meals*), 1.5 *m.*, from which is a view of the Greenbrier Hotel and the valley of Howards Creek. Kate's Mountain was named for Kate Carpenter, wife of the first owner of White Sulphur (*see above*), who about 1750 took refuge here with her small daughter during an Indian raid, later making her way to the nearest fort some 30 miles distant. On the mountain grows Kate's Mountain clover, said to be found at few other places in the world; here also are found the box huckleberry, which some botanists declare to be the oldest known living plant, and specimens of virtually all flora native to West Virginia.

US 60 passes the GREENBRIER AIRPORT, 6.8 *m.*, and the GREENBRIER POLO FIELD, 7.5 *m.*

Rising on a short steep grade, the highway overlooks the rugged wooded spurs of WHITE ROCK MOUNTAIN (L) and GREEN-

BRIER MOUNTAIN (R), and descends between hillsides covered with dogwood, pine, elm, and poplar.

CALDWELL, 10.8 *m.* (1,693 alt., 110 pop.), on the east bank of the Greenbrier River, is a village of farmhouses with post office and country store.

LEWISBURG, 14.1 *m.* (2,084 alt., 1,293 pop.), seat of Greenbrier County and trading center of the rolling bluegrass country known as the Big Levels, has retained much of the appearance and many of the customs of a leisurely village of the Old South. The stock-breeding gentry of the fertile valley come into town frequently to buy supplies, swap horses, talk politics, and exchange gossip. Except during the annual fair week in August, the tempo of life is unhurried and sedate.

From the small business district radiates an orderly network of shady streets and unpaved lanes, along which stand Georgian Colonial houses—some of frame, some of brick, others of local limestone—all mellowed with time and weather. Many of the old houses have been restored by summer residents, attracted by the charm of the town and its proximity to White Sulphur, and many new houses have been built in styles that harmonize with the old. Family and genealogy are still matters of concern in social life, and the conservative traditions of the town are reflected in its two private schools, the Greenbrier Military School and the Greenbrier College for Women.

Lewisburg was named for Andrew Lewis, who in 1751, while surveying for the Greenbrier Land Company, camped with his father near the spring behind the courthouse. Under orders from General Braddock he erected Fort Savannah here in 1755 for the protection of the few settlers who had ventured into the Big Levels. Although the region was depopulated during the French and Indian Wars, settlement began again in 1769 with an influx of Scotch and English from eastern Virginia. In 1774 General Lewis was able to muster 1,000 militiamen here at Fort Union, as it was renamed, and marched them against the Indians in the campaign that culminated in the Battle of Point Pleasant (*see Tour* 14).

Strategically situated at the junction of the Seneca Trail and the Kanawha Trail, Fort Union was chosen as the seat of Greenbrier County on its formation in 1778; the first courthouse was a temporary structure near Lewis' Spring. In 1782 the town was incorporated as Lewisburg, and in the same year a wagon road was completed from the east. By 1786 it had been extended to the Great Kanawha, and Lewisburg became an important way station on the westward route of migration. A log church was erected by a Presbyterian congregation organized in 1783, the first west of the Alleghenies. A Masonic lodge was chartered in 1796, and the Lewisburg Academy was founded by the Presbyterians in 1810. Lewisburg became 'the western capital of Virginia' when the State Supreme Court of Appeals began holding sessions here in 1833 to accommodate litigants west of the mountains.

The attendance of litigants, lawyers, and six justices at these sessions, the only ones of the tribunals not held in Richmond, increased the town's political and social importance. Several large hotels, including the Old Long Ordinary, nicknamed the 'Old Long Ornery,' were filled to overflowing at such times.

With the outbreak of the War between the States, the Supreme Court of Appeals ceased to meet here and the court's library was removed to Richmond. The academy closed its doors, and civilian travel on the turnpike came to a standstill. An hour's battle occurred in May 1862, when Confederates attempted to drive Federal forces from the town but were defeated.

Because of its Southern sympathies, Lewisburg lost much of its political importance during the Reconstruction era. But the reopening of the academy as the Lewisburg Female Institute in 1876, and the founding in 1890 of a school for boys, now the Greenbrier Military Institute, brought the town revenue and stability; these institutions and the influx of summer residents have made Lewisburg something more than the usual rural county seat.

The OLD STONE CHURCH, Church St., erected in 1796 to replace a log structure built in 1783, is constructed of limestone blocks said to have been brought on horseback from the banks of the Greenbrier River, four miles away, by the women of the Presbyterian congregation. A small bell cupola rising from the center of the shingled hip roof tops the rectangular, two-story building. Green shutters flank the many-paned sash windows. The interior has been rearranged, but the original pews, the balcony in which slaves sat, and the pulpit with sounding board have been preserved.

The GREENBRIER COLLEGE FOR WOMEN, opposite the church, was founded as the Lewisburg Academy in 1810 by the Reverend John McElhenney, pastor of the Old Stone Church. It was a mixed school of academy grade until 1876, when it became the Lewisburg Female Institute. In 1925 it was chartered as the Greenbrier College for Women. Some of the buildings were destroyed by fire in 1901 and again in 1921. The main building, a four-story structure of red brick, with a white-columned portico rising the entire height of the building, was erected in 1922. The President's House, formerly the Frazier Tavern, was erected about 1818 and remodeled in 1925, the original lines and woodwork being retained. The OLD LODGE, across the road from the campus, was built about 1836; the two-story square brick building served as the library of the Supreme Court of Appeals of Virginia until the War between the States terminated its sessions in Lewisburg. It was then used by the Masonic Lodge for more than 50 years, and is now the college laundry.

The GREENBRIER MILITARY SCHOOL, Lee St., was founded by Thomas Gilmore in 1890 as an academy for boys and became a military school in 1891. Known as the Lee Military Academy, from 1896 until 1899, it offered college preparatory courses under 'ideal' conditions, advertising that there was 'no saloon in town; no distractions.' In 1906 the Presbyterian Church purchased the academy and again conducted it as a school for boys until 1920, when it became a privately owned military school. Its buildings are new and modern, for fire destroyed the school in 1925.

The GREENBRIER COUNTY COURTHOUSE, Market St., erected in 1837, was the first structure built especially for this purpose; the court had previously used three temporary buildings. Although the exterior of the red brick Georgian structure has remained unchanged, wings were added and extensive interior alterations were made in 1938. The jail, Jefferson Street, is in two sections. The limestone section, built about 1800, is nicknamed the 'stoney lonesome'; the brick addition was probably built between 1820 and 1830. Its bricks have become so softened with age that a teaspoon is an adequate implement for digging through them, as many escaped transgressors can testify.

LEWIS' SPRING, locally known as the Town Spring, near the jail, pours into a large round concrete watering trough. During court sessions and fair week, traders gather here to swap horses, pacing their animals up and down to display their points and spirit.

The LEWISBURG HOTEL, Randolph and Market Sts., is a long building, part limestone and part frame, with first and second story galleries running the entire length of the structure. The limestone section was formerly the Mays Hotel, erected about 1800.

The GENERAL LEWIS HOTEL, Main St., at the eastern end of town, is a modern building, classical in style, furnished with authentic Colonial furniture from old houses in the neighborhood; it has a collection of warming pans, fire irons, stirrup irons, pokers, and other relics of pioneer life. The east wing was constructed around a house built in 1798; the rough-hewn ceiling beams of the main hall are from an even older cabin.

The LEWIS OAK in the garden of the General Lewis Hotel is alleged to have been blazed by Andrew Lewis in 1751 to mark the southeast corner of a grant surveyed for the Greenbrier Land Company; his 'L' is still faintly discernible under a protective glass covering.

The JOHN WESLEY METHODIST CHURCH (*Negro*), German St., was erected before the War between the States by a white congregation and was taken over by the trustees of the Methodist Episcopal Church, South, when the Methodist Church split on the slavery issue. The trustees were later ordered to surrender the building by the West Virginia Supreme Court of Appeals in its first decision on the ownership of the property.

Lewisburg is at the junction with US 219 (*see Tour 8b and c*).

West of Lewisburg the highway traverses the wide grain fields and the bluegrass pastures of the fertile Big Levels. Fields are dented with the sink holes characteristic of limestone country; here underground streams have leached out limestone strata and formed many caverns.

On a farm (L), 17 *m.*, is a WEST VIRGINIA UNIVERSITY CATTLE EX-PERIMENT STATION (*open*).

MORLUNDA (L), 18.1 *m.*, a large estate on which blooded Hereford cattle and Percheron horses are bred, was named for the owner's old home in Sweden. The rectangular two-story house, with a two-story white portico, was designed and built in 1800 by Colonel Samuel Mc-Clung of handmade brick imported from England. Two wings were later added. The interior woodwork is hand carved, every room has a mantel of elaborate design. On either side of the fireplace in the dining room are deep presses of walnut and mahogany extending from floor to ceiling. The oak floors, duplicates of the originals, are laid with pegs; on the doors are the original locks, opened with keys as huge as the ceremonial 'keys to the city.' Behind the house is a one-story building, once the slave quarters. The old smokehouse, which has slate floors, has been converted into a guest house.

RICHLAND, 20.3 *m.* (2,100 alt., 65 pop.), is a minor trading cen-ter of a rich agricultural section.

At 21.1 *m.* is the junction with a dirt road.

Right on this road to the SITE OF FORT DONNALLY 6 *m.*, built by Andrew Donnally sometime prior to 1771. In May 1778 a large band of Indians, out to avenge the death of Chief Cornstalk at Point Pleasant (*see Tour* 14), attacked this supposedly weak garrison. Warned by messengers from Fort Randolph, neighboring settlers gathered here, and a call for help was dispatched to Fort Savannah (Lewisburg). Only four men were killed by the Indians. A force of 68 men under Colonel John Stuart arrived the second day of the siege and routed the Indians. After this decisive victory, almost as important as the Battle of Point Pleasant, no more attacks were made on the settlers in Green-brier Valley.

Throughout this section outcroppings of blue limestone appear on the grass-covered hillsides and in the rolling pastures.

A small bell tower rises above the hipped roof of the rectangular SAM BLACK CHURCH (L), 30.4 *m.*, a white frame structure erected in 1902 in memory of the Reverend Sam Black, an early Southern Meth-odist circuit rider. His name is written in large letters across the door-way of the building. On his horse, Shiloh, Black traveled through Greenbrier, Fayette, Clay, Nicholas, Webster, and Kanawha Counties, organizing congregations and building churches with money obtained by selling gloves and socks made by women of the church.

At 34.6 *m.* is the junction with a dirt road.

Right on this road to GLENCOE (*private*), 1.5 *m.*, known locally as the McFarland House, the one-story central unit of which was erected in 1822. The work of clearing the grounds and building the house was done by slaves, who hauled stone for the foundation, cut the lumber, and manufactured nails in a blacksmith shop built by them. The log house is now weatherboarded and painted white. At either end two-story towers rise to a hip roof, topped with a white wooden spire. Two cabins formerly occupied by slaves stand (R) near the house. In the open field a short distance from the cabins is the site of a whipping post used by McFarland in punishing his slaves.

Crossing LITTLE CLEAR CREEK, 36 *m.*, and BIG CLEAR CREEK, 38 *m.*, the highway enters RUPERT, 38.5 *m.* (2,436 alt., 110 pop.), headquarters for anglers and hunters in the western Greenbrier country.

For several miles west and south of CHARMCO, 42 *m.* (2,401 alt., 75 pop.), US 60 skirts (L) the MEADOW RIVER ROADSIDE PARK (*camp sites, picnic facilities*).

EAST RAINELLE, 43.7 *m.* (2,404 alt., 1,272 pop.), is the trading center of small mining and lumbering villages in the vicinity.

RAINELLE, 45 *m.* (2,425 alt., 920 pop.), in the Meadow River Valley at the foot of Big Sewell Mountain, is crowded on Saturday and pay-day nights with miners from the coal fields, farmers from outlying valley farms, tourists from several States, and 'wood-hicks' from near-by logging camps wearing denim trousers clipped to the top of calked boots, which strike sparks as the lumberjacks stride along the cement sidewalks.

The MEADOW RIVER LUMBER COMPANY PLANT (L), established by John and W. T. Raine, for whom the town was named, is one of the largest hardwood plants in the East, employing 500 men; its triple bandsaws can cut some 35,000,000 feet of lumber annually, or five carloads daily. Logs are transported to the mill twice daily by rail from the upper Meadow River Valley. In the lumber yard, which has more than three miles of docks, lumber is stacked to a height of 20 or 30 feet. After the stacked lumber is thoroughly seasoned, it is put through the finishing mill, where it is smoothed and converted into building materials, furniture stock, or flooring. The plant produces annually more than 4,000,000 women's wooden shoe heels.

The highway begins a gradual ascent of Big Sewell Mountain; laurel and dogwood form a background for a ROADSIDE DRINKING FOUNTAIN, 47.2 *m.*

At 47.9 *m.* is the junction with a dirt road.

Right on this road 0.5 *m.* to the summit of BIG SEWELL MOUNTAIN (3,170 alt.), where General Robert E. Lee established headquarters during the autumn of 1861; the wind-swept height overlooks miles of mountains and rolling farmlands. A bronze tablet here marks the SITE OF LEE'S TREE, a large sugar maple which stood until 1937. Under it Lee is said to have received his beloved horse, Traveller, which had been born and raised near Blue Sulphur Springs in Greenbrier County. As a colt it was named Jeff Davis and took first prize at the Lewisburg fairs in 1859 and 1860. Lee first saw the spirited young horse when it was a four-year-old and he spoke of it admiringly as 'my colt,' but declined to accept it when it was offered to him as a gift by Major Thomas L. Broun and Captain Joseph M. Broun. Lee rode the horse for a month, however, and became so attached to the animal that he purchased him for $200 in Confederate currency. Renamed Traveller, the horse served the Southern leader throughout the war; later, when Lee became president of Washington and Lee University at Lexington, Virginia, he often rode Traveller about town. On Lee's death in 1870, Traveller, saddled and bridled, walked behind the coffin to the grave. Some years later, while grazing on the campus, he stepped on a rusty nail, tetanus developed, and he died in the brick barn near the President's House on the campus. A feather bed had been placed under him by Washington and Lee students. His skeleton is preserved in Lee Museum at Lexington.

At 55.6 *m.* is the junction with State 41.

Left on State 41 is the entrance (R) to BABCOCK STATE PARK, 4 *m.*, a 3,231-acre tract developed around a deep Y-shaped gorge cut through the mountains by two swift streams (*fishing in season*). Motor roads and more than 25 miles of trails wind through the forest, along the rim of a canyon 1,100 feet deep, and up the mountainsides to picnic tables, ovens, and shelters. The administration building contains the park offices, a restaurant, a bathhouse, and several overnight lodging rooms; cabins furnished with all necessities for a week can be rented (*apply State Conservation Commission, Charleston*). At the foot of a waterfall in Glade Creek is a swimming pool. ISLAND IN THE SKY, a headland with a stone shelter, overlooks the surrounding valley and peaks. At its base is a cave, once the haunt of a bandit gang, which in earlier days, say the hill folk, robbed the pay-roll trains on the narrow-gauge logging railroad that wormed its way through the park area; the railroad is now used to haul coal to Sewell near by.

LOOKOUT, 60.7 *m.* (2,316 alt., 210 pop.), is dominated by SPY ROCK (L), 61.5 *m.*, used first by the Indians and later by the Union army as an observation post. West of Lookout the highway follows a rolling course between stake and rider fences bordering cultivated fields and pasture land. On hillsides, flowering dogwood gleams white in May.

ANSTED, 71.9 *m.* (1,310 alt., 1,404 pop.), is the headquarters of the Gauley Mountain Coal Company and the trading center for their mines in the vicinity. The highway splits the business section of the town and the gray miners' houses lined up in rows on the hill slopes. Ansted was settled in 1790 by Baptists. The settlement was first named New Haven by a colony of Spiritualists who came here from New England in 1830, but in 1831, when the town became the seat of Fayette County, it was renamed Ansted for Professor David T. Ansted, British scientist, who was instrumental in interesting English capitalists in the development of coal here. The town's growth dates from 1873 when coal operations were opened near by.

In Westlake Cemetery (R), which covers the crest of a small knoll overlooking the main part of town, is the GRAVE OF JULIA NEALE JACKSON, mother of General Stonewall Jackson. The grave was visited by Major Jackson in 1855, who noted in a letter to an aunt that the grave was unmarked. After the War between the States a marble monument was erected by Captain Thomas D. Ranson, a veteran of the Stonewall Brigade; later the grave was enclosed within an iron fence mounted on a stone coping.

HAWKS NEST STATE PARK (L), 73.7 *m.*, a 41-acre recreational area (*paths, picnic grounds and shelter, parking space, benches*), centers on HAWKS NEST (L), a towering rock overlooking (L) the NEW RIVER GORGE. The steep-walled canyon, in summer brilliant with thick growths of oak, maple, dogwood, and rhododendron, rises 585 feet above New River. From the rock, named for the fish hawks that once nested there, is a view (R) of the waters of the New River impounded by the HAWKS NEST DAM, part of a large hydroelectric plant. The dam, a graceful structure of 14 concrete arches, with steel wickets between them, is topped with a 14-foot highway (*private*). On the south side of the dam is the inlet of the HAWKS NEST TUNNEL, a conduit varying in diameter from 32 to 44 feet, which carries the entire flow of New River three miles through Gauley Mountain to the power plant.

During the construction of the tunnel, begun in 1930 and completed in 1933, the 5,000 workers encountered a stratum of pure silica. The fact that many contracted silicosis and died resulted in protracted litigation.

On the top of a knoll overlooking the parking space is HAWKS NEST MUSEUM, reached by a steep climb up a footpath, a stained log structure on a pinkish stone base. Three one-story wings branch from a story-and-a-half central unit. The building houses the park custodian and a two-room museum containing a large collection of pioneer rifles, knives and ammunition, and numerous Indian relics.

In CHIMNEY CORNER, 76.3 *m.*, is a junction (L) with US 19 (*see Tour 10c*). The highway follows a winding course, frequently within view of the New River, which between the Hawks Nest Dam and the power plant is almost dry, except when melting snows and protracted rains send the overflow from the dam churning down the boulder-strewn canyon bed.

SCENIC VIEW (L), 77.5 *m.*, on the edge of the gorge, overlooks an oasis of well-kept greensward around the concrete oval of the overflow basin, marking the halfway point of the Hawks Nest Tunnel. The basin checks the tremendous force of the water in the tunnel when, because of some emergency at the power plant, the mighty valves that control the turbines are suddenly closed. It is one of several devices to protect the tunnel and the penstocks that feed the turbines from the destructive force of the imprisoned river. An electric power line, following a cleared right-of-way through thickets of scrub oak and dogwood, marks the course of the tunnel under the mountain.

The ELECTRO-METALLURGICAL COMPANY POWER PLANT (L), 79.6 *m.*, a modern industrial structure with tall arched windows, has four turbines, each of which develops 35,000 h.p. from the swift stream that rushes through the tunnel.

GAULEY BRIDGE, 80.8 *m.* (677 alt., 516 pop.), lies in a narrow, steep-walled valley at the confluence of the New and Gauley Rivers, which unite to form the Great Kanawha.

In 1822, during the construction of the James River and Kanawha Turnpike, an $18,000 covered bridge was built across the Gauley here against the vigorous protests from ferrymen up and down the river. The bridge stood until July 11, 1826, when it was destroyed by a fire attributed to 'persons interested in the ferry at that point.' Until construction in 1828 of a new bridge—uncovered, this time, to guard against fires—ferrymen were paid a third of all tolls collected by the State for passage across the Gauley. During the War between the States the town had great strategic value as the gateway to the Kana-

wha Valley. In November 1861, General W. S. Rosecrans defeated
General John B. Floyd here in the last of a series of battles that left
the Union forces in secure control of the valley.

The old MILLER TAVERN (R), Main St. northeast of the Virginian
Railway overhead crossing, is a two-story white frame building with
a two-story portico. Here, during the War between the States, was
the headquarters for officers of the Union Army, among whom were
William McKinley and Rutherford B. Hayes, both destined for the
presidency of the United States. Near the bridge (R) over the Gauley
are the crumbling stone piers of the bridge destroyed by retreating
Confederate forces in 1861.

Gauley Bridge is at the junction with US 19 (*see Tour* 10*b*).

Section b. GAULEY BRIDGE to CHARLESTON, 35.8 m. US 60.

This section of US 60 follows the Great Kanawha River from its
beginning at the union of the New and Gauley Rivers to Charleston,
the State capital. Through a valley alternately cramped and spacious,
steeped in frontier tradition and rich in historical incident, the highway passes coal towns, in a field past its zenith of production, to enter
a region indebted for life and livelihood to the chemical industry, attracted here by a concentration of coal, natural gas, and salt brine.

West of GAULEY BRIDGE, 0 *m.*, the highway is shadowed by
steep rocky banks, broken by small cool grottoes in narrow ravines
down which miniature cataracts splash from rock to rock. The Kanawha River (L) is bordered with willows and dotted with wooded
islands.

GLEN FERRIS, 1.7 *m.* (669 alt., 306 pop.), was known until 1895
as Stockton, for Colonel Aaron Stockton, who settled here in 1812.
During the early days of the James River and Kanawha Turnpike,
over which the last stagecoach rolled in 1873, Stockton kept a popular
tavern here, now the GLEN FERRIS INN (L), a two-story red brick
structure with a high white-columned porch running the length of the
front and extending along one side. The central unit is the original
section of the building, the wings on both sides being later additions.
The genial host was described by one of his patrons as 'a good-natured
chunk of a man who cast a shadow of almost the same altitude when
lying down as when standing up.'

From Glen Ferris Inn is a fine view of KANAWHA FALLS, extending
in a jagged line across the river, with a drop of 22 feet. A 10-foot
dam has been built above the falls to generate power. The waters
slip smoothly over the lip of the dam in a swirling confusion of white
foam on the broken ledge of the falls. From VAN BIBBER LEAP, a crag
overhanging the whirlpool below the falls, on the opposite side of
the river, Reuben Van Bibber, a pioneer, jumped into the river and
escaped pursuing Indians, according to tradition. Here also, according to some historians, Thomas Batts and Robert Fallam, leaders of

an expedition 'for the finding out the ebbing and flowing of ye South Sea,' took possession of the Mississippi Valley in the name of the king of England.

On both sides of the highway are low mounds of purplish iridescent blocks, similar to congealed tar, finished ferrochrome alloy from the smelters of the ELECTRO-METALLURGICAL COMPANY PLANT (L), the oldest of four plants operated by the company in the production of ferro-alloys and metals. Constructed in 1898 to utilize power generated from Kanawha Falls, the operations of this plant have been largely taken over by a new works opened in 1932 at Alloy (*see below*).

FALLS VIEW (L), 4.9 *m.* (653 alt., 350 pop.), is an attractive residential village built for the officials at the Electro-Metallurgical Company plants. Comfortable modern houses with spacious grassy lawns are screened from the highway by a half-mile row of Lombardy poplars.

ALLOY, 6.8 *m.* (675 alt., 219 pop.), is the central unit of a string of small towns that depend chiefly upon the plants of the Electro-Metallurgical Company here and at Glen Ferris for a livelihood. Up to 1932 the town was a coal camp with a cluster of small unpainted frame shanties. Squatting in the center of a web of power lines, conveyors, and railroad tracks, the ELECTRO-METALLURGICAL COMPANY PLANT (L) was built in 1932 to utilize the power generated by the Hawks Nest hydroelectric system (*see above*). Half hidden by heaps of ore and silica, the plant houses high-voltage furnaces in which ore brought from South Africa is transformed into ferrochrome alloy, a combination of iron and chromium, used in chromium plating and in toughening steels for special purposes. Chrome steel, a stainless and rust-resisting metal, is used in the manufacture of turbine blades, golf clubs, cutlery, marine and architectural fittings, and apparatus for the dairy, food, and chemical industries.

The town stands on the SITE OF THE PADDY HUDDLESTON FARM, where Daniel Boone often stopped on his hunting and fishing expeditions. Huddleston and Boone used to trap beaver together at Kanawha Falls. Two stone chimneys (R) are all that remain of the comfortable log house built by Paddy's father, which later became the Travelers Inn, a favorite stopping place on the James River and Kanawha Turnpike. On one of the chimneys is a bronze memorial plaque to Daniel Boone (1773–1820), 'pioneer, hunter, explorer, frontiersman, Indian fighter, and pilot of civilization.'

Although never a member of any church, Paddy was an upright man and in a small way compensated for his lack of interest in churches by not charging his guests for Sunday entertainment. On six days of the week he charged the legal tavern rate: 'warm diet dinner,' 16⅔¢; 'cold diet dinner,' 10½¢; 'lodging, good beds and clean sheets,' 8⅓¢; the rate was cheaper for sharing a bed with 'one or more bedfellows,' or taking a 'chaff' instead of a feather bed; but on the Sabbath day all entertainment was free.

BOOMER, 7.8 *m.* (670 alt., 1,213 pop.), was a coal town until 1938 when the Electro-Metallurgical Company bought the site to build a residential village for plant employees at Alloy.

West of Boomer the highway crosses a thickly populated mining and industrial area. A long row of beehive coke ovens (L), 8 *m.*, each spouting flames from the round opening at the top, casts a lurid and eerie light against the night sky.

In an abandoned railroad station, 11 *m.*, is RESCUE STATION No. 11, of the State Department of Mines (*see Tour 18a*).

Left from the Rescue Station on a bridge spanning the Kanawha River to MONTGOMERY, 0.2 *m.* (650 alt., 2,906 pop.), a coal town in the heart of the Kanawha and New River coal fields. First known as Coal Valley, it was incorporated in 1891 and named for its founder, James C. Montgomery.

The NEW RIVER STATE COLLEGE, a coeducational institution specializing in vocational courses, occupies a hillside at the southern end of town. The Main Building, a three-story rambling structure of red brick, contains dormitory rooms, offices, a gymnasium, and classrooms. In the one-story Physical Education Building, constructed of brick and concrete, are a gymnasium-auditorium, locker rooms, and chemistry laboratories. A print shop and classrooms are in the Annex, a one-story frame building. A shop building contains a woodworking shop, forge room, machine shop, physics laboratory, and a classroom. A three-story apartment building for faculty members was erected in 1936 with PWA funds. In addition to the usual college curriculum leading to a degree of Bachelor of Arts, courses are offered in engineering, printing, woodworking, machine and forge work, and automobile mechanics. The school was founded in 1895 as the Montgomery Preparatory Branch of West Virginia University; the annual enrollment approximates 900.

1. Left from Montgomery on State 61 is MOUNT CARBON, 41 *m.* (675 alt., 475 pop.); at the summit of the mountain (R), reached by a stiff climb of several hundred feet through underbrush, are the remains of a prehistoric wall built by the mound builders or a contemporary race. Following the contour of the mountain, the loosely constructed stone wall forms an enclosure from 100 yards to a mile in width. In places it is almost obliterated by vines and weeds. The antiquity of the structure is indicated by the huge trees, some estimated to be 500 years old, that have pushed their way through the stones, displacing sections of the wall. The purpose of the enclosure is unknown.

2. Right from Montgomery on State 61 is PRATT, 4.6 *m.* (660 alt., 325 pop.), where walls similar to that on Mount Carbon extend for almost 800 yards along the side of the mountain above the mouth of Paint Creek. At the base of the mountain, near the mouth of the creek, is an extensive burying ground, marked by cairns of loosely piled stones; skeletons unearthed indicate that those who built the walls were a race of unusually large size; one skeleton measured more than seven feet.

U. S. LOCK No. 3 (L), 13.7 *m.*, is one of a series of three locks and dams completed in 1938 at a cost of $25,000,000 to maintain a nine foot stage in the Great Kanawha River (*see Tour 14*) between Point Pleasant and Kanawha Falls. The highway passes in quick succession through four small coal camps; thin seams of coal streak the rock face of the highway cuts. Several blackened tipples span the highway, carrying coal from mine openings high up on the mountain side to coal barges on the river.

CEDAR GROVE, 18.5 m. (605 alt., 1,110 pop.), on the banks of Kellys Creek, is the oldest settlement in the Kanawha Valley. Walter Kelly came from North Carolina in 1773 and built a cabin here near the mouth of the creek. Warned that the Indians were on the warpath, he sent his wife and children to Fort Savannah, but remained to plant his crop. Only a few hours after the departure of his family, Indians attacked the cabin and scalped Kelly and a Negro servant. The next year William Morris took up the Kelly claim, and with his seven grown sons and several daughters built Kellys Fort and established a permanent settlement. Soon other settlers came and Morris built a church and a school, the first in Kanawha Valley. For many years Boat Yards, as the village was called, was the end of the road for those who came on foot or horseback over the Lewis Trail and later for the westward travelers who came in wagons over the Old State Road. Here they loaded their goods onto flat boats, or into bateaux and poled them down the river to settlements farther west. Boat yards sprang up, and the village became a busy frontier settlement, where the hammering in the boat yards mingled with the excited cries of embarking immigrants. When the turnpike was completed to the Ohio River, boat building was no longer profitable, and the town's chief industry gradually died. Cedar Grove was incorporated in 1902 when coal operations stimulated the growth of the town.

The MORRIS MEMORIAL CHURCH (L), on the highway on the eastern edge of town, is a small rectangular red brick building erected in 1853 on the site of the first church in Kanawha Valley, a Baptist church built by William Morris, first settler. Above the doorway, which is surmounted with a broad fanlight, rises a white-painted octagonal bell tower. Three long narrow windows on either side of the building rise to sharply angled arches. The church is furnished with heavy straight-backed wooden benches, smooth and polished from long wear. In the grassy churchyard is the WILLIAM MORRIS MEMORIAL BOULDER, with a bronze plaque inscribed to the founder of the town and the 'first permanent settler in the Great Kanawha Valley.' On the west exposure of the building is a memorial plaque to his oldest son, William Morris, Revolutionary War soldier.

Right from Cedar Grove on a dirt road to the MOUNT DESERT FIRE TOWER (*open*), 10 m., affording a view of the surrounding country.

Across the river (L), 22 m., rise the stacks of a power plant at the mouth of CABIN CREEK, along which occurred in 1912–13 one of the most violent conflicts in the history of American labor.

DICKINSON, 23.3 m. (619 alt., 350 pop.), is a railroad village on the New York Central, named for John Q. Dickinson, owner of a salt works at Malden (*see below*). The Kanawha Valley broadens into a smooth grassy flood plain here, used to pasture blue-ribbon Hereford cattle.

In BELLE, 26.5 m. (620 alt., 217 pop.), is (L) the huge E. I. DU PONT DE NEMOURS AMMONIA PLANT, and the smaller BELLE AL-

KALI COMPANY PLANT; the latter established in 1920, employs 200
men in the manufacture of liquid chlorine, caustic soda, calcium chloride, and other chemicals from salt brine. The du Pont plant employs
2,000 men in the manufacture of anhydrous and aqua ammonia, men-
thanol, anti-freeze products, commercial solvents, Nylon, and similar
products from coke and nitrogen taken from the air. When constructed
in 1925, this was the second largest chemical plant in the United States;
it sells its products to fertilizer, refrigeration, and other chemical plants.

At 29.1 *m*. is (L) DAM AND LOCK No. 2 in the Kanawha River, one
of the three new roller-type dams constructed to aid navigation, the
others being at London and Winfield (*see Tour* 14).

A marker in LEVI, 29.8 *m*. (610 alt., 100 pop.), indicates the SITE
OF BURNING SPRING, discovered in 1775 by the pioneer Van Bibbers,
who found gas bubbling through its waters and reported that when it
ignited, it would burn 'until put out by a high wind.' A 125-acre tract
here was patented two years later by George Washington, who recorded
in his will that it 'was taken up by General Andrew Lewis and myself
on account of a bituminous spring which it contained, so that it burns
as freely as spirits and is as difficult to extinguish.'

In 1843 a salt well was sunk near the spring and struck gas, which
rushed from the well with a great roar, hurling a column of salt water
150 feet into the air; so great was the pressure that a 1,500-pound
iron sinker shot from the well like an arrow from a cross-bow. The roar
of the gas and water as they gushed from the well could be heard several miles, and stage drivers on the James River and Kanawha Turnpike stopped to let their passengers view the sight. On one occasion a
Harvard University professor was among the passengers; 'being a man
of investigating and experimenting turn of mind,' he lighted a match
near the well to see 'what chemicals the vapor contained.' The atmosphere instantly burst into flames, and the well frame and enginehouse
caught fire. The professor saved himself by jumping into the Kanawha
River, and then crawled back to the stagecoach. When the owner of
the well heard of the damage done to his property, he sent a friend to
Charleston to find the unknown passenger and have him arrested for
'willfully and wantonly burning property—unless you find the fellow
is a natural damn fool and didn't know any better,' he added. The
professor was found in a Charleston hotel, his hair and eyebrows singed,
his hands and face blistered. In plain language the messenger stated
his instructions, including the codicil. 'It seems a pretty hard alterna-
tive,' sighed the professor, attempting a faint smile with his parched
lips. 'However, under the circumstances, I feel it my duty to take
advantage of the last clause and escape.'

MALDEN, 31.4 *m*. (613 alt., 900 pop.), originally called Terra Salis
and later known as the Kanawha Salines, was the metropolis of Kanawha Valley and the center of an extensive salt industry during the first
half of the nineteenth century. Rambling old brick houses with shaded

lawns border the narrow winding highway that splits the town, now little more than a residential village.

The salt came from springs known to early settlers as the Big Buffalo Licks (*see below*), near the mouth of Campbells Creek just west of Malden. By 1815, 30 furnaces dotted the valley on both sides of the river, and Malden boomed as people swarmed in to seek work in the salt furnaces, or in the boat yards and tub mills that grew up around them. Salt was a common medium of exchange; local newspapers advertised land and houses to be sold for 'salt or money.' More than 3,000 persons were employed in one phase or another of the salt business.

Production reached a peak of 3,000,000 bushels in 1850, but during the following decade the industry declined and salt makers turned to the exploitation of coal, timber, oil, and gas in the valley. After the War between the States, salt makers attempted to resume operations, but found that producers in other fields had captured the market. During the hard times of 1876, all but one of the furnaces closed down. Today only one plant continues to operate, the JOHN Q. DICKINSON COMPANY SALT FURNACE (*open: inquire locally*).

Near the center of the town is (R) the SITE OF BOOKER T. WASHINGTON'S BOYHOOD HOME, a garden plot on which stood the log cabin in which the renowned Negro educator lived with his mother and stepfather. Booker T. Washington (1858–1915) was born in a slave cabin on a plantation at Hales Ford, Virginia, and lived there with his mother, brother, and sister until he was six years old. Booker's stepfather escaped to West Virginia and sent for his family after the Emancipation Proclamation. At Malden both he and Booker worked in the salt furnaces.

Freedom for the Negroes brought with it a desire for knowledge and advancement, and young Booker daily joined groups of neighbors as they clustered attentively around a young Ohio Negro as he read the day's news. Later a Negro school was opened, and Booker attended while working night shift in the furnaces. After a year in the coal mines, he became a servant in the home of General Lewis Ruffner, having meantime assumed the name of Washington, simply because he had no other and everybody else had two names.

A year and a half later he left General Ruffner to enter the Hampton Normal and Agricultural Institute at Hampton, Virginia; en route he had his first experience with racial discrimination when an innkeeper refused him a room for the night. Graduated from Hampton in 1875, he returned to Malden and taught school here for two years, witnessing several conflicts between whites and Negroes, fomented by the Ku Klux Klan; in one of these riots General Ruffner defended several Negroes from attack and received injuries from which he never fully recovered. After a term of study at Wayland Seminary, Washington, D. C., Washington returned to Hampton as instructor in 1879, departing in 1881 to organize and become principal of a Negro normal school at Tuskegee, Alabama. Intermittently he returned to Malden, and was welcomed by whites and Negroes alike; known as 'Bookah Tee' to every-one, he was a favorite son of the town. At Tuskegee his school grew from a single frame building and a church to a modern institution of more than 40 buildings, the foremost school of Negro industrial edu-cation and training in the world. Washington continued to write and lecture, counseling his people to seek 'hard work and enlightenment,' and in 1896 Harvard conferred on him an honorary A.M., and Dart-mouth an honorary D.C.L. in 1901. He died at Tuskegee on Novem-ber 4, 1915, and a monument has been erected there to honor him as one of the outstanding American leaders since the War between the States.

REED, 32 m. (609 alt., 20 pop.), is a shipping point for coal brought from near-by mines and loaded here into barges and railroad cars. Known also as Campbell Creek, the hamlet was once a bustling com-munity with activities centered around BIG BUFFALO LICK, a salt spring near the mouth of the creek. Indians had made salt here long before the whites learned of the spring from Mary Ingles after her escape from the Shawnee, who had brought her here as a captive after their attack on the Ingles-Draper settlement in Virginia. In 1794 Joseph Ruffner bought 502 acres around the springs, but, being a farmer, leased the springs to Elisha Brooks, who built the first salt furnace in 1797. The Brooks furnace consisted of 24 kettles set in a double row, with a chimney at one end and a fire box at the other. To obtain better brine, he sank hollow 'gums' made of bark into the earth and dipped up the brine as it flowed to the surface. With his crude apparatus Brooks manufactured 150 pounds of salt a day, selling it for 10¢ a pound at the furnace. People came from 100 miles around to buy salt, carrying it away in pack-saddles or flatboats.

In 1806 Joseph and David Ruffner began to refine salt on a large scale. For 'gums' they used hollow sycamores, four feet in diameter; two men, with pick, shovel, and crowbar, worked on the inside of the gum to dig the well. When a sufficient depth was reached, a platform and well-sweep was erected. A whisky barrel was sawed in two and used to dip the brine from the well. Salt was packed in seven-bushel hogsheads, shipped by flatboat down the Kanawha, and sold to the river-valley dwellers of Ohio, Indiana, Illinois, and Kentucky, who needed it to make 'hog and hominy,' their dietary staples.

Larger furnaces were built, which greatly increased production, with the result that the price of salt fell to 4¢ a pound. Cutthroat compe-tition among the salt makers and poor transportation facilities threat-ened the future of the industry in 1816, and the salt makers met at the Kanawha Salines in 1817 to form America's first trust; control of prices and production was placed in the hands of an elected board of governors. Production of salt by each furnace was pro-rated, and a sale price was set and maintained, except during occasional price wars to discourage importers of salt from England and the West Indies.

By 1820 coal and gas had largely replaced wood as fuel in the furnaces, and eight years later the steam engine took the place of the mules in working the pumps. In 1831 William Morris invented a tool called the 'slips,' known in the oil fields as 'jars,' which made deep drilling practical; wells were sunk to depths of 2,000 feet. With deep boring came oil, regarded at the time as a nuisance to salt makers. Wells driven beyond the 40-foot level almost invariably brought in oil, with some wells yielding from 25 to 50 barrels a day. The oil was allowed to fill the salt cisterns and overflow into the river, where it formed 'slicks,' big patches of iridescence, which gave the Kanawha its name of 'Old Greasy,' and salt producers cursed the 'devil's grease' that spouted from shafts sunk for salt brine.

The Indians had long known of springs from which petroleum and water emerged together. They skimmed the oil from the surface of standing pools, boiled it until the water evaporated, and used it externally to toughen their skins and ward off insects. A German traveler in 1789 noted that the Indians took the oil 'inwardly, and it has not been found to do harm,' and further remarked his surprise that 'it will burn in a lamp.' Under the name of 'Seneca Oil,' the pioneer whites used the oil as a sovereign remedy for rheumatism and similar ailments.

In 1841 gas was struck by drillers, and for several years the natural flow was so powerful it was used to force the brine from the well, boil it, and light the works at night. The salt makers' only complaint against the gas, said a contemporary, was its inability to 'pack the salt in barrels.'

From time to time the trust encountered difficulties due to poor management, inefficient operation, and dishonesty among the directors; in fact, the trust was reorganized 9 times in 60 years. Disruption began in 1852 with the opening of salt wells in the Ohio Valley, where the brines were stronger and costs of operation and transportation less. Fighting a losing battle, the Kanawha salt men took to 'dead-renting' their properties—that is, closing down their furnaces for six months' periods in return for stipulated sums paid them by Eastern capitalists interested in developing salt wells elsewhere. One by one the Kanawha salt men entered into such agreements, accepted advance payments, closed their furnaces, and then waited in vain for another payment at the close of the first six months' period. They discovered too late that they had been tricked into abandoning the market to competitors. The Reconstruction era after the War between the States sounded the death knell of the Kanawha salt industry; the sole plant that continues to operate is at Malden (*see above*).

In SNOW HILL, 33.7 *m.* (605 alt., 75 pop.), is (R) the DANIEL BOONE CAVE, said to have been used as a shelter by 'the pilot of civilization' on his hunting expeditions in the vicinity. On the bluff across the river he built a cabin in 1788 or 1789 and lived there several years; nothing remains of the cabin.

CHARLESTON, 35.8 *m.* (598 alt., 60,408 pop.) (*see Charleston*).

Charleston is at the junction with US 21 (*see Tour* 13), US 35 (*see Tour* 14), and State 4 and 13 (*see Tour* 11*a and b*).

Section c.   CHARLESTON to KENTUCKY LINE, 61 m.   US 60.

This section of US 60, a heavily traveled highway between two of the State's largest centers of population and industry, links the chemical manufacturing area in and around Charleston with Huntington, the State's chief commercial city. The highway traverses low hills and gently undulating farm country, with corn and high-grade leaf tobacco as the most important crops. Between Huntington and the Kentucky Line the highway parallels the Ohio River.

On the outskirts of CHARLESTON, 0 *m.*, near the northern end of the Patrick Street Bridge spanning the Kanawha, is (R) the KELLEY AXE AND TOOL WORKS (*open on application at office*), 1.8 *m.*, consisting of 50 sprawling brick, sheet iron, and frame buildings along the river bank, one of the largest factories in the world producing edged tools. Established here in 1904, the plant was acquired by the American Fork and Hoe Company in 1930.

Axes, scythes, hatchets, and other edged tools are hammered, cut, and trimmed into shape by goggled workmen, who swing heavy tongs from forge to anvil in a steady rhythm as showers of crimson sparks fly up a fireworks display. After the forging and stamping process, the tools are loaded on conveyors and drawn through normalizing furnaces; they are then bathed in oil, a process that insures uniform tempering. After final tests, the tools are either polished to a high gloss on emery wheels or given baked enamel coatings in electric ovens. Handles for the various tools are smoothed and finished in the carpentry shop; the tools and handles are fitted, wrapped, and packed in wooden boxes in the assembly room.

SOUTH CHARLESTON, 3.9 *m.* (600 alt., 5,904 pop.), on the south bank of the river, is a chemical manufacturing center, as evidenced by pungent odors of chlorine and alcohol. Bordering the highway for more than a mile are (R) a series of chemical plants (*not open to visitors*).

The CARBIDE AND CARBON CHEMICALS CORPORATION PLANT, largest in the group, occupies 160 acres of land with its red brick and opaque glass buildings, circular metal tanks, and square steel framework towering as high as a three-story building, encasing clusters of valves, pipes and gauges. The main works and laboratories are on BLAINE ISLAND (R), a mile-long sliver of land in the middle of the river. The plant is wreathed in fogs of steam and white smoke by day, and bathed in blazing incandescence by night as 2,500 employees produce alcohols, ethers, esters, ketones, aldehydes, amines, chlorinated hydrocarbons, resins, and acids. The basic raw material, natural gas, is supplemented with air, water, chlorine, sulphuric acid, and limestone to make such products as anti-freeze liquids, thermoplastics for victrola records, dentures, and unbreakable ware, and such intermediates as ethers, oxides, glycols, ketones, amines, and aldehydes used in the textile, chemical, printing, rubber, and explosives industries. A subsidiary of the Union Carbide and Carbon Corporation was opened at Clendenin in 1920 as an experimental manufactory, and the plant was moved to South Charleston in 1925; the Blaine Island works was erected here in 1928.

In the BARIUM REDUCTION CORPORATION PLANT, a group of bulky sheet-iron buildings between two parts of the Carbide and Carbon Corporation plant, 200 men are employed in producing barium sulphide, blanc fixe, barium carbonate, sodium sulphide and dulphydrate, hydrogen sulphide, strontium peroxide, and allied chemicals. The plant was established in 1913.

The WESTVACO CHLORINE PRODUCTS PLANT, established in 1914 at the western end of the Carbide and Carbon plant, is the largest plant of its type in the country. It employs 350 men in the manufacture of liquid chlorine, caustic soda, carbon bisulphide and tetrachloride, and sulphur chloride. More than 90 per cent of its production is chlorine, made from salt taken from wells inside the building; almost all of the chlorine is piped into the neighboring Carbide and Carbon Chemicals Corporation plant.

In STAUNTON PARK (L), a triangular park near the western end of the town, is a conical Indian Burial Mound, 175 feet in circumference at the base and 30 feet high. Ornaments, stone weapons, fragments of pottery, and 14 human skeletons—one more than seven feet long—were found when the mound was opened by the Federal Government in 1883.

A U. S. NAVAL ORDNANCE PLANT (L), 4.2 m. (*open to visitors on Navy Day and Armistice Day*), was erected immediately after the United States' entry into the first World War.

A detachment of marines, housed in white frame barracks, guards the reservation and the building housing machinery for the manufacture of steel armor and 14-inch guns. Idle since the war, the plant was turned over to the National Youth Administration in 1939 as a resident training school for 500 boys from West Virginia and neighboring States. Opposite the plant is (R) ARMOUR PARK, with rows of two-story stucco houses lining several concrete avenues. Formerly the quarters of naval officers assigned to the plant, they are now occupied by civilians.

ST. ALBANS, 10 m. (595 alt., 3,254 pop.), at the mouth of Coal River, serves a coal and lumber area and the rich farmlands of Teays Valley; it was known successively as Coalsmouth, Philippi, and Kanawha City before assuming its present name.

Thomas Teays explored and pre-empted land in this section in 1774 but failed to settle it. Fort Tackett, erected here about 1787 by Lewis and John Tackett, was attacked and destroyed by Indians three years later, and almost all the inhabitants were killed. John Young, Lewis Tackett's son-in-law, escaped and carried his wife and day-old son to a canoe, which he paddled through the rain and darkness up the river to Fort Lee. The first permanent settlement was made in the 1790's by Stephen Teays, son of Thomas, on his father's land. In 1799 he was authorized to operate a ferry 'across Coal River from the land of Stephen Teays to the land of General George Washington, and across the Kanawha River . . . to the land of Fry and others.' He constructed a tavern at the mouth of the Coal River; the old building was destroyed by floods in 1861.

Crossing Coal River, the highway passes (L) RIVERLAWN, 11.5 *m.*, a white, two-story structure with portico, the original part of which was built about 1832 as a tavern to serve travelers on the James River and Kanawha Turnpike. James Teays erected the tavern, an eight-room building of whip-sawed tongue-and-groove construction; two later additions have made it into a rambling structure of 16 rooms; it is now a tourists' home. The furnishings include a cedar chest made in 1778, a century-old 'squire's chair' with a broad armrest containing a drawer for writing materials, and four-poster beds from the old tavern.

A marker (R), 14.5 *m.*, commemorates the Battle of Scary Creek, fought three miles north on July 17, 1861. Confederate forces under General Henry A. Wise here won their first victory in the Kanawha Valley, but General Jacob D. Cox soon received reinforcements and drove the Confederates up the valley, and the Union army assumed complete control of the region.

Westward the highway gradually ascends COAL MOUNTAIN (935 alt.), 17.2 *m.;* descending, it winds between low hills, their slopes cleared for pasture or cultivation. The road is bordered with fields of burley tobacco, with stalks two to three feet high, which bear a tiny white bloom in midsummer. Old log houses and modern red barns are used for drying the tobacco. When harvested, the stalks are split and placed on long poles suspended in tiers across the barn, the sides and ends of which are so arranged as to expose the tobacco to the sun. After three months, when the tobacco is cured, the leaves are stripped from the stalks and graded. Buyers usually come to the tobacco sheds and purchase the entire crop, after which it is delivered to the warehouse in Huntington to await transportation to factories making highgrade chewing tobacco, cigars, and cigarettes. The average annual yield of burley tobacco in the Teays Valley section is 1,000,000 pounds.

LAKE WASHINGTON (L), 23.3 *m.*, is a 60-acre artificial lake maintained by the Mount Vernon Country Club (*private*); the highway skirts the lake for almost a mile.

HURRICANE, 26 *m.* (667 alt., 1,293 pop.), is a trading and residential town for tobacco growers and other agriculturalists of the valley. It wears an air of dusty somnolence except on Saturdays, when the sidewalks of its main street overflow with farmers in overalls who, while their wives throng the stores, carry on political arguments and talk of tobacco prices.

West of Hurricane the valley widens into a billowing plain, across which geologists believe the Great Kanawha River once flowed, many miles south of its present course, to join the Ohio.

At 30.7 *m.* is the junction with an improved dirt road.

Left on this road is the MORRIS MEMORIAL HOSPITAL, 1.5 *m.*, an institution for the treatment and care of crippled children, founded in 1931 by Walter T. Morris. The group of sandstone buildings stands on a high knoll in the center of a 200-acre tract of fertile farming land. The hospital maintains a dairy, orchards, poultry flocks, and vegetable gardens. The hospital is being enlarged with Work Projects Administration funds to increase its capacity from 75 to 150 children. On the grounds are two pools filled with water from a brine well. One is used by children able to play, and the other is fitted with a platform that can be lowered into the water for treatment of helpless patients.

MILTON, 33 *m.* (583 alt., 1,305 pop.), on Mud River, is known locally as Milton-on-the-Mud. It provides shopping facilities for farmers and workers in near-by gas fields.

The BLENKO GLASS COMPANY PLANT (*open*), Florida St. and Washington Ave., employs about 20 highly skilled glassworkers in the manufacture of handblown sheet glass for stained-glass windows. The company, established in 1922, is an independent concern owned and operated by William G. Blenko. Master craftsmen, trained in Europe to a high degree of proficiency in an extremely intricate process, supervise the training of young men selected for their deftness and delicacy of touch. Glass and glassware from the plant were used in the restoration of Williamsburg, Virginia.

Left from Milton on an improved dirt road to the old UNION CHURCH, 1 *m.*, erected in 1848 and occupied during the War between the States by Federal troops. On the pine columns in the interior and in the slave balcony are marks made by the soldiers' bayonets.

ONA, 37 *m.* (632 alt., 66 pop.), was formerly the home of William Jennings Bryan's grandparents, who are buried here. On a knoll (R), stands the CABELL COUNTY HOME FOR THE OLD AND INFIRM, a long two-story red brick building on 200 acres of broad, rolling grounds planted with fruit trees.

Right from Ona on a graveled road to the PRITCHARD SCHOOL, 3.4 *m.*, a home for orphan children. The large two-story building of sandstone, Norman in design, stands on a high knoll overlooking the countryside. Three tall chimneys rise from the gable roof, and the main entrance is under a broad portico with three arched doorways.

A monument set in a niche in the roadside embankment (L), 41.7 *m.*, marks the point where the highway enters the Savage Grant, a tract of 28,627 acres given to John Savage and others in 1772 by George III, for their services under George Washington in the French and Indian Wars.

At 41.9 *m.* is the junction with a concrete-paved road.

Left on this road is BARBOURSVILLE, 0.4 *m.* (586 alt., 1,508 pop.), once a bustling little frontier city. From 1813 to 1888 it was the seat of Cabell County and an important shipping point. The Guyandot River was locked and dammed above the town, and stagecoaches on the James River and Kanawha Turnpike stopped here to transfer passengers to the large packets that churned their way up and down the Ohio River. The locks were destroyed during the War between the States. Upon removal of the county seat to Huntington, the courthouse was converted into a conference school for the Methodist Episcopal Church, South, and named Barboursville College. Renamed Morris-Harvey College, it was removed to Charleston in 1935. With the rerouting of US 60 to by-pass the town, Barboursville was left with little but memories of its former glories.

The GUYAN COUNTRY CLUB (R), 44.8 *m.*, has a clubhouse, a swimming pool and an 18-hole golf course (*open to U.S.G.A. members*).

The WEST VIRGINIA COLORED CHILDREN'S HOME (L), 47.3 *m.*, is a State institution for the care and education of orphaned and neglected Negro children. It has a fully equipped 200-acre farm; the main building, a three-story brick structure trimmed with Indiana limestone, accommodates 65 children. The first six grades are taught here; older children are sent to Huntington schools.

HUNTINGTON, 52 *m.* (564 alt., 75,572 pop.) (*see Huntington*).

Huntington is at the junction with State 10 (*see Tour 17b*) and US 52 (*see Tour 18b*).

The SPRING VALLEY COUNTRY CLUB (L), 56.3 *m.*, has an 18-hole golf course (*greens fee, 75¢–$1.50*).

CAMDEN PARK (R), 57.1 *m.*, is a commercial amusement park (*adm. free*).

CEREDO, 58.7 *m.* (554 alt., 1,164 pop.), is a town of two distinct sections: one, occupied by residential commuters from Huntington and retired merchants; the other, an older farming community of substantial frame homes on generously shaded streets. Established in 1857 by Eli Thayer, an abolitionist from Massachusetts, the town was named for Ceres, goddess of grain and harvests, because of the fertile soil of the area, but the first settlers hoped to make it an industrial community. Their hopes were blasted by the War between the States and the rapid expansion of Huntington after the coming of the Chesapeake & Ohio Railway.

KENOVA, 59.8 *m.* (567 alt., 3,680 pop.), at the mouth of the Big Sandy River in the western corner of the State, is the junction point of three railroads, on which it ships petroleum products, cement, and chemicals from its own plants. Its name is a combination of the abbreviations of Kentucky, Ohio, and Virginia. Founded in 1889 with the opening of timber operations up the Big Sandy River (*see Tour 18b*) and incorporated in 1894, it was for a decade a bustling town, the hangout of a vast army of raftsmen in the days when wages were high and work plentiful. The air rang with the improvised songs and fantastic oaths of the hard-working loggers. Their physical courage and prowess were respected, and their daring deeds were the talk of young and old. The choice timber was soon gone, and with the advent of the railroads the rafters vanished.

At the western city limits, 60.7 *m.*, is (R) DREAMLAND POOL (*swimming: open May 30–Sept. 7; 9 A.M.–12 P.M., 20¢ and 25¢*).

US 60 crosses the KENTUCKY LINE, 61 *m.*, on a bridge (*toll*, 20¢) spanning the Big Sandy River, 5 miles east of Ashland, Kentucky (*see Kentucky Guide*).

ʃʃʃ

Tour 16

(Covington, Va.)—Sweetsprings—Union—Hinton—Beckley—Racine—Yawkey—West Hamlin; State 3.
Virginia Line to West Hamlin, 189.1 *m.*

Bituminous surface throughout.
Route is paralleled by Chesapeake & Ohio Ry. between Alderson and Hinton, Beckley and Racine; by Virginian Ry. between Harper and Surveyor.
Accommodations at short intervals between Virginia Line and Beckley; limited between Beckley and West Hamlin.

No West Virginia tour offers greater contrasts than this one, which follows State 3 across the southern part of the State. At the Virginia Line, close to the once famous Old Sweet Spa, now abandoned and decayed, there is nothing to indicate that one has left the Old Dominion.

The tour then sweeps into industrial Hinton, into the 'Black Knight' coal country around Beckley, then dodges among oil derricks to emerge into the fertile level country of the Guyan Valley, not far from the junction of the Guyandot with the Ohio.

Section a. VIRGINIA LINE to BECKLEY; 85.1 m. State 3.

This section of State 3 winds over and around the mountains of southern West Virginia through the Sweetsprings Valley to the coal-mining area about Beckley.

State 3, a continuation of Va. 311, crosses the VIRGINIA LINE, 0 *m.*, 23 miles southwest of Covington, Va. (*see Virginia Guide*).

SWEETSPRINGS, 0.5 *m.* (2,023 alt., 250 pop.), in its day a fashionable spa, one of the oldest in the South, now drowses by the roadside, lost in dreams of a glamorous past. Renowned as Old Sweet, it opened as a watering place in 1792. Set in spacious grounds the first Sweetsprings hotel, built by William Lewis, son of John Lewis (*see below*), contained 72 rooms and 72 fireplaces, but no baths. The resort reached its height of popularity after 1833 with the erection by the Lewises of a second larger hotel, which still stands although now closed. Georgian Colonial in style, with a great dining hall and reception room, it was based upon a design by Thomas Jefferson. Above the many arches of the flagstoned ground-floor promenade is a deep veranda, level with the second story, which runs the full length of the long three-story red brick building; it looks across a semicircular lawn to a pavilion, the springs, and a long low building that housed a swimming pool. Under the old elms and maples the uncut bluegrass lawns and flower beds have taken on new life. George A. Washington, a nephew of General Washington, visited the spa, as did John C. Calhoun, Henry Clay, Millard Fillmore, Franklin Pierce, and Martin Van Buren in its heyday before the War between the States. It continued to be well patronized until the first World War, after which its popularity waned; the resort was closed in 1930. In recent years the novel, *Glorious Betsy*, adapted for both stage and screen, has revived interest in Old Sweet, which is described in the story as the locale of the romance between Jerome Bonaparte, brother of the first Napoleon, and Elizabeth (Betsy) Patterson of Baltimore. The romance is pictured against a conventional background of stately mansions, fine old furniture, beautiful women, handsome men, liveried servants, and mint juleps, much as they might have been when Old Sweet was a center of fashion.

Near Old Sweet was the home of Major William Royall, Revolutionary soldier, who became one of the wealthiest men of the region. In 1786, Major Royall, a widower, brought the Widow Newport to his mansion as a scrub woman, with her two daughters to help in the house and fields. In 1797 Major Royall married one of the daughters in Botetourt County, and for 16 years Ann Newport Royall (1769–1854) ruled the household in which she had been a servant. The marriage from all accounts was a happy one, and on his death in 1813 Major Royall left the bulk of his estate to his wife. Relatives contested the will and brought suit against the widow, claiming that the will was a forgery.

While the suit was in court Ann Royall lived lavishly, residing in Charleston for two years or more, traveling a great deal in the South. On one visit she received word that the suit had been decided against her. Friends paid her stagecoach fare to Washington where she applied for a pension for the Revolutionary War services of her husband. On her journey she took notes for a travel book that later brought her a measure of fame, *Sketches of History, Life and Manners in the United States,* in which she was very critical of western Virginia and its inhabitants. In Washington, application for a pension was rejected because the pension act did not cover widows who had married after the year 1794. Although a special act of Congress later amended the Act, no pension was granted her until she was past 80 years of age.

Desperately in need, Ann Royall was aided by a friend, Sarah Stack, in establishing in Washington in 1831 a newspaper called *Paul Pry,* a highly critical but honest journal, in which she published pen portraits of members of Congress and other public characters; some portraits were complimentary, but others certainly were not. In 1836 *Paul Pry* was succeeded by *The Huntress* (*see Newspapers*). As the pioneer woman publicist at the national Capital, she 'watched Congress as a cat watches a rat hole' for three decades, her writings causing much anguish and gnashing of teeth. She was the first woman to force an interview with a President of the United States. Dignified John Quincy Adams refused her an interview on the State bank question and denounced her as a 'virago-errant in enchanted armor.' The resourceful Ann discovered the spot where Adams liked to swim in the Potomac; she strolled to the spot one morning, seated herself on his clothes, and refused to budge until the President, treading water, expressed his mind on the State banks.

In an era when ladies were expected to be pale and interesting and a woman with a career was viewed askance, Ann Royall had her troubles. The mildest epithets applied to her were 'Holy Terror' and 'the Widow with the Serpent's Tongue.' Anguished males attempted to thwart her in many ways.

'The Senate has adopted a rule *excluding females from the floor,* and (would you believe it?) I am included in the interdiction,' she wrote on one occasion with great indignation. 'I give the Senators fair warning now of my intentions. If they don't repeal that rule—that odious law—that Gothic mandate, I mean to appeal to the people that made them, and by the blood of the Royalls, we shall unmake them—unfrock them and unsenator them. What right have a set of musty old bachelors, as some of them are, and others merely led by their wives, to exclude from their carpet, the Madam de Stael of the age?'

Dishonest and stupid congressmen had a healthy fear of 'Godless Anne Royall,' who, though she had a sharp and sometimes cruel tongue, never wanted courage, ever preserved her integrity, and always stood for fair play; her name has outlived that of the majority of those who were so shocked by her 'improprieties' and 'indiscretions.'

At 0.8 *m.* is the junction with State 311.

Left on State 311 up PETERS MOUNTAIN (3,050 alt.) to the Virginia Line, 3.2 *m.,* where the highway becomes Va. 311, 49 miles northwest of Roanoke, Virginia (*see Virginia Guide*). From the parking space at the State Line the fields along meandering Sweetsprings Creek are seen far below. To the north appears the level ridge of GAP MOUNTAIN, flanked (R) by the rounded dome of HIGH HEAD MOUNTAIN (3,347 alt.); southward, the mountains stretch away in long parallel ridges.

LYNNSIDE (R) 0.9 *m.*, was the home of the Lewis family. The low red brick house, with round-topped windows trimmed in white, was built in 1845. It was the home of the Lewis family for five generations. John Lewis came from Ireland to Virginia in 1720 and settled at Belfonte, in Augusta County, where he was the first white resident. He married Margaret Lynn, daughter of the Laird of Lock Lynn, a descendant of the chieftains of a once powerful clan in the Scottish Highlands. Their son, William Lewis, was the founder of the Old Sweet (*see above*).

The GRAVE OF JOHN FLOYD (1783–1837), eighteenth governor of Virginia (1830–34), is in the old Lewis cemetery on the estate. Governor Floyd died here of a heart attack while visiting his daughter, Letitia Preston Floyd, the wife of William Lewis.

Floyd was a member of the U. S. House of Representatives from 1817 to 1829. A leader in the House, he opposed President John Quincy Adams, and his influence contributed to the election of Andrew Jackson to the presidency in 1828. In 1832, during Jackson's administration, the question of States' rights flared high with the passage of a tariff obnoxious to the South and particularly to South Carolina. The South Carolina legislature declared the tariff act 'null and void, and no law, not binding on the State, its officers or citizens.' President Jackson issued a forceful proclamation that the tariff act would be enforced by arms if necessary, which loosed in Congress a flood of oratory from the lips of Webster, Clay, Calhoun, and others. Governor Floyd sent several messages to the Virginia legislature strongly condemning, the President's Proclamation, recommended a convention of the States of the Union to set aside the tariff act, but rejected the idea of secession.

GAP MILLS, 10.9 *m.* (2,343 alt., 62 pop.), was the birthplace of Andrew Summers Rowan, who during the Spanish-American War performed the feat celebrated in Elbert Hubbard's *A Message to Garcia.* At the outbreak of hostilities in 1898, the U. S. War Department required certain secret information from General Garcia, leader of the Cuban insurgent forces hidden somewhere in the vast, tropical, Cuban jungle from which they were waging guerrilla warfare against Spain in a war for independence. Young Lieutenant Rowan, a graduate of the U. S. Military Academy in 1881, started from Washington on his dangerous mission and landed from a small boat at Turquino Peak, a secluded spot on the Cuban coast, on April 24, 1898. Under cover of darkness he made his way through enemy territory and dense jungle to the camp of General Garcia, delivered his message, received the needed information, and returned to Washington a month later. For his exploit Rowan later received the Distinguished Service Cross. Retiring from the Army with the rank of lieutenant colonel in 1912, Rowan has made his home in San Francisco for many years.

The highway follows the gentle descent of SECOND CREEK through the gap for which Gap Mountain was named.

At 17.5 *m.* is the junction with a dirt road.

Right on this road is the REHOBOTH CHURCH, 0.3 *m.,* a log meeting house erected in this shady dell in 1784, the oldest extant Methodist church building west of the Alleghenies. It was dedicated in 1786 by the Reverend Francis Asbury, first Methodist bishop in America, who later visited it frequently, holding annual conferences here in 1792, 1793, and 1796. Worshippers attended services with their rifles stacked close at hand. The site of the church and the adjoining cemetery was donated by Edward Keewan, who is buried here 'for as long as grass grows and water flows.' The centennial of Rehoboth was celebrated on July 30, 1886. Thousands came from far and near to attend the services.

In a new church near by is the original communion table. Services are no longer held in the old church, which is dedicated to Francis Asbury, who arrived from England on October 27, 1771, and spent the remainder of his life preaching Methodism in the wilds of America.

UNION, 21.1 *m.* (2,070 alt., 331 pop.) (*see Tour 8c*), is at the junction with US 219, which is united with State 3 for 4.1 miles (*see Tour 8c*).

West of the junction (R) with US 219 (*see Tour 8c*), 25.2 *m.*, State 3 slowly ascends to the top of a low ridge, passing occasional small farms on steeply canted hillside clearings.

ALDERSON, 38.9 *m.* (1,555 alt., 1,458 pop.), is a tri-county town bisected by the Greenbrier River: south of the river, in Monroe County, near the Summers County line, is the small business district; north of the river, in Greenbrier County, is the residential section of shaded avenues and comfortable houses. Alderson has no industry. Except for a few merchants and workmen who commute to Hinton, Lewisburg, or the limestone quarries at Snowflake, most of the population are of independent means.

The townsite was settled in 1777 by the Reverend John Alderson, a Baptist minister, who four years later erected here the first church in the region. The town was incorporated in 1871 and grew steadily after the coming of the Chesapeake & Ohio Railway the following year. The Greenbrier Male and Female Seminary was established in 1885 and flourished for several years. Alderson Collegiate Institute was opened in 1888 and continued until 1925. The Alderson Baptist Academy, founded in 1901, was merged with Broaddus College at Philippi (*see Tour 22b*) in 1931.

Right from Alderson on a paved road to the FEDERAL INDUSTRIAL INSTITUTION FOR WOMEN (open 9 A.M.–4 P.M. weekdays), 1 *m.*, a $3,000,000 innovation in penal institutions, showing no trace of the traditional prison atmosphere. The modern brick structures include 17 cottages, each designed to accommodate 30 women; the administration building, Katherine Bement Davis Hall, Jane Addams Hall, Elizabeth Fry Cottage, two-story brick dormitories, Willebrandt Hall, school building, industrial arts building, hospital, laundry, and power plant are scattered over an upper and lower campus. On the 500-acre farm are a dairy, plant experiment house, greenhouse, henhouse, and other necessary farm outbuildings.

The institution was established by Congressional Act in 1926, after a campaign led by Assistant Attorney General Mabel Walker Willebrandt had forced Federal penitentiary officials to acknowledge that the incarceration of women criminals in county jails and State penitentiaries was a contributing factor in the increase in crime. The Government decided to build a new type of institution designed less to confine inmates behind bars than to educate them and stimulate a desire in them to become worthy members of society. The architect broke all precedents to give the institution the appearance of a young ladies' preparatory school, and from the beginning the policy was adopted of treating each inmate as an individual. Inmates are employed in garment making, gardening, and dairying. Classes are conducted in commercial studies, homemaking, hygiene, dressmaking, and similar subjects. The illiterate and foreign-born are taught English and elementary subjects. The United States Public Health service provides medical, mental, surgical, and psychiatric care. Although 95 per cent of the women are free to come and go as they please, attempts at escape are almost unknown; of the 600 women released on parole up to 1934, only 3 per cent had their paroles revoked.

PENCE SPRINGS, 46.9 *m.* (1,521 alt., 107 pop.), with its business center (L) across the river, is a small resort built around a pavilion-covered spring.

At 47.4 *m.* is the junction with a dirt road.

Right on this road is CLAYTON, 4.1 *m.* (2,028 alt., 46 pop.), named for Richard Clayton, who in 1838 landed here on the first balloon flight west of the Alleghenies, having ascended at Cincinnati, 250 miles distant.

The GRAHAM HOUSE (R), 49.6 *m.*, a two-story log structure with loopholes in the walls to permit rifle fire, was built by John Graham about 1772; today, overgrown with rambler roses and surrounded by an attractive lawn, it gives no hint of the Indian attacks it once withstood.

TALCOTT, 51.1 *m.* (1,519 alt., 450 pop.), is a crossroads hamlet.

· Left from Talcott on a graveled road to a path, 0.9 *m.;* R. on this path 0.5 *m.* through open fields to BACON'S FALLS, on the Greenbrier River, and to BACON'S MILL, built in 1855 by Robert Bacon and Jacob Fluke.
GREENBRIER SPRINGS (R), 3.5 *m.*, formerly known as Barger's Springs, were owned about 1800 by Isaac Carden, who built the old log house (R), one of the first fur-trading posts in this region. Summer cottages line the road and river (*swimming, fishing*). A hotel built beside the sulphur spring in 1903 closed its doors in 1929.
STONY CREEK GORGE (L), 3.6 *m.*, is a rugged chasm through which Stony Creek tumbles on its way to join the Greenbrier.

The highway passes just above the Chesapeake & Ohio tracks at their entrance into the TWIN BIG BEND TUNNELS (6,500 feet), 52.2 *m.* The first tunnel was driven in 1873, the second in 1934. The construction of the first, which was driven by hand, occasioned the ballad 'John Henry,' now part of world literature (*see Folklore*); for it was here that John Henry, the giant Negro steel driver, one of West Virginia's contributions to the gallery of American folk heroes, performed his great feat of driving steel faster than the then newfangled steel drill.

Many old Negroes swear that they have seen John Henry's hammer embedded in the rock above the tunnel. From the highway here is a broad view of the Greenbrier River, cultivated fields, and wooded hills. The highway crosses a shoulder of BIG BEND MOUNTAIN (1,768 alt.) and descends through dense woods.

At 60.2 *m.* is (L) a PICNIC GROUND AND BATHING BEACH.

HINTON, 61.7 *m.* (1,382 alt., 6,654 pop.), seat of Summers County, is a railroad town built on one flank of the mountains that here form a gigantic cup, as the New River Valley widens to receive the Greenbrier River. Its streets scramble uphill from the foaming New River cataracts and from the railroad shops and yards which support the town. Settled and laid out by John Hinton in 1831, the town grew slowly until 1871, when the construction gangs of the Chesapeake & Ohio Railway blasted a path through the New River Gorge and the railroad officials made Hinton a division terminal. Large shops and yards were established and skilled labor imported from neighboring States, with the result that less than 1 per cent of the present population is foreign-born. Hinton, incorporated in 1880, is the shipping amalgamation point of the produce and livestock from surrounding farms.

Residents of Hinton are all railroaders in spirit, being conscious of the railroad from childhood; they grew up singing such ballads as 'The Wreck of the Old 97,' and telling and retelling the stories of yesterday's heroes of the steel ribbons. They know every detail of the schedule, running time and past records of the fast C. & O. de luxe flyers, and are more familiar with their appointments than with the arrangement of furniture in their own parlors. They honor the grizzled engineer and the weather-beaten brakeman above all men, and to them a man who has worked his way to a position at the throttle is a man whose judgment is beyond question.

The CONFEDERATE MONUMENT, First and James Sts., is a 15-foot metal statue of a Confederate soldier mounted on a granite base, in the center of a small triangular park dotted with flowering shrubs. Erected in 1914, the monument bears an embossed likeness of General Robert E. Lee, and commemorates the Confederate soldiers of Greenbrier and New River Valleys who followed Lee and Stonewall Jackson.

The MIKE FOSTER MONUMENT, Forest Hill Cemetery, a ten-foot shaft of white marble erected in 1907, commemorates the Confederate soldier, a native of the New River Valley, whose bravery under fire is legendary in this region.

CONEY ISLAND, Main and Pleasant Sts., is a picnic ground and bathing beach. On the outskirts of Hinton the highway crosses the New River and climbs the steep grades up BEACH RUN to a wide plateau that extends westward for twenty miles.

In JUMPING BRANCH, 68.6 m. (2,290 alt., 155 pop.), is an old tavern, now a residence, built before the War between the States. Westward, as the highway winds and climbs, offering frequent views across Jumping Branch Valley, WHITE OAK MOUNTAIN (2,950 alt.) lifts its bulk above the plateau. Here and there on its thickly wooded flanks stands the gaunt skeleton of a chestnut tree, one of millions of victims of the devastating blight that about 1910 swept the forests of the country and all but exterminated the species.

In SHADY SPRING, 77 m. (2,675 alt., 367 pop.), a roadside FIRST AID STATION marks the junction with US 19 (see Tour 10c), which unites with State 3 for six miles (see Tour 10c).

Just west of the junction (R) with US 19 (see Tour 10c), 83 m., is (L) the BLACK KNIGHT COUNTRY CLUB, with a nine-hole golf course (open to members of other clubs; greens fee, $1.50).

BECKLEY, 85.1 m. (2,400 alt., 9,357 pop.), is the hub around which revolves the life of more than 200 small mining towns, farming communities and railroad junctions. Called the 'smokeless coal capital of the world,' Beckley is the center of a large area, which annually produces 50,000,000 tons of the finest steam and domestic coals. Beckley lies out on a high plateau, surrounded by lush valleys and distant peaks. Streets, business buildings, and houses are all new, for the community's active growth dates from 1900. Employment is limited to coal mining, affiliated industries and commercial establishments serving the mining towns. As the demand for smokeless coal is fairly constant, the depression has had little effect on the city.

When General Alfred Beckley came west to settle here on the plateau in 1838, he envisaged his settlement as a grain and livestock center. The community was slow to develop and was jeered at as 'Beckley's paper town'; not until 1850 was the first business establishment opened, a blacksmith shop. In that year the Virginia General Assembly created Raleigh County and made Beckley the county seat. At the outbreak of the War between the States the little village, containing 'not more than 50 heads of families,' found itself besieged and occupied in turn by both armies, although it was actually shelled only once, by Union troops in 1863. Beckley's first newspaper editor made a plea for developing local coal seams in 1868, but the sedate little farming community ignored him. So slow was the community's growth that when Collis P. Huntington built the main line of the Chesapeake & Ohio Railway down the New River Valley in 1873, he constructed it 10 miles east of the town.

The presence of coal here was known as early as 1774, when a soldier in General Andrew Lewis's expedition wrote in his diary of a fuel that burned easily and with a minimum of smoke, but it was not until 1890 that the first shipment of coal was made. Production was slightly stimulated by the completion of a Chesapeake & Ohio branch line to the town in 1901. In 1907 the great Winding Gulf field, which now produces 12,000,000 tons annually, opened at Beckley's doorstep. Production doubled, then tripled, after the Virginian Railway completed a line from southern West Virginia to tidewater in 1909. The first World War made smokeless coal a standard bunker fuel, and mines opened rapidly along the Virginian's route, increasing from 4 to more than 100 by 1918.

Increased coal operations brought an influx of population. Schools and churches were built, and in 1906 the Carter Opera House opened with a gala presentation of *The Merry Widow,* and twice each week thereafter townspeople applauded such plays as *The Fighting Parson,* in which the hero saved the blonde and lisping heroine from a crew of ruffians by drawing his trusty six-shooter and bellowing magnificently, 'Back there, you rabble, or we'll let daylight through you.' Beckley became civic-minded in 1916, when an intensive street-paving campaign was instituted.

In 1938 Beckley celebrated three decades of steady growth with parades, concerts, dedicatory addresses, and a giant pageant; a monument was unveiled to General Alfred Beckley.

BECKLEY COLLEGE, 105 S. Kanawha St., an accredited junior college opened in 1933, is housed in a single red brick building, two stories high in front, four stories in the rear, in which the 300 or more students pursue studies leading to standard normal or elementary teaching certificates or do preliminary work for degrees in the arts, sciences, medicine, engineering, business administration, or nursing.

RALEIGH COUNTY COURTHOUSE, Heber, Fayette, Prince, and Main Sts., a square two-story structure of dressed limestone in variegated shades, strikes a note of modified modernism in the prevailing conservation of business architecture. Completed in 1938, the $450,000 PWA-aided courthouse is the third to occupy the same site. General Alfred Beckley deeded a lot to the town in 1850, specifying that the ground was to be used 'for a house of Justice,' and the first courthouse was finished in 1852. This small brick structure was declared unsafe in 1890, and three years later a second courthouse had been completed. The present building was begun after city officials declared the courthouse to be inadequate in 1934. On the courthouse lawn, near the corner of Fayette and Main Sts., is the MONUMENT TO GENERAL ALFRED BECKLEY. The structure, which was dedicated June 21, 1938, is of concrete, 18 feet high and 12 feet across the base.

The SOLDIERS AND SAILORS MEMORIAL BUILDING, N. Kanawha and Howe Sts., is a massive two-story edifice of red brick and heavy limestone block. Completed in 1932, the building commemorates the Raleigh County men who lost their lives in the World War, and is headquarters for the Boy Scouts, ex-service men's organizations, and the local 4-H club. The public library, an auditorium seating 825, and meeting rooms for fraternal and civic organizations, occupy the remainder of the building.

Beckley is at the junction with US 19 and US 21 (*see Tour 10c*).

Section b. BECKLEY to WEST HAMLIN; 104 m. State 3.

West of BECKLEY, 0 m., State 3 traverses a region that is a representative cross-section of West Virginia—coal mines operated both by primitive and highly mechanized means, occasional small sawmills, derricks above oil and gas wells, and, farther west, fields of corn, soy beans, sorghum cane, tobacco, and alfalfa.

ECCLES, 6.7 m. (2,087 alt., 1,027 pop.), is a mining town dependent largely for income on two shaft mines (L), equipped with modern machinery for cutting, loading, and cleaning coal.

The highway makes a wide horseshoe curve high on the hillside, 20.9 m. Far below (L) the MARSH FORK cascades over tumbled rocks; for nearly 15 miles the road parallels this wild stream, now far above it, now so close as to be washed by its occasional freshets. From the high ridges are magnificent views of jumbled wooded ridges sloping steeply into canyon-like valleys.

From the highway, 31.4 m., appears EDWIGHT (1,000 alt., 117 pop.), a coal camp (L) across the river, with two mines, one high up on the mountain, the other lower down, the two served by a common conveyor line to a modern tipple at the base. Perched high on the mountain (L), 37.5 m., is the headhouse of another mine. A long conveyor of corrugated metal slopes steeply down the hill to the tipple.

State 3 crosses the COAL RIVER, 38.5 *m.*, lined with sycamore, birch, poplar, and willow, and for many miles follows the level narrow valley; between coal towns and expiring lumber camps are wide stretches of cornfields and meadows.

WHITESVILLE, 39.1 *m.* (816 alt., 1,225 pop.), a railroad and trading center for near-by mining camps, is strung out for more than a mile along the narrow valley of Coal River. The business district consists of one- and two-story red brick buildings; a residential area of frame cottages, painted dark red, lies (L) on a hillside.

The COAL RIVER GOLF CLUB (L), 41.9 *m.*, has a nine-hole golf course (*greens fee* $1.00), a picnic ground, tennis courts, and facilities for swimming or fishing.

BIG ROCK appears (L), 47 *m.*, a formation with a long spout-like projection, often called the Devil's Teapot. West of Big Rock the highway passes through the southern tip of the Cabin Creek oil field; derricks dot the ridges and valley.

SETH, 53.1 *m.* (714 alt., 214 pop.), the ghost of a once booming lumber town, was established in 1899 and grew rapidly around a large sawmill which cut from 60,000 to 80,000 feet of lumber a day.

In RACINE, 58 *m.* (675 alt., 56 pop.), is the JOHN PETER SALLEY MEMORIAL MARKER, commemorating the discovery of coal here in 1742, the first to be reported in West Virginia. Salley, a German settler in Virginia, was one of the party of six who set out in March 1742 on an exploring expedition westward to the Mississippi under a commission from the governor of Virginia, who had promised them 10,000 acres of land as recompense. The signing of the agreement, Salley remarked in the record of his journey, was 'a very unlucky hour to me and my poor family.' The party did not return until May 1745, 'having been absent three years two months and one day from my family,' Salley complained, 'having in that time by the nicest calculation I am able to make, traveled by land and water four thousand six hundred and six miles, since I left my house till I returned Home again.'

Entering the region here, Salley wrote, 'Where we came to this river, the country is mountainous, but the farther down, the plainer; in those mountains we found great plenty of coals, for which we named it Coal River.' Today the outlying seams of coal along the river are tapped by so-called truck mines, in which primitive cars are pushed by hand, often along wooden rails, from the face of the coal to the mouth of the mine. The seams are so thin here that miners have to work them lying down.

The highway crosses COAL RIVER, 59.6 *m.,* on the banks of which (R) is PEYTONA (669 alt., 214 pop.), the site of the first large mining operations in the Coal River field, instituted in 1856 by a company organized by General William S. Rosecrans. The large stone building (R) housed the offices and commissary of the company, which, lacking railroad facilities, decided to float coal down the river to market, building a series of eight locks and dams, traces of which remain.

TIGER ROCK (R), 60.1 *m.*, is a striped formation on a roadside cliff. At DRAUDY FALLS (R), 100 yards west of Tiger Rock, Draudy Creek drops in a white spray over two ledges (*picnic grounds*). The highway climbs DRAUDY MOUNTAIN (1,116 alt.), 65.6 *m.*, and descends into a gas and oil field.

YAWKEY, 86.7 *m.* (700 alt., 210 pop.), is the trading center of the oil and gas field. Derricks and tanks stand in small hillside clearings. Gas street lights illuminate the one thoroughfare.

Yawkey is at the junction with State 13 (*see Tour 11b*).

GRIFFITHSVILLE, 88.5 *m.* (685 alt., 264 pop.), is an agricultural village centered around a flour mill.

HAMLIN, 98.8 *m.* (642 alt., 844 pop.), seat of Lincoln County, was incorporated in 1833 as Hamline in honor of Bishop Leonidas L. Hamline of the Methodist Episcopal Church; the postmaster later dropped the final 'e' from the name, which letter had been added to the family name by the Reverend Mr. Hamline himself.

WEST HAMLIN, 104 *m.* (595 alt., 210 pop.), on the Guyandot River and a branch line of the Chesapeake & Ohio Railway, is a buying and shipping center for neighboring farmers.

West Hamlin is at the junction with State 10 (*see Tour 17b*).

Tour 17

Junction with US 19—Matoaka—Logan—West Hamlin—Huntington; State 10, 149.4 *m.*

Stone and macadam surface, except one graveled stretch west of Arista.
The Virginian Ry. parallels route between Matoaka and Pineville; the Norfolk and Western Ry., between Matoaka and Arista; the Chesapeake & Ohio Ry., between Logan and Huntington.
Few accommodations except in Logan and Huntington.

State 10 traverses one of the largest and most recently developed coal regions of West Virginia, linking the smokeless bituminous fields of Mercer, Raleigh, and Wyoming Counties with the newer fields of highly volatile coal about Logan. The road winds over ridges and through deep V-shaped mountain coves, passing numerous coal camps, the newer of which are laid out according to plan, with sidewalks and freshly painted houses. Huge tipples flank the road, their inclines reaching far back on mountains bearing marks of coal and timber operations. Around the mines the countryside has been stripped of everything but brushy undergrowth; dumps of culm and slate scar the hills and valleys. Away from the mines the region is wild and undeveloped, covered with large stands of second growth timber and underlaid with oil and gas, and coal seams containing an estimated reserve of 12,000,000,000 tons. West of Logan the high hills that wall the Guyandot Valley gradually give way to rolling knolls dotted with small farms as the route approaches the Ohio Valley.

State 10 branches west from US 19 (*see Tour 10c*), 0 *m.*, 4.7 miles north of Princeton (*see Tour 10c*).

The highway crosses the BLUESTONE RIVER, close to which appears (R) SHAWNEE LAKE (*see Tour 10c*), and climbs and descends a series of small ridges in a fertile agricultural district.

MATOAKA, 6.6 *m.* (2,340 alt., 929 pop.), built in the narrow winding valley of Widemouth Creek, is a trading and banking center for near-by mining communities and small lumber camps. The town was named for Pocahontas, daughter of the Chief Powhatan; Matoaka was her secret, or 'sacred,' name. The business district lies on both sides of the highway; attractive frame houses are perched on sloping hillsides above the rocky creek bed. Near the center of town are two railroad stations; the Virginian Railway station stands just a few yards above that of the Norfolk and Western Railway. Both railroads were extended into this region during a period of feverish development, each seeking to obtain the largest possible share of the traffic resulting from the average annual production of 8,000,000 tons of coal in this area. West of Matoaka the rival roads cross, recross, and jostle one another in a narrow valley scarcely wide enough to provide passage for them and the highway.

North of GIATTO, 7.7 *m.* (2,373 alt., 1,009 pop.), a residential suburb of Matoaka, the highway passes through HIAWATHA, 9.5 *m.* (2,390 alt., 118 pop.); SPRINGTON, 11.3 *m.* (2,407 alt., 121 pop.); and ARISTA, 12.6 *m.* (2,450 alt., 520 pop.); all are mining towns. Here and there on the hillsides are small cornfields and garden patches. From Arista the road climbs steeply up FLAT TOP MOUNTAIN (3,150 alt.) to BURTONS GAP, 14.4 *m.*

> Right from Burtons Gap on a dirt road, which winds through a dense stand of second-growth timber, to PILOT KNOB (3,300 alt.) 0.3 *m.*, a cone-shaped elevation capped with a fire tower (*open*), offering a fine view of surrounding mountains and zigzag valleys. In spring the landscape is bright with redbud, white dogwood, and thickets of pinkish rhododendron.

Northwest of COVEL, 18.4 *m.* (1,950 alt., 165 pop.), a mining camp on the outskirts of the Winding Gulf field, the road descends into the narrow tortuous valley; the Virginian Railway clings to the opposite slope, up which the grade is so steep that steam trains of more than seven cars cannot climb it. Powerful electric locomotives, built in three units for use on sharp curves, pull heavy coal trains over this division.

HERNDON, 19.7 *m.* (1,879 alt., 725 pop.), is a trading town for farmers who till the surrounding ridges; until 1927 it was a lumber camp with a large sawmill; piles of rotted sawdust attest the herculean labors that ceased with the depletion of the timber.

From the hillside, 22.2 *m.*, the highway overlooks (R) the frame houses of BUD (1,594 alt., 500 pop.), the home of miners who work in near-by mines. Their houses face a narrow street strung out along the Barkers Creek Valley. In the early 1880's the town was a large logging camp; poplar, pine, and cherry were hauled here from near-by mountains and floated down the Guyandot to sawmills at its mouth.

ALPOCA, 24 *m.* (1,518 alt., 263 pop.), is a town of faded brown and white company houses occupied by miners working two local seams of coal. The coal from the top seam is lowered down the mountainside on a tram road in large monitor hoppers; that from the lower seam is hoisted to the tipple on a conveyor line from below the valley level.

In TRALEE, 27 *m.* (1,396 alt., 165 pop.), are (R) the steam locomotive shops and roundhouse of the Virginian Railway. Smoke and coal dust have long since killed all grass and flowers in the vicinity; dingy houses and an unused coal tipple (L) are surrounded by piles of coal refuse and bare coal-black earth. Over the network of tracks and the huge brick pile of the roundhouse hangs a pall of smoke and steam, dimming the view (R) of the V-shaped valley and the hills. The air is filled with the whine of machinery, the clanking of engines, and the hiss of escaping steam.

Right from Tralee on State 12 is MULLENS, 2.5 *m.* (1,419 alt., 2,356 pop.), in the narrow valley where Slab Fork joins the Guyandot River. A railroad and trading town for coal and lumber camps in the area, Mullens is built around Tater Hill, a high potato-shaped elevation that rises from the semi-circular valley in which the business district lies. Attractive houses stand well back on the slopes overlooking the valley.

A post office established in 1904 was named for A. J. Mullins, who bought and cleared a farm here in 1896. A misspelling of his name became officially established as the name of the town. With the coming of the Virginian Railway in 1907 and the opening of coal mines, the settlement grew steadily. The Mullins farm was divided into lots and sold; in 1912 the town was incorporated.

On the north side of Tater Hill are the electric locomotive shops and yards of the Virginian Railway. Here at the western terminus of the road's electrified section, giant electric locomotives exchange long strings of 'empties' for cars loaded with coal brought from the mines on Bearwallow Mountain, north of the town, and from the headwaters of the Guyandot River.

ITMANN, 27.8 *m.* (1,400 alt., 75 pop.), once a coal camp, was named for I. T. Mann, president of the company that initiated mining operations here. Two large Gothic structures of granite (R), separated by a driveway and connected by an arcaded bridge, were constructed to serve as company offices; their castle-like magnificence stands in marked contrast to the rows of ill-tended company houses now used by employees of the Virginian Railway. The granite buildings now house (1941) the local post office and the offices of the Wyoming County Department of Public Assistance.

Highways and Byways

FISHING IN THE SOUTH BRANCH OF THE POTOMAC, NEAR ROMNEY

Photograph by courtesy of Chesapeake & Ohio Lines

THE GREENBRIER, WHITE SULPHUR SPRINGS

SPRING HOUSE, WHITE SULPHUR SPRINGS

GARDEN, CLAYMONT COURT, NEAR CHARLES TOWN

BLACK KNIGHT COUNTRY CLUB HOUSE, BECKLEY

STONE FACE AT BECKWITH CUT-OFF, NEAR CHIMNEY CORNER (US 19 AND 21)

NEW RIVER GORGE FROM HAWKS NEST

COUNTRY ROAD, THROUGH GERMANY VALLEY

Photograph by courtesy of Wheeling Chamber of Commer

BARGE SHIPMENT ON THE OHIO (WHEELING IN BACKGROUND)

TU-ENDIE-WEI-PARK, POINT PLEASANT

Photograph by courtesy of Bolling

BLACKWATER CANYON

SWIMMING POOL AND RECREATION CENTER, BABCOCK STATE PARK

BASS FISHERMAN

The BLUE HOLE (L), 30 *m.*, is a popular swimming and picnic spot along the Guyandot River. Across the road from a FOREST RANGER STATION, 37.5 *m.*, are (L) picnic grounds between the road and a wide bend in the river.

PINEVILLE, 37.9 *m.* (1,323 alt., 462 pop.), a county seat and trading town for surrounding mines, is crowded on court days with mountain farmers who loiter about the lawn of the gray stone WYOMING COUNTY COURTHOUSE, west Main Street, a two-story building with a Doric portico and a balustrade around the roof. On the courthouse lawn is the W. H. COOK MEMORIAL, a gleaming white statue of the Reverend W. H. Cook, 'soldier, statesman, minister,' one of the first settlers. The Pineville High School, a modern brick structure on landscaped grounds along the Guyandot River, is flanked (R) by a new Recreation Hall, constructed by the National Youth Administration's Wyoming County unit of boys, the first structure of its kind in West Virginia. Built of logs contributed by local people, it has a large garage in the basement for instructing youths in automobile mechanics; it also has sewing rooms, a kitchen for training girls in the domestic sciences, and a large hall suitable for dances and meetings of all kinds. The upper floor serves the Masonic Order as a lodge room. The use of an old wagonwheel for a chandelier is in keeping with the semirustic character of the building. The stretch of river back of the school and hall is to be developed for swimming and boating. At the base of CASTLE ROCK, a stone mass towering 90 feet above the river, is a swimming hole and a sandy beach.

West of Pineville the highway leaves the river and traverses an undeveloped section, passing an occasional weathered cabin on a small hilly farm. Rocky cornfields slant steeply to stony creek bottoms. Mountain scenery is at its best here as the road ascends a high hill or sweeps in long graceful curves around precipitous bluffs.

At 50 *m.* is a junction with an improved road.

Right on this road is KOPPERSTON, 5.6 *m.* (1,300 alt.), a model coal camp built by the Koppers Coal Company. Completed in November 1938, the 100 houses are strung along a level valley (L) between the road and a steep hill. Streets at regular intervals separate the rows of one-story houses painted gray, tan, and white. East of the residential section is the company store; beyond is the huge gray tipple equipped to run and clean all grades of coal from three seams opened in the mountain (L). Steep inclines branch to the different seams; the coal is carried by conveyors to the surface and dumped into giant monitor hoppers that lower it to the tipple. Chutes direct the different grades of screened coal into railroad cars on tracks under the tipple.

OCEANA, 52 *m.* (1,259 alt., 275 pop.), established in 1850 as the first seat of Wyoming County, was originally known as Cassville and later as Sumpterville; in 1855 Thomas Dunn English (*see below*) persuaded the county court to change the name to Oceana in honor of the youngest daughter of Chief Cornstalk (*see Tour* 14). The first house built in the town still stands (R), a two-story frame structure with a double porch supported by large Doric columns, built in 1849.

In 1907 the county seat was moved to Pineville; a year later the old courthouse was destroyed by a fire that wiped out the business district. A modern high school occupies a slight rise (L) beyond the river, here used for bathing at several points.

The highway crosses HUFF MOUNTAIN (1,973 alt.), 53.6 *m.;* on both slopes a heavy cover of mature second-growth timber is broken here and there by upland clearings, each with its tiny cabin.

MALLORY, 68 *m.* (780 alt., 212 pop.), one of the larger coal camps operated by a company of the same name, has two long conveyor inclines that form a 'V' in reaching from a single tipple up the hillside to separate seams, one near the top of the mountain, the other half way up. The tipple (R) straddles the four-track switch of the railroad, and large chutes direct the coal into the cars. The company store, painted white with a deep red trim, makes a gay splash of color in the midst of the barren country and the dull white, tan, and green company houses.

MAN, 70.5 *m.* (729 alt., 835 pop.), trade center for several mining camps on Buffalo Creek, spreads along Guyandot River at the base of a steep bare cliff. In 1904, Man was a busy logging camp. Logs were cut in the near-by mountains, rafted down Buffalo Creek, thence down the river to sawmills.

On the outskirts of the village is a roundhouse of the Chesapeake & Ohio Railway; rows of company houses occupy a narrow strip of land between the river and hill, far below the road which crowds the edge of the cliff. As it proceeds along the cliff, high above the railway tracks and river, the highway is protected by a railing of stone posts, joined by light steel rails commonly used in mines. Northwest of EARLING, 72.9 *m.,* a small coal camp, the highway passes several small mining settlements, with miners' houses of the older type, of one or two rooms, perched on stilts on the steep hillside above the railroad tracks.

LOGAN, 82.7 *m.* (682 alt., 4,396 pop.), seat of Logan County and the busy trading center of a mining area, has a business district of large brick buildings along two narrow streets that parallel the river for almost a mile. On pay day and on Saturday, usually a holiday in mining camps, Logan is crowded with miners down from the hills to shop and amuse themselves in town. On a hill (L) across the Guyandot River mine owners and managers have their homes, large brick houses set on terraced lawns sloping gently to the river.

The town was known as Lawnsville when it became the county seat in 1824. Later it was named for Aracoma, eldest daughter of Chief Cornstalk, who came here in 1765 to live with Bolling Baker, her white husband. The wigwams of her small tribe stood on an island in the river just south of the business district. In a battle in 1780 with settlers from the Greenbrier Valley, Aracoma was fatally wounded and before expiring requested that she be buried here; a monument on the site of the old Baptist Church, 425 Main Streeet, marks the GRAVE OF ARACOMA.

Thomas Dunn English, author of 'Ben Bolt' and the town's first mayor (1852–7), persuaded the town to adopt Aracoma's name; in 1907 it was rechristened in honor of Logan, chief of the Mingo (*see Tour 21a*), for whom the county was also named. Although the song was not written in Logan, residents still point out the grove of elms under which, so they say, English penned these lines:

> Don't you remember sweet Alice, Ben Bolt,
>   Sweet Alice, whose hair was so brown,
> Who wept with delight when you gave her a smile,
>   And trembled with fear at your frown?
> In the old churchyard in the valley, Ben Bolt,
>   In a corner obscure and alone,
> They have fitted a slab of the granite so gray,
>   And Alice lies under the stone.

Jack Dempsey, former world's heavyweight champion, spent his boyhood here and worked in the mines. He returns occasionally to referee wrestling matches and revisit the scenes he knew in the hurly-burly days of the mining region.

The LOGAN COUNTY COURTHOUSE, set in spacious grounds, is a two-story stone structure, surmounted with a narrow dome.

The APPALACHIAN ELECTRIC POWER COMPANY PLANT, at the western limits of Logan, is a huge red brick building topped with a tall stack and surrounded by a complicated maze of metal grids and transformers. Across the river stretches a network of pipes from which steam and hot water spray into the stream in numerous fountains. Completed in 1937, the plant supplies light and power to Logan, neighboring towns, and mines in the surrounding area.

In 1850 the town was the center of extensive logging operations in the mountains along the Guyandot River and its tributaries, which were dammed so that millions of feet of poplar, cherry, and white oak could be rafted downstream to the Ohio. Coal mining began in 1904 with the entry of a railroad. Production increased rapidly from 2,000,000 tons in 1910 to 30,000,000 in 1925.

Left from Logan on US 119 to the junction with a paved road, 0.7 *m.*

1. Right on this road is HOLDEN, 3.4 *m.* (734 alt., 2,046 pop.), a model coal town with a modern water system and recreational facilities, including a theater, tennis courts, Y.M.C.A. building, swimming pool, and a clubhouse in English half-timbered style, on a landscaped lawn overlooking the main street of the town. The streets are lined with trees, and the houses surrounded by lawns, flower beds, and shrubbery. Although the houses are identical, some of the monotony has been relieved by painting them alternately green, gray, and yellow, with no two houses of the same color side by side. Here are the railroad yards of the railroad that serves the Island Creek coal section.

Left from Holden on a paved road, which passes several shaft mines and runs through an area where the trees have been blighted and killed by smoke from burning piles of mine waste, to the junction with a graded road, 4.8 *m.*; R. here 1 *m.* to (L) the SITE OF THE MINGO WHITE OAK TREE, in its day the largest white oak tree in the United States. In 1938 the tree, which had far outlived the average life of white oaks, was pronounced dead by State foresters, when for perhaps the first time in 500 years it failed to bear leaves. A fungus, which usually attaches itself only to dead trees, was discovered on the gnarled giant, and the tree was felled amid ceremonies attended by State officials and several hundred spectators. Its girth at the ground was 30 feet, its height 145 feet; from it was cut a 90-foot merchantable log. A cross-section of the tree was placed in the State Museum.

2. Left (straight ahead) on US 119 through a series of coal towns is OMAR, 8.7 m. (900 alt., 1,230 pop.), the largest of these. The town differs from the ordinary coal camp in that its streets are lined with Lombardy poplars, along which the houses are alternately of stucco and of frame.

In the HATFIELD CEMETERY, 12.9 m. (*open upon application to J. D. Hatfield, 500 yards N. on US 119, or at house at foot of hill*), reached by a stiff climb (R) up the hillside, is the GRAVE OF 'DEVIL ANSE' HATFIELD, a leader of a Hatfield faction in the bitter Hatfield-McCoy feud. A life-size statue of Devil Anse stands on a four-foot granite base. The statue, modeled from photographs taken after Anse's death, was imported from Italy at a cost of $3,000. The bareheaded and bearded figure, in frock coat and riding leggings, stands stiffly with hands at side, gazing into the distance. The back of the base is inscribed: 'Capt. Anderson Hatfield, 1839–1921. Levicy Chafin, His Wife, 1842–1929'; on the front is this inscription: 'Johnson, William A., Robert L., Nancy, Elliot R., Mary, Elizabeth, Elias, Troy, Joseph D., Rose, Willis E., Tennis S., Their Children.'

The Hatfield-McCoy feud, best known of the mountain feuds of the Southern highlands, was precipitated by Johnse Hatfield's attempt to elope with Rosanna McCoy in 1882 during an election in Pike County, Kentucky. Tolbert McCoy quarreled with Elias Hatfield, a Hatfield intervened, and other McCoys joined in, then shot Ellison Hatfield, who had intervened. The three McCoy brothers were arrested, but as they were being taken to jail at Pikeville, armed Hatfields led by Devil Anse took them from the sheriff and carried them to the West Virginia side of the river. On Ellison's death they rowed the McCoys back across the river and shot them dead on Kentucky soil.

Ambushes were laid for members of the hostile clans, and Hatfields and McCoys were shot on sight. Hatfields arrested in Logan County, where every other deputy and officer was a Hatfield, were invariably acquitted; McCoys arrested in Pike County likewise went free. Governor Buckner of Kentucky sought to extradite the Hatfields, who had been indicted for murder of the three McCoy brothers, but Governor Wilson of West Virginia refused to honor the request, and the two governors exchanged heated and lengthy letters.

On New Year's night, 1888, the Hatfields surrounded the house of Randall McCoy, the leader of his clan, and shot his son Calvin. Led by the mother, the McCoys, sick of feuds and killing, moved to Pikeville, and as time went on many more people settled in Logan and Pike Counties with the development of coal fields and timber lands. Hatfields and McCoys found their feud regarded with less tolerance. 'Cotton Top' Mounts, Hatfield supporter, was arrested, tried at Pikeville for murder, and hanged. Johnse Hatfield, oldest son of Anse, was arrested, tried for murder, and sentenced to life imprisonment. The last outburst of violence occurred in 1896 when 'Cap,' the second son of Devil Anse, was shot by John Rutherford, a McCoy connection; the former's stepson, Joe Glen, not yet in his teens, drew a gun and shot Elliot Rutherford as he came to his brother's aid and, in the excitement, also shot a bystander. Cap was arrested but released by relatives, and took refuge in the hills, but in the end was allowed to return in peace to his home. Both families were now tired of bloodshed, and in time the bitter antagonism between the two families weakened and died.

At 18.1 m. is the junction with US 52 (*see Tour 18a*).

The Guyandot Valley, through which State 10 runs west of Logan, is scarred for several miles by coal mines, and beyond is dotted with small fertile farms and oil and gas derricks. The high hills that border the valley gradually give way to low rolling hills as the Ohio Valley is approached.

HATFIELD ISLAND, 83.2 *m.*, a popular picnic spot, is used also as a landing field for light airplanes; on this island James, Joseph, and Nimrod Workman, the first settlers in the valley, built their cabins and planted their crops in 1794.

PEACH CREEK, 86 *m.* (700 alt., 421 pop.), is a residential community centered around the shops and roundhouse of the Chesapeake & Ohio Railway. The LOGAN COUNTRY CLUB (L), 96.1 *m.*, between the road and the river, has a nine-hole golf course (*greens fee* $1).

In BIG CREEK, 100 *m.* (500 alt., 463 pop.), is (L) an old WATER MILL, with an overshot wheel, still used to grind grain brought from near-by farms. Truck farming is the principal occupation in this section.

The highway traverses a distinctly backwoods section; occasional log cabins and crude shacks appear in small clearings on the steep hillsides; ragged children and the family livestock gambol in the bare yards, while the hill folk sit on the porches staring at passing traffic.

MIDKIFF, 120 *m.* (615 alt., 122 pop.), is the distributing center of an oil and gas section.

WEST HAMLIN, 130 *m.* (595 alt., 210 pop.), an agricultural trading center, is at the junction with State 3 (*see Tour 16b*).

SALT ROCK, 134 *m.* (590 alt., 93 pop.), is built around a country store, a church, and a school.

West of Salt Rock, State 10 traverses a hilly, sparsely populated stretch of country. Outcroppings of shale and limestone make farming unprofitable.

HUNTINGTON, 149.4 *m.* (564 alt., 75,572 pop.) (*see Huntington*).

Huntington is at the junction with US 60 (*see Tour 15b and c*) and US 52 (*see Tour 18b*).

ↀↀↀ

Tour 18

(Wytheville, Va.)—Bluefield—Welch—Williamson—Wayne—Huntington—(Ironton, Ohio); US 52.
Virginia Line to Ohio Line, 189.3 *m.*

Macadam and stone surface, with short graveled and concrete stretches.
Norfolk & Western Ry. parallels route between Maybeury and Welch, Williamson and Crum; roughly parallels it between Welch and Iaeger.
Good accommodations at Bluefield, Welch, Williamson, and Huntington.

US 52 closely follows the southwestern boundary of the State, traversing the Pocahontas coal field around Bluefield and the Mingo coal basin centering on Williamson, joining them with Huntington, West Virginia's largest city, a bustling industrial and commercial center on the Ohio River. Early settlers along this route, as in other sections of West Virginia, depended upon game and such produce as could be grown on 10 or 15 acres cleared around their rough cabins on the hillsides, usually in coves or on flat benches of ground to minimize erosion. Buckwheat, corn, and beans were staple crops; corn shuckings were festive occasions. Neighbors came to assist in hauling corn from the fields on sleds drawn by a yoke of oxen and heaping it up in great stacks. To this gathering came bright-eyed girls and brawny youths in their homespun best. Dinner was prepared by the women folks. Shucking was speeded by hiding a jug of apple brandy, or 'corn likker,' at the bottom of the stack. He who found the jug was not only the first to quench his burning thirst with fire-water but was privileged to kiss 'the best lookin' gal what attends this corn shuckin'.' When the day was done, they often sang under the moon:

> Heap high the farmers' wintry hoard,
> Heap high the golden corn.
> No richer gift has autumn poured
> From out her lavish horn.

The frolic ended with a square dance in the cabin.

The section along the Tug Fork of the Big Sandy River, which the route follows northwest of Williamson, was a bloody battleground between early settlers and Indians; later, fights and brawls among the pioneers were frequent, precipitated by disputes on matters ranging from finer points of religious doctrine to the merits of 'houn' dawgs.' Lumbering was the chief industry of this section until the Norfolk and Western Railway blasted a way through the mountains to the Tug Fork in 1892, opening up the Pocahontas and Mingo coal fields and transforming a primitive farming and logging country into a modern industrial area within two decades.

Section a. VIRGINIA LINE to WILLIAMSON; 107.8 m. US 52.

This section of US 52 traverses a territory given over to small coal camps and slightly larger coal towns, almost indistinguishable except for different colors of paint on the houses and varying degrees of disintegration and decay. But between the camps the beauty of the hill country is unspoiled. Only a quarter-century has elapsed since this section was wilderness, yet ghost towns are to be found here, abandoned when coal seams were depleted. Two hundred thousand people occupy the hill country along this trail, and on Saturday nights a large part of the population crowds the small and narrow streets of the towns.

US 52 crosses the VIRGINIA LINE, 0 *m.*, on the summit of EAST

RIVER MOUNTAIN (3,480 alt.), 47 miles north of Wytheville, Va. (*see Virginia Guide*).

BLUEFIELD, 4.1 *m.* (2,558 alt., 19,339 pop.), in two shallow valleys and along intervening ridges at the foot of East River Mountain, is the larger of two incorporated towns of the same name, separated only by the West Virginia-Virginia boundary line. The high surrounding hills are carpeted with fields of chicory, a native wild flower, that gave the city its name. The immediate vicinity of Bluefield shows little evidence of the 1,400-square-mile Pocahontas coal field, eight miles west, to which the community owes its birth and rapid growth.

For four and a half miles of its length Bluefield is split by the 21 tracks of the Norfolk and Western Railway yards, always filled with hundreds of loaded coal cars and switching engines. The business district is separated from the yards by a four-foot stone wall, topped with concrete flower pots—an esthetic gesture in the midst of much smoke, steam, and noise. The noise, however, is an index to local prosperity; when the mines are active the valley is filled, night and day, with the clink of heavy car wheels passing over the maze of switches and the whistles of yard locomotives as they shuttle the heavy coal gondolas from track to track. Princeton Avenue, paralleling the yards and grimy with smoke, gives Bluefield the appearance of a much older city than it really is; only a block away, the remainder of the business section looks like a modern and comparatively new city. South Bluefield, separated from the commercial area and the railway yards by a high ridge running east and west, spreads over park-like knolls and shallow vales that cling to the foot of East River Mountain; higher up the slopes are orchards and dairy farms. North of the railroad yards is a residential section, with streets extending up steep hillsides. Here lives much of Bluefield's large Negro population. Bluefield State Teachers College, in the western end of this section, is the cultural center of more than 30,000 Negroes employed in the mines and other industries of Bluefield and its environs.

The city has had considerable development since 1930. The PWA constructed in 1937 a concrete bridge for Cherry Street and Route 52 to span the Norfolk & Western yards. In the same year the PWA completed new sewerage disposal plants for both Bluefields, and the one in the West Virginia city has since been used as a model for similar projects in much larger cities. During 1937-8 an extensive housing program, in which new residential sections were added to the city, was carried out in South Bluefield.

Bluefield is largely a railroad town, the chief wholesale and retail distributing center of the coal field, but has a few small plants manufacturing flour, lumber, mattresses, electrical and mechanical equipment for the mines. The city is headquarters of many coal companies, coal associations, wholesale firms, and distributing houses of various kinds. At one time the city had the highest per capita ownership of automobiles in the nation.

Bluefielders are joiners and doers; the tranquillity of more reflective citizens is broken by the ceaseless activities of the Chamber of Commerce, Rotary, Kiwanis, Lions, Quota and Better Service clubs, American Legion, Veterans of Foreign Wars, and the Red Cross. Tourists and new residents are bombarded with information on 'Bluefield, the Air-Conditioned City,' which is a half-mile above sea level. The community entertains scores of conventions each year, and it goes out of its way to aid the unfortunate—as in 1937, when it received, fed, and housed several hundred flood refugees from the Ohio Valley, 200 miles away.

In 1777 John Davidson and Richard Bailey, early settlers, erected the Davidson-Bailey fort for protection of their families against the Indians. Surrounding claims were taken over by the children of the two families, but the region remained sparsely settled for a century. In 1791 Indians raided the home of Andrew Davidson, killed his three children, burned his house, and took his wife captive. She was sold to a French Canadian farmer, but several years later was ransomed by her husband. John Davidson was killed by Indians in 1793 while crossing East River Mountain after having sold some property in Virginia.

In 1883, when the first mines of the Pocahontas coal field were opened, the site of Bluefield consisted of two large farms owned by the Davidson and Higginbotham families. The Norfolk and Western Railway, construction of which began in 1881–2, began shipping coal from the area in 1883. A post office serving a scattered population of about 50 persons was established in 1887 on the site of the present city. In 1888 the Norfolk and Western Railway made the village a flag stop. In December of that year the railway purchased the Higginbotham farm and erected a station, roundhouse, and machine shops. Sidings and yards were laid out. With the opening of the mines and the building of the railroad yards, growth was rapid. The town of Bluefield was incorporated in 1889 with a population of 1,775. Within 10 years the population had more than doubled; by 1920 it exceeded 11,000. In 1921, the neighboring town of Graham, Virginia, changed its name to Bluefield; in 1924, at ceremonies held on the Bluefield College campus, the governor of Virginia stood at the boundary line and clasped the hand of the governor of West Virginia, and the sister cities pledged co-operation. In 1930 the two cities had a combined population of 23,245.

BLUEFIELD COLLEGE (*all buildings open during school hours*), a Baptist college with an enrollment of 275, is situated at the southwestern end of College Avenue, largely in Virginia. The campus of 100 acres occupies high rolling ground and extends into West Virginia. The principal buildings are a three-story red brick classroom, a three-story red brick boys' dormitory, a dining hall, and six faculty houses. Courses are offered in pre-law, pre-medicine, pre-dentistry, pre-engineering, and business. The school is coeducational, but a majority of the students are boys. The college was organized in 1922 by Dr. Renaldo Addison Lansdell as a junior college and until 1935 offered preparatory work.

The SITE OF THE DAVIDSON-BAILEY FORT, 200 yards north of the Bluefield College classroom building, is marked by a tall granite boulder with a bronze plaque. The boulder is said to have been used as a door prop of the fort at night and during Indian raids. About 150 yards northwest of the boulder stands a small cabin built of logs, said to have been taken from the old fort.

BLUEFIELD STATE TEACHERS COLLEGE (*open during school hours*), western end of Pulaski St., is a coeducational teachers-training institution for Negroes. In the center of the 22-acre campus, which overlooks the railroad yards and the western end of Bluefield from a steep hillside, is CONLEY HALL, the administration building, a three-story red brick structure, with a Corinthian portico, completed in 1930. West of Conley Hall is the two-story LIBRARY of red brick, with a recessed entrance fronted by four Ionic columns. Southwest of these two buildings is a three-story red brick dormitory, completed in 1938 with PWA funds, and a one-story auditorium and gymnasium, under construction in 1938. Other buildings include a dormitory for women and faculty houses. The school was established by the State legislature as Bluefield Colored Institute in 1895, and when opened in 1896 offered only high school work. In 1933 the name was changed to Bluefield State Teachers College. The school has an annual enrollment of about 350 and is State-supported.

The old DAVIDSON HOUSE (*private*), 504 Pulaski St., the oldest in Bluefield, is a two-story rectangular structure, weatherboarded and painted brown. Brick chimneys rise at the gable ends. The eastern end of the house was built of logs in 1811 by Colonel Joseph Davidson, son of the first settler and Revolutionary War soldier; deep window sills reveal the thickness of the logs covered by the weatherboarding. The western section of the house, the porch, and an addition at the rear are of more recent construction.

Bluefield is at the junction with US 19 (*see Tour 10c*).

After a gradual ascent from the rolling valleys, the road rounds a curve, 8.2 *m.*, high on a slope that overlooks (L) Lick Branch Valley and the village of Nemours, with its long rows of houses like square beads on a string.

PINNACLE ROCK (2,764 alt.), 10.8 *m.*, resembling a giant cockscomb almost a half mile long, stands (R) on the crest of a ridge; the highway passes through a gap cut in the rock. PINNACLE ROCK STATE PARK, a 31-acre tract around this landmark, provides a popular Sunday playground. The rock and surrounding area have recently been purchased by the Conservation Commission. The area is under development by the Commission and the WPA as a roadside park.

FREEMAN, 12.4 *m.* (2,250 alt., 1,036 pop.), known locally as Simmons, the name of the railroad station here, is a village, which is all that remains of an abandoned coal camp.

Left from Freeman on a concrete-paved road is BRAMWELL, 1 *m.* (2,250 alt., 1,574 pop.), established in 1888 with the opening of a near-by coal field. In the ensuing boom the town became a residential center for wealthy operators and officials of the coal companies. Large and often ornate houses line the streets.

In MAYBEURY (L), 18 *m.* (2,050 alt., 2,027 pop.), a mining center, rows of houses, monotonously alike, radiate up narrow hollows into the hills. Near the store is the tipple, from which rise clouds of coal dust to settle on houses and yards. Life for the miner's wife is a continuous chore of dusting and washing; few of the yards are brightened with flowers.

Along the highway, 20 *m.*, is a row of crumbling beehive coke ovens, abandoned when it was found that the by-products they wasted were worth more than the coke they produced. Today scientifically constructed coke ovens produce thousands of materials used in making such articles as combs, phonograph records, household appliances, explosives, dyes, soaps, oils, aspirin, and even perfumes.

A typical modern by-product plant is composed of a block of ovens, from 40 to 60 in number. Around each group, or battery, are assembled the various units for collecting and refining by-products—usually gas, coal tar, sulphate of ammonia, and motor benzol. To insure a good quality of coke and by-products, the coal must be low in sulphur content and rich in volatile matter, the element from which by-products are extracted, and the coal must contract when subjected to high heat. In 1937 the State stood second in the Union in the production of coke.

ELKHORN, 20 *m.* (1,900 alt., 1,285 pop.), one of the first coal camps to be established on the Elkhorn River, which parallels the road, draws its livelihood from two large coal operations; UPLAND, 21 *m.* (1,875 alt., 312 pop.), although a part of Elkhorn, consists of a small separate group of houses.

POWHATAN, 22 *m.* (1,800 alt., 480 pop.), named for the renowned Indian chief, and the headquarters of a coal corporation of the same name, consists of simple box-type wooden houses strung along the highway.

NORTHFORK, 24.5 *m.* (1,725 alt., 494 pop.), at the junction of the North Fork and the main Elkhorn Creek, is a coal town rather than a coal camp, being the trade center of the camps on the upper Elkhorn and in North Fork Hollow. Across the creek from upper Northfork is the coal camp of ALGOMA (1,713 alt., 310 pop.), continuously in operation longer than any other camp in the field.

KEYSTONE, 25.2 *m.* (1,645 alt., 1,897 pop.), is no longer the busy center it was in early years when the railroad was the only roadway through this section, and vehicles, if any, used the river bed as a highway. The main support of the town comes from neighboring coal operations. Here in this bottom the outlaw of song and story, John Hardy, 'killed his man,' a Negro, during a crap game.

Below the road and across the river (R), 25.6 *m.*, are the ECKMAN

Yards of the Norfolk and Western Railway; a large roundhouse services the huge mallet locomotives that haul coal over the steep grades of the surrounding hills. On the hill beyond the yard is the KEYSTONE-ECKMAN NEGRO HIGH SCHOOL, a modern brick building, with many large windows.

ECKMAN, 26 m. (1,600 alt., 1,050 pop.), lies (L) below the new highway bridge that spans both the old highway and the railroad. Its old houses are in disrepair. High on the hill is a small church. An abandoned theater and a partially abandoned company store flank the dilapidated railroad station.

LANDGRAFF, 27 m. (1,575 alt., 337 pop.), has two Negro residential sections—one (L) in a bottom filled with coal slack and bone; a second (R) on the hillside above the road. Its modern and newly painted houses stand in neat and ordered rows. A tipple stretches up the mountain side to receive the black diamonds brought from the drift mines by trams. Bordering the road are railway switches filled with cars awaiting an engine to haul them north or east.

The highway passes above VIVIAN (L), 29 m. (1,500 alt., 650 pop.), the post office address for persons living in Tidewater, Bottom Creek, and Peerless. A new consolidated grade school building shares the open level ground in the valley below the road with the company store, also a modern brick building.

In KIMBALL, 30 m. (1,475 alt., 1,467 pop.), is a large car repair shop of the Norfolk and Western Railway. The town's Negro population almost equals its white. The two-lane concrete highway forms the main street of the town, sweeping in a curve around the residential hill section.

The first all-Negro American Legion building in the United States, the LUTHER PATTERSON WAR MEMORIAL, on the hill above the highway (R), was dedicated in 1927. A brick building with Doric columns, the center of community life, it has recreation rooms, a dance hall, and is used for meetings both by Negroes and whites.

At Kimball, in the near-by Carswell plant of the Koppers Company, is one of the West Virginia Department of Mines' 21 Mine Rescue Stations. The State is divided into five districts with a full-time State Mine Rescue Director over each. These directors conduct two classes a month for the members of each rescue team in their districts. A team consists of six members, with a possible alternate or two. Members are paid $1 an hour for time spent in classes, which last two hours. Instruction covers the entire field of mine rescue and safety work. Almost all mine employees are now proficient in first aid, but none is allowed to assume the risks of rescue work until he has had additional mine rescue training provided by the State to a limited number; this lessens the possibility of additional tragedy after a major catastrophe.

Equipment is provided by the State Department of Mines and is stored by the mining companies. Classes are held in warehouses, basements, or any available space. For the work, 64 separate items are always on hand—manometers, nod and shake goggles, reducing valves, head cradles, nose clips, breathing bags, cartridge springs, brackets, and cardoxide cans, in addition to timers, gas masks, glycerine, safety lamps, stretchers, inhalators, fumigators, screw drivers, wrenches, coolers, gaskets, safety valves, and supply tubes. Teams are drilled in the use of every instrument until the handling of them becomes almost automatic. A careful check is maintained on all equipment, and at a moment's notice the teams are prepared to assemble under the direction of their captains to carry out whatever orders are given by the district director. Mine rescue work has the support and co-operation of all connected with mining.

Passing BIG FOUR, 31.5 *m.* (1,440 alt., 527 pop.), which lies along the river on the opposite bank of the Elkhorn, the highway skirts steep hills until it drops suddenly and sharply downward to SUPERIOR, 33.5 *m.* (1,361 alt., 500 pop.), an active coal operation sprawled along the narrow valley floor.

MAITLAND, 35 *m.* (1,340 alt., 271 pop.), adjoins Superior and is separated from it only by the railroad and underpass. On a leveling of the hill across the river (L) is the MAITLAND-SUPERIOR JUNIOR HIGH SCHOOL, a modern building with a large playground. For two miles the highway parallels the river bed and traverses the valley without passing a house. The STEVENS CLINIC (R), 38.1 *m.*, a three-story brick structure in the modern manner, is one of three hospitals serving Welch and surrounding coal camps.

WELCH, 37.5 *m.* (1,303 alt., 5,376 pop.), the seat of McDowell County, is built at the confluence of Elkhorn Creek and Tug River. The business section occupies a level area in the narrow Elkhorn Valley, and the residential section is scattered on surrounding hills. Welch, the trade center of the surrounding coal fields, is served by the Norfolk and Western Railway. Narrow streets provide a traffic problem, and except for the pleasantly suburban residential area, Welch is a congested town, so much so that it has been called 'Little New York' by the *New York Times*.

On Saturday nights thousands of coal miners from dozens of operations descend upon the town to shop and find amusement; among them are Negroes, Japanese, Chinese, and Europeans of every nationality. Race prejudice is conspicuously absent.

Welch was settled in 1885 on lands acquired by John Henry Hunt. I. A. Welch, for whom the town was named, together with J. H. Bramwell and J. H. Juring, bought the site for $40. Furs and ginseng were the chief products of the region. There were no bridges and no wagons until 1880; transportation remained difficult until the completion of the Norfolk and Western Railway in 1891, which opened up the surrounding coal seams. The town was laid out in 1893 and incorporated in 1894.

The first court in McDowell County was held at the house of George W. Payne on the Dry Fork of Tug River. In the War between the States the county seat was removed to Tug River, near the site of Wilcoe, where the first courthouse was built. In 1872 the county seat was removed to Perryville, now English. After a bitter fight in September 1891, a popular election made Welch the permanent county seat. In October 1892 the records were placed in a two-story frame house in Welch, once used as a saloon, on the site of the present courthouse. This old building was replaced with the present courthouse in 1895 (*see below*).

GRACE HOSPITAL, on Maple Terrace, is a three-story brick structure with two sections joined on opposite sides of the street by an overhead passageway.

The McDOWELL COUNTY COURTHOUSE, corner McDowell and Court Sts., is a three-story stone building set amid spacious landscaped grounds.

The WORLD WAR MEMORIAL BUILDING, north of the courthouse, facing the railroad station and Elkhorn River is a yellow-brick structure of colonial design, facing two high school buildings on the mountainside across the river.

The WELCH HIGH SCHOOL, JUNIOR HIGH SCHOOL and GYMNASIUM, Virginia Ave., all three-story structures of gray brick, are on the mountainside overlooking Elkhorn River and the World War Memorial Building.

WELCH EMERGENCY HOSPITAL NO. 1, Stewart St., a State institution, just inside the corporate limits, is a red brick two-and-a-half-story building with spacious lawns, shade trees, and graveled walks and driveways, enclosed within a stone wall.

In IAEGER, 52 *m.* (980 alt., 1,066 pop.), the western terminus of the electrified section of the Norfolk and Western Railway, is (L) the COMMUNITY CENTER (*swimming pool, wading pool, courts, game rooms, dance hall*), recently constructed under the auspices of the National Youth Administration.

The highway crosses INDIAN RIDGE (1,610 alt.), 60.8 *m.*, and follows a twisting course down the valley of the Guyandot River (L).

GILBERT, 71 *m.* (833 alt., 451 pop.), is the junction point for branches of the Chesapeake & Ohio Railway, Norfolk and Western Railway, and the Virginian Railway. On the bank of HORSEPEN CREEK, 76.8 *m.*, a marker indicates the site where Bolling Baker, the renegade horse thief who married Aracoma (*see Tour* 17), Chief Cornstalk's daughter, is said to have concealed horses stolen from white settlers.

On HORSEPEN MOUNTAIN (1,880 alt.), 83.8 *m.*, an arm of Mingo Mountain, is the junction with a dirt road.

Left on this road to the MINGO MOUNTAIN FIRE TOWER, 1.7 *m.*

At 84.9 *m.* is (L) a RED CROSS FIRST AID STATION. The highway begins a steep and sharply winding ascent of two ridges, 98.9 *m.*, through a dense growth of evergreens. The WILLIAMSON GUN CLUB RANGE (R), 105.3 m., adjoins a State Police station.

At 105.9 m. is a junction with State 49.

Left on State 49, 8 m., to the MINGO COUNTRY CLUB (*private*). Its frame clubhouse and cottages, a nine hole golf course, and swimming pool occupy a setting of natural beauty.

WILLIAMSON, 107.8 m. (660 alt., 9,410 pop.), seat of Mingo County, stands on a hilly area along the north bank of the Tug Fork of Big Sandy River, which forms part of the boundary line between Kentucky and West Virginia. Williamson lies in the center of what is known as the 'Billion Dollar Coal Field'; there are more than 100 mines in operation within a radius of 20 miles. An air of brisk business activity characterizes the city.

The site of a cornfield in 1891, Williamson was incorporated as a town in 1892 and named for Wallace J. Williamson, son of pioneer settlers and a dominating figure in community life for many years, amassing a large fortune in timber and real estate. The town grew rapidly, after the main line of the Norfolk and Western Railway was extended through it to tap the vast coal resources of the area, and was chartered as a city in 1905.

In 1890 a charge of illicit distilling against a moonshiner led to the formation of Mingo County. When arraigned, the prisoner challenged the jurisdiction of the court, asserting that the still was in Lincoln County. The judge ordered a survey of the boundary line, which had long been in dispute between the two counties. The survey revealed that a large strip of territory on which Lincoln County had been collecting taxes for years was in Logan County, and that Logan County was large enough to form two counties. Agitation led to the formation of Mingo County, of which Williamson became the county seat.

The CITY HALL AND FIRE STATION, corner Harvey St. and 3rd Ave., a red brick structure, houses all municipal offices and the fire department.

The COAL HOUSE, west corner of Courthouse Square, is a one-story building occupied by the Williamson Chamber of Commerce; the side walls are constructed of coal.

The MINGO COUNTY COURTHOUSE, 2nd Ave. between Court and Logan Sts., has a tall clock tower, with a heavy ribbed dome, rising above the two-and-a-half-story brick and stone structure. Before the entrance is a Doric portico. A STATUE OF LOGAN, the Mingo chief, stands in the spacious courtyard.

The WORLD WAR MEMORIAL BUILDING, corner First Ave. and Logan St., is a three-story brick building, with a large auditorium and assembly rooms.

WILLIAMSON MEMORIAL HOSPITAL, Alderson St. on Reservation Hill, is a four-story structure of light brick.

Section b. WILLIAMSON to OHIO LINE; 81.5 m. US 52.

Northwest of WILLIAMSON, 0 *m.*, US 52 follows the Tug Fork of the Big Sandy River through a region of high and rugged hills. As the route approaches the Ohio Valley, the country gradually becomes gently rolling and is devoted to agriculture.

The Tug Fork was the course followed by an ill-fated expedition led by Major (later General) Andrew Lewis against the Indians of Ohio in 1756. Winter overtook them and their supplies gave out. In their extremity they boiled the tugs, or thongs, of their boots, and from this unhappy episode the river received its name.

Lumbermen early cast their eyes on the virgin forests of this section of West Virginia. With its sharp drop and spring floods the Tug Fork allowed them to float logs down to Catlettsburg, or Ironton, where they were rafted down the Ohio to Cincinnati. Yellow poplar, cucumber, oak, bird's-eye maple, black walnut, and other hardwoods were in great demand.

CHATTAROY, 4.3 *m.* (654 alt., 526 pop.), is a mining camp that extends up a hollow (R) for nearly two miles.

BORDERLAND, 5.7 *m.* (625 alt., 262 pop.), another mining community, has a conveyor that crosses Tug River (L) and a long tram line that encircles the mountain to bring coal almost a mile from the mouth of a large mine.

At 6.2 *m.* (L) is the WILLIAMSON AIRPORT (*day service only*), a commercial field with one small hangar.

HATFIELD, 6.6 *m.* (620 alt., 62 pop.), once a prosperous mining town, is still inhabited by a few families who cultivate small corn patches on the hillsides.

NOLAN, 7.8 *m.* (648 alt., 160 pop.), is a trading center for farmers and miners in the vicinity.

In KERMIT, 21.3 *m.* (625 alt., 749 pop.), the center of a rich gas and oil field, is (L) the UNITED FUEL GAS COMPANY COMPRESSOR STATION, which pumps gas to Louisville and Pittsburgh.

CRUM, 28 *m.* (615 alt., 390 pop.), is a scattering of stores and houses with small truck gardens. Turning abruptly from the river, the highway begins a steep ascent of BULL MOUNTAIN (800 alt.), 29.8 *m.* Along Bull Creek the highway traverses an area of second-growth timber, with tiny clearings behind dilapidated shanties along the road.

MISSOURI BRANCH, 38.4 *m.* (705 alt., 25 pop.), consists of a few scattered houses, the remains of an abandoned coal camp.

Right from Missouri Branch on a dirt road to the entrance of CABWAY-LINGO STATE FOREST, 2.5 *m.*, containing 6,705 acres, situated amid high peaks, from which the hilltops of Kentucky and Ohio can be seen in the distance. Thirteen cabins (*for rentals apply to State Conservation Commission*) have been built in secluded spots on the banks of Twelvepole Creek (*swimming, fishing*). The forest has two picnic and play areas, with open fireplaces, tables, and benches. Trails wind around flower-strewn cliffs into more remote regions where rabbits, quail and squirrels abound.

Left from the entrance 0.8 *m.* is CAMP ANTHONY WAYNE, a CCC Camp.

1. Left from the camp 1.1 *m.* is a picnic ground; at 1.3 *m.* is the lake, and at 2.4 *m.*, the SPRUCE PICNIC GROVE.

2. Right from the camp 2 *m.* to TICK RIDGE FOREST FIRE TOWER (1,250 alt.); on Tick Ridge, a quarter of a mile north of the tower, just outside the boundaries of the forest, is a farm surrounded by cliffs so steep that the farmer has to climb a ladder to get to his cornfield.

North of Missouri Branch the road passes through several small towns, each the center of community life for a small area, with stores, a school, and a church.

WAYNE, 63.1 *m.* (707 alt., 675 pop.), seat of Wayne County, is perched on a hill almost 200 feet above a horseshoe bend of Twelvepole Creek, so called because it is 99 miles and 12 poles long. Named for 'Mad Anthony' Wayne, the town was settled in 1842 and incorporated in 1882.

DICKSON, 71.4 *m.* (550 alt., 119 pop.), grew up around an old mill, and the mill pond is still a popular swimming hole.

HUNTINGTON, 80.5 *m.* (564 alt., 75,572 pop.) (*See Huntington*).

Huntington is at the junction with US 60 (*see Tour 15c*) and State 10 (*see Tour 17*).

US 52 crosses the OHIO LINE, 81.5 *m.*, on a modern suspension bridge (*pedestrians 5¢, cars 25¢*) spanning the Ohio River, 0.8 miles east of Ironton, Ohio (*see Ohio Guide*).

ꝼꝼꝼ

Tour 19

(East Liverpool, Ohio)—Chester—Weirton—Wheeling—Moundsville —New Martinsville—Parkersburg; US 30, State 2. Ohio Line to Parkersburg, 133 *m.*

Concrete roadbed throughout.
Route paralleled by the Pennsylvania R.R. between Chester and Wheeling; by the Baltimore & Ohio R.R. between Wheeling and Parkersburg.
Accommodations at short intervals.

This route runs the length of the Northern Panhandle of West Virginia, a narrow and highly industrialized strip between the Pennsylvania Line and the Ohio River. Beyond this smoky region of mines and mills the highway winds along the wooded banks of the broad and shining river through many old towns, settled more than a century ago when the Ohio was the main artery of travel to the newly opened West. Water-borne traffic declined with the building of the railroads, but many of the river ports survived to become prosperous trading centers when oil and gas fields were later discovered in the vicinity.

The Indians who occupied the forested Ohio Valley at the arrival of the first white men called the river Ohiople (*river of white caps*), a name corrupted by the whites to Oyo, and later to Ohio. The settlement and exploitation of the valley by restless pioneers and empire-builders marked the first step forward by the new Nation after it had achieved its independence. The story of the development of West Virginia is in large part the story of the Ohio Valley. It was the pioneer route to the west and the early tradeway to the south. Broad and placid, the stream still contributes to progress, although on occasion it asserts its wild power in floods that devastate many of the valley towns from Wheeling to Huntington. The story of the Ohio is the story of bloody strife among the British, French, Indians, and later the Colonists; of plots and treason, as when Aaron Burr and a few others schemed to set up an independent empire in the West; of arson, pillage, torture, and murder; of crude log forts and cruder cabins, tiny bulwarks of civilization in the wilderness, and of the brave men and women who built and maintained them.

Eastern manufactures were floated down the Ohio on flatboats to the western and southern settlements, where they were exchanged for the frontiersmen's flax, ginseng, beeswax, and hides. Today the same route is followed by Diesel-powered towboats, each pushing a dozen or more 2,000-ton barges, laden with iron, steel, metal products, coal, oil, ore, gasoline, naphtha, or other goods, through a channel maintained at a uniform depth by Government dams. The red flames of the giant mills, under pillars of acrid black smoke, illuminate the soot-covered hills once lighted only by campfire. Here are dank odors of mine pits and the blue haze of potteries and glass plants. The clank of the oil derrick, the chug of the compressor, the roar and grind of metal fabrication processes, the thunder and crunch of foundry machinery, the rattle of mechanized farming equipment, the swish and rumble of highway transportation, the assorted wails and shrieks of factory whistles —all have drowned out the last echoes of the frontier along the narrow valley of the stream known to the first French explorers as La Belle Rivière.

Section a. OHIO LINE to WHEELING, 47 m. US 30, State 2.

In this section of the route along the Northern Panhandle of the State, man-made mountains of slag and ore surround the blackened sheds and chimneys of steel mills; red and yellow banks of clay form a background for the bulging kilns of pottery, brick, and tile works;

and the lofty stacks of glass plants reach as high as the surrounding hills, in the bowels of which coal is mined.

On the western bank of the river, at the limits of East Liverpool, Ohio (*see Ohio Guide*), US 30 crosses the OHIO LINE, 0 *m.*, on a toll bridge (15¢ *one way*, 25¢ *round trip*).

CHESTER, 0.8 *m.* (704 alt., 3,701 pop.), a predominantly residential town, has a small business district, several potteries, and no hotel accommodations. Laid out in 1896 and incorporated in 1907, it was called Chester by its founder, J. E. McDonald, 'solely because it was a short name, easy to remember.'

ROCK SPRINGS PARK (R), a municipal amusement center, has a roller coaster looming high above the street.

Right from Chester on State 66 is NEWELL, 1 *m.* (710 alt., 1,042 pop.), a pottery town. The HOMER LAUGHLIN CHINA COMPANY PLANT (*open*), one of the largest in the country, manufactures dinnerware, kitchenware, colored pottery, and china novelties. A pioneer pottery established here about 1830 used clay from the neighboring hills to make crude yellow ware for the local market. In addition to native clay, the present plant uses raw materials imported from far and wide—ball clay from Cornwall, feldspar from Maine, silica from Pennsylvania, cobalt from Canada, zinc from Missouri, white lead from Colorado, gold from Alaska, kaolin and whiting from the chalk cliffs of Dover.

At 3.8 *m.* is the junction (R) with State 2, which the route now follows.

Left (straight ahead) on US 30 to the Pennsylvania Line, 0.9 *m.*, 38.9 miles west of Pittsburgh, Pennsylvania.

PUGHTOWN, 9 *m.* (1,196 alt., 418 pop.), formerly known as Fairview and New Manchester, now a tranquil country town, once fought bitterly with New Cumberland for possession of the county seat. In the course of three hotly contested elections the seat was removed to New Cumberland, returned here, and again removed to New Cumberland. The old courthouse, erected in 1849 and now a private residence, is Pughtown's sole trophy of these battles.

Right from Pughtown on an improved road to TOMLINSON RUN STATE PARK (*trails and picnic shelters*), 1 *m.*, 1,224 acres of woodland.

At 11.5 *m.* is a junction with State 66.

Right on State 66 is HARTFORD'S MILL, 1 *m.*, the first in the State to manufacture gunpowder (1795).

At 3 *m.* is the SITE OF THE LOGAN MASSACRE, one of the incidents that precipitated Lord Dunmore's War (*see History*). In 1774, in the absence of Logan, chief of the Mingo, the keeper of a grog shop here invited some of the chief's family to a drinking party. In the course of a brawl the whites attacked and killed all the Indians, which so enraged and embittered Logan that he led his tribe on the warpath, he himself taking 30 scalps in revenge. At the close of Dunmore's War, Logan was among the Indian chiefs invited to the peace conference. He refused to attend, but sent a bitter speech that has survived as a notable example of Indian eloquence:

'I appeal to any white man to say if he ever entered Logan's cabin hungry that I gave him not meat; if ever he came cold and naked I gave him not warmth and clothing. During the course of the last long and bloody war Logan remained in his tent, an advocate for peace. Nay, such was my love for the whites, that those of my own country pointed at me as they passed by and said, "Logan is a friend of the white man." I had even thought to live with you but for the injuries of one man. Colonel Cresap, then last spring, in cold blood and unprovoked, cut off all the relatives of Logan, not sparing even my women and children. There runs not a drop of my blood in the veins of any creature. This called on me for revenge. I have fully glutted my vengeance. For my country, I rejoice at the beams of peace. Yet, do not harbor the thought that mine is the joy of fear. Logan never felt fear. He will not turn on his heel to save his life. Who is there to mourn for Logan? Not one.'

NEW CUMBERLAND, 12.2 *m*. (671 alt., 2,300 pop.), seat of Hancock County, a quiet town with old houses set in large shady lawns surrounded by iron and stone fences, was formerly known as Brick Bend because of its numerous brickyards and pottery works. Platted in 1839 on the site of Fort Chapman, erected in 1784, the town was first named Cuppytown in honor of John Cuppy, its founder.

The highway crosses KINGS CREEK, 18.3 *m*., where in 1794 Peter Tarr built the first iron furnace west of the Alleghenies. Cannonballs cast here were fired from the guns of Commodore Perry's fleet in the Battle of Lake Erie, 1813. Campbell Tarr, a grandson, served as treasurer of the Restored Government of Virginia and was treasurer (1863–7) of the new State of West Virginia.

WEIRTON, 19.5 *m*. (640 alt., 8,572 pop. in 1930, estimated 18,000 in 1940), the largest unincorporated town in the country, is the 'Topsy' of West Virginia industry. Once a cornfield cramped between the hills, the town has grown rapidly since 1910 when the first steel mill opened and its flames against the night sky heralded a new era; it has steadily expanded in area and population to keep pace with the ever-growing number of mills that squat grimly (R) behind a reinforced wire barrier stretching along the highway for a mile and a half.

In 1905 Ernest T. Weir and J. R. Phillips bought a bankrupt tin mill in Clarksburg and put 150 men to work manufacturing tin plate. Five years later, having increased their business by new methods, they decided to manufacture sheet steel and bought a site here on the Ohio River. The properties of the company now include 26 rolling mills producing 1,260,000 tons of slabs, billets, and bars annually; 12 open hearth furnaces, with a yearly ingot capacity of 1,410,000 tons; two blast furnaces smelting 666,000 tons of pig iron; 111 by-product coke ovens, with an annual capacity of 7,000,000 tons; and finishing mills for hot and cold rolled steel, galvanized and black sheets, tin plate and structural shapes, aggregating 1,400,000 tons each year. Employing 10,000 men, the plant also produces such by-products as coke, tar, sulphate of ammonia, and light oils, while the rolling mill at Clarksburg employs 1,000 men in the production of tin plate. In 1930 the Weirton Steel Company merged with the Great Lakes Steel Company to form the National Steel Corporation, with Weir as chairman.

A hard-bitten community of heavy-muscled men and strong-limbed women, Weirton is a study in contrasts. Its residents enjoy municipal conveniences, but pay no local taxes. Its daily life is American but colored by the customs of 25 nationalities. Weirton is a company town in that the steel corporation provides the town's economic lifeblood and exercises a dominant influence in its political and social life. Workmen and merchants alike find their lives regulated by the smoke from the mill stacks; times are good when great sooty clouds indicate that the mills are working at capacity; brows are wrinkled with anxiety when stacks rise starkly into a smokeless sky. But Weirton is not a company town in the usual sense, for the corporation owns only the mill property; workmen do not live in company houses or buy at the company store; the community has a high percentage of individually owned homes, yet all discussion of individual or group activity is prefaced with the reservation, 'if the mill works.'

For years American steel towns were known as 'damn goot place make money, no place live.' Workmen immigrated from Europe to labor in the mills for a few years before returning to the 'old country' to live in relative comfort. E. T. Weir sensed that decent living conditions would not only make millworkers more than mere transients but would also produce greater working efficiency and higher profits. The steel company established the Weirton Improvement Company to provide the usual municipal services, such as street repair, sewage disposal, and public utilities. The fire department is volunteer, and deputy sheriffs and constables of Hancock County police the community. These services are furnished without tax, so that there has been no strong movement to incorporate the community. Sports and recreations are sponsored by the company, and certain holidays are celebrated with special programs, elaborate parades and pageants; the Festival of the Nations on Labor Day attracts as many as 25,000 visitors.

Poles, Greeks, Italians, Serbs, Croats, Slovenes, and Turks have come to work in Weirton, creating a potpourri of foreign customs, a Babel of strange tongues, including English with a curious accent and idiom. Quick to anger, gay, hard-working, courageous, and thrifty, they form a polyglot held together by steel's demands for a strong body and a great endurance. Although their lives are dominated by the steel company, they are not servile, and other years have seen the streets alive with restless crowds, resolute in defense of their rights, as their understanding of these was clarified by long discussions in coffee houses and social clubs.

Since 1937 Weirton has received considerable public attention because of a hearing before the National Labor Relations Board involving the steel company and its company union, the Employees Security League.

Weirton is at the junction with US 22.

Left 5 *m.* on US 22 to the Pennsylvania Line, 5 miles west of Florence, Pa. (*see Pennsylvania Guide*).

HOLLIDAYS COVE, 21.4 *m.* (742 alt., 4,480 pop.), a residential city inhabited by steel workers employed in the mills at Weirton, was settled in 1776 by John Holliday, who built a blockhouse here which served neighboring forts as an arsenal. Weirton and Hollidays Cove combine under the name of the Weir-Cove Community for sports, celebrations, and other activities, having a joint community chest and safety council; large signs on the highways warn motorists entering the cities: 'Go slow. You only die once, but please not here.'

Hollidays Cove is at the junction with US 22.

Right on US 22 across a toll bridge (*one way* 15¢; *round trip* 25¢) to the Ohio Line, 1.3 *m.*, on the northern limits of Steubenville, Ohio.

FOLLANSBEE, 26.2 *m.* (673 alt., 4,841 pop.), a steel town, is built around the FOLLANSBEE BROTHERS COMPANY MILL along the river. At night the furnaces here and at Mingo Junction across the Ohio cast a bright glow, revealing in silhouette the tall stacks and long sheds of the steel mill and the network of a railroad bridge spanning the river.

The river here narrows and the navigation channel twists to avoid rock ledges and subsurface sand bars. Although now dredged and marked with buoys by Federal maintenance craft, this stretch of river was long a hazard to steamboats. It was here that the *Scioto* rammed the *John Lomas* head on, July 4, 1882, with great loss of life. Here, too, the great coal tows cautiously inched their way south under the power of the *Sprague, Joseph B. Williams, Duquesne,* and other steamboats. Through this channel and down the entire length of the Ohio the *Joseph B. Williams* once bulldogged a tow of barges 1,009 feet long, the longest on record. Her contemporary, the *Sprague,* most powerful towboat of her time, set a record on the lower Ohio in 1907 by making a trip with 60 barges loaded with 70,000 tons of merchandise.

WELLSBURG, 30.4 *m.* (661 alt., 6,398 pop.), seat of Brooke County, is an unromantic-looking industrial town; but for a long time it was more widely known for its 'gin weddings' and 'marrying parsons' than for its glass plants and large paper mills producing great quantities of paper bags.

A town of narrow streets and smoke-begrimed old buildings, Wellsburg thrived as a Gretna Green for many years. Its enterprising ministers and accommodating county clerk married 10,000 couples a year up to 1937, when the legislature enacted a law requiring a three-day notice on the part of those intending to wed. As the law did not require the notice to be filed in person, the taxi-cab companies that worked with the ministers on a commission basis undertook to salvage part of the Dan Cupid business by offering to make all advance arrangements for bright-eyed brides and grooms. Business has fallen off lamentably, however, although some parsonages still seek to attract custom by signs, 'Marriages Performed Here.'

Jonathan, Israel, and Friend Cox, the first settlers here, built a cabin on the river bank in 1772. In 1788 they sold 500 acres of the bottom land to Charles Prather, who, in selling lots, included a proviso in the deeds restraining buyers from operating a ferry across the Ohio River in competition with himself and his family. The ferry that still plies between Wellsburg and Brilliant, Ohio (*car and driver*, 25¢; *with passengers*, 30¢), operates under the original Prather charter signed by John Adams, second President of the United States.

The settlement was platted in 1790, chartered as Charles Town the following year, and became the county seat in 1797. In 1816, to avoid confusion with two other towns of the same name, it was renamed Wellsburg in honor of Alexander Wells, Prather's son-in-law. The town grew rapidly and for a time rivaled Wheeling as a commercial center, being a serious contender in the fight to become the western terminus of the National Road (*see Tour 23*). As it had an excellent river landing, boatyards were established, and huge warehouses were built in which to store flour and liquor awaiting shipment to New Orleans. Several ships built in the yards were sea-going vessels and carried cargoes of flour to Glasgow and Liverpool. The first glass plant in the State was established here in 1813 by Isaac Duval. The local manufacture of paper began in 1835. Distilleries, most prosperous of Wellsburg's early plants, were closed before 1845 by temperance agitation.

Wellsburg made probably the first attempt at flood protection along the Ohio River. By 1829 a large part of the bottom land, including the site of the Cox cabin, was under water as a result of erosion and periodic floods. In that year, with the permission of the Virginia assembly, townspeople raised $25,000 by lottery and erected two parallel flood walls. They still stand along the river front; they do not wholly protect the town from flood but have prevented much damage.

Left from Wellsburg on State 27 is FOWLERSVILLE, 2.5 *m.* (1,100 alt., 50 pop.), where the original Grimes Golden apple tree was discovered in 1832 on the farm of Thomas Grimes. The Grimes Golden is a yellow apple, mellow in flavor and popular both for cooking and eating. The origin of the first tree is unknown, but legend asserts that it sprang from a seed planted by Jonathan Chapman, better known as Johnny Appleseed, who wandered up and down the Ohio Valley distributing appleseeds, reading religious tracts to settlers and Indians, planting his seeds wherever he thought an orchard could thrive; the seeds he planted between 1806 and 1847 started many of the better orchards in the Ohio Valley. The original Grimes Golden tree blew down about 1900, and the wood was used to make gavels for the West Virginia Agricultural Society; two stone pillars and a watering trough mark the spot where the tree stood.

At 31.7 *m.* is a junction with State 67.

Left on State 67 is BETHANY, 7 *m.* (932 alt., 439 pop.), which owes its existence to BETHANY COLLEGE, a nonsectarian institution sponsored by the Disciples of Christ Church. Seven buildings of Gothic design occupy a 50-acre campus. An additional area of 535 acres is used for experimental farming. Since 1881 it has been a coeducational school, and in 1938 had an enrollment of 375. Chartered in 1840 by Alexander Campbell, founder of the Disciples of Christ Church, the college succeeded a similar school, Buffalo Academy, conducted by Campbell from 1818 to 1823.

The CAMPBELL HOMESTEAD, which adjoins the campus, is maintained by the Campbell Historical and Memorial Association as a memorial to the religious leader. The white frame mansion contains the furniture used by the Campbell family and has been restored in part to its original condition. Behind the mansion stands the schoolhouse attended by Campbell's 14 children and a few of the neighbors' boys and girls. In the yard in front of the house, surrounded by a few huge old pine trees, is a small octagonal brick structure in which Campbell read and composed his sermons. Campbell's bookshelves, books, and a large chair with an arm table have been preserved here.

Near by stands the old BRUSH RUN MEETING HOUSE (*open upon application*), a one-story, white frame structure with a shingled gable roof, erected in 1811. This meeting house, in which Campbell preached many of his early sermons, is not used now, and was removed to its present site as a part of the Campbell Memorial.

Alexander Campbell, son of a Presbyterian minister, came to the United States from Scotland in 1809 and soon became affiliated with the Baptist Church. Until 1830 Campbell and his followers remained nominally Baptists, but shortly thereafter a new congregation was formed and the Disciples of Christ church was founded. The main tenets of the Disciples are simplicity of organization and doctrine, freedom of the will, no distinction between laymen and clergy, and a union of God's people on the basis of the Bible alone.

BEECH BOTTOM, 35.2 *m.* (660 alt., 309 pop.), has a large steel plant. An INDIAN MOUND (R) was opened and explored by the University of Pennsylvania in 1929; skeletons, bits of pottery, weapons and ornaments of stone and copper were found. During the Indian attacks of 1777 and 1789, Fort Beech Bottom, erected here about 1775, sheltered many of the settlers of the section.

The WHEELING STEEL CORPORATION PLANT (R) consists of long, slender, A-type structures of brick and corrugated iron, covering the larger part of a 1,160-acre tract of land surrounded by a bristling steel fence. These smoke-streaked red buildings house 7 mechanized hot mills, with an annual capacity of 72,000 tons of sheet steel; the mills add a rumbling threnody to the song of industry which rises high above the whistling winds that sweep down the valley. Bars of metal brought from the furnaces at Benwood and Steubenville are here heated and rolled by 'roughers' and 'catchers,' who feed the bars through roughing mills until the sheets reach the proper thickness for finishing. A 'charger' then guides them to the furnace conveyor, where the sheets are re-heated and again rolled until they reach four or five feet in length. A 'matcher' then shapes the sheets for final rolling, and a 'doubler' folds the sheets into four thicknesses called a 'pack.' Again reheated and passed between the rolls of the mill until they reach the desired size and thickness, the sheets are stacked by a 'piler,' and each pack is shaped to size by 'shearmen' operating great electrically powered knives capable of slicing four thicknesses of steel in a split-second; after the sheets have been separated, they are pickled, annealed, cold rolled, or terne-coated, depending upon the specifications of the order. Each mill is under the supervision of a 'roller,' who, with two helpers, is responsible for the proper operation of the mill.

Adjoining the Beech Bottom rolling mill is the STEELCRETE EXPANDED METAL PLANT of the Wheeling Steel Corporation, in which steel fence and metal lath are made from flat-rolled steel. The sheets are cut by guillotine shears and then stretched to leave diamond-shaped openings; finally they are sheared to the size desired.

POWER, 35.8 *m.* (665 alt., 1,532 pop.), lives under a modified form of corporate paternalism; it was named for and is largely dependent upon the large power plant here. Neat white frame houses line the streets of the company town in the shadow of the bluff along the river; at the southern boundary of the community a seven-story coal tipple spouts coal from the company's 'captive' mine, which taps the coal strata underlying 11,000 acres of land. A belt conveyor crosses the highway on steel stilts, emptying the coal into towering piles close to the plant.

Crouched (R) between the road and the river like some tawny beast, the WINDSOR POWER COMPANY PLANT, a square brick structure topped with lofty black chimneys, houses the furnaces, boiler, turbines, and other equipment used to generate 800,000,000 kilowatt-hours annually. Coal by the carload is dumped automatically into the red hell of tremendous furnaces, tended by goggled furnacemen who rake the fires with long steel pokers and face the blasting heat to free the furnace grates of clinkers. Water from the river is converted into steam in the boilers, and the steam propels turbines shaped like mammoth snail shells, while dozens of alert engineers and workmen trained by a lifetime of service in the plant carefully check the dials of countless gauges. From a control room lined with panels, on which colored lights blink intermittently to record every variation in the mad whirl of machinery, electricity is dispatched along transmission lines in all directions, serving not only the homes and industries of the Ohio Valley, but also the rubber plants of Akron and the steel mills of Canton and Youngstown.

. SHORT CREEK, 37.5 *m.* (668 alt., 421 pop.), an unincorporated town, occupies the approximate site of Fort Van Meter, erected about 1774. Major Samuel McCulloch (*see Wheeling*) was killed here by Indians in 1782 while in command of the fort.

WHEELING, 47 *m.* (678 alt., 61,659 pop.) (*see Wheeling*).

Wheeling is at the junction with US 40 (*see Tour 23*) and US 250 (*see Tour 22b*).

Section b. WHEELING to PARKERSBURG; 86 m. State 2.

This section of State 2 parallels the course of the Ohio River through a valley framed by low hills. Industrial development hides much of the beauty of the route south of Wheeling. Between Moundsville and Parkersburg, long stretches of green countryside alternate with neat small towns; the broad shining river, bordered with trees, is almost always in view. At intervals the route passes through river towns, settled between 1774 and 1810, which became suddenly prosperous near the close of the nineteenth century with the local discovery of oil and gas. Scattered through the valley are many round burial mounds left by the Indians.

Between WHEELING, 0 *m.*, and Moundsville (*see Tour 22b*), State 2 and US 250 are one route (*see Tour 22b*).

South of Moundsville the highway runs close to the river in the shadow (L) of a high rocky bluff (*danger of falling rocks*) and then emerges into the open land of ROUND BOTTOM, patented by George Washington in 1784 and sold to Archibald McClean in 1798. The sale was followed by years of litigation, for the land was claimed also by the Tomlinson and Cresap families who had settled on the tract between 1771 and 1784, and had built homes and planted crops. The Tomlinsons claimed that the survey made by Colonel Crawford, upon which Washington's patent was based, had been made in violation of 'tomahawk rights,' established by notching with a tomahawk or axe the trees bounding a plot of ground. Such claims were recognized by other settlers and in most cases were upheld as prior claims in case of dispute. The Supreme Court of Appeals at Richmond upheld Washington's patent in 1834, however, and the original settlers were forced to relinquish their claims.

Across the river rise shale and slate cliffs, which tower above shaft mines dwarfed by piles of slag; the narrowness of the valley here amplifies the siren blasts of towboats. Through the years these austere bluffs have echoed the warning signals of craft famous in river lore—the *Rebecca,* which rammed a bridge pier at Parkersburg in 1869 and sank in a few minutes, with appalling loss of life; the *John Porter,* victim of an outbreak of cholera, cut loose to drift because no pilot would board her, rechristened the *Transporter,* but ever after shunned as a pariah by rivermen; the pretentious *Great Republic,* which passed most of her life on the Mississippi, although built on the Ohio in 1867 and considered the ultimate expression of the steamboat builder's skill.

CRESAPS GROVE, 20.5 *m.* (680 alt., 65 pop.), on the site of a blockhouse erected by Captain John Baker in 1784, was a favorite lookout of scouts intent on preventing Indians from crossing the Ohio to raid settlements on this bank. The fort was never attacked, but numerous clashes between Indians and scouts occurred near by, in one of which Captain Baker and John Wetzel, brother of Lewis Wetzel (*see Wheeling*), were killed. The victims were buried at the fort, and the little stream that here flows into the Ohio still bears the name of Graveyard Run.

A marker, 20.6 *m.*, points (L) to ROSBYS ROCK, 5 miles to the east, at which point the final spike on the Baltimore & Ohio Railroad tracks between the Atlantic seaboard and the Ohio River was driven on Christmas Eve, 1852, just 25 years after work had been begun in Baltimore. The last 200 miles of track across the Alleghenies were laid from Cumberland to Wheeling in four years, at a cost of $6,500,000, after legal and financial difficulties and the hostility of the legislature and the people of Virginia had stopped construction at Cumberland for six years. Service was instituted in May 1830, when the 13-mile stretch from Baltimore to Ellicott's Mills was completed. A horse furnished motive power, but a steam engine was employed later in the year, after Peter Cooper had successfully demonstrated his *Tom Thumb*, the first locomotive built in this country. In 1834 the line reached the Potomac River opposite Harpers Ferry, and two years later the bridge across the Potomac was completed. Meanwhile, in 1835, a branch line had been built to Washington. During the following eight years the railroad pushed on 97 miles to Cumberland. When construction was resumed six years later, the territory between Cumberland and the Ohio River presented problems that challenged the greatest engineers of the time. The awesome Cheat River chasm was bridged, and 11 tunnels were driven through the mountains. The first train to cross the Alleghenies arrived in Wheeling on January 1, 1853, crowded with company officers and State and Federal officials.

CAPTINA, 21.7 m. (640 alt., 100 pop.), is a mining camp of frame houses. While on his way to his inauguration at Washington, President-elect Zachary Taylor was stranded here in 1849, when the *Telegraph II*, the packet on which he was traveling, stuck fast in the icebound river, forcing his party to disembark and proceed by sled to Wheeling.

The gently sloping flood plain here encouraged the construction of boat landings in the heyday of the packets during the 1840's and 1850's, when the economic life of the valley centered on river traffic. From 1843, when the first regular Pittsburgh-to-Cincinnati packet service was instituted, these landings were piled high with farm and dairy products, picked up for delivery at the larger valley towns, or with cordwood for boiler fuel. Outstanding among the luxurious express boats, which made limited stops at large cities, was the *J. M. White*, most palatial packet on western waters, the pride of all rivermen; her record run from New Orleans to St. Louis in 1844 stood unequaled for 30 years. By 1855 travel had so increased that the packets carried 3,000,000 passengers in that year. River travel was favored by such celebrities of the day as Jenny Lind, the 'Swedish Nightingale,' Charles Dickens, and P. T. Barnum, with his traveling menagerie. Henry Clay, Andrew Jackson, and Abraham Lincoln traveled by packet on their way to Washington and welcomed stops at rural landings to explain national issues.

WOODLANDS, 22.7 m. (637 alt., 35 pop.), occupies the site of a blockhouse erected by Presley Martin (*see below*) during the Indian wars.

NEW MARTINSVILLE, 36.7 m. (630 alt., 2,814 pop.), seat of Wetzel County, is a river town with large frame and brick houses built by farmers who suddenly found themselves well-to-do with the discovery of oil on their lands. Rather ornate houses elbow one another in neighborly fashion along the shady streets; their ample bay windows and porches are neither too far back from the street nor too heavily shaded to obscure the view of passing traffic.

Edward Doolin, the first settler here, patented 800 acres of river bottom in 1780. Two years later he was killed on his doorstep one morning by Indians returning from an unsuccessful foray on Fort Henry. His wife and new-born baby were not harmed. Instead, the Indians promised Mrs. Doolin, a beautiful woman, that they would return for her when she was able to travel and make her the wife of the chief. Mrs. Doolin was not flattered and fled to a fort up the river; in 1810 she sold the site to Presley Martin, who settled here the next year. Platted in 1838, the town was named Martinsville in his honor; 'New' was prefixed later to avoid confusion with another town of the same name.

A ferry (*tolls: car and driver 25¢, trucks 40¢–50¢, trailers 15¢, pedestrians 10¢*) connects New Martinsville with Ohio State 7 (*see Ohio Guide*).

New Martinsville is at the junction with State 7 (*see Tour 21b*) and State 20 (*see Tour 20a*).

The 'Poor Man's Highway,' as the river was known during the post-bellum years when packets vied with railroads for dominance, is broad, smooth, and passive along these miles, offering few problems to river captains. The channel is marked with buoys, and shore lights mounted on white metal tripods outline the banks. Heavy tows make up time here, toiling south with steel, pipe, and metal manufactures, just as their predecessors hauled farm produce, timber and coal. Recent years have seen a great increase in river transportation especially of inflammable liquids, gasoline, oil, naphtha, and benzine, for one barge has the capacity of a dozen tank cars, and the danger of fire or explosion is slight on metal barges partly submerged in water. Fleets of barges carry bulk shipments under the guidance of such mighty towboats as the *Duncan Bruce, Plymouth, W. A. Shepherd,* and *George T. Price*—squat formidable craft that generate as high as 70,000 horsepower each and can handle in a single tow a volume of merchandise equal to the capacity of three trains.

PADEN CITY, 43 *m.* (630 alt., 2,281 pop.), an orderly and spacious river town, specializes in the manufacture of bottles. In 1790 Obadiah Paden patented 2,000 acres of hill and river bottom here and in succeeding years fathered 10 children, who in turn fathered the town. PADEN ISLAND (R) was acquired by Obadiah, according to family tradition, through outscheming the Indian chief, Munsie, who lived on it. Munsie much admired and coveted a gun and powder horn owned by Paden, and one morning came to tell him how, in a dream, these things had been presented to him by Paden. As Indian custom required that Paden make the dream come true, he did so but was very thoughtful for several days. A week later he told Munsie of a dream that he had had, in which the chief had given him the island. Munsie surrendered the island he loved, but told Paden no more of his dreams.

SISTERSVILLE, 47.4 *m.* (648 alt., 3,072 pop.), was a quiet river village until the 1890's when oil was discovered under it. Houses, churches, and schools were quickly moved so that wells might be drilled. Oil derricks still standing in backyards and forming additional hazards on the local golf course testify to the mad rush for 'liquid gold' in those years. The boom is over, but several gasoline refineries are still in operation here.

Sistersville was settled in 1802 by Charles Wells, who built his cabin on what is now the golf course. Wells had 22 children; a tenant named Scott had 22; Gordon, a neighbor, had 28; in 1811 the *Navigator* solemnly commented: 'The banks of the Ohio seem peculiarly grateful to the propagation of the human species.' Wells named his 20th off-spring Twenty and his 21st Plenty. Evidently despairing of the efficacy of symbolical names, he named the 22nd Betsey. Known as Wells Landing for a number of years and then for a short time as Ziggleton, the settlement was incorporated in 1839 as Sistersville, in honor of Well's 18th and 19th children, Sarah and Deliah, upon whose property the town was platted. Wells Street perpetuates the name of this prolific family; Chelsea Street was once known as Brown Betty Street for their favorite mare.

FRIENDLY, 52.3 *m.* (650 alt., 170 pop.), named for Friend Cochran Williamson, grandson of Thomas Williamson who settled here in 1785, is situated at the head of a long straight stretch of river valley known as the Long Reach since the days of Washington's explorations.

At LONG REACH, 54.7 *m.* (612 alt., 25 pop.), are the remains of PREHISTORIC WALLS (R), two parallel earthen ramparts, about 120 feet apart and 3 miles long, extending down the valley to Bens Run. Believed to have been 12 feet high originally, the walls have been eroded and are now so covered with vines and weeds that they are scarcely distinguishable. They enclose an area of 400 acres, divided near the center by a cross wall; the southern half is additionally divided by two parallel curving walls running north and south. The northern enclosure contains two burial mounds as yet unexplored. Near the walls are two stone platforms, one on top of a knoll. The purpose of the walls has puzzled archeologists.

The Long Reach, a broad stretch of river deceptive in its placidity, has been known to rivermen since the first steamboats pioneered the route from Pittsburgh to Louisville. In 1816 a series of shifting bars at this point almost caused disaster for Captain Henry M. Shreve and his steamboat *G. Washington,* en route from Wheeling to New Orleans. Constructed at Wheeling, the *G. Washington* was the initial double decker on the western waterways, being the first steamboat to float on the water rather than in it. Her sumptuously appointed cabins were named for the States. Shreve's voyage to New Orleans was undertaken to test the legality of the claims of the Robert Fulton interests, who had been granted the exclusive right of operating steamboats on the lower Mississippi by the legislatures of several States, following the successful voyage of their *New Orleans* in 1811. Shreve was arrested in New Orleans but was released under bond; later, a decision by the U. S. Supreme Court opened the Mississippi to all comers. The *G. Washington* was the first steamboat to demonstrate the practicability of river navigation by making the voyage upstream from New Orleans to Louisville in 25 days.

RAVEN ROCK, 59.8 m. (647 alt., 132 pop.), settled in 1810 by Basil Riggs, who erected a gristmill here, was named for the large flocks of ravens that once nested on the rocks east of the village.

SPRING RUN, 60.8 m. (718 alt., 75 pop.), contains the WEST VIRGINIA TRAINING SCHOOL (L), a State institution for feeble-minded children, occupying a 694-acre farm settled by Robert Browse in 1810. Opened in 1932, the school consists of a modern two-story dormitory building, housing 80 children, and the remodeled three-story Browse mansion. In an endeavor to instruct children in some occupation that will fit them to take care of themselves as adults, boys are taught farming, dairying, and manual training, while girls receive instruction in domestic science, hand and machine sewing, rug and basket weaving.

SAINT MARYS, 64.3 m. (623 alt., 2,182 pop.), seat of Pleasants County, depends largely for subsistence on neighboring oil and gas fields and the manufacture of glass. The courthouse and residential district occupy a high bench overlooking the business section along the river. Two Frenchmen, Isaac and Jacob La Rue, settled here in 1790 on land granted them for their services in the Revolutionary War. Their graves are on MIDDLE ISLAND (R), reached by a ramp leading down from the toll bridge across the Ohio River.

Saint Marys owes its existence and name, legend has it, to Alexander Creel, who was passing on a steamboat when the Virgin Mary appeared to him in a vision and said, pointing to the shore, 'There you behold the site of what will some day be a happy and prosperous city.' Creel bought the land in 1834 but seemed somewhat dubious about the vision, for he soon sold his holdings and settled at Vaucluse (*see below*). In 1849, when the question of selecting a county seat arose, he realized that Pickens Bottom, as the land here at the mouth of Middle Island Creek was called, offered more room for expansion than the narrow valley at Vaucluse. He repurchased the land, had the town platted, and named it Saint Marys.

Saint Marys is at the junction with US 50-Alt. (*see Tour 4c*).

A marker (R), 66.2 m., indicates the SITE OF VAUCLUSE, settled by Alexander Creel and named for the French town celebrated by Petrarch, the Italian poet.

EUREKA (Gr., I have found it), 69 m. (654 alt., 212 pop.), was so named when, after many difficulties, a gusher was struck here amid great jubilation in 1885, opening the rich Eureka-Belmont oil field. A fire and the loss of tools down the hole had delayed operations for two years and almost caused abandonment of the enterprise.

Below Eureka the Ohio winds in a series of broad sweeping curves, with the sharp rubble banks of the upper valley giving way to swampy spongy shores on both sides. As fishing is good here, the stretch is a frequent port of call for shanty-boaters. These boats, generally flat bottomed, but often built to resemble an ark, cruise the thousand miles between Pittsburgh and Cairo each year. The shanty-boater lives in the small cabin on his craft; the river and its banks provide his food; driftwood for heating and cooking is to be had for the taking, while a little backdoor begging at farmhouses usually provides him with castoff clothing. More energetic shanty-boaters work a few days each week ashore; they are invariably jacks-of-all-trades, their footloose life developing in them both an amazing versatility in handicrafts and an earnest desire to practice these crafts as seldom as possible.

Not all houseboat dwellers are shanty-boaters, this term being applied mainly to those whose wanderlust keeps them from settling in one spot for any great length of time. Cheerful, hospitable with what little he has, shiftless and slovenly, the typical shanty-boater leads a fairly carefree existence. His whims and moods are dictated by the vagaries of the river, which gives him sustenance and transportation. When left high and dry, he shores up his boat and waits for high water to put him afloat again—a few months of waiting mean nothing in his life of leisure. He is generally law-abiding, but his neighbors include a few elements who impart a bad reputation to all shanty-boaters by distilling and selling cheap whisky, and by hiding criminals until all trace of them is lost in the vague peregrinations and trackless wanderings of the boats. Yet his fellow boatmen include a number of Gospel preachers—elderly men, as a rule, who have grown weary of worldliness and dedicated themselves to the regeneration of the water gypsies. These preachers travel continuously, and their boats are welcome wherever shanty-boatmen congregate.

PARKERSBURG, 86 *m.* (615 alt., 29,623 pop.) (*see Parkersburg*).

Parkersburg is at the junction with US 50 (*see Tour 4c*) and US 21 (*see Tour 13*).

〽〽〽

Tour 20

New Martinsville—Clarksburg—Buckhannon—Webster Springs; 138.2 *m.*, State 20.

Alternating stretches of concrete, brick, macadam, and gravel.
Baltimore and Ohio R.R. parallels route between New Martinsville and Clarksburg.
Accommodations limited, except in Clarksburg.

State 20 runs southeastward across the sparsely settled divide separating the Ohio and the Monongahela valleys, and proceeds south through farm and pasture lands into country that grows increasingly rugged as the route near its junction with State 15 in Webster Springs, a hunting and fishing center.

Section a. NEW MARTINSVILLE to CLARKSBURG; 59.4 m. State 20.

This section of State 20 climbs from the Ohio River up the winding course of Fishing Creek, past oil and gas fields into a more populous coal-mining area along the Monongahela. A few villages with white frame houses have grown up around oil refineries and compressor stations. Few roads penetrated this isolated and heavily forested region until the advent of the railroad in 1902.

In NEW MARTINSVILLE, 0 m. (630 alt., 2,814 pop.) (see Tour 19b), are the junctions with State 2 (see Tour 19b) and State 7 (see Tour 21b), which runs jointly with State 20 for 3.2 miles.

PORTERS FALLS, 9.5 m. (672 alt., 29 pop.), on the edge of oil and gas fields, draws income also from trade with neighboring farms. On the outskirts of the hamlet is (R) one of many compressor stations in the valley. Here the waters of FISHING CREEK tumble over a low ledge to form the falls for which the settlement was named.

READER, 13.3 m. (693 alt., 65 pop.), surrounded by oil and gas fields, was named for Benjamin Reader, who traded a bay mare and a ten-gallon copper kettle for a claim staked out here in 1788 by James Troy. Reader in turn sold it for a flintlock gun to Morgan Morgan, grandson of the State's first settler (see Tour 11). Known as 'Spy Mod' for his exploits as an Indian scout, Morgan continued to live on his farm a few miles up the valley and sent Negro slaves to work the land here. That part of the hamlet in which the slave cabins stood is still known as the 'Negro quarters.'

HASTINGS, 18 m. (720 alt., 86 pop.), has an oil refinery, with a capacity of 40,000 gallons of gasoline a day, and a compressor station, in which natural gas is cooled, compressed, and pumped to Cleveland, Columbus, Youngstown, and other Ohio cities. The aluminum-painted buildings of the two plants extend for several miles along Fishing Creek, which here spreads out in a wide silvery pool behind a small dam (L).

SMITHFIELD, 30.3 m. (828 alt., 609 pop.), a trading center for neighboring oil, gas, and agricultural areas, was incorporated in 1904, three years after Henry Smith had opened a store here during a local oil boom.

FOLSOM, 33.5 m. (990 alt., 617 pop.), consists of a single street of frame houses occupied by oil and gas workers. The highway begins a long ascent along low ridges, with many pastures and grain fields on their slopes.

WALLACE, 38.8 m. (1,001 alt., 500 pop.), is the trading center of an agricultural district lying between the oil and gas fields to the west and the coal mines to the east.

State 20 descends along LITTLE TENMILE CREEK into gently rolling country, at times following the slopes of low rounded hills, then dipping into narrow valleys with small cornfields and unpainted farmhouses.

LUMBERPORT, 49.2 m. (992 alt., 1,289 pop.), born of the logging industry and suckled on oil and gas, now sustains itself on coal and farm products. In the Saturday crowds that gather in the few stores and throng the single business street, farmers in overalls, or 'Sunday best,' and miners, many of them wearing the 'hard hats' of their trade, now outnumber oil and gas workers and lumbermen. Up to 1,800 logs were floated down Tenmile Creek, cut and dressed in mills here, and then rafted down the Monongahela to Pittsburgh. With the development of the oil and gas fields of the vicinity, the town was incorporated in 1901.

At 50.7 m. is the junction with US 19 (see Tour 10a), with which State 20 unites for 8.7 miles (see Tour 10a).

CLARKSBURG, 59.4 m. (1,007 alt., 28,866 pop.) (see Clarksburg).
Clarksburg is at the junction with US 19 (see Tour 10a) and US 50 (see Tour 4b and c).

Section b. CLARKSBURG to WEBSTER SPRINGS, 78.8 m.
State 20.

This section of State 20 crosses a rolling countryside of farms and pastures into a rugged region of craggy mountains, cut by deep gorges.

Southeast of CLARKSBURG, 0 m., the highway curves over and around low hills, worn and smooth, cleared of trees to provide rich pasture.

NUTTER FORT, 2 m. (1,020 alt., 1,825 pop.), an industrial town producing pottery and glassware, was settled in 1770 by Thomas Nutter, a captain in the Revolutionary War, who two years later erected the fort for which the town was named.

QUIET DELL, 5.1 m. (1,025 alt., 220 pop.), a peaceful agricultural community that seldom belies its name, was the scene in 1930 of five 'bluebeard' murders by Harry Powers, who conducted a Clarksburg matrimonial bureau. He was convicted and hanged for the crimes.

The CHALET, 11 m., reached by a private driveway, was built in 1914 by Melville Davisson Post (1871–1930), author of mystery novels, many of which were written here. The house, typically Swiss in design, has foundations and a lower story of stone, with an upper story and projecting eaves of wood, intricately carved.

PEEL TREE, 14.6 m. (1,068 alt., 170 pop.), an unincorporated village named for a near-by creek of that name, was formerly known as Scoop Town because two men working on an old mill here drove home their points in a heated argument by pounding each other with scoop shovels.

HODGESVILLE, 20.2 *m.* (1,433 alt., 180 pop.), is a crossroads village in the midst of grazing country.

At 24.5 *m.* is the junction with a dirt road.

> Left on this road to the SITE OF THE PRINGLE TREE, 1 *m.*, marked by a granite shaft. In the hollow of this tree, said to have been so large that an eight-foot fence rail could have been rotated in it like the hands of a clock, John and Samuel Pringle took refuge in 1764 after they had deserted in 1761 from the garrison at Fort Pitt (Pittsburgh). After three years of trapping and hunting with John Simpson (*see Clarksburg*), the three quarreled and the Pringle brothers crossed the mountain westward and followed Turkey Run to its confluence here with the Buckhannon River, where they came upon the large hollow sycamore in which they lived for nearly four years. In 1767 John returned to the South Branch Valley with a load of furs, and finding that the French and Indian War was over, he made himself known to friends and persuaded several families to come with him and settle on the Buckhannon River. Samuel later married and established his home in the tree. In 1790 the original sycamore fell and a second grew from its roots. The present small tree is the third to grow on the site.

At 25.3 *m.* is the junction with an improved dirt road, known locally as the Post Road.

> Left on this road is an old BAPTIST CEMETERY, 0.6 *m.*, where in 1790 white settlers under the leadership of Jesse Hughes, border scout (*see Tour 10a*), ambushed a band of Indians and repulsed them with heavy losses. The settlers had been warned of the impending attack by Jacob Reger, Jr., who, according to some accounts, ran from the Ohio River, a distance of 125 miles, in 24 hours.
>
> In the HEAVNER CEMETERY, 1.3 *m.*, are the graves of Captain William White, John Fink, and Jacob Brake, pioneers and Revolutionary War soldiers. The graves of White and Fink, victims of the Indians in 1782, are marked by rudely lettered sandstone slabs set up in 1816 by an 11-year-old boy who had heard stories about these men. Also buried in the cemetery is Laura Jackson Arnold, a sister of Stonewall Jackson (*see Clarksburg*), and D. D. Farnsworth, governor of West Virginia for four days—February 27, 1869, to March 3, 1869.
>
> Across the road (R) from the cemetery a granite marker indicates the SITE OF BUSH'S FORT, built in 1773 by John Bush.

BUCKHANNON, 26.1 *m.* (1,433 alt., 4,374 pop.) (*see Tour 7b*), is at the junction with US 33 (*see Tour 7b*).

In TENNERTON, 27.9 *m.*, a suburb of Buckhannon, the Upshur County Singers Convention is held each August. Soloists, quartettes, and choirs from the scattered mountain communities of this section gather here in Jackson Grove to 'promote Social Fellowship among the people of Upshur County, and to create more interest in vocal music.' People from miles around begin to gather at nine in the morning, the hour at which the program opens with hymns and devotions. Some sit quietly on benches near the platform to hear the singing; others wander through the grove renewing old acquaintances; all later assemble around huge basket lunches spread under the trees. Above the singing, which 'must be sacred and in keeping with the day,' rises the sound of laughter and a thousand conversations.

South of Tennerton the road winds upward through mountainous country.

HINKLEVILLE, 31.5 *m.* (1,600 alt., 80 pop.), a scattering of frame houses on a ridge top, was settled in 1867 by Abraham Hinkle, who operated the first portable sawmill in this part of the State. The view (L) from the ridge extends over jagged crests of other ridges to a distant range of mountains.

ADRIAN, 33.4 *m.* (1,426 alt., 653 pop.), is a prosperous coal-mining town on Bull Run; two mines employ the majority of villagers.

In FRENCH CREEK, 35.4 *m.* (1,438 alt., 321 pop.), a small shop sells split-bottom chairs and peavey handles fashioned from timber cut in the near-by mountains. Settled about 1808 by Aaron Gould's party from Massachusetts, this vicinity received its name from a local legend that three Frenchmen came prospecting for gold here in 1725.

The STATE GAME FARM (*free*), 38 *m.*, is a 327-acre game refuge in which wild turkeys, quail, ring-necked pheasants, and deer are propagated; bears and other native animals are on exhibition.

ROCK CAVE, 40.1 *m.* (1,736 alt., 265 pop.), is a mountain village surrounded by forests. Seventy members of the Upshur County Militia, under Captain Daniel Gould, were drilling here unarmed in 1863 when surprised by a force of Confederates and captured without a shot; 7 escaped and 25 were paroled, but the majority perished in Confederate prison camps.

ARLINGTON, 42.1 *m.* (1,502 alt., 60 pop.), consists of a group of frame buildings in a grassy hollow on the banks of the Little Kanawha River, here a small mountain stream with steep slopes wooded with poplar and pine.

South of Arlington the highway ascends PRITT MOUNTAIN (1,800 alt.), 44.6 *m.*, where a parking space (R) overlooks a precipitous drop into the gorge-like valley of the Little Kanawha.

KANAWHA HEAD, 46.2 *m.* (1,705 alt., 40 pop.), is a scattered village of weather-beaten unpainted houses surrounded by meager cornfields in the valley between Pritt and Cleveland Mountains.

At 57.9 *m.* is the junction with an improved dirt road.

Left on this road, which descends into the green hollow of Hacker Valley, to a stone registration and information booth at the entrances to the HOLLY RIVER STATE PARK, 1.1 *m.*, approximately 6,000 acres of wild and rugged country set aside as a park in 1938. Secluded among the trees and the rhododendron and laurel thickets are picnic shelters, a swimming pool, and 10 log and stone cabins (*apply to State Conservation Commission, Charleston, for rentals*). Formerly the Kanawha Head Project, established by the Resettlement Administration of the Federal Government to demonstrate proper use of submarginal and non-productive land, the area has many roads and trails winding over the mountains and through the narrow valleys and ravines. Deer, bear, wildcats, and birds of many kinds find cover in the forest, which is second-growth for the most part.

HACKER VALLEY, 59.4 *m.* (1,501 alt., 150 pop.), lies at the foot of Cleveland Mountain where Laurel Fork joins the Left Fork of Holly River.

Crossing HODAM CREEK, 61.2 *m.*, State 20 begins a winding ascent of HODAM MOUNTAIN, passing over a high shoulder (2,537 alt.), 63 *m.*, with the rocky bulk of the mountain rising steeply (R) and falling away (L) in an almost sheer drop of 1,000 feet to Hodam Creek in its pinched valley below.

Between small farms, unpainted cabins, scrubby pasture lands, and wooded stretches, the highway winds up MILLER MOUNTAIN (2,333 alt.), 75.6 *m.* From its heights distant ranges form a blue background for the deep green valleys. At times the lower slopes of the ridges are hidden by swirls of fog, with only the higher peaks emerging from the mists like islands in a phantom sea.

WEBSTER SPRINGS, 78.8 *m.* (1,509 alt., 976 pop.) (*see Tour* 9), is at the junction with State 15 (*see Tour* 9).

Tour 21

(Oakland, Md.)—Terra Alta—Kingwood—Morgantown—New Martinsville; State 7.
Maryland Line to New Martinsville, 110.5 *m.*

Concrete roadbed, except for 20 miles of rough graveled highway west of Knob Fork.
Baltimore & Ohio R.R. roughly parallels route between Corinth and Terra Alta, Kingwood and Morgantown; Monongahela R.R., between Morgantown and Blacksville.
Accommodations of all types between Oakland and Morgantown; none between Morgantown and New Martinsville; filling stations scarce between Westover and New Martinsville.

From the Maryland Line, high on the Alleghenies' western slopes, State 7 courses north and west across the north central part of the State. Hill farms with grazing herds and high-altitude crops are left behind as the highway descends the blue foothills that roll away in waves toward sharp peaks farther south. Stumps and rotting timber, scrawny saplings on rock ledges, and rusted machinery supplant the beauty of the hills. Only 40 years ago a railroad was built through this region of 'the 800 square miles of virgin forest,' with enough timber to supply 'traffic for the railroad for 30 years.' The 30 years have come and gone, and the virgin forest is no more, leaving posterity a mute reminder of ruthless exploitation. West of the Monongahela River, State 7 traverses the Scotts Run coal field, and then forsakes the sound of drill and crusher for the soft murmur of lazy streams and the earthy smells of agriculture, following Fishing Creek Valley to its junction with the Ohio River.

Section a. *MARYLAND LINE to WESTOVER*, 40.1 *m.* State 7.

State 7 crosses the rolling plateau of the 'buckwheat belt' of Preston County, which annually produces almost 40 per cent of the State's buckwheat crop. Between Masontown and Morgantown the route follows the course of Deckers Creek, which tumbles noisily down its narrow rocky gorge. The iron mines of pioneer days have been abandoned; today coal tipples, glass sand mines, the ruddy glow of coke ovens, and the smoking stacks of factories indicate the region's diverse industrial activities.

A continuation of Md. 39, State 7 crosses the MARYLAND LINE, 0 *m.*, 6.4 miles west of Oakland, Maryland.

CORINTH, 0.4 *m.* (2,400 alt., 118 pop.), is a coal town served by the Baltimore & Ohio.

HOPEMONT SANITARIUM (R), 2.7 *m.*, a State hospital for tubercular patients, occupies three brick hospital buildings and nine many-windowed dormitories on the crest of a hill; the institution has a farm and a dairy, which supply much of its food.

TERRA ALTA (Lat., high ground), 5 *m.* (2,559 alt., 1,474 pop.), once known as Cranberry Summit because of the many cranberry bogs in the high marshlands of the region, adopted its present name in 1885. Off the highway (R) is the MUNICIPAL PARK.

> Right from Terra Alta on a dirt road to LAKE TERRA ALTA, 2 *m.*, an abandoned mill pond, a half-mile long and 150 feet wide, with summer camps and cottages along its shores. Summer camps are maintained here by the Staunton Military Academy of Staunton, Virginia, the Oglebay Park Institute of Wheeling, and the College of Engineering of West Virginia University.

SNAGGY MOUNTAIN FIRE TOWER, 7 *m.* (3,000 alt.), offers a far-reaching view of the mountain country.

The highway ascends BRIERY MOUNTAIN, 8.4 *m.* (2,735 alt.); rolling farm country stretches away to distant low ranges, a hazy blue background for green meadows and tawny fields of buckwheat.

On the eastern bank of the CHEAT RIVER, 11.7 *m.*, is (L) DUNKARDS HOLLOW, the site of the first white settlement in the vicinity. Fleeing from the community established in Pennsylvania by a sect of German Baptists known as the Dunkards or Dunkers, Dr. Thomas Eckarly and two brothers built a cabin here in the wilderness in 1753. Several years later Eckarly recrossed the mountains to obtain salt, ammunition, and clothing; on his return he was detained at Fort Pleasant on the South Branch of the Potomac as a spy and confederate of the Indians. He finally persuaded the officers in command to send an armed escort with him to verify his claim that he was a peaceful settler in the wilderness. The party arrived here to find the cabin in ashes and Eckarly's brothers killed and scalped. Cleared of the charges against him, Eckarly accompanied the military guard back to Fort Pleasant. CAMP DAWSON, a training camp of the National Guard, occupies many acres in the southern part of Dunkards Bottom.

KINGWOOD, 14.7 *m.* (1,862 alt., 1,709 pop.), seat of Preston County, is built around a spring, from which the streets of the town climb steeply in all directions. The COURTHOUSE (L) is of iron-bearing sandstone, which at a distance appears to be marble. The town was established in 1811, although a few settlers had built cabins here before the turn of the century, and was incorporated in 1853. Mining, lumbering, and agriculture are its chief support, although during the last decade tourist trade has been attracted by Kingwood's cool summer weather. The town was named for the grove of tall stately trees, called 'forest kings' or 'king woods,' which once stood in the center of town.

In REEDSVILLE, 22.1 *m.* (1,817 alt., 345 pop.), a farm trade center, is the PHILLIPS-JONES ELECTRIC VACUUM CLEANER PLANT (*open on application*), in which many people of Arthurdale (*see below*) are employed.

Left from Reedsville on State 92 is ARTHURDALE, 1.5 *m.* (1,797 alt., 650 pop.), one of three Federal resettlement projects in West Virginia, established in 1934 to rehabilitate selected families. The settlement offers each homesteader a house, a combination barn and poultry house, and three acres of land. The fireproof dwellings of concrete block have five, six, and seven rooms, and have been arranged in a semicircle around the meadows which slope from the hilltop crowned with the 20-room ARTHURDALE INN (*open all year*) of modified Colonial design. Handicraftsmen of the resettlement project have fashioned the furniture, draperies, and linens of the inn, which has become nationally known through the frequent visits of Mrs. Franklin D. Roosevelt.

Arthurdale occupies a 1,017-acre tract, formerly the plantation of Colonel John Fairfax, one of George Washington's close associates. The land was later sold to Richard Arthur, of Pittsburgh, whose name it now bears. The project consists of 165 individual houses, and a general farm, poultry farm, dairy, gristmill, general store, automobile service station, barber shop, and motion picture house. Homesteaders grow buckwheat, corn, and potatoes, while the products of the dairy and poultry farm successfully compete in the open market with those of neighboring farms. Craftsmen manufacture period furniture in a woodworking shop and iron wrought articles at the community forge, products which find a ready market. The project's affairs are managed by the non-profit Arthurdale Association on a co-operative basis. Other homesteaders are employed in a shirt factory and in the vacuum cleaner factory at Reedsville, while a tractor factory under construction is expected to solve whatever employment problems may arise.

MASON TOWN, 25.1 *m.* (1,752 alt., 924 pop.), is an industrial and coal-mining center built along a main street lined with plain two-story business houses of concrete block.

Left from Mason Town on an improved dirt road to CORNWELL CAVE (*adm. free, parking* 50¢), 6 *m.*, an extensive series of partially explored limestone caverns in which are numerous strange labyrinths, stalagmites, and stalactites. The cave is unlighted (*guides available at Mason Town or near-by farmhouses*).

West of Mason Town the highway follows the course of Deckers Creek, which dashes tumultuously down a narrow boulder-strewn ravine, along which are several small settlements clustered about coal tipples, limestone quarries, and rows of beehive coke ovens.

Reaching CASCADE, 27.5 *m.* (1,650 alt., 120 pop.), a once thriving mining town, the highway ascends a series of gentle grades, passing

(R) hill meadows dotted with tortured masses of gray rock, scattered far and wide, as if a mad Gargantua had turned sculptor and then destroyed his work in a sudden frenzy. Far across the valley (L), 29.5 *m.*, are the buildings of a glass sand mine, with tipples, chutes, and conveyors mounted above high piles of sand, tan spots on a carpet of green.

GREER, 28.7 *m.* (950 alt., 28 pop.), a daub of color on the landscape, is the child of the Greer Limestone Company; a red tipple spans State 7 to empty limestone slabs into the crushers, which reduce the rock to fine powder or nugget-size ballast. Little green and white houses nestle close to tremendous piles of crushed limestone, gray heaps that loom imperiously over steam-shovels and cranes working in the loading yards.

ROCK FORGE, 35.4 *m.* (884 alt.), the ghost of a twice-born town, has a double row of deserted houses that sag on their foundations beside weed-grown mine dumps and crumbling coke ovens. Iron fathered the town in 1796 when a furnace and forge were erected here. The settlement prospered until the development of the Lake Superior ore deposits checked iron-mining operations in West Virginia. By 1848 little trace of Rock Forge remained. Coal revived the dead town in 1905 when a large mine was opened, and the village thrived until the depression following the first World War forced the mine to close. Rock Forge may enjoy a third life if geologists are correct in predicting that the iron in the West Virginia hills will be mined again when the Lake Superior fields are depleted.

SABRATON, 37.5 *m.* (867 alt., 1,717 pop.), on the site of the settlement founded by Thomas Decker in 1758, was destroyed by a party of Mingo the following year. The sole survivor of Decker's settlement spread the news of the Indian invasion, so the story goes, and a force of 30 men was sent from Fort Pitt to intercept the raiders. Headed by a Captain Gibson, the frontiersmen missed the raiding party, but intercepted and fought a small Indian band under the Mingo chief Kiskepila, or Little Eagle. Gibson decapitated Little Eagle with one mighty stroke of his sword, and the fleeing Mingo arrived home to speak in awe of the 'Long Knife' with which Little Eagle was slain. The Indians later hesitated to go on the warpath, explaining that they 'feared no Redcoats, but could not cope with the Ashalecoa, or Great Knife,' a name they applied to the Virginians generally. Sheet steel, tin plate, and varied glass products are manufactured in this predominantly industrial town.

MORGANTOWN, 39 *m.* (892 alt., 16,186 pop.) (*see Morgantown*).

Right from Morgantown on US 119 is EASTON, 3.5 *m.* (1,000 alt., 76 pop.), a rural crossroads community, the site of Fort Pierpont, built in 1769 by John Pierpont, Revolutionary soldier and son-in-law of Zackquill Morgan, for whom Morgantown was named. Easton was the birthplace of Francis H. Pierpont, governor of the Restored Government of Virginia 1861–7 (*see History*).

Right from Easton on State 73 is CHEAT LAKE, 3.7 *m.*, formed by the Cheat River Dam, the largest artificial body of water in the State, which State

73 crosses on a slender steel bridge to the eastern shore, lined with cabins and summer cottages nestling beneath the wooded cliffs of Cheat River Gorge, which tower more than 1,000 feet above the silvery lake waters. At the eastern end of the bridge are two millstones, one standing edge-wise on the other and bearing a plaque marking the birthplace of David Adam Ice, 'the first white child born in West Virginia,' a claim questioned by historians. The lake now covers the SITE OF ICE'S FERRY, where Washington crossed the Cheat River on his exploration of 1784. Until 1848 the village flourished as one of the country's important iron centers, having three furnaces, a foundry, a machine shop, and a nail factory.

State 73 swings sharply east, 4.3 m., to lay a black asphalt ribbon through ravaged timberlands, with acres of rotting stumps, mute evidence of nineteenth-century 'empire building.' At 5.2 m. lies (R) an expanse of gray boulders and limestone outcroppings in fields stripped of timber, bearing a resemblance to the monoliths of Stonehenge in England. State 73 crosses the western boundary of COOPERS ROCK STATE FOREST, 5.5 m., a 12,915-acre tract developed as a recreational center and game refuge and for reforestation about a ridge of rock overlooking the wild Cheat River Gorge. The section was named for a cooper, a fugitive from justice, who hid here, according to local legend, and whiled away his time making oak barrel staves. When at last he acquired a boat, he loaded it with staves and escaped down the river.

The HENRY CLAY FURNACE (L), 5.8 m., a crumbling pile of handcut stone blocks cemented with clay and lined with a core of stones fitted together without adhesive materials to resist the heat of the fires, once smelted crude iron for the use of village forges, foundries, and arsenals. From a square base the furnace rises 20 feet to a circular apex, now crowned with shrubs. Built by Leonard Lamb in 1834, the furnace was one of four operated along the river by the Cheat River Iron Works between 1792 and 1868; at one time they employed 1,200 ironworkers. The Henry Clay, the only furnace still standing, produced iron up to 1847; its output was shipped by flatboat to Pittsburgh. The furnace smelted 4 tons of iron every 24 hours; it was driven by steam generated by burning charcoal; the charcoal was made by igniting piles of logs covered with earth and allowing them to smolder to a point just below combustion.

The paved road ends at 6.3 m., giving way to a dirt road virtually impassable in winter and extremely slippery in wet weather.

WESTOVER, 40.1 m. (950 alt., 1,633 pop.), a residential satellite of Morgantown on the west bank of the Monongahela, is a community of middle class homes built along streets that climb directly up the hillside.

Westover is at the junction with US 19 (see Tour 10a).

Section b. WESTOVER to NEW MARTINSVILLE, 70.4 m. State 7.

State 7 passes through the Scotts Run coal field and follows the course of Dunkard Creek through an isolated agricultural section with long stretches of slanting pasture lands and grain fields, dotted with occasional oil wells. A historical marker or unpretentious monument here and there indicates the path followed by early settlers in fighting their way westward into the wilderness against hostile bands of Indians.

Northwest of WESTOVER, 0 m., State 7 and US 19 (see Tour 10a) are united as far as RANDALL, 2.4 m. (920 alt., 165 pop.); the route closely parallels the smooth green waters of the Monongahela River.

West of Randall the highway is lined for several miles with railroad tracks, coal tipples, and grimy buildings. The many small mining camps in the Scotts Run field are crowded so closely together and are so uniform in character that they can be distinguished only by the signs indicating the boundaries between them. Typical are LIBERTY, 5.2 *m.* (850 alt., 200 pop.), where coal dust has transformed the creek into a writhing black serpent, and JERE, 6.1 *m.* (900 alt., 250 pop.), remarkable for frame dwellings painted a mustard color rather than the gray or white, with green trim, characteristic of most mining towns.

Paralleling the highway and Scotts Run are the tracks of the Monongahela Railroad, the construction of which opened this coal field in 1890. Johnson N. Camden (*see Tour* 9) and associates built the road after a survey had convinced them that the upper Monongahela valley was rich in high quality coal suitable for the Great Lakes trade. The railroad survived the panic of 1893, and Camden sold it to the Baltimore & Ohio in 1899, which took a lease on the coal holdings of Camden and his associates. Oil derricks replace mine tipples for a short distance, and then State 7 enters the rich farming and grazing country of the Little Fishing Creek valley.

CORE, 9.7 *m.* (952 alt., 112 pop.), a small oil center with a compressor station (L), was named for Michael Core, who settled here in 1770. From a well (L) drilled during the oil boom of 1865 flows a copious supply of mineral water (*free*). Although early drillers missed their mark in this first well, they were soon rewarded when oil was struck near by.

This region was the scene of much bloodshed between 1760 and 1790 when the Indians fought a bitter rearguard action as the whites forced them westward. On DOLLS RUN, 10.6 *m.*, a roving band of Indians in 1778 ambushed a group of settlers on their way back from their fields to Statlers Fort (*see below*) and killed 18 of them. A MONUMENT TO ELIZABETH BOZARTH, 13.1 *m.*, commemorates the bravery of a woman, widowed by the ambush, who withstood an attack on her cabin the following year. Wielding an ax, she killed three of the attackers and drove off the others, who in their retreat killed the Bozarth children, who had been unable to reach home. In PRINCE MEMORIAL CEMETERY (R), 13.4 *m.*, is a tablet erected to the memory of the 18 men killed in the Dolls Run ambush. Their bodies are believed to have been interred here, although all trace of the graves has long since been lost.

Left from the cemetery on a dirt road to (R) the SITE OF STATLERS FORT, 3 *m.*, within a sharp bend on Dunkard Creek. Erected in 1770, it served as a haven of safety for settlers of this section until the end of the Indian disturbances in 1794. The stockade stood until 1850, and for many years was used as a church and a schoolhouse. In the 'bloody year of the three 7's' (1777), Captain John Minor, a commander of the fort, wrote to Zackquill Morgan at Morgantown:

'This minute Alexander Clegg came in great haste, who escaped the shot of a number of Indians. While we were getting ready to go after them, John March and Jacob Jones came, and say they think they saw at least twenty, and followed them, but they escaped. The Indians fired at Jacob Farmer's house. Two men and a boy were killed. A young woman and two children missing. It is supposed that she is killed, and Nathan Wirley [Worley] and two of Jacob Jones' children, and a daughter of Farmer's.'

PENTRESS, 15.2 *m.* (938 alt., 35 pop.), had its beginning in 1766 when Bruce Worley built a cabin here on Dunkard Creek.

BLACKSVILLE, 18.9 *m.* (956 alt., 269 pop.), was also settled by the Worleys, Bruce and Nathan. Baldwin's blockhouse stood here from 1770 to 1776. Platted in 1829, the hamlet was named for David Black, who sold lots by lottery.

In WADESTOWN, 27.6 *m.* (1,015 alt., 96 pop.), is (L) a Covered Bridge across the West Virginia Fork of Dunkard Creek.

At 33.7 *m.* is the junction with US 250 (*see Tour 22c*), which unites with State 7 for 2.1 miles.

West of the junction State 7 is known as the Lewis Wetzel Trail, for the Indian fighter of that name (*see Wheeling*), whose father, John Wetzel, owned farmlands along Fishing Creek Valley. The smooth concrete gives way to a rutted graveled roadway, 43.2 *m.*, which shows little evidence of improvement since Wetzel's moccasins trod Fishing Creek valley in advance of pioneers' wagons.

KNOB FORK, 42.4 *m.* (787 alt., 92 pop.), and WILEYVILLE, 52.7 *m.* (801 alt., 160 pop.), are quiet crossroads communities. West of Wileyville State 7 plays hide-and-seek with the crests of a half dozen summits of worn hills, where the earth wrinkles in whorls like the skin on the face of an ancient mountain woman; the highway then descends to Fishing Creek Valley to dodge oil wells and creep past drowsing farmlands. Houses on slopes across the creek are connected with the road by wire-and-slat swinging footbridges or fallen trees. Natives in this quiet section contentedly fish in the creek, dogs sun themselves in the middle of the road, and the tourist finds pleasure in the total absence of billboards and filling-station architecture; barns and outbuildings are not painted to proclaim the merits of several brands of chewing tobacco.

At 65.3 *m.* State 7 unites with State 20 (*see Tour 20a*), 3.1 miles southeast of NEW MARTINSVILLE (630 alt., 2,814 pop.) (*see Tour 19b*).

Tour 22

(Monterey, Va.) — Huttonsville — Elkins — Grafton — Fairmont — Moundsville—Wheeling; US 250.
Virginia Line to Wheeling, 176.6 m.

Concrete roadbed with long stretches of bituminous-macadam surface.
Route paralleled by Western Maryland Ry. between Huttonsville and Belington;
by Baltimore & Ohio R.R. between Belington and Wheeling.
Tourist accommodations at frequent intervals; hotels in larger towns.

From the Blue Ridge Mountains along West Virginia's eastern border, US 250 drops to the valley of the Tygarts River and follows its course northward into rolling farm and mining country. Climbing through the hills, past oil and gas fields, it plunges into the Ohio Valley lined with tumultuous industrial towns in the heart of a great coal, iron, and steel region.

Section a. VIRGINIA LINE to HUTTONSVILLE, 32.4 m. US 250.

This section of the route trails through the Monongahela National Forest. West of the forest, the highway dips to the fertile fields of Tygarts River valley, which it follows along the approximate course of the old Seneca Trail. Skirting the now silent Roaring Creek coal fields, it winds through a hilly region of upland farms and descends to the Monongahela River at Fairmont.

US 250 crosses the VIRGINIA LINE, 0 m., and climbs the rugged and densely forested slope of ALLEGHENY MOUNTAIN (4,271 alt.); the broad ribbon of highway winds down the slopes into the Greenbrier Valley.

At 7.7 m. is a junction (R) with State 28 (see Tour 6), which unites with US 250 for 2.2 miles; the white buildings of the forest village of Thornwood (see Tour 6b) glimmer (R) through the trees.

At 9.9 m. are the junctions (R) with State 28 (see Tour 6), and (L) a section of the old Staunton-Parkersburg Turnpike.

Left on the paved turnpike to TRAVELER'S REPOSE (lodging and meals), 0.1 m., once a popular stagecoach stop. On the hills south of the inn are the grass-grown trenches of a Confederate camp of 1861. Low unmarked mounds on lands now used for pasture are the last resting places of hastily buried soldier dead. This is the 'Tol'able David' country pictured in the novels of Joseph Hergesheimer and the weird tales of Ambrose Bierce.

BARTOW, 10.2 m. (2,872 alt., 29 pop.), a village of white frame houses in a broad, green, mountain-girded valley, was named for General F. S. Bartow, a Confederate officer who was killed at the first Battle of Bull Run. A minor skirmish was fought here in December 1861.

Between Bartow and Huttonsville, US 250 follows the approximate route of the old Staunton-Parkersburg Turnpike. In 1855-8 the contract for carrying the mails along the route was held by the Trotter Brothers of Staunton. During the hard winter of 1856 the service became irregular and one postmaster complained to Washington several times about the matter. A post office official sent a sharp letter to the Trotter Brothers, reminding them of their duties, to which he received the following reply:

> Mr. Postmaster General,
> Washington, D. C.
>
> Sirs:
> If you knock the gable end of Hell out and back it up against Cheat Mountain and rain fire and brimstone for 40 days and 40 nights, it won't melt the snow enough to get your damned mail through on time.
>
> Trotter Bros.
> By JAMES TROTTER

FRANK, 11.7 *m.* (2,740 alt., 300 pop.), draws its livelihood from the POCAHONTAS TANNING COMPANY PLANT (*open*), one of the largest in the United States, established here because of its proximity to large supplies of oak and hemlock bark used in the tanning process. The plant produces leather, glue, and greases, as well as floor coverings, insulation felts, and padding made of cattle hair.

In DURBIN, 12.8 *m.* (2,730 alt., 498 pop.), a lumber town and district shipping center, is the U. S. FOREST RANGER STATION of the Greenbrier District (*inquire for information on fishing, hunting, and camping in Monongahela National Forest*).

The highway crosses the GREENBRIER RIVER, 13.4 *m.*, and begins a twisting ascent of SHAVERS MOUNTAIN. A break in the screen of close-growing trees, 14 *m.*, opens a view to the head of Greenbrier Valley. Plunging again into the woods, the road climbs between walls of dark pine, spruce, and hemlock, splashed with lighter foliage of oak. For miles no habitation breaks the isolation of the forest, which opens here and there in gladelike bluegrass pastures.

US 250 crosses Shavers Fork of the CHEAT RIVER, 19.8 *m.*, a stream running swiftly northward to join the Monongahela. A scant 4 miles away and 1,000 feet below, the Greenbrier flows southward, following a tortuous route, and mingling with the New and Kanawha Rivers before joining the Ohio at Point Pleasant (*see Tour 14*). Thickets of spruce, hemlock, and laurel grow to the water's edge. The highway follows a wide bend in the Cheat River and skirts (L) the foot of WHITE TOP MOUNTAIN (4,006 alt.), on the summit of which, reached by a steep foot trail, is the SITE OF FORT MILROY, used by Union troops during the War between the States. Climbing CHEAT MOUNTAIN (3,802 alt.), 23.8 *m.*, the highway descends along Riffle Creek through a widening valley of cleared fields. In the rock face of a deep highway cut, 29.4 *m.*, appear fossil trees estimated by geologists to be between three and five hundred million years old, being of the same geologic age as those in David Reger Fossil Park (*see below*).

HUTTONSVILLE, 32.4 *m.* (2,030 alt., 303 pop.) (*see Tour 8a*), is at the junction with US 219, which unites with US 250 as far as ELKINS, 49.9 *m.* (1,930 alt., 7,343 pop.) (*see Tour 8a*).

Elkins is at the junction with US 33 (*see Tour 7a and b*) and US 219 (*see Tour 8a and b*).

Section b. ELKINS to FAIRMONT, 65.6 m. US 250.

West of ELKINS, 0 *m.*, US 250 is united with US 33 for 7.6 miles. On the outskirts of the city the highway passes (L) BLUEGRASS PARK, 1.2 *m.*, where annual horse shows are held during the Mountain State Forest Festival.

The DAVID REGER FOSSIL PARK, 3.2 *m.*, consists of a narrow strip (R) at the base of a cliff, in the steeply canted rock strata of which appear the fossilized remains of trees that flourished here three to five hundred million years ago and were later buried under the silt of an inland sea. Although less distinct elsewhere, outcroppings of the formation occur over an area of 50 square miles.

On the outskirts of NORTON, 7.6 *m.* (1,885 alt., 1,037 pop.) (*see Tour 7b*), is the junction (L) with US 33 (*see Tour 7b*).

HARDING, 7.9 *m.* (1,860 alt., 136 pop.), was the scene of great activity in the 1870's, when thick seams of lower Kittanning coal were discovered along Roaring Creek. A huge block of coal from this seam was exhibited at the Centennial Exposition at Philadelphia in 1876 and attracted the attention of U. S. Senator Henry Gassaway Davis, through whose influence the Coal and Coke Railroad was built into this section (*see Tour 8a*). When the superior Sewell seam along New River in southern West Virginia was discovered, activity in the Roaring Creek district subsided. Many of the dingy green cottages of the miners stand vacant.

BELINGTON, 15.3 *m.* (1,896 alt., 1,571 pop.), is a trading town for farmers and miners and a shipping point for mine timbers cut in adjacent woodland. Near the center of town, at the corner of Crim Avenue and Watson Streets, is a marker commemorating the Battle of Laurel Hill, fought in the vicinity during the War between the States.

On the southern edge of town, skirting the Tygarts Valley River, is a five-acre MUNICIPAL PARK, equipped with picnicking facilities and tennis courts (*no charge*). The spot is popular in summer as a place for family reunions.

1. Right from Belington on Watson Street to a junction with a dirt road, 2.1 *m.;* R. on this road to LAUREL HILL, 5 *m.*, crowned with a fire tower offering a magnificent view of the rolling countryside. In an apple orchard on the hillside are the remains of Confederate breastworks, thrown up in an attempt to block General George B. McClellan's relentless advance into Virginia. On July 10, 1861, McClellan moved forward quickly, leaving an artillery unit to bombard Laurel Hill as he hurried his main force southward

against Colonel John Pegram's smaller force on Rich Mountain (*see Tour 8a*). The ruse deceived General Robert S. Garnett, in command at Laurel Hill, who did not discover until too late that he had been outflanked. He retreated to the east and north, and when the weary survivors of the Confederate rout at Rich Mountain fell back to Laurel Hill, they found the fortified camp abandoned. Cut off from supplies, faced with the prospect of hunger and a dangerous retreat through hostile territory, 555 soldiers and officers of Colonel Pegram's command surrendered to McClellan when he offered them wagon-loads of bread.

2. Right from Belington on State 92 to MEADOWVILLE, 8 *m.* (1,569 alt., 125 pop.), a quiet country village widely known for its blackberry jam. Founded by New Jersey colonists on the site of a fort built in 1784, the town, with its taverns, stores, and near-by mills, was the bustling trade center of the valley for more than 100 years.

Northwest of Belington the highway runs through broken ridge country with a blue mountain range in the background R. setting off its green fields.

PHILIPPI, 27.7 *m.* (1,311 alt., 1,767 pop.), in the level valley of the Tygarts River, is the seat of Barbour County; the town is strung out along the one main street. The town was first settled in 1780 by Richard Cottrill and Charity Talbott. Originally called Anglin's Ford, the name was later changed to Booths Ferry and finally renamed Philippi for Philip Pendleton Barbour, for whom the county also was named. Here was the scene of an important early battle in the War between the States, known as the 'Philippi Races,' because of the speed with which Confederate forces under Colonel George A. Porterfield retreated when routed at dawn by Federal troops under Colonel B. F. Kelley. The attack was launched by the Federals to protect and retain control of the Baltimore & Ohio Railroad, the main line of communication between Washington and the West. The battle is described on a marker at the entrance to Alderson-Broaddus College (*see below*) as the 'First land battle between the North and South.'

In Philippi a two-way COVERED BRIDGE spans the Tygarts River. Built in 1852 by Chenoweth (*see Tour 8b*), the bridge was widened and reinforced in 1937 by the State road commission.

ALDERSON-BROADDUS COLLEGE, on the crest of Broaddus Hill overlooking the town, is a coeducational Baptist institution established in 1931 when Alderson Junior College was removed here from Alderson and merged with Broaddus College; the latter institution was founded in 1871 by the Reverend E. J. Willis at Winchester, Virginia; it was removed to Clarksburg in 1876 and to Philippi in 1909. In addition to the usual curriculum leading to a bachelor of arts degree, the college offers theological training. The moral code of the Baptist Church is strictly enforced among the students.

The three-story brick MAIN BUILDING, with a portico supported by columns with Corinthian capitals, contains classrooms, offices, and dormitory rooms. The boys' dormitory, WHITESCARVER HALL, is a three-story building of brick.

US 250 crosses and recrosses a section of Baltimore & Ohio tracks built in 1936 when its old right-of-way was flooded by waters backed up by the Tygarts Reservoir Dam (*see below*).

GRAFTON, 44.4 *m.* (996 alt., 7,737 pop.), seat of Taylor County and commercial center for the surrounding grazing country and scattered mining camps, spreads over the steep slopes of high hills that rise abruptly from a rugged cup-shaped valley along the Tygarts River. The shops and yards of the Baltimore & Ohio provide the chief industrial activity of the town, which is the terminus of four divisions of the railroad.

William Robinson pre-empted 400 acres of Buffalo Flats here at the mouth of Three Forks Creek in 1773. The land was never cultivated, however, and when Irish construction crews on the Baltimore & Ohio pitched their tents here in 1852, the entire countryside was a tangle of grapevines and wild berry briars. With the completion of the railroad a village sprang up, incorporated in 1856. It received its name, so it is said, because construction crews referred to it as the 'graftin' on' point, for here many branch lines were joined to the main line. Because of its railroad facilities, Grafton had strategic importance during the War between the States, being occupied at various times by Union and Confederate troops. In June 1861, General Thomas A. Morris with 4,000 Federal troops camped here before marching southward to the battle of Philippi (*see above*); later in the same year General McClellan established headquarters in the town, but no fighting occurred.

As the railroad extended branch lines into surrounding coal and timber regions, Grafton became the mercantile and transportation center for near-by coal and lumber towns. In 1870 a sawmill began cutting lumber on a large scale from logs floated down the Tygarts River.

In 1872 Grafton aspired to become the State's capital. Delegates from near-by counties, presided over by Joseph Johnson (*see Tour 4b*), convened here and drafted resolutions instructing their delegates to the Constitutional Convention at Charleston (*see History*) to seek the removal of the capital from Charleston. Although it failed in this, it succeeded in becoming the county seat in 1878.

Right from Grafton on Park Road to the $15,000,000 TYGARTS RESERVOIR DAM, 3.2 *m.*, designed to regulate the waters of the Tygarts and Monongahela Rivers, prevent floods, and provide navigation on the Monongahela during dry seasons. Two 15-foot openings on the west bank provide for the future diversion of the flow for generation of power. One of the openings is now used by the Baltimore & Ohio as a passageway through the dam. Grafton's water supply is provided by the 3,860-acre storage lake. The dam, completed late in 1937 after three years of work, is 1,900 feet long, with a spillway 209 feet high, and at the time of completion was the highest dam east of the Mississippi River. A 30-foot auxiliary dam impounds part of the flow from the spillway and forms a cushion basin to prevent the undermining of the large dam.

On a high knoll above the east bank of the river is a parking area with the commissary and residences of caretakers. From this point is a fine view of the dam and surrounding hills and valley.

On the outskirts of Grafton is the junction with US 50 (*see Tour 4b*), which unites with US 250 for 5.5 miles (*see Tour 4b*).

The highway begins a curving ascent of CURRY RIDGE (1,555 alt.), on both sides of which stretch the broad worn tops of rolling hills, checkered with fields, divided by heavily wooded ravines. Descending into Tygarts Valley, the road passes (R) the FAIRMONT GUN CLUB, 63.7 *m*.

FAIRMONT, 65.6 *m*. (883 alt., 23,159 pop.) (*see Fairmont*).
Fairmont is at the junction with US 19 (*see Tour 10a*).

Section c. FAIRMONT to WHEELING, 78.6 m. US 250.

West of FAIRMONT, 0 *m*., US 250 follows a winding course through the narrow valleys of an oil and gas region, rises to follow a skyline route along a series of ridges through peaceful farming country, and then descends into the smoke and grime of a congested industrial section along the Ohio River.

At 1.7 *m*. is the junction with a paved road.

Right on this road is BARRACKVILLE, 1.3 *m*. (980 alt., 260 pop.), founded in 1785–6 by the four sons of Frederick Ice, of Ice's Ferry (*see Tour 21a*). One of the sons, Adam, is buried in the cemetery on the hill, with his wife and son David.

Near the center of town, on the banks of Buffalo Creek opposite the railroad station, stands the old ICE GRIST MILL, erected in 1797 by Adam Ice and still used as a storage house by one of his descendants. The white oak frame and the 12-inch poplar planks of its original vertical siding, now covered with weatherboard, were joined with wooden pegs. The old water wheel has rotted away, but several millstones lie near by.

Downstream from the mill is a COVERED BRIDGE built by Chenoweth (*see Tour 8b*) in 1852. During the War between the States retreating soldiers threatened to burn the structure, but one of the Ice family dissuaded them by pointing out that pursuers could cross the creek on a near-by dam, and destruction of the bridge would serve no purpose.

Along Buffalo Creek, hemmed in by rugged ridges, small groups of miners' cottages are scattered along the highway, but no mines are visible.

FARMINGTON, 7.1 *m*. (936 alt., 819 pop.), trading center for an agricultural, mining, and oil district, was laid out by William Willey early in the nineteenth century and named Willeytown. His son, Waitman T. Willey, a leader in the movement to make West Virginia a state, was born in a log cabin here in 1811. The WILLEY HOUSE, a stone structure built in 1833 by the elder Willey, stands on Chatham Hill.

In the thinly settled valleys west of Farmington, oil derricks rise in groups of twos and threes; aluminum-painted compressing and pumping stations, surrounded by complicated networks of pipes and tanks, appear at short intervals along the road. In the intervening spaces corn patches and vegetable gardens occupy every moderately level piece of ground.

MANNINGTON, 14.5 *m*. (975 alt., 3,261 pop.), lying in a triangle of bottom land at the confluence of Pyles Fork and Buffalo Creek, is the center of oil and gas operations in the vicinity. In addition to gasoline plants and compressing stations, the city has a pottery, a glass factory, and a plant manufacturing tools. Much of its income, however, is derived from trade with surrounding farms. The Mannington District Fair is held here annually in September.

METZ, 19.6 *m.* (1,002 alt., 165 pop.), and GLOVER GAP, 22 *m.* (1,039 alt., 200 pop.), are clusters of white frame buildings in the cleft-like valley of Pyles Fork, each with a tiny red railroad station.

At 25.8 *m.* is a junction with State 7 (*see Tour 21b*), which unites with US 250 for 2.1 miles.

BURTON, 26.5 *m.* (1,016 alt., 275 pop.), is a crossroads oil town, with buildings and derricks scattered along an opening in the valley.

HUNDRED, 28.6 *m.* (1,019 alt., 788 pop.), a prosperous oil and gas town, was named for an early settler, Henry Church, better known as 'Old Hundred.' While serving under Cornwallis during the Revolution, Church was captured by American troops led by Lafayette. Church died here in 1860 at the age of 109; his wife lived to be 106 years old. When his second daughter died at the age of 63, 'Old Hundred' is said to have consoled himself with the remark, 'She allus was a puny child, and we know'd we'd never raise her.'

LITTLETON, 34.6 *m.* (939 alt., 648 pop.), another oil town, has streets cramped and twisted by converging hills and railroad tracks (*dangerous diagonal crossing in center of town*).

West of LITTLETON US 250 follows a skyline route along a series of ridges; for miles in all directions farms appear on rounded hilltops, checkered in midsummer with tawny squares of ripening grain and greener squares of pasture.

BELLTON, 39.8 *m.* (888 alt., 319 pop.), listed as Denver in railroad timetables, is the center of an agricultural area in the midst of oil and gas fields.

The highway crosses the North Fork of Fish Creek and leaves derricks and compressor stations behind as it ascends from Bellton into farming country. The highway winds up and over CULLEY HILL, 44.4 *m.*, and descends in a series of looping curves.

CAMERON, 47.2 *m.* (1,170 alt., 2,281 pop.), a prosperous farm town at the headwaters of Grave Creek, has streets that climb the steep hillsides in stairlike fashion; houses on the slanting lots are supported on one side by stilts. The Himes brothers, Joseph, Christopher, and John, erected a blockhouse here in 1788, but soon discovered that the good-natured surrender of a hog or a timely donation of a side of bacon provided better insurance against Indian attacks than a fort. The town grew steadily after the coming of the railroad in 1852; destroyed by fire in 1895, it was rebuilt in more substantial form the following year.

The BEELER STATION CHRISTIAN CHURCH, 54 *m.*, stands (L) near the site of Beeler Station, a fort erected about 1779. Indians attacked the stockade in 1782, but were repulsed by its defenders, among whom were Lewis Wetzel and his brother Martin (*see Wheeling*), renowned Indian fighters and scouts.

LIMESTONE, 59.6 m. (1,377 alt., 30 pop.), a scattered rural community, was settled late in the seventeenth century on land granted to John Zane in 1782 by Governor Patrick Henry of Virginia.

MOUNDSVILLE, 65.7 m. (689 alt., 14,411 pop.), seat of Marshall County, stretches along the Ohio River at the mouth of Little Grave Creek; it was named for the Grave Creek Mound (see below) that stands in the heart of the city. Scattered along the river are several plants manufacturing glass, zinc, and enamel products. The city is also a coal center but has maintained a more leisurely air than other industrial communities of its size.

Joseph, Samuel, and James Tomlinson came from 'east of the mountains' in 1771, took up land on the flats along Grave Creek, and built a cabin about 300 yards from the mound. The following spring more of the family arrived at the settlement then known as Grave Creek. In 1798, Joseph Tomlinson, Jr., divided the tract into lots and renamed the settlement Elizabethtown in honor of his wife. A rival community was established on the banks of the Ohio by Simon Purdy in 1831, who named his settlement Mound City. The two towns were consolidated and incorporated as Moundsville in 1865.

The GRAVE CREEK MOUND (open daily until 9 p.m.), 9th St. between Jefferson and Tomlinson Aves., is 79 feet high, 900 feet in circumference at the base, and 50 feet across the top, one of the largest Indian burial mounds in America. Acquired by the State in 1907, the mound has been landscaped by prison labor. Before the installation of electric lights in 1938, this ancient burial ground had long been a favorite rendezvous of lovers.

The STATE PENITENTIARY (10 a.m.–2 p.m. workdays; 25¢ adm.), 10th St. and Jefferson Ave., occupies two five-acre tracts enclosed within 30-foot walls. Its construction was begun in 1866 with convict labor. The four-story administration building, flanked by the two-story north and south cell blocks, is of modified Gothic design and serves as the west wall of the double enclosure. The building has three arched entrances, and high above the central entrance is a reproduction of the great seal of West Virginia, with its motto, somewhat ironic here: Montani Semper Liberi (mountaineers are ever freemen). Close by are the buildings in which the prisoners manufacture their own clothing. Prison labor was formerly hired out to private contractors who maintained shops here for the manufacture of clothing, brooms, and whips, but the practice was stopped in 1937.

Prisoners write and print Work and Hope, a monthly magazine, copies of which are on sale in the prison. A recreation program includes boxing and wrestling matches and an annual minstrel show (public) usually presented late in November.

The penitentiary was designed to accommodate 800 prisoners but has housed three times that number. To relieve overcrowding, the legislature appropriated $250,000 in 1937 for a 200-acre prison farm at Huttonsville, designed to handle prisoners with good records. A coal mine on the farm supplies the institution's entire fuel needs.

The MUNICIPAL PLAYGROUND, Tomlinson Ave. between 3rd and 5th Sts., constructed in 1922 with funds raised by Dr. B. M. Spurr and other citizens on what was then a quagmire, has three swimming pools (*20¢ for large pool; 10¢ for medium-sized pool; small pool free*), tennis courts, swings, slides, roller-skating rink, merry-go-round, and a recreation room, in which children play quoits, pingpong, and shuffleboard on rainy days. On Friday nights in summer a 'community sing' is held in the large amphitheater, seating more than 6,000. Many families from the surrounding countryside attend, arriving before sundown with their picnic suppers. The children march around the amphitheater to open the program, which consists of the 'sing,' a band concert, and two hours of motion pictures.

The CAMP MEETING GROUNDS, left from 1st St. on Fostoria Ave., swarm with thousands of visitors at the annual camp meeting each August; exhorters, circuit riders, and evangelists have preached here since 1787. On the grounds are the auditorium, summer cottages, and picnic facilities.

Moundsville is at the junction with State 2 (*see Tour 19b*), which unites with US 250 for 12.9 miles.

In GLENDALE, 69.3 *m.* (640 alt., 1,493 pop.), a pleasant residential town with many trees and spacious lawns, is (R) the REYNOLDS MEMORIAL HOSPITAL, founded by the Reverend B. M. Spurr in 1899 to care for discharged convicts and persons in distress. Financed largely by Mrs. James Banks Reynolds, the hospital was named in memory of her husband, a physician, and her two sons, victims of typhoid fever. Two wings have been added to the original unit until the hospital now has 100 beds. The MARX TOY COMPANY PLANT (*open on application*), housed in a group of buildings on the edge of an emergency landing field (R), manufactures electrical and mechanical toys of all types.

US 250 enters THE NARROWS, in which the highway and the railroad are squeezed tight between the Ohio River and overhanging cliffs. After a heavy rain, falling rocks occasionally block the highway here. At the northern end of the narrows, 71.6 *m.*, a marker indicates the site where Captain William Forman and 21 of his Hampshire County Militia, while on their way to aid border forces at Wheeling, were ambushed and killed by Indians in September 1777. Buried here in a common grave, their bodies were removed 40 years later to Mount Rose Cemetery, Moundsville.

McMECHEN, 72.5 *m.* (648 alt., 3,710 pop.), is largely a residential city inhabited by workers in the industrial plants between Wheeling and Moundsville. Red houses, shoulder to shoulder, line the highway, their doorsteps flush with the narrow sidewalks.

BENWOOD, 74.3 *m.* (688 alt., 3,950 pop.), succeeds McMechen with no perceptible break in the rows of smoke-grimed houses. The

WHEELING STEEL CORPORATION PLANT (R), with cindered yards, railroad tracks, and piles of steel tubing, stretches along the highway for blocks, being the largest of the city's industrial plants. Just north of the plant is (L) an electrically lighted pedestrian tunnel almost a mile long, once part of a coal mine, now used as a short cut between Benwood and the Boggs Run section on the opposite side of the steep hill.

On April 28, 1924, the third largest mine explosion in West Virginia occurred here in a drift mine, one of the oldest in the State, operated by the Wheeling Steel Corporation. Gas and coal dust caused an explosion just after the morning shift had gone to work. Trains carrying United States Mine Rescue teams rushed to the scene from Fairmont and Pittsburgh. Rescue work began on the opposite side of the hill, for the main tunnel at Benwood was blocked with heavy slate. The entire shift of 119 men was found dead, many burned beyond recognition, when the rescue crews reached them two days later.

WHEELING, 78.6 *m.* (678 alt., 61,659 pop.) (*see Wheeling*).

Wheeling is at the junction with US 40 (*see Tour 23*) and State 2 (*see Tour 19a*).

ⵉⵉⵉ

Tour 23

(Washington, Pa.)—Triadelphia—Wheeling—(Bridgeport, O.); US 40. Pennsylvania Line to Ohio Line, 15.4 *m.*

Concrete roadbed.
Baltimore & Ohio R.R. parallels route throughout.
Tourist accommodations plentiful; hotels in Wheeling.

US 40, in its brief passage across the Northern Panhandle of West Virginia, follows the approximate route of the old National Road, the first highway over the Allegheny Mountains to the western frontier. Now part of a coast-to-coast highway, the turnpike carries automotive traffic past old taverns at a speed that would have astounded even Dan Gordon, whose run of 32 miles in 2 hours and 20 minutes was the best record established by the old stage expresses on the Pike, as the road is locally known.

The National, or Cumberland, Road was authorized in 1806 when the future of the young republic was still in doubt. Britain's cross of St. George and St. Andrew floated with sullen hostility on the heights of Quebec to the north, and events threatened to embroil the Nation in the Napoleonic wars involving all Europe. Washington had realized that the Alleghenies formed such a barrier between the eastern and western sections of the country that they might drift apart to become separate nations, and he had urged the necessity of building a highway between them.

When Ohio was admitted to statehood in 1803, the United States Government had agreed to construct a road to connect the new State with the Atlantic seaboard; funds were to be raised by the sale of Government lands within Ohio's boundaries.

As originally planned, the road was to run from Cumberland, Maryland, to a point on the Ohio River opposite Steubenville, Ohio; but the commissioners appointed to lay out the route chose Wheeling (*see Wheeling*) as its western terminus—partly because of obstructions in the river near Steubenville, which at certain seasons interfered with navigation, but largely because of the efforts of Henry Clay, the 'Cock of Kentucky' and spokesman of the West, who preferred Wheeling. The road closely followed Nemacolin's Path, one of five great Indian trails from east to west; along this trail Braddock had pushed through the wilderness on his disastrous campaign against Fort Duquesne during the bloody French and Indian War.

Contracts for building the turnpike were let in 1811, but the War of 1812 intervened and construction did not begin until 1815. By 1818 it had been completed to Wheeling, which grew rapidly as streams of settlers poured through it on their way down the Ohio Valley. Stagecoaches drawn by four and six horses were soon traveling the National Road, diverting much westward traffic from Pittsburgh to Wheeling. By 1822 one large commercial house in Wheeling had unloaded 1,081 wagons, averaging 3,500 pounds each, for which the freightage totaled $90,000. While only 15 miles of the turnpike were in West Virginia, its construction greatly stimulated the development of the northern part of West Virginia. The National Road played an important role in the history of the country, helping to put an end to all separatist tendencies in the West, tying it firmly to the Union.

US 40 crosses the PENNSYLVANIA LINE, 0 *m.*, 16 miles west of Washington, Pennsylvania.

The RAY MARKER, 4 *m.*, honors the memory of Joseph Ray, who was born near this place. Ray was the author of *Ray's Arithmetic*, long a standard textbook in many schools of the country.

An old MILESTONE OF THE NATIONAL ROAD, 4.9 *m.*, indicated to early travelers that they were still 10 miles from Wheeling. Today, the city has so grown that its corporate limits are less than four miles distant. The mileages that appear on the iron mileposts, now painted white, are inaccurate because of the rerouting of the highway in many places.

RONEYS POINT, 5.1 *m.* (830 alt., 213 pop.), a shipping center for the Ohio County Farmers' Co-operative Association, was a lively spot in the days when stagecoaches of the Good Intent and Sims lines carried gay parties of travelers to the OLD STONE TAVERN (R), which remains much as it was when built in 1818. A sunburst transom over the door, the old woodwork, and the massive fireplaces are still in place. Originally a two-story stone building with 11 rooms and a large hall, it was enlarged years later with a 9-room addition.

TRIADELPHIA (Gr., three brothers), 6.3 m. (745 alt., 302 pop.), is a quiet old village with few reminders of its early importance as a stagecoach stop and summer resort. Incorporated in 1829, it was named for three intimate friends, Colonel Josias Thompson, Amasa Brown, and John D. Foster, who settled here about 1800 and donated the townsite.

The old GREEN HOTEL (R), abandoned years ago to village idlers who lounge on its long veranda, served statesmen and other travelers on the National Road for more than a century. The two-story, T-shaped frame building, first known as the Lawson House, was erected about 1800 by Colonel Josias Thompson. Until the day of the automobile the hotel was a popular summer resort, known the length of the pike as much for the genial hospitality, flowing whiskers, and broad-brimmed hat of its genial manager, Joseph Green, as for the menagerie he kept in the back yard. Beside the hotel stands a weathered and crumbling monument, representing four angels with uplifted arms, carved by Roman Catholic masons in honor of a priest who journeyed from Pittsburgh each Sunday to say Mass for the workers constructing the highway. Placed here about 1811 to await the building of a church, it had so crumbled by 1861, when a church was finally built, that it was left to molder away here.

The highway crosses MIDDLE WHEELING CREEK, 7.3 m., on a bridge constructed in 1936 to replace the hazardous S-bridge (L). The natural route for the National Road was the old trail along the northern bank of the creek, but the capricious and charming Lydia Shepherd, wife of Moses Shepherd, was determined to have the road pass her house on the southern bank. She appealed to Henry Clay, who had often been a guest at the Shepherd mansion (*see below*), and persuaded him to use his influence in having the highway routed as she desired, even though it necessitated the difficult construction of an S-bridge here and of another in Elm Grove.

The FLORENCE CRITTENDEN HOME FOR UNFORTUNATE GIRLS (L), 7.4 m., erected in 1910 to care for unmarried mothers in need, is supported by State and private funds.

MONUMENT PLACE (*open*), 8.2 m., a large Georgian Colonial mansion of gray stone erected by Moses Shepherd in 1798, stands (L) on elm-shaded grounds sloping down to the northern bank of Wheeling Creek. Two slender Corinthian columns support a small portico with pediment. The heavy wooden door, joined with pegs, has a three-inch keyhole through which to operate the bolt, a huge bar. Over the doors are sunburst transoms. The interior woodwork, mantels, cornices, and paneling are hand carved in a distinctive pattern for each room. The

Mystic Shrine of the Masonic lodge, which now owns Monument Place, has restored with originals and reproductions the furnishings of the library, dining room, ballroom, master bedroom, and guest room, in which many distinguished persons slept on their visits to the Shepherds. From the high ceilings hang crystal chandeliers, originally lighted with candles. Silken cords are looped over the doorways to the Henry Clay room and to the ballroom where General Lafayette, John C. Calhoun, Andrew Jackson, President James K. Polk, and others were feted.

David Shepherd, father of Colonel Moses Shepherd, came to this section in 1777 to settle a large tract of land granted him by Governor Patrick Henry, and erected Fort Shepherd, which was destroyed by Indians in the same year. The Indians spared the gristmill because the revolving water wheel fascinated them. The fort, rebuilt in 1786, stood until 1798 when Moses Shepherd tore it down to erect his mansion on the site. Shepherd made a fortune as contractor on the National Road, and he and his wife, Lydia, entertained lavishly. Henry Clay was a frequent visitor even before the building of the highway, and this friendship is said to have been responsible for Clay's sponsorship of Wheeling as the terminus of the route. After her husband's death, Lydia Shepherd managed the estate until she died, at the age of 110, having outlived her second husband, General Daniel Cruger.

On the grounds stands a MONUMENT TO HENRY CLAY, a sandstone figure representing the Goddess of Liberty, erected by the Shepherds in honor of their friend; the base of the monument is inscribed, 'Time will bring every amelioration and refinement most gratifying to rational man, and the humblest flower plucked under the tree of Liberty is more to be desired than all the trappings of royalty.' Near the driveway is a SUNDIAL, erected by the Shepherd family, with this inscription:
The noiseless foot of Time steals softly by,
And ere we think of manhood age draws nigh.

The old STONE MILL (L), 8.5 m., was erected about 1826 by Daniel Cruger, second husband of Lydia Shepherd, and has been in continuous operation since that time. The old STONE HOUSE (R), 8.6 m., a square two-story structure used as a lunch room, was erected about 1820 as a stagecoach station and was known successively as the Gooding House, the French House, and the Roeteger House.

At the entrance to the WHEELING MUNICIPAL PARK (R), 9.2 m., stands the MADONNA OF THE TRAIL MONUMENT, erected by the D.A.R. as a memorial to the mothers of covered wagon days. One of hundreds of identical statues scattered from the Atlantic to the Pacific, the white granite monument represents a woman in pioneer dress, with a baby in her arms and a small child clinging to her skirts. In the park are two lakes, a swimming pool, tennis courts, picnic grounds, 9-hole golf course, and a dancing pavilion.

ALTENHEIM (L), 11.3 m., a home for dependent older women, founded in 1896 by Anton Reymann, a Wheeling philanthropist, occupies a large red brick building, once the Bellview Hotel, popular in the early nineteenth century as a stagecoach station.

On the crest of Wheeling Hill is the McCulloch's Leap Marker (L), 13.2 *m.*, a tablet commemorating the feat of Major Samuel McCulloch, Indian scout and soldier, who, according to tradition, rode his horse down the precipitous 150-foot cliff into Wheeling Creek (L) to escape a band of Indians. Leading reinforcements from his fort at Short Creek to the aid of besieged Fort Henry, McCulloch was cut off from his company and forced to ride for his life to Fort Van Meter. When Indians blocked this avenue of escape, he took refuge on the summit of this hill. Confident that they had him cornered, the Indians closed in for the kill, but McCulloch spurred his horse over the cliff and a few minutes later rode safely from the creek.

The Mingo, 13.3 *m.*, a bronze figure of an Indian warrior standing on a stone base with right arm outstretched, was erected by the Kiwanis Club in commemoration of the Mingo whom the whites supplanted in the Ohio Valley.

West of the statue US 40 descends to the business center of Wheeling.

WHEELING, 13.9 *m.* (678 alt., 61,659 pop.) (*see Wheeling*).

Wheeling is at the junction with US 250 (*see Tour 22c*) and State 2 (*see Tour 19a and b*).

The Suspension Bridge, 14 *m.*, which spans the Ohio River between Wheeling and Wheeling Island, was the longest single span in the country at the time of its construction in 1856. This bridge and its predecessor, destroyed by a storm in 1854, occasioned long and bitter controversy between Wheeling and Pittsburgh (*see Wheeling*).

WHEELING ISLAND, 14.3 *m.*, a large suburb of Wheeling, is often swept by floods; in 1884, 1913, and 1936, the island was completely inundated. After the regular annual flood the islanders clean up the wreckage, rebuild their houses, and calmly go about their business until the waters rise again the next spring. The island was bought from the Indians by Ebenezer Zane, who, it is said, gave them a barrel of whisky for it.

On the island is Wheeling Downs, S. Penn St., a half-mile race track opened in 1937 on the grounds of the State Fair Park. Races are held here from late May to late June, and from late August to late September. The pari-mutuel system of betting on horse races, legal in West Virginia, is used here.

US 40 crosses the Ohio River on a steel bridge (*automobiles*, 5¢; *pedestrians*, 1¢) to the OHIO LINE, 15.4 *m.*, at the eastern limit of Bridgeport, Ohio (*see Ohio Guide*).

PART IV

Appendices

Chronology

<table>
<tr><td>1607</td><td>First permanent English colony in America established at Jamestown, Virginia, by 105 English colonists.</td></tr>
<tr><td>1641</td><td>New River discovered by Walter Chiles, Rice Hoe, Walter Austin, and Joseph Johnson.</td></tr>
<tr><td>1669–70</td><td>Crest of the Blue Ridge reached near Harpers Ferry on two occasions by John Lederer, a German physician.</td></tr>
<tr><td>1671</td><td>Batts-Fallam expedition, sent out by Colonel Abraham Wood 'for the finding out the ebbing and flowing of ye South Sea,' reaches Falls of Great Kanawha.</td></tr>
<tr><td>1716</td><td>Lieutenant Governor Alexander Spotswood and Knights of the Golden Horse Shoe penetrate western Virginia to peaks of the Alleghenies.</td></tr>
<tr><td>1725</td><td>John Van Meter, of the New York Dutch settlers, visits valley of South Branch of the Potomac.</td></tr>
<tr><td>1726–7</td><td>Morgan Morgan made first permanent settlement of record in western Virginia at Bunker Hill on Mill Creek (Berkeley County).</td></tr>
<tr><td>1726–30</td><td>Germans from Pennsylvania settle at Mecklenburg, now Shepherdstown.</td></tr>
<tr><td>1730</td><td>Isaac and John Van Meter, sons of John Van Meter, receive patent for 40,000 acres, much of it in what are now Jefferson and Berkeley Counties, West Virginia.</td></tr>
<tr><td>1742</td><td>John Peter Salley and others discover coal on Coal River.</td></tr>
<tr><td>1744</td><td>All territory between Allegheny Mountains and the Ohio River ceded to English by Six Nations for 400 pounds.</td></tr>
<tr><td>1746</td><td>Fairfax stone placed (four miles north of Thomas, Tucker County) to mark western limit of the Fairfax Estate.</td></tr>
<tr><td>1747–8</td><td>George Washington surveys land in western Virginia for Lord Fairfax and visits 'Ye famed Warm Springs at Bath' (Berkeley Springs).
Draper and Ingles families found settlement of Draper's Meadows in New River Valley near what is now Blacksburg, Montgomery County, Virginia.</td></tr>
<tr><td>1749</td><td>Captain Peter Joseph Celeron, Chevalier de Bienville, makes expedition down Ohio River and buries plates, taking possession for the King of France.
Jacob Marlin and Stephen Sewell build cabins at mouth of Knapp's Creek in present Pocahontas County.</td></tr>
<tr><td>1750</td><td>Christopher Gist travels along Clinch, Bluestone, and New Rivers while on exploration trip to the Ohio country.</td></tr>
</table>

Dr. Thomas Walker, while traveling down Greenbrier River, writes in his journal, 'There are some inhabitants on the branches of Green Bryer but we missed their plantations.'

First frontier fort, Fort Ohio, built at Ridgeley, in present Mineral County.

1751   The Greenbrier Company authorized by English government to locate 100,000 acres on Greenbrier River.

1753   First mention of school in what is now West Virginia is mention of schoolmaster named Schrock in Hampshire County, then created.

1754   Baptist Church organized at Opequon in present Berkeley County.

1755   July 8, Draper's Meadows settlement in New River section attacked by Shawnee Indians and nearly all settlers killed or captured.

Mrs. Mary Ingles and other white captives of Indians credited with making first salt in state at Campbells Creek, east of Charleston, while being taken to Ohio following Ingles-Draper massacre.

1756   Lord Fairfax granted acreage and springs at Bath (Berkeley Springs) to Virginia, that 'these healing waters might be forever free to the publick, for the welfare of suffering humanity.'

1762   Romney and Mecklenburg (Shepherdstown) established as towns by Virginia assembly in act signed December 23 by Governor Francis Fauquier. Virginia General Assembly authorizes an Agricultural and Mechanical Fair at Mecklenburg (Shepherdstown).

1763   French and Indian War terminated by Treaty of Paris.

1764   John and Samuel Pringle lived in a hollow sycamore tree near Turkey Run on Buckhannon River near present site of Buckhannon.

1765   Mathew Arbuckle of Greenbrier settlement explores the Great Kanawha Valley.

1766   Survey of Mason-Dixon Line reached western boundary of Maryland.

1768   Nearly all of western Virginia north of the Little Kanawha River ceded to the King of England by the Six Nations in Treaty of Fort Stanwix.

First flood of record in Ohio River.

1769   Settlement at mouth of Wheeling Creek by Colonel Ebenezer Zane and brothers, Jonathan and Silas.

1772   George Washington patents 10,990 acres of land, south side of Great Kanawha, two miles above confluence of Ohio and Great Kanawha Rivers.

George Rogers Clark explores Ohio and Great Kanawha Rivers.

1773   First family settlement in the Great Kanawha Valley made at Cedar Grove at mouth of Kellys Creek by Walter Kelly from North Carolina.

1774   Dunmore's War precipitated by murder of Chief Logan's family by party of white men at mouth of Yellow Creek, April 30.

Battle of Point Pleasant (considered by some as first battle of Revolution).

Fort Fincastle, later renamed Fort Henry, erected at Wheeling by Captain Angus McDonald.

General Andrew Lewis, with 1,100 men, leaves Fort Savannah (Lewisburg) en route to Point Pleasant to oppose Indians.

Lord Dunmore arrives at Fort Fincastle (Wheeling) with 1,200 men.

1775 First regular troops raised in Virginia for Continental service mobilized at Morgan's Springs and Winchester.

1776 Virginia adopts its first constitution.

1777 Cornstalk, his son Elinipsico, and Red Hawk murdered by whites at Fort Randolph.

Indians led by Simon Girty, renegade white man, unsuccessfully besiege Fort Henry.

1782 Mason-Dixon Line continued to southwestern corner of Pennsylvania.

Second siege of Fort Henry at Wheeling, sometimes called the last battle of the Revolution.

1784 James Rumsey demonstrates model of a mechanically propelled boat near Berkeley Springs on Potomac in presence of George Washington.

Permanent survey of Mason-Dixon Line completed.

1785 The Potomac Company incorporated to build a canal to connect Potomac River with Cheat River; the James River Company incorporated to construct a canal to connect James River with the Great Kanawha.

George Washington made president of both companies.

1788 Six new western counties send representatives to the Virginia convention which ratified the Constitution of the United States.

1789 Daniel Boone commissioned a lieutenant colonel of Kanawha Militia.

1790 Population of western Virginia reported at 55,873, and demands for equality in representation in assembly made.

Potomack Guardian and Berkeley Advertiser first newspaper in western Virginia, was printed by Nathaniel Willis at Shepherdstown. It was removed to Martinsburg in 1797.

1792 Kanawha County represented in the Virginia assembly at Richmond by Daniel Boone and George Clendenin.

1794 December 19, Charlestown (Charleston) established as a town.

Iron furnace erected by Peter Tarr at Kings Creek.

Post office established at Wheeling.

1795 Treaty of Greenville makes Virginia frontier safe from Indian attacks.

Daniel Boone and family leave Kanawha Valley permanently.

1796 Old Stone Presbyterian Church erected at Lewisburg.

1800 Population of western Virginia increases to 78,592, and discontent because of unequal representation reiterated in a petition to Virginia assembly citing that Warwick with 614 white population and Berkeley with 17,832 had the same number of representatives in the assembly.

1806   First salt well bored in Great Kanawha Valley at Great Buffalo Lick near Malden by Joseph and Daniel Ruffner.

National or Cumberland Road authorized by Congress.

Blennerhassett Island and Mansion confiscated by Virginia Militia as a result of alleged Burr-Blennerhassett plot.

1810   Western Virginia with 312,626 white inhabitants and four senators protest unequal representation of eastern Virginia with 338,826 and 20 senators.

Parkersburg established as a town.

Blennerhassett Mansion destroyed by fire.

Oil discovered in gravel beds along Hughes River in Wood County.

1814   Monongalia Academy at Morgantown, forerunner of West Virginia University, incorporated.

1815   James Wilson, boring for salt near Charleston, brings in first natural gas well in America.

1816   Newspapers propose division of state into North Virginia and South Virginia at line of the Rappahannock River, thence to the confluence of the Greenbrier with the New and down the Kanawha to the Ohio.

1817   First trust in United States, the salt trust, formed by salt manufacturers of Kanawha Valley.

1818   National Road opened to Wheeling.

1819   First steamboat on Great Kanawha River ascends stream to Red House.

1824   James River and Kanawha Turnpike completed from Lewisburg to Falls of Great Kanawha.

Staunton and Parkersburg Turnpike authorized.

1827   Northwestern Turnpike authorized.

Baltimore and Ohio Railroad chartered by Virginia Assembly.

1830   Discussion of abolition of Negro slavery assumed alarming sectional aspect.

Second Virginia constitution ratified but western Virginians, dissatisfied, hold mass meeting at Wheeling to consider annexation of Maryland.

1841   First industrial use of natural gas in United States at Burning Springs (Kanawha County).

1842   Public meetings held in western counties to deliberate 'our restoration to equal political rights of which we are deprived.'

1847   Jefferson County adopts free school system, the first in western Virginia.

Western Virginia studies means of ridding that part of state of Negro slavery. Dr. Henry Ruffner publishes pamphlet.

1851   Ratification of third Virginia constitution; it extended suffrage to all white male adults. For the first time western Virginia has a majority in the House of Delegates.

1853 January 1, first through train from Atlantic Ocean to the Ohio River reached Wheeling over Baltimore & Ohio Railroad.

1859 John Brown's raid at Harpers Ferry. Brown convicted of treason and hanged at Charles Town.

1860 First commercial oil well in state drilled at Burning Springs, Wirt County.

1861 April 14. Fall of Fort Sumter begins War between the States.
April 17. 29 of 46 western Virginia counties vote against secession.
April 21. Harpers Ferry garrison burns arsenal and flees to Maryland.
May 13. First Wheeling convention, with 26 counties represented, opposes secession.
June 3. Confederate outposts defeated at Philippi.
June 11. Second Wheeling convention opens; delegates from 40 counties take oath of loyalty to the Union.
June 13. Convention adopts Declaration of Rights.
June 19. Convention adopts ordinance to recognize State government; and next day votes unanimously to set up Restored Government of Virginia on loyal basis, with Francis H. Pierpont as governor. Submits ordinance to people.
July 1. First Virginia Legislature held in western Virginia meets at Wheeling.
July 9. John S. Carlile and Waitman T. Willey elected United States Senators.
July 11. Confederates driven from Rich Mountain.
July 13. Engagement at Corrick's Ford.
July 17. Skirmish at Scary Creek.
August. Wheeling convention resumes its work.
Sept. 10. Engagement at Carnifex Ferry.
Sept. 12–13. Battle of Cheat Mountain; Lee defeated.
Sept. 25. Engagement at Kanawha Gap.
Oct. 3. Engagement at Greenbrier.
Oct. 24. People ratify new State ordinance.
Nov. 26. Constitutional convention opens at Wheeling.
Nov. 27. Convention chooses name 'West Virginia.'
Dec. 13. Engagement at Buffalo Mountain.

1862 April 3. Constitution of West Virginia ratified by voters.
May 6. Legislature of Restored Government of Virginia approves formation of new state.
Sept. 10. Engagement at Fayetteville.
Sept. 15. Capture of Harpers Ferry by Jackson.

1863 June 20. West Virginia admitted as 35th state of the Union.
June 20. First legislature of West Virginia convenes at Wheeling.
Aug. 5. Berkeley County transferred from Virginia to West Virginia.

Aug. 26–7. Engagement at Rocky Gap.

Sept. 26. State seal adopted.

Oct. 18. Engagement at Charleston.

Nov. 2. Jefferson County transferred from Virginia to West Virginia.

Nov. 6. Engagement at Droop Mountain.

Dec. 10. Present free school system created by legislative act.

1864   Jan. 29–Feb. 1. Cavalry skirmishes at Medley.

July 4–7. Confederates under General Early in engagements about Harpers Ferry.

1864   The West Virginia Hospital, State's first public institution, opened at Weston, established by Virginia assembly, 1859.

1865   April 9. War between the States ends, when Lee surrenders.

The first public free school in the State is opened at Charleston. First railroad bridge over the Ohio River completed at East Steubenville.

1866   May 24. Voters ratify constitutional amendment barring from citizenship all who had given aid to the Confederacy.

Virginia demands payment of $15,000,000 from West Virginia as its part of debt at time of separation.

1867   Jan. 16. Legislature ratifies Fourteenth Amendment.

West Virginia University chartered February 7, 1867, under name of Agricultural College of West Virginia; absorbs Monongalia Academy (incorporated January 4, 1858) and Woodburn Female Seminary (incorporated January 4, 1858).

1868   Dec. 4. Legislative act changes name of West Virginia Agricultural College at Morgantown to West Virginia University.

1869   Feb. 20. Charleston designated as seat of government by legislature 'on and after April 1, 1870.'

March 3. Fifteenth Amendment ratified by legislature.

1870   Population (U. S. Census) 442,014.

State School for Deaf and Blind established at Romney.

State capital moved to Charleston.

1871   April 27. The Flick Amendment, enfranchising all persons disfranchised in 1866, becomes effective.

1872   Jan. 16–April 9. Constitutional Convention drafts new constitution. Ratified by people August 22.

1875   Feb. 20. Legislature passed an act designating Wheeling as the seat of government.

May 21. Wheeling becomes the capital.

1880   Population 618,457.

First telephone exchange in State erected in Wheeling.

1881   Jan. 6. Nathan Goff appointed Secretary of the Navy.

1885   The second capitol building at Charleston is erected.

Seat of state government removed from Wheeling to Charleston.

1886   Wesleyan Seminary, now West Virginia Wesleyan College, established at Buckhannon.

1890   Population 762,794.

1891   Stephen B. Elkins appointed Secretary of War.

1895   William L. Wilson appointed Postmaster General.

1898   West Virginia furnishes two regiments of volunteer infantry in Spanish-American War. Neither regiment saw active service, although many West Virginians saw active service in other organizations.

1900   Population 958,800.

West Virginia's oil production for year 16,195,675 barrels.

1901   Office of Commissioner of Banking created.

1903   Jan. 23. Rhododendron adopted by state legislature as State flower.

West Virginia State Federation of Labor organized 60 craft unions.

1904   State Department of Archives created.

1907   Five mine explosions cause 537 deaths.

1910   Population 1,221,119.

1911   State Department of Agriculture created.

1914   State prohibition law becomes effective.

1915   West Virginia-Virginia debt case decided by United States Supreme Court, holding West Virginia's share of the debt to be $12,393,929.

1917–18   World War: West Virginia Selective Service registrants numbered 323,383; 45,648 enter active service; 624 killed in action; 375 died of wounds or other causes overseas; 722 died of disease or other causes in this country.

1918   A Government explosives plant, costing about $75,000,000, erected at Nitro.

State Department of Public Safety created.

1919   West Virginia University placed under control of State Board of Education.

Legislature authorized payment of Virginia debt by issuance of 20 year bonds and cash payment of $1,062,867.

1920   Population 1,463,701.

Constitutional amendment passed for issuance of $50,000,000 in road bonds to 'lift West Virginia out of the mud.'

1921   Jan. 3. State Capitol at Charleston destroyed by fire.

Logan County coal fields invaded by 4,000 armed miners who fought battle of Blair Mountain with 500 deputy sheriffs and State police. Force dispersed by Federal troops.

1923   A hard-surfaced road constructed between Charleston and Huntington. Tax on gasoline becomes effective.

1924   Howard M. Gore of Harrison County appointed Secretary of Agriculture.

1927   Federal prison for women erected at Alderson.

1929   March 7. New State flag design adopted by legislature.

West Virginia ranks first in production of bituminous coal.

1930   Population 1,729,205.

Glass production of 17 counties valued at more than $50,000,000.

1932   June 30. Dedication ceremonies held for new State Capitol at Charleston; building and grounds cost $9,491,180.

Levy limitation and property classification amendment adopted by referendum.

1933   Legislature declared 5 per cent beer 'non-intoxicating.'

County unit plan of school administration adopted.

1934   State Prohibition Law repealed.

1938   The Mingo Oak, largest and oldest white oak tree of record in the United States, declared dead and felled with ceremony.

State Treasurer announced funds on hand for last payment of Virginia Bond Debt (due July 1, 1939).

1939   Miners certificate law, requiring six months' apprenticeship in West Virginia mines to establish eligibility for work, enacted by legislature.

State Road Commission reports 13,068 miles of surfaced highways out of a total of 34,350 miles of state roads, largely constructed during past 10 years.

1940   Explosion of mine at Bartley, McDowell County, claims the lives of 92 miners.

WEST VIRGINIA COUNTIES WITH DATES OF CREATION

Bibliography

GENERAL INFORMATION

American Automobile Association. *Northeastern Tour Book.* Washington, D. C., 1939. 656 p., illus., maps. See p. 318–38. Issued annually.

Anderson, Hugh Edgar. *Facts of West Virginia* . . . Charleston, Woodyard Commercial Printers, 1936. 197 p., bibl.

Conley, Phil, editor in chief. *The West Virginia Encyclopedia.* Charleston, West Virginia Pub. Co., 1929. 1,052 p., illus., plates, ports.

Gannett, Henry. *A Gazetteer of West Virginia.* Washington, Govt. Print. Off., 1904. 164 p. (U. S. Geological Survey. Bulletin no. 233).

West Virginia. *West Virginia Blue Book.* Comp. and ed. by Charles Lively, clerk of the Senate. Charleston, 1938. 794 p., col. front., plates, ports., maps.

DESCRIPTION AND TRAVEL

Cain, James M. 'A Mine-Field Melodrama.' (In Gruening, Ernest, ed. *These United States.* 2d series. New York, Boni & Liveright, 1924. p. 80–92.)

Conley, Phil. *West Virginia Yesterday and Today: a Textbook in the Geography, History, Resources, Industries, and Government of West Virginia.* Rev. ed. Charleston, West Virginia Pub. Co., 1937. 446 p., front., illus., maps. Collaborators, Boyd B. Stutler, Mary Yost Sandrus.

Kennedy, Philip Pendleton. *The Blackwater Chronicle, a Narrative of an Expedition into the Land of Canaan, in Randolph County, Virginia* . . . By 'the Clerke of Oxenforde.' With ill. from life by Strother. New York, Redfield, 1853. 223 p. incl. plates, front.

Royall, Mrs. Anne. *Sketches of History, Life, and Manners, in the United States.* By a Traveler. New Haven, Printed for the Author, 1826. 392 p., front. One of America's first newspaperwomen here portrays the lives and customs of early West Virginia residents.

Rucker, Mrs. Maude A., comp. *West Virginia, Her Land, Her People, Her Traditions, Her Resources.* New York, W. Neale, 1930. 257 p., front., plates, ports., facsim.

Schaeffer, John Randolph. *Over the Alleghenies by the Northwestern Turnpike. Now the Great Scenic Federal Highway.* Strasburg, Va., 1928. 144 p. incl. front., illus.

Strother, Gen. D. H. *Virginia Illustrated: Containing a Visit to the Virginian Canaan, and the Adventures of Porte Crayon and His Cousins.* Ill. from drawings. By Porte Crayon. New York, Harper, 1857. 300 p.

West Virginia State Road Commission. *West Virginia Historic and Scenic Highway Markers* . . . Charleston, 1937. 247 p. incl. front., illus. (incl. maps).

RESOURCES AND THEIR CONSERVATION

Conservation Commission of West Virginia. Reports. Charleston, 1935 to date. Illus., tables, diagrs.

Hennen, Ray Vernon. *Important Resources of West Virginia.* New York, Phillips & Van Brunt, 1919. 20 p.

Summers, George W. *The Mountain State. A Description of the Natural Resources of West Virginia* . . . Charleston, M. W. Donnally, printer, 1893. 259 p., front. (fold. map), fold. tab.

HISTORY
General

Ambler, Charles Henry. *A History of West Virginia.* New York, Prentice-Hall, Inc., 1933. 622 p., col. front., illus., bibl. (Prentice-Hall history series, C. Wittke, editor.)

————*West Virginia: Stories and Biographies.* New York, Chicago, etc., Rand McNally & Co., 1937. 600 p., front., illus. (incl. ports., maps).

Boyd, Peter. *History of Northern West Virginia Panhandle.* 2 v. Topeka, Indianapolis, Historical Pub. Co., 1927. 1050 p., illus., plates, ports.

Callahan, James Morton. *History of West Virginia, Old and New.* Chicago and New York, Am. Historical Society, Inc., 1923. 3 v. Front., illus. (incl. maps), plates, ports. Vols. 2 and 3, biographical.

Fast, Richard Ellsworth, and Hu Maxwell. *The History and Government of West Virginia.* 3d ed. Morgantown, Acme Pub. Co., 1906. 518 p., front., illus. (incl. ports.), plates, bibl.

Kercheval, Samuel. *A History of the Valley of Virginia.* 4th ed. Strasburg, Va., Shenandoah Pub. House, 1925. 405 p. First pub. 1833.

Lewis, Virgil A. *History and Government of West Virginia.* New Century ed. New York, Cincinnati, etc., Am. Book Co., 1922. 416 p., front., illus. (incl. map). (State Government series.) First pub. 1896.

Miller, Thomas Condit, and Hu Maxwell. *West Virginia and Its People.* New York, Lewis Historical Pub. Co., 1913. 3 v. Fronts., plates, ports., maps. Vols. 2 and 3, family and personal history.

Myers, Sylvester. *Myers' History of West Virginia* . . . Wheeling, News Lithograph Co., 1915. 2 v. Illus., port.

Shawkey, Morris Purdy. *West Virginia, in History, Life, Literature and Industry,* by Morris Purdy Shawkey . . . assisted by an advisory council; West Virginia biography by a special staff of writers. Chicago and New York, Lewis Pub. Co., 1928. 5 v. Fronts., illus. (incl. maps, facsims.), ports. Vols. 3–5 contain biographical material.

Early Period

Allman, Clarence B. *The Life and Times of Lewis Wetzel.* Scottdale, Pa., Mennonite Pub. House, 1932. 140 p., illus.

Ambler, Charles Henry. *George Washington and the West.* Chapel Hill, Univ. of North Carolina Press, 1936. 270 p., illus. (incl. maps), plates, ports., bibl.

——*Sectionalism in Virginia from 1776 to 1861.* Chicago, Univ. of Chicago Press, 1910. 366 p., maps, bibl.

Beveridge, Albert J. *The Life of John Marshall.* Boston and New York, Houghton Mifflin, 1919. 4 v. Col. fronts., plates, ports., facsims.

Dandridge, Mrs. Danske. *American Prisoners of the Revolution.* Charlottesville, Va., Michie Co., Printers, 1911. 504 p., front., bibl.

Doddridge, Rev. Joseph. *Notes on the Settlement and Indian Wars of the Western Parts of Virginia and Pennsylvania from 1763 to 1783* . . . Pittsburgh, 1912. 320 p., front., ports. First pub. 1824.

——*Frontier Defense on the Upper Ohio 1777–1778.* Compiled from the Draper manuscripts in the library of the Wisconsin Historical Society . . . Madison, 1912. 329 p., front. (fold. map), plates, ports., facsims. (Draper series, vol. 3.)

Gist, Christopher. *Christopher Gist's Journals* . . . Pittsburgh, J. R. Weldin & Co., 1893. 296 p., maps. Describes three expeditions—the first and second in the interests of the Ohio Company, the third in company with Major George Washington.

Hale, John Peter. *Daniel Boone. Some Facts and Incidents Not Hitherto Published. His Ten or Twelve Years' Residence in Kanawha County* . . . Wheeling, L. Baker & Co., printers (188–). 18 p.

——*Trans-Allegheny Pioneers; Historical Sketches of the First White Settlers West of the Alleghenies 1748 and After.* 2d ed. Charleston, W. Va., Kanawha Valley Pub. Co., 1931. 340 p., illus. (facsim.), plates, ports., maps. First pub. 1886.

Hughes, Josiah. *Pioneer West Virginia.* Charleston, The Author, 1932. 186 p.

Lederer, John. *The Discoveries of John Lederer . . . Begun in March, 1669, and Ended in September, 1670* . . . Tr. from the Latin by Sir William Talbot. Charleston, S. C., Walker, Evans & Cogswell Co., 1891. 47 p., map. First pub. London, 1672.

Lewis, Virgil A. *Life and Times of Anne Bailey, the Pioneer Heroine of the Great Kanawha Valley.* Charleston, Butler Print. Co., 1891. 90 p., front.

McWhorter, Lucullus Virgil. *The Border Settlers of Northwestern Virginia from 1768 to 1795* . . . With preface by William Elsey Connelley . . . Hamilton, O., Republican Pub. Co., 1915. 509 p., front., illus., plates.

Ruffner, Henry. *Address to the People of West Virginia: Showing That Slavery is Injurious to the Public Welfare* . . . Louisville, printed at the *Examiner* office, 1847. 32 p.

Thwaites, Reuben Gold, and Louise Phelps Kellogg, ed. *Documentary History of Dunmore's War, 1774.* Compiled from the Draper manuscripts in the library of the Wisconsin Historical Society . . . Madison, 1905. 472 p., front. (port.), maps, facsim. (Draper series, vol. 1.)

Virginia (Colony). Lieutenant Governor, 1751–58 (Robert Dinwiddie). *The Official Records of Robert Dinwiddie* . . . Richmond, The Society,

1883–4. 2 v. Fronts. (ports.), fold. map, facsim. (Half-title: Collections of the Virginia Historical Society. New series. Vol. 3–4.)

Washington, George. *Journal of Colonel George Washington, Commanding a Detachment of Virginia Troops . . . in 1754 . . .* Ed., with notes, by J. M. Toner, M.D. Albany, N. Y., J. Munsell's Sons, 1893. 273 p., plans.

——*Journal of My Journey over the Mountains . . . in 1747–48.* Ed., with notes, by J. M. Toner, M.D. Albany, N. Y., J. Munsell's Sons, 1892. 144 p., maps.

——*Washington and the West; Being George Washington's Diary of September, 1784, Kept during His Journey into the Ohio Basin . . .* with commentary by Archer Butler Hulbert. New York, Century, 1905. 217 p., front., plan, maps.

West Virginia. Point Pleasant Battle Monument Commission. *Battle of Point Pleasant, First Battle of the American Revolution . . .* By Mrs. Livia Simpson-Poffenbarger. Charleston, Jarrett Print. Co., 1936. 22 p.

Withers, Alexander Scott. *Chronicles of Border Warfare . . .* New ed., edited and annotated by Reuben Gold Thwaites. Cincinnati, R. Clark Co., 1895. 447 p., front. (port.). First ed., Clarksburg, Va., 1831.

Civil War and Statehood

Ambler, Charles Henry. *Francis H. Pierpont, Union War Governor of Virginia and Father of West Virginia.* Chapel Hill, Univ. of North Carolina Press, 1937. 483 p., front., illus. (incl. facsims.), plates, ports., maps.

Battles and Leaders of the Civil War. The Century Company, New York, 1884–7, 4 v. 3,097 p., fronts., plates, illus., ports.

Bierce, Ambrose. *Battlefields and Ghosts . . .* Palo Alto, Calif., Harvest Press, 1931. 16 p., front. (port.) Recollections of the Civil War.

Cook, Roy Bird. *The Family and Early Life of Stonewall Jackson.* 2d ed. Richmond, Old Dominion Press, Inc., 1925. 109 p., front., plates, ports., facsims., bibl.

Eckenrode, Hamilton J. *The Political History of Virginia during the Reconstruction.* Baltimore, 1904. 128 p. (Johns Hopkins Studies in Historical and Political Science . . . Series 22, nos. 6, 7, 8.)

Egan, Michael. *The Flying, Gray-Haired Yank: or, The Adventures of a Volunteer . . . A True Narrative of the Civil War.* Philadelphia, Hubbard Bros., 1888. 414 p., incl. front., plates, ports.

Fremont, John C. *Reports of the Operations . . . While in Command of the Mountain Department, during the Spring and Summer of 1862.* New York, Baker & Godwin, printers, 1866. 40 p. Describes military operations in West Virginia.

Hall, Granville Davisson. *Lee's Invasion of Northwest Virginia in 1861.* Chicago, Mayer & Miller, 1911. 164 p.

——*The Rending of Virginia, a History.* Chicago, Mayer & Miller, 1902. 630 p., illus., plate, port.

Hotchkiss, Major Jed. *Virginia.* Atlanta, Confederate Pub. Co., 1899. 1,295 p., ports., plans, maps. (Evans, C. A., ed. *Confederate Military History.* v. 3.)

Johnson, Reverdy. *Virginia vs. West Virginia.* Argument of Hon. Reverdy Johnson, in the Supreme Court of the United States, delivered in behalf of the defendant, Wednesday, May 8, 1867. Washington, printed at the *Globe* office, 1867. 18 p.

Leib, Charles. *Nine Months in the Quartermaster's Department: or, The Chances for Making a Million.* Cincinnati, Moore, Wilstach, Keys & Co., printers, 1862. 200 p., front., plates, port. Reminiscences of a Union soldier.

Lincoln, Abraham. *Complete Works of Abraham Lincoln.* Ed. by John G. Nicolay and John Hay . . . New and enl. ed. New York, F. D. Tandy Co., 1905. 12 v. See index under West Virginia.

McClellan, Major-Gen. George B. *Report on the Organization and Campaigns of the Army of the Potomac: to Which is Added an Account of the Campaign in West Virginia* . . . New York, Sheldon & Co., 1864. 480 p., maps.

MacCorkle, William Alexander. *The Recollections of Fifty Years of West Virginia.* New York, London, Putnam, 1928. 633 p., front., illus. (coat of arms), plates, ports., facsims. The author was governor of West Virginia, 1893–7.

McGregor, James C. *The Disruption of Virginia.* New York, Macmillan, 1922. 328 p., fold. map, bibl.

Summers, Festus P. *Johnson Newlon Camden: a Study in Individualism.* New York, London, Putnam, 1937. 605 p., front. (port.), bibl.

Taylor, Walter H. *General Lee, His Campaigns in Virginia, 1861–1865, with Personal Reminiscences.* Brooklyn, N. Y., Braunworth & Co., 1906. 314 p., fold. maps.

Warren, Robert Penn. *John Brown: the Making of a Martyr.* New York, Payson & Clarke, Ltd., 1929. 474 p., front. (port.), plates, map, bibl.

Willey, Waitman P. "The Final Crisis in Our Struggle for Statehood." *West Virginia Historical Magazine,* Jan. 1901, p. 20–24.

Willey, William P. *An Inside View of the Formation of the State of West Virginia* . . . Wheeling, News Pub. Co., 1901. 245 p., port.

POLITICS AND GOVERNMENT

Atkinson, George Wesley. *Bench and Bar of West Virginia.* Charleston, Virginian Law Book Co., 1919. 543 p. incl. ports. The author was governor of West Virginia, 1897–1901.

Callahan, Mrs. Maud L. *Evolution of the Constitution of West Virginia.* Morgantown, 1909. 40 p. (West Virginia Univ. Studies in West Virginia History. J. M. Callahan, ed. Constitutional History, nos. 1 and 2.)

Chandler, Julian A. C. *The History of Suffrage in Virginia.* Baltimore, 1901. 76 p. (Johns Hopkins Univ. Studies in Historical and Political Science. Series 19, nos. 6–7.)

Donnelly, Thomas C. *The Government of West Virginia.* Huntington, W. Va., Marshall College Book Store, 1935. 86 p., front., illus. (maps), bibl.

McDougal, Henry Clay. *Recollections, 1844–1909.* Kansas City, F. Hudson

Pub. Co., 1910. 466 p., front. (port.). Describes lawyers of West Virginia.

Pulliam, David L. *The Constitutional Conventions of Virginia from the Foundations of the Commonwealth to the Present Time.* Richmond, J. T. West, 1901. 180 p.

AGRICULTURE

Atkeson, Mary Meek. *The Woman on the Farm.* New York and London, Century, 1924. 331 p. (Century Rural Life Books.)

Dadisman, Andrew Jackson. *Farm Organization and Management of Typical West Virginia Farms* . . . Morgantown, West Virginia Agricultural Experiment Station, 1924. 75 p., illus., diagrs. (Thesis [Ph.D.] Cornell Univ.)

West Virginia Farm Bulletin. Morgantown, Agricultural Extension Dept. of College of Agriculture, West Virginia Univ., 1913 to date. Illus.

INDUSTRY, COMMERCE, AND LABOR

Lane, Winthrop D. *Civil War in West Virginia: a Story of the Industrial Conflict in the Coal Mines.* With int. by John R. Commons. New York, B. W. Huebsch, Inc., 1921. 128 p. (On cover: The Freeman Pamphlets.)

Morris, Homer Lawrence. *The Plight of the Bituminous Coal Miner.* With foreword by Joseph H. Willits. Philadelphia, Univ. of Pennsylvania Press; London, H. Milford, Oxford Univ. Press, 1934. 253 p., front., illus. (facsims.), plates. Deals with conditions in Kentucky and West Virginia.

Owings, C. W. *West Virginia's Coal-Mine Accident Costs and Data, July 1, 1929, to June 30, 1934.* Washington, Govt. Print. Off., 1937. 51 p. incl. tables (U. S. Bureau of Mines. Technical paper 580.)

Ross, Malcolm Harrison. *Machine Age in the Hills.* New York, Macmillan, 1933. 248 p., front., plates. 'The effects of technology . . . in the coal fields of Kentucky and West Virginia.'

TRANSPORTATION

Albig, W. Espey. 'Early Development of Transportation on the Monongahela River.' Ohio Valley Historical Assn. *Report,* 1914, v. 8: 66–74.

Ambler, Charles Henry. *A History of Transportation in the Ohio Valley* . . . Glendale, Calif., Arthur H. Clark Co., 1932. 465 p. incl. front., plates, maps.

Hulbert, Archer Butler. *The Ohio River: a Course of Empire* . . . New York and London, Putnam, 1906. 378 p., front., plates, ports., maps, plan.

Hungerford, Edward. *The Story of the Baltimore & Ohio Railroad, 1827–1927.* New York and London, Putnam, 1928. 2 v. Fronts., plates, ports., facsims., maps.

Reniers, Perceval, and Ashton Woodman Reniers. *The Midland Trail Tour in West Virginia* . . . New York, Midland Pub. Co., 1926. 31 p., illus., maps.

Turner, Ella May. *James Rumsey, Pioneer in Steam Navigation.* Scottdale, Pa., Mennonite Pub. House, 1930. 245 p., front., plates, ports., facsims., bibl.

THE NEGRO

Harris, Abram L. 'The Negro in the Coal-mining Industry.' *Opportunity: Journal of Negro Life and History,* Feb. 1926, v. 4: 45–8.

Johnson, Charles S. *The Negro in American Civilization: a Study of Negro Life and Race Relations in the Light of Social Research.* New York, Holt, 1930. 538 p., diagrs., tables, bibl. See especially p. 48–9, 114, 219–21.

Posey, Thomas E. *The Negro Citizen of West Virginia.* Institute, W. Va., Press of West Virginia State College, 1934. 119 p., plates, ports., diagrs., bibl.

Spero, Sterling D., and Abram L. Harris. *The Black Worker.* New York, Columbia Univ. Press, 1931. Tables, bibl.

Taylor, A. A. 'Making West Virginia a Free State.' *Journal of Negro History,* April 1921, v. 6: 131–73.

Washington, Booker T. *Up from Slavery; an Autobiography.* New York, Doubleday, Page & Co., 1900. 330 p., front. (port.). Also in later editions.

West Virginia. Bureau of Negro Welfare and Statistics. Biennial Reports. Charleston, 1922–38. Tables, maps.

Woodson, Carter G. 'Early Negro Education in West Virginia.' *Journal of Negro History,* Jan. 1922, v. 7: 23–63.

———'Freedom and Slavery in Appalachian America.' *Journal of Negro History,* April 1919, v. 1: 132–50.

EDUCATION

Ash, Irvin Oda. *West Virginia Educators.* Shepherdstown, The Author, 1936. 216 p., ports., bibl. Includes Waitman T. Barbe, Virgil Anson Lewis, Thomas Condit Miller, etc.

National Child Labor Committee, New York. *Rural Child Welfare; an Inquiry* . . . *Based upon Conditions in West Virginia.* New York, Macmillan, 1922. 355 p., front., plates, tables, diagr. Folks, Gertrude H., 'Rural School Attendance' (p. 94–139). A study of 183 rural schools in 17 counties.

West Virginia. Dept. of Free Schools. *History of Education in West Virginia.* Prepared under direction of State superintendent of free schools (Thomas C. Miller). Charleston, Tribune Print. Co., 1904. 319 p., front., illus., ports.

West Virginia. Dept. of Free Schools. *Survey of Education in West Virginia.* Charleston, 1928–9. 3 v. Tables.

RELIGION

Asbury, Francis. *The Journal of the Rev. Francis Asbury, Bishop of the Methodist Episcopal Church, from August 7, 1771, to December 7, 1815.* New York, N. Banks & T. Mason, 1821. 3 v.

Colhouer, T. H. 'Hon. F. H. Pierpont.' (In his *Sketches of the Founders of the Methodist Protestant Church.* Pittsburgh, 1880. p. 456–7.)

Henkel, Paul. 'Rev. Paul Henkel's Journal. His Missionary Journey in the State of Ohio in 1806.' *Ohio Archeological and Historical Quarterly,* 1914, v. 23: 162–218.

LITERATURE AND JOURNALISM

Atkeson, Mary Meek. *A Study of the Literature of West Virginia, 1822–1922.* Washington, D. C., 1922. 24 p.

Jones, Col. Buehring H. *The Sunny Land; or, Prison Prose and Poetry, Containing the Productions of the Ablest Writers in the South, and Prison Lays of Distinguished Confederate Officers.* Ed., with preface, biographies, and stories, by J. A. Houston. Baltimore, Innes & Co., printers, 1868. 540 p.

McMurtrie, Douglas Crawford. *The Beginnings of Printing in West Virginia . . .* Charleston, Press of Charleston High School, 1935. 20 p., front. (facsim.), bibl.

——*West Virginia Imprints; Being a First List of Books, Pamphlets and Broadsides . . . 1791–1830.* Charleston, Charleston High School Print. Shop, 1936. 24 p.

The *West Virginia Review* (monthly). Charleston, Conley-Teter Pub. Co., etc., 1923 to date. Illus.

Wood, Warren. *Representative Authors of West Virginia.* With foreword by Dr. Tucker Brooke. Ravenswood, Worth-While Book Co., 1926. 322 p., front., illus. (incl. ports.), plates.

ARCHITECTURE

Thruston, Mynna. *The Washingtons and Their Colonial Homes in West Virginia.* Charles Town, 1936. 29 p., illus. (incl. map), fold. geneal., table.

Ware, W. R. *The Georgian Period.* New York, U. P. C. Book Co., 1923. 6 v. plates. Vol. I contains information on the Home of Charles Washington, Charles Town, and on 'Harewood,' home of Richard Washington.

Wayland, John Walter. *Historic Homes of Northern Virginia and the Eastern Panhandle of West Virginia.* Staunton, Va., McClure Co., Inc., 1937. 625 p., illus. (incl. ports., maps).

FOLKLORE

Cambiaire, Celestin Pierre, comp. *East Tennessee and Western Virginia Mountain Ballads (the Last Stand of American Pioneer Civilization).* London, Eng., Mitre Press, 1934. 179 p.

Chappell, Louis W. *John Henry, a Folk-Lore Study.* Jena, Germany, Walter Biedermann, 1933. 144 p., bibl.

Combs, Josiah Henry. *Folk-Songs du Midi des Etats-Unis* . . . Paris, Les Presses Universitaires de France, 1925. 230 p. 'Bibliographie' at end of each chapter.

Cox, John Harrington. *Folk-Songs Mainly from West Virginia.* Introductory Essay and Supplementary References by Herbert Halpert. American Folk-Song Publication #5. New York: National Service Bureau, 1939.

Cox, John Harrington, ed. *Folk-Songs of the South, Collected under the Auspices of the West Virginia Folk-Lore Society.* Cambridge, Harvard Univ. Press, 1925. 545 p., plates, ports., fold. map.

Halpert, Herbert, ed. *Traditional Ballads, Mainly from West Virginia.* With int. essay and supplementary references by Herbert Halpert. New York, National Service Bureau, 1939. 109 p.

Johnson, Guy B. *John Henry; Tracking Down a Negro Legend.* Chapel Hill, Univ. of North Carolina Press, 1929. 155 p., front. (facsim.), bibl. (Half-title: The University of North Carolina. Social Study Series.) Includes music.

Montague, Margaret Prescott. *Up Eel River.* New York, Macmillan, 1928. 225 p., incl. front., illus.

CITIES, COUNTIES, AND POINTS OF INTEREST

Barry, Joseph. *The Strange Story of Harper's Ferry* . . . Martinsburg, Thompson Bros., 1903. 233 p., plates.

Callahan, James Morton. *History of the Making of Morgantown, West Virginia; a Type Study in Trans-Appalachian Local History.* Morgantown, W. Va., 1926. 330 p., fold. front., illus. (incl. maps), plans, bibl. (West Virginia Univ. Studies in History.)

Cook, Roy Bird. *The Annals of Fort Lee.* Charleston, West Virginia Review Press, 1935. 119 p., illus. (incl. ports., facsim.), plates.

Gibbens, Alvaro Franklin. *Historic Blennerhassett Island Home, near Parkersburg, W. Va.* Parkersburg, Globe Print. & Binding Co., 1914. 111 p., illus., plates, ports. First pub. 1899.

Haymond, Henry. *History of Harrison County, West Virginia* . . . Morgantown, Acme Pub. Co., 1909. 451 p., illus., fronts., plates, ports.

Laidley, W. S. *History of Charleston and Kanawha County, West Virginia, and Representative Citizens.* Chicago, Richmond-Arnold Pub. Co., 1911. 1,021 p. incl. illus., plates, ports.

MacCorkle, William Alexander. *The White Sulphur Springs; the Traditions, History, and Social Life of the Greenbrier White Sulphur Springs.* New York, Neale Pub. Co., 1916. 410 p., front., plates, ports., maps, facsims.

Musser, Clifford S. *Two Hundred Years' History of Shepherdstown.* Shepherdstown, printed by the *Independent,* 1931. 199 p., front., plates, fold. maps.

Wingerter, Charles A., ed. *History of Greater Wheeling and Vicinity.* Chicago and New York, Lewis Pub. Co., 1912. 2 v. Front., illus., ports.

1940 Census Figures

(The following are the final figures for all incorporated cities, towns, and villages.)

CITIES OF 10,000 OR MORE

	Population 1940	Population 1930		Population 1940	Population 1930
Beckley	12,852	9,357	Martinsburg	15,063	14,857
Bluefield	20,641	19,339	Morgantown	16,655	16,186
			Moundsville	14,168	14,411
Charleston	67,914	60,408			
Clarksburg	30,579	28,866	Parkersburg	30,103	29,623
Fairmont	23,105	23,159	South Charleston town	10,377	5,904
Huntington	78,836	75,572	Wheeling	61,099	61,659

2,500 TO 10,000

	Population 1940	Population 1930		Population 1940	Population 1930
Benwood	3,608	3,950	Montgomery	3,231	2,906
Buckhannon	4,450	4,374	Mullens	3,026	2,356
Charles Town	2,926	2,434	New Martinsville	3,491	2,814
Chester	3,805	3,701	Nitro	2,983	...
Dunbar	5,266	4,189	Oak Hill	3,213	2,076
Elkins	8,133	7,345	Piedmont	2,677	2,241
Follansbee	4,834	4,841	Point Pleasant	3,538	3,301
			Princeton	7,426	6,955
Grafton	7,431	7,737	Richwood	5,051	5,720
Hinton	5,815	6,654			
Hollidays Cove	6,137	4,480	St. Albans	3,558	3,254
			Salem	2,571	2,943
Kenova	3,902	3,680	Shinnston	2,817	2,802
Keyser	6,177	6,248	Sistersville	2,702	3,072
Keystone	2,942	1,897			
Logan	5,166	4,396	Welch	6,264	5,376
			Wellsburg	6,255	6,398
McMechen	3,726	3,710	Weston	8,268	8,646
Mannington	3,145	3,261	Williamson	8,366	9,410

LESS THAN 2,500

	Population 1940	Population 1930		Population 1940	Population 1930
Addison	1,133	976	Fairview	831	836
Albright	334	343	Falling Spring	388	355
Alderson	1,493	1,458	Farmington	880	819
Ansted	1,422	1,404	Fayetteville	1,347	1,143
Athens	682	628	Flat Woods	308	299
Auburn	168	166	Flemington	690	617
			Fort Gay	645	664
Barboursville	1,550	1,508	Franklin	613	431
Bayard	585	743	Friendly	148	170
Belington	1,517	1,571			
Berkeley Springs	1,145	1,039	Gassaway	1,429	1,618
Bethany	410	439	Gilbert	490	451
Beverly	484	431	Glasgow	725	614
Blacksville	261	269	Glendale	1,348	1,493
Bolivar	628	616	Glenville	588	799
Bramwell	1,494	1,574	Grantsville	1,052	1,018
Brandonville	113	82			
Bridgeport	1,581	1,567	Hambleton	394	368
Bruceton	165	116	Hamlin	850	844
Buffalo	338	316	Harman	184	114
Burnsville	851	868	Harpers Ferry	665	705
			Harrisville	1,338	1,192
Cairo	532	607	Hartford City	467	423
Camden-on-Gauley	373	435	Hedgesville	403	361
Cameron	1,998	2,281	Henderson	398	330
Capon Bridge	201	192	Hendricks	539	484
Cass	597	708	Hillsboro	224	220
Cedar Grove	1,411	1,110	Hundred	706	788
Ceredo	1,212	1,164	Hurricane	1,103	1,293
Chelyan	1,397	...	Huttonsville	308	303
Clark	715	787			
Clay	511	444	Iaeger	986	1,066
Clendenin	1,200	1,217			
Cowen	539	491	Jane Lew	505	445
			Job	184	61
Danville	417	486	Junior	533	560
Davis	1,454	1,656			
Durbin	533	498	Kermit	811	749
			Kimball	1,580	1,467
Eastbank	601	476	Kingwood	1,676	1,709
East Rainelle	1,515	1,272			
Elizabeth	685	716	Layopolis	252	198
Elk Garden	342	299	Leon	219	283
Ellenboro	277	330	Lester	909	609
			Lewisburg	1,466	1,293

	Population	
	1940	*1930*
Littleton	539	648
Lumberport	1,285	1,289
Mabscott	1,473	1,260
Madison	1,205	1,156
Man	1,342	835
Marfrance	875	1,066
Marlinton	1,644	1,586
Marmet	1,814	1,200
Mason	795	691
Masontown	869	924
Matewan	905	932
Matoaka	926	929
Meadow Bridge	477	476
Middlebourne	733	769
Mill Creek	732	723
Milton	1,641	1,305
Monongah	1,790	1,909
Montrose	122	114
Moorefield	1,291	734
Mount Hope	2,431	2,361
Newburg	696	745
New Cumberland	2,098	2,300
New Haven	606	...
Northfork	387	494
Nutter Fort	1,803	1,825
Oakvale	273	261
Paden City	2,215	2,281
Parsons	2,077	2,012
Paw Paw	990	781
Pax	631	608
Pennsboro	1,738	1,616
Petersburg	1,751	1,410
Peterstown	467	388
Philippi	1,955	1,767
Pine Grove	841	820
Pineville	769	462
Pratt	417	325
Pullman	204	184
Rainelle	985	920
Ranson	1,171	1,002
Ravenswood	1,061	1,189
Reedsville	324	345
Reedy	329	405

	Population	
	1940	*1930*
Rhodell	995	...
Ridgeley	1,907	1,972
Ripley	759	669
Riverside	1,043	940
Rivesville	1,552	1,700
Romney	2,013	1,441
Ronceverte	2,265	2,254
Rowlesburg	1,452	1,573
Sabraton	1,810	1,717
St. Marys	2,201	2,182
Shepherdstown	945	888
Smithers	2,232	...
Smithfield	455	609
Sophia	1,160	611
Spencer	2,497	2,493
Star City	1,175	1,121
Summersville	643	536
Suncrest	238	...
Sutton	1,083	1,205
Terra Alta	1,471	1,474
Thomas	1,449	1,660
Thurmond	339	462
Triadelphia	359	302
Troy	133	101
Tunnelton	552	595
Union	346	331
Vienna	2,338	...
War	1,277	1,392
Wardensville	195	189
Wayne	801	675
Weirton Heights	2,476	...
West Milford	389	349
Westover	1,752	1,633
West Union	1,020	984
White Sulphur Springs	2,093	1,484
Whitesville	942	...
Williamsburg	177	148
Williamstown	1,687	1,657
Winfield	318	294
Womelsdorf	417	373
Worthington	507	405
Yolyn	245	422

Index

F